Revolution and Its Past

Revolution and Its Past is a comprehensive study of China from the last quarter of the eighteenth century through to 2018.

A fascinating and dramatic narrative, the book compels interest both as a history of an ancient civilization developing into a modern nation-state and as an account of how the Chinese as a people have struggled and continue to work to find their identity in the modern world. Beginning in the last two decades of the reign of the Qianlong emperor (1736–1795), the book provides a baseline that allows readers to understand China's rapid decline in the nineteenth and part of the twentieth century, and extends into the present day, a time when China has the second largest economy in the world and aims to become a leading global power by 2050. The vast changes that have swept over China between these times are probed through the lens of the broad and important theme of "identities." This fourth edition has been updated throughout, providing a more thorough examination of recent history since 1960, and increasing coverage of such topics as "new Qing history," frontier and ethnicity, women and their roles, environmental concerns and issues, and globalization.

Supported by maps, images, tables, online eResources and suggestions for further reading, and written in an engaging, concise, and authoritative style, *Revolution and Its Past* is the ideal textbook for all students of the history of modern China.

R. Keith Schoppa is Professor Emeritus at Loyola University Maryland in Baltimore, Maryland, USA. From 1998 to 2014, he served as the Doehler Chair in Asian History. His research focused on the political, social, and cultural history of the first half of the twentieth century. His major research works include *Chinese Elites and Political Change* (1982); *Xiang Lake—Nine Centuries of Chinese Life* (1989); *Blood Road* (1995), for which he won the Association for Asian Studies Levenson Award; and *In a Sea of Bitterness* (2011).

Revolution and Its Past

Identities and Change in Modern Chinese History

Fourth Edition

R. Keith Schoppa

Routledge
Taylor & Francis Group

NEW YORK AND LONDON

This edition published 2020
by Routledge
52 Vanderbilt Avenue, New York, NY 10017

and by Routledge
2 Park Square, Milton Park, Abingdon, Oxon, OX14 4RN

Routledge is an imprint of the Taylor & Francis Group, an informa business

© 2020 Taylor & Francis

The right of R. Keith Schoppa to be identified as author of this work has been asserted by him in accordance with sections 77 and 78 of the Copyright, Designs and Patents Act 1988.

Every effort has been made to contact copyright-holders. Please advise the publisher of any errors or omissions, and these will be corrected in subsequent editions.

First edition published by Pearson Education Inc. 2002
Third edition published by Pearson Education Inc. 2011
Third edition reprinted by Routledge 2016

Library of Congress Cataloging-in-Publication Data
Names: Schoppa, R. Keith, 1943– author.
Title: Revolution and its past : identities and change in modern Chinese history /
R. Keith Schoppa.
Description: 4th edition. | New York, NY : Routledge, 2020. | Includes
bibliographical references and index. |
Identifiers: LCCN 2019007097 (print) | LCCN 2019014706 (ebook) |
ISBN 9781315182025 (Ebook) | ISBN 9781138742161 (hardback : alk. paper) |
ISBN 9781138742185 (pbk. : alk. paper) | ISBN 9781315182025 (ebk.)
Subjects: LCSH: China—History—19th century. | China—History—20th century. |
China—History—21st century. | Revolutions—China—History. | National
characteristics, Chinese.
Classification: LCC DS755 (ebook) | LCC DS755 .S294 2019 (print) | DDC 951—dc23
LC record available at https://lccn.loc.gov/2019007097

ISBN: 978-1-138-74216-1 (hbk)
ISBN: 978-1-138-74218-5 (pbk)
ISBN: 978-1-315-18202-5 (ebk)

Typeset in Garamond
by codeMantra

Visit the eResources: www.routledge.com/9781138742185

To Beth—

with love and gratitude

CONTENTS

FIGURES

MAPS

PREFACE

Context: The 1920s in one of the most modernized and developed zones of Zhejiang province along the coast of Hangzhou Bay.

The inside of all thatched roof farm houses … were the same: black rafters, gray walls, a dirt floor, a kitchen table, a bench, farm implements, and amulets from the local temple. The walls were bare. The floors were covered with chicken shit, and people walked through it with their bare feet. The constant lament in the village: "Nothing to eat, nothing to wear—everything goes to the landlord."

Context: 2018, almost a century after the scene above and 40 years into the post-Mao Reform era.

During the period 1989 to 2017, the annual growth GDP rate (the total value of everything produced by all the people and companies in a country) averaged a remarkable 9.69 percent. It was the fastest sustained expansion by any major power in all of history. Statistics from the World Bank showed this stunning economic progress through GDP per capita from 1978 (185.4 USD), to 2016 (8,123.2 USD) and projected to 2022 (12,834.7 USD). World Bank statistics revealed that up to 2017, 800 million Chinese were pulled out of poverty level as the poverty rate dropped from 88 percent in 1981 to 3.1 percent in 2017. Not many, if any, thatched roof houses exist. Instead, in many modernized areas, there are attractive modern two-story homes with double garages, satellite dishes, and all modern conveniences. The wealthy often own three or more cars, among which would probably be a Lexus or BMW or both.

In the international sphere the economic success was equally spectacular as China became the world's second largest economy in 2010 and the largest trading nation in the world in 2013. Its Gross Domestic Product in 2016 made up 14.9 percent ($11.2 trillion) of the global output, which was second only to that of the United States (25 percent, 18.6 trillion). China became the world's largest exporter of goods in the world in 2009. Data from 2011–2013 show that in the world economy China produced 90.6 percent of all personal computers; 80 percent of all air conditioners; 70.6 percent of all mobile phones; 63 percent of all shoes; 50 percent of all DVDs; and 43.1 percent of all clothing.

Not surprisingly, China's rise to a position of global power in the forty years since the disaster known as the Great Proletarian Cultural Revolution (1966–1976) has been described by different writers as *amazing, astonishing, awesome, phenomenal, spectacular*, and *staggering*. While these adjectives contain some truth especially when posed against the depths of degradation, ridicule, weakness, shame, and humiliation that China experienced in the 140 years from 1850 to 1990, they overlook the fact that these years were, in fact, for China an aberration in the last two millennia, when China was consistently one of the world's largest economies.

It is a truism (though one frequently forgotten in the presentist American culture) that one cannot understand the present and its identities without understanding the past. This book, which is comprehensive in scope, examines the fundamental aspects and developments of the Chinese past. How does a society develop in a century from those dark thatched hovels to brightly-lit skyscrapers and neon-lit streets? To modern homes with multiple TVs, computers, and dishwashers? From sedan chairs and carts to the Lexus and BMW? I have used the broad and important theme of "identities" to help shape much of the presentation—analyzing traditional identities and the array of modern identities that the Chinese have tried to shape or have experimented with. It is a natural theme, given the fact that the discourses of history and identity both attempt to delineate a meaningful past for a particular present. Further, in the making of history, individual and state actions depended in large part on how the individual and the state perceived their identities and how they were perceived by others with whom they had to interact.

This study begins in the last two decades of the reign of one of China's greatest emperors, the Qianlong emperor (1736–1795). Although early textbooks of "modern" China had often treated the salvoes of the Opium War (1839–1842) as the beginning of the modern period, recent work has shown that important changes foreshadowing developments in the nineteenth and twentieth centuries were already underway in the late seventeenth and eighteenth centuries. Starting then, we see the dynamics that gave rise to the late-eighteenth-century developments when Chinese wealth and power were at their imperial peak. Analyzing that era also provides a baseline for understanding China's rapid decline in the nineteenth and part of the twentieth century. In that period of decline and throughout its twentieth-century revolution, one of the most important problems facing individual Chinese and China as a nation was choosing appropriate political, social, cultural, and economic identities as contexts and situations changed.

Above all, this is a story of men and women whose choices shaped modern Chinese history in the often-startling directions in which it lurched. It is a dramatic story filled with some triumph but, more often than not, tragedy. It is a tale frequently bloody and violent, alternately soaring with hope and plunging into bleak despair. It compels our interest both as a history of an ancient civilization developing into a modern nation-state and as an account of how the Chinese have struggled and are continuing to work to find their identity in the modern world.

NEW TO THE FOURTH EDITION

In this fourth edition, I have completely rewritten some chapters, substantially expanded on and enlarged the scope of coverage, and probed more deeply some topics that were unfortunately given rather short shrift in the third edition. Responding to readers who suggested that I bolster certain themes or issues in the post-Mao Reform Era, I have added two new chapters, which allowed me to survey recent history more thoroughly and thereby pave the way for readers to place current events into a more coherent context. In addition, I have devoted much more time to women and their roles in every time period from elite women in the lower Yangzi region up through the effects of the post-Mao reforms on women's lives. I have focused on some environmental concerns, including coverage of the Great Famine in north China from 1876 to 1879 and environmental issues under Communist control. Finally, I have explored questions of ethnicity with special attention to Xinjiang and Tibet.

I have discussed at some length the nature of the rule of Xi Jinping, his Belt and Road Initiative, and his policies in the East China and South China seas and their environmental ramifications. Whatever for good or for ill, his rule promises, as of this point, to make major and qualitative impacts on China today and in the future. My discussion on Taiwan in Chapter 23 zeros in on the ever more unavoidable question of unification or independence. The success of the DPP in three recent presidential elections makes the question more critical, as does the import of the PRC's wealth and power.

R. Keith Schoppa
Baltimore, Maryland

NOTES ON PRONUNCIATION

In writing about Chinese developments before 1949 and in the People's Republic since that time, I use the pinyin system of romanization in general use today. Names in pinyin are pronounced generally as written, with vowels often taking on the phonetic value of vowels in European romance languages and German. Consonants are generally pronounced as consonants in English, but there are three exceptions:

Q is pronounced as *CH*—as in the name of the last Chinese dynasty, Qing, pronounced as if it were written Ching.
X is pronounced as *HS*, in effect a softer version of *SH*, with the *H* producing a slight hiss—as in the name of China's late-twentieth-century reformer Deng Xiaoping.
C is pronounced as *TS*—as in the name of the important cultural leader Cai Yuanpei.

I have not used pinyin for Sun Yat-sen and Chiang Kai-shek, who are better known by these names than by their names in pinyin (Sun Yixian and Jiang Jieshi, respectively).

In writing about Chinese developments in Taiwan and about those men and women closely involved with Chiang Kai-shek's government in the 1930s, I have used Wade-Giles romanization. This choice was made to respect the fact that the regime in Taiwan has not adopted the pinyin system and generally uses Wade-Giles, though romanization in Taiwan tends to be highly variable. Vowels, as in pinyin, generally take on the value of vowels in Spanish, Italian, and German. Most consonants are pronounced as in English, with these exceptions:

When the following consonants have an apostrophe after them, they are pronounced as in English: *ch', k', p',* and *t'*. When they do not have an apostrophe, *ch* is pronounced as *j*, *k* is pronounced as *g*, *p* is pronounced as *b*, and *t* is pronounced as *d*. Further, *j* is pronounced as *r*.

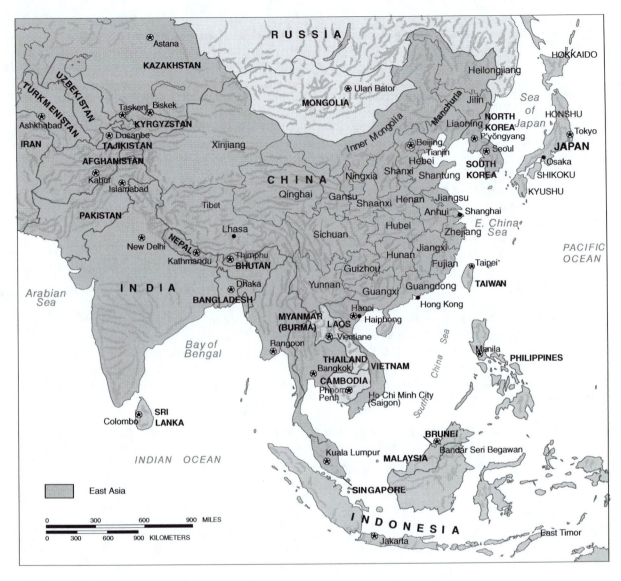

MAP 0.1   East, South, and Northeast Asia, 2018.

Part 1

From the Heights to the Depths

Challenges to Traditional Chinese Identities, 1780–1901

1

Identities

There are almost 1.4 billion Chinese living in the People's Republic of China today. In Western minds over the years, images of these masses have often focused on the sameness—the "hordes" moving in "human wave" assaults in the Korean War, the "blue ants" mindlessly carrying out the bidding of their Communist overlords in mass campaigns of the 1950s, the mobs of Red Guards screaming in demonstration marches in the 1960s, enraged students attacking the U.S. embassy in 1999, and so on. Indeed, in all these images, all Chinese seemed to look alike. But the identities of Chinese, like people of every country and ethnic group, are as different as the number of Chinese who exist. Thumbnail sketches of a quartet of Chinese figures point to the stark individuality seen amid the masses throughout China's modern history.

Zeng Guofan (1811–1872) was a stolid Confucian conservative. With the highest civil service degree under his belt, he became perhaps the most important Chinese official serving the alien Manchu dynasty. What mattered to him most were his family, his family's farm, and his culture. He organized an army to defend his home province, Hunan, against the threat of the Taiping rebellion led by a man who claimed to be the younger brother of Jesus Christ. During his leadership of this army, he, as the elder brother, wrote letters to his brothers in Hunan, urging them, in good Confucian terms, to pay attention to their duties at home. Although he was impressed with modern Western technology, when he was old and infirm he refused to seek Western medical treatment, preferring to be treated with traditional Chinese medicine.

Qiu Jin, a thirty-two-year-old woman, was beheaded at dawn on July 15, 1907. She had left her husband and children several years earlier to go to Japan to study. With a reputation for wearing men's clothes and riding horses in men's style, she was photographed wielding an unsheathed dagger and antagonized locals by having female students at her school train in military drills. She became involved in an elaborate plot that included assassinating the governor of a province and staging an uprising against the government. But she was arrested before she could rebel and paid the bloody price.

Soong Meiling (1898–2003), the daughter of a wealthy Chinese merchant, attended Wellesley College in Massachusetts, spoke excellent English, and was a Christian. In 1927 she was married to Chiang Kai-shek, who would become the leader of the Republic of China, first on the mainland

(1928–1949) and then on Taiwan (1949–1975). Madame Chiang became the darling of the American press and political elites during World War II, when she addressed a joint session of Congress stressing China's plight. Though she maintained a home in Taiwan after Chiang's death, she lived in New York City until her death in October 2003.

FIGURE 1.1   Known as thoroughly Confucian, Zeng Guofan was China's most outstanding scholar-official in the third quarter of the nineteenth century.
Source: Historic Images/Alamy Stock Photo.

FIGURE 1.2   China's first feminist, Qiu Jin wrote, "We, the 200 million women of China, are the most unfairly treated objects on earth".
Source: via Wikimedia Commons.

Born in 1961, Cui Jian is China's most famous rock star. Beginning his career as a trumpet player in the Beijing Symphony Orchestra, he started experimenting with rock in the mid-1980s. His musical genres merged Chinese folk music and traditional Chinese instruments with guitar, sax, and Western percussion instruments. Although the government tried to keep him off television and attempted to cancel his concerts, this long-haired, often open-shirted cultural rebel became a hero to the youth of China. His song lyrics scandalized government leaders and censors. An American journalist commented that Cui's "raspy outbursts of alienation [became] the anthems of his generation."[1]

Zeng, Qiu, Soong, and Cui all put the lie to the stereotype that Chinese were faceless and colorless masses with minds benumbed by powerful authorities, whether emperors, generals, or Communist ideologues. As the world entered a new millennium and China found itself in the midst of vast change, three questions were raised with increasing frequency: What does it mean to be Chinese? What attributes, ethical and cultural values, attitudes, and worldviews are typically Chinese? Most important here, what is the shared history of the Chinese that gives them their identity?

This book focuses on the history of modern China, that is, China's history from the late eighteenth century to the present. It is concerned with Chinese characteristics, customs, idiosyncrasies, past experiences, and relationships. It probes the identities that China and the Chinese have assumed and the identities that others have ascribed to it and to them. It analyzes the changes seen over time. Above all, this is a story of people—men and women who shaped China's identity and history and who, in turn, were shaped by them. This chapter sets the stage for the study of Chinese identities by focusing on the cultural commonalities that were the foundation for Chinese society and the dynamics of social relations, actions, and interactions. Because these cultural elements often played key roles in historical events and developments, understanding them is the first step in understanding the Chinese and their past.

FIGURE 1.3 Noted for her grace and eloquence, Soong Meiling (Madame Chiang Kai-shek) speaks on the radio during one of her trips to the United States.
Source: Keystone/Getty Images.

HISTORY AND IDENTITY

A person's identity comes from many sources. Contextual sources are important: time and place of birth, ethnic heritage, parents' occupations and socioeconomic status, the nature of the local community, schools, and friends. Perhaps equally significant components are personal characteristics—appearance, personality, and habits. But people's identities are fundamentally their personal history, what has happened to them during their lifetime; that history has created each person as he or she is at the present time. Understanding someone's past or the past of any institution or political and social body—nation, town, neighborhood, school, church, company, organization, sports team—is recognizing a person's or group's identity. In other words, the shape of the past gives meaning to the present.

There are three important corollaries to seeing the relationship between history and identity. Take, as an example, a college senior in a fraternity. On an individual level, he has his own characteristics, personality, habits, and history that give him an identity through which he sees and understands himself. But ultimately, in the outside world, his identity is given or bestowed by others; a fraternity brother, a freshman classmate, a girlfriend, or a professor would likely all bestow on our hypothetical fraternity man substantially different identities. Sometimes how he is perceived might be as or perhaps more important for those around him than what he really is.

So it is with China's past and its identity. Over the past 250 years, China has acted on its own for its own reasons and according to its own standards. But the outside world has often perceived Chinese actions and motivations in entirely different ways, sometimes through direct reactions to Chinese events, policies, or actions, and sometimes, unfortunately, through bias and stereotype. Thus, the violent crackdown of the Chinese government on student demonstrators in 1989 continued for many years to shape and color views of American politicians and journalists about the goals and motives of the Chinese government. This particular coloration remained despite changes in Chinese political leadership and several decades of staggering economic and consequent attitudinal changes. In the first years of the twenty-first century, that economic success itself may

FIGURE 1.4 Cui Jian's 1986 song "Nothing to My Name" has been called the biggest hit in Chinese history and was the beginning of Chinese rock music. Cui gave a Thirty-Year Retrospective Concert in Beijing in September 2016 and played in Sydney in August 2017.
Source: VCG/VCG via Getty Images.

produce new, challenging images of the Chinese as cheap laborers taking outsourced American jobs and as workers whose products stock the shelves at Wal-Mart.

Second, a person's identity may be bestowed by people with biases and ulterior motives as well as by those seeking to truly understand what kind of person he or she is. Thus, our fraternity man may be judged on the basis of race, ethnicity, religion, gender, sexual orientation, or social group. Because different people with different agendas are bestowing different identities, it follows that every individual will have many identities—so too with China and the Chinese. Thus, in the early twenty-first century, China can be seen primarily as an ambitious economic power and soon-to-be global leader, or a country awash in corruption and money-hungry greed, or a state facing huge demographic and environmental problems, as the main regional power in East Asia, or as a country marked by a gaping, perhaps nation-rending economic inequality, or a country where dissenters are harshly oppressed. Just as in any perception of an individual's identities, some of the many identities or all of them may apply in a variety of combinations.

Third, because identity comes in large part from history and because a person's present and future will become a part of that history, the person's identity is continually evolving and developing. He or she might react to a new situation in a way that would be seen as totally out of character with the expectations of others. Yet that reaction would help others redefine that person and give him or her a new identity. Identity is therefore very fluid, provisional, and tentative. Again, such is the case with China and the Chinese. Each new event and reactions to events shape anew our understanding of Chinese attitudes and goals. My work as a historian—and the goal of this book—is to try to reach and present an understanding of Chinese historical identities that reflects as closely as possible China's culture and past experiences.

ASSOCIATIONAL IDENTITIES: LINEAGES AND FAMILIES

It is a truism that whereas the basic social unit in the modern West is the individual, in China that foundational unit is the group. There is probably no clearer illustration of the relationship of the Chinese individual to the group—and here the most important group, the family—than the nature of Chinese names. Many Chinese personal names are composed of three characters and pronounced as three syllables. Traditionally the surname came first, pointing clearly to the priority of the surname group, the family, or, taken more largely, the lineage (sometimes called a "clan"), that is, all Chinese descendants of a single patriarch. Take the name Zeng Guofan. The surname is Zeng. The second name, Guo, is a generational name. For those families deeply rooted in the Chinese tradition of the extended family, all brothers and cousins of one generation should ideally share a common name. Thus, Zeng's brothers were named Zeng *Guo*quan, Zeng *Guo*hua, and Zeng *Guo*huang.[2] It follows that only the last character in the three-character name is the individual's own—the family, the generation, and then *and then only* the individual—a marked difference from the modern West, where the individual name precedes all others.

Such a Chinese naming pattern suggests the role of the individual in the family; he or she was submerged in the group, with implicit responsibilities to that group. There was no concept of an individual's rights within the family in the traditional cultural view: when Qiu Jin's parents arranged her marriage to a bland, conventional man with whom she had little in common, she did not assert herself against the family's decision (though, later showing considerable spunk, she eventually left him). An assertion of individual rights would immediately jeopardize family harmony and solidarity. Elder brother Zeng Guofan set off bitter quarreling with his brothers by insisting that they remain at home, tending family needs, instead of serving in the military campaigns against the Taiping. At least two brothers saw him as blocking their individual careers and possible paths to higher status and prestige.[3] This situation reveals an important facet of family structure: it was hierarchical, and, as in any hierarchy, there were superior and subordinate ranks. Elder brother Zeng Guofan could tell his younger brothers what to do, and they were expected to comply. The elder brother–younger brother relationship was one of five "Confucian bonds" that defined cardinal relationships in Chinese society. Three were familial. Joining elder brothers in the superior ranks were fathers and husbands, who could direct and control sons and wives, respectively. Clear in these bonds was that maleness and age outranked femaleness and youth.

Within the family, "responsibility" was the watchword. Both superiors and subordinates had responsibilities: superiors to direct, train, provide for, and control and subordinates to obey, comply, and respect. For sons and daughters the proper family ethic, filial piety, had a number of aspects. First and foremost, it meant doing whatever was necessary to provide for the physical and psychological needs of parents in a spirit of respectful obeisance. Stories abound, many likely apocryphal, about the dimensions of such action. There was the filial son who cut off flesh from his own thigh to feed a starving parent; there was the filial daughter who breast-fed an elderly parent for nourishment; there was the seventy-year-old son who clowned around on the floor to lift his elderly parents' depression. There was the story of one Guo Ju, desperately poor and trying to support his wife, son, and mother. When there was no way for all to survive, he decided it best for his son to die so that his mother might have enough to eat. But this extreme solution was aborted, for while digging the grave for his son, he dug up buried treasure, which allowed all to live and prosper. The moral: upholding filial piety will bring solutions to a family's bleakest plights and ultimately happiness and prosperity.

A second component of filial piety was protecting one's body as a gift from one's parents. A Confucian disciple once fell off a porch and injured his leg; from that point on, he walked around with a continual hangdog expression on his face. When someone asked him why, he replied that his fall showed that he had not been properly filial, that one should not forget one's parents in taking a single step or in saying a single word. Although it is unlikely that any Chinese were so totally constrained, such teachings probably produced some hesitance before one acted recklessly and, as a consequence, helped give rise to a markedly conservative Chinese social culture.

A third aspect of filial piety was carrying on the family line. The second-generation Confucian thinker Mencius argued that the most unfilial thing was to have no children, for it meant that the ancestors who ultimately had produced the present generation would have no one to remember them properly. This remembrance of deceased family members constituted a fourth important aspect of filial piety. Remembrance came in various ways. The best-known method of remembering ancestors was ancestor reverence: rituals were held on birthdays and death days of parents and key ancestors where food was presented for their sustenance in their other life. The graves of ancestors were traditionally swept on the Qing Ming festival (April 5 or 6).

Mourning periods for one's parents lasted for up to three years. Marked by various restrictions in lifestyle, they were taken very seriously and were obligatory even for men in important positions. In the middle of the campaigns against the Taiping, Zeng Guofan had to retire twice, once on the death of his mother in 1852 and then following his father's death in 1857, the latter retirement lasting almost two years. Remembrance also involved the most auspicious siting of the graves; if the graves of the deceased were sited poorly, the spirits of the dead might play a negative role in the lives of their descendants. So it was that in 1858, because of a series of family mishaps and tragedies, Zeng and his brothers relocated the graves of their parents to try to change their fortune for the better.[4] It was a task for Daoist geomancers, or specialists in the art of *fengshui* (literally "wind-water" and pronounced something like "fung-shway"), to discover the best burial sites.

Daoism was an indigenous Chinese philosophical and religious tradition that focused on nature and on aligning oneself in various ways with the forces of nature and the natural state of things.

Though the extended or joint family (including grandparents, parents and siblings, children and cousins) was the ideal, financial realities probably made it quite rare. An estimated 60 percent of the Chinese in late imperial times lived instead in small or nuclear families composed of parents and their unmarried children. Another ideal was the lineage, in which all the descendants of one patriarch lived in the same area and provided a support base for their relatives. Ideally, the lineage owned joint property; the proceeds of harvests from that land provided an economic safety net for lineage members or money for special projects or undertakings. Most lineages periodically published genealogies as a way to express their unity and significance.

The strength and importance of lineages varied across China. They were strongest in the South. Anthropologists argue over the reason. Some say that strong lineages developed there to deal with the labor-intensive irrigation facilities crucial in southern rice paddy agriculture. Others suggest that since the South was China's frontier area, strong lineages developed for protection in an often violent and unpredictable context. Whole villages in southern areas were—and today still are—composed of members of one lineage. Often the lineage surname simply became the name of the village; thus, in East-Central China, a village inhabited mostly by the Sun lineage was known simply as Sun Village on the Lake. If lineages were a source of solidarity in South China, they were also a scourge in some areas, when one strong lineage might be pitted against another in bloody and costly feuds. Feuds, especially common in the southeastern provinces of Fujian and Guangdong, could begin over any issue but were often ignited by disputes over water rights and boundaries.

ASSOCIATIONAL IDENTITIES: SOCIAL CONNECTIONS

Basic social identity comes not only from a person's family and his or her place in it, but also from social connections and the networks that develop from them. An American journalist has written that the Chinese

> instinctively divide people into those with whom they already have a fixed relationship, a connection, what the Chinese call *guanxi*, and those that they don't. These connections operate like a series of invisible threads, tying Chinese to each other with far greater tensile strength than mere friendship.[5]

Connections and their next step, networks, were established in various ways.

Some of the connections were surefire. Friends obviously had close connections; the only one of the five Confucian bonds that neared equality rather than hierarchy was friendship. For this reason, friendship was more celebrated in Chinese literature than any other social relationship. Friendship also provided connections to the friend's family. If a person came from the same hometown or county or even province (called in Chinese "native place"), he or she had an automatic connection with anyone else from that place; the connection was stronger the more local the common place—county or town or village, for example. Thus, among all the Chinese students living in Japan during the first decade of the twentieth century, Qiu Jin (executed for her role in the 1907 assassination plot) developed her most important revolutionary ties to two men from her native place of Shaoxing, men whom she had not known previously.

Academic and scholarly ties were also significant sources of connections. The men who received civil service degrees in the same year shared an alumni connection. An example of the

power of such a connection: in a famous sixteenth-century case, an official who received his degree the same year as a murdered fellow official became a surrogate father to the victim's son, even
to the point of coaching him for a revenge attack on the guilty.[6] Teacher–student relationships provided connections for life, taking on an almost master–disciple dynamic. When he chose someone
to lead the Anhui provincial army against the Taiping, Zeng Guofan, not surprisingly, selected one
of his former students and protégés, Li Hongzhang.[7]

Though social connections are important in every culture, Chinese culture has developed them
to the utmost. They are immensely practical social realities; put more bluntly, they are a *must* to get
things done. From the bureaucracy of the traditional state to the bureaucracies of the Communist
and post-Communist states, people have used their personal social connections to get what they
want or need. Li Hongzhang nurtured his connections to Zeng Guofan, theoretically his superior, by
performing various acts of kindness and by supportive actions. Zeng, in turn, responded with acts
of kindness, generosity, and support to Li (a key example was selecting Li to head one of the provincial armies). In the process, Li's social debts to Zeng increased. His repaying those debts through
reciprocal actions further nurtured the connection that they shared, making its "tensile strength"
very great indeed. The accumulation and repayment of obligations was a continual social reality.

China's most famous twentieth-century sociologist, Fei Xiaotong, wrote about the importance
of connections and networks for the working of Chinese society. Networks might encompass many
people, but their structure was based on the connections of two people, and then two others, and
so on. The strength of any two connections varied. Similarly, individuals found themselves to be
part of a number of networks, and the strength of the personal connections to people in each network also varied. This situation had definite ethical implications. Noting that Chinese society was
structured as "webs woven out of countless personal relationships," Fei argued that "[t]o each knot
in these webs [was] attached a specific ethical principle." In this society,

> general [ethical] standards [had] no utility. The first thing to do [was] to understand the specific
> context: Who [was] the important figure, and what kind of relationship [was] appropriate with
> that figure? Only then [could] one decide the ethical standards to be applied in that context.[8]

Thus, there was no universal ethic to be applied across the board to all people and in all situations.
Ethics in China were traditionally determined by connections, and they varied with particular people and situations.

These social realities gave Chinese social life considerable fluidity. Not only did a person's
place in society largely depend on those to whom he was connected, but the way he treated others
and the way he was treated depended on those connections. In addition, the power of connections
was such that a person might be moved to act in ways or participate in efforts that he might ordinarily have been reluctant about. In the end, the disheartening fact was that if the person with
whom he had spent years establishing and cultivating connections was kicked out of power, lost
his job, was incapacitated, or died, he would be back to square one in trying to establish his own
social position. Developing and nurturing personal connections was understandably a full-time,
lifetime undertaking, for it was those connections that gave a person his social identity.

ASSOCIATIONAL IDENTITIES: RELATIONS TO THE "OTHER"

In a real sense, if a person's social identity depended largely on those with whom he or she was
connected, the obverse was also true. Identity came in a negative way from those with whom a

person had no connections—call them the "Other." By lifestyle, habits, religious practices, and language, a person shows or tells society in various ways, "I am not one of them; I am different from the Other." Since one had no connections to the Other, there were no special ethical responsibilities to them. Thus, for example, a person could cut in line in front of them or push and shove them while getting on or off the bus. Fei notes the wretched state of many public toilets as an example of the lack of a sense of ethical responsibility to the public with whom one has no special connections. It must be stressed that this is a general cultural tendency, not a necessary inevitability. The Buddhist concept of "karma," that a person's deeds in this life determine how he or she will be reborn in the next life, may have played a role in the ethical views of many. In traditional Chinese social thought, there was no sense of equality among people, only connections or their lack. The philosopher Mencius put it this way: "That things are unequal is part of their nature. … If you reduce them to the same level [that is, to equality], it will only bring confusion to the empire."[9]

The Other was potentially frightening, possibly dangerous, and almost always an object of suspicion precisely because one did not owe any special concern or treatment to those with whom one had no connections. Thus, the Other had best be kept at arm's length. In the world of folk spirits, the most threatening beings were the "hungry ghosts," ancestors who were no longer remembered and revered; that is, no one living was providing them with the necessities for existence in the spirit world. In the language of connections, no one in the world of the living was maintaining the proper connections with them. These ghosts were reported to be mean and dangerous, more than willing to create all sorts of misfortune for those who were not providing them with their needs. As with connections and the Other in the land of the living, the spirits of ancestors revered by one family were for another family the "Other," in this case ghosts to be avoided.

In society, strangers were always suspect. Short-term transients—beggars and vagrants—and more long-term drifters and uprooted—the homeless and refugees—were potential threats. Their presence, and their passing through an area suffering a famine or experiencing the violence of banditry, rebellion, or war, only heightened the fluid danger latent in society. Even more serious than these passing strangers were permanent Others with whom Chinese had to deal: ethnic minorities. Whereas one might avoid transient strangers, state and society had to determine how to deal with the permanent Others.

China is a country with fifty-six sizable ethnic minorities recognized by the government. In 2010, there were approximately 94,580,000 people in these minority groups. The home of many of these—Mongols, Tibetans, Uighurs—has been and continues to be near the periphery of the Chinese nation. Yet groups such as the Zhuang, Hui, Miao, and Yi have remained more within the Chinese geographical core, living scattered among the Han people, those considered the ethnic Chinese (about 92 percent of the total population). Contemporary social scientists have pointed out that terms like "race" and "ethnicity" do not describe discrete or even meaningful categories; there is much fluidity and complexity in these concepts. Instead of being in one or another ethnic group, there is a large spectrum of possible ethnic identities. Ethnicity today is seen more as a system of relationships. In the words of one historian, "ethnicity, or ethnic belonging, is not something that one is but something that one does."[10] The rock star Cui Jian, a native of North China, is ethnically Korean by birth; but given his role as a national, even international, star, his natal Korean ethnicity is not "something [that he] does."

And yet, the traditional Chinese state and the Han Chinese elite continued to see the Other as a noun, not as a verb in process; and as a noun, Others were to be classified and then controlled as the "barbarians" they were until they could be assimilated into Han Chinese culture. From early in Chinese history, ethnicity—based more on language, customs, and culture than on race—was a rationale for keeping the ethnic Other separate. It is important in this regard to realize that the category of Han Chinese itself was not homogeneous. Some Han Chinese, like the Hakka, who centuries earlier had migrated from the North into central and southern areas; the Hui, who were Muslim Chinese; and people from Subei, the northern part of Jiangsu province, were treated with suspicion and contempt.

SPATIAL IDENTITIES: NATIVE PLACE

A person's native place was crucial to his or her identity. It was generally the site where a person's ancestors were buried and where eventually he or she would be interred as well. It provided a "home," a retreat from life beyond: people returned to mourn for parents, to renew old ties, between career positions, and at stressful and traumatic periods of life. Native place was and is the indispensable information provided in newspaper accounts and biographies in local histories and yearbooks. It is one of the first things a Chinese asks about when meeting someone else.

As we have seen, shared native place is one of the most important bases for connections and, by extension, networks. In turn, native place connections and networks played crucial roles in politics, culture, and the economy. In the economy, certain native places became associated with particular trades and professions and sent men out, in some cases, around the country to carry on their activities. In the late empire, merchant bankers from Shanxi province, for example, dominated the world of banking, becoming as it were bankers for the central government. The city of Shaoxing in Zhejiang province became known as a supplier of lower officials and clerks who staffed many government offices and the central government boards. Merchants from the city of Ningbo, also in Zhejiang province, came to dominate the economic and social life of the city of Shanghai.

Even in the realms of the non-elite and non-rich, native place came to be connected with particular roles. In the central Zhejiang river port of Quzhou, where docks stretched almost 2 miles along the bank, men from two relatively nearby counties in Zhejiang and one in neighboring Jiangxi province dominated stevedoring. In the city of Shanghai, people from northern Jiangsu (Subei) provided the bulk of unskilled labor.

When elites and non-elites alike traveled to or "sojourned" away from their native places in other cities or ports, they could often depend on "native place associations" there as a home away from home to provide lodging, meals, advice, and a general helping hand. When a person sojourned or traveled, he or she became the Other in relation to the native populace. The native place associations in a sense softened that Other status; they provided assistance both to anyone from the native place passing through and to sojourners, such as merchants, who lived semi-permanently in their non-native place. Native place associations could serve people from whole provinces, or they could serve a particular city or county or prefecture. Take as an example the river city of Quzhou, where in the early twentieth century sojourning outsiders dominated the commercial population—bankers, merchants, stevedores, freight brokers, commission agents, and warehousemen. Altogether there were sixteen native place associations in the county; in the city itself there were six, four of them by the 1930s nearing the end of their second century of existence: two provincial associations, Jiangxi (established in 1746) and Fujian (1801); one two-prefecture association, Ningbo and Shaoxing (1752); and one prefectural association, Huizhou (1756).

Native place identities were also part and parcel of politics. Networks in which native place was often a critical component flourished in political decision making and action. In the fluid world of politics where connections were the name of the game, networks, especially if they were tightly cohesive, tended to become factions or cliques. When Chiang Kai-shek, who hailed from the province of Zhejiang, assumed control of the country in 1928, men from Zhejiang appeared in many positions of importance. Political factions in Chiang's Nationalist Party—the CC clique and the Western Hills faction—were based in large part on native place. The Guangxi clique was a military faction from that southern province that became a potent political force and a frequent antagonist of Chiang Kai-shek. Other considerations—kinship, friendship, personality, ideology, and context—certainly played important roles in politics, but native place was a basic building block.

Cultural developments were also often linked to locality and the native places of those instrumental in these developments. Studies, for example, have shown that the "evidential research" scholarship that marked Confucianism in the seventeenth and eighteenth centuries was centered in the Lower Yangzi (Jiangnan) region. Various subsets of this "school," like the Zhedong (eastern Zhejiang) school, developed in different geographical subregions.[11]

SPATIAL IDENTITIES: VILLAGE AND MARKETING COMMUNITIES

Before the late 1960s, social scientists studying China generally considered the village to be the basic geographical unit in Chinese society. In the countryside, the usual housing pattern was the village; only in Sichuan province did one find the pattern of the solitary farm home sited on the farm itself. Farmers then generally lived together in villages and went out to farm their lands, which were typically divided among several small plots not at all contiguous with each other. Villages ranged in size from a few households to several thousand, with a common range between perhaps 200 and 400 inhabitants. Because they were generally quite small and because of the relatively large population in most areas, villages tended to be clustered fairly closely. Nevertheless, in his study of rural China in the first half of the twentieth century, sociologist Fei Xiaotong painted a picture of villager isolation. Village life centered on the village; there was not much interaction with other villages nearby. Villagers did not tend to travel, and there was little contact with the world beyond the village confines. The focus of life was the village and the life and affairs of villagers. It was, in Fei's words, "a society without strangers,"[12] a social and cultural world that would perhaps predispose its inhabitants to see what was at hand as the norm, and as good, and consequently to be fearful and distrustful of the Other. When, especially in villages in the South, villagers were all members of the same lineage or clan, the tightness and closedness of the village to outsiders might tend to be even stronger. If one were to ask a villager with this sort of life about his or her spatial identity, he or she would almost certainly have responded with the name of the village.

But many scholars today believe that the most basic geographic unit shaping the horizons of the Chinese villager was what has been called a "marketing community." If this is the case, then, contrary to the views of Fei, the world of the villager did extend beyond the village. A market town served a marketing community composed roughly of six to forty villages whose population was too small to support a market; further, since many traditional village families were almost self-sufficient, even the market town did not have to maintain a market all the time. Part of a hierarchy of market towns stretching from large city all the way down, the lowest-level marketing town, often called the "standard market," tended to hold its market on mornings according to certain patterns. Traditional China did not use a seven-day week, having instead a basic time frame of ten days. A market town thus might open its market on days one, four, and seven of the ten-day cycle; or on days two, five, and eight; or on days three, six, and nine.

Imagine Li Village on the first cycle, Wang Lane on the second, and Lin Lake on the third. On the first day of the cycle, Mr. Sun, who lived in a small village 2 miles away from Li Village, would walk there early in the morning. Traveling merchants would have already arranged their goods in stalls along streets or on the temple grounds. Others selling services—doctors, dentists, barbers, fortunetellers—would set up booths. Local restaurants, teahouses, and taverns would be open for the villagers who came to buy and in some cases to sell goods. On the next day, Mr. Xiao, whose village was oriented to Wang Lane, would do his marketing, and the following day Mr. Jiang, whose village was oriented to Lin Lake, would follow suit. Because of the rather close clustering of villages in populated areas, even the village farthest from the market town was probably only 3 miles away.

All three villages would be a part of the larger intermediate marketing community, say, of Greenfield. As an intermediate marketing town, Greenfield would have a larger population, and the goods at its market would include more specialized and harder-to-get products. Whereas the standard market generally served only retailing functions, the intermediate market town served both wholesaling functions for the standard market traveling merchants and retailing functions for its own merchants' businesses. The other higher-level marketing centers shared these wholesaling-retailing functions. If Sun, Xiao, and Jiang were unable to find what they needed at the standard market, they could travel to the intermediate market or make arrangements with an itinerant merchant to bring the item from the intermediate market on the next standard market day.

Apart from its obvious commercial and economic significance, the marketing community provided the general social and cultural horizons for the farmers in its villages. It is likely that Sun, Xiao, and Jiang did not go beyond the standard marketing community many times in their lives. When they went to the market, not only did they buy and sell, but they also likely conversed with friends and acquaintances along the streets or in teahouses. They caught up on the news from neighboring villages, asking questions about spreading rumors from other villages and passing on the latest gossip from their own. They talked about the weather, political news, and new farming techniques. In the marketing community, the same dialect was spoken and village inhabitants generally shared the same culture. It is not, of course, that people never ventured beyond their marketing community, but for many it defined their economic, social, and cultural world.

SPATIAL IDENTITIES: MACROREGIONS AND PROVINCES

Provinces were the largest political and administrative units in the Chinese system, composed (moving down the administrative ladder) of prefectures, counties, and townships. (Provinces were roughly the size of states in the United States, and Chinese counties and townships were roughly equivalent to their U.S. counterparts.) In the Qing (1644–1912), there were eighteen provinces within (i.e., south of) the Great Wall, a sporadic 2,000-mile structure built at various times in the Chinese past to try to keep the Other out. Provincial boundaries had largely been set in Ming times (1368–1644); many of their names reflected their geographical situation (e.g., Hubei [north of the lake] and Hunan [south of the lake], Shandong [east of the mountains] and Shanxi [west of the mountains]). Provinces were the largest native place to which Chinese could claim residence, and thus they were still a source of connections—even though much weaker than connections formed in the village, town, county, or prefecture. As such, they were an important part of the constellation of attributes making up the Chinese identity.

In the 1970s, anthropologist G. William Skinner, whose earlier work had focused on the standard marketing community, argued that Chinese economic, social, cultural, and perhaps political history might be better understood in terms of the history of natural economic regions than in terms of artificial political units (provinces, prefectures, and counties). Skinner described a number of "macroregions," many of them structured around the basin(s) or valley(s) of a river or of several rivers and often surrounded by mountains. The scope and boundaries of these macroregions have little relationship with provinces; in fact, some provinces are divided into different macroregions (on the second map, see the province of Zhejiang, for example). Skinner argued that these large natural regions were more coherent systems, where transportation and communication links as well as social and political networks were denser than those between macroregions or within provincial borders drawn by humans, often with political purposes in mind. Thus, to understand Chinese historical trends and developments more systematically and therefore more realistically, a student should look at the past of macroregions.

For purposes of analysis, macroregions have been divided into "cores"—areas of denser population, greater commercial activity, and higher degrees of urbanization and economic development—and "peripheries"—areas of sparser population, less commercial activity, and lower levels of urbanization and economic development. The nature of life in the cores and peripheries of each macroregion varied considerably and certainly affected how resident Chinese elites at least saw themselves and their world.

A brief survey of the nature of each macroregion will set the stage for our study of the key patterns and trends of Chinese history. I discuss them in no particular order, though I start with North China, which held the capital city for almost the entire time; then I move to the south along the coast and into the interior; the survey ends with areas around the periphery. As you read the description of each region, try to imagine the key or pressing issues of life in that area and how they may have given a person's identity a particular flavor. Note such things as the natural environment, the topography, the crops, and the growing season. How easy would it have been to make a living? Note the social realities—the existence or nonexistence of kinship groups (lineages) and whether there was ethnic homogeneity or diversity. Note the orientation of the region: to the sea, to the interior, to an important river, to a city. The purpose of this section, other than to set the context for our study, is to underscore in your mind from the beginning that there are many Chinas, and that to understand China of the past and of the present, we must begin to see it in its fascinating diversity. Though many of these characteristics endure to the present, the presentation uses the past tense.

The original description of macroregions analyzed the territory within China proper (China south of the Great Wall). Areas around the periphery—Taiwan, Manchuria, Xinjiang, Tibet, and Mongolia—are today a part of China or have special relationships with China. This survey of regions will conclude with them, though I make no attempt to analyze any macroregional properties such as cores and peripheries.

North China

In part because it contained Beijing, the capital city throughout most of the late imperial and modern periods, the North China region, bordered on the north by Manchuria and Mongolia, played a central role in China's history. Its most prominent topographical feature was its large plain constituting large parts of three provinces—Zhili (now called Hebei), Shandong, and Henan—bordered by mountains on three sides and low-lying swampy land to the south. Its most prominent natural waterway was the Yellow River. Traditionally this river has been called "China's sorrow" because of its propensity to flood. Early in its journey to the sea, it traversed loess lands, where it picked up huge amounts of silt. East of Xi'an, after it made its greater than right angle turn toward the sea, the gradient of the riverbed became very slight, dropping less than a foot per mile as it flowed the 500 miles to the sea. Thus, the velocity of the water dropped precipitously, and with it immense quantities of silt, something in the order of 100 million tons a day, sank to the riverbed. Because of this continual buildup of sediment, the river flowed between 10 and 40 feet above the floodplain; therefore, dike building and repair to prevent flooding at times of heavy rains required constant vigilance. Inevitably, at times of state economic weakness, political crisis, or administrative corruption, the dikes were not adequately maintained. The price was disastrous floods, destroying people and property and devastating cropland. Like the Yellow River, most other rivers and streams in this region were not navigable. The most important north–south waterway was the human-constructed Grand Canal, which ran from the South-Central city of Hangzhou to near Beijing.

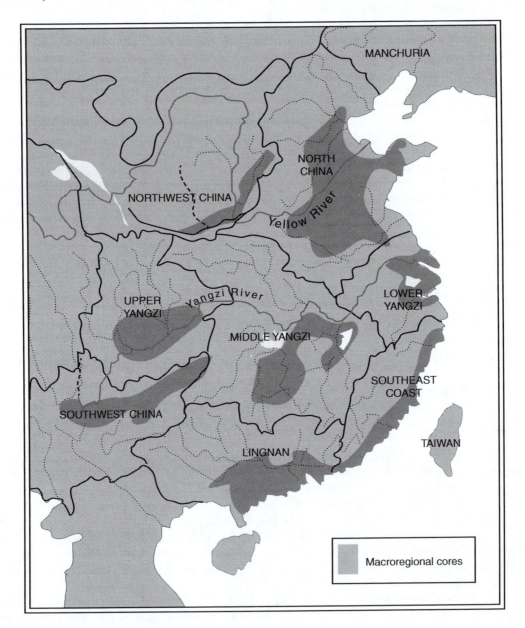

MAP 1.1   Late Imperial China, Its Macroregions and Their Cores.

Because of the general absence of abundant water resources, farmers depended on rain for the key crops—wheat, barley, millet, and sorghum. Draft animals were horses, mules, and even camels. The settlement pattern was in small clustered villages. Differences in dialects across the region were small. Compared to other regions, subethnic differences were minor, and there was consequently less violence. As might be expected in relatively consistently flat terrain, there was considerable mobility in the population. Because of the presence of the country's capital and the trade on the Grand

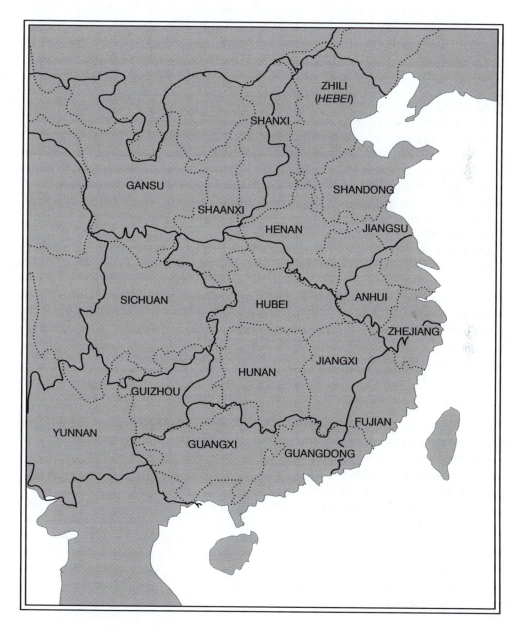

MAP 1.2 Macroregions in Relation to Provinces.

Canal and between the North China region and the steppe to the north, there were many sojourning merchants. The region had many native place associations from around the country.

Lower Yangzi

Mostly flat plains, the Lower Yangzi had in abundance what the North China region did not: sufficient water resources for irrigation and for easy transportation. Composed of southern Jiangsu, northern Zhejiang, and southern Anhui, it was, in the late imperial and modern periods, the region with the highest level of urbanization and the densest population. The Yangzi River, which for this area did not constitute the same kind of flood threat as the Yellow River, produced the delta that has made the region one of China's most significant rice baskets. It produced not only great quantities of rice but also tea, silk, and wine, which were sent to markets across much of the country. A measure of its economic centrality was that in the Qing dynasty over a quarter of the land tax that was paid to the government came from this region. Its economic importance was more than agricultural and commercial, for it was an important industrial base since the Ming and Qing dynasties, when silk and cotton textile mills flourished.

The region's generally high level of wealth allowed more families here than perhaps in other regions to set aside and use resources to help talented young men study for the famous civil service examinations; if they passed, they might rise to become officials in the Chinese governmental bureaucracy (see Chapter 2). Education and the scholarly tradition were therefore emphasized. It is then perhaps not surprising that six of the nine prefectures in the whole country producing the largest number of PhD-equivalent degrees (*jinshi*) were in this region.

Villages, generally larger than in North China, were often clustered along canals and waterways. Many villages were made up of a single lineage. Although regional lineages published more genealogies than other regions, lineage roles here seemed "softer-edged" than in regions to the south, where lineage power frequently led to violence. There were small ethnic groups, islands in the sea of Han Chinese in this region, but they did not play a major social role. Because of the trade and the general wealth of the region, merchant sojourners were abundant. A very large number of native place associations set up alongside restaurants, teashops, taverns, and gardens helped make the style of life, especially in cities, sophisticated and eminently livable.

Southeast Coast

The Southeast Coast was a mountainous region composed of the valleys of several rivers. It included the province of Fujian, southern Zhejiang, and eastern Guangdong. It had several hallmarks. Although two crops of rice could be grown in areas along the coast, its most famous product was tea. The region's many mountains had necessitated intensive use of the land. Tea was often produced on mountain and hillside terraces, with villages clustered in opportune sites.

Another hallmark was the involvement of the region in high-volume trade, both with other regions along the coast and especially with overseas ports. Chinese who ventured abroad, whether in late traditional or modern times, to Southeast Asia or to Chinatowns in the United States and Europe generally came from this region or from that of Lingnan to its south. The advanced degree of trade helped foster the relatively high degree of urbanization in the Southeast Coast core; overall, there was also a high population density.

The society here was much more disparate and violent than in North China or the Lower Yangzi. There was a larger number of ethnic groups; though some were partially assimilated, such groups tended to separate themselves and maintain a coherence that could intimidate and perhaps fend off opponents. The most serious troubles often involved Hakkas, Han Chinese who, nevertheless, maintained their own identities through their occupations, customs, language, and dress. They clashed with other Han Chinese and ethnic minorities. Another stimulus of social unrest was the power and unruliness of lineage groups, whose feuds over such things as property boundaries and water rights were notorious throughout the country. In addition, this region was the origin of various blood brotherhoods, such as the Triads, who might function as mutual support groups but could transmute in gang-like fashion to involvement in organized crime. It is little wonder that in such a violence-prone situation, walled villages and even fortresses were not uncommon.

Lingnan

Lingnan was the drainage basin of the East, North, and West Rivers in the provinces of Guangxi and most of Guangdong. Just as North China was dominated by the capital, Beijing, there was a dominant city in Lingnan as well—Canton (in Chinese, Guangzhou). A city that in the eighteenth and nineteenth centuries became a symbol of overseas trade with the West, Canton underscored the importance of overseas trade for the region. As indicated above, Lingnan and the Southeast Coast were the regions most oriented to the sea and those beyond the sea; Lingnan joined the Southeast Coast in contributing the largest number of Chinese from all the regions to settle abroad.

Its mild subtropical–tropical climate joined with rich alluvial soils in the Pearl River delta to produce flourishing crops and bountiful harvests; rice, for example, could be triple-cropped. Agriculture in the interior mountains and their river valleys was, however, markedly poorer. The contrasts between production and lifestyles in the two areas were stark.

As on the Southeast Coast, society in Lingnan was diverse and often rancorous. In addition to the fact that people in the region spoke six major dialects of Chinese, there was a heterogeneous population of Han Chinese, Zhuang, Yao, Tanka, Miao, Hakka, and Muslim. As in the Southeast Coast, Hakkas often found themselves in disputes with the locals. Although single-lineage villages in Lingnan were as common as in much of Southern China, there were also single-ethnicity villages. Lineages were strong social forces and often based their power on estates owned by the lineage as a type of corporation. So strong was the emphasis upon kinship that in this region so-called clans were organized to join all persons having the same surname on the basis that, ultimately, they shared the same ancestor.

Northwest China

This corridor for trade with Central Asia and the upper valley of the Yellow River was separated from the rest of China by mountains to the east and south. Composed of Gansu, Shaanxi, and western Shanxi provinces, this region, semiarid in nature, was often the site of severe drought. With few navigable waterways, transport was difficult and costs were high.

Population density was one of the lowest in China. Even so, diverse ethnicities and religions, as well as dialects, gave rise to considerable internal disunity. Han Chinese, Hui (Han Chinese Muslims), Mongols, and Tibetans intermingled, often with notable antagonisms. The Han Chinese population was heaviest in cities and river valleys. Muslims comprised over a third of the population in Gansu province by the end of the nineteenth century. Many Muslims had outwardly assimilated into Han Chinese culture, choosing Chinese names and adopting Chinese speech and habits of dress, but they retained their own neighborhoods, their religious leaders, and their restriction on eating pork.

On the whole, life was hard here. In traditional times, Han Chinese and Muslims often lived in caves carved into the loess hillsides, whereas Tibetans and Mongols made their homes in tents. In this region, lineages were not strong. As a result in part of the bleak economic situation, this region did not produce large numbers of scholars.

Middle Yangzi

In contrast to the aridity of Northwest China, the Middle Yangzi was focused on water. The region, including parts of no fewer than nine provinces, derived its identity from the over 500 miles of the Yangzi River that flowed through it and from the Yangzi's four major tributaries. Those tributaries and the mountains that border them formed clearly defined subregions, yet all were oriented to the Yangzi. Water was a focus in three ways. Its abundance meant irrigated paddies, in contrast to the dryland farming of North and Northwest China. On the downside, it often experienced serious flooding; severe floods in 1998, 2010, and 2016 for example, left many dead and many more homeless. Finally, the Yangzi, cutting west to east across central China, and its tributaries, running north and south, were important arteries of trade. Merchant groups involved in flourishing trade dominated the political, social, and cultural life of many riverine cities. In late imperial times, because of the Middle Yangzi's commercial importance, the role of the government was perhaps less than in other regions.

Ethnic conflict marked the region. Before the Han Chinese migrated into the area in the third and fourth centuries, non-Chinese inhabited it. These immigrants pushed the non-Chinese up into the mountains during their settlement of the area. Like the relationship between settlers and Native Americans in the American West, the relations between the Han and non-Han remained uneasy, with sporadic outbreaks of violence. The situation was exacerbated by the presence of large numbers of Hakkas in the South who often feuded with others.

Upper Yangzi

Known as "heaven's storehouse" because of its favorable climate and rich productive farmland, the Chengdu basin was the core of the Upper Yangzi region. In this area, which included the eastern two-thirds of Sichuan province and contiguous mountains in Gansu to the north and Yunnan and Guizhou to the south, the chief products were agricultural—rice, wheat, potatoes, maize, and timber products. Yet this region on the periphery of the Chinese state was tied to other, more central regions through trade on the Yangzi. The river indeed served as the lifeline to the province: the only natural entrances into this mountain-contained region were the Yangzi River gorges and a pass to the northeast.

The population was diverse—a large Muslim population, Tibetan tribes living in the west, sojourning merchants, and other ethnic groups. Yet hostilities were a less important feature than in other regions, and the cities were noteworthy for lack of animosity among their ethnic groups. Following massive depopulation in bloody early-seventeenth-century unrest and rebellion, this region was one of the least urbanized in late imperial times.

Southwest China

Composed mostly of the provinces of Yunnan and Guizhou with a small portion of southern Sichuan, Southwest China was peripheral in many ways. Its rivers were mostly unnavigable, making travel and transportation difficult and expensive. Population settlements were small. The region was not well incorporated into the Chinese cultural mainstream; indeed, there was more fundamental cultural diversity than in any other region. Tribal peoples made up roughly half of the population in late traditional times; they were joined by a host of ethnic and subethnic groups.

The most important nonagricultural occupation was mining deposits of copper, silver, zinc, lead, cinnabar, coal, and iron. This was a lure to Han Chinese from outside the region. Male sojourners, coming into the area to make their fortune, dominated the Han Chinese population. For the indigenous population, these immigrants were a destabilizing force in the local economy and society; conflicts between them and the locals were prevalent and frequently bloody.

Taiwan

The island of Taiwan, 90 miles from the mainland, was the eastern frontier of the Southeast Coast. Chinese, mainly from Fujian province across the strait, had begun to migrate to the island in the sixteenth century; many of the first immigrants were sojourning men. The island was not brought firmly under Chinese government control until 1683, the year the Manchus defeated the Ming loyalists who had fled there in the 1640s. In that year, there were approximately 100,000 aboriginal peoples of Malayo-Polynesian stock from over a dozen ethnolinguistic groups who were mostly hunters but who also cultivated rice and millet; there were also approximately the same number of Han Chinese immigrants. By the end of the eighteenth century, the number of Han Chinese had reached about a million, including large numbers of Hakkas. As in the Middle Yangzi area, the Han Chinese settlement pushed the aboriginal groups into the mountains of the central and eastern parts of the island, where they remain to the present. The presence of Han Chinese, Hakkas, and aborigines created the same combustible ethnic mix apparent in such other regions as the Southeast Coast and Lingnan.

As more settlers came from the mainland, they transformed the wild grasslands of the western part of the island into the richly productive coastal plain that came to resemble the rice paddy terrain of Southeast China. Taiwan would remain under the firm control of the Manchu government until it was taken as a war trophy by Japan in 1895.

Manchuria

Like the frontier of Taiwan in late imperial China, Manchuria, the homeland of the Manchus, remained largely a frontier until the twentieth century. A region of rich soil and important natural resources—minerals, timber, and water—Manchuria was off limits to Chinese immigration from 1668 on. The Manchus, in their concern over maintaining their identity, restricted Chinese migration in order to preserve the area as their haven.

The fertile core of the region in the south was the valley of the Liao River, which entered the Bo Hai west of the Liaodong peninsula, less than 70 miles from the Shandong Peninsula. In other words, this area was easily accessible to Chinese merchants, who, despite the closed-off political status of the region, were able to link it commercially to other regions of China. Its bordering on Korea made it strategically important to the Chinese regime, as was the more remote northern area of Heilongjiang that bordered on Russia.

Xinjiang

Yet another frontier area was China's far west, known in traditional times as the "Western regions."[13] Though "far west" in China's perspective, it was "not a remote, isolated region, but the crossroads of the Eurasian continent." Thus, when it was won militarily by troops under the Qianlong emperor in 1759, the conquest, in the words of one historian, actually constituted "a world historical event."[14] This immense area, three times the size of France, was composed of two large basins that essentially were deserts; they were separated by the rugged Tianshan Mountains. The northern basin was called Zungharia; successful farming occurred only in mountain river valleys and at the base of the mountains. The southern basin, called most often the Tarim Basin and sometimes Chinese Turkestan, has been called "one of the most forbidding places on earth" (see map, Chapter 22). The Taklamakan Desert at the basin's center has an average annual rainfall of less than two-thirds of an inch and towering sand dunes ranging from over 300 to 1,000 feet. Yet where irrigation is possible near the mountains, agriculture has been productive. Two main passes through the Tianshan mountains link the two basins. The most agriculturally productive part of Xinjiang was the so-called Eastern March between Urumchi, which became the region's main economic center, and Suzhou (today named Jiuquan). There, sometimes using underground aqueducts for irrigation, farmers produced cotton, melons, grapes, and other fruit.

The mostly Muslim population of Xinjiang consisted predominantly of Turkic-speaking Uighurs (pronounced "we-gur"). Although Xinjiang had held most of the famous oases along the old silk route, it was not until after the 1759 conquest that Chinese merchants became actively involved in what developed as thriving commercial activity. After the Qing made Xinjiang a province in 1884, Chinese immigration increased substantially. At the establishment of the People's Republic in 1949, only 5.5 percent of Xinjiang's population were Han Chinese; by 1970 that proportion had skyrocketed to 40 percent. During that period, the Tarim Basin became the main site for China's nuclear weapons testing.

Inner Mongolia

Until the twentieth century, both Outer and Inner Mongolia fell within the Chinese sphere. By 1924, Outer Mongolia was independent but within the sphere of the Soviet Union. Inner Mongolia is now the third largest Chinese province (technically an "autonomous region"). Located south of the Gobi Desert and north of the Great Wall, it has been described as "flat, featureless plains," immense grasslands with some deserts in the eastern sector (where the handful of cities and towns are located), and large deserts in the west. Life is harsh: eight months of the year see a cold, often brutal winter; winds are characteristically strong, creating a yellow haze with clouds of dust; and herdsmen have to move frequently to find the short grass to feed their flocks. These animals, in turn, provide mutton, dairy products, and fuel (in the absence of wood, animal dung must be used instead). Indeed, it is said that common greetings are "Is the pasturage with you rich and abundant?" and "Has rain fallen in your neighborhood?" It is ultimately the presence of water that makes life possible, but the area sees only 8 to 12 inches of rain per year.

The ecological boundary between pastoral Mongolia and agricultural China is not specifically fixed; thus, throughout Chinese history, this "inner Asian" zone has often served as a meeting place between the two cultures. However, the climate and generally poor soil quality of Mongolia militated against its deep penetration by Chinese farmers. Inner Mongolia is sparsely populated, with only about 2.2 people per square kilometer. Yet it is composed of many ethnic groups, including Mongolian, Daur, Orogen, Ewenki, Hui, Han, Korean, and Manchu. Its people practice the Tibetan Buddhism known as Lamaism.

Tibet

Although linked to China since the eighteenth century, Tibet is distant geographically and culturally from Han China. Lhasa, its capital city, is some 800 miles due west of Chengdu, the capital of the western province of Sichuan. As a measure of Tibet's general isolation and the difficulty of transportation, its first railroad was not operational until July 2006; because of the thin air at high altitudes, trains had to produce a flow of enriched air of 40 percent oxygen and provide individual oxygen nozzles. Sandwiched between the Kunlun Mountains on the north and the Himalayas on the south, the Tibetan plateau is largely a forbidding frozen desert. The northern sector is lower in elevation and less rugged but arid. Most of the population of this autonomous region lives in the lower valleys in the south around Lhasa, but even these "lower" valleys are at an elevation of 10,000 feet.

Whereas the Mongols practice horizontal nomadism, it is said that the Tibetans, who depend on their herds of goats and yaks, engage in vertical nomadism, moving up and down mountains to seek the alpine grasses for their flocks. Tibetan society is divided into Tibetan and non-Tibetan tribes and family groups; there are clearly understood boundaries dividing these groups territorially. As part of the religion of Lamaism, headed by the Dalai Lama, one son per family is required to enter a monastery. Historically, these lamaseries became major centers of wealth and important nodes on trade routes.

The cultural and regional stage has now been set for historical action.

Notes

1 Nicholas D. Kristof, "China: The End of the Golden Road," *New York Times Magazine* (December 1, 1991). https://timesmachine.nytimes.com/timesmachine/1991/12/01/062791.html
2 William James Hall, *Tseng Kuo-fan and the Taiping Rebellion* (New York: Paragon Book Re-print Corp., 1964), pp. 417–19.
3 Ibid., pp. 164, 209, 335–6.
4 Ibid., pp. 146, 200, 344.
5 Fox Butterfield, *China: Alive in a Bitter Sea* (New York: Times Books, 1982), pp. 74–5, cited in Ambrose Yeo-chi King, "Kuan-hsi and Network Building," *Daedalus* 120, no. 2 (Spring 1991): 64.
6 R. Keith Schoppa, *Xiang Lake—Nine Centuries of Chinese Life* (New Haven, CT: Yale University Press, 1989), pp. 46–54.
7 Frederic Wakeman, Jr., *The Fall of Imperial China* (New York: Free Press, 1975), p. 173.
8 Fei Xiaotong, *From the Soil: The Foundations of Chinese Society* (Berkeley, CA: University of California Press, 1992), pp. 78–9.
9 Ibid., p, 79.
10 Robert E. Gamer, ed., *Understanding Contemporary China* (Boulder, CO: Lynne Rienner, 1999), p. 231.
11 Benjamin Elman, *From Philosophy to Philology: Intellectual and Social Aspects of Change in Late Imperial China* (Cambridge, MA: Harvard University Press, 1984), pp. 91, 233.
12 Fei, p. 41.
13 This description is based upon James A. Millward, *Beyond the Pass* (Stanford, CA: Stanford University Press, 1998), pp. 20–5.
14 Peter Perdue, *China Marches West: The Qing Conquest of Central Eurasia* (Cambridge, MA: Harvard University Press, 2005), p. 9.

Suggestions for Further Reading

Brownell, Susan, and Jeffrey Wasserstrom, eds. *Chinese Femininities, Chinese Masculinities: A Reader* (Berkeley, CA: University of California Press, 2002). An anthology dealing with issues of gender, sexuality, and ethnicity from the late eighteenth century to the present.

Fei Xiaotong. *From the Soil, The Foundations of Chinese Society,* trans. Gary G. Hamilton and Wang Zheng (Berkeley, CA: University of California Press, 1992). This must-read 1947 work by China's most famous sociologist is key in understanding traditional Chinese culture.

Kristoff, Nicholas, and Sheryl Wudunn. *China Wakes* (New York: Random House, 1994). This is a well-written description of actions and attitudes of Chinese under the reforms.

Skinner, G. William, ed. *The City in Late Imperial China* (Stanford, CA: Stanford University Press, 1977). All of the essays in this lengthy book are worth reading, but the highlights are Skinner's own essays ("Regional Urbanization in Nineteenth-Century China" and "Cities and the Hierarchy of Local Systems") that set forth his macroregional thesis.

Williams, Dee M. *Beyond Great Walls: Environment, Identity, and Development on the Chinese Grasslands of Inner Mongolia* (Stanford, CA: Stanford University Press, 2002). This anthropological study of a village explores contemporary Mongolian identity vis-à-vis the Chinese state and in the midst of drastic environmental changes.

2

Chinese, Manchus, and Others

From China's earliest history there had been a continual *pas de deux* between Chinese within the Great Wall and those outside, the peoples of the steppe—Mongols, Turks, Jurchens, and Manchus. In certain periods the steppe dwellers pursued an aggressive China policy, initiating raids and outright invasions. In the tenth century C.E., a more active pattern of outsider involvement began, with various ethnic groups from outside the Wall taking and holding parts of North China. Then in the late thirteenth century all of China fell into the hands of the great Mongol conquerors Genghis and Kublai Khan. Although the Mongols controlled China for less than a century, throughout the subsequent Han Chinese Ming dynasty (1368–1644), Mongols from the North and West sporadically continued to threaten the Chinese political order. When outsiders from northeast of the Ming frontier took power in China in 1644 and established the Qing dynasty, it was therefore not the first time that non-Chinese had donned imperial yellow court clothing. Traditional interpretations of the conquest and its aftermath was that it was a project of ethnic Manchus, well-established in their ethnicity but whose rule was successful because they became Sinified, thoroughly embedded in Han Chinese culture, traditions and practices. Recent scholarship, incorporating new understandings of the concept of ethnicity, has presented views that challenge the older interpretation of Sinification and are much less Manchu-centered.

Contemporary anthropologists and historians do not tend to see ethnic identity "as an objective, static, 'primordial' *condition*," or as "immutable givens." Rather, an ethnic group came to be defined by the 1980s as "a group conscious of its own solidarity,"[1] a consensus resulting from dynamic *processes* over time, where the group constructs its identity through social and cultural transactions, relationships, and contingencies, thereby negotiating its own cultural identities. The newer interpretation sees many diverse tribes in the region, governed by tribal chieftains who led the way in using ethnic institutions of genealogical lines, language, religion, and cultural traditions to identify themselves vis-à-vis "others." Indeed, recent revisionist views have suggested that the Manchus did not exist *as Manchus* before the conquest. Rather, a powerful clan, the Aisin Gioro, from among the Jurchen tribes rose to create a multi-ethnic military organization specifically for the conquest of the Ming.

In the late sixteenth and early seventeenth centuries, two exceptionally able leaders emerged from the Aisin Gioro. Nurhaci (1559–1626) and his son Hong Taiji (1592–1643) put in place the organizational framework—the banner system—that made possible the military seizure of China.

Specifically, these rulers assigned Jurchen (among them, Manchus), Mongol, and even Han Chinese warriors to various "banners," groups identified by particular colored flags that would serve as units both for military and civilian bureaucratic mobilization. It is important to note that despite ethnic identities (for the Jurchens: shared descent and territory, similar clothing, food, hairstyles, family rituals, and austere lifestyles), decisions to place anyone from one ethnic group into a banner were often politically based: some Mongols, for example, were placed into Manchu banners. Having a common language was crucial as the foundation of ethnic identity; the Manchus did not have one. In 1599 Nurhaci commissioned the drawing up of a Manchu alphabet with letters ultimately based on the Mongolian alphabet with phonetics based on Jurchen. Scholars have suggested that by 1635 the Jurchens had the look of an ethnic group; but that "Manchu identity ... [was] created largely after the conquest itself."[2] When the conquest came, the invading banners army was a multi-ethnic force not simply a Manchu army.

This growing and organized force from outside the Wall emerged at the same time as a Ming dynasty tailspin, with all the ills traditionally associated with a dying regime: governmental inertia and corruption, factionalism, the exercise of arrogant power by imperial eunuchs (the keepers of the harem), the depletion of the national treasury, and rebellion. When one of the rebels succeeded in taking the capital in the spring of 1644 and the last Ming emperor dramatically hanged himself on a hill immediately north of the Forbidden City, it seemed as though another Han Chinese dynasty would emerge. But then the banner army charged into China through the pass between the Great Wall and the sea, sweeping before them the would-be emperor rebel and seizing the Dragon Throne for themselves. By 1683, the minority Manchus had become masters of the majority Han Chinese (who outnumbered them by about one hundred to one) and the realm's various ethnic minorities. Their full ethnic Manchuness was realized only during their 268-year reign.

PATTERNS IN THE EARLY QING

The Manchus had won the kingdom, as the cliché put it, "on horseback." But it took much more to establish long-term successful rule: at the heart of doing so was the tricky and precarious balancing act of adopting sufficient aspects of Chinese cultural identity to be acceptable to the Chinese majority while maintaining enough distance to develop and preserve their own cultural legacy. At the heart of a person's identity are the cultural values that he or she lives by. The Aisin Gioro were clan-based peoples who stressed martial values based on horsemanship and archery—a stark contrast to Chinese society, which stressed civilian values based on skills of the writing brush. The first Manchu leaders were "gripped with this anxiety [:] ... that hereafter our sons and grandsons will forget the old regulations and do away with horseback riding and archery in order to copy Han customs."[3] From the beginning, the fear of the diminution of native identity was strong. But if the fear was strong, so, too, was the knowledge that they could not rule China without the assistance of the Chinese.

The dynasty began (as it would end) with a minor king whose power was wielded by a regent. When the Shunzhi emperor took direct control at age thirteen in 1651, he was surrounded by bitterly feuding factions of Manchu princes. Yet his short reign (he died of smallpox at age twenty-three) was notable for several reasons. Like his regent before him, he openly sought out the suggestions and thinking of Chinese advisors. He also cultivated an ongoing dialogue with the Jesuits, who had been at the court since the late Ming. He developed a deep friendship with the German head of the Jesuit mission, Adam Schall von Bell, with whom the young emperor discussed astronomy, philosophy, and religion. On his deathbed, the emperor was, reportedly,

FIGURE 2.1 A Buddhist pagoda in southern China provides the backdrop for a group of Manchu bannermen. Their military training emphasized archery and horsemanship.
Source: Wellcome Collection.

tortured by the identity question: had he listened too much to Chinese advisors and the Jesuits, thereby diminishing his own ethnic identity?

His most important contribution to the dynasty's success was naming his third son to be his heir apparent. Though a minor when named (a situation that necessitated another regent—this one, quite power hungry), this emperor became probably the greatest of the dynasty and perhaps in all of imperial China, the Kangxi emperor (1661–1722). He too grappled with the dilemma of identity. He was a role model in holding to the Manchu traditional identity by preserving the martial vigor and skills that had made the conquest possible. He insisted that the military ethos be preserved symbolically through hunting expeditions he led north of the Wall throughout his reign, and he championed mounted archery, shooting contests with guns, and the pleasures of vigorous exercise. He saw the hunt as "training for war, a test of discipline and organization."[4] In his war mode, he masterminded the final military campaigns that ended the Ming resistance. He personally led military campaigns against Mongol forces in the mid-1690s. He commanded forces moving into Tibet in 1720 to install the Seventh Dalai Lama, whom the Kangxi emperor had sponsored.

But he also reached out to the Chinese, many of whom were embittered by Manchu terror and brutality during the conquest. The Qing had offered triennial *jinshi* examinations (the highest-level examinations) since 1646, with special examinations sometimes added; but some Chinese scholars boycotted the regular civil service exams. As gesture of his benevolence, the Kangxi emperor offered them a special examination in 1679 as an enticement to join the Manchu regime. At one point in his reign, he declared in an edict that he saw no difference between Manchus and Chinese and their ability to serve the state.

He made it a point of showing his concern for the welfare of the people by visiting areas where flooding had occurred and where dikes were being repaired. He showed his benevolence for the people quite remarkably when, in 1712, he froze land tax assessments, the most important government levy. In many ways he seemed the quintessential "modern" politician. He took six grand tours to the southeast during his reign to show publicly his concern for the people and their problems and to display his prestige and power, in what one historian has called "a form of political theater that drew huge crowds and rendered the social order visible."[5] He took the lead in furthering the state's "civilizing [literally, instructing and transforming] mission," an effort that was nothing less than the moral "ordering of the state."[6] In 1670, the Kangxi emperor issued a list of sixteen moral maxims that were to be read in every community twice a month, following a tradition begun by his father. This key function cast the emperor as teacher-propagandist.

PRESERVING A MANCHU IDENTITY

A key to upholding Manchu martial identity was to maintain the integrity of the banner forces, the vehicles of their military success. After the Manchus defeated the Ming forces, they preserved those defeated enemies as the Army of the Green Standard, a constabulary force assigned to garrisons around the country. Though the 500,000 Green Standard forces were at least double the size of the Manchu banners, the banner forces were positioned more strategically: for example, whereas in the eighteenth century there was only one banner garrison in the commerce-focused Middle Yangzi region, there were many garrisons in the newly conquered Central Asian frontier territory of Xinjiang—where numbers of bannermen were clearly a major factor in China's political control. While civil officials controlled the Green Standard, military governors controlled the banners.

Yet another strategy for maintaining martial values was to set aside Manchuria as a permanent Manchu homeland. That had been the military base from which the conquest proceeded; the territory itself was thus inextricably linked with the source of the Manchus' military prowess. Further, by making Manchuria off limits to the Han Chinese, the leadership may have been saying that even if life among the Han Chinese within the Wall might dull Manchu military ardor, Manchuria would always remain as a place where military values could be revived and rejuvenated.

Once in control in China, the Manchus also continued to maintain and promote their native shamanism, a policy that clearly differentiated them from Chinese ways and the Chinese themselves. A shaman was thought to have had a spiritual death and rebirth and could thus easily pass into the world of the supernatural, where he or she could influence events. Using spirit poles to symbolically connect heaven and earth in order to communicate with clan spirits, Manchus conducted shamanic state rituals, processions, and dances in the Forbidden City into the twentieth century.

In addition, the Manchus patronized Yellow sect Lamaism in Mongolia and Tibet. In Mongolia, patronage of Lamaism became a method of controlling Mongol tribes that had converted to that religion in the seventeenth century. Lamaism was overseen by the Dalai Lama in Lhasa, Tibet; thus, Manchu interests in exercising control in Mongolia through this religion naturally fostered its interests in exercising control in Tibet from the 1720s on. From the late seventeenth to the late eighteenth century, the Manchu regime constructed or restored thirty-two Tibetan temples in Beijing and eleven in the Manchu summer capital of Chengde, north of the Great Wall.

The Manchu regime tried to prevent close association between Chinese and themselves by forbidding intermarriage and outlawing business partnerships. They stepped into the realm of customs so as to differentiate Manchus from Chinese physically, forbidding, for example, Manchu women to bind their feet, as most proper Chinese women did (see Chapter 4). They also ordered a physical change of customs among Chinese men as a pointed expression of Manchu overlordship; they commanded all Chinese men to adopt the Manchu hairstyle: shave the front parts of their heads, let the hair in the back grow longer, and then plait that hair into queues or pigtails. In essence, that hairstyle physically marked the Chinese as subjects of the Outsider Manchus. The order was particularly scandalous to Chinese men who had been used to growing their hair long; it has been suggested that many saw the new hairstyle as something like "tonsorial castration," a mutilation of their physical wholeness and their manhood.[7]

In the arena of official rule, the Manchus gave themselves preferential treatment in the examination system, in official appointments, and in the justice system. Although their small numbers relative to the Chinese population meant that they had to work with the Chinese, appointment to governmental positions went more or less equally to Manchus and Chinese. If there was balance in that way, the fact remained that the Manchus were careful to check Chinese power. Although Chinese might be appointed to serve as governors of provinces, governors-general, who oversaw two or three provinces, tended to be Manchu. The trump card, of course, was that the ultimate arbiter and decision maker—the emperor—was always Manchu.

BUYING INTO CHINESE CULTURE

The Civil Service Examination and the Crucial Role of Women

The Qing, for all their Manchu identity, accepted the heart of the Chinese political, social, and cultural system—the imperial civil service examination and the Confucianism on which it was based. Developed over many centuries, this system aimed to bring into government positions the best and the brightest men (women could not participate in the examination system), who brought to their ruling tasks both wisdom and virtue. China's government personnel system was then not generally based on birth but rather on merit measured through an examination system grounded in what today we would call the humanities—Confucian philosophical texts and commentaries, history, and literature. Thus, it produced generalists, not specialists. In normal times the vast majority of men who served took the examination, but at times of economic crisis men might enter the civil service "irregularly" by purchasing degrees or positions. In 1800, when the Qing government had hit harder times, an estimated 350,000 had purchased degrees.

Confucianism, the foundation of the Han Chinese cultural system, was based on the teachings of Confucius (Kong Fuzi [551–479 B.C.E.]) and his key followers—especially, in late imperial times, on Mencius (Mengzi [372–289 B.C.E.]). Confucius and Mencius both taught at a time when Chinese society and politics were in disarray. Their prescription for a more harmonious, smoothly functioning polity was to attract wise and virtuous men who could transform politics and society and restore the situation to what it had been in the golden age of a mythic past. These men would be motivated to rule the state benevolently through high principles, a profound sense of morality, and a thorough empathy with the people. In Confucius's eyes, education was the key to developing sages who could so rule the state.

If a Chinese family had a son with strong intellectual abilities, it might attempt to hire a tutor who could oversee his preparations for taking the examination. This decision certainly depended in part on the family's economic situation. Poor farm families, for example, would have had less cash available for such an undertaking and would have likely been unwilling to lose an extra farmhand to the long study necessary to succeed. In areas where strong lineages dominated, lineage estates might provide precocious young men, even of poorer families, the money to study for the examination.

The exams themselves took several days. Candidates were ushered into tiny cubicles placed in long rows in the examination area. There they wrote essays and poetry in answer to various questions. In different periods, the examination's substance differed; for example, questions relating to practical administration were dropped in 1757, but they were added again by the late nineteenth century. The form of the answer was important: essays had to follow a particular format of presentation; the essay's length was prescribed. Poetry was stressed: a provincial director of studies said that inferior ability in writing poetry carried with it the "smell of village mediocrity."[8] Calligraphy was also important because it was seen as indicative of a person's morality. Throughout the centuries, questions were raised about how these examination practices could produce men who were capable of handling the messy problems of day-to-day governance. But, despite these concerns, the examination remained central into the twentieth century.

Success in major examinations, offered at three levels, brought degrees. Preceded by a preliminary exam at the county seat, the lowest-level exam was offered twice every three years in prefectural capitals. Successful candidates received the *shengyuan* (government student) degree; studies have shown that the vast majority received these degrees between the ages of twenty and thirty. Pass rates for all examinations were only about 1 to 2 percent. Receiving the *shengyuan* degree did not entitle the degree-holder to an official position; however, it brought him and his family considerable status and marked him as an elite member of his resident community. The *juren* (provincial graduate) degree was bestowed on those passing the second-level examination at the provincial capital, which was offered once every three years; the average age for this accomplishment in the nineteenth century was about thirty-one. This degree provided an entryway into officialdom, not to the highest positions but to magistracies of counties, prefects of prefectures, and sometimes ad hoc appointments. The highest degree, the *jinshi* (metropolitan graduate), came from success at the imperial capital; here, the written examination was followed by an oral examination at the palace administered by the emperor himself. In the nineteenth century, the average age for attaining this degree was thirty-three to thirty-six. It opened all official career doors immediately—from governorships to important imperial commissionerships to membership in the Hanlin Academy, the government's policy-making think tank.

Attaining any of these degrees brought legal, economic, and social privileges. Degree-holders could be judged in a legal case only by someone who was educationally superior. They were legally protected from insults by commoners and could receive no corporal punishment. They were freed from official labor service that was required of all commoners. All degree-holders had buttons on their hats that indicated their particular degree—the *jinshi* and *juren*, plain gold; the *shengyuan*, plain silver. They wore black gowns bordered in blue and they alone were allowed to wear furs, brocades, and fancy embroidery. However, despite the personal privileges and the status that attaining a degree brought generally to the candidate's family, he could not pass the honor on to his son; if his son wanted such status, he had to pass the examination himself. At any time in the nineteenth century there were somewhat over 800,000 *shengyuan* degree-holders (roughly 1.8 to 2.4 percent of the population), 18,000 to 19,000 *juren* degree-holders, and about 2,500 *jinshi* degree-holders.

A crucial aspect of the examination system for the governance of the Chinese state was that it required all potential officials to be trained in the same body of principles, rules, and norms. Although such a common educational base could never produce uniformity of thought, it did provide a common base of learning with clearly understood standards for ruling and strategies for governance. Since the pass rate on the examinations was so small, many more Chinese men were trained in the classics than those who held degrees; one historian has estimated that classically educated men numbered at the very minimum 5 million in the early eighteenth century (10 percent of the population).[9]

What about women with regard to the examination system? One important social development especially in elite families in the Lower Yangzi region was the emergence of educated women who had been trained by family members in Confucian thought and values from little on. Studies have shown that already in the seventeenth century, "[t]hrough writing and reading, elite women developed new spheres of influence, expanding the domain of kinship and friendship beyond domestic space, mastering the tools of learning that had been the domain of men."[10] The emergence of elite women through their learning and by their writing indicates that the idea of a highly educated woman was respected by at least a part of elite society.

Shifts in gender relations were underscored by debates about the degree of learning that women in scholarly families should endeavor to attain. Many of these women wrote excellent and thoughtful poetry that delved into domestic issues and beyond. During the Qianlong emperor's reign, for example, in the city of Changzhou between Shanghai and Nanjing, there were 281 women writers, "an essential part of Changzhou's prestige."[11] Through their writings, women sought "to assert and extend their authority in the family and to reach beyond the domestic realm to criticize the commercial sex markets of their time."[12] They also wrote to make connections to other women to share "what they valued, to celebrate what they admired, and to lament what they lost."[13]

Educated and elite women's roles enabled the successful working of the examinations system. The system required a man frequently to sojourn away from his household perhaps to study for and definitely sit for the examinations and to cultivate connections to attain success. If the candidate were not successful in gaining a degree, he often had to seek employment elsewhere, perhaps as a peripatetic teacher. In the absence of a male wage earner, his wife became the pillar that held the household together, being in charge of the family's education and comity. Most important, she financed her husband's necessary travels through selling commodities produced in the household: decorative arts and fashion design, embroidery, and calligraphy. In this capacity, she learned how to produce goods, services, and artwork, to invest money and earn interest, and collect commercial profits. All of these accomplishments rested on her social skills—cultivating individual relationships and building networks. "In sum, if the governing class of scholar-officials was the bedrock of the Qing imperial system, then womanly virtue and womanly managerial skills were central to it."[14]

The Bureaucratic Veneer

With a few major exceptions, the Qing emperors bought into the traditional government ideal: "a minimum state with maximal reach: that is, a relatively small state apparatus that succeeded in extracting substantial revenues and labor from a large population."[15] Minimalist government meant a relative stagnancy in the number of county magistrates over time. During the late seventeenth century, there were 1,261 counties and magistrates. While the population tripled in size in the century from 1680 to 1780, there were only 1,303 counties and magistrates in the late nineteenth century.[16] Taking the population in 1700 to be about 150 million and that of 1900 to be about 420 million (both reasonable projections), the average number to which one man served as magistrate in 1700 was about 119,000 but was over 320,000 in 1900. By contrast, in China today, there are county level officials for about every 2,000 people.[17]

Though counties varied widely in size and population, the figures from imperial China—estimates though they are—nevertheless, suggest the minimalist reality. Clearly, imperial official presence was only the thinnest of veneers, insufficient for serving the population well. Furthermore, county governments were under-funded to a point where monies were clearly insufficient for the execution of prescribed duties. In the locality, the government was only "tenuously in control."[18] Indeed, the Chinese proverb had a profound truth about the relationship between the government and the people: "Heaven is high; the emperor is far away."

This system worked well when it did so because of two elements: the county magistrate and the support and help of local elites. The power and the responsibility of the magistrate, often called the "father–mother" official, were especially great; equally great was the trust implicitly placed in him by the state. Its own reputation in counties all across China could rise or fall with the leadership of the magistrate as the state bureaucrat with whom people most had to deal. The state recognized that the key to good government was the magistrate and local government. Their trust in magistrates came because of their belief in the validity and general transcendence of the state system, based as it was on ethics and education, and out of a sense that these civil service degree-holders were men "who, through learning and self-cultivation, ... lived their lives according to the rules of propriety ... and transformed those around them through the power of their moral example."[19] The comprehensive and holistic vision of state-society was part of the political genius of the system.

But the magistrates could not do it alone. They had to rely on local elites to be essentially political and social associates who contributed to the management and well-being of the community. In this system, the center had to trust local elites to act in its place at the community and county levels in the public "arena of non-state activity that contributed to the supply of services and resources in the public good."[20] Local elites played key roles in funding, constructing, and managing "schools, academies, city walls, granaries, bridges, ferry docks, hydraulic systems, orphanages, temples to state-sanctioned gods, shrines to local figures, even Buddhist monasteries."[21] The state's trust in local elites had to be based on the assumption that these local leaders would accept and support the state's legitimacy and mission.

Rituals, Religion, and Values

The adoption of Ming state rituals was crucial for Manchu rulers to assert their legitimacy by linking themselves to the former imperial state. There were no fewer than 256 state rituals in the Qing period. These included sacrifices to gods and the imperial ancestors; political rituals, such as receiving envoys and reviewing troops; and imperial household and lineage rituals focusing on marriage and death. Through these state rituals—displays of pomp and power—the emperor underscored his legitimacy as Son of Heaven, promoted order and harmony, asserted his sovereignty vis-à-vis the bureaucracy, and impressed people with his splendor. All rituals—state, community, and family—validated the sense of hierarchy and order, so crucial in the Confucian worldview.

Whether Confucianism was a religion or a philosophy depends on one's definition. Though Confucius himself had refused to get involved in questions about an afterlife ("We do not yet know about life; how can we talk about what happens after death?"), his teachings on the continuity of the family over generations and of ancestors raised issues often thought of as religious. Central here was ancestor reverence. The Qing erected both their ancestral tablets for state sacrifices in Beijing and their familial tablets within the Forbidden City. The practice especially pointed to the value of filial piety, or filiality, to which Qing emperors had explicitly committed. The Kangxi emperor (1661–1722) noted, "We rule the empire with filial piety. That is why I want to exemplify this principle for my ministers and my people—and for my own descendants."[22] Such a central Confucian conception seemed to resonate in the actions of the most important Qing emperors—from the care of the Kangxi emperor for his beloved grandmother to the Yongzheng emperor's (r. 1722–1736) filiality to his father to the Qianlong emperor's (r. 1736–1795) ostentatious show of filial piety for his mother, which included building in the capital replicas of her beloved Southern China streets that she could putter around in.

The patronage of Lamaist Buddhism not only was a way of controlling ethnic subjects but also linked the regime with Buddhism, borrowed by the Chinese from India over 1,500 years earlier. Though the power of Buddhism in Chinese society had greatly diminished after the ninth century, it was still a part of many Chinese lives. The construction of Buddhist temples by the regime in both Beijing and Chengde was a visible linkage of the Manchu outsiders with an important Chinese religious tradition.

DEALING WITH THE OTHER

Since they themselves were Other to the Chinese, the Qing regime in its policies toward China's Others seemed to be acutely aware of differences in those Others. It developed two starkly different approaches to dealing with those outside the Chinese cultural realm. Even before it established its rule in China, in 1638 it organized the Court of Colonial Affairs (*Lifanyuan*) to handle its relations with the Mongols. This court became the organ in charge of relations with the peoples north and west of "China within the Wall"—Mongols, Uighurs (Turkish Muslims), Tibetans, and Russians. Han Chinese were almost completely excluded from the membership of the Court; indeed, Court meetings were generally conducted in non-Chinese languages. Triumphant mid-eighteenth-century military campaigns extended Chinese control into the Central Asian Tarim Basin, bringing control over Xinjiang in 1759 and 6 million square miles of grasslands, desert, and scattered oases into the empire. The Qing considered it a "strategic frontier zone" and did not allow Chinese colonization. Three interventions in Tibet from the 1720s to the 1750s made that state a Chinese protectorate. The *Lifanyuan* supervised the affairs of Lamaist organizations in Qing efforts to control both the Mongols and the Tibetans through their patronage of Lamaism. Sinification was not the name of this game. On the contrary, Qing policies toward the peoples of this region, as one historian suggests, brought economic, social, and cultural changes "that encouraged the growth of ethnic identities" among these peripheral peoples.[23] Doing so fit into the self-chosen identity of the Qing emperors, ethnic outsiders themselves. They were not simply the Chinese Sons of Heaven but also emperors of an Asian multi-ethnic, multicultural empire.

Over the centuries, the Chinese state had developed a different system of dealing with foreigners who did not come from the northern and western steppes; the Qing regime inherited it. Though the Chinese themselves had no name for its various procedures, Western scholars have called it the "tributary system." In surveying the barbarians who ringed the country, Han Chinese elites saw China as the Civilized Country. Early in China's past, the country had been known as Everything Under Heaven (*tianxia*)—that is, everything that was worth anything. Another name often used was Central Country (*Zhongguo*)—central specifically in terms of culture. The Chinese believed that their role was to train and educate the Others, not by physically forcing them to accept the Chinese way but as elder brothers to younger brothers, making it possible for them to participate in certain controlled ways in the blessings that Chinese believed their culture had to offer. As with any connections, the strength of China's ties to various countries and peoples varied in intensity. Relations with the kingdoms of Korea and Vietnam, located along Chinese borders, were strongest.

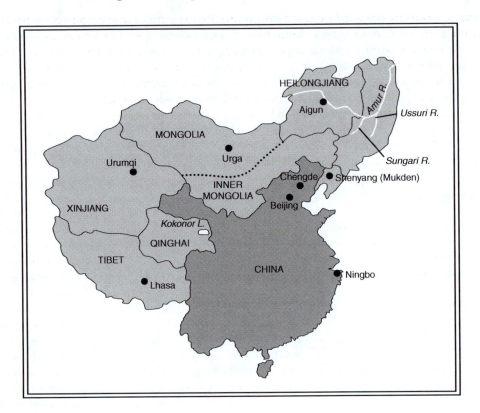

MAP 2.1   The Qing Empire, Early Nineteenth Century.

But for the present, as an example of the tributary system, let's take Japan, a close tributary state of China during the Ming dynasty. As with traditional ethnic minorities (and as with elder brothers treating younger brothers), a crucial goal was control. The Board of Rites, not the Court of Colonial Affairs, managed this system, for the core of the system was ritual. The Ming regime allowed Japan to send to China one mission every three years. It brought tribute—silks, aromatic woods, precious stones, horses, gold-decorated screens, fans, sheets of thin Japanese paper, and tons of sulphur—whatever the Japanese ruler deemed appropriate. The Chinese specified the port of entry, in this case Ningbo, south of Shanghai on the East China Sea. The Japanese mission was met at Ningbo by a Chinese delegation that accompanied them to Beijing via the Grand Canal. Along the way, the Japanese were repeatedly banqueted and showered with costly gifts of silk and jade. Once they arrived in the capital, they had to bide their time until the arrival of the most auspicious date, when they would be ushered into the presence of the Chinese emperor.

At that meeting they would perform various rituals, the most famous being the kowtow (*ketou*), in which they prostrated themselves on the floor three times and, with each prostration, knocked their heads on the floor three times—three prostrations, nine head knockings. It was a ritual of extreme obeisance, one that, at least theoretically, every Chinese child performed before his or her parents each New Year's Day. Apart from the deep meaning of submission evident in the kowtow, the performance of this ritual by children for their parents in a sense connected the foreigners, the Others, with the larger Chinese "family" and its culture. After the rituals, the foreign mission was allowed to remain in Beijing and trade for a period before being accompanied back to Ningbo and the trip home. For the Others, the episode offered the bestowal of expensive presents and the lucrative opportunity to trade, continual rounds of feasting and celebrations, and probably what was the experience of a lifetime. For the Chinese, it provided corroboration of their view of themselves as the superior, generous, paternalistic elder brother, offering the Other the opportunity, as the Chinese phrase went, "to come and be transformed [*laihua*]."

IDENTITY AND CHANGE: THE QIANLONG EMPEROR IN THE LATE EIGHTEENTH CENTURY

Historians frequently assert that traditional China reached the height of its power and wealth during the reign of the Qianlong emperor (1736–1795). His successful military conquest of inner Asian frontiers more than doubled Chinese territory. With peace and prosperity the order of the day within China, South, Southeast, and East Asian states regularly sent tributary missions. Economic prosperity, prompted by efficient and effective government in the earlier reigns of the dynasty, flourished. The state treasury in the first year of the Qianlong emperor's reign had a surplus of 24 million taels of silver; fifty years later, the surplus had more than tripled. Probably nothing reveals the extraordinary fiscal situation better than the fact that the Qianlong emperor was able to cancel the collection of annual taxes four times.

Although traditional China's economic cornerstone was its agricultural base, the country experienced a commercial revolution from the mid-sixteenth to the end of the eighteenth century. By the Qianlong era, "China was possibly the most commercialized country in the world."[24] Agricultural diversification and the increasingly significant availability of regional cash crops—cotton, tea, and tobacco—stimulated the expansion of trade between regions. By the end of the eighteenth century, over 10 percent of its grain, over 25 percent of raw cotton, more than 50 percent of cotton cloth, over 90 percent of raw silk, and almost all the tea were for sale in the markets.[25] Commercialization reached down to the lowest levels of society. As the number of markets increased, farmers in villages were linked to towns and cities in new commercial relationships: in the rice-exporting county of Xiangtan in Hunan province, for example, the number of market towns soared from three in 1685 to over one hundred in 1818.[26]

Commercialization brought many socioeconomic changes. Taxes were now usually paid in money rather than in kind (as in earlier dynasties), underscoring the increasing importance of money in the economy. The credit and transfer needs of long-distance interregional trade fueled the development of native banks and new fiscal institutions. Elite status came to depend more and more on wealth; occupational differentiation gave rise to new opportunities; merchants and those associated with businesses, always low on the social totem pole, thrived in the general economic well-being and abundance.[27] In the view of one eighteenth-century writer, "Houses cluster together like fish-scales and people are as numerous as ants. ... everywhere [i]n the fields, mulberry, hemp, and various cereal crops are grown; the streams abound with carp and other fish."[28] The reality of environmental and historical differences in macroregions, however, requires us to draw back a bit and keep in mind that this picture of China is generalized from one or several areas. Despite general prosperity, many areas were not sites of plenty and wealth. One historian has noted, "One did not have to travel far from the commercialized cores to find abject poverty, unemployment, and disorder."[29] Our knowledge of the variety, diversity, and complexity of China's macroregions, cores, and peripheries must also temper this generalized view of prosperity.

Foreign trade also thrived: southeastern coastal provinces traded on a large scale with Southeast Asia and Taiwan. The glories of China were sought for and emulated in the late eighteenth-century

West. Chinese products—silk, cloisonné, porcelains, fans, tea, rhubarb—were not simply sought: many things Chinese became the European rage. Europeans copied Chinese wallpaper, interior decor, and furniture; elite homeowners in Versailles and London created Chinese gardens with Chinese pavilions. European royalty and Enlightenment philosophers were enthusiastic about the perceived Chinese model of rule, "enlightened" or "benevolent" despotism. Unfortunately, it is likely, as an American historian suggested, "literate Westerners knew more about China in the eighteenth century than they [did] in the twentieth."[30]

IDENTITY CRISIS

The Emperor's Roles

The issue that loomed larger and larger for the Qianlong emperor in the years after the Qing's last act of expansion, the seizure of Xinjiang in 1759, was his growing malaise over Manchu identity. Were the Manchus simply outsiders who, in their capacity as leaders of a Chinese dynasty, were becoming Sinified? Or, were they primarily rulers of a multi-ethnic empire in which the Chinese were only one part and in which Manchu dealings with other ethnic groups in newly won territories gave them varied and pragmatic outlooks of governance important for all those they ruled?

In many ways, as we have seen, the Manchus accepted and supported Chinese traditions, upholding the examination and political systems, Confucianism, filial piety, ancestor reverence, and the body of family and state rituals. The Qianlong emperor himself performed rituals before ancestral tablets in the Forbidden City and in Manchuria at the reputed site where the Manchus originated. In addition, he took on the scholarly and artistic roles of the Chinese sage, serving as patron to Chinese scholars and artists. He collected about 8,000 paintings and works of calligraphy in an imperial collection, on a number of which—as indicative of his questionable lack of taste and judgment—he made notations on the works themselves. He added fifty-four inscriptions to one hand scroll and pressed his seal thirteen times on a single painting. His tastes, which leaned to the showy, theatrical, and monumental, had a great impact on the artistic trends of his day. He was also enormously productive himself, though quantity is no obvious indicator of quality. He wrote about 43,000 poems and, it is said, ninety-two books of prose. That he took the abilities of and devotion to the role of a Chinese scholar seriously is underscored by his daily schedule. Rising at 6:00 a.m., he spent the morning reading official reports and memorials, consulting with his advisers, and receiving and dispatching officials. Afternoons, however, he devoted to reading, painting, and writing poetry.

It is abundantly clear that the Qianlong emperor had not become thoroughly Sinified despite his Chinese interests. But in years after the Qing's successful imperialism in Xinjiang, he launched various initiatives to reinvigorate Manchu traditions. He was, in the words of one historian, "bent on authentic Manchuness."[31] There are two ways to interpret the reason for the emperor's "reinvigoration" agenda. If one takes the traditional interpretation of Manchu origins and the conquest of China, his agenda was containing the extent of Sinification by emphasizing Manchu traditions. On the other hand, if one supports the revisionist view that Manchu ethnic identity was not determined until the Qing reign itself, then his agenda was to structure and enhance Manchu identity. Either reason led to the same end.

The emperor first turned to the Manchu elites, the bannermen scattered around the realm in city-based garrisons, who had been the foundation of the conquest and imperial power. The emperor saw that the livelihood of bannermen in those garrisons was in general economic decline,

FIGURE 2.2 Castiglione painted this portrait of the twenty-one-year-old Qianlong Emperor. It is placed in a larger work depicting the emperor, empress, and eleven imperial consorts and is titled, *In My Heart There Is the Power to Reign Peaceably.*

Source: Lang Shih-ning (Giuseppe Castiglione), Chinese, 1688–1768, Qing Dynasty, "Inauguration Portraits of Emperor Qianlong, the Empress, and the Eleven Imperial Consorts," 1736. Handscroll, ink and color on silk, 52.9 × 688.3 cm. © The Cleveland Museum of Art. 2003. John L. Severance Fund, 1969.31.

a serious situation producing low morale. In fact, garrison commanders had begun to allow bannermen to live outside the garrison, purchase homes and businesses there, and participate in city life. For the emperor, such a change opened the bannermen to a slippery urban diversity that threatened the integrity of Manchu identity. This necessitated an active revival of the Manchu language among bannermen, especially among the imperial Aisin Gioro clan; it involved establishing standard tests for military skills; and it included rejuvenating the spiritual and cultural roles of the clans. For all bannermen, the government promoted education that stressed the reading and writing of Manchu, astronomy, mathematics, riding, and shooting.

In addition to his concern with the bannermen, the Qianlong emperor chose to uphold the Manchu character of the imperial household and clans. Whereas his grandfather, the Kangxi emperor, had participated in autumn hunts north of the Great Wall, his father, the Yongzheng emperor, had never done so. The Qianlong emperor restored the practice, developing the hunting "preserve to its fullest extent."[32] He insisted on sponsoring archery contests for both banner and Green Standard troops and boasted about his ability to kill deer with one shot. He directed the publication of Manchu genealogies, the writing of a history of the eight banners, and the laying out in detail of myths about the origins of the imperial Aisin Gioro clan. Fearful that shamanism was disappearing and desiring to preserve this traditional Manchu religion, he ordered that its practices be written down and disseminated among the Manchus.

The Qianlong emperor also asserted his Manchuness as a ruler of the multi-ethnic empire by championing Tibetan Buddhism. He continued the construction of Tibetan Buddhist temples in Beijing and in Chengde, site of the summer palace. He sponsored the translation of Buddhist sutras, which he then distributed to temples and monasteries. He had a Buddhist chapel built in the Forbidden City and reportedly practiced meditation every day. He had himself painted by court painters not only as a great warrior and a sage, but also significantly as the Buddha and as a Buddhist monk. At the summer palace, he built a replica of the Potala, the Dalai Lama's residence in Lhasa. Most persuasive of his commitment to Buddhism was the tomb that he designed for himself. On the ceiling of the crypt directly over the place where his coffin was laid was a symbol of the *cakravartin*, "the wheel-turning king"—"an earthly ruler who by his conquests in the name of the Buddha would move the world toward the next stage in universal salvation."[33] In addition, he had Sanskrit prayers for the wheel-turning king carved on the tomb walls.

Clearly, in his religious efforts he was trying to impress the non-Han Chinese in the empire and to assert his multicultural moral legitimacy. His multilingualism was also part of this effort. He began to learn Mongolian in 1743, Uighur in 1760, and Tibetan in 1776. In his description of his language ability, he stated,

> In 1780, because the Panchen Lama [the chief spiritual adviser of the Dalai Lama] was coming to visit, I also studied Tangut. Thus, every year when the [emissaries] of Mongols, Uighurs, and Tibetans came to the capital for audience, I used their own language and did not rely on an interpreter.[34]

Literary Inquisition

The question of Manchuness and Chinese-ness became most strained and dangerous when posed in the context of the Manchu conquest. In some areas of China and some sectors of Chinese society, bitterness about the conquest and the violence with which it was carried out (e.g., walled cities burned with all inhabitants slain) did not lie far beneath the surface. The Manchus were alert from the beginning to any writings that hinted at resistance or insurrection; occasional cases emerged.

One that served as a harbinger of sorts for a spectacular literary inquisition from 1772 to 1782, and that underscores the identity obsession that the Qianlong emperor developed, was the case of Zeng Jing. During the reign of the Qianlong emperor's father, Zeng had read the anti-Manchu writings and rantings of a Han Chinese scholar named Lu, who had died in the 1680s. Zeng had been so agitated by what he read that he contacted a general in the area to try to persuade him to launch a rebellion against the government. The general promptly turned Zeng in, and in 1730 the case reached the Yongzheng emperor. The emperor's response was an exhibition of the benevolence of the Confucian sovereign: he ascribed Zeng's actions to the gullibility and naiveté of youth, taken in by Lu's abusive and overdrawn rhetoric. Zeng's interrogation was printed and published, along with his recantation and an essay by court scholars on Lu's errors. Zeng was released and, as a mark of the emperor's mercy, was even given a minor local position. In his response, the emperor had suggested that Lu's original attack on the Manchus was misplaced because the Manchus had been transformed by their long-term exposure to the civilizing force of Confucianism.

This position had apparently rankled the soon-to-be Qianlong emperor. As one historian wrote on the subject,

> [W]as it really necessary that the emperors of the great Qing empire continue to humble themselves before the image of Confucius, still placidly denying the culture of their ancestors in order to curry favor with those whom they had conquered?[35]

On taking the throne, the Qianlong emperor reopened the Zeng case, ordering the destruction of the published record of the interrogation and recantation. Zeng was retried, found guilty of sedition, and sentenced to death by slicing. The case revealed that the Qianlong emperor was determined, as soon as he took the throne, both to stifle anti-Manchu expressions and to reassert the Manchu nature of the regime.

In 1772 the emperor ordered the collection of all existing books and manuscripts, whether held in libraries or owned privately. The goal was to bring them to the capital, review them, and recopy the most outstanding ones in new editions in order to ensure the preservation of important, valuable, and, in some cases, rare literary and historical treasures. The collection, known as the *Four Treasuries* because it was grouped into four sections—classics, history, philosophy, and miscellaneous literary works—was immense. Fully 3,593 works were recopied, filling 36,000 manuscript volumes; in addition, the *Four Treasuries* included an annotated catalogue of 10,680 extant titles. In initiating this vast undertaking, the emperor was clearly giving evidence of his Chinese persona: here are the opening lines of his edict. "[In our rule] We have always been mindful of precedent, revered the writings of the past, [and] relied on the brush to govern and ruled in accordance with principle."[36]

The huge project was facilitated by intellectual trends of the late eighteenth century, when a philosophical movement called Han learning, or "evidential research" (*kaozheng*), was the rage. Beginning in the seventeenth century, this movement emphasized getting at the truth by analyzing old texts and, if need be, revising them on the basis of skills that scholars had gained from such fields as epigraphy, philology, historical investigation, and textual criticism. The goal was to abandon speculation and to search for the truth in actual facts (*shishi qiushi*), in effect to reestablish classical learning on a firmer foundation. In the *Four Treasuries* project, *kaozheng* scholars played the leading role. Because of their interests, many such scholars in the Lower Yangzi macroregion were tied to networks of bookstores and booksellers, a fact that eased the collection of books. Many books for the project, for example, came from Hangzhou libraries. But, more important, these scholars controlled the editorial process in combing through the texts and therefore in shaping the project's outcome.

Although not abundantly clear from the beginning, the project became a full-blown campaign of censorship or, as it has been called, a "literary inquisition." In this regard, the Qianlong emperor was acting in his Manchu persona. A little more than a year after inaugurating the project, the emperor noted that some provincial governors had not sent many books to the capital and wondered whether this might be because they were of a "rebellious or seditious nature."[37] This speculation is indicative of the emperor's Manchu-defensive assumptions. By late 1774, these assumptions were declared forcefully: the fact that no book thus far collected expressed any hint of sedition suggested to him that books were being hidden; they had to be found. From 1776 on, more and more time of the men involved in the project was spent examining books closely for an indication of anti-Manchu thoughts or language; the censorship campaign seemed to develop its own momentum. From 1780 until 1782, the central government took firmer control of the effort, establishing

centralized censorship boards and issuing lists of banned books and criteria for determining sedition. Up to 2,400 works were destroyed in this literary inquisition, and an estimated 400,000 to
500,000 were edited following official decree. This movement reflects the almost schizophrenic
government attitude toward Chinese and Manchu identities; it also likely reflects growing tension
at the court between Chinese and Manchu factions. It clearly highlights the late eighteenth-century
identity crisis epitomized in the policies of the Qianlong emperor.

EMERGING PROBLEMS

For subsequent Chinese, the literary inquisition left a bitter taste of Manchu autocracy, certainly a
dark experience amid what many have perceived as traditional China's most glorious period. There
were, in addition, other political, economic, and social indicators that pointed to a host of emerging
problems, some fraught with danger as China headed unawares into confrontation with the West.

Although the expansive military campaigns in Central Asia had ended, the country was faced
with an increasing number of social explosions. A 1774 religion-inspired rebellion in Shandong
province was followed in the 1780s by a secret society-based uprising in Taiwan, by two Muslim
revolts in Gansu province, and by rebellious Miao tribesmen in Southwest China. The military's
efforts to douse the flames of rebellion began to erode the full treasury. The strongest test for the
Chinese military was the White Lotus Rebellion (1796–1804), a religious-based movement to establish a utopia on earth that raked across north-central China. It took eight long years for the Chinese
military to quell this threat. Not only did the state reportedly spend 100 million taels (or 30 percent
more than the government's annual revenue) in suppressing this rebellion, but, perhaps even more
serious, the Chinese military response was tentative and ineffective.[38] Corruption and poor morale
had already substantially weakened the banner forces by the mid-eighteenth century. The Green
Standard forces, though battling the same social problems, seem to have maintained somewhat
better fighting ability. Nevertheless, an undisciplined and generally incompetent military coupled
with a weakening economy did not bode well.

The greatest long-term danger not only for the Qing dynasty but for China itself was a monumental increase in population. Data reveal that the population rose sharply, from over 177 million
in 1749 to over 301 million in 1790, an increase of 70 percent in little more than forty years.[39]
What gave rise to such a soaring population is not completely clear, though the general prosperity,
new food crops (sweet potatoes, maize, and peanuts) from the Western Hemisphere, and techniques such as double cropping helped support it. Other factors may have included a declining
mortality rate, a rising birth rate, a decline in the rate of infanticide, and the control of smallpox
through inoculation. Scholars have seen population growth as both a "reflection of—and a contributor to—prosperity."[40] It contributed to prosperity, for example, by providing more field workers
to increase harvest yields and more immigrants to develop regions of previously non-arable or
under-populated land.

The negative impacts of the population explosion? The population increase far exceeded what
could be supported by the newly cultivated crops from the Western Hemisphere. Estimates suggest
that the population tripled from about 1685 to 1780, but during that time the amount of cultivated
land only doubled. The problem of too many people and not enough land was worsened by Chinese inheritance customs. The Chinese practiced a partible inheritance system whereby land was
divided equally among all the sons. Landholdings in China tended to be tiny to begin with; in the
North China macroregion, for example, in the late eighteenth century the average farm was only
2.5 acres. Given that figure and a hypothetical farmer on the North China plain with three sons,

each son would inherit only .83 acre of land. With the huge population increase, land per capita was shrinking dangerously; when coupled with partible inheritance, the odds of once economically viable farmers falling into bankruptcy and poverty escalated sharply.

Various regions of the country were differentially affected by the population increase, since demographic growth occurred at different rates. It is also likely that economic problems were more serious in the peripheries, which had far fewer human and natural resources, than in the cores. But the demographic situation affected to a greater or lesser extent the whole country, not only with economic but also political implications. The larger population put greater strain on an already fiscally weakened government to provide various services for the people. Two crucial services were public works and the distribution of charitable grain relief at times of poor harvest or famine. In the last years of the Qianlong emperor's reign, public works were not being maintained as they should have been; sections of the Grand Canal, for example, were clogged with silt. Floods were in the offing. More serious, charitable relief granaries often contained little grain.

The political implications were perhaps even more crucial than the short-term economic effects. In ascending the throne, the Chinese emperor was said to have received the Mandate of Heaven. As part of the mandate to rule as the "Son of Heaven," he had to rule benevolently and carry out his proper ritual functions. Natural disasters—droughts, floods, earthquakes, insect plagues—were interpreted as signs that the emperor was not performing his functions properly and that his Mandate was in jeopardy. Emperors who were believed to be inattentive to the people's needs were in danger of losing the Mandate, that is, being overthrown. When poor harvests in an area created hunger and even starvation, empty relief granaries were visible and potent evidence that the emperor was not meeting the needs of those over whom Heaven had given him charge.

Part of the difficulties of the last decades of the eighteenth century however, can be chalked up to the personal decisions of the Qianlong emperor himself. Emulating his grandfather, the Kangxi emperor, he took a number of tours down the Grand Canal to the Lower Yangzi area. At least two of these were undertaken for his mother's sake, a notably public display of filial piety. But the expenses of these Southern Tours were ten times those of his grandfather, and they were accompanied by significant disruptions of life along the Grand Canal. Triumphal arches and temporary palaces were built; the Grand Canal had to be repaired to ensure the safety of crowds; grain that ordinarily would have been shipped north was kept for the imperial retinue in the south. Such conspicuous display of government power was generally for the glory of the emperor (and his mother). Yet, the Yellow River overflowed some twenty times during the Qianlong emperor's reign, and not once did he make a personal visit to perform a ritual inspection of the dikes or to express concern for the flood victims. In short, the emperor's sense of perspective on both the appearance and the substance of rule seemed to be wanting.

Perhaps nothing illustrates what might best be called a loss of perspective than his doting on a handsome court favorite, Heshen. Beginning in 1775, when he was sixty-five and Heshen was twenty-five, the emperor handed over much power to this man, who was said to have reminded him of his father's concubine, with whom as a youth he had been infatuated. Whether this was a homosexual relationship or not, Heshen was able to parlay his ruler's patronage into extensive personal power. He held many important posts, including minister and vice-minister of key boards and director of the *Four Treasuries* project. His son was married to the emperor's daughter. He was able to appoint cronies to key bureaucratic posts throughout the empire; he and they engaged in many corrupt activities from which they made millions of taels to enrich themselves. When the Jiaqing emperor, the Qianlong emperor's son, forced Heshen to commit suicide in 1799, his personal treasury held the equivalent of two years of the realm's revenue. Corruption had a way of spreading like a cancer on the body politic, metastasizing far beyond Heshen and his gang, in the end harming the people themselves. When each level of the bureaucracy took more and more from the levels below, it ultimately not only stole economic resources but also eroded the people's respect for their rulers.

THE DAOGUANG EMPEROR

After he returned to the Forbidden City from the summer palace in early October 1813, the thirty-one-year-old prince who would become the Daoguang emperor in 1821 encountered a remarkable scene. With the help of unscrupulous eunuchs, a rebel band had entered the Forbidden City. Once the alarm had sounded, the prince acted quickly and courageously, grabbing a pistol and shooting two rebels as they tried to scale a wall. He then assisted in the roundup and capture of the remaining rebels. Such decisive action might lead one to think that as emperor he would, in the words of one biographer, be "one who could be relied on to restore the dynasty's fortunes in the face of crises spawned by the Heshen scandals and the fiscal strains unleashed by demographic crisis."[41] But the Daoguang emperor was of different mettle from his grandfather, the Qianlong emperor, and, above all, the times and the context were different.

The Daoguang emperor as a boy and teenager had participated in hunts north of the Great Wall with his grandfather and his father, the Jiaqing emperor (1796–1820); on a hunt at the age of nine he killed a deer with his bow and arrow, reportedly greatly pleasing his grandfather. He thus knew his Manchu roots, being trained in martial skills and military values. He was also adept in the customary activities of a Chinese sovereign/Confucian sage: studious and especially knowledgeable about Chinese literature, he was the author of ten volumes of prose and twenty-four volumes of poetry. The obsession with the Manchu–Chinese identity crisis had generally diminished after the Qianlong emperor's reign. Like his father, the Daoguang emperor was less concerned about the Manchu identity of bannermen and more concerned about keeping them in the garrison compounds and away from opium, the black market, and banditry. The word best describing Manchu life among the banner population even at the center of the Manchu world in Beijing was "decline": dilapidated housing, general poverty, and spreading opium usage.

In the realm at large, at the beginning of his reign, the Daoguang emperor had some military success in putting down a Muslim uprising in Turkestan (1825–1828), but he did not pursue Muslim allies in further western campaigns, likely because it would have been too costly. The crucial reality that he faced was the depletion of the treasury, which meant an ongoing financial crisis that prevented any government attempts to act forthrightly. Many important public works, for example, were now largely in disrepair. Whereas his grandfather's gaze had ranged from the multi-ethnic empire of the forests of Manchuria to the Mongolian and Tibetan grasslands to the Xinjiang deserts, the eyes of the Daoguang emperor had to focus on developments within the Wall.

It is not that this emperor had no ability. Though earlier studies had suggested that he was weak, conservative, and unimaginative, more recent accounts have shown him to be conscientious, flexible, and even innovative. He was ready to experiment in trying to deal with the financial crisis. He repeatedly admonished bureaucrats to tighten their fiscal belts and set an example by cutting back on his own expenditures. In trying to find ways to finance crucial public works, he worked closely with regional and local officials, cajoling bureaucrats to take the initiative and working toward consensual center–local arrangements.

The most important of these public works for the overall health of the state was repairing the crucial waterway, the Grand Canal. The Grand Canal had been constructed in the Sui (589–618) and Ming (1368–1644) dynasties to link the northern capital region to the Lower Yangzi macrore-gion, one of China's chief rice baskets. It had been constructed because China's main rivers ran from west to east and the sea route along the coast was notoriously treacherous. Running from Hangzhou to near Beijing, the canal served as an essential artery not only for commerce but espe-cially for the transport of tax grain, important at any time but especially at this time of financial desperation. The Grand Canal system was extraordinarily complex, composed of the canal itself, tributary streams, dikes and embankments, floodgates, and drainage channels. At one place the canal briefly joined the Yellow River; at the junction site there was an elaborate system of embank-ments, locks, and lock gates. The whole system was in disrepair, with the canal itself shallow and silting up. Indeed, the basic problem was that the Yellow River itself was in the process of shifting its channel from south of the Shandong peninsula to its north—a disaster that has happened about once every 600 years.

The emperor's technique in ruling was to listen to men in the field, to compromise and work toward consensus, and to be flexible: "I manage the country as a whole and search out information from everyone. Then I select a good plan and follow it. Moreover, I do not go into the planning process beforehand with a prejudiced view."[42] He came to see that he could not control the project from Beijing and that, although the fiscal realities called for central government–regional collabora-tion, the careful analysis and actual repair of the waterworks systems had to be conducted by men on the scene. This was a less assertive and autocratic approach than the one the Qianlong emperor had used, say, in the *Four Treasuries* project, but the reality of the times called for different tac-tics. In this crisis, however, the Daoguang emperor did take a generally bold initiative in pushing for a one-year experiment of transporting the grain by the sea route; that effort was successfully designed (enlisting Shanghai merchant vessels) and carried out in 1826.

If the concerns and contexts of the Daoguang emperor's reign bore little resemblance to those of his grandfather, neither did his style. The arrogance and ostentation of the reign in the late eighteenth century were replaced by humility and frugality. In his will, the emperor requested that no tablets praising his accomplishments be set up at his tomb and that his clothing be distributed to his courtiers (in contrast to the usual custom of preserving imperial clothes in sealed chests). During his reign, he made it known that he even wore mended clothes as part of his effort to hold down expenditures. One wonders whether the Daoguang emperor ruled at a time that was indeed more difficult than it had been for his grandfather, who had full treasuries, military triumphs, and unprecedented prosperity. The Daoguang emperor's original name, Mianning, means "unbroken peace." Unfortunately, his reign would forever come to be associated with war; it was his fate "to be the first Emperor of China to be humiliated by a Western power."[43]

Notes

1 Mark C. Elliott, "Ethnicity in the Qing Eight Banners," in *Empire at the Margins: Culture, Ethnicity, and Frontier in Early Modern China*, ed. Pamela Kyle Crossley, Helen F. Siu, and Donald Sutton (Berkeley, CA: University of California Press, 2006), pp. 34–35. The words "objective, static, and primordial condition" come from the writings of Norwegian anthropologist Fredrik Barth in a path-breaking 1969 essay. "Im-mutable Givens" are in Elliott, p. 34.
2 Wiliam T. Rowe, *China's Last Empire: The Great Qing* (Cambridge. MA: The Belknap Press of Harvard University Press, 2009), p. 6.
3 Quoted in Frederic Wakeman, Jr., *The Great Enterprise* (Berkeley, CA: University of California Press, 1985), Vol. 1, p. 209.

4 Jonathan D. Spence, *Emperor of China: Self-Portrait of K'ang-hsi* (New York: Vintage Books, 1974), pp. 12–13.

5 Michael G. Chang, *A Court on Horseback: Imperial Touring & the Construction of Qing Rule, 1680–1785* (Cambridge, MA: Harvard University Press, 2007), p. 1.

6 See William T. Rowe, *Saving the World: Chen Hongmou and Elite Consciousness in Eighteenth Century China* (Stanford, CA: Stanford University Press; 2001), pp. 331–5 and 406–7.

7 Wakeman, *The Great Enterprise*, pp. 648–50.

8 Quoted in Chang Chung-li, *The Chinese Gentry* (Seattle, WA: University of Washington Press, 1955), p. 177.

9 David Johnson, "Communication, Class, and Consciousness in Late Imperial China," in *Popular Culture in Late Imperial China*, ed. David Johnson, Andrew J. Nathan, and Evelyn S. Rawski (Berkeley, CA: University of California Press, 1985), pp. 58–9.

10 Susan Mann, *Precious Records* (Stanford, CA: Stanford University Press, 1997), p. 7.

11 Susan Mann, *The Talented Women of the Zhang Family* (Berkeley, CA: University of California Press, 2007), p. 46. Hereafter, *Talented Women*.

12 Mann, *Precious Records*, p. 120.

13 Ibid., p. 226.

14 Mann, *Talented Women*, p. 199.

15 John Bryan Starr, *Understanding China: A Guide to China's Economy, History, and Political Structure* (New York: Hill & Wang, 1997), p. 42.

16 H. Lyman Miller, "The Late Imperial Chinese State," in *The Modern Chinese State*, ed. David Shambaugh (Cambridge, UK: Cambridge University Press, 2000), p. 34.

17 Calculated from Yu Keping, *Globalization and Changes in China's Governance* (Leiden: Brill, 2008), p. 29.

18 Philip A. Kuhn, *Origins of the Modern Chinese State* (Stanford, CA: Stanford University Press, 2002), p. 22.

19 Jonathan K. Ocko and David Gilmartin, "State, Sovereignty, and the People: A Comparison of the 'Rule of Law' in China and India," *Journal of Asian Studies* 68, no. 1 (February 2009): 60.

20 Timothy Brook, "Family, Continuity and Cultural Hegemony: The Gentry of Ningbo, 1368–1911," in *Chinese Local Elites and Patterns of Dominance*, ed. Joseph W. Esherick and Mary Backus Rankin (Berkeley, CA: University of California Press, 1990), p. 43.

21 Ibid., p. 46.

22 Quoted in Evelyn S. Rawski, *The Last Emperors* (Berkeley, CA: University of California Press, 1998), p. 208.

23 Ibid., p. 301.

24 Rowe, *China's Last Empire*, p. 122.

25 Ibid., p. 123.

26 Ibid., p. 127.

27 See the discussions in Susan Naquin and Evelyn S. Rawski, *Chinese Society in the Eighteenth Century* (New Haven, CT: Yale University Press, 1987), especially Chapters 1, 2, 4, and 6.

28 Quoted in Frederic Wakeman, Jr., "High Ch'ing: 1683–1839," in *Modern East Asia: Essays in Interpretation*, ed. James B. Crowley (New York: Harcourt, Brace & World, 1970), p. 5.

29 Philip A. Kuhn, *Soulstealers: The Chinese Sorcery Scare of 1768* (Cambridge, MA: Harvard University Press, 1990), p. 39.

30 Ibid., p. 94.

31 Pamela K. Crossley, *Orphan Warriors: Three Manchu Generations and the End of the Qing World* (Princeton, NJ: Princeton University Press, 1990), p. 21.

32 Rawski, *The Last Emperors*, p. 21.

33 Pamela K. Crossley, *The Manchus* (London: Wiley-Blackwell, 2002), p. 112.

34 Quoted in Rawski, *The Last Emperors*, p. 255.

35 Crossley, *The Manchus*, p. 111.

36 Quoted in R. Kent Guy, *The Emperor's Four Treasuries* (Cambridge, MA: Harvard University Press, 1987), p. 35.

37 Ibid., p. 159.

38 Naquin and Rawski, *Chinese Society*, p. 219.

39 Jonathan Spence, *The Search for Modern China: A Documentary Collection* (New York: W. W. Norton, 1990), p. 94. These figures come from Ho Ping-ti, *Studies on the Population of China, 1368–1953* (Cambridge, MA: Harvard University Press, 1959), p. 281.

40 Naquin and Rawski, *Chinese Society*, p. 223.

41 Jane Kate Leonard, *Controlling from Afar* (Ann Arbor, MI: University of Michigan Press, 1996), p. 54.

42 Ibid., p. 195.

43 Arthur W. Hummel, *Eminent Chinese of the Ch'ing Period* (Washington, DC: U.S. Government Printing Office, 1943), p. 575.

Suggestions for Further Reading

Elliott, Mark C. *The Manchu Way: The Eight Banners and Ethnic Identity in Late Imperial China* (Stanford, CA: Stanford University Press, 2001). This analysis credits the Qing success to the "coherence and constancy" of banner forces. In contrast to Crossley, Elliott argues that ethnic identity was important in forging a common identity and heritage.

Leonard, Jane Kate. *Controlling from Afar: The Daoguang Emperor's Management of the Grand Canal Crisis, 1824–1826* (Ann Arbor, MI: Center for Chinese Studies, 1996). This account reveals much about a little-studied emperor but even more about the pragmatic approaches of the Qing state in dealing with crises at the beginning of its decline.

Mann, Susan. *The Talented Women of the Zhang Family* (Berkeley, CA: University of California Press, 2007). This eye-opening, revisionist work shows the crucial role educated women in elite families played in the success of the examination system.

Perdue, Peter. *China Marches West: The Qing Conquest of Central Eurasia* (Cambridge, MA: The Belknap Press of Harvard University Press, 2005). This groundbreaking work puts the Qing conquest of its western reaches into a global context, thus transcending what has been the prevalent Sinocentric focus.

Rowe, William T. *Saving the World: Chen Hongmou and Elite Consciousness in Eighteenth Century China* (Stanford, CA: Stanford University Press, 2001). This magisterial study of Chen (1696–1771), perhaps the most influential Chinese official of the eighteenth century, opens up the rich world of "on-the-ground" governance framed by a state-projected mission to "save the world."

3

The Opium War and the Treaty System
Challenges to Chinese Identity

I f only in terms of territorial size, the drive of European states to establish colonies in Asia seems quite surprising. China and India are huge countries on the Eurasian landmass, whereas Europe is only a small peninsula on that same body of land. But European expansion was impelled by imperialism's three M's: merchants, missionaries, and the military. Commercial motives drove the merchant class that had emerged during the rise of capitalism; they sought to profit from bringing commodities—such as rice, spices, sugar, and cotton—from East Asia, items that were not naturally prolific in the narrow span of European latitude (from 35 to 55 degrees north). Convinced that it possessed the Truth, the Christian church sent out missionaries to gather in the souls of benighted heathens like so many crops to be harvested. In many countries the merchant and the missionary were the advance men, preparing the way for the military, the arm of state power, to come for the biggest harvest of all: territory and people. All three groups were propelled by a missionary-like urge to spread the gospels of Western capitalism, Western religious truth, and Western state power.

THE EARLY WESTERN ROLE

What Might Have Been: the Jesuit Mission in China

One of the most promising periods of Western–Chinese interchange was the almost century-and-a-half-long Jesuit mission (1579–1724). The secret of Jesuit success lay in their efforts "to put [themselves] fully into a Chinese frame of reference,"[1] that is, by mastering the Chinese language and understanding how Chinese society and culture worked. Mastery of the Chinese language was an immense feat at a time when there were no Chinese–Portuguese or Chinese–Italian dictionaries. While they had first donned the robes of Buddhist monks in an effort to convey the religious nature of their undertaking, famed Italian Jesuit Matteo Ricci and others were perceptive enough to note that Buddhist monks did not get great respect in Chinese society at the time. In contrast, the literati, civil-service degree-holders, were admired and respected; thus, the Jesuits adopted the dress of the literati.

It was not only their dress: the Chinese were impressed by these foreigners who spoke Chinese and who clearly understood the tenets of Confucianism. But even more, the Jesuits had a message that grabbed the attention of the literati and the imperial court (both Ming and Qing): their enormous store of knowledge about science, math, astronomy, philosophy, and religion and their attention-getting instruments: European books, oil paintings, maps, prisms, globes, and clocks.

One goal of the Jesuit mission early on was to reach the imperial court and impress and make connections with officials, who then might provide protection for them and the mission. Ricci achieved that goal in 1601 and the Jesuits generally retained official protection until the mission ended. In only two periods, 1616–1623 and 1664–1670, did the Jesuits experience persecution, in both cases caused by officials who accused them of propagating a heterodox way; but these were only temporary setbacks. Though it has frequently been thought that the Jesuits only targeted literati and those at the court for conversion, the Jesuits were far more successful in converting commoners than they were those at the court. In 1700, they were also actively proselytizing in twenty cities around the realm and in rural areas around those cities. Estimates of numbers of baptized in 1700 range from 70,000 to more than 100,000.[2]

In the end, it was probably the source of their success that led to the demise of the mission. Over the years the Jesuits were dogged by problems of financing the undertaking and of getting sufficient numbers to work in China ("the sea voyage alone caused the deaths of half of the prospective missionaries"[3]). But the chief reason for their demise was "their efforts to create a mission church deeply rooted in Chinese society."[4] Part of being "deeply rooted" was the Jesuits' allowing converts to participate in rituals at Confucian temples and to carry on ancestor reverence. To the Jesuits, participation in rituals at the Confucian temple annually was simply a "solemn expression of remembrance for a revered master." Similarly, the Jesuits contended that keeping ancestral tablets in the home was also only an indication of respect; there was no sense that the dead ancestor resided in the tablet. After much study and careful thought, the Jesuits allowed these practices to be continued, not wanting to "[force] their converts to divorce themselves from their society."[5]

But in the 1630s the Franciscans and Dominicans, Catholic orders who had proselytized in the Philippines, came to China. Motivated by a more fundamentalist Catholicism and likely by some jealousy of and dislike of the Jesuits, these other orders claimed that rites in Confucian temples and ancestor reverence amounted to "idolatry." In 1692, the Kangxi emperor had declared by edict that the Throne granted toleration to Christianity so long as converts could participate in "Confucian rites." The papacy believed that the emperor was trying to trump the Church in matters of doctrine; Rome sent an emissary to investigate and discuss the issues. Hostile meetings in 1705 and 1706 produced a "do-or-die" struggle between emperor and pope. The pope prohibited Catholic missionaries from following the emperor's order and threatened excommunication if they did so. In turn, the emperor ordered all missionaries to sign an agreement to follow his order on pain of expulsion from the country. The Jesuit mission was mortally wounded. The Yongzheng emperor gave it the coup de grace in 1724 when he outlawed Christianity and expelled the missionaries. It was a tragic instance of "what might have been."

The Lure of Commerce

In 1600 the British government granted the East India Company a monopoly on trade east of Africa's Cape of Good Hope to South America's Straits of Magellan, that is, all trade in the Indian and Pacific Oceans; made perpetual in 1609, this monopoly lasted until 1834. Others had come before without such grandiose dreams. In 1517 the Portuguese made a horrific start in southernmost China when they followed their African practice of kidnapping adolescents to take as slaves; the Chinese forbade them to return. The Spanish arrived in the 1570s, trading along the southeast coast and setting up a base in Taiwan. The Dutch came in the early seventeenth century, supplanting the Spanish by the 1640s.

Most of the West's most active early phase of exploring East Asian waters came during the collapsing Ming regime and the bloody Manchu conquest, a disorienting and chaotic time for the Chinese state. The threat of Ming loyalists, based in Taiwan, compelled the Qing to close coastal ports in 1662; but when the threat was suppressed in 1685, four ports were reopened. Traditional state cultural and economic attitudes had denigrated merchants and trade, as Confucianism had called agriculture the root of the state. In contrast, commerce was simply trying to profit from what others had produced. In that respect, merchants thus exhibited parasitic characteristics and were ranked as the lowest legitimate social grouping, following scholars, farmers, and craftsmen. Further, in its own self-perception, China was "everything under Heaven," by definition self-sufficient, and therefore needing nothing from the outside. China's allowance of trade probably came in small part from its traditional paternalistic outlook toward barbarians, but more likely it resulted from the government's desire to profit from the trade even as it outwardly frowned on it.

Even with the opening of four ports, much of the trade gravitated to Canton (Guangzhou). Beginning in the 1720s, Canton merchants dealing with Western trade established their own guild, the Cohong (from *gonghang*, or cooperative merchant companies), to monopolize trade; the guild was composed of thirteen "hong" (from *hang*, or company) merchants. The government made them guarantors for the behavior of foreigners and payment of transit fees. In 1759, the East India Company sent James Flint to undertake talks with the government about the trading situation at Canton. Flint violated Chinese restrictions by sailing to northern ports and presenting petitions using incorrect procedures. In retaliation, the court decreed that Canton from that time would be the only open port and that Europeans could trade only with the Cohong under the general control of a Superintendent of Maritime Customs (the "hoppo"). If the government were compelled to trade, it would make certain that it gained some profit. In this case, the profit came from the hong merchants, who both had to buy their positions and then make extensive annual gifts and contributions as well. In 1834, for example, what they paid totaled over 456,000 taels. Hong merchant willingness to pay such a sum points to the lucrative nature of the monopoly and their ability to profit from it.[6]

Over time, a procedure of trade and barbarian management called the "Canton system" evolved. Essentially it was an effort to fit Western merchants into the traditional tributary state framework; as such, the system set various rules and regulations that outsiders had to follow. They had to pay cash for any purchased goods. They could not enter the walled city of Canton, could not ride in sedan chairs, could not learn the Chinese language, and could not bring weapons or women to the thirteen Western "factories" or trading posts located on the bank of the Pearl River outside the city walls. They could only deal with hong merchants and could attempt no direct communications with Chinese officials; any communication with officials went first to the Cohong and had to include the character for "petition." Finally, if a regulation were violated or other problems developed, the Chinese halted all trade, as in the traditional tributary system—until the outsiders came to their senses and followed Chinese directions. The Westerners were generally willing to dance to the tributary tune that the Chinese played and thus were able to continue to purchase the tea, silk, and porcelains that European and American customers desired.

By the turn of the nineteenth century, tea made up 80 percent of Chinese exports to Europe. From the picking of tea buds and leaves to the delivery of tea chests in British ports, the tea trade was an arduous and lengthy undertaking. Black teas were harvested in Fujian province, approximately 400 miles northeast of Canton; green teas came from even farther away, 500 to 600 miles, in Zhejiang, Jiangxi, and Anhui provinces. From an economic perspective, limiting Western trade to Canton made the tea business more difficult and costly. The tea had to be carried by porters over mountain trails until rivers could be reached to boat the tea to Canton; in addition to transport costs, money had to be paid out to toughs along the routes to protect the cargo. There were at least three tea pickings per year, in March–April, May, and June. The early spring harvest began to arrive in Canton in October, with most arriving from November to January. It was stored in warehouses near the Western factories until Western ships picked it up. Western ships generally left London in the early spring for the four-to-six-month voyage to Canton. They were usually at that port in October and out to sea again by January. The round trip from London to Canton took over a year.

Despite such a long haul and the hassles of the Canton system, the eighteenth and early nineteenth centuries saw trade continually expanding; from 1719 to 1833 the tonnage of foreign ships increased more than thirteen times. And, little wonder, given the fact that in the late 1820s enough tea was imported into England to give every man, woman, and child two pounds a year. But despite the flourishing trade, Westerners were unable to change the terms and procedures of the trade. In 1793, the British East India Company sent Lord George Macartney to try to expand trading privileges, open more trading ports, and establish diplomatic residence. But the Qianlong emperor treated the effort as a tributary mission, and there were no changes in Chinese policy. An 1816 follow-up mission, led by Lord William Amherst, was not even formally received.

Recent studies have cautioned against seeing what happened in encounters between the representatives of China and those of foreign countries, such as in the Macartney mission, as a clash of cultures or of civilizations.[7] Just as we have been reminded repeatedly that there are many Chinas, so there were many Western countries with their own structures, outlooks, and practices. And there were, to focus on Macartney's land, many British who would have had their own approaches, outlooks, and styles. Historical analysis must dissect the realities of each moment and not assume that one abstracted variable, say culture, explains what happened. Thus, in any close study of the 1793 mission, Macartney should be seen as "an exemplar of a specific stratum of late eighteenth-century British society rather than a 'Westerner' in some undifferentiated, timeless sense."[8] These points are especially important in understanding people trying to deal with the Other, for the prevailing tendency was to over-generalize and make the Other undifferentiated.

CHINA AND THE WEST: MUTUAL PERCEPTIONS

To the Chinese, Western merchants and diplomatic emissaries coming to the east coast of the country were first simply eastern barbarians. Indeed, in the 1860s, after two decades of treaty making, the British ambassador was still referred to in Chinese sources as the "English barbarian chieftain."[9] There was great confusion in Chinese minds over the separate identities of Western countries, likely in part a reflection of Chinese inability to perceive much physical difference among Westerners. They all looked alike—with their big noses, generally light-colored eyes and hair, ruddy complexions, and hairy bodies. The last contributed to their repulsive body odor, especially after months on board ships in the tropics; it was a sickening smell that the Chinese, who had comparatively little body hair and odor, had trouble tolerating. Rumor had it that because of their light-colored eyes, Westerners could not see at night. Matteo Ricci's colleague Diego de Pantoja was a blue-eyed Spaniard; he reported in a letter, "The Chinese find them very mysterious, and normally say that my eyes spy where to find precious stones and the like ... claiming even that they have characters written inside them."[10]

Some Chinese claimed that Westerners could not bend their knees or stretch out their legs or feet, as Chinese could. It is surely the case that the confusion and ignorance came from lack of contact, lack of interest, and strong repugnance—realities that also gave rise to reporting only superficial characteristics that seemed strikingly different from Chinese attributes. One writer, for example, noted that

> their flesh is dazzling white, and their noses are lofty … their custom is to esteem women and think lightly of men. … The men are violent and tyrannical and skilled in the use of weapons. They wear short coats and tip their black felt hats as a sign of politeness. The Swedes and the Englishmen like to take snuff, which they carry in little containers made of golden thread.

At best, Westerners were quaint curiosities; at worst, they were morally and intellectually inferior or even savages—foreign devils—who lived "as a herd of cattle." An important Manchu official reported on England: "This is naturally a country of barbarians, with the nature of dogs and sheep, fundamentally ignorant of rites and of modesty; how can they know the distinction between ruler and subject, and upper and lower?"[11]

Views of China in the abstract among Western intellectuals and some statesmen in the late eighteenth century, as we have seen, had been positive, even enthusiastic. Once merchants and then missionaries went to China to deal with Chinese on a day-to-day basis, the labor and stresses of cultural interaction began to color the views of some, though not all. One with negative views, whose musings were published and who allegedly helped create growing anti-Chinese feeling in the West, was British Commodore George Anson. Anson asserted that he had been treated badly by Chinese—given the bureaucratic runaround and overcharged—when he had entered Canton harbor in 1743 for repair work on his ship. As a result, he paid the Chinese back with bitter assessments of the people: "Indeed, this much may undoubtedly be asserted, that in artifice, falsehood, and an attachment to all kinds of lucre, many of the Chinese are difficult to be paralleled by any other people."[12] Anson accused the Chinese of being innately dishonest, of being second rate in handicraft arts, and of suffering confusion due to the "infinite obscurity" of their language. Missionaries, as we will see, brought their own brand of verbal abuse. Suffice it to say that the perceptions that developed on both sides when Westerners interacted with Chinese helped to shape actions and reactions then and later, sometimes tragically so.

OPIUM: THE PROBLEM AND THE WAR

The serious trade problem for Western merchants was that they had nothing that the Chinese wanted to buy. At Canton, stevedores would unload the cargo: from Britain, woolens and lead; and from goods picked up in India and stops in Southeast Asia (in what was known as the "country trade"), camphor, tin, cotton piece goods, rattan, birds' nests, fish maws, and spices. Had it not been for the South Asian and Southeast Asian items, the British position would have been a complete disaster. Woolens, the main British export, hardly appealed to Chinese in tropical Canton and its environs. Even with the country trade, there was a severe trade imbalance. British ships arrived in Canton with 90 percent of their stock composed of bullion, mostly silver. The annual flow of silver into China reached over 3 million taels in the 1760s but soared to 16 million twenty years later. But then opium came to Britain's rescue.

The Chinese had begun to smoke opium in the seventeenth century, first mixing it with tobacco in a regular pipe, a practice perhaps first introduced by the Dutch in Taiwan. Smoked in this way, each pipe gave the smoker about 0.2 percent of morphine by volume. By the mid-eighteenth century, Chinese had begun to smoke pure opium by heating refined opium paste and inhaling it through a long-stemmed pipe; this method provided the smoker with 9 or 10 percent of morphine. Opium smoking renders its users inert and dormant. The French writer Jean Cocteau described the drug as "the only vegetable substance that communicates the vegetable state to us."[13] Those who sought some kind of escape from stress and boredom were most attracted to the drug. Its use stretched across the social landscape from rich to poor, from high officials to clerks and runners in county government offices, from eunuchs and bureaucrats in the Forbidden City to peasants, from merchants and coolies to soldiers. The most serious implications for China's political and social health was the reported high number of smokers in the military and in government offices—the first, because inert soldiers cannot fight; and the second, because secretaries, clerks, and runners were the government bureaucrats with whom most people came into contact on a daily basis: finding them incapacitated by opium would not have filled people with great confidence in their government.

Estimates of the number of smokers vary, though about 10 percent of the population was a commonly accepted figure; the number of addicts may have reached 3 to 5 percent of the population.[14] The personal tragedy was addiction. Without daily fixes, the user experiences the hellish misery of withdrawal, with a variety of wretched physical and psychological symptoms. Cocteau, himself an addict, wrote that the person experiencing withdrawal should "bury his head in his arm, to glue his ear to that arm, and wait. Catastrophe, riots, factories blowing up, armies in flight, flood—the ear can detect a whole apocalypse in the starry night of the human body."[15] In patterns well known from contemporary society, it is apparent that the addict would do whatever it took to get opium—from using all of his household's money to various criminal activities. Addiction, then, led to a host of social problems.

In 1800 and 1813, new imperial edicts (which followed earlier prohibitions in 1729 and 1796) forbade opium importation, production, and consumption. Although the Cohong had handled the purchases of opium until then, the new edicts made it impossible for such aboveboard purchases. Consequently, opium importation became opium smuggling. Western ships anchored off the marshy delta, with its many small bays and crisscrossing creeks and streams, unloading opium chests either onto a receiving ship that served as a floating warehouse or onto well-armed but shallow draft Chinese boats that delivered the goods to networks in the delta and beyond Canton. The number of chests smuggled into the country grew dramatically, from 4,000 to 5,000 around 1820 to 18,000 in 1828 to 40,000 in 1839.[16] The smuggling got a huge boost when the East India Company's trade monopoly was abolished in 1834; then more individual shippers got into the smuggling business. Other countries joined in the trade; U.S. firms, for example, picked up opium in Turkey. There were many sides to the developing tragedy. Perhaps the most ironic was that some—large numbers of Chinese *and* the British nation as a whole—were becoming economic addicts of the drug, as it were. As the number of chests increased, the number of Chinese involved in the smuggling trade grew, becoming increasingly dependent on it for their economic livelihood. For the British, the opium trade meant that their unfavorable trade balance had been righted; now the trade imbalance was on the Chinese side, with silver bullion leaving Chinese coffers to pay for opium.

The outflow of silver has been estimated at up to 9 million taels annually in the early 1830s, an almost fivefold increase from the 1820s. Such a huge outflow destabilized the Chinese economy, because it was based on a bimetallic system of silver and copper. As silver left the country, it became more expensive in terms of copper. Although daily purchases were made in copper, copper coins had to be changed into silver for the payment of taxes. In the province of Shandong, far from the site of the smuggling, in 1800 it took between 1,450 and 1,650 copper cash to equal one silver tael; in 1830, it took 2,700.[17] Thus, taxes were dramatically driven up by the outflow of silver. This growing economic pressure was worsened by years of bad harvests in the first half of the 1830s, a situation that created food shortages and rising prices.[18] The crisis of international relations and the opium-induced social and cultural crisis thus helped create an economic crisis as well.

The Daoguang emperor, having successfully fended off the takeover of the Forbidden City by rebels in 1813, could not so easily and decisively beat back the opium crisis. He had issued anti-opium edicts in 1821, 1822, 1823, 1828, 1829, 1831, 1832, 1834, 1835, 1838, and 1839. This year-by-year listing suggests the persistence of the throne's actions, but they were to little avail. The emperor was especially angry to learn that the imperial clan, key banner officers, and high civil servants were opium users. The court debated its course of action. Some advocated legalizing the drug so that it might be traded and taxed, with the goal of taxing it so greatly that the expense might decrease some of its use; at the least, such a policy would make up for the outflow of silver. Others opposed legalization, arguing that it would only worsen the social problems stemming from opium use.

In the end, in early 1839 the emperor decided that the opium trade had to be wiped out. He had found the advice of an official, Lin Zexu, persuasive—that the importers and distributors of the drug, rather than the users, had to bear the principal force of government actions. To suppress the opium traffic, the emperor in March appointed Lin as imperial commissioner. It was an appointment that seemed a good bet to deal with the problem successfully, for Lin had the highest credentials and a reputation for incorruptibility—for which he was known as Lin, the Blue Sky. In trying to quash the distribution system, Lin rapidly mobilized gentry and local officials to name opium dealers and distributors. By July 1839, he had arrested about 1,700 Chinese and confiscated 44,000 pounds of opium and over 70,000 opium pipes.

In trying to deal with the problem of importation, Lin demanded that the foreigners turn over their opium stocks. He tried to reason with the British and use shame to get them to surrender the drug. His plaintive words in a message to Queen Victoria:

> The wealth of China is used to profit the barbarians. ... By what right do they then in return use the poisonous drug to injure the Chinese people? Even though the barbarians may not necessarily intend to do us harm, yet in coveting profit to such an extreme, they have no regard for injuring others. Let us ask, where is your conscience?[19]

Such appeals had little effect: the British first ignored the order, then refused. Following the logic of the tributary system, Lin then stopped all trade and set up a siege of the factories and their 350 foreigners. They held out for six weeks, blasting the action as a "piratical act against British lives, liberty, and property."[20] When they finally delivered over 21,000 chests to Lin, he had 500 laborers dig three immense trenches—7 feet deep, 25 feet wide, and 150 feet long, line them with flagstones on the bottom and timber on the sides, fill them with 2 feet of water, put in the more than 2.6 million pounds of opium, decompose it using salt and lime, and flush it out to the sea. This monumental task took twenty-two days to complete. He composed a prayer to the God of the Sea, apologizing for polluting the waters and endangering sea creatures. He had won what seemed a moral victory over the opium-smuggling foreigners.

But it was a pyrrhic victory. Because the British superintendent of foreign trade had been, since 1834, a representative of the crown and not a merchant company, the British treated the siege and the seizure of opium as a national affront and a cause for war. Hostilities began with clashes between war junks in fall 1839 after incidents in the summer had ratcheted up tensions. The Daoguang emperor, who had been impressed with Lin Zexu's memorials on the opium problem, was infuriated by the results of his policy. In comments on Lin's explanation of what had gone wrong, the emperor wrote that Lin had "caused the waves of confusion to arise" and "a thousand interminable disorders" to grow. "In fact you appear as if your arms were tied, without knowing what to do. It appears that you are no better than a wooden image."[21] With that, the emperor sent Lin into exile in Turkestan for four years.

The war itself was an on-again, off-again struggle against a backdrop of negotiations between the two sides. Serious talks began in the fall of 1840, with a settlement reached in early 1841. But both the Daoguang emperor and Prime Minister Henry Palmerston were upset that the settlement was too lenient for the other side. The fighting then dragged on for a year and a half longer before the signing of the Treaty of Nanjing in August 1842 ended it with the surrender of the Central Country to the English barbarians.

For the Chinese, it was a military disaster, underlining the reality that the imperial forces were desperately outmoded. The British not only had large, traditional men-of-war but also steam-driven, shallow-draft crafts that could glide up inland streams. The Chinese, in stark contrast, had no navy at all. There was simply no way that they could compete with the steam-powered warship that one day in early 1841, with withering long-distance artillery, destroyed nine war junks, two military stations, five forts, and a shore battery. In land fighting it was the same. The British, sporting the latest in technology, fought the Chinese with self-firing rifles. The banner forces had matchlocks, in which the gunpowder had to be ignited by hand; most troops had only cold weapons—knives, swords, clubs, and spears. The mid-century official Zuo Zongtang probably summed it up best: "the land troops could neither ride nor shoot and the water troops could not sail or fire a cannon."[22]

The Opium War was the opening salvo of a century of aggression by Western nations against China, a century of conflict between very different cultures with sharply differing values; yet each clash would have its own particulars and realities. An eventual war may have been likely, but it was particularly tragic that this first conflict centered on questions of international morality, specifically England's demand that it had a right to smuggle opium into China no matter what the drug was doing to China or many of its people. For a number of Chinese this pivotal first confrontation with the West marked the West as amoral, if not immoral: the plaintive question of Lin Zexu echoes—"Let us ask, where is your conscience?" One consequence of the war was that foreign nations continued to import opium into the country despite Chinese laws forbidding its sale and use. Whereas the number of chests smuggled into China in 1839 was about 40,000, by 1884 the number brought into the country had more than doubled to 81,000.[23]

THE UNEQUAL TREATY SYSTEM AND ITS IMPACT ON CHINESE IDENTITY

The Treaty of Nanjing, which ceded Hong Kong Island to Great Britain, was the first of many treaties between China and foreign nations that were called "unequal" because China did all the giving and received nothing in return. The treaties began to erode China's sovereignty. In the beginning, the Chinese deluded themselves by rationalizing that their "generosity" matched their traditional tributary benevolence. It was only over time that they realized the insidious nature of the treaties. A cornerstone of the system was the application of the most-favored-nation principle, put in place in a supplementary treaty Britain and China signed in 1843. It promised that each country would receive every right and privilege that every other country received even if it was not specified in its particular treaty. For example, the Treaty of Nanjing did not contain a provision for renegotiations. The U.S.–Chinese Treaty of Wangxia of 1844 did, however, provide that possibility in ten years' time. The British then used the most-favored-nation clause to claim that right and demanded renegotiation of their treaty in 1852. From the Chinese perspective, as benevolent tributary elder brother, it was simply providing the same privileges magnanimously to all Western countries.

The early treaties were signed under the leadership of a group of Manchus at the court who had come to favor greater conciliation in dealing with the West. Led by the chief councilor, Mujangga, this group dominated diplomacy relative to the West from 1840 to 1850 under the policy of avoiding at all costs actions that might incite a new military conflict. They were opposed by groups of Han Chinese literati who supported stronger resistance against the West and opposed any treaty that would give the West more trading rights. During the opium crisis, these groups were strong proponents of Lin's cutting off trade with Britain in 1838 and of fighting the British with local militia units that allegedly had a more resistant and determined spirit than the banner forces. The Manchu–Han Chinese hostility at the highest level of the government was also apparent in Lin Zexu's exile, which Mujangga demanded and which the Han Chinese opposed. This difference in policy outlook should not be taken to suggest that the Manchus were easy on the West because they were outsiders themselves. For the Manchus, it was a choice over which strategy was least dangerous for the country until it could more effectively meet the challenge of the West. For the Han Chinese, who saw themselves as upholding the principle of protecting the morality of the state and culture against the attack of immoral barbarians, the Manchu policy was disgustingly weak and had to be morally censured.

When the Daoguang emperor's son, the Xianfeng emperor, took power in 1850, he dismissed Mujangga, whom he personally detested, as well as his allies. As if to underscore the shift from his father, he appointed Lin Zexu to deal with the growing social unrest in the South and brought back to policymaking positions Han Chinese whom Mujangga had earlier ousted. Once in power, they did not try to undo the treaty system under construction, but they downplayed appeasement in their dealings with the West.

Foreign Concessions

The series of treaties opened up more ports for trade and foreign residence. The Treaty of Nanjing, for example, opened up four new ports (Xiamen [Amoy], Fuzhou, Ningbo, and Shanghai) to join Canton as a site for foreign settlements and continuous trade. Each port was chosen for its role in the already existent maritime trade. Xiamen was a center of the junk trade with Southeast Asia; Fuzhou was the main tributary port for Taiwan and the Ryūkyū Island tributary missions; Ningbo was the traditional port involved in trade with North China, Korea, and Japan. Shanghai was a developing port near the Yangzi's mouth. Other treaties opened more ports, first along the coast, then on inland rivers, especially the Yangzi.

Foreign concessions were areas carved out of existing Chinese cities where foreigners now became the rulers. In these areas where many Chinese still lived, foreigners assessed the taxes and collected them; foreign police and troops patrolled there; foreign law was the authority there. Thus, Chinese residents of foreign concessions were uprooted from their native country without moving an inch, and Chinese sovereignty over these former citizens was ended. Yet the Chinese did not react strongly to the situation; they could point to the precedent in past dynasties when Arab traders in particular lived with their own laws in designated parts of port cities.

The number of foreigners was small, growing at the five ports from about 450 in 1846 to around 600 in 1854. Most of these people had been resident for some time before the war at Canton, so there was a sense among the treaty port foreigners of being one community, a sense that may have been heightened by some Chinese cultural hostility. The British, having "opened" China, led the way in the creation of the treaty system and in the life of the ports. Approximately half of the foreign populace, predominantly men, was from the British Isles, with another quarter from India, so that treaty port life was reflective of the British–Indian culture of the time.

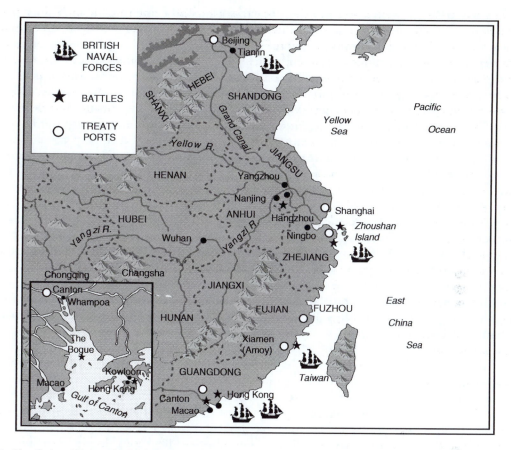

MAP 3.1   The Opium War and Initial Treaty Ports.

The foreign population was made up mostly of merchants, with a fairly small number of missionaries. The most important merchant houses were two British firms—Jardine, Matheson and Company and Dent and Company; the major American firm was the Boston-based Russell and Company. All three had been involved in the opium trade; in the new treaty ports, they still brought in opium but participated as well in legal commerce and expanded their interests into such areas as banks and insurance, go-downs (warehouses), and shipyards. The head of a foreign firm had to rely completely on a Chinese middleman, or comprador, who spoke enough pidgin English (a mixture of Portuguese, Chinese, and English) to converse with the foreigner and who could fulfill the needs of the firm through his contacts in the Chinese community, overseeing transactions and being responsible for the firm's Chinese personnel. Many compradors became extremely wealthy.

Extraterritoriality with Consular Jurisdiction

Another treaty right established by the West was extraterritoriality with consular jurisdiction, by which a foreigner accused of a crime would be tried not in a Chinese court but in one presided over by the consul of his nation. The Western rationale was that Chinese law was barbaric. Western culture had made law the centerpiece of its political, social, and economic life ever since the deity had handed it down. Chinese culture had denigrated law as the last recourse for people who could not deal with their fellow men in proper moral fashion. China had no independent profession of law, nor were there lawyers. No independent judiciary existed. The county magistrate investigated cases, presided as court judge, and delivered judicial decisions. In criminal cases, punishments were prescribed; since extenuating circumstances were not considered, magistrates had to follow them. Suspects were presumed guilty and were treated severely; torture and beating were expected if the suspect did not confess. Those who had passed even the lower-level civil service examination were exempted from physical punishment in such cases. At times of local social disturbances, those involved in the action might be subject to summary execution. In homicide cases, the Chinese system firmly upheld an "eye for an eye" policy. There was little consideration if the death was an accident, and there was no possible lesser charge, as in the West, of involuntary manslaughter. If a life was taken, a life must be given. If the killer could not be found, then a family member or someone connected to the killer could substitute.

Western experience with the Chinese legal system stretched back to the early eighteenth century, but the two most famous cases related to two ships, the British ship *Lady Hughes* in 1784 and the Baltimore-based American ship *Emily* in 1821. The country-trading *Lady Hughes* sailed up to Canton with very important people on board. The gunner fired a salute, the discharge from the shot killing two Chinese. When the ship's captain refused to tell the Chinese which gunner fired the shot, they arrested the ship's business manager, who was then threatened with punishment as an associate, as it were, of the gunner. When the gunner was eventually turned over to the Chinese, he was, in accord with China's eye-for-an-eye homicide law, strangled. His execution following the deaths that most British considered accidental underscored in foreign minds the barbarism of the Chinese legal system. In a similar case, a sailor on the *Emily* was responsible for the death of a Chinese woman on a boat; though there are different accounts of the nature of the death, the sailor was seized and executed. Because of these experiences, when drunken British sailors went ashore near Hong Kong and beat a Chinese villager to death in the summer of 1839, the British refused to turn them over to Chinese authorities. The episode ratcheted up tensions already high over the opium crisis. Westerners took the position that extraterritoriality was necessary until the Chinese amended their legal system.

Initially there was no strong Chinese reaction to this loss of control over foreign citizens. For one thing, it meant that the Chinese did not have to burden themselves with learning all the languages of these barbarians. As with the establishment of foreign settlements, China could find a precedent for such an arrangement: they had allowed Tang dynasty Arab traders in Canton to hold extraterritoriality. But difficulties surfaced quickly when, as in foreign settlements, some Chinese also gained a measure of protection in their own courts from Westerners protected by extraterritoriality. This happened among different groups. For example, when a comprador or another key Chinese personnel of a Western business firm was accused of a crime, the officers of the firm understandably became highly agitated. Without their intervention, there was the possibility that he would be found guilty. With imprisonment or worse, he would then be lost to the firm. Since compradors were the key to business success, performing the crucial middleman role, in such cases Western firms faced financial losses or even bankruptcy. To find a new comprador would take much time, and for a new comprador to make the required business connections and arrangements would take much longer. Thus, officers of Western firms began to intervene in court cases, pressuring Chinese courts to be more lenient to the firm's protégés than they otherwise might be.

Western missionaries also offered such protection to their accused protégés, Chinese converts. Missionaries may have worked many hard years for only a dozen or so converts. Imagine the chagrin when, say, the first convert and leader of the congregation was accused of a crime. Missionaries would have wanted to vouch for the man, and in many instances they intervened in Chinese court cases or prevailed on their foreign consul to do so for them. When, as it happened more than once, missionaries resorted to having their consuls dispatch gunboats to force their way in difficult cases, the matter became not simply a legal dispute but one of brute force. In episodes where the missionary was successful, it almost seemed as though he was able to impart some measure of extraterritoriality to his convert; in any case, there came to be a category of Chinese who were more privileged than others, a particularly galling situation for the non-privileged.

According to the treaties, China also lost its sovereign right to set, control, and collect its own tariffs. Tariff rates were set at about 5 percent of the value of the goods, not raising a red flag in Chinese minds because they were not notably out of line with traditional tariff rates. But the times were not traditional. Unable to raise tariffs, the Chinese could not, for example, keep out unwanted items. Perhaps more important, China's enforced paralysis relative to tariffs had serious implications for China's efforts to industrialize. During the Opium War, China came face-to-face with modern technology in the form of ships and weapons; the experience was a catalyst, spurring some Chinese to begin to think initially about buying them from the West and ultimately to consider manufacturing them themselves. But Chinese efforts to establish modern industry, both heavy and light, were hampered by their inability to raise tariffs to protect their infant industry. In the twentieth century, Communist thinkers and activists were especially condemnatory about the loss of tariff control, for they argued that it prevented China from entering the capitalist era, thereby short-circuiting China's passage through the "scientific" evolution of history described by Marx.

Not only did China lose control of its tariffs, it also lost the right (of any sovereign state) to collect those customs duties. In the 1850s, in the middle of the turmoil of the Taiping Rebellion in the vicinity of Shanghai, the British began collecting customs duties to ensure their collection. This collection became institutionalized in the Chinese Maritime Customs Service. Even though the long-time director, Robert Hart, was effective and dedicated, seeing himself essentially as part of the Chinese bureaucracy, the collection of customs for one country by another was a humiliating loss of sovereignty. China would not gain control of tariffs or their collection until 1933.

Another sovereign right of a nation is to control its rivers and streams, specifically to control who can sail up those waterways into its interior regions. This right is obviously critical for a country's security and defense. Yet, according to the treaties, China could not make any inland waterway off limits to foreign ships, nor could it prevent ships of any nation from penetrating its space via its rivers.

Foreign Ambassadorial Residence

The main structure of the treaty system was completed by the Treaty of Tianjin (1858) and its follow-up, the Convention of Beijing (1860). These agreements came in the midst of another war waged by Britain and France against China. Called the Arrow War and sometimes the Second Opium War, this struggle began with the British accusation that a Chinese ship (the *Arrow*) under British registry had been illegally searched by Chinese officers pursuing a Chinese pirate. Overreactions to a series of incidents led to fighting and to British calls for upholding the honor and interests of Great Britain abroad. In the end, France joined the campaign, using as an excuse the murder of a French missionary in an area that was off limits to foreigners. It is hard to avoid the conclusion that both countries were simply looking for a pretext to force further political and economic demands on China.

The British and French took Canton in December 1857 and then sailed north, seizing in summer 1858 the coastal Dagu forts that provided strategic protection for key cities in the capital region and taking the city of Tianjin. Negotiations ensued, producing the treaty that bears the city's name. It expanded the treaty system and established two more exceptionally significant rights. As for expanding the system, it opened ten new treaty ports, four of them on the Yangzi River. It allowed anyone with a passport to travel anywhere in the country, and passports were not even required for travel up to 30 miles from treaty ports.

One of the new rights set forth in the treaty was that ambassadors of foreign states would reside permanently in Beijing. An important aspect of the tributary system had been to designate ports of entry far away from the capital in order to keep the Chinese home port at a distance for foreigners. They were escorted to the capital and, following the prescribed rituals, were allowed to remain in Beijing for only a specified period. There was no ongoing presence of foreigners in the capital or anywhere else in China. Now diplomatic representatives from all barbarian nations could live near the Forbidden City. This, the Chinese could not abide. Even after the treaty was signed, they continued to fight. In the summer of 1859 the British again attacked the forts but were repulsed. When a British negotiating team was sent to Beijing, it was arrested and some members were killed. The British commander, Lord James Elgin, decided that strong measures must be taken in revenge and to force compliance with the treaty. He sent his troops to occupy Beijing; the emperor fled the capital for his hunting lodge north of the Great Wall. In October 1860, Elgin's troops marched northwest of the city to the Summer Palace (Yuan Ming Yuan), a complex of over 200 pavilions and pagodas built during the reign of the Qianlong emperor. There they looted its thrones, furniture, porcelains, and robes; then Elgin gave orders for them to burn the whole 10-square-mile area. Chinese resistance against aggressive Western armies had turned beauty to ashes. The words of an Englishman with Elgin's army:

> But whenever I think of beauty and taste, of skill and antiquity, while I live, I shall see before my mind's eye some scene from those grounds, those palaces, and ever regret the stern but just necessity which laid them in ashes.[24]

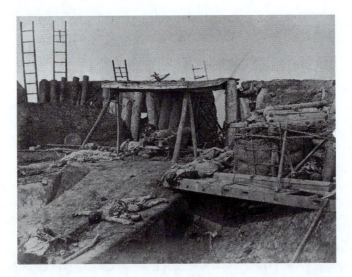

FIGURE 3.1   The British took the strategic Dagu fort in May 1858, but they were repulsed by the Chinese when they tried to take it back in June 1859. Here many Chinese lie dead after the first attack.
Source: Felice Beato/Getty Images.

Six days after the torching, the Chinese agreed in the Convention of Beijing to the permanent residence of foreign ambassadors in the capital. One minor stipulation of the treaty was that from that time on, China could no longer use the character for "barbarian" (*yi*) in referring to the British. What underlay this stipulation and the demand for permanent diplomatic residence was the Western state model of equality among nations, a model with which the traditional tributary system with its hierarchy of superior/subordinate could never coexist. Though it would take decades for the system to die in Chinese thinking, for all practical purposes the centuries-long tributary system was dead. Although China never became a full-fledged colony, its loss of sovereignty over its own territory and people created what has been called a "semicolony," subject to the demands and pressures of not one but many foreign nations.

THE MISSIONARY AND CULTURAL IMPERIALISM

The Treaty of Tianjin granted another crucial right to Western nations: the guarantee that Christianity could be openly taught and practiced. Missionaries could travel anywhere, purchase property for church and school, and spread their message at will. The record of the impact of nineteenth-century missionaries is complex: each missionary naturally had personal motives; they came from a variety of countries, each with its own approaches to China and attitudes toward the mission effort. Yet missionaries shared one thing: their conviction that they possessed absolute Truth. Largely because of this, the story of the relationship between missionaries and Chinese was by and large not a happy one. The political and social landscape of the dynasty's last half century is marked by episode after episode of turmoil and violence touched off by the actions of missionaries in communities across China.

As we have seen, the Yongzheng emperor (1722–1736) outlawed Christianity. From that time on, Christianity had to operate underground; in the early nineteenth century, persecutions with arrests, punishments, and executions were frequent. As a measure of the control exercised in this area, only one new missionary entered China during the years 1801–1829—the Protestant Robert Morrison, who entered Canton with the protection of the East India Company. Beginning in the late 1810s, Catholic missionaries began to build Catholic communities around the country; the first American Protestants came in 1830. Others followed. One, the German Karl Gutzlaff, is not a symbol of all missionaries at the time, but his actions point to something all missionaries shared—a willingness to use any means necessary to spread the gospel. Gutzlaff became a translator on opium ships plying the China coast. From these ships dispensing opium, Gutzlaff also distributed Christian tracts. The message the Chinese ultimately picked up from this mix of Christ and opium must at the least have distorted the Christian intent.

In viewing the Chinese, the missionaries were convinced of their own superiority and the unimpeachable Truth of their message. The Chinese, in their estimation, were benightedly superstitious, greedy, and materialistic. In that state, they desperately needed what the Christian message offered. But these early missionaries were frustrated by the prohibition against the open practice of Christianity and frequently attacked Chinese policies regarding the West and Western merchants. By the late 1830s, some missionaries were calling for armed invasion by the West "to break down the barriers which prevent the gospel of Christ from entering China."[25] Once the Opium War broke out and battles led to the slaughter of Chinese, one missionary opined: "I regard such scenes . . . as the direct instruments of the Lord clearing away the rubbish which impedes the advancement of Divine Truth."[26] Although this missionary saw the Chinese people as "rubbish," others used other adjectives: "imbecilic," "ignorant," "conceited," "weak," "heathen," "pagan." It does not take much imagination to realize how these conceptions of the people they wanted to save would affect their approach.

In 1844, as part of a general treaty with France, the Qing government removed its proscription against Christianity. The 1860 treaty further solidified the toleration of the Western religion. The number of missionaries entering China grew quickly. By 1870, 250 Catholic missionaries represented a number of orders; at least 350 Protestant missionaries were in China by that year. Yet the Catholics, who had a long history of mission work in China, were far ahead of the Protestants in terms of conversions. In 1870 there were approximately 400,000 Catholic converts as opposed to about 6,000 Protestants. The Catholic mission at that time had spread throughout China, whereas the Protestant effort was concentrated in treaty ports mostly along the coast.

Unhappily, the missionaries retained the same attitudes toward the Chinese people that they had shown during the Opium War period. Their approach in all daily matters was that they were the privileged, who had to have their own way in every matter—especially in dealing with the rabble Chinese. That approach raises the question of whether a missionary could be sincerely tolerant of a society that he or she wanted to change to some degree; even if sympathetic, was it not the case that rejection of that society as it existed was at the heart of his or her approach? Missionaries frequently wanted to protect their converts by intervening in their legal cases; they felt they could rely on the support of their national consuls, who had the treaties behind them. In extreme situations, a missionary called for his consul to send a gunboat for a show of force or firepower if he was thwarted by local officials in his demands. The government of France, which saw the Catholic establishment in China as the vehicle for furthering its national interest, became the demanding protector of the Catholic mission. In one famous case, the governor of Guizhou province was accused of ordering various anti-Christian moves. The Catholic bishop lobbied French diplomats to have them pressure the Chinese government first to have the governor removed and then to have him executed; the French legation in Beijing did so. From the perspective of the French, they still had to rid themselves of the "rubbish" impeding their way. From the perspective of the Chinese government, here were foreigners demanding the transfer and execution of a Chinese provincial governor, a matter over which outsiders should have no say in another sovereign state.

The Chinese reaction to missionaries and their work grew out of reactions to foreigners in general and to the missionaries' message and approach in particular. Although Chinese elites did not necessarily speak for all Chinese, elite attitudes filtered down to the masses, affecting their reactions. Educated Chinese generally saw all non-Chinese and their ideas as barbarian. Whereas the Chinese saw themselves as grounded in realistic pragmatism, some Christian teachings, such as a virgin birth and a father allowing his son to be crucified, seemed not only superstitious but downright scandalous. Further, the Chinese saw missionaries in their daily activities maneuvering to purchase the best sites for their churches and pronounced them materialistic and grabbing. Many Chinese scholar elites found missionaries to be direct threats in their local communities. Products of the Chinese civil service examination system, scholar-gentry were the locality's teachers, mediators, authorities, and charity providers. When missionaries moved into an area and converted Chinese, they were the obvious leaders of their congregations. In that capacity, they performed the same functions for their congregations—teaching, mediating, and providing charity—which gentry did for society at large. Therefore, not only were gentry upset by this usurpation of their roles, but, just as the treaties had done with foreign concessions and extraterritoriality, the missionary presence and roles separated some Chinese from others.

Chinese elites did not have access to gunboats or instruments of force to deal with offensive missionaries, but they did wield the writing brush. They wrote propaganda tracts about missionaries and their work with the intent to tar the missionary with the broad brush of sexual immorality. This was a tactic that traditionally had been an important weapon in the Chinese political attack repertoire. Here is a sample from a tract, "A Record of Facts to Ward Off Heterodoxy" (*Bixie zhishi*), first published in 1861 but reprinted many times in the decades following:

> During the first three months of life the anuses of all [Christian]
> infants—male and female—are plugged up with a small hollow tube,
> which is taken out at night. They call this "retention of the vital
> essence." It causes the anus to dilate so that upon growing up
> sodomy will be facilitated. At the junction of each spring
> and summer boys procure the menstrual discharge of women
> and, smearing it on their faces, go into Christian churches
> to worship. They call this "cleansing one's face before paying
> respects to the holy one" and regard it as one of the most
> venerative rituals by which the lord can be worshipped.
> Fathers and sons, elder and younger brothers, behave licentiously
> with one another, calling it "the joining of the vital forces." …
> There are all sorts of things of this nature that cannot be fully related.
> Hard as it may be to believe, some of our Chinese people also
> follow their religion. Are they not really worse than beasts?[27]

Such scatological tracts were widely circulated, painting for elites and non-elites who heard the tales pictures of despicable depravity and perversity. They certainly helped incite suspicion, anger, and fear among the Chinese populace. Indeed, Chinese authorities in at least three provinces, sensing its incendiary possibilities, banned this particular tract. Missionaries blamed such tracts for anti-Christian violence that erupted in numerous localities against themselves and their converts.

A paroxysm of violence in the northern treaty port city of Tianjin on the afternoon of June 21, 1870, underscores the cultural gulf and the fragility of relations that existed between foreign missionaries and Chinese. Tianjin was a city where relations with the West had set Chinese nerves on edge. It was there, following the signing of the 1858 treaty, that French and British troops had been based from 1860 to 1863. Having seized a former imperial mansion to serve as a consulate and having built a cathedral on the site of a former Chinese temple, the French were seen as arrogant and especially detested by the local populace. As if the latent animosity were not enough, in 1869 and 1870 anti-Christian writings had appeared in the area.

French Catholic nuns managed an orphanage in the compound of the large new cathedral of Notre Dame des Victoires. They were especially eager to be able to baptize sick children and administer last rites to those who might be near death. The orphanage thus saw a higher mortality rate than normal, a reality made worse by an epidemic that raced through the orphanage in June 1870. Suspicion spread about goings-on behind the compound's walls. Rumors abounded: orphans, it was said, were being killed, with their body parts used to make aphrodisiacs for priests and nuns in their alleged sex play. Chinese mistrust of French motives was heightened because the nuns had a policy of giving a small sum of money to people who turned children into the orphanage. In addition, once children were placed under the nuns' control, the nuns did not allow them to be reclaimed by anyone, even if they represented themselves as parents or relatives. This situation helped fuel the rumor that scoundrels were kidnapping children to turn them in to make some cash. The confession of a man arrested on June 18 that he had kidnapped several children and sold them to a janitor who worked for Catholic institutions in the city raised tensions to an almost palpable level.

As rumors swirled, Chinese began to demand to search the orphanage. The search of the premises by a high local official, his disproval of the kidnapper's confession, and his announcement that all seemed in order at the orphanage did not still the increasing agitation. When a fight broke out at the cathedral between converts and onlookers, the official dispatched soldiers to quash the disturbance. At the same time, the French consul and his chief secretary charged into the official's office, the consul carrying two pistols. Incredibly, the consul shot at the official. When he missed, attendants seized him. The official calmly advised that he not go back on the streets, where a huge, angry crowd was forming. Saying that he was not afraid of any Chinese, the consul walked into the crowd. When he spotted the local magistrate coming toward him, he totally lost control, opening fire again; he missed the magistrate but hit and killed his attendant.

The killing transformed the crowd into an angry mob that killed the consul and his officer on the spot, as well as nineteen others, including twelve priests and nuns. The French victims were mutilated: after being raped, the nuns had their breasts sliced off and their eyes gouged out before they were burned alive. Several dozen Chinese converts were also killed. The cathedral, along with four American and British churches, was burned. French demands followed. The settlement included a large sum for reparations, the execution of eighteen mob leaders and hard labor for twenty-five others, the exile of the high official and magistrate of Tianjin, and the sending of a mission of apology.[28] This violent episode often stands as a symbol of the seeming impossibility of amicable relations between these two sides.

If the faces of imperialism in its 3M onslaught—merchants, missionary, and military—differed as to motive, approach, and national and individual purpose, they all had some common features. They all believed that what they had to bring to the Chinese was infinitely better than what the Chinese had. Acting for the capitalist countries of the West, the merchants believed that they could shake China awake from its self-sufficient dream world into the system of multistate trade and that they could take advantage of the fabled China market. The military, with its power, had no doubt that it could blast apart the neanderthalic and outmoded Chinese regime and culture, thereby making possible the expansion of "enlightened" Western civilization. The missionary had the Truth to save Chinese from eternal damnation.

But they were dealing with a culture that gloried in its long history and vaunted traditions, with an intellectual elite that was absolutely certain of the superiority of its culture. In the depth of their commitment to their transcendent civilizational goals, these cultures were seemingly two immovable forces. The difference for the two sides in this confrontation was the timing of the Western arrival. The West's military power came in force at a time when China's military power was on life support. The historical game of "what if" often provides insights: *what if* the West's military had come during the military heyday of the late eighteenth century? We will never know for sure, but it is likely that the course of world history would have been markedly different, and it is likely that China's modern history would not have been so tragic.

Notes

1 See Liam Matthew Brockey, *Journey to the East: The Jesuit Mission to China, 1579–1724* (Cambridge, MA: The Belknap Press of Harvard University Press, 2007), p. 44.

2 Ibid., p. 171.

3 Ibid., p. 37.

4 Ibid., p. 419.

5 Ibid., pp. 106–7.

6 See Chang Hsin-pao, *Commissioner Lin and the Opium War* (Cambridge, MA: Harvard University Press, 1964), p. 14.

7 James Hevia, *Cherishing Men from Afar* (Durham, NC: Duke University Press, 1995), pp. 24–6.

8 Paul Cohen, "Review of *Britain in China* by Robert Bickers," *Journal of Asian Studies* 59, no. 2 (May 2000): 401.

9 This discussion is based on John King Fairbank, *Trade and Diplomacy on the Chinese Coast* (Cambridge, MA: Harvard University Press, 1954), pp. 9–20.

10 Quoted in Brockey, *Journey to the East*, p. 50.

11 Ibid., p. 19.

12 Quoted in Jonathan D. Spence, *The Chan's Great Continent* (New York: W.W. Norton, 1998), p. 53.

13 Quoted in Peter Ward Fay, *The Opium War, 1840–1842* (Chapel Hill, NC: University of North Carolina Press, 1975), p. 9.

14 Ibid., p. 154.

15 Ibid., p. 10.

16 Jonathan Spence, "Opium Smoking in Ch'ing China," in *Conflict and Control in Late Imperial China*, ed. Frederic Wakeman, Jr. and Carolyn Grant (Berkeley, CA: University of California Press, 1975), p. 151. A chest usually contained 133 English pounds.

17 Chang Hsin-pao, *Commissioner Lin*, p. 39.

18 James Polachek, *The Inner Opium War* (Cambridge, MA: Harvard University Press, 1992), p. 79.

19 "Lin Zexu's Moral Advice to Queen Victoria, 1839," in *China's Response to the West*, ed. Ssu-yu Teng and John K. Fairbank (Cambridge, MA: Harvard University Press, 1954), p. 25.

20 The phrase is Immanuel C.Y. Hsu's in *The Rise of Modern China* (New York: Oxford University Press, 1970), p. 228.

21 Fay, *The Opium War*, p. 268.

22 Paraphrased in John K. Fairbank, Edwin O. Reischauer, and Albert M. Craig, *East Asia, The Modern Transformation* (Boston, MA: Houghton Mifflin, 1965), p. 142.

23 Spence, "Opium Smoking in Ch'ing China," p. 151. He notes that by 1900 the imports had leveled off at about 50,000 chests per year.

24 Quoted in Frederic Wakeman, Jr., *The Fall of Imperial China* (New York: Free Press, 1975), p. 158.

25 Stuart Creighton Miller, "Ends and Means: Missionary Justification of Force in Nineteenth Century China," in *The Missionary Enterprise in China and America*, ed. John K. Fairbank (Cambridge, MA: Harvard University Press, 1974), p. 252.

26 Ibid., p. 255.

27 Paul Cohen, *China and Christianity* (Cambridge, MA: Harvard University Press, 1963), p. 51.

28 The amount of reparations varies with the source. Jonathan Spence, *The Search for Modern China* (New York: W.W. Norton, 1990), says that they totaled 250,000 taels (p. 205). Immanuel Hsu, in *The Rise of Modern China*, puts the sum at 400,000 (p. 363). Cohen, in *China and Christianity*, notes that a total of 280,000 taels of reparations were paid (250,000 to France and 30,000 to Russia), with an additional 212,000 taels to France and England to pay for property losses (p. 246).

Suggestions for Further Reading

Brockey, Liam Matthew. *Journey to the East: The Jesuit Mission to China, 1579–1724* (Cambridge, MA: The Belknap Press of Harvard University Press, 2007). This recent study of the Jesuit mission provides a cogent revisionist view of the missionary efforts; it is rich in its details and insights.

Cohen, Paul. *China and Christianity* (Cambridge, MA: Harvard University Press, 1963). This is the best analysis of the cultural divide between Western missionaries and Chinese elites.

Fay, Peter. *The Opium War, 1840–1842* (New York: W.W. Norton, 1976). A well-written and thorough study of the war; reviews often call it "classic."

Polachek, James. *The Inner Opium War* (Cambridge, MA: Harvard University Press, 1992). This important study focuses on Chinese domestic policy debates and factions in decision making in the 1840s and 1850s.

Wong, John Y. *Deadly Dreams: Opium and the Arrow War (1856–1860) in China* (Cambridge, UK: Cambridge University Press, 2002). A provocative meditation on imperialism, gauging British and Chinese agendas but including the roles of personalities, opinions, and the press.

4

An Age of Rebellion
Defiance of and Commitments to Traditional Chinese Identities

Beset and besieged by Western powers, the Qing government faced an even more desperate threat in a series of mid-nineteenth-century domestic rebellions that one scholar says "constitute[d] what was probably the greatest wave of peasant wars in history."[1] The devastation wrought by the largest of these, the Taiping War (1851–1864), was almost unfathomable: in the words of one observer,

> smiling fields were turned into desolate wildernesses; "fenced cities into ruinous heaps." The plains ... were strewn with human skeletons; their rivers polluted with floating carcasses; wild beasts descending from their fastnesses in the mountains roamed at large over the land, and made their dens in the ruins of deserted towns.[2]

Not only were foreigners destroying Chinese life and property, but Chinese themselves were also turning productive land into moonscapes and slaughtering each other in vast numbers.

TRADITIONAL REBELLIONS

The nineteenth century was born in domestic rebellion, mostly of the guerrilla variety. The rebellion of ethnic Miao tribesmen (the modern Hmong) in Guizhou against the ever-increasing encroachment of Han settlers lasted over a decade (1795–1806), primarily because Heshen, who was given the job of putting down the rebellion, prolonged the campaign to draw more military funds that he could siphon off for himself or his clique. Buddhism gave rise to the White Lotus Rebellion (1796–1804), which strove to establish a utopia on earth and also straddled the turn of the century, and to the 1813 rebellion of Lin Qing, which reached the Forbidden City in its aim to assassinate the Jiaqing emperor. Though each had its own context and meaning, there were similar patterns of setting, historical actors, agenda, and Qing dynasty responses. They prefigured patterns in the great mid-century rebellions.

Setting

These traditional rebellions were born in provincial border regions. Practically, such a setting made sense since bandits and rebels could quickly cross the boundary to another province if they were being pursued. Although authorities in the other province might eventually pursue them, it is obvious that the rebels did not cross the border where there were military garrisons or police posts. Many provincial border regions were known for their natural wildness—mountains, forests, deserts, areas where the population might be less sedentary and stable, often (especially in Central, South, and Southwest China) where the population was ethnically mixed. If there were ethnic diversity and accompanying language differences, ethnic consciousness often produced among each group a strong sense of the Other's presence. Maintaining order or bringing peace in areas marked by such social diversity and such environmental challenges often necessitated a substantial degree of militarization. The mix—ethnically diverse peoples, with a consciousness of that diversity, militarized, and potentially in trouble with the law—could easily become combustible if ignited.

The Miao Rebellion began along the mountainous border between Hunan and Guizhou but, even more significant, along the border between the Middle Yangzi and both the Upper Yangzi and Southwest China macroregions. At higher altitudes, they practiced slash-and-burn agriculture; at lower elevations, they farmed. The rebellion was ignited by the Qing dynasty's efforts to extend its political control in the area, a policy accompanied by a large influx of Han Chinese settlers. The White Lotus Rebellion took shape in the mountainous and forested lands on the borders of Hubei, Sichuan, and Shaanxi—or, again, more telling, on the borders of three macroregions: Northwest China, the Upper Yangzi, and the Middle Yangzi. A utopian Buddhist ideology fueled this rebellion. Lin Qing's 1813 rebellion that the Daoguang emperor helped to quell does not fit the macroregional border pattern and thus points to the range of possibilities for rebellious activity. It erupted with the impetus of Buddhist beliefs in Shandong and near Beijing in the plains of the North China macroregion; but the world of its leader, Lin Qing, was the economically peripheral world of the poor North China peasant and the poverty-stricken urban underclass.

The Historical Actors and Their Agendas

Any rebellion required leaders. A leader might emerge from almost any social type—peddlers, Daoist or Buddhist monks, laborers, failed examination candidates, boatmen, charcoal burners, or geomancers. Yet all leaders had compelling messages or were charismatic or both. During his life, Lin Qing had many odd jobs: night watchman, clerk, coolie, construction worker—nothing, in short, to indicate exceptional talent. Yet after his arrest, a relative told the Qing authorities that the secret of his success was his convincing description of how he would succeed and why people should contribute money to his cause. White Lotus Rebellion leader Liu Zhixie was reportedly charismatic, an able strategist who mobilized many numerous congregations of White Lotus followers.

In addition to leaders, of course, a rebellion needed masses of people who were organized and mobilized at least to some degree. The social structures and substance of rebellions varied geographically. In North China during the late Qing, a number of such social upheavals, including the White Lotus Rebellion, were inspired by a belief in the coming of the Buddha of the Future, who, it was thought, would establish a paradise on earth. At times of social trouble and disorder, local communities (in the case of the White Lotus sect, based on congregations) joined in defensive efforts by forming militia groups; in this way they quickly became the building blocks for rebellion. For disturbances to grow into major rebellions, leaders of these communities had to have links to other groups who were involved in the world of violence—for example, groups that practiced traditional martial arts. The White Lotus Rebellion spread in the beginning because of the links that sect congregations and communities had to bandits who lived in the forests of the three-province border region.

In South China, the building blocks of rebellion tended to be "lodges" in a secret blood brotherhood called the Triads. The Triads spread throughout the Southeast Coast and Lingnan macroregions in the eighteenth century and to the Lower Yangzi by the early nineteenth century. Composed mostly of the underclasses—laborers, pirates, smugglers, yamen clerks and runners, boatmen, and peasants—Triad organizations did not seek to overthrow legitimate society but to exploit it. A slogan put it this way: "The people of the top class owe us money; those of the middle class should wake up. Lower classes come with us! It is better than hiring an ox to plow poor land!" There was nothing revolutionary about the Triads. They looked back to the Ming and, with anti-Manchu venom, called for restoring the Ming to power. Like the White Lotus sects in the North, the Triads found a ready audience because of the growing social malaise brought on by changes coming from urbanization, migration, and expanding networks of domestic and foreign trade. In time of peace they served as mutual assistance organizations; they readily accepted women as members. In the South, the presence of strong and often feuding lineages further encouraged the growth of the Triads.

Qing Government Response

In the White Lotus Rebellion, the government sent regular banner forces against the guerrilla enemy. A key goal was to capture the leaders, the theory apparently being that a leaderless movement could be dealt with more quickly. The struggle then turned into what in the twentieth-century French and American wars in Vietnam were called "search-and-destroy" operations, with destruction often falling most heavily on civilians in their villages. The war dragged on, with local congregations and communities often left in charge of their own defense. There were two elements to the defense. First was utilizing an old tradition of "strengthening the walls and clearing the countryside"—that is, building to fortify the walls of urban settlements, bringing people and grain from the countryside into these "strategic hamlets." Such a policy brought more security to the civilian population and deprived the rebels of food. The second element of defense was the establishment of local militia units by local elites who also served as militia heads. Both these policies relied on local solutions which eventually successfully met the threat of the rebellion.

THE TAIPING WAR (1851–1864): ATTEMPTING TO REVOLUTIONIZE IDENTITY

Though traditionally called a rebellion, this largest and most destructive such explosion in world history might best be considered a civil war that devastated much of East Central and South China and militarily embroiled to a greater or lesser degree sixteen of the eighteen provinces within the Great Wall. A rebellion is defined by the established power holders whom rebels endeavor to unseat. A civil war, in contrast, pits armies composed of combatants without necessarily presuming that one is in a privileged position.[3] Even more pertinent to the themes of this book is the revolutionary threat of the Taiping to traditional Chinese cultural identity: Taiping ideology and practice struck at the very heart of the Confucian framework and substance that were central to the Chinese identity. The Taiping War also underlined in blood one pernicious effect that Western Christianity came to have in the social tinderbox of South China. For the rebellion was the brainchild of Hong Xiuquan, whose sickbed visions left him with the conviction that he was the younger brother of Jesus Christ and that he had a holy mission.

Regional Context

The historical and spatial contexts provided Hong with the people and the support that made his movement a threat not only to the ruling Manchus but to traditional Chinese civilization as well. The Taiping movement was born in the Canton region in the troubled years following the Opium War; it grew in large part because of the destabilization of the region from the opium scourge and the war itself. For several decades, opium smuggling, trafficking, and smoking had been major problems in the region. In their daily lives, people in the area had experienced the full impact of ballooning taxes caused by the currency instability that resulted from the outflow of silver to pay for the opium. There were other longer-term political problems for some in this region. Two centuries earlier, this had been the last region conquered by the Manchus, and many areas had not—even after all that time—ever reconciled themselves to the control by these outsiders. In that context of distrust and contempt, this area had then watched the pitiful performance of the regime's military forces in the Opium War. It is almost certainly the case that such a humiliating defeat brought to some people in the region thoughts and perhaps talk about the Mandate of Heaven. Was it beginning to slip from the dynasty's grasp? Further, the treaty system itself opened up to Westerners not only the walled city of Canton (which had been off limits to the West earlier) but also the interior; to see "foreign devils" was an immediate reminder that the Manchus had not been strong enough to keep them out. Given such a reality, Manchus, their military, and their bureaucrats could become obvious targets.

The new treaty system itself made the possibility of social unrest in the region more likely. In the rapid growth of trade with the West in the late eighteenth century, tea and silk had been the West's prime objectives. Though some were produced in the Canton area, the main tea- and silk-producing regions were in Zhejiang, Jiangsu, and Fujian provinces. During the approximately eighty years (1760s–1842) when Canton was the only port open to the West, overland and riverine trade routes had developed from the Lower Yangzi and Southeast Coast macroregions to Canton. Shippers and brokers were involved along these routes, as were local toughs who were enlisted to protect the expensive commodities; they all made their living from this domestic trade. They were generally men who, by the nature of their occupations, knew how to deal with dangerous situations and handle themselves amid potential violence and criminal behavior. With the opening of the treaty ports of Ningbo (Zhejiang province) and Shanghai (Jiangsu province) in the Treaty of Nanjing, tea and silk could much more easily and quickly be carried to these closer new ports. No longer needed, the old trade routes dried up and, with them, the livelihood of the transporters and security guards who had worked the routes. The unemployment of these transport workers—many of whom were roughnecks at best—created a new, potentially destabilizing factor in the region.

The introduction of another unsettling population increased the tinderbox situation. Pirates had been a traditional threat along the Southeast Coast. Because the ports opened with the Treaty of Nanjing were along this coast, Western ships plying these waters became the objects of pirate raids and attacks. The British therefore began a policy of suppressing the maritime pirates. This campaign was on the whole successful, allowing safer ocean travel, but it forced the now-unemployed maritime pirates into the interior, where they were transformed into land- and river-based bandits who preyed on the local Chinese population.

In addition to these new forces, there were old ethnic rivalries that tore at the region's social amity. There were Hakkas, "guest people," Han Chinese immigrants from North China centuries earlier, who remained separate from the locals. They spoke their own dialect. Hakka women did not bind their feet, as respectable and sophisticated Han Chinese women did. Thus, women joined men in working the fields. Hakkas often worked the poorer land since the area had already been settled when they moved in; there were frequent clashes with locals over land use and irrigation rights and even over patterns of residence. Yet even Hakkas fit in more easily with the longtime resident Han Chinese than the Miao and Yao tribesmen who inhabited the mountainous areas. Hakkas often found themselves in competition and skirmishes with the Miao and Yao peoples. The ethnic diversity in the area increased the likelihood of social unrest.

Thus, considerable social tensions had arisen from ethnic divisions, poverty, the presence of a variety of unruly and criminal types, and contempt for the Manchus and Westerners. But until there was some vehicle to express this malaise and give it shape, it was amorphous and aimless. Beginning in the mid-1830s, those vehicles began to appear in the form of secret societies and religion-based sects. An 1836 rebellion led by a Yao minority tribesman who was also the leader of a White Lotus community was only the first of several uprisings that eventually involved the Triad society. Like this one, mini-rebellions in 1847 and 1849 were put down. When secret societies and religious sects became involved in the increasingly bitter rivalry between Hakkas and locals, social tensions and violence threatened to explode in social fragmentation.

THE REBELLION TAKES SHAPE

It was into this world that Hong Xiuquan, a Hakka, the son of a poor farmer, was born in 1814. Since he seemed to be a bright child, his family arranged for Hong to be tutored so that he might take the civil service examination. He failed in his first two attempts. In 1836, when he was in Canton to try again, he was handed a collection of biblical passages and explanatory sermons called "Good Words for Exhorting the Age." The author was one Liang Afa, a convert to Christianity early in the century, who had become an evangelist. The work was explicit in asserting that moral decline was putting Chinese society in great peril; its "stark fundamentalist message hammer[ed] home the omnipotence of God, the degradation of sin and idolatry, and the awesome choice between salvation or damnation."[4] Hong reportedly did not read the material but took it home and set it aside. The next year he failed the examination yet again. Overcome with humiliation and shame, he reportedly spoke at length to his parents about his feelings of worthlessness. And then he fell ill; it is not certain to what extent his illness was physically related and to what extent it was a nervous breakdown.

During his illness, he had a vision. He ascended to Heaven, where he was purified and his body regenerated with new internal organs. A venerable man with golden hair and beard dressed in black robes handed him a sword and emblems of royalty, instructing him to kill the demons. Feeling as righteous and powerful as he had felt worthless before, Hong set out on quests that spanned the cosmos, carrying out the golden-haired man's orders. Accompanying him on these missions was a middle-aged man whom Hong thought to be his older brother. When his illness abated, Hong turned to teaching in the village school, though he clearly remembered his hallucinatory vision. In 1843 he tried to pass the civil service examination once more, and once more he failed. Angry with himself but more so with the system, he returned home.

At this point he apparently read the Christian tracts that he had brought home seven years earlier. It was a eureka experience that explained his earlier vision. The venerable old man was none other than God, and the middle-aged man was Jesus. God addressed Hong as the heavenly younger brother; he was, in effect, God's Chinese son. And it was God who had instructed Hong to slay the demons. Yet, in his comprehension of the vision, Hong did not immediately see any political import. His writings in the years after 1843 depicted his charge as one of converting Chinese to Christianity. Further, Hong seemed to want to merge the Christian message, which in his hands meant primarily worship of the One God, with Confucianism, especially an emphasis on living an upright and morally orthodox life. Hong's impassioned beliefs led him to begin to convert family and friends and to antagonize his community by destroying statues of gods in the local temple.

In 1844 Hong and one of his earliest converts, his close friend Feng Yunshan, left his native village and journeyed to the hill country of southern Guangxi to begin proselytizing. Hong returned to his home village later that year and spent the next two years writing and teaching about his beliefs; he studied for two months in 1847 with the American Baptist missionary Issachar Roberts in Hong Kong. Feng in the meantime proved to be a master missionary and organizer, by 1850 converting many Hakka communities. He organized local congregations and linked them together in multi-village networks stretching over a dozen counties; they comprised the God Worshipping Society.

In many ways, this organization was a secret society, founded, like the White Lotus sect, on religious ideas. The context of communal struggle and vendettas among ethnic groups, serious famines in 1847 and 1849, and the consequent appearance of many bandits helped fuel the spread of the God Worshippers. God Worshippers, who were in the main Hakkas and Miao tribesmen, began to set up their own militia units for self-defense; in the tense atmosphere, they frequently fought with militia units formed by non-Hakka, non-Miao local inhabitants. Members of the Triad Society began to join the God Worshippers, adding a contingent to the organization that actively called for the overthrow of the Manchus. It was in this context that Hong's message began to become politicized, with many coming to see that the demons God had ordered exterminated were Manchus.

History often turns on contingencies. In late 1848 Feng was seized by a local militia leader, accused of sedition, and sent to Guangdong to the governor-general's office; Hong left also to argue Feng's case. They were gone for seven months, a critical period in the movement's development because it allowed other leaders to emerge. Probably the most powerful was a local bully from Thistle Mountain, the headquarters of the God Worshippers—Yang Xiuqing, an illiterate charcoal maker. His crony, Xiao Chaogui, was also a charcoal maker. Two others came from wealthier backgrounds: Wei Changhui, of aboriginal stock, came from a landlord pawnshop-owning family and Shi Dakai from a wealthy farm family. Of these four, only Shi had some education. Yang and Xiao took a page from the divinity book of Hong Xiuquan. Whereas Hong was the Heavenly Younger Brother, Yang announced—as an obvious reflection of his ambition—that when he spoke it was the voice of God the Father, and Xiao alleged that his voice was the voice of Jesus. These developments had all the makings of future trouble: when divinity clashed with divinity, who could mediate?

In July 1850 the leaders called all God Worshippers, about 20,000 strong, to Thistle Mountain. They had left their homes behind; all their movable possessions they put into a common treasury. They had been farmers, charcoal makers, miners, Triads, and pirates. Now they made up a vast military camp. The Qing government recognized the threat as serious: a Christian cult had militarized and was now forming an army. In response, it sent the state's army, which was promptly defeated by the God Worshippers in several engagements. With victories under their belts, in January 1851 the God Worshippers declared the establishment of a new dynasty, the Heavenly Kingdom of Great Peace (*Taiping tianguo*). As a visible symbol of their anti-Manchu identity, they abandoned the Manchu hairstyle, letting their hair grow long all over their heads; people called them the "long-haired rebels." So coifed, they set out on a military campaign to realize the Heavenly Kingdom on earth now.

The year and a half between the Taiping seizure of the small city of Yongan in Guangxi province and the capture of Nanjing in March 1853 saw the rapid growth of the movement, in many cases because the Qing armies, disorganized and poorly disciplined, could not execute any coordinated military strategy. The Taiping suffered serious defeats; in one, the movement's most prolific proselytizer and best organizer, Feng Yunshan, was killed in summer 1852. Then in the fall, Xiao Chaogui, the voice of Jesus, died of wounds suffered in battle, a death that, taken on its face, should have created a theological crisis of major proportion. But no one seemed to notice.

In the God Worshippers' march north to the Yangzi River, a key was crossing over from the Lingnan macroregion, with its east-flowing rivers, to the Middle Yangzi, with its vast Yangzi River tributary network. As transportation was made easier after the crossing, triumphs seemed to come the same way. They took the Hunan provincial capital, Changsha, in September 1852; the Hubei provincial capital, Wuchang, on the Yangzi River in January 1853; and then Nanjing. With each victory the number of Taiping swelled: after Changsha, an estimated 120,000; after Wuchang, possibly 500,000; after Nanjing, perhaps 2 million. On the taking of Nanjing, the Taiping leadership followed the orders the golden-haired man had given Hong long ago back in his native village: they began to exterminate the demons. In an act that might be called the first Nanjing massacre, all of the 40,000 Manchus who lived in Nanjing who were not killed in the fighting were stabbed to death, drowned, or burned alive.

THE TAIPING REVOLUTION

The Qing dynasty had enough problems with the Taiping Rebellion that exploded out of the Guangxi hills and transformed itself into the Taiping War once it gathered momentum in the Yangzi River valley. But it was the Taiping ideology and its political, social, and economic systems making up the Taiping Revolution that posed the most serious threat to the regime and eventually gave rise to the forces that would crush the whole Taiping movement.

Underlying Taiping Christianity was the basic idea of the equality of human beings before God, creating a universal brotherhood–sisterhood. The world and all in it belonged to God. It followed that the brotherhood–sisterhood used the natural world and its products but that there was no private ownership. Further, economic competition, exploiting the world's resources, and acting selfishly were condemned. Implicit, of course, was a clear economic leveling that made extremes of poverty and wealth untenable. The social ideal was embodied in the 1853 land system, which specified that all men *and women* receive equal shares of land. The land grants were not owned but rather cultivated in common by a grouping of twenty-five families, the basic social-political unit in Taiping society. In keeping with the primitive economic communism that was a hallmark of the new regime, each grouping of families shared a common treasury. The grouping was headed by a "sergeant" who performed multiple roles. He kept records of production and of the common treasury. He mediated disputes and served as judge. He managed the education of the families' children. As the grouping's military leader, he selected militiamen to serve for the unit's defense. He oversaw church services on the Sabbath. The structure of this commune-like system came in large part from an old traditional Chinese work, the *Rituals of Zhou*; but since much of the ideology was based on Christian idealism, the system was clearly a hybrid. It is perhaps not surprising, given the commune-like structure and the primitive form of economic communism, that twentieth-century Communists saw the Taiping movement in a positive light.

The social roles and position of women in Taiping society were markedly superior to those of women in Qing society. That women could be allotted land is the first indication of the gender revolution that the Taiping were ready to engineer. Women were also allowed to take the new civil service examinations based on the Bible and the various writings of Hong Xiuquan. Women could, as a result, hold some offices in the bureaucracy. In addition, women could actively participate in military units. This near-revolution in gender relations scandalized those with traditional Confucian sensibilities.

As part of the Hakka heritage, the Taiping forbade footbinding. That custom had begun centuries earlier when fascination with a ballerina of the court led many young women to desire tiny

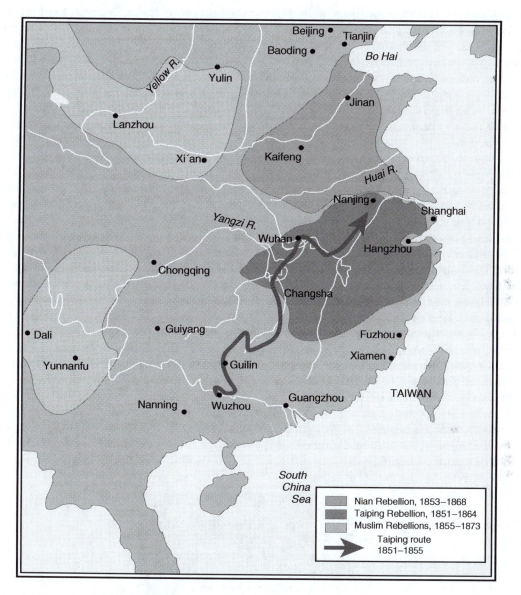

MAP 4.1 Mid-Nineteenth-Century Rebellions.

feet, no more than three inches long, known as "golden lilies." Girls, roughly five to eight years old, had their feet tightly bound with cloth so that the arches were broken and pushed upward.

As the arch [was] gradually broken, the flat of [a girl's] heels and the balls of [her] foot … [were] gradually moved from horizontal to perpendicular, facing each other, so that an object like a silver dollar [could] be inserted in the narrow space between them. The result [was] that [she would] never run again and [could] walk [only] on the base of [her] heels … with [great] difficulty.[5]

This cruel and curious custom supposedly lent sophistication to its victim, making a good marriage match more likely. The patriarchal family system defined by male domination perpetuated the custom, though, as has been pointed out, "without the cooperation of the women concerned, foot-binding could not have been perpetuated for a millennium." It has been called "a central event in the domestic women's culture," "an exclusively female affair."[6] Be that as it may, it hobbled women, keeping them from gallivanting. Golden lilies even became used in sex play. Though not all Chinese women in all places bound their feet, footbinding continued into the twentieth century. The Manchus had chosen to differentiate their women from Chinese women through their prohibition of footbinding.

In some areas of social policy, the puritanism of fundamentalist Christianity reinforced a native Chinese puritanism. The use of alcohol, tobacco, and opium was forbidden. Gambling, witchcraft, prostitution, and adultery were taboo. With regard to sexual relations, the Taiping instituted a policy of strict abstinence, even between husbands and wives. If one thought of a universal brotherhood and sisterhood, sexual relations of any sort would be incestuous. It is obvious that the Taiping could not end sexual intercourse permanently, for no newborn Taipings ultimately would mean the end of the movement. But leaders wanted chastity to be the rule in order to preserve order and discipline until after the heavenly kingdom was firmly established. Therefore, men and women lived in strictly segregated housing; having sex brought with it the penalty of execution. Not surprisingly, this policy gave rise to massive morale problems; the policy of sexual segregation was thus abandoned by 1855.

The Taiping Revolution was a potent threat to the traditional Chinese Confucian system. Taipingism provided an all-embracing cosmology, linking the three components of the traditional Chinese universe—Heaven, earth, and humans—in a new way. God in a Christian Heaven replaced the impersonal force of Heaven that endowed the Chinese emperor with his mandate to rule and that reflected events on earth by the forces of nature (e.g., storms, plagues, and earthquakes). Now earth and its resources were to be shared by humans equally in a universal siblinghood—a startlingly different framework for thought and society from the traditional Confucian vision of a social hierarchy, with elites dominating society and its resources. Further, specific social and political policies undercut traditional Chinese norms. The centrality of the family disappeared into

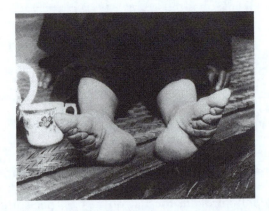

FIGURE 4.1 Footbinding began in the Song dynasty, probably in the late eleventh century. Although the big toe was not bound, the rest of the foot was wrapped in long bindings. A woman's feet therefore became a private body part, to be seen only by herself, her mother, and later her husband.
Source: AP Photos/Shutterstock.

the twenty-five-family grouping, with the power of the father taken by the sergeant and the family losing its economic and social preeminence. As we have seen, the roles and status of women were markedly enhanced. Economic competition was abolished. The new state received a new kind of legitimacy—from the Christian God—and delved deeper into personal lives than ever before: prescribing daily economic, social, and religious roles for people, even forbidding sexual intercourse between husbands and wives. It is little wonder that some Chinese, trained in the glories of traditional Confucianism, might have begun to feel their cultural identity and that of China threatened by the Heavenly Kingdom.

Why the Revolution Failed

Historians speculate on whether the Taiping could have swept the Qing away if they had maintained their remarkable military momentum and marched to the north. But they did not know where to proceed, so Nanjing became their capital. In the end, it became their tomb. During their eleven-year stint in the city, they tried, generally unsuccessfully, to implement their vision of politics and society even as they wreaked havoc and destruction on forays in all directions but especially in the Lower Yangzi region.

The eventual collapse came for many strategic reasons—probably most important was the disintegration of the central leadership. In the days at Thistle Mountain, six men had emerged as leaders, first called "marshals," but after reaching Nanjing, "kings." Two, the South King (Feng) and the West King (Xiao), had been killed in the campaign. That left the powerfully ambitious East King (Yang), the North King (Wei), the Assistant King (Shi), and the Heavenly King (Hong). While egalitarianism was prescribed for the masses by the Taiping kings, the kings themselves had numerous perks and privileges, perhaps the most notable being heavily populated harems, in which they could have sex whenever they wanted. Living luxuriously in palaces that took years to construct, the kings could expect commoners to fall on their faces in a show of obeisance whenever they passed in their sedan chairs. If a commoner did not comply with this expectation, he could become a "celestial lamp," that is, burned alive; alternatively, he might be torn apart after being tied to five horses.

Because political power was so concentrated at the top, problems that developed among the kings had life-and-death import for the whole movement. Almost from the time of reaching Nanjing, bad blood developed between Hong and Yang, the East King. In a moment of rage, Hong had kicked one of his concubines. Yang, claiming that God the Father spoke through him, demanded that Hong be punished by beatings with a bamboo rod. Later, when Hong agreed to submit, God graciously canceled the sentence. But from that time on, there was bad blood between them. Yang continued to try to one-up Hong, letting it be known that he was not only the voice of God the Father but also the incarnation of the Holy Ghost. In 1856, he (in his voice of God the Father incarnation) demanded that Hong give him the title of "10,000 Years," the traditional title of the Chinese Son of Heaven. This was too much for Hong, who could see a coup in the making. He enlisted Wei, the North King, to kill Yang. Wei's actions were like using a bomb to kill a fly: in a bloody massacre, he slaughtered not only Yang and his family but 20,000 followers to boot. Shi, the Assistant King, was horrified and denounced Wei's actions, but then discovered that he was next on Wei's list. Though Shi escaped over the city wall, Wei wiped his family out. Hong, now fearing the madman he had unleashed, had Wei and 200 of his supporters killed. Although there was a regime revival of sorts with the appointment of a raft of new kings, "[i]n this arena of carnage, greed, and paranoia perished whatever remnants of its original vision the Taiping movement might have retained."[7]

Another reason for the failure of the Taiping Revolution was that the land reform and commune-like grouping systems were never really put in place in areas that the Taiping controlled. The Taiping, however visionary, were not skillful administrators. The envisioned revolution faced huge practical obstacles, not the least of which was insufficient time to install so radical a program. Even if there had been time, there was not enough manpower to penetrate to the local level where entrenched social patterns had to be eradicated. Thus, those people who staffed most of the local governments had been there before the Taiping and had little loyalty to the regime or its program.

A basic reason for the failure can be found in the very identity of the Taiping effort. It was a fanatical totalitarian religious movement that promised utopia but delivered nothing beyond hard work, strict discipline, no sex, and a harsh existence. Once the bloodshed between the kings started, once one's friend became a celestial lamp, once the discrepancy between the lifestyles of the kings and their entourages and those of the masses became known, resentment began to replace the hope that had driven the movement. In short, when promises of future rewards, which had given the movement aim and direction, were not fulfilled, the commitment of people to the regime vanished. In some areas, especially those to which the Taiping came late in the life of its regime, there was not much commitment to the Taiping anyway.

Strategically, the Taipings can be faulted in many ways. Instead of keeping their substantial momentum and moving to the north, where Qing political power lay, they had holed up in Nanjing—where the movement eventually was snuffed out. They were not adept at enlisting possible collaborators who might join in a common drive to overthrow the Manchus. For example, there were two other serious uprisings that occurred concurrently with the Taiping, the Nian in North China and the Red Turbans in South China. There was frequent cooperation with the Nian but never any efforts to pursue the possibility of a long-term strategic alliance, which, in any case, was probably doubtful, given the religious nature and claims of the Taiping. Similarly, one can point to the Taiping lack of foresight in trying more directly to curry favor with Western nations. Initially, Western missionaries were interested and intrigued by the possibility of a Christian revolutionary movement seizing power. When many of them visited Nanjing, however, they were shocked by the substance of Taiping Christianity. In addition, just as the Chinese in various tracts had alleged that Western missionaries and their converts practiced sodomy, now Western missionaries claimed that Taiping leaders were involved in homosexual activities. Taiping ideology and alleged practices repulsed Western missionaries; they wanted nothing to do with Hong and his followers. Western merchants were put off by the Taiping refusal to allow opium into their realm. Western nations, which initially might have been interested in the Taiping as a regime that could possibly be more open to the West and its demands than the Qing, rallied instead to the Qing. Late in the rebellion, Western-led mercenary troops, the "Ever-Victorious Army," led first by the American Frederick Townsend Ward and then by Charles "Chinese" Gordon, fought Taiping troops in their efforts to take the treaty port of Shanghai.

Despite the multiple internal faults and weaknesses that help explain the Taiping collapse, the most important reason for the failure of the Taiping Revolution was military defeat at the hands of Chinese civil servants who were deeply committed to traditional Chinese culture and who saw the Taiping as spearheading an attack on their way of life. In 1852, the Xianfeng emperor named some militia commissioners whose role was to bring together gentry-led local militias into federations that could protect local society from the rebels. This was notably an admission that banner and Green Standard forces could not do the job and a decentralization of military authority to the provincial and local levels—a crucial indicator of Manchu military weakness.

The important official Zeng Guofan accepted the appointment as militia commissioner. He was outraged by the Taiping threat to traditional culture. His proclamation against the Taiping in 1854 reads in part:

> Scholars may not read the Confucian classics, for they have their so-called teachings of Jesus and the New Testament. In a single day, several thousand years of Chinese ethical principles and proper human relationships, classical books, social institutions and statutes have all been completely swept away. This is not just a crisis for our Qing dynasty, but the most extraordinary crisis of all time for the Confucian teachings."[8]

With the permission of the court, Zeng took his appointment and ran with it straight to the formation of his own provincial (Hunan) army, which he recruited from his networks of gentry connections. Throughout the chain of command, Zeng's army was built on Confucian principles—"duty to one's neighbors, piety to one's family, and personal loyalty to one's commander."[9] It was largely funded by a new tax, the *lijin*, collected on shipped commercial goods at customs barriers along key routes. Zeng's protégé, Li Hongzhang, set up a counterpart provincial army in Anhui province. Both men purchased some foreign cannon and arms for their forces. These armies played the key role in battles leading to the final Taiping collapse. It was Zeng's Hunan army that was the key in the seizure of Nanjing in July 1864. The Heavenly King had died a few weeks earlier; none of the original leaders of the movement were around at the end.

Yet, despite the insanity of some of its assumptions and some of its leaders, the movement had great historical significance apart from the horrific death toll and destruction.

> More than any other rebellion of their day, [the Taiping] addressed themselves directly to the crisis of the times and offered concrete measures for resolving it. Their vision of a new system of property relations, a new mechanism of local control, and a new relationship between the individual and the state was an authentic response to the distinctive problems of the late imperial age.[10]

A Taiping Post-Mortem

One scholar has argued that the "Taiping War was the most destructive war in human history to that time, and in the twentieth century only the Second World War appears to have surpassed it."[11] The Lower Yangzi macroregion, the economic core of the Qing empire, was laid waste. The destruction wrought by the rebellion was appalling. Population estimates for just the Lower Yangzi macroregion suggest that the population in 1843 had reached 67 million but that a half-century later it had dropped to 45 million.[12] Fully fifty years after Hong's capital went up in flames, a reporter from a Shanghai newspaper described the great destruction still apparent in the Zhejiang prefectural capital of Yanzhou: "At the southeast corner of the city what are today grazing lands were once the site of a bustling, crowded quarter."[13] In the aftermath, people in this region, that had been most prominent in scholarship, produced many officials through the examination system, and celebrated its women writers, felt as if they had been transported to another world where simple survival became the paramount necessity. The lively academic communities in the macroregion disappeared; as a contemporary writer commented after the Taiping on how a great many scholars were turning to the military.[14]

Also destroyed in the Taiping War were the records of women writers describing in detail their personal lives. Many women stopped writing after the war; indeed, it has been noted that, especially after the Taiping, "'women' as figures of controversy or as subjects of historical change were almost invisible" and that until the 1890s women were rarely referred to in Chinese or other language sources.[15] During the seventeenth century, Manchu conquest of the Lower Yangzi had experienced more terror, killing, and fire than other macroregions. In the years after the Taiping War, anti-Manchu sentiment emerged and would continue to grow. In such a context, women, who continued to write, often turned to poetry with political themes, as they had done during the Opium War. This was likely a result of their connections to male relatives who were "in-the-know" about the political crises of the time.[16]

GUERRILLA WARFARE: THE NIAN REBELLION (1853–1868)

The Nian Rebellion was the only one of the four major mid-century rebellions that did not have a religious dynamic. It developed in the bleakly poor, sandy Huaibei region of North Central China along the Anhui–Henan–Jiangsu border, an area subject to severe flooding and drought. As in the Taiping, the region was populated with a huge cast of potential rebels. Some were the "human debris of the White Lotus Rebellion":[17] White Lotus adherents and perhaps rebels themselves, but, more important, mercenary soldiers who had been recruited in Huaibei to fight the White Lotus rebels farther in the interior and who returned to the area after the rebellion. Other potential elements of the population that might have had a predilection to social violence included peasants propelled toward belligerence by their harsh existence and by the ruffian-like salt smugglers and guards for the salt traffickers. A prized and essential commodity produced along the Jiangsu seacoast, salt was a government monopoly. There were always large numbers of men who attempted to make money by smuggling outside the bounds of the monopoly. Studies have also shown that the rate of female infanticide in the area was higher than in some other areas of China and that as many as 20 percent of marriage-age men remained unmarried. The availability of large numbers of such unattached males (called "bare sticks"), free to participate in social unrest, was also a destabilizing factor.

In this perennially poverty-stricken area, disaffected types joined groups in various predatory practices—banditry, smuggling, theft, plunder, kidnapping, and organized feuds. Some of these groups were Nian bands that began to appear around the turn of the nineteenth century; in the beginning, they were often structured around families and lineages. Although the origins of the word *nian* remain somewhat unclear, the term came to be applied to groups of bandits who took a blatantly Robin Hood approach: a folk song of the time put it this way: "The poor men's hearts are happy to see him [the Nian leader], and the moneybags' bones go soft with terror."[18] By about 1850, Nian bands had become firmly ensconced in villages across the Huaibei area, with whole communities participating in banditry and plunder. Natural disaster helped to weld these bands together in what became known as the Nian Rebellion. Severe floods in 1851 heralded the beginning of the tragic shift of the Yellow River from the south to the north of the Shandong peninsula; though the major collapse of the dikes did not occur until 1855, the years from 1851 on brought famine and economic calamity. In the context of crisis, more and more people joined Nian bands. In guerrilla strikes they plundered for their livelihood as they protected and fortified their home communities.

In 1852, Zhang Luoxing, a local landlord and member of a powerful local lineage involved in salt smuggling, was chosen to lead a federation of Nian communities. When he was elected "Lord of the Alliance" in 1856, the Nian organized themselves in five units under red, yellow, blue, white, and black banners; each may have contained up to 20,000 men, though the total number of Nian is unknown. Later the number of banners was increased, but the organization remained loose.

Though Zhang's leadership never approached the centralized control of Hong Xiuquan, the banner system did bring greater coherence to the movement. As an indicator of the still-haphazard nature of the revolt, however, some Nian bands in Henan province did not even join the federation.

The first phase of the rebellion until about 1864 took the form of what one writer has called "seasonal militarization." Even after the formation of the alliance, the Nian continued to fight in small guerrilla units, notably mobile on horseback. Like any guerrilla force, they were dependent on the local populace for support. Rebels maintained their fortified base communities and tended to be sedentary in the summer and winter months. In the spring and autumn they moved into the military phase of banditry, raiding, and plunder. They utilized the traditional policy the Qing regime had used in fighting the White Lotus Rebellion, "strengthening the walls and clearing the countryside." This meant keeping rebel communities protected, sometimes with cannon, while gathering all the grain and other food items from the countryside and bringing them into the earth-walled settlements.

This policy created a scorched earth situation in the countryside, which deprived government troops of what they needed to subsist on during their efforts to quell the rebellion. A French missionary who accompanied government troops in the early 1860s talked about that reality. He reported that in their area of operations, if the troops did not sufficiently intimidate villagers, the locals refused to let the troops water their horses. If they offered to buy grain—millet or corn—to feed the horses, the response was always that the villagers had none to sell. The missionary noted, in contrast, that when rebels approached the same villages, local residents rushed out to greet them and readily provided whatever the rebels wanted.

Most of the rebellion's plundering occurred in Shandong, Henan, and northern Jiangsu in an area of about 100,000 square miles. The Qing regime began to take the movement very seriously when in the mid-1850s Zhang assumed threateningly suggestive titles such as "Great Han Prince with the Heavenly Mandate"; when the rebels adopted secret society symbols, oaths, and rituals; and when the rebels cooperated on an ad hoc basis with the Taiping on a number of occasions.

The Qing government first utilized troops from the Army of the Green Standard who had difficulty coping with the Nian's guerrilla warfare. When the Mongol prince Senggerinchin, a descendant of Genghis Khan, was appointed imperial commissioner to deal with the Nian in late 1860, he brought with him not only Green Standard troops but also banner cavalry and infantry. Known for his aggressive leadership, he ordered that those he captured have their ears and noses cut off, to be sent to Beijing as war trophies. Under his direction, Zhang Luoxing was captured in 1863. In his confession before his execution, Zhang noted the handful of times he had cooperated with the Taiping in joint military operations and, at age fifty-three, resignedly recognized his fate and the rebellion's rather dire straits:

> In these past few years I have plundered too many places to remember all of them clearly. My wife has been chased off by government troops and I do not know where she is. My son and adopted son have both been captured together with me. My brother Zhang Minxing, leading several thousand men, has taken off for the Southwest and I do not know his whereabouts. As for [four other leaders], they have all been killed by the government troops.[19]

In 1864 a second, more dangerous phase of the rebellion began—a war that ranged sporadically over the North China plain, fought by an increasingly expert Nian cavalry. This second wind of the Nian may have been fueled in part by erstwhile Taiping troops who survived the defeat at Nanjing. The ambush death of Senggerinchin in May 1865 led the Qing government to appoint

Zeng Guofan, the scholar-official hero of the Taiping War, to lead the suppression of the Nian movement. Zeng focused first on the central Nian base. His goal was to establish a water block-ade formed by rivers and canals and to establish four major government bases on all sides of the nest area. Having thus isolated the Nian base, government troops invaded it, digging ditches and trenches in order to hamper the Nian use of horses and painstakingly separating each walled vil-lage from its neighboring settlements. The goal was to register the population, appoint new village chiefs, and quarantine each "cleansed" village from Nian rebels.

Government forces attempted to turn the tables on the Nian and utilize the strategy that the rebels had used so successfully—scorched earth and fortified settlements. The former denied rebels their resources; the latter protected villages from rebel seizure. In the end, Zeng was less successful than in his struggle against the Taiping. He had trouble getting the cooperation of the governors of the provinces involved; and, having demobilized many of his best Hunan provincial forces, he was dependent on troops from the Anhui army of his protégé, Li Hongzhang, many of whom were not personally loyal to Zeng. In the end, it was simply Nian mobility that allowed many of the rebels who were still in the base area to escape.

Because of these difficulties, the government appointed Li to finish the job in late 1866. The rapid mobility of Nian forces and their effective guerrilla activity still produced two more years of fighting before Li's forces were finally able to wear the rebels down. Eventually victory came through the use of modern British-made guns that Li purchased and the importation of 4,900 experienced and skillful cavalrymen from Manchuria and Inner Mongolia. In contrast to the Taip-ing, the Nian were no challenge to the traditional value system or to traditional cultural identity. The nature of their warfare, diffuse guerrilla attacks, made them very difficult to suppress: Li had reported that they moved "as freely as mercury." Whereas the Taiping had moved in large mili-tary campaigns to take new territory, the Nian were embedded in local villages among lineages, intimately linked to local society. Their rebellion was not so much an attack on Qing political and ideological legitimacy as it was an attempt in the Nian nest area to cast off government authority.

MUSLIMS VERSUS CHINESE: CLASHES IN ETHNIC IDENTITY

Muslims had lived in China for many centuries. Since the Tang dynasty (618–907), Muslims had settled in communities at the eastern end of the Silk Road in the northwestern provinces of Gansu and Shaanxi. The other site of great Muslim population concentration was in the far southwestern province of Yunnan, which had been settled first in the thirteenth century. But there were Muslims elsewhere as well. Muslim Arab traders since the Tang period had lived in ports along the Guang-dong and Fujian coasts. By the mid-nineteenth century, there were an estimated 1 million Muslims in the region of the Nian rebellion. Han Chinese Muslims were called *Hui*. Although they main-tained their own mosques and religious practices, Muslims saw themselves as subjects of Chinese authorities. Muslims could take the civil service examination and receive bureaucratic posts. The early Qing emperors had handled relations with Muslims and their communities with respect.

Beginning in 1762, however, the Qianlong emperor announced a series of anti-Muslim laws; this policy stemmed from Muslim rebellions in the late 1750s, one of which was "the most serious rebellion by ... Mongols against Qing rule until the end of the dynasty."[20] According to the new laws, penalties for crimes committed by Muslims became harsher than those for Han Chinese who had committed the same crimes. Problems began to develop when Han Chinese started to move into areas where Muslims had been the majority population and controlled the region's resources. Competition between Han Chinese settlers and Hui over land and commercial opportunities led to animosity and heightened tensions. Court cases over disputes relating to these issues usually found the Muslims on the losing side, discriminated against by Han Chinese and Manchu alike.

Panthay Rebellion (1855–1873)

Concurrent with the Taiping and Nian conflagrations were two bloody rebellions waged by Muslims in Southwest and Northwest China. The Panthay rebellion in Yunnan province grew from a mix of ethnic and religious tensions, but the spark that ignited it was economic rivalry. Yunnan's greatest natural resources were its copper, gold, and silver mines, which had long been controlled by Muslims. Han Chinese settlers had worked some mines, which over the years had become depleted. By the beginning of the nineteenth century, they thus lusted after the Muslim mines, a desire that escalated into feuding and violence. In 1856, at the behest of a Manchu official, between 2,000 and 3,000 Muslims in the provincial capital of Kunming were massacred. Han Chinese in the countryside began to form militias to kill Muslims. Muslims fought back, assassinating Chinese officials and capturing the city of Dali. There, an educated devout Hui named Du Wenxiu established the kingdom of Panthay, claiming for himself the title of sultan. Du oversaw a bureaucracy manned primarily by Han Chinese officials and a military with a strong minority of Han Chinese officers. He believed that Islam was compatible with Confucianism; indeed, he proclaimed that all three religions in Yunnan—Islam, Confucianism, and the folk religions of aboriginal tribes—should be revered. Du's forces controlled almost half of Yunnan. He was challenged until 1862 by another Muslim faction that controlled much territory in central and southern Yunnan.

The Qing military response was weak and incompetent. The terrain was rugged and military campaigning rigorous. In the end, the government was able to play opposing Muslim factions off against each other and militarily depend especially on local forces and leaders. The rebellion continued in the western part of the province until 1873, where it was marked by siege warfare of over fifty walled cities that Du controlled. Most of the seizures of the cities resulted in bloody massacres by Qing troops. Du was captured and executed.

Northwest Muslim Rebellion (1862–1873)

The northwest rebellion that spread from near Xi'an in Shaanxi province westward into Gansu province was more serious from a strategic viewpoint than the Panthay rebellion. Located between Mongolia and Tibet, regions crucial, as we have seen, in the Qing empire, and reaching to the Russian border, this area was the main corridor between Beijing and Xinjiang, the vast region won by conquest in the mid-eighteenth century. It was also the main passageway through which Chinese Muslims could have contact with the Islamic world to the west. Thus, it was here, more than in Yunnan, that Islamic currents from the west continually reinvigorated or challenged religious thought and faith.

In the mid-eighteenth century, a Chinese Muslim introduced into the area a practice from the mystical Muslim school of Sufism. Known as the New Teaching, it challenged the traditional method of "ridding the mind of all thinking except that focused on God." In the 1780s it inspired several uprisings against the Qing, who put them down, executing the sect leader and banning the sect, actions that turned the leader into a saint and sowed the seeds of a bitter ill will. It was Muslim networks of supporters of the New Teaching that became the main factor in the rebellion that erupted in 1862. Yet it was not so much the New Teaching that was at the root of the violence, but rather simple Muslim–Han Chinese antagonism.

In that year, a brief Taiping expedition close to Xi'an had set off unrest. It was the pretext for both Han Chinese and Muslim communities to engage in the rapid formation of militias ostensibly for defense. But the volatile situation quickly led to each side attacking the other, burning villages and murdering their inhabitants. The Qing military was able to suppress the violence in Shaanxi province by early 1864, in part because so many Muslims had fled west to Gansu, carrying the message that the Qing was planning a huge massacre of Muslims. The number of adherents of the New Teaching sect, now led by Ma Hualong, was greater in Gansu. Joined by other rebels not of the New Teaching sect, they quickly mobilized. By 1867 all of Gansu save for a few cities and the provincial capital were in Muslim hands; Qing power had been effectively overthrown.

In the fall of 1866, the Qing court appointed Zuo Zongtang (1812–1885) to be governor-general of Shaanxi and Gansu provinces. A scholar who had failed three times in his attempt to pass the highest-level civil service examination, Zuo was a serious student of geography and agriculture. In the 1840s he had bought a farm to experiment with methods of producing tea and silk. In the first years of the Taiping he became involved in military affairs, rising rapidly in the esteem of fellow officials; and in 1860 he was ordered by the court to raise his own army to fight the Taiping, alongside the armies of Zeng Guofan and Li Hongzhang. Named governor-general of Zhejiang and Fujian provinces in 1863, he was an excellent administrator and showed his forward-looking approach by experimenting with steamboats and selecting the site for the Fuzhou shipyard (see Chapter 5). On his way to the Northwest to deal with the Muslim uprising, he received orders to help in the final campaigns against the Nian.

Much of the struggle that Zuo faced was siege warfare, attacks on walled urban centers for which his army, most of which were provincial forces who had had experience fighting the Taiping or the Nian, had large siege guns, including some imported from the German firm of Krupp. In approaching the Muslims, Zuo was guided by the Qing policy: "The only distinction is between the innocent and the rebellious, there is none between Han and Muslim."[21] Because he likened the New Teaching to the heterodoxy of the White Lotus sect, he refused to grant clemency to any active supporter of the New Teaching. As Zuo and his forces moved west in the campaign, there was great loss of life. His campaign was focused on Ma Hualong's stronghold of Jinjibao near the border between Gansu and Inner Mongolia, supposedly protected by more than 500 forts. Zuo tightened the noose, slowly starving the walled city; by the time Ma surrendered and the siege was lifted, Jinjibao's inhabitants had been reduced to eating grass roots and the flesh of the dead. Ma and adult men from his family were executed by slicing, and almost 2,000 of his staff and troops were massacred. Zuo then continued the campaign, the final walled city siege coming in October 1873. The campaign took five years, and it saw widespread slaughter of the inhabitants of the besieged cities. But with this suppression, the country was generally free of rebellion and at peace for the first time in over two decades.

All in all, the four midcentury rebellions created vast devastation in six macroregions, killed tens of millions of people, and destroyed hundreds of towns and cities. They all reflected the ballooning crisis that China faced. Three of the rebellions raised issues of identity. The Taiping championed a completely new identity for China that would have constituted a revolution had it been successful. The Muslim rebellions brought to the fore issues of ethnic identity, a crucial fact in the Qing multi-ethnic empire and an extremely volatile factor with potential not only to rip the fabric of society but also to gut state control. Two of the rebellions openly challenged the Qing dynasty with calls for a new dynasty: the Taiping's Heavenly Kingdom of Great Peace and the

Nian's guerrilla campaigns against the government. With the exception of the Panthay rebellion, the midcentury rebellions were suppressed not by Qing generals but by scholar-officials, civilians who had advanced degrees in the civil service system. They were military generalists, not professionals, who applied Confucian moral and political principles, insisted on serious training for and discipline among their troops, and used some Western technology, particularly guns and ships. They looked both to the Chinese past, trying to save their culture from the Taiping version of Christianity, the Nian plunderers, and the Muslim crusaders, and to the Chinese future, taking the first gingerly steps toward what became known as "self-strengthening," that is, using Western technology to bolster the Chinese defense. In one sense, the military actions of the scholar-officials were cases of ethnic Chinese saving Manchu overlords; but more accurately, they were efforts of scholar-administrators imbued with Chinese culture aiding their rulers also committed to that culture.

Notes

1 Jean Chesneaux, *Peasant Revolts in China, 1840–1949* (New York: W.W. Norton, 1973), p. 23.

2 Thomas W. Kingsmill, "Retrospect of Events in China and Japan during the year 1865," *Journal of the North China Branch of the Royal Asiatic Society* 2 (1865): 143.

3 In using the term "civil war," I am following the lead of Pamela Crossley in *The Manchus* (Oxford: Blackwell, 1997) p. xv.

4 Philip A. Kuhn, "The Taiping Rebellion," in *The Cambridge History of China, Vol.10: Late Ch'ing, 1800–1911, Part 1*, ed. John K. Fairbank (Cambridge, UK: University of Cambridge Press, 1978), p. 267.

5 John King Fairbank and Merle Goldman, *China, A New History* (Cambridge, MA: Harvard University Press, 1998), p. 174.

6 Dorothy Ko, *Teachers of the Inner Chambers* (Stanford, CA: Stanford University Press, 1994), pp. 149–50.

7 Kuhn, p. 295.

8 Zeng Guofan, "A Proclamation against the Bandits of Guangdong and Guangxi, 1854," in *The Search for Modern China: A Documentary Collection*, ed. Pei-kai Cheng and Michael Lestz with Jonathan Spence (New York: W.W. Norton, 1999), pp. 147–8.

9 Frederic Wakeman, Jr., *The Fall of Imperial China* (New York: Free Press, 1975), p. 170.

10 Kuhn, p. 317.

11 Pamela Kyle Crossley, *The Wobbling Pivot: China Since 1800* (Chichester, Sussex, UK: Wiley-Blackwell, 2010), p. 116.

12 G. William Skinner, "Regional Urbanization in Nineteenth Century China," in *The City in Late Imperial China*, ed. G. William Skinner (Stanford, CA: Stanford University Press, 1977), p. 229.

13 *North China Herald*, August 8, 1914, p. 336.

14 The commenter was Jin Wuxiang. His remarks are noted in Susan Mann, *Talented Woman*, p. 194.

15 Mann, p. 196.

16 Ibid., p. 195.

17 Kuhn, p. 310.

18 Quoted in Chesneaux, p. 33.

19 Quoted in Elizabeth J. Perry, *Rebels and Revolutionaries in North China, 1845–1945* (Stanford, CA: Stanford University Press, 1980), p. 266.

20 Peter Perdue, *China Marches West: The Qing Conquest of Central Eurasia* (Cambridge, MA: The Belknap Press of Harvard University Press, 2005), p. 276.

21 Quoted in Kwang-ching Liu and Richard Smith, "The Military Challenge: The North-West and the Coast," in The *Cambridge History of China, Vol. 11, Late Ch'ing, 1800–1911, Part 2*, ed. John King Fairbank and Kwang-ching Liu (Cambridge, UK: Cambridge University Press, 1980), p. 228.

Suggestions for Further Reading

Atwill, David. *The Chinese Sultanate: Islam, Ethnicity, and the Panthay Rebellion in Southwest China, 1856–1873* (Stanford, CA: Stanford University Press, 2005). This revisionist study focuses on ethnic identities and the complexity of reality in the Panthay rebellion.

Kuhn, Philip. *Rebellion and Its Enemies in Late Imperial China: Militarization and Social Structure, 1796–1864* (Cambridge, MA: Harvard University Press, 1970). A pathbreaking study that showed how patterns of local military organization "were related to long-term political and social trends in modern China."

Lipman, Jonathan. *Familiar Strangers: A History of Muslims in Northwest China* (Seattle, WA: University of Washington Press, 1998). A richly detailed history of the Muslims, including the 1862–1873 rebellion, this work explores the identity of a people whom the author sees as "Sino-Muslims."

Perry, Elizabeth J. *Rebels and Revolutionaries in North China, 1845–1945* (Stanford, CA: Stanford University Press, 1980). This excellent study analyzes rebellions ranging from the Nian rebellion to the Red Spears of the early twentieth century in their ecological context of North Central China's Huaibei region.

Spence, Jonathan. *God's Chinese Son: The Taiping Heavenly Kingdom of Hong Xiuquan* (New York: W.W. Norton, 1996). In the words of one reviewer, this is "[a] spellbinding narrative, [and] a masterpiece of careful and creative historical scholarship" on the leader of the Taiping movement and the movement itself.

5

Crises and Choices

For a culture so deeply rooted in the glories of the past, the bloody and violent nightmares of the mid-nineteenth century were wrenching, for they seemed such a cataclysmic rupture from that past. Chinese culture had always focused on the past. Even for Confucius the golden age had been in that past, a time when society was harmonious and the country was peaceful. The goal of statesmen throughout the centuries was to restore something of that splendid past, even though no one thought that it could ever really be done. The past framed the present, so any change in state and society had to be rationalized in terms of that past, whether the particularly relevant past was the policies of a recent emperor or one's family traditions.

Previous foreign invaders had come to China on horseback, wielding bows and arrows. To a greater or lesser degree, China had been able to rein them in, incorporating them into the Chinese cultural world, even as those cultural forces often served to modify or supplement Chinese culture in turn. But these foreign invaders had come by sea with big ships and powerful cannon. They offered no indication that they would ever accept the Chinese cultural tradition. The break with the past was dramatically clear. The Central Country was being buffeted by radical challenges that it could not control; humiliation seemed to grow by the day. The crises of the nineteenth century therefore presented Chinese leaders with a life-and-death decision: how to overcome their military and strategic impotence so that they could begin to compete with these foreigners on a more equal playing field.

Scholar-officials varied considerably in their reactions and in their prescriptions about what should be done. Yet no one believed that the Chinese political system or its institutions might somehow be too weak or ill arranged or at fault. All reactions were defensive. Even the most liberal reaction, the move to self-strengthening, was based on the premise that the system and its institutions must be saved.

UNWILLING TO CHANGE (OR HOLDING ON TO THAT OLD-TIME IDENTITY)

Some argued that China's only road to restored strength was revitalization of its incomparably great culture, which had given rise to the glories of the past. Above all, these culturalists argued, barbarian weapons and machines were not the answer. Use of such implements of war would contaminate the Chinese hands that wielded them. If tools of war were to be part of the answer to China's problems, then Chinese should use those from the Chinese repertoire of warfare from the past.

One of these archconservatives and a famous teacher, official, and man of letters, Yu Yue (1821–1907), looked at China in the late nineteenth century and wrote about his three fears. His first fear brings us face to face with the issue of China's identity: if the current involvement of Western nations in China continued, Yu was afraid that "it will not be long before she loses her identity as the 'Central Nation.'"[1] Second, if scholars began to study Western things, "Confucianism will be undermined and eventually destroyed." Third, with technology beginning to use up natural resources, "the universe as we know it may end soon." The common denominator in these fears was fear of change and the impact it might have on the world that Yu, holder of the highest civil service degree and member of the Hanlin Academy, had come to know.

Yu was not alone in his fears. A host of influential men in the Beijing bureaucracy and in positions of power came to oppose any compromise in dealing with the West or adopting Western things. Perhaps the most influential in the 1860s was the famous Mongol official Woren. Like Yu Yue, he held the highest degree and served in the Hanlin Academy. In addition, he held a variety of high official posts—Grand Secretary and president and vice president of several boards (or ministries), where he established connections with and enjoyed considerable influence over key figures in the capital. He has also been called "one of the two or three great transmitters" of Neo-Confucian thought during the nineteenth century.[2] And he was probably the staunchest opponent of any official dealing with the West. He is said to have wept when he was appointed to serve in a new governmental body, the Zongli Yamen, set up to deal with the West. When his attempt to resign was not permitted, he intentionally threw himself from his horse on the first day on the job, injuring himself. He then used the injury as an excuse that he could not walk and thus could not serve on the Yamen; although he received several sick leaves, he did not recover until he was allowed to resign.

Woren (and others) advanced arguments like the following. "The foundation of a nation lies in the virtues she possesses" rather than in technology; no nation, he claimed, "has ever become strong by relying on achievement in technology."[3] At the heart of the answer for the crises facing China was dependence on Confucian moral principles and unfailingly continuing to exhort the people to follow these principles. Anathema to Woren was dealing with the West, which he described as treacherous, as consisting of mere technicians—"foreigners have always been our enemies." If we have to be taught this science, math, and technology, Woren asserted, find Chinese experts to do the job: "Why do we have to employ foreigners? Why do we have to honor them as our teachers?" Foreigners were devoid of civilization—simply put, barbarians; many archconservatives even saw them as closer to beasts—dogs and sheep—than to men.

But, the arguments on technology went on, we should not have to borrow at all. China had never borrowed from the West; why begin now? Just because technology was good for the West did not mean that it would have the same meaning in China, for China had different values and realities. The West, for example, might need machines to make up for a labor shortage; but move the machines to China, with its vast population, and the machines would only make unemployment a greater problem.[4] Even if China could be convinced that it must borrow technology from the West, would not the West, for military reasons, sell China only obsolete guns and cannon? In that case, China would be cheated as well as humiliated. A number of officials claimed that the benefits of technology had clearly been exaggerated. Further, they argued that the use of technology would deplete the natural resources that were used to power and feed machines. Finally, they worried that introduction of Western technology and Western things in general would interfere with and wreck the existing cosmic order. Since the cosmic and human worlds were intimately connected and mutually reflective, Western imports such as railroads and telegraph poles, for example, would by their nature make the "spirits of wind and water" (fengshui) go awry, with negative and perhaps catastrophic results.

SELF-STRENGTHENING

Rationale and Fallacy

The so-called self-strengtheners, those who wanted to strengthen China with a view to fending off Western imperialists, had a far different line on technology. Li Hongzhang, the commander of the anti-Taiping Anhui army, minced no words: "I firmly believe that to strengthen herself as a nation, China must learn Western technology."[5] Although self-strengthening involved a multi-pronged effort in the spheres of diplomacy, education, technology, and the military, advances in military technology—guns, ships, and armaments—were usually taken as a yardstick of successful self-strengthening, for they were most clearly related to defense.

But how to rationalize these changes that to archconservatives only raised fears? Self-strengtheners started with the premise that Western weapons and ships were simply inanimate machines, culture neutral, as it were. They argued that foreign weapons and ships could therefore be bought or manufactured without cultural pollution. Indeed, they argued that in the extreme crisis facing China, foreign military implements were the means (yong) by which the crucial end—protecting traditional Chinese culture or essence (ti)—could be achieved. In other words, Western guns and ships were the techniques by which the substance of Chinese civilization could be protected and maintained. By this formula, self-strengtheners rationalized change as the only way to protect the culture of the past and to realize some restoration of that past. Even for these "reformers," the past was the lens making possible appropriate views of the present.

Simply stated, this formula seemed tame enough, but it contained a serious logical fallacy. Foreign machines might look culture neutral (i.e., anyone can turn a switch, pull a trigger, or pilot a ship), but they came with a host of culture-specific scientific views and worldviews. To build ships and weapons at the new Jiangnan arsenal or the recently constructed Fuzhou shipyard would require the study of engineering and technology. Reading these scientific texts would take the student into a new world where old assumptions about the natural world would almost certainly be challenged. If a Chinese entered that world and then returned to the Chinese classics, he would again almost certainly see those classics in a broader context and ask new questions of them. For that student, their meaning and indeed the substance of Chinese culture would have been changed. In short, means do affect ends.

Or, taking up more practical issues, if arsenal and shipyard schools were established with engineering and foreign-language courses, how could they attract able young men to study these barbarian things? After all, the ladder to success in imperial China remained the civil service examination. Li Hongzhang had an answer: "One of the measures we can take is to introduce a new category in the civil service examination, namely the category of technology." But that strategy would mean that a traditional degree that had always been based on the classical humanities tradition could now be based at least in part on something from outside that tradition. Clearly, if this were the case, the practical requirements for successful self-strengthening revealed that means had an immense impact on ends. Borrowing Western technology had a way of undercutting traditional

Chinese cultural substance. The logical fallacy of the self-strengtheners was one that would begin to open China up to new, often unpredictable forces. It was also one that would appear again more than a century later, when China opened itself up to computers and high technology in the 1980s and 1990s.

The Self-Strengtheners

In the bureaucracy at Beijing, the key supporters of self-strengthening were the Manchu leaders Prince Gong and Wenxiang. Prince Gong was the sixth son of the Daoguang emperor. He negotiated, at age twenty-five, the 1858 Treaty of Tianjin and the 1860 Convention of Beijing; his conduct of foreign affairs from the 1860s to the 1880s was known for its conciliation. In 1861, after the death of his brother, the Xianfeng emperor, he played a key role in the coming to power of the late emperor's concubine, Cixi, who emerged in a coup d'état as regent for her young son, the Tongzhi emperor. Though considered spoiled and not averse to seeking bribes from office seekers, Prince Gong was especially close to Wenxiang, one of the most talented, conscientious, and respected Manchu metropolitan officials. A jinshi degree-holder, Wenxiang became a member of the Grand Council, the most important policy and personnel body in the central government.

Among Chinese officials, the triumvirate that had been instrumental in suppressing the mid-century rebellions—Zeng Guofan, Li Hongzhang, and Zuo Zongtang—were important leaders in the self-strengthening effort. Zeng was a model of the Confucian official, the most important Chinese official at midcentury. A jinshi degree-holder and member of the Hanlin Academy, he served with distinction in various capacities. His Hunan army, which he formed in the conscientious way that was his hallmark, was the chief agent of the Qing victory over the Taiping. He became a Grand Secretary in 1867 and governor-general of Zhili province in 1868. Known for his foresight, incorruptibility, and great perseverance, he was an excellent judge of men: many of the more than eighty men who served on his personal staff later became famous in their own right.

Li was a protégé of Zeng, though in many ways Li was as flashy as Zeng was gray in his stolidity. A jinshi degree-holder, Li became the most powerful official in the last thirty years of the nineteenth century and was involved in many of the major events and developments of the times, including every important international issue. His most important official post was governor-general of Zhili province (the capital province) from 1872 until his death in 1901. He amassed great power and wealth; in the process, he was often awash in a sea of corruption. (A brief biographical vignette of Zuo, the central hero in the suppression of the northwest Muslim rebellion, is presented in Chapter 4.) There was a host of second-tier reformers of whom one other should be mentioned: Feng Guifen, a Hanlin Academy scholar and local administrator, who might be called the best publicist for self-strengthening. In 1860, he published a collection of about fifty essays discussing the political, social, and economic issues facing China and calling for reform. He noted especially the rationale for self-strengthening—that Western learning was useful in a framework of Chinese values. Feng had considerable influence in Li's self-strengthening thinking and proposals.

Reforms

Though self-strengthening did not call for institutional change, emphasizing instead already existing institutions and policies, an important new institution was created in 1861. Established principally at the initiative of Prince Gong and opposed by the conservatives, the Zongli Yamen (Office for General Management) was the general coordinating bureau for all "Western affairs" (*yangwu*). These included diplomacy and trade, missionary problems, and, most important in the context

FIGURE 5.1   The able Prince Gong in his early dealings with Westerners treated them with "disdain mingled with hatred and fear." But after negotiating with them following the Arrow War, he began to approach them with some respect.
Source: Beinecke Rare Book & Manuscript Library via Wikimedia Commons.

of reform, overseeing and managing all projects and programs that involved Western matters or technology. Prince Gong headed the Zongli Yamen for twenty-seven years (1861–1884, 1894–1898). Indicative of its centrality in governmental decision making was the fact that from 1861 to 1884, it functioned in reality as a committee of the Grand Council, with Grand Councilors serving concurrently on the Yamen.

In the sphere of diplomacy, the Zongli Yamen sponsored the establishment of a school to train diplomats to handle relations in the new international order China had to face. The Tongwenguan (Interpreters College) was formed in 1862 to offer foreign-language instruction. When Prince Gong and Wenxiang undertook an initiative to seek out Western science teachers for the school in 1866, conservatives shot down the trial balloon. However, in 1869, the school developed an eight-year course of study with a curriculum focused on languages and science. Most of China's diplomats were trained there. It was headed by the American missionary W. A. P. Martin, who also co-translated a major work on international law, Henry Wheaton's *Elements of International Law*. Published under the auspices of the Zongli Yamen, translations like this began to acquaint diplomats and the Zongli Yamen's members with Western concepts and practices of international relations. Robert Hart, the longtime inspector-general of the Imperial Maritime Customs Service, served as the leading foreign adviser to the Yamen.

The major diplomatic step managed by the Zongli Yamen was the sending of diplomats abroad, not a small accomplishment, given the shame and contamination that many Chinese associated with dealing with Western barbarians. Zongli Yamen members were frequently referred to as "devil's slaves." The first "Chinese" ambassador sent abroad in 1868, on the urging of Robert Hart, was actually an American, Anson Burlingame, who had been serving as the U.S. minister in China. Burlingame's mission was to dissuade Western nations from being too insistent in upcoming treaty revision talks. Traveling to the U.S. and European capitals with Chinese and Manchu co-envoys, Burlingame was able to achieve the mission's objective: countries were at least temporarily moderate in their approach to treaty revision. Burlingame himself was not so fortunate; he died of pneumonia in Russia. His co-envoys made it back to China in late 1870, but they were treated as if the trip had contaminated them. Both were sent far away from Beijing, almost as if in exile—one to a position in Mongolia and the other to a remote post in Western China.

That treatment paled in contrast to the treatment received by Guo Songtao, the first Chinese ambassador, sent abroad in 1877. Guo had been a Hanlin Academy scholar who had thought long and hard about China's dealings with the West. He became an adviser to Li in the early 1860s. In the self-strengthening camp, he wanted to discover the secrets of Western wealth and power. He was also persuaded that a successful policy toward the West could only come when Western realities were understood; he firmly believed that the application of long-held Chinese principles in any crisis would end negatively if they were used without reference to the specific circumstances of the crisis. When he accepted an appointment to serve as minister to Great Britain, he was roundly condemned for his decision by conservative officials. One wrote in his diary, "Guo Songtao stands out for his learning and literary talents, but he should not have accepted the mission to the West! I am truly regretful for him."[6] He was leaving the world of Confucian sages to serve the devils. In Guo's hometown in Hunan province, people felt that he had brought such shame on his native place that they attempted to demolish his house.

During his two-year stay in London, Guo was awed by the British system of governance and especially by the modernization begun in the Industrial Revolution. His letters back to China extolled the virtues of railroads, telegraphs, machines, and electricity. He talked of Great Britain's Great Leap Forward in a letter to Li:

> From the beginning of England's rise [following the Industrial Revolution], it has been only several decades; while China was weak and declining, they covered a distance of 70,000 li in the wink of an eye. ... Chinese scholars and officials are presumptuous in their sanctuary and are trying to obstruct the changes of the universe; they can never succeed.[7]

The vituperation and threats that Guo received led him to cut short his service as ambassador. Although he had intended to publish his diary under the auspices of the Zongli Yamen, the court, under great pressure from the ultraconservatives, ordered the seizure and destruction of the printing blocks. Fearful for his life, Guo retired—and might as well have been in exile for all the impact he had on Chinese developments. Permanent diplomatic missions were sent to the United States, Japan, Russia, Germany, and France for the first time in 1879, fully eighteen years after Western ambassadors had begun to live in Beijing, a time gap that underscores the difficulty, acrimony, and sense of shame that underlay China's movement into the international arena. It was a question of identity: China's identity as the Central Kingdom had been lost forever. China had been decentered and was now simply one in a large group of nations.

In his arguments about self-strengthening, Feng had asserted, certainly with tongue in cheek: "what we then have to learn from the barbarians is only the one thing, solid ships and effective guns."[8] Certainly, weapons for defense were first on China's borrowing priority list. The first steps toward attaining military technology were through the Zongli Yamen with the establishment of arsenals, shipyards, and machine shops. Key here were also the scholar-administrator heroes of rebellion suppression. In 1865 at Shanghai, Zeng and Li established the Jiangnan Arsenal, which produced ships, gunboats, muskets, howitzers, shrapnel, ammunition, tools, and machinery. The following year Zuo built the Fuzhou Shipyard, at which 2,000 Chinese craftsmen, 900 laborers, and an administrative staff of 150 labored to produce fifteen larger ships than did the Jiangnan Arsenal in the half-decade from 1869 to 1874.

Educational programs were established at both the shipyard and the arsenal. The shipyard school was established in 1867, having enrolled over a hundred pupils under thirteen years of age. For the sake of political correctness, they had to take a Chinese curriculum and enter either a French or an English division. In the English division, cadets took courses in nautical astronomy, plane and spherical trigonometry, geography, and English, all under a three-year "major" of theoretical navigation. Then they went on board a training ship. The French division focused on naval construction and design, with courses in analytical geometry, calculus, physics, mechanics, and French. After five or six years, the students took on major responsibilities at the shipyard. The arsenal had a more varied educational program. A translation department published manuals, textbooks, and treatises on science and technology; at least fifty-four volumes were published by 1877. There were various courses of study, including Chinese studies, English, French, math, and science, but the study was more haphazard and was not directed to specific ends as the program at Fuzhou.

Finally, part of the self-strengthening educational program involved sending students abroad for training so that they could return and assist in China's modernizing effort. The most famous of these was the mission of Yung Wing, a Cantonese who had been educated at Yale with the support of missionaries. Between 1872 and 1875, with the approval of Zeng, Li, and the Zongli Yamen, four groups of thirty boys, ages twelve to sixteen, went to the Connecticut Valley. They were slated to stay for fifteen years, attending school, living with local families, and spending two weeks every three months at Hartford being tutored in a Chinese curriculum. The last did little to prevent the boys from becoming thoroughly Americanized. The program was ended in 1881 for many reasons, including the growing anti-Chinese movement in the United States. On their return, many of the students, then adults, made contributions in the technological and business sectors.

For the technological, diplomatic, and educational progress made under the leadership of the self-strengtheners from the early 1860s to the 1880s, the speed of progress and the possibility of bolder initiatives were greatly hampered by the ultraconservatives. Many officials on all levels dragged their feet in carrying out policies. Conservatives attacked the famous self-strengthening proponents and secondary figures as traitors. As we have seen, just dealing with foreigners could bring the wrath of the conservatives. Cultural inertia held back change. Feng's collection of essays on reform, published in 1860, was not presented to the emperor for his reading until 1889. Another key early work explaining the West, Wei Yuan's 1843 *Illustrated Treatise on the Maritime Kingdoms*, was not presented to the court until 1858.

If one needs further evidence of the negative and destructive impact of the ultraconservative culturalists, one need only look at the course of railroad development. In 1876, a less-than-20-mile line from Shanghai to Wusong was started by Westerners. In 1877 Chinese officials purchased the line and ripped up the tracks. Railroad construction from Beijing to the town of Qingjiangpu planned by the official Ding Richang, who worked closely with both Zeng and Li, was aborted because of conservative opposition. Likewise, a plan as late as 1889 to run a line from Tianjin to Tongzhou, about 10 miles east of Beijing, was forcibly discarded. Guo Songtao rightly predicted the outcome of such outmoded thinking:

> After several decades foreigners will arrive and then they will gradually build railroads and develop (natural resources) for us. ... Then both the ownership and the profits will fall into the hands of foreigners and China will have nothing to depend upon.[9]

FAMINE RELIEF, FACTIONALISM AND SELF-STRENGTHENING

Beyond the general Confucian moral and ethical philosophizing about opposing the goals of self-strengthening, there was a specific existential crisis that challenged the wisdom of self-strengthening at the time. While droughts and floods, leading to famine, were a perennial problem for China's farmers, the famines in the late nineteenth and early twentieth centuries were the most frequent and intense of those at any time in the Chinese past.[10] The so-called Incredible Famine (1876 to 1879) followed three years of drought in Shanxi Province, spawned by a strong El Niño episode in the waters of the tropical Pacific, which produced almost no monsoons, the usual source of rain for Shanxi.[11] The severe drought reduced people to eating grass, tree bark, and each other; starving families often had to decide which family members could eat and which would be abandoned. The Incredible Famine took between 9.5 and 13 million lives.

Traditionally, the government handled famines by providing relief grain from its ever-normal granary system. The Qing had perfected the system, which stored in the late eighteenth century up to 48 million piculs of grain; a picul is 133.33 pounds so that up to 6,399,840,000 pounds were stored in the High Qing. But by the 1870s, for the Qing state military expenses to deal with the mid-nineteenth-century rebellions, the now-continuous threat of imperialists at its shore, and the reconquest of Xinjiang totaled nearly 75 percent of all government expenditures.[12] The granary system, declining since the 1790s, was by 1850 storing less than 20 million piculs; and by the 1870s had deteriorated into a makeshift system because of the dearth of grain. Early in 1877, the Board of Revenue allocated relief money to Shanxi, but the actual relief program was not inaugurated until that November. In the end, between 1877 and 1879, the government sent a little over 10.7 million taels of relief silver and about a million piculs of relief grain to Shanxi. In comparison, Zuo Zongtang's reconquest of Xinjiang in 1877 cost 52.3 million taels.[13] The issue of government spending priorities became a political-economic battleground between the two factions.

The self-strengthening faction (the Foreign Affairs faction) was often opposed by the Qingliu (Pure Stream) faction. This group offered *qingyi* ("pure discussion"), which was heavily weighted with the sense of "moral critique." "Pure discussion" was a reflection of a Daoist concept of "pure conversation" in the early imperial era, where the group had purportedly cut themselves off from material concerns and personal and social connections so that their discussion would contain no partisanship, no special interests, and no mundane concerns. Theoretically it would thus express policies that were "pure," that is, restoring true Confucian ideals that would lead to the benevolent rule of the people and insure the public interest. The faction was based in the Hanlin Academy, the think tank composed of *la crème de la crème* of *jinshi* degree-holders still waiting their official appointments. This group, made up of men mostly born at about the time of the Opium War, was carrying on the tradition and positions of men who had called for a strong anti-British stand in the 1830s and 1840s and who had opposed the conciliatory stand of the Manchu negotiators during treaty negotiations in the 1850s, thus making it conservative and idealistic. Most of the group had no experience in foreign policy or in military affairs. The faction often stressed the special morality of China and that battles are not determined by weapons but by men's hearts. Thus, they gave little to no support to self-strengthening. They argued that the horrific Shanxi famine, not foreign affairs, was the transcendent crisis facing China; they stressed the Confucian idea that the people were the foundation of the state, that they were due benevolent rule and policies from above. Worrying that the people's extensive suffering and anxiety might give rise to uprisings, even rebellions, some *qingyi* proponents memorialized the court to temporarily stop self-strengthening to use money to feed the hungry; to ban railroad construction and to call all ambassadors home from their posts to save money for famine relief; to order Li to shift up to 400,000 taels from coastal defense funds to famine relief (he transferred 200,000); and to explore ways of collecting funds for famine relief, including taxation or seeking a foreign loan.[14] There were suggestions to purchase rice from Vietnam to be sent as relief and as a tool for price stabilization in the affected area; some argued that the famine occurred because of the huge amounts of land devoted to opium cultivation and not to grain or other foodstuffs, and that too much of the grain was taken for the distillation of liquor.

In the end, the initial government relief in silver taels and grain and Li's shift of 200,000 taels was the total amount of relief that Shanxi received. In the struggle between self-strengtheners and *qingyi* culturalists over funds and projects, the self-strengtheners had the upper hand, having solid support from the Zongli Yamen and, after some waffling, from the court as well. The voices of pragmatism or realism in this case overcame hard-core Confucian traditionalism.

WOMEN AND FAMINE

Women in the ancient Daoist conception of yin-yang, interactive forces that produced all change in the world and ultimately the course of history, were the yin force, associated with darkness, weakness, the moon, and, most appropriate during the famine, "wetness." Some contended that the famine was caused by evils brought on by women's lack of chastity and filiality and by their extravagance, wastefulness, and laziness. Other critics, in contrast, argued that because of their association with wetness, women might play a special role in ending the drought.

The Chinese traditionally used various images of women to signify the trauma and terror of mass starvation; and they are not alone in that among countries of the world. Images of the Great Irish Famine (1845–1852), of the twentieth century's Bengali famine (1943–1944), and of the South Sudan famine (1988–1994, 1998–1999, 2017) also focused on the plight of women.[15] Women became the "bearers of meaning" of the misery of starvation; for example, in sketches and woodblock prints of a baby sucking at the breast of its dead mother; or of a desperate mother trying to breast-feed her dead baby; or of a married woman being attacked with a knife by her father-in-law who, because of his and his wife's impending death by starvation, has decided to kill and eat their daughter-in-law; or of a mournful woman being photographed with her starving, dying children.

During a serious famine, for example, women (both mothers and daughters) suffered more than men. Daughters could become victims of infanticide or sold to some man (to get money and get rid of an extra mouth to feed). Wives could be killed by their husbands, or, more likely, sold to traffickers in women that flourished during this period. The Qing government tried to control women trafficking during the famine but found it was impossible, given the pressures that families faced. The sale of women or the selling of the woman by her own choice was horrifying to traditional Confucians (and to the *qingyi* group) because such women were thereby losing their most important moral attribute, chastity. An eleventh-century Neo-Confucian philosopher had made the matter crystal clear: "To starve to death is a small matter; to lose one's chastity is a great matter."[16] Thus, a woman could keep her most cherished chastity by starving to death in her home or on the road—and many did.

The feminization of famine, that is, representing the horrors and humiliations of famine through images of women, is a cross-cultural phenomenon. In China, women become synecdoches for the sufferings of all who were caught up in the misery of the disaster. Why women? The practice "represents a ... tradition in which images of women are used because they have great power to move the reader or spectator." Repeatedly, "images of women are used to figure moments of breakdown or crisis—in the social body, in political authority, or in representation itself."[17] Often represented in Chinese sketches or prints was a woman breastfeeding her infant or being unable to do so "because the mother's milk is a 'central metaphor of the gift of life', her dry breast is 'one of famine's deepest horrors', expressive of a primal fear, where the 'fountain of life' is now death-giving."[18] (See print by Feng Zikai in Chapter 14 of a mother nursing an infant who, while nursing, is instantaneously decapitated by Japanese bombs.) Despite women's second class social role in Confucian thought, "women are most often selected to embody 'the purported authenticity of the nation.'" Such representation of women has been "a very significant site upon which regimes and elites in China, responsible for charting the destiny of the nation, have sought to locate the unchanging essence and moral purity of that nation."[19] Two beacons of Confucian morality during the Incredible Famine, female chastity and filiality, speak pointedly to the unchanging essence and moral purity of Chinese culture, as the Pure Stream faction understood it. The self-strengtheners in contrast were downplaying the culturalism with its essences and morality and beginning to see China threatened by other nations, as a Chinese nation vying with other nations in the new international arena.

THE LOSS OF TRIBUTARY STATES: THE LIUQIUS, VIETNAM, AND KOREA

In the twenty-one years from 1874 to 1895, China lost its three most important tributary states: the Liuqiu Islands (Ryūkyūs in Japanese), Vietnam, and Korea. Aggressive actions by Japan in the first and third and by France in the second pointed to a new wave of imperialism in the closing quarter of the nineteenth century. All three cases underscore how deeply the tributary mentality continued even though on paper it had been dead since 1860 and even though in Korea, China had merged it with imperialism. For the Chinese, the treaty system and the tributary system coexisted, relating to each other in various ways in different places and situations.

The Loss of the Liuqiu Islands

For China, the Liuqius were an important tributary state; since 1372, China had regularly received tribute missions from the islands. But China was completely unaware of the islands' relationship to Japan. In 1609 the feudal lord of the Japanese domain of Satsuma on Kyushu's southeast coast had conquered the islands. From that point—even before the establishment of the Qing dynasty—Japan ruled the northern part of the islands directly, with the rest indirectly under the titular control of the Ryūkyūan king. The islands thus paid tribute to Satsuma and even to the shogun in Edo. Since Satsuma wanted to participate in trade with China, however, it ordered the Liuqius to continue to participate in the tribute system with China.

Late in 1871, over fifty shipwrecked sailors from the Liuqiu Islands were killed by aborigines in eastern Taiwan. In 1873, the Japanese claimed that they had the sole right to speak for the islands and in 1874 undertook a naval expedition to Taiwan to punish the aborigines. China responded in amazement, declaring that both Taiwan and the Liuqius were Chinese. The Japanese asserted that they had had to act because the aborigines' action clearly revealed that the Chinese did not in fact exercise sovereignty over the island. When face-to-face diplomacy did not achieve a solution to the dispute, the British minister served as arbiter. In the end, China paid 500,000 taels for the victims of the killings, and for some Japanese barracks built in Taiwan, and also promised not to condemn the Japanese expedition. Both actions pointed to diplomatic obtuseness: going along with the expedition was basically a recognition of Japan's sovereignty over the islands, and the payment to Japan, in the words of the British ambassador to Japan, amounted to a "willingness to pay for being invaded."[20] In 1879, Japan annexed the islands, and they became Okinawa prefecture.

Troubles in Korea

Korea was one of China's closest tributary states. Whereas many tributary states sent tributary missions once every so many years, in the Qing Korea sent four tributary missions every year. China had occupied the northwestern part of the peninsula during the Han dynasty and had tried without long-term success to seize the country again in the Sui and Tang dynasties. Despite that history of aggression, the Koreans took Chinese institutions as the models for their cultural and political institutions; by the Choson dynasty (1392–1910), Korea was in many ways a small replica of the Chinese system. Koreans called their relations with China "serving the great," whereas their relations with others, for example Japan, were denoted "neighborly relations."

A tragic fact of Korea's history has been its geographical position. Caught between Japan and the huge land powers of China and Russia, Korea has served as the bridge for land powers to Japan (in the thirteenth-century Mongol invasions) and for Japan to the land powers (in the late sixteenth-century invasion of the Japanese leader Hideyoshi). Viewed in the context of potential threats from the mainland, Japan, in a stock phrase, contended that Korea was a "dagger pointed at its heart." It is not surprising that in the nineteenth century Korea tried to isolate itself for protection, turning itself into what became known as the "hermit nation."

From 1866 to 1873 Korea had been ruled by a regent for the minor king, who had been adopted into the line of succession because there was no direct heir of the preceding king. The regent, known as the Taewon'gun, was in reality the king's biological father and would remain one of the political lightning rods around which many would rally from the 1860s to the 1880s. The king had in his early teens been married off to an ambitious older woman of the powerful Min family who emerged as the other political lightning rod. Since the rivalry between China and Japan in Korea would be played out in the context of the struggle between the Taewon'gun and Queen Min, their positions regarding foreign affairs are important.

> The Taewon'gun had a simple foreign policy: no treaties, no trade, no Catholics, no West, and no Japan. He viewed Japan's progressive reforms as yet more evidence of how far it had fallen from the Way, how little the island people really understood the virtues of a Sinic [Chinese] world order.[21]

But the king came of age and took over in 1873, and, with his assertive wife, was more open to dealing with the outside world.

In the first half-decade following the overthrow of the Tokugawa shogunate in 1868, some government leaders in the new Meiji regime saw Korea as an opportunity. By military action in Korea, Japan could establish itself on the continent, prevent other countries from gaining territory or a colony so close to Japan, and provide a chance for former samurai to get the fighting blood out of their system by turning them on Korea as retaliation for a Korean rebuff to Japanese vessels. Though that plan came to naught, Korea, located only 100 miles across the Tsushima Strait, began to become important in Japan's conception of its role in Northeast Asia.

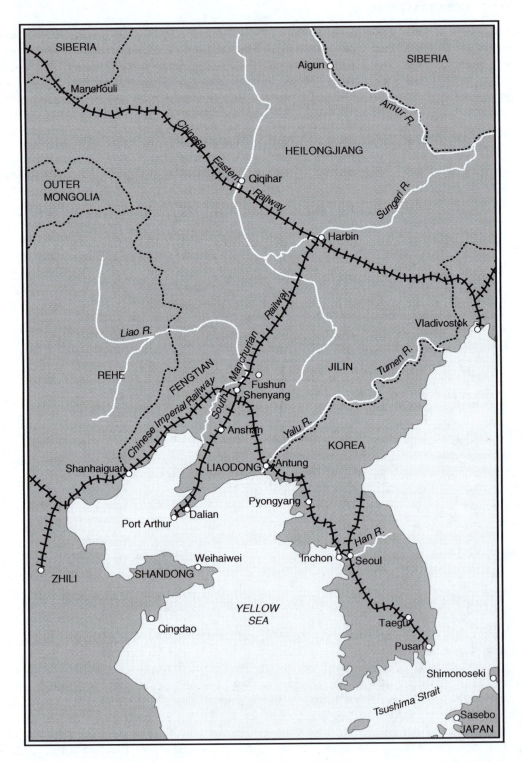

MAP 5.1 Northeast Asia, Late Nineteenth and Early Twentieth Centuries.

In 1875, Japan sent emissaries to sound out China about its reactions to greater Japanese involvement in Korea. Li Hongzhang's tributary-framed answer was that "though Korea is a dependent country of China, it is not a territorial possession; hence in its domestic and foreign affairs, it is self-governing." Emboldened by China's implicit permission to talk to Korea about opening trade, the Meiji government proceeded to "open" the hermit nation by signing a treaty in 1876. As to Korea's status, the treaty stated, "Korea, being an independent state, enjoys the same sovereign rights as does Japan." China interpreted "independent" as "autonomous," but it is clear from subsequent events that Japan saw things differently.

When Japan annexed the Liuqiu Islands in 1879, China seemed to suddenly realize the threat that an unchallenged Japan posed in Korea. In 1880 Korean relations were taken away from the Board of Rites, which oversaw the tributary system, and given to Li who encouraged the Korean government to sign treaties with Western powers and thereby to encourage a foreign policy of using barbarians to control barbarians. Indeed, when there was some hesitance on the Korean part, Li negotiated the U.S.–Korean treaty and presented it to the Koreans to sign: in this way, the tributary elder brother acted to pull the younger brother into the international community. Seen another way, Li had taken over Korean foreign policy, a view underscored by the fact that he followed up the American treaty by treaties with the British and the Germans. It was a role that went beyond the "elder-brotherliness" of the tributary system, mixing it with more than a shade of imperialism. Indeed, in dealings with Korea, China used some tactics that reflected those of Western nineteenth-century imperialists: treaties and international law, a customs service under Chinese control, and the technology of empire—gunboats, steamships, and the telegraph. Essentially China worked imperialistically to set up a multilateral imperialist system to protect its own interests in Korea.[22]

Because of China's continuing involvement in Korea and Japan's new interests, the 1880s and 1890s saw increasing tensions between China and Japan on the Korean peninsula; with both keeping some nationals in the country, the situation was always ripe for problems. Firmly in power, Queen Min supported reform, specifically hiring Japanese military officers to train the nucleus of a modern Korean military. The Taewon'gun was determined to break her power. In 1882, he reportedly incited a Korean army mutiny over the better provisions that the Japanese-trained unit received. The mutineers attacked the palace (with Queen Min barely escaping) and burned the Japanese legation. The Taewon'gun again took the reins of government. Both China and Japan sent forces "to restore peace."

The Chinese then performed the big brother act once again. Informed of the Taewon'gun's complicity in the mutiny, the Chinese arrested him and threw him in jail in China because he had moved against the queen, whom the Chinese had recognized as the proper authority. This act, the arrest of a Korean leader by Chinese diplomats and his incarceration in China, trumpeted the tributary mentality for the world to hear, but also had strains of imperialistic action. Clearly not dead, the tributary system continued to function through the cultural inertia that was so much of the response to reform or, more accurately, to change. The upshot of the crisis was that the Japanese maintained a permanent guard at their legation in Seoul; the Chinese kept 3,000 soldiers in the country, sent arms and Chinese instructors to the Korean military, and posted advisors to the Korean government. These actions too were those of the elder brother.

In the mid-1880s, different Koreans looked in different directions for the path that their country should follow, some to China, some to the United States, some to Japan. A number of youthful Koreans had gone to Japan to study and had become passionately enthusiastic about the course of Meiji reforms. In 1884, they attempted a coup against a Korean regime that now seemed clearly in the Chinese camp. The Japanese ambassador participated in the conspiracy, readying Japanese legation guards for action. The plan: take advantage of a large public gathering—a dinner attended by foreign diplomats and key Korean officials in celebration of the opening of the new post office—to assassinate important leaders. The reformer-conspirators were successful in murdering seven people. They then set fire to the city; Japanese guards rushed the palace and seized the king and queen. But at Queen Min's urgent appeal, the Chinese military leader Yuan Shikai advanced on the palace, freed the monarch and his spouse, and suppressed the coup. But Japan sent forces and demands for both an indemnity and an apology over damage to the Japanese legation (which had, in fact, been torched by the fleeing Japanese ambassador). The Japanese leader Itō Hirobumi was sent to China to negotiate an end to the crisis with Li. Each country withdrew its forces and promised to notify the other if it was planning to send forces in the future. Presumably if that happened, joint consultations would mean that cooler heads would prevail and another crisis could be averted. This Li–Itō convention brought another decade of peace, in which the new Chinese Resident General, Yuan Shikai, sought to preserve the forms of Chinese suzerainty. But the agreement also made Korea a virtual co-protectorate of China and Japan. The trouble was not over.

French Imperialism in Vietnam

Vietnam, the northern part of which China had controlled directly from the Han through the Tang dynasties, was a close tributary in the Ming and Qing dynasties. Though it fought off Chinese political control, it continued in the Chinese cultural orbit, like Korea, borrowing its most important political and cultural institutions. From the Chinese perspective, the tributary relationship with Vietnam was a crucial reality. China established Vietnamese emperors in office and sent troops to help its tributary younger brother put down unrest. By the 1880s, after China's experience with foreign invasion and pressures and its tributary concerns, China was well aware of the strategic importance of Vietnam for its own security. In the words of one official,

> The border provinces are China's gates; the tributary states are China's walls. We build the walls to protect the gates, and protect the gates to secure the house. If the walls fall, the gates are endangered; if the gates are endangered, the house is shaken.[23]

French interest in Vietnam began with Jesuit missionaries in the seventeenth century, but the French Revolution and the Napoleonic wars put East Asian involvement on hold. At the turn of the nineteenth century, the French became briefly involved, offering crucial support for Nguyen Anh in the establishment of the Nguyen dynasty (1802–1945). The Nguyen emperors championed and emphasized Chinese cultural models and forbade trade and intercourse with the West and the spread of Christianity. In the late 1850s the French began to take more concerted action to extend their interests, beginning with a military campaign in southern Vietnam as revenge against anti-missionary riots. By 1862, they had taken Cochin China, the three southernmost provinces of the country, and forced the Vietnamese government to cede it to them.

A treaty in 1874 further extended French influence, permitting French shipping on the Red River in the country's northernmost section, Tonkin, and seizing control of Vietnamese foreign relations. Part of France's intention in this treaty was to try to establish the independence of Vietnam from China, an obvious precondition if France was taking control of Vietnam's foreign affairs. Thus, the treaty recognized "the sovereignty of the King of Annam [Vietnam] and his complete independence of all foreign powers."[24] The Chinese responded to this treaty by saying that Vietnam had been a tributary state of China for centuries and that China would look into the matter, but it did not do so. Even worse, the Chinese response was translated in the French past perfect tense ("had been a tributary"), implying that the tributary relationship was completely over. Therefore, the French took this as Chinese tacit acceptance of what was essentially a French protectorate. Feeling free to act forcefully, the French stepped up their aggressive actions in northern Vietnam, whereupon the Vietnamese government, in the role of tributary younger brother, sent a tributary mission to China and asked the Chinese for help. With the situation "as precarious as piled eggs," the Chinese sent in irregulars known as the Black Flags, groups of former Taiping and Panthay rebels, who began to skirmish with French troops in 1882.[25] The next year the Chinese, without fanfare, dispatched regular troops.

MAP 5.2 Southeast China and Vietnam.

THE WAR WITH FRANCE AND THE IMPACT OF SELF-STRENGTHENING

As war clouds thickened, Chinese policy was halting and uncertain. A rancorous policy dispute over the proper reaction to the Vietnamese crisis had broken out. On one side were so-called realists such as Li, who contended that Chinese self-strengthening, specifically coastal defenses and the naval program, had not yet reached the point where China could realistically repel France. This group called for negotiations since, they argued, China could not annul the treaties France had signed with Vietnam, nor could it force France from Vietnam. Open war would only end in certain Chinese defeat and French demands on China itself. Though Li had the support of the Zongli Yamen's Prince Gong, the opposition was shrill and vociferous. The Pure Stream faction emerged as a pro-war faction and attacked Li's position as appeasement. Essentially their argument was "enough is enough": if China made one great effort, then all of China's foreign policy humiliations would come to a halt. In practical terms, this meant that if China made a huge concerted effort to fight the French until they were defeated, that action would so deter other foreign nations that they would cease bullying China.

It seems clear that the Empress Dowager was to some degree immobilized by the clashing policy lines of the Foreign Affairs faction and the Qingliu faction. The court let the skirmishing in Vietnam continue even as it ordered Li to negotiate. In the next few months two potential peace treaties were scuttled, the first by the French and the second by the French and the pro-war Qingliu faction, which flooded the court with almost fifty calls for Li's removal. On the reception of a French ultimatum that Chinese forces withdraw from Vietnam and with the threat of a French attack on China, the Empress Dowager went over to the side of the pro-war faction, appointing two of its leaders to key positions in South China, one to the command of the Fujian fleet based at the city of Fuzhou.

In August 1884, the skirmishing between the Chinese and French became a war. French ships sailed up the Min River 20 miles to Fuzhou, homeport of one-quarter of the Chinese navy and site of the Fuzhou Shipyard. All the ships, including their largest vessel in Chinese waters, sailed past numerous Chinese batteries with modern guns and cannon purchased from European firms, all exhibits of the self-strengthening program, but none of them fired a shot. Early on the afternoon of August 23, the French fleet made target practice not only of the Chinese fleet but also, disastrously, of the shipyard itself. In a quarter of an hour, all but two of the twenty-three Chinese war junks and men-of-war were sunk or were burning; the shipyard was demolished. Approximately 3,000 Chinese were killed. The pro-war faction commander of the Fujian fleet was one of the first to flee and watched the conflagration from hills overlooking the port. For that debacle he was exiled.

That summer afternoon had revealed the emptiness of the self-strengthening efforts: without organization, coordination, and leadership, all the modern machines and weapons that might be manufactured or bought were ineffectual. The presence of the French fleet at Fuzhou at a time of an increasing likelihood of war in the area should have alerted Chinese authorities to the imminent danger. Garrisons along the riverbank should have been prepared to prevent the ships from sailing upstream. The tragic irony was that the court had attempted to force two of its other fleets to participate in actions against the French, but their leaders, one of whom was Li, refused. Li's refusal can be seen as a statement of displeasure at having the Empress Dowager side with the pro-war faction or, more certainly, as a desire to keep his fleet out of a battle (that he believed would almost certainly be a defeat) and intact so that it might be ready if necessary in Korean waters.

The disaster at Fuzhou brought the Empress Dowager more solidly into the pro-war faction's camp. But when, three months later, there were no gains and fears began to spread that Japan would take advantage of the situation by wreaking havoc in Korea, the Empress Dowager went back to the negotiating route. The end of the war came with an agreement in mid-1885 in which China ended its centuries-long tributary relationship by recognizing French control over Vietnam. Part of the blame for the loss had to be placed on the pro-war Qingliu faction and its naiveté; only one of its proponents, Zhang Zhidong, survived to play any important public role in the years following the war.

The self-strengthening movement had been an ignominious failure to this point: China seemed not in the least capable of fighting off aggressors. Political decision makers had not been able or willing to make the institutional and personnel decisions that could have provided the appropriate context for self-strengthening success. Moreover, they did not take the necessity for institutional and personnel changes as the main lessons of the war. The incorrect lesson they learned instead was that there had simply not yet been enough self-strengthening.

Therefore, the decade following the loss of Vietnam saw an expanded menu of self-strengthening. A key figure in the effort was none other than the pro-war faction leader Zhang Zhidong, who, anti-foreign as he continued to be, was converted by the war into a forceful self-strengthener. He wrote,

> If we wish to make China strong and preserve Chinese learning, we must promote Western learning. But unless we use Chinese learning to consolidate the foundation and to give our purpose a right direction, the strong will become rebellious leaders and the weak, slaves. The consequence will be worse than not being versed in Western learning.[26]

In Zhang's thinking, China had to emphasize both the old and the new: only if Chinese maintained a firm grounding in Chinese traditional thought would self-strengthening using Western technology and science not eradicate Chinese identity.

Although Zhang established an arsenal and a mint in Canton, his main base was the metropolis of Wuhan (made up of the three cities of Wuchang, Hankou, and Hanyang) in the Middle Yangzi, where he served as governor-general of Hunan and Hubei provinces from 1889 to 1894 and from 1896 to 1907. At Wuhan he set up an iron foundry, and he founded two schools of Western studies, one focusing on the sciences and international law, the other on commerce and Western languages. In keeping with his conviction that the old must be studied as well as the new, he established a traditional academy that became involved in publishing over 175 volumes written during the Qing period.

One institutional innovation that especially portended greater changes was the establishment of military academies. Li had set up a naval academy at Tianjin in 1880 and 1881 modeled on the school that functioned at the Fuzhou shipyard. Its first dean was Yan Fu, a graduate of the Fuzhou school and soon to become China's most important translator of major Western works. Apparently prompted largely by the Sino–French War, Li in 1885 established the Tianjin Military Academy, where men selected from his Anhui army were trained in military affairs. Li hired German officers as teachers in the two-year curriculum that included science, mathematics, surveying, fortifications, and military drilling; classes were conducted mostly in German. Approximately 1,500 men received training from 1885 to 1900. Li added a special five-year officers' training program in 1887. In 1885, Zhang Zhidong also established a military training school, the Guangdong Naval and Military Officers' Academy. Whereas the military innovations in midcentury, the founding of Zeng's and Li's personal provincial armies, had been established under a Confucian ethos, these institutional changes were the first steps toward the establishment of a modern Chinese military, setting up curricula focusing on military science. Significantly, many important military leaders in the early twentieth century were trained at these academies.

In the wake of the naval disaster at Fuzhou, the government established a Board of Admiralty to centralize navy functioning and build naval power. But this board was soon moribund because of the system of personal connections and corruption that sank any efforts to reform. Efforts to centralize the fleets foundered on the desires of men in charge of specific fleets to maintain their own control; Li created the strongest fleet, the Beiyang or northern fleet. The naval self-strengthening program was also undercut by lack of funds, a problem made worse by actions of the Empress Dowager. In a story that has become classic in its disturbing irony, much of the appropriation earmarked for naval expansion was used by the Empress Dowager for rebuilding the Summer Palace, which had been destroyed during the Arrow War. Apparently, part of that naval appropriation was used to fund the renovation of the infamous Marble Barge on which the Empress Dowager liked to picnic: at a time when no ships whatsoever were added to the main Chinese fleet, she poured money into one that would not float.

IDENTITY AND PERCEPTION: THE ROLES OF THE EMPRESS DOWAGER

From her emergence in 1861 to her death in 1908, the Empress Dowager, Cixi, was the most powerful and controversial figure in modern Chinese history. Part of her reputation most certainly came from the traditional Chinese negative attitude toward female rulers. Women should not rule: "The hen does not herald the coming of the morning." Female rulers in the past, like the Tang dynasty's Empress Wu, have been morally tarred with salacious stories about their sexual appetites and promiscuity. There have been sexual whisperings about Cixi as well. Another part of her negative reputation stemmed from her unscrupulous political manipulation (and worse) of the two emperors for whom she served as regent and her unwillingness to relinquish power. Yet another part of her reputation arose from the disastrous problems that China experienced on her watch. Domestic turmoil, state bankruptcy, humiliation by foreign powers, and war have been blamed to a greater or lesser degree on her narrow-mindedness, authoritarian nature, and corruption. Others besides Cixi were certainly to blame. To take the wretched state of China's finances as an example: already by 1850, over a decade before she took power, the Qing government was taking in only about 10 percent of what it was spending. In the end, all the criticisms and rumors about her indeed make it difficult to disentangle her actual identity from her perceived or attributed identity.

In 1861, she became regent for her son, the Tongzhi emperor, who ascended the throne at the age of five. For twelve years she ruled outright for him, and after he began to rule for himself she constantly interfered in matters of state and in his private life. He apparently resented her actions and in turn enraged her by choosing for his bride someone other than her own choice. Rumor had it that she or at least eunuchs close to her encouraged the young emperor to visit brothels and adopt a dissolute lifestyle. Some accounts have suggested that he may have contracted venereal disease. In November 1874, however, he became ill with smallpox, which may have been the cause of his death in January 1875. Without either a son or a brother, the Tongzhi emperor's demise left Cixi again in the driver's seat.

She chose her nephew, who was four years old at the time and who was indeed her closest male relative, to become the Guangxu emperor. This choice infuriated some conservatives at the court because it violated the precedents and tradition of dynastic succession, particularly that the next emperor come from a generation younger than the deceased emperor. The ideal of filial piety necessitated such a choice. The new emperor was, however, from the same generation as the Tongzhi emperor. Cixi was able to survive the criticism, and she achieved her main goal—to serve as regent once again, in effect to serve as the sole ruler.

FIGURE 5.2   One of the most powerful figures in modern Chinese history, the Empress Dowager Cixi began her rule as a thoroughgoing conservative traditionalist but ended her career embracing progressive reforms.
Source: Hulton-Deutsch Collection/CORBIS/Corbis via Getty Images.

When the Guangxu emperor achieved his majority in 1889, Cixi officially retired to the Summer Palace, where she could loll away her afternoons on her Marble Barge. But she had held power too long to give it up. She insisted, for example, that all memorials be sent to her for her perusal; she retained decision-making power in key appointments to the six boards and to the Grand Council. Reportedly, at moments of crisis she held court with the emperor. Just like the earlier relationship between mother and son (the Tongzhi emperor), the relationship between aunt and nephew became very strained. The Guangxu emperor's ideas about China and the West began to diverge sharply from Cixi's, and feelings of suspicion and mistrust grew between them.

What were the sources of Cixi's power over the emperor and her continued centrality at the court? First, as the Empress Dowager, she was the emperor's official mother even if not his biological mother. Therefore, the emperor had to treat her with the proper respect and filial piety; certainly he could never show her open hostility. Further, the emperor was not the natural heir; Cixi had selected him. Beholden to her for his position, he could not rid the court of her presence or do away with her efforts to control him. Any such actions would only incense many of the high court officials who were also beholden to Cixi for their positions; their connections to her made most of them personally loyal to her. The emperor could not have taken any bold action in his relationship with the Empress Dowager because he would have alienated the very people he needed in order to rule. Since the court was filled with her supporters, it made her continued involvement all the easier. As one other indication of Cixi's stranglehold, it was traditional for a new emperor to make his own appointments to the Grand Council. But for four years after the Guangxu emperor took power, only Cixi's appointees staffed the Council; and even after that, those who were appointed to the Council had started their careers with her patronage.

Thus, as China entered the 1890s, a decade that would come to take on the terrifying aura of a nightmare, at the top of the government there was an ominous split. The fifty-five-year-old Empress Dowager, who was used to being in control, was now trying to hold on to as much power as possible and was continuing to cultivate ties to those at the court and in the top ranks of the bureaucracy. The nineteen-year-old emperor, on the other hand, had, as a child, been so fearful and timid (perhaps because of Cixi's overbearing qualities) that, on hearing the sound of thunder, he reportedly hid his head in his tutor's lap. Now, however, he had begun to try to assert himself, to take up the responsibilities of the Son of Heaven, and to stake out his own intellectual and political positions. The troubles of the 1890s would only make their mutual resentment and distrust more intense.

Notes

1 Quoted in Dun J. Li, *China in Transition, 1517–1911* (New York: Van Nostrand Reinhold, 1969), p. 164.
2 Ting-yee Kuo and Kwang-ching Liu, "Self-Strengthening: The Pursuit of Western Technology," in *The Cambridge History of China, Vol. 10: Late Ch'ing, 1800–1911, Part 1*, ed. John K. Fairbank (Cambridge, UK: Cambridge University Press, 1978), p. 529.
3 These quotations from Woren are taken from Li, *China in Transition*, pp. 162–3.
4 This example comes from Yen-p'ing Hao and Erh-min Wang, "Changing Chinese Views of Western Relations, 1840–1895," in *The Cambridge History of China, Vol. 11: Late Ch'ing, 1800–1911, Part 2*, eds., John King Fairbank and Kwang-ching Liu (Cambridge, UK: Cambridge University Press, 1980), p. 174.
5 Li, *China in Transition*, p. 142.
6 Hao and Wang, p. 183.
7 "A Letter of Guo Sungtao from London, 1877," in *China's Response to the West*, eds., Ssu-yu Teng and John K. Fairbank (Cambridge, MA: Harvard University Press, 1979), p. 99.
8 Feng Guifen, "On the Manufacture of Foreign Weapons," in Teng and Fairbank, p. 53.
9 "A Letter of Guo Songtao from London, 1877," p. 102.
10 Lillian Li, *Fighting Famine in North China* (Stanford, CA: Stanford University Press, 2010).
11 Mike Davis, *Late Victorian Holocausts: El Niño Famines and the Making of the Third World* (London: Verso, 2001), 6, 13–14, 61–2, 213–17, 230–8, 256–9.
12 Kathryn Edgerton-Tarpley, *Tears from Iron: Cultural Responses to Famine in Nineteenth Century China* (Berkeley, CA: University of California Press, 2008), pp. 38–40.
13 Ibid., p. 31.
14 Ibid., pp. 93–108.
15 The referenced work is Margaret Kelleher, *The Feminization of Famine: Expressions of the Inexpressible?* (Cork, UK: Cork University Press, 1997). Taken from Edgerton-Tarpley, *Tears from Iron*, pp. 161–2.
16 Quoted in Edgerton-Tarpley, p. 173.
17 Kelleher, pp. 6–8, 23–4, 29. See Edgerton-Tarpley, p. 162.
18 Julia Kristeva, "Stabat Mater," in *The Julia Kristeva Reader*, ed. Toril Moi (Oxford: Basil Blackwell, 1974–82). Quoted in Edgerton-Tarpley, p. 285, endnote 3.
19 Prasenjit Duara, "The Regime of Authenticity: Timelessness, Gender, and National History in Modern China," *History and Theory* 37, no.3 (October, 1998): 296.
20 Fairbank and Liu, *The Cambridge History of China*, p. 88.
21 Bruce Cumings, *Korea's Place in the Sun* (New York: W. W. Norton, 1997), p. 100.
22 See Kirk Larsen, *Traditions, Treaties, and Trade: Qing Imperialism and Choson Korea, 1850–1910* (Cambridge, MA: Harvard University Asia Center, 2008).
23 Quoted in Lloyd E. Eastman, *Throne And Mandarins: China's Search for a Policy during the Sino–French Controversy, 1880–1895* (Cambridge, MA: Harvard University Press, 1967), p. 38.
24 Ibid., p. 33.
25 This phrase was used by the governor-general of Yunnan and Guizhou. It is cited in Lloyd E. Eastman, "Ch'ing-I and Chinese Policy Formation During the Nineteenth Century," *Journal of Asian Studies* 24, no. 4 (August 1965): 602.
26 Zhang Zhidong, "Exhortation to Learn," cited in J. Mason Gentzler, *Changing China* (New York: Praeger, 1977), p. 102.

Suggestions for Further Reading

Chu, Samuel C., and Kwang-ching Liu, eds., *Li Hung-chang and China's Early Modernization* (Armonk, NY: M.E. Sharpe, 1994). The most complete work on this important Chinese official; its various essays detail his roles as self-strengthener and diplomat.

Cumings, Bruce. *Korea's Place in the Sun: A Modern History* (New York: W. W. Norton, 1997). This insightful and vibrantly written history puts the Chinese interests and actions in Korea in essential perspective.

Eastman, Lloyd. *Throne and Mandarins: China's Search for a Policy during the Sino–French Controversy, 1880–1885* (Cambridge, MA: Harvard University Press, 1967). This book is essential in analyzing the struggle between China and France over Vietnam.

Edgerton-Tarpley, Kathryn. *Tears from Iron: Cultural Responses to Famine in Nineteenth-Century China* (Berkeley, CA: University of California Press, 2008). This fascinating study of Shanxi's "Incredible Famine" (1876–1879) covers telling skirmishes between the self-strengtheners and the Qingliu faction and discusses the "feminization of famine," especially the role of women in the very conception of famine.

Larsen, Kirk. *Tradition, Treaties, and Trade: Qing Imperialism and Choson Korea, 1850–1910* (Cambridge, MA: Harvard University Asia Center, 2008). This revisionist work sees China's adoption of imperialist strategies in Korea to accompany a lingering tributary mentality.

6

The Devastating Nineties
Destroying Traditional Identities

Bookends of a tragic decade.

In 1891, a brilliant thirty-three-year-old *jinshi* degree-holder, Kang Youwei, dropped the intellectual equivalent of a bomb on the Chinese intellectual community. He argued in a book that the version of the Confucian classics that had been considered the philosophical canon and used for centuries as the basis for the civil service examination was a forgery. The fallout was the same as if a Western scholar were to prove that the Bible as the West has known it is a forgery. Kang had shattered the Chinese intellectual identity; how was it to be re-formed?

In 1900, a scene in Tianjin.

> On this day someone saw a corpse on the slope. … It was a man who had been killed by the [Boxer] bandit chief Cao Futian. His testicles had been cut off and his head severed and placed between his thighs, facing upward stiff and motionless. These people regard life as a trifling matter. When they kill a person, they rarely dispatch him with a clean blow of the sword; more often they slash indiscriminately with their swords and chop the body into pieces. The horror of the slaughter they perpetrate is even worse than that of the punishment of death by dismemberment.[1]

In many ways, the 1890s saw the bitter culmination of challenges to traditional Chinese identities and self-perceptions and reactions to the presence of imperialists unchecked. From the intellectual shocks brought by Kang and others to the bloody terror of the Boxers, the question that kept coming was "What does it mean to be Chinese?" In between there were other shocks—a startling military defeat, Western nations coming to carve up the "Chinese melon," and an aborted political reform effort that ended with the Empress Dowager putting the Guangxu emperor under permanent house arrest. It was a decade that at last proved to most Chinese that for China to survive, radical changes had to occur.

IDEOLOGY FOR CHANGE: KANG YOUWEI'S INTELLECTUAL BOMB

Rationalizing change in the name of the past was the quintessential Chinese way of looking to the future. The self-strengtheners were out to protect the past by using modern Western technology.

In addition to the ideas of the self-strengtheners, there were other, more mechanical ways of using the past to validate change. One argument, based on patterns of cyclical change, asserted that it had been 2,000 years between the time of the ancient sage kings of Yao and Shun and the establishment of the empire in 221 B.C.E. Because the late nineteenth century was about 2,000 years after that axial event, it was thus cyclically appropriate for a new momentous change to occur. Another argument proposed that Western science and technology could be legitimately borrowed from the West because mathematical and chemical ideas current in the West had first appeared in early Chinese history. This approach brought up the question of why and how, if this knowledge was so critical for the development of modern science, China had somehow lost it.

A key motive force in the modern Western world, emerging in the Enlightenment in the late eighteenth century, was the idea of progress. Humans, using their brains and the realities of modern technology and science, had the power to make progress inevitable. It was a view of history that was ever onward, ever upward, a strong contrast with the Chinese view of history, which envisioned a trend cyclically downward from a past golden age. Above all, the Chinese worldview was marked by an acceptance of fate—not, as in the modern West, by the potentiality of human action. In the 1890s, the scholar Kang Youwei gave the Chinese intellectual world its own idea of progress, building a rationale, as always *based upon the past*, for radical institutional change. Notably, his prescribed changes went far beyond self-strengthening. They were no longer to preserve traditional Chinese culture (as the self-strengtheners wanted to do) but, most basically, to preserve China. Put another way, Kang moved beyond what is often called "culturalism" (loyalty to a particular culture) to the borders of a modern "nationalism" (loyalty to a particular geographic entity).

In order to build new ideological structures, Kang first had to destroy the old edifices. The shocking forgery thesis in his 1891 book was a major part of that demolition. Kang claimed, based on textual criticism, that the true Confucian teachings were not found in the texts that had been the basis for the School of Han Learning since the seventeenth century. Rather, they were found in the so-called New Texts from the earlier Han dynasty. Kang's purpose was to undermine the School of Han Learning, whose textual and philological focus he believed had taken serious thinkers away from the central point of Confucianism, which should be political concern and institutional reform. Though today Kang's interpretation is not seen as credible, the impact on the intellectual world of the 1890s, already buffeted by realities of imperialism and rebellion, was shattering. If the traditional canon was shown to be false, there was no firm intellectual ground on which to stand.

A second major ideological contribution was Kang's 1897 book *Confucius as a Reformer*, which he began in 1886. It contributed both to the demolition of the old and to the construction of something new. During his lifetime, Confucius himself had claimed that he was not a creator but simply a "transmitter" from the past. This idea Kang tried to demolish. In its place, he structured a new Confucius as a great innovator, "a messianic, forward-looking 'sage king,'" a man who used the past to call for major institutional change in the present. Kang was not only proposing a new Chinese identity; he was questioning the meaning of China's traditional identity. In another work, he then set forth his rationale for progress, using primarily ideas from the West but placing them in categories that he found in the "real" Confucian New Texts.[2] His ideas set forth a unilinear view of history similar to that in the post-Enlightenment West. He found three axial ages through which history moved: the Age of Disorder, the Age of Approaching Peace, and the Age of Universal Peace. He argued that the world had been stuck in the Age of Disorder but that it could move to the next axial age, that of Approaching Peace, if his reform ideas were adopted. In essence, Kang was using the past to break away from the past. His reform proposals advocated basic institutional change, which included a state constitution and assemblies where rule by the people might be exercised.

Although many in the intellectual and political worlds judged him a heretic from Confucian orthodoxy, his proposals for institutions based on and infused with Western ideas began to excite, as nothing had before, an interest in Western things beyond simply guns and ships. Kang's works thus began to prime the pump for greater change. Perhaps even more significant, Kang's reinterpretation of Confucianism had a major impact, the shock waves of which would continue for decades. The reason? Kang's treatment of Confucius and his thought essentially changed Confucianism from "what so far had been the unquestioned centre of faith into an ideology, the basic character of which was problematic and debatable."[3] Once Confucianism became an ideology, for example, it could be interpreted as a tool that elevated certain social types (fathers, husbands, parents, elder brothers) and degraded other social types (sons, wives, children, younger brothers). Kang's work in essence was the revolutionary first step, however little he intended it, in deposing Confucius and his thought as the foundation of Chinese culture, the first step in dismantling the traditional Chinese identity.

One Chinese identity that both Kang and Liang challenged was the traditional view of women and their roles in society. One historian has asserted that Kang "should rank at the top of the list of Chinese male champions of women's emancipation."[4] He called for gender equality and made clear his feminist views before any Western feminist books appeared in China. He advocated women's education, legal equality with men, rights to serve in public office, wives keeping their maiden name after marriage, freedom of marriage via contract, unisex clothes for men and women, and the ending of footbinding. Indeed, in 1883, he established the first anti-footbinding association in Nanhai county, Guangdong province, his natal home. Susan Mann finds a "turning point" in the conception of the role of women in society with Liang's 1897 essay "General Discussion on Reform," wherein he addressed women's education.

Liang's sweeping blueprint for saving the empire located "the very source of China's cumulative weakness" in the lack of women's education. It was this salvo that opened the discourse on the "woman problem" that occupied China's twentieth-century reformers and revolutionaries.[5]

POLITICAL AND CULTURAL EARTHQUAKE: DEFEAT BY THE "DWARF PEOPLE"

From the mid-1880s an uneasy calm between China and Japan existed on the Korean peninsula. Their agreement in 1885 to abstain from sending troops without notification to the other had held into the 1890s. Chinese Resident General Yuan Shikai had developed close relations with powerful Queen Min. But Japanese determination to act decisively in any future crisis had become firmer.

Beginning in the 1860s, an eclectic religion called *Tonghak* (Eastern Learning) had begun to grow in southwest Korea. In many ways, especially in its promise of a utopian regime, it was reminiscent of the Taiping movement. In the early 1890s, it gave rise to a rebellion that grew out of an array of political, social, and economic problems besetting the Korean countryside. In the summer of 1894, with the rebellion spreading, the Korean government, still operating under its tributary mentality, asked the Chinese government to send troops to help quell the disturbance. Following the guidelines of the Li–Itō convention, the Chinese government notified Japan of its plan to send 1,500 troops but to withdraw them as soon as the rebellion was suppressed. The Japanese answered by sending around 8,000 troops. Li desperately tried to negotiate a settlement; he was well aware that any war would be fought with his Anhui army and Beiyang navy. But when his efforts to use Britain and the United States as mediators went nowhere, he decided that reinforcements had to be sent. On July 25, the Japanese sank a British steamer that had been chartered by the Chinese, drowning 950 Chinese soldiers. Both countries declared war on August 1.

The war was the first test for the Chinese military after ten years of what might be called "accelerated self-strengthening." In the climactic naval battle off the Yalu River on September 17, of the twelve Chinese ships involved, four were sunk, four were crippled beyond repair, and four fled. All twelve of the more up-to-date Japanese ships survived without major damage. The results, in short, were the same as those in the war with France a decade earlier: complete and humiliating defeat on both land and sea. A nation comprised of what earlier Chinese had contemptuously dismissed as "dwarf people" had smashed the Central Country. Many nations were astonished by the outcome, having assumed that the land giant would overwhelm the tiny island nation. But the result should not have been surprising. Japan had been rapidly modernizing since the 1870s, and its war effort was driven by national fervor. China's efforts at modernizing had been fitful, eroded by factionalism and counterproductive policies. When war came, it was indeed fought mostly by Li's Beiyang fleet and his provincial army. "China had no clear demarcation of authority, no unity of command, and no nationwide mobilization. Conflicting advice from the Tsungli [Zongli] Yamen, provincial authorities, and irresponsible [pro-war] officials rendered the court indecisive."[6] The same postmortem could have been written about the Sino–French War.

The settlement might have been even worse from the Chinese perspective had two events not occurred. First, peace envoy Li was shot in the head by a Japanese terrorist. Though he survived, the Japanese were horrified and most of all frightened that this insane act might jeopardize their spoils of victory. They thus withdrew some of their most overweening and expansive demands, specifically that they be given control of three cities in the Beijing area. The second unexpected development came after the conclusion of the Treaty of Shimonoseki, which ceded Taiwan and the Liaodong peninsula in southern Manchuria to Japan. Russia, Germany, and France joined in what became known as the Triple Intervention to force Japan to return the Liaodong peninsula to China. In spite of that return, China lost Taiwan and had to give up forever any tributary-related claims to Korea.

With the Sino–Japanese War, imperialism entered a far more perilous phase. The cession of Taiwan was the first major loss of Chinese territory. Japan acquired the right to build and operate factories in the treaty ports, a right that was soon taken by all the Western nations. More ominously, Japan successfully imposed a huge indemnity (200 to 230 million taels) on China to defray the costs of the war—an action that deepened China's financial crisis (its annual revenue was only about 89 million taels) and thereby further eroded the government's chances to undertake any needed policy initiatives. It also meant the necessity of borrowing money from foreign firms. From 1895 to 1898, loans were arranged from Russia, a French–Russian consortium, and an Anglo–German consortium; they were secured against customs revenues. From this point until the establishment of the People's Republic of China in 1949, China was continuously deep in debt to foreign countries.

No event to this point in the nineteenth century had created such widespread shock and such deep humiliation as the loss of this war to a people whom many Chinese had traditionally scorned. Any critically-thinking Chinese could no longer believe that things could go on as they had or that business as usual would somehow allow them to muddle through. Had there been protest demonstrators carrying signs emblazoned "The end is near," they would likely have captured the despair felt by many Chinese. As it was, there was a protest in Beijing following the signing of the treaty. Because it was the time for the metropolitan examination for the highest degree in the civil service system, large numbers of candidates thronged the capital. Kang and his closest disciple, Liang

Qichao, drew up a long memorial calling on the government to repudiate the treaty, to continue the war and move the capital farther into the interior, and to institute reforms. Thirteen hundred examination candidates signed the petition. But the government did not respond. The country apparently had to be abased even further before the government would recognize its abject shame and humiliation.

A NEW PHASE OF IMPERIALISM: CARVING THE MELON

In the aftermath of one foreign policy disaster came another crisis between China and the foreign powers. It initially involved Germany and Russia. Since it was Russian interest in Manchuria and Korea that in part drove Japan to fight China for predominant rights in Korea, and since it was Russia that spearheaded the Triple Intervention, a look at the Russian role and interests with regard to China is essential. The Sino–Russian relationship seems most atypical when it is compared to China's other international relationships.

Russia had been active in East Asia since the seventeenth century, a logical extension of its interests in Siberia. Treaties in 1689 and 1727 had established the border between China and Russia and essentially regularized their relations. From the beginning, China treated Russia differently from other Western nations. The treaties were signed as between equals; the tributary system did not seem to come into play. Although Chinese documents indicate that Russian ministers kowtowed to the Chinese emperor, Qing records never officially named Russia as a tributary state. Russia "was the only foreign country with which China maintained treaty relations, the only 'Western' state to which China sent diplomatic missions, and the only foreign power granted religious, commercial, and educational privileges" in Beijing.[7] From 1693 on, Russian merchants were permitted to come to Beijing every three years. In addition, the Chinese government authorized and paid for the travel of Russian priests to Beijing every ten years in order to minister to Russians in the capital; the government also picked up the cost of living expenses for the priests. Following the treaty in 1727, Russia was allowed to send students to learn Chinese and Manchu at a language school in Beijing; the Chinese government helped pay the costs of travel and, once in the capital for decade-long stays, it subsidized living expenses, including providing clothing and food at no charge. Although the Qing bestowed these special concessions and considerations in order to ensure Russian neutrality as Beijing tried to strengthen its hold on the North and Northwest frontiers, the special grants continued long after those frontiers had been stabilized. Russia monopolized this special status in Beijing until the Treaty of Tianjin in 1860 opened the capital to general diplomatic residence.

In that treaty, in fact, the Russian ambassador helped mediate disputes between Prince Gong and British and French representatives. He also had his own goals to further the Russian agenda in Central and Northeast Asia. From the early 1850s, the Chinese had allowed Russians to trade, build storage facilities, and set up consulates in northern Xinjiang. The Russians had also been pushing into eastern Siberia, building garrisons along the Amur River. In a treaty concluded in 1860, Russians showed themselves as aggressive as the Western Europeans, demanding and receiving land north of the Amur River and all land east of the Ussuri River, the latter comprising what became known as the Maritime Province. Altogether these territorial gains totaled between 300,000 and 400,000 square miles. In addition, more cities in Xinjiang were opened to Russians: these chickens came home to roost when the Russians seized the northern part of Xinjiang in 1878, but negotiations led in 1881 to their withdrawal and a reduction in the number of their consulates in the region.

But Russian interests in Northeast Asia did not diminish. The terminus of the Trans-Siberian Railway, begun in 1891, was to be Vladivostok on the Sea of Japan. The Russians could have chosen a route totally in Russian territory, that is, running along the north bank of the Amur River. But that route was about 350 miles farther and with much rougher terrain than a route that would cut across Manchuria in a straight line from Chita. For the less expensive route, the Russians obviously needed Chinese permission. This they received in negotiations with Li, sent to St. Petersburg in 1896 as China's imperial commissioner at the coronation of Nicholas II. With their railroad, the Chinese Eastern Railway, cutting through Manchuria, Russian interests and commitments in the area were substantially enhanced.

It was at about this same time that other European powers in their late-nineteenth-century race for empire around the world also began to enhance their own standing in China. It was Germany that put into motion what has been called the "scramble for concessions" or the establishment of "spheres of influence" or, more graphically, "carving up the Chinese melon." Germany had been interested in establishing a Chinese naval base for some time; by 1896, it had focused its lustful eyes on Jiaozhou Bay on the southern coast of Shandong both because of its excellent deep-water port and because of its location generally near Shandong's mineral resources. All it needed was a pretext to act with demands and, if need be, force. This came in November 1897, when two German missionaries of a particularly aggressive Catholic order were hacked to death by a band of Chinese while visiting a third missionary. In response, Germany occupied the bay and its city, Qingdao. In March 1898, it forced the Chinese government to lease the port and its surrounding area for ninety-nine years; the leasehold included Germany's right to build two railroads and hold mining rights.

Driven by imperialist rivalry, the other nations followed suit. Russia used the pretext of protecting China from Germany to occupy Port Arthur and Dalian on the tip of the Liaodong peninsula in December 1897 and signed a twenty-five-year lease in March 1898. As part of the leasehold, Russia also acquired the right to build a railroad from these two ports up to the Chinese Eastern Railway; it would come to be called the South Manchurian Railway and would play a crucial role in China's subsequent history. To check the Russians, Britain countered with a twenty-five-year lease of the port of Weihaiwei directly across the Bohai Straits from Port Arthur and Dalian; in June 1898, it also leased the so-called New Territories of Hong Kong for ninety-nine years. France forced a lease of Guangzhou Bay for ninety-nine years in April 1898, thus setting up its sphere of influence in Lingnan and Southwest China. Italy, the United States, and Japan were frozen out of the carving competition: Italy's late demands were refused; the United States was interested in a particular site but was occupied in its war with Spain; Japan was focusing on its role in Korea.

In the aftermath of the scramble and with no sphere of influence of its own, the U.S. government issued the Open Door notes, statements by which it hoped to ensure continuing and equal commercial opportunity. Not an altruistic policy, it was obviously intended to ensure that countries with spheres would not freeze the United States out of treaty ports or areas of natural resources that were within those spheres. Though no country obligated itself to the notes, U.S. Secretary of State Hay asserted that they all had. In any case, the fact that the land grab had stopped did not develop from this policy but rather "because the imperialists feared rivalry and conflict among themselves. The resultant equilibrium saved the [Qing] empire from immediate collapse."[8]

At the time, of course, the Chinese were not aware that the Westerners would cease their carving competition. The establishment of treaty ports had thus escalated to the seizure of considerable territory with substantial economic rights. In this scramble for more and more of China and its resources following so closely the disastrous war with Japan, imperialism had thus reached a more virulent strain that boded greater danger for China's future. It is not surprising that alarm about the incipient demise of the Chinese nation spread among elites all over China.

THE REFORM MOVEMENT AND THE HUNDRED DAYS: CLASHING IDENTITIES

The scramble for concessions formed the backdrop for one of the compelling dramas of the late nineteenth century—the Hundred Days from June to September 1898, when breakneck, breathtaking reforms promised a new China but instead delivered beheadings, forced flight, and imprisonment. The Hundred Days reform effort did not emerge suddenly full blown. The ideas that infused the movement and the institutions that gave it momentum had developed in the aftermath of the loss of the war with Japan. Its leaders were Kang and Liang.

Liang's writings are important because many elements of his thought remained central in the discourse of change throughout much of the twentieth century. He believed that self-strengthening efforts had focused too narrowly on technological innovations at a time when the essential agenda necessitated political reforms. His prescription for the foundation of such change was the traditional cultural approach of educational reform, specifically fostering the spread of literacy. This goal could clearly not be accomplished through the traditional examination system. Since it was obvious that as long as the examination system remained in place no other system could be successfully carried out, Liang favored abolishing the examination system and moving toward the establishment of a national school system. In that system, with students studying both ideas from the West and Chinese traditions, intellectual development and political consciousness would be fostered.

Beyond educational reform, Liang supported Kang's emphasis on the essentiality of significant institutional change to move China forward. A cardinal concept in Liang's thought about what China needed to do was "grouping"—an idea that involved several aspects of change.[9] At its most basic level, it meant the formation of associations of concerned elites who would meet to study and discuss the political and social changes that had to be undertaken; in a real sense, such associations would *mobilize* the intellects and energies of China's leaders.

But the concept had a deeper, more revolutionary thrust as well. China's predicament necessitated national solidarity and a commitment of the people as a whole to solving their desperately urgent problems. Implicit in Liang's arguments was the belief that traditional Chinese political culture and institutions, with their emphasis on individual identity and personal connections and networks, discouraged and inhibited a more general social solidarity and any sort of energetic commitment to wider goals. In addition, the traditional state was authoritarian: Its policies constrained and even repressed the people and prohibited the free flow of information. If China was ever to be able to compete with the West, Liang contended, such constraints had to be shattered so that Chinese political culture could develop an all-important "collective dynamism."

There was certainly a strong flavor of nationalism here, even if he did not use the word. Further, Liang called for a new political community to be the center of a reconceived and restructured state. This new state would not be founded on the rule of a monarch over his subjects but would feature a shared participation of rulers and ruled in a system of popular sovereignty. For the first time, Liang brought the language of democracy into Chinese political discourse. The concept of grouping thus encapsulated in a fundamental way ideas of political community, the nation, and democracy. Liang's radical political discourse, which championed mobilizing the people, the collective and the community, and installation of a system of popular sovereignty, would become the watchwords of subsequent Chinese reformers and revolutionaries from Sun Yat-sen to Mao Zedong.

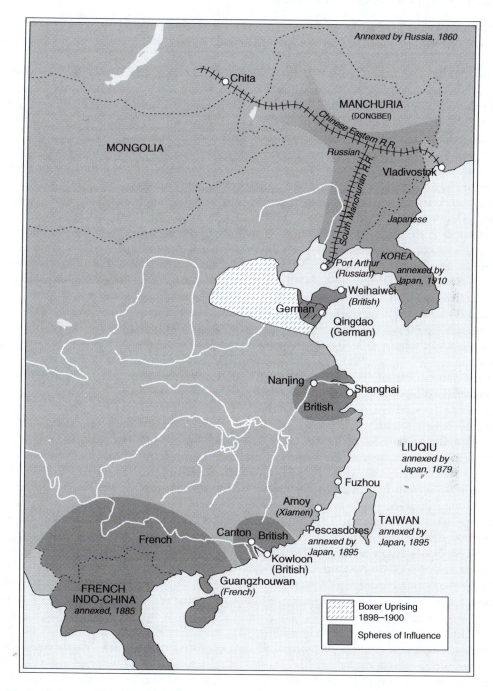

Annexed by Russia, 1860

Chita

MANCHURIA
(DONGBEI)

MONGOLIA

Chinese Eastern R.R.

Russian

Vladivostok

South Manchurian R.R.

Japanese

Port Arthur
(Russian)

KOREA
annexed by
Japan, 1910

Weihaiwei
(British)

German

Qingdao
(German)

Nanjing

Shanghai

British

LIUQIU
annexed by
Japan, 1879

Fuzhou

Amoy
(Xiamen)

TAIWAN
annexed by
Japan, 1895

French

Canton

British

Pescasdores
annexed by
Japan, 1895

Kowloon
(British)

Guangzhouwan
(French)

FRENCH
INDO-CHINA
annexed, 1885

Boxer Uprising
1898–1900

Spheres of Influence

MAP 6.1   Foreign Spheres of Influence and the Boxer Uprising.

The practical efforts of institutional reformers, led by Kang and Liang, began with the estab-lishment of groupings in particular study associations. The ultimate goal was to remake China by giving it a new national identity. As a first step, the study associations were to facilitate greater contact and social integration among official and nonofficial elites and, through the study process, to educate elites and mobilize their energies. The first study societies were established in Beijing and Shanghai in the second half of 1895. Since the Manchus had forbidden the formation of private societies in the 1650s and this ban still held, the study societies' establishment was illegal; indeed, by the next spring, the government banned both study societies.

But it was Hunan province in central China that became the incubator for reform that would come to fruition in the Hundred Days. There a reform-minded provincial administration sponsored in mid-decade the formation of a number of important new industrial, commercial, and educa-tional institutions. In the provincial capital of Changsha, for example, electric lights were installed and paved (macadamized) roads became a reality. A telegraph line was erected between Changsha and the important Yangzi port of Hankou. With encouragement and sometimes loans from the government, local elites established a match factory and a steamship line to link Hunan and Hubei.

A fervent champion of reform in Hunan was Huang Zunxian, a leading expert on foreign affairs. Huang prompted administrative, judicial, and prison reforms, as well as setting up in 1897 a School of Current Affairs. Sponsored jointly by the provincial government and elites, the school had a mixed curriculum of Western studies (sciences, history, and politics) and Confucian classics. Its teaching staff were advocates of radical reform. Liang was named head lecturer; three other young disciples of Kang became his assistants. The study of seventeenth-century texts condemning despotism and describing the Manchu massacre at the city of Yangzhou during the Manchu con-quest helped plant seeds of anti-Manchu thought. It is not surprising that the Qing state tolerated such a potentially dangerous situation for only a few months.

The most famous Hunan study association was the Southern Study Society, founded by the more radical reformist gentry; it was the largest of the fourteen study societies founded in Hunan in 1897 and 1898. At its height, it had over 1,200 members, both official and nonofficial elites. Nominally a private voluntary organization, it escaped being banned because the Changsha gov-ernment had supported its formation and even participated in its functioning. Provincial officials received proposals from its members on matters of public policy for consideration and possible implementation; and in researching current issues, members could petition the government to see public records. Commenting on the Society after it had closed, Liang noted that "though nominally a study society, the Southern Study Society had all the makings of a local legislature."[10]

Another crucial aspect of the reform activity was the publication of newspapers, most short-lived but almost all focusing on questions relating to the identity of the new China. The early Beijing, Shanghai, and Hunan study societies published their own newspapers, which became crucial vehicles for publicizing and propagandizing reformist and radical thought. Most of Liang's essays appeared in Hunan newspapers. They were distributed mostly free of charge, not only in Hunan but along the Southeast Coast as well.

In early 1898, the teachings of Liang and newspapers linked to the Southern Study Society became notably radical, taking staunchly nationalistic positions with a considerable anti-Manchu slant. Conservatives and even moderate reformers who had been involved in provincial reform ac-tivities became apprehensive. A struggle erupted between reformers and more conservative forces. The question at issue was "What is the Chinese identity?" Whereas for the reformers the answer was increasingly becoming Han Chinese nationalists subordinated to a depraved and ineffective Man-chu minority. For the conservatives the answer was simple: adhering to traditional Chinese cultural values—which they felt duty bound to protect against the heterodox views of reformers. The abrasive staying power of the past was at work, eroding the possibilities of institutional change.

A bitter ideological attack on Kang and Liang spread as streams of accusations poured into the court, condemning both their ideology and their reform agenda as heresy from the Confucian orthodoxy. Kang and Liang were condemned for their open criticism of Chinese political culture and tradition and for their negative treatment of the Manchus. Kang's reinterpretation of Confucius and the classics was especially upsetting. The call in the writings of Liang and others for people's rights and equality clashed head-on with the traditional Confucian bonds and the Confucian ideas of social hierarchy. For those in the camp of the anti-reformers, the reformers were as much cultural enemies of Chinese traditions as the Taiping had been forty years earlier. By the summer, most reformers had been expelled from Hunan, with the majority of Hunanese gentry mobilized not for the construction of a new state and society but against the reformers. By late summer, the governor of Hunan petitioned the court in Beijing to destroy the printing blocks for Kang's *Confucius as a Reformer* and to ban its publication.

At the very time that Kang and company were bearing the attacks in and being hounded out of Hunan, he was to come closest to wielding substantial national power. The surprising development was that Kang had found a powerful supporter in the Forbidden City—the Guangxu emperor himself. The twenty-seven-year-old emperor had been won over to the cause of reform through his long-time tutor, Weng Tonghe. In 1889, Weng had encouraged the emperor to read Feng Guifen's 1860 collection of essays on reform. The emperor was so impressed with the possibilities of using Western learning for Chinese benefit that in the early 1890s he studied English in the Forbidden City with teachers from the Interpreters College. He was especially interested in the contemporaneous writings of advocates of reform. In 1895, the Empress Dowager, well aware of the emperor's burgeoning interests in Western things, halted his language study and allowed him to have tutorials only on traditional Chinese materials.

Weng Tonghe's interests in reform had naturally led him to Kang as the leader in calls for institutional change. Kang had sent memorials to the court as early as 1888 pointing out the need for reform. When Kang formed the eventually banned study society in Beijing in 1895, Weng Tonghe had been a member. Weng was not an advocate of radical reform, but the radical nature of Kang's ideas came to be known only gradually: many of Kang's most extreme views and positions were set forth only in 1898. In any event, Weng recommended Kang to the emperor, who established direct communications with the reformer. On January 24, 1898, the emperor arranged an open meeting at the Zongli Yamen between Kang and high officials at the court, including Weng, Li, and Ronglu, one of the Empress Dowager's trusted Manchu confidants. An exchange revealed Kang's goal of remaking the Chinese identity.

RONGLU: "The institutions of the ancestors cannot be changed."
KANG YOUWEI: "We cannot preserve the realm of the ancestors; what is the use of their institutions?"
LI HONGZHANG: "Shall we abolish all the Six Boards and throw away all the existing institutions and rules?"
KANG: "The laws and governmental system ... have made China weak and will ruin her. Undoubtedly they should be done away with."[11]

After the meeting, Kang sent three memorials to the emperor detailing his plan of action. They included following the reform models of Meiji Japan and Russia under Peter the Great and establishing a constitution and a national assembly. To facilitate change, the emperor should announce openly that reform was the order of the day and he should establish new bodies to work to that end, thereby avoiding working through the cumbersome and conservative government bureaucracy. On June 11, the emperor showed whose camp he was in, announcing, as Kang had suggested, that reform had become state policy. Five days later, Kang had his first audience, a five-hour marathon, with the emperor. The emperor appointed Kang to the Zongli Yamen and permitted Kang to submit memorials directly to him instead of through the regular bureaucratic channels. From June 11 to September 21, in what has come to be known as the Hundred Days, the emperor, with Kang providing the agenda, issued over a hundred decrees calling for institutional reforms in almost every policy arena. It is certainly the case that the national context in early 1898—the Western scramble for concessions through the new approach of "leasing" territory—created in the minds of many the sense that some kind of substantial change was necessary to keep the country from being eaten alive.

Taken as a whole, the political, economic, military, and educational reforms called for in the wave of reform edicts would have drastically restructured the Chinese polity and society. They included revamping the examination system and establishing a national school system; prohibiting footbinding; restructuring the government and abolishing sinecure positions; modernizing the military, police, and postal systems; setting up new institutions to promote agriculture, commerce, and industry; and establishing rewards for inventions. Significantly, the emperor did not decree the centerpieces of Kang's plan—a constitution and a national assembly—presumably because he saw them as too radical for the current political context.

But even so, the reforms threatened the entire status quo, specifically the world of the Empress Dowager and her supporters. Changing the examination system was unsettling to all those already in the examination pipeline. Suggestions that Buddhist temple complex buildings might be used as schools stepped on the toes of Buddhists. Restructuring the government threatened those in current positions, as did abolishing those posts for which men were paid yet for which they did little or no work. Military reforms meant changing or perhaps abolishing existing armies. It also did not help the cause with Manchus that the only Manchu involved in the effort was the emperor. The Empress Dowager's continuing power at the court was the crucial reality that would end the efforts at reform.

From the opening of the Hundred Days, the Empress Dowager revealed her opposition to the emperor and the reform group. Already on June 15, she had dismissed Weng Tonghe. She then bided her time, let antireform bitterness fester, and made certain of her support. Then on September 21, with the help of the military under Yuan Shikai, she staged a coup d'état, seizing all power from the emperor and putting him under house arrest. She then began her third regency, one that would last to her death a decade later. Five days after the coup, all the reform edicts were revoked. Although Kang was able to escape to Hong Kong and Liang to Japan, six young reformers, including Tan Sitong, were executed. Tan, a brilliant thirty-three-year-old intellectual, had been a leader of the reform efforts in Hunan. He was assigned to be a secretary to the Grand Council in order to facilitate the reforms only on September 5. When the Empress Dowager's coup came, he had been on the job for less than three weeks. He refused to flee, saying, "I wanted to kill the robbers, but lacked the strength to transform the world. This is the place where I should die. Rejoice, rejoice!"[12] He was beheaded for treason on September 27.

The reform effort was put down quite easily, a fact that is often used to argue that in China change at this time could not likely come from the top. Chinese political leaders seemed unable to change the system in order to deal effectively with the crises; perhaps they were not yet able to realize the state's dire peril. And yet, despite the coup against it, the reform movement had considerable historical import. It did, as one historian argues, "usher in a new phase of Chinese culture—the era of ideologies." The ideas of Kang and Liang, which took Western thought seriously and dethroned Confucianism from a way of life to an ideology, "raised the curtain on the cultural crises of the twentieth century."[13]

Elites began to join together in associations, debating issues and starting to deal with problems in new contexts; since many involved political activity, the amount of political participation on the part of elites increased. Newspapers sprouted up and proliferated, in the stock Chinese phrase, "like bamboo shoots after a spring rain"; perhaps their most outstanding feature was evidence of a growing sense of nationalism. The discourse they began was essentially the beginning of modern Chinese public opinion. Elites placed educational reform at the center of the public agenda, and that reform would be realized in the next decade. Finally, the reform era gave rise to the birth of the modern intelligentsia; unlike the old scholar-gentry, the new intelligentsia were "free-floating intellectuals,"[14] not tied to localities and lacking the traditional symbiotic relationship with the government. Further, the new intelligentsia, unlike the old scholar elites, struggled with problems of alienation from the government and above all of cultural identity, caught between the old and the new, East and West.

THE BOXER CATASTROPHE: WHICH IDENTITY NOW?

The collapse of traditional state and civilization was punctuated at century's end by an outrageous constellation of events in North China. From a culture of poverty in Shandong province came a social explosion. Led by so-called Boxers, a name taken from the martial art rituals, or boxing, that they performed, the movement was composed of mostly young farmers, laborers, and out-of-work drifters. The roving Boxer groups also included women's groups (called Red Lanterns).

Natural disasters—flood and drought—formed the context for the rise and spread of the Boxer movement. In August 1898, a month before the Empress Dowager's coup against the reformers, a flood broke the Yellow River dikes in three places, sending torrents of water into 34 counties, covering over 2,000 villages, and making at least temporary refugees of millions. Crops were ruined, and in some places the devastation wrought by the flood was so severe that crops could not even be planted the next spring. Government corruption in the dispersal of relief grain meant that large numbers of people, even those living relatively close to cities, did not receive any aid. "Many peasants were still huddled on the dikes [where they had taken refuge] eating leaves, bark, or weeds fully three months after the flooding began."[15] In such cases, anti-government or anti-official feelings began to rise quickly. Drought was a factor in expanding the Boxer movement, as we will see.

Anti-Christian hostility was a crucial cause of the uprising. In the area where the Boxer movement began, German Catholic missionaries of a stridently militant order had been very active. The killing of the two missionaries that had served as Germany's pretext to seize Jiaozhou occurred in this area. A missionary named Georg Stenz, whom the two were visiting at the time of their murders, escaped death—ironically, since Stenz was the likely object of the armed attack. A word about him reveals some dynamics behind the anti-Christian hostility. Stenz revealed the aggressive nature of the missionizing approach of his order in his autobiography: he described his "mission cross which was to be at once weapon and banner in [his] fight for the Kingdom of God." His contempt for the Chinese drips from his description of Shanghai:

An entirely new world now opened before us. Crowds of slit-eyed Chinese swarmed about the harbor—prominent merchants in their rustling silks and poor coolies in ragged clothes that did not hide their filthy bodies. ... Cunning, pride, and scorn flashed from the eyes that met our inquiring looks."[16]

But more upsetting to Chinese than attitudes of superiority, arrogance, and contempt for those they were trying to save were the actions of missionaries with regard to their converts. They were particularly active in interfering in their converts' lawsuits, frequently pressuring magistrates. They also demanded that magistrates punish people for alleged offenses against the church or church property. They forbade converts from participating in or contributing to village festivals, which often featured processions following a statue of the local god; such participation the missionaries called idolatry. In the name of preventing that evil, they were rupturing the Chinese community by asserting their own values and in the process in effect taking away at least a part of the Chinese identity of their converts. Non-converted Chinese were offended and embittered by this action.

Therefore, from their start in 1898 and 1899, Boxers attacked the property and persons of Christian converts and missionaries. Most pockets of Boxer activity in the beginning were in Shandong. But the governor of the province, Yuxian, was able generally to settle the unrest in southern Shandong by the spring of 1899. Growing Boxer activity in the province's northwest, along with Western pressure on the government, got him cashiered in late 1899. Yuan Shikai succeeded him in Shandong and was able to crush the Boxers there.

In the winter of 1899–1900 the movement began to spread and grow—into Zhili, Henan, Shanxi, and even Inner Mongolia and Manchuria. There was no central leadership; Boxer bands coalesced, attacked Christian converts, then faded away. One historian has argued that in part the movement spread quickly because of the dynamic of spirit possession.

> The empowerment possession conferred made it enormously attractive to those at the bottom of the Chinese social scale, regardless of locale. Also, the possession ritual [which involved boxing, incantations, breathing through clenched teeth, and foaming at the mouth], by placing individuals in direct communication with their gods and enabling them, when in a possessed state, to in effect become gods, placed a major barrier in the way of the creation of a more centralized, structured, and perhaps durable movement.[17]

The expansion of the movement also depended on the attitude of the officials. Yuan Shikai's no-nonsense approach in suppressing the northwest Shandong Boxers contrasted sharply with Yuxian's encouragement of the Boxers in Shanxi in the summer of 1900.

But perhaps the most important dynamic in the Boxer growth was the drought that began after the Yellow River floods in late 1898. It freed up many young men who ordinarily would have been working in the fields to join the Boxers. An attraction of the Boxers, as food became scarce, was that they usually had good supplies of grain, gained in their pillaging of Christian households and sometimes their extortion from the wealthy. Psychologically, the drought created a problem of hunger anxiety, of growing nervousness, restlessness, and hopelessness. And the drought became linked in many Chinese minds with the presence of the Westerners, particularly the missionaries.

> In one placard after another, the Chinese people are enjoined to kill off all foreigners and native Chinese contaminated by foreigner or foreign influence. Only after this process of physical elimination of every trace of the foreign from China has been completed will the gods be appeased and permit the rains once again to fall.[18]

It is little wonder that missionary anxiety moved in the direction of panic over the continuation of the drought.

Western nations, frightened by the continuing attacks on and murder of missionaries, as well as property losses, demanded that the Qing court act to suppress the uprising. Since the Boxers had championed a slogan supporting the Qing ("Revive the Qing; destroy the foreigner"), the Empress Dowager was reluctant to undertake such suppression. Wall posters hung up in villages and towns shouted the Boxer goal:

> When at last all the Foreign Devils
> Are expelled to the very last man,
> The Great Qing, united, together,
> Will bring peace to this our land.[19]

The Empress Dowager echoed the Confucian line, "Heaven sees as the people see; Heaven hears as the people hear," alluding to the Mandate of Heaven. The whole situation had turned her into something of a populist; in that vein, she argued that "China is weak; the only thing we can depend upon is the hearts of the people. If we lose them, how can we maintain our country?"[20] With Western pressure on the court becoming stronger, the Empress Dowager quite incredibly threw her support behind the Boxers—slowly at first, in January 1900, ordering local authorities to distinguish between lawful local militia formation and bandit activity. The Qing did send military forces against the Boxers, but there was no concerted or sustained action that might have halted the unrest. Nearing Beijing in late spring, Boxers attacked railroad lines, ripping out track and burning stations, and tore down telegraph lines. The political and policy bankruptcy of the Qing, in permitting and even condoning this action, was clear.

Western nations and Japan determined that they would have to act to save missionaries and stop the bloodshed. On June 10, 1900, Boxers beat back a British relief force, marching from Tianjin; they were eventually joined by Qing imperial troops. On June 17, pro-Boxer Manchus told the Empress Dowager that the foreign nations were demanding that she retire and that the Guangxu emperor be returned to the throne. If there had been any question about her siding with the Boxers before, there was not anymore. On June 20, the German minister, on his way to a meeting with the Zongli Yamen, was shot dead on the street. The next day, in a scene that conjures up the theater of the absurd, the Empress Dowager declared war on the eight foreign powers. Having been repeatedly defeated by one country at a time, the Qing had now decided to battle eight at once. The Manchus, who throughout their dynasty had identified themselves with Chinese and Chinese culture, were now identifying themselves and putting their fate in the hands of adolescent warriors. Two of the emperor's brothers were reportedly seen leading Boxer forces in their attacks.

The ambassadorial legation quarters in Beijing and the Northern Cathedral two miles northwest of the legations had become the havens to which missionaries and converts fled. In late June, the Boxers besieged the legation quarters and cathedral, acts that gave rise in the Western press to the phrase "yellow peril." The worst Boxer violence occurred in Shanxi province, where Governor Yuxian, having lost his Shandong governorship due to Western pressure, encouraged Boxer attacks on Westerners. In early July he called forty-four missionaries and their families—men, women, and children—to Taiyuan, the provincial capital, for their protection. On July 9, under his personal supervision, he had them executed. Other missionaries in the province suffered similar fates, along with some 2,000 Christian converts.

The war was localized in the North because of the actions of key central and southern governors-general and Yuan serving as Shandong governor. They simply ignored the declaration

FIGURE 6.1   German soldiers with spiked helmets enter the Forbidden City during the eight-nation expedition to lift the Boxer sieges. Because the German minister had been killed on the streets of Beijing in June 1900, Germany had a heightened interest in how the Chinese would be treated.
Source: Keystone-France/Gamma-Keystone via Getty Images.

of war. An 8-nation force of about 20,000 men arrived in the capital on August 14 to lift the siege. Most Boxers disappeared into the North China countryside. The Empress Dowager fled to the southwest, deciding as well that the emperor had to be taken. When the emperor's favorite consort suggested that he be allowed to remain in Beijing in order to negotiate peace, the Empress Dowager had her thrown down a well for her presumptuousness. Disguised and under armed guard, the Empress Dowager and the emperor took flight in a cart. En route, edicts were issued in the emperor's name in which he took full blame for the disaster. In late October, they reached the ancient capital of Xi'an in Shaanxi province, some 800 miles from Beijing. They would remain there until January 1902.

Over the next six months, Western troops joined missionaries in making raids on surrounding cities and towns, pillaging Chinese property. The missionaries were quite enthusiastic about revenge. One missionary, D. Z. Sheffield, wished that more American troops would be sent:

It is not bloodthirstiness in missionaries to desire to see further shedding of [Chinese] blood, but an understanding of Chinese character and conditions, and a realization that the policy of general forgiveness means the loss of many valuable native [Christian] and foreign lives.[21]

Sheffield's remarks were par for the missionary course. But for sheer outrageousness, the essay "The Ethics of Loot," written by the missionary Gilbert Reid for *Forum* magazine in 1901, takes the cake. Reid argued,

> To confiscate the property of those who were enemies in war may be theoretically wrong, but precedent had established the right. For those who have known the facts and have passed through a war of awful memory, the matter of loot is one of high ethics.

He even said he was sorry that he had not looted more himself. In his capacity as a conspicuous Christian, he had the audacity to ponder the question of "whether the sacking and burning of the entire city of [Beijing] might not 'have been the greatest good for the greatest number.'"[22]

By late 1900, 45,000 foreign troops were in North China. They spent their time on search-and-destroy missions, trying to ferret out Boxers and kill them. But, as in any guerrilla-type action, how does one identify the enemy? The upshot was many innocent persons killed. One American commander noted, "it is safe to say that where one real Boxer has been killed since the capture of [Beijing], fifty harmless coolies or laborers on the farms, including not a few women and children, have been slain."[23] Troops staged "punitive picnics," affairs that featured menus of arson, rape, and looting.

The signing of the Boxer Protocol in September 1901 brought the lowest point of the Qing court in its relations with the West. The West, like its missionaries, was out for revenge: they called for the execution and punishment of officials who had participated in the war; the Manchu Yuxian, who had egged the Boxers on in Shanxi, was executed; and five others were allowed to commit suicide. The foreign nations punished the whole elite class of would-be officials by suspending the civil service examinations for five years in forty-five cities. They ordered over two dozen forts destroyed and a dozen railroad posts occupied so that Western troops could have ready access to

FIGURE 6.2   Foreign troops stand in rather blasé fashion among bodies and heads of decapitated Boxer prisoners. Note the Japanese soldier wiping blood off his sword.
Source: Wellcome Library via Wikimedia Commons.

Beijing. They expanded the legation quarters and ordered it permanently fortified. They put a two-year prohibition on China's importation of arms.

But most disastrous was an indemnity that was staggering in its immensity.[24] For damage to foreign property and lives, the Chinese were forced to pay 450 million taels (about $333 million in 1901), a sum truly *staggering* since, by this time, the complete annual Qing income was only 88,200,000 taels. The indemnity was to be paid annually in thirty-nine installments in gold, with interest rates that by the date of the full payment of the debt (the end of 1940) would total about 1 billion taels. For a government that could not move with any certainty into the modern world in part because of lack of money, the indemnity was a crushing burden.

The extremely harsh nature of the protocol, the miserable showing of the Chinese military, the insane policy of attempting to use the Boxers as instruments of policy, and the mortifying overland flight of the country's sovereigns were on view for the whole world to see. The apex of Qing wealth and power under the Qianlong emperor had been just a century earlier, yet the state now entered the twentieth century in degradation, poverty, and humiliation.

Notes

1 Cited in Paul Cohen, *History in Three Keys* (New York: Columbia University Press, 1997), p. 174.
2 Hao Chang, "Intellectual Change and the Reform Movement, 1890–98," in *The Cambridge History of China, Vol. 11, Late Ch'ing, 1800–1911, Part 2*, ed. John K. Fairbank and Kwang-ching Liu (Cambridge, UK: Cambridge University Press, 1980), p. 288.
3 Ibid., p. 290.
4 Wang Zheng, *Women in the Chinese Enlightenment: Oral and Textual Histories* (Berkeley, CA: University of California Press, 1999), p. 36.
5 Mann, *The Talented Women of the Zhang Family* (Berkeley, CA: University of California Press, 2007), p. 197.
6 Immanuel C.Y. Hsu, "Late Ch'ing [Qing] Foreign Relations, 1866–1905," in Fairbank and Liu, *The Cambridge History of China, Vol. 11, Late Ch'ing, 1800–1911, Part 2*, p. 109.
7 Immanuel C.Y. Hsu, *The Rise of Modern China* (New York: Oxford University Press, 1970), p. 163.
8 Hsu, "Late Ch'ing [Qing] Foreign Relations, 1866–1905," p. 115.
9 This discussion of Liang Qichao's thought is based on Hao Chang, *Liang Ch'i-chao and Intellectual Transition in China, 1890–1907* (Cambridge, MA: Harvard University Press, 1971), pp. 73–120.
10 Quoted in Hao Chang, "Intellectual Change," p. 308.
11 John K. Fairbank, Edwin O. Reischauer, and Albert M. Craig, *East Asia, the Modern Transformation* (Boston, MA: Houghton Mifflin, 1965), pp. 391–2.
12 Quoted in Jonathan Spence, *The Gate of Heavenly Peace* (New York: Viking Penguin, 1981), p. 53.
13 Ibid., p. 329.
14 The wording is from Hao Chang, "Intellectual Change," p. 337.
15 Joseph Esherick, *The Origins of the Boxer Uprising* (Berkeley, CA: University of California Press, 1987), p. 179.
16 Ibid., p. 125.
17 Cohen, *History in Three Keys*, p. 34.
18 Ibid., p. 89.
19 Esherick, *Origins of the Boxer Uprising*, p. 300.
20 Fairbank, Reischauer, and Craig, *East Asia*, pp. 397, 400.
21 Stuart Creighton Miller, "Ends and Means: Missionary Justification of Force in Nineteenth Century China," in *The Missionary Enterprise in China and America*, ed. John K. Fairbank (Cambridge, MA: Harvard University Press, 1974), p. 274.
22 Ibid., pp. 279–80.
23 Quoted in Esherick, *Origins of the Boxer Uprising*, p. 310.
24 See as examples, ibid., p. 403; Jonathan Spence, *The Search for Modern China* (New York: W.W. Norton, 1990), p. 235; and Frederic Wakeman, Jr., *The Fall of Imperial China* (New York: Free Press, 1975), p. 221.

Suggestions for Further Reading

Bickers, Robert and R.G. Tiedemann. *The Boxers, China, and the World* (Lanham, MD: Rowman & Littlefield, 2007). This collection of cogent essays on various topics is notable for its providing a fittingly international context and an account of some global consequences of this historical episode.

Chang, Hao. *Liang Ch'i-ch'ao and Intellectual Transition in China, 1890–1907* (Cambridge, MA: Harvard University Press, 1971). This is a meticulous study of the thought of a key intellectual whose impact was felt in Chinese politics and society for much of the twentieth century.

Cohen, Paul. *History in Three Keys: The Boxers as Event, Experience, and Myth* (New York: Columbia University Press, 1997). This prize-winning meditation focuses on the Boxer movement to explore the nature of history, memory, and myth.

Esherick, Joseph W. *The Origins of the Boxer Uprising* (Berkeley, CA: University of California Press, 1987). This revisionist study of the Boxer movement explores its cultural and ecological bases.

Karl, Rebecca, and Peter Zarrow, eds. *Rethinking the 1898 Reform Period: Political and Cultural Change in Late Qing China* (Cambridge, MA: Harvard University Asia Center, 2002). This book of wide-ranging essays sees the period 1895–1898 as laying the groundwork for the New Policy reforms of 1901–1911.

Part 2

"No Checking the Tides of Change"

Reconstructing Social, Cultural, and Political Identity, 1901–1928

7

Revolutionaries
Manchu and Anti-Manchu

During their exile in Xi'an, the Empress Dowager reported,

> We [the emperor and I] were both clad in the meanest of garments, and to relieve our hunger we were scarcely able to obtain a dish of beans or porridge. Few of our poorest subjects have suffered greater hardships of cold and hunger than befell us in our pitiful plight."[1]

Despite its laughable exaggeration, Cixi's description probably reflected much of what she felt. Taken together, her Xi'an experience of over a year and the memory of the Boxer nightmare and subsequent Western revenge had awakened her to China's danger with all the subtlety of a bucket of icy water thrown into her face. The total experience changed Cixi from what appeared an obstructionist conservative into a leading reformer, initiating change in all the areas that the reformers of the Hundred Days had dreamed about.[2] The reforms focused openly and without apology on adopting the strong points of foreign countries in order to make up for China's weaknesses. In substance they varied from mildly reformist to quite radical, even revolutionary. When the Manchus' world ended with the emperor's abdication in early 1912, it was after a decade-long bang of activity rather than the whimper of those who, resigned to the forces of history, did nothing.

THE STIRRINGS OF A NEW CHINA IN MACROREGIONAL CORES

During the course of the reforms up to the 1911 revolution, the first signs of a new China began to appear—from modern economic developments to outbursts of nationalism to the appearance of new social forces. Certainly, if the Manchu reform effort was stimulated by China's plight vis-à-vis the outside world, it was also prompted by the increasing evidence of marked internal developments and change.

From the start, it should be noted that the stirrings of a new China were spatially uneven. Macroregional core areas of greater urbanization and higher levels of economic development, often situated along the coasts or on important river systems, exhibited the greatest degree of modern change; peripheral backwaters, the least. The rate of change tended to create different experiences, attitudes, and worldviews among the people in areas of varying development. Cities were always the sites of greatest change. They were now being paved, lighted, and policed. They were the homes of wide-ranging reformist voluntary associations dealing with social problems like footbinding and vices such as opium smoking and gambling. Newspapers and magazines were being produced in greater number, focusing on current issues and developments. With regard to social change during these years, it has been estimated that the number of letters, newspapers, and magazines sent and received in 1910 was twenty-five times that in 1901.[3] Such an increase came primarily in the macroregional cores.

Increasingly common in the cores during these years was evidence of nationalism, expressed often as fears of national dismemberment and even of the obliteration of the Chinese people. Public meetings and demonstrations dotted the political landscape—about British threats to Tibet and, by extension, even the province of Sichuan; Russian influence in Mongolia and Manchuria; and French pressure in the Southwest. School songs and plays urged the government to stand up to all foreign pressure. Nationalism as resistance to foreign powers perhaps reached its high point in the 1905–1907 anti-U.S. boycott for its immigration restriction law and its mistreatment of Chinese who attended the 1904 World's Fair in St. Louis.

Nationalism was also expressed against Western intrusion into matters within China. A growing number of rancorous treaty port incidents exploded from cases of Westerners' right of extraterritoriality. Though some provinces had eliminated the cultivation of opium, the British argued that until the drug was completely eradicated from the country at large, it still could import it. In an angry response, there was talk in some Chinese circles of another opium war. A dramatic "rights recovery" movement developed to win control over mines that were foreign-owned and railroads that were foreign-built and foreign-controlled. Recovering the railroads seems to have captured the attention of core society as a whole. People from all social classes in pertinent core zones—from gentry and rich merchants to students and shopkeepers to coolies and even beggars—pledged and contributed money to recover China's railroad rights. Key railroads targeted included the Canton–Hankou line, the Shanghai–Ningbo line, and lines in Sichuan province. Some contributors, increasingly upset by foreign control, even threatened to commit suicide in front of foreign embassies in Beijing. Their patriotic shout: "To die for one's country is glorious."

Another important group in the recovery movement, and in Chinese politics and economics in general, was overseas Chinese, particularly those in Southeast Asia (but also in the United States and Europe), who came to be seen by elites in China as a source of considerable financial and moral support for reformist and revolutionary causes. One feature of the Chinese diaspora had always been the continuing interest in their homeland of those abroad and especially their desire to be buried in their ancestral native place. The early twentieth century saw the birth among overseas Chinese communities of a more committed political interest in developments in the "home country," which would remain a reality throughout the twentieth century and into the twenty-first.

In these public displays of nationalism, new social groups for the first time were finding public voices, joining the old leaders of society, the scholar gentry, and a new group that appeared in the last years of the nineteenth century: the gentry-merchants. Youth emerged as a vocal and enthusiastic force, specifically the students who went to Japan, Southeast Asia, the United States, and Europe. China had sent students to Japan beginning in the late 1890s, many on provincial government scholarships: in 1899 there were 200; by 1903, about 1,000; and by 1906, some 13,000. In Japan, students formed associations, many of them based on common provincial origin; there were, for example, associations for students from Jiangsu, Hubei, and Zhejiang that published their own newspapers. Seeing rapidly modernizing Japan, already a growing world power, these students naturally asked what was wrong with China. One student newspaper noted, "Japanese schools are as numerous as our opium dens, Japanese students as numerous as our opium addicts."[4] Those who studied in Japan and Southeast Asia became enamored of Western liberal and radical ideas and returned to China ready to reshape the world. Those who studied in Europe and the United States tended to concentrate on more technical subjects; although they might not have reentered the Chinese scene with the political commitment that others evidenced, they were still affected by life in more modern states.

Another traditionally subordinated social group, women, emerged from 1901 to 1910 in over forty associations or groups established by women and that focused on women's rights and on initiatives to better society. Many groups had their own journals, which, however short-lived, had women involved in all phases of the publication process. *New Chinese Women's Magazine*, founded in Tokyo in 1907 had a circulation of up to 5,000 printed issues. The women's associations were most successful in fighting footbinding and in making progress in female education. As publicity involving footbinding spread, fewer women bound their feet, especially in urban areas; some local governments in all areas of China forbade footbinding. Newspapers reported on the suicides of women whose mothers-in-law forbade them to unbind their feet. As for education, by 1909 there were 308 girls' schools, with a total of 14,564 students. It was a small start, but there were still many Chinese men and women who saw no need for female education.[5]

Some male intellectuals continued to support gender equality. In 1903 Jin Tianhe published a lengthy tract, "The Women's Bell," to urge women to seek their rights and to offer "a blueprint for making new Chinese women in the twentieth century."[6] Some historians suggest that Jin's tract "may well have been the first systematic championing of women's right to education, to suffrage, to employment and livelihood, and to human dignity."[7] His tract brought the term *nuquan* (women's rights) into China's sociopolitical discourse and was extremely popular among anti-Qing revolutionaries. Whether it played a large role or not, the fact was that women in the cores did step into the world of public affairs as never before. They joined in nationalistic demonstrations, organized patriotic societies, contributed jewelry for the revolutionary cause, and joined Sun Yat-sen's anti-Qing, pro-republic organization, the Revolutionary Alliance (*Tongmenghui*). They ran the gamut from the upper crust (court women read *Peking Woman*, which talked about the equality of all human beings) to the masses (Canton boatwomen went to the revolutionary front line in 1911 to serve as the first nurses ministering to combat troops).

Female spokespersons advocated the feminist and revolutionary ideas they saw in Qiu Jin (1875–1907). Born into a lower gentry family, she was educated at home with her brother and sister. Her parents arranged her marriage, much to Qiu's chagrin. In a poem she expressed her unhappiness: "Alas they sent me off by force to be mere 'rouge and powder'—How I despise it! My body will not allow me to join the ranks of men, but my heart is far braver than that of a man." In 1903, she left her husband and children to go to Japan to study; there she frequently posed in men's clothes with an unsheathed dagger or sword. She saw herself as knight-errant and a model feminist revolutionary. On her return from Japan, in 1906 she founded the *Chinese Women's Journal* in which she published a poem, "Promoting Women's Rights." Significant lines include

Equality between men and women is endowed by Heaven. How can we be content to lag behind? ... Our fair hands are needed in order to recover our [Chinese] rivers and mountains. ... we citizen heroines must never fail to live up to our expectations.[8]

The same year as Qiu's death, another feminist, He Zhen, organized the Society for the Restoration of Women's Rights and began publishing *Tianyi* (Natural Justice) in Tokyo where she and her scholar-husband had gone to study. Despite the fact that it was published for less than two years, some scholars have seen it as the early twentieth century's "foremost and most influential medium for the articulation of radical ideas: feminism, socialism, Marxism, and anarchism."[9] Feminists have pointed out He's powerful prose and analytical perspicuity in *Tianyi* as "one of the significant achievements of Chinese feminism before the 1911 Revolution."[10] For thinkers such as Jin Tianhe and other male intellectuals, feminism was part of a larger political and economic framework of nationalism and capitalist modernization. But for He Zhen, feminism could not be subordinated to these larger struggles. She resisted and opposed intellectuals who were prescribing for women what they thought women needed: "They attempt to acquire distinction by promoting women's liberation; but their original intention is not to liberate women but to treat them as private property,"[11] raising their own stature as they prescribed the way for women. He Zhen's basic belief and platform were that women must liberate themselves, for feminism was about the beginning of a complete social revolution that would do away with the state and private property and usher in true gender equality. The role of male intellectuals in feminist projects continued to be problematic for women during the Republic.

The caveat in all this is that these sweeping revolutionary-sounding changes were largely restricted to macroregional cores. There was a huge gap between the cores and peripheries in the extent of political, social, and economic change; that gap would continue to have a substantial impact on the life of the populace in each zone and on the rate and nature of change in the future.

THE MANCHU REFORM MOVEMENT: EDUCATION

As the Empress Dowager took the Qing into the reform arenas, this flurry of activity in cities and core zones must have been part of the reality prompting her to act. Reform was necessary to build Chinese strength to fend off the West and to maintain leadership in China. In its reformist efforts, the government turned first to education, at the heart of any change that Confucian China might try to undertake.

Examination Reform

It is clear that the Empress Dowager and her officials meant business. Traditionally, the function of education had been to train future officials, inculcating them with Confucian values. The proof was in the examination, which had varied considerably over the years in the coverage of questions (sometimes more relevant to current issues, other times not). A hallmark of the examinations since the Ming period, however, was that the essays had to be written in a formulaic format known as the "eight-legged essay," a structure that straitjacketed the writer's presentation and creativity. From Xi'an in August 1901 came Cixi's edict banning the eight-legged essay and calling for examinations that would in part test knowledge of foreign governments and sciences. Note that this was less than three years from the end of the Hundred Days reform attempt. The reformers—some dead, some in exile, with their emperor-supporter under house arrest—may ultimately have had much more impact on subsequent political thinking and developments than the events of September 1898 might at first suggest.

One Chinese historian has described the significance of these changes as "epoch-making." Indeed, the following questions and topics asked on the "foreign" portion of the 1903–1904 civil service examination for the *jinshi*, or highest degree, tend to show that the thought and actions of Kang, Liang, and others had substantially altered the thinking of conservative Qing officials.

> *Topic 1:* "Western countries attach great importance to foreign study tours. How can we define the purpose and contain the time span [of such tours] in order to obtain the maximum benefits with the least costs?"
>
> *Topic 2:* "Japan Westernized its system of learning with great rapidity. In its initial rush to change, Japan invariably encountered problems from deliberately skipping over normal steps. Yet Japan can still be called a Confucian country. What are suitable goals [for Japan] that preserve strengths while rejecting weaknesses?"
>
> *Topic 3:* "Chambers of commerce and modern banks are the main features of a modern fiscal system for which budgeting and balancing accounts are fixed practices. In order to put [modern fiscal practices] into effect, the[se] fundamental components are necessary."
>
> *Topic 4:* "A modern police system is closely linked to a modern political system. We should obtain foreign police codes and proceed to implement their practice."
>
> *Topic 5:* "Industry, modern shipping, and railways augment military strength. All countries that have achieved wealth and power have done so using these means. Should we therefore adopt these things? What about the foundational values of a nation?"[12]

It is likely that the bodies of archconservatives such as Woren were spinning in their graves with the reality that Western institutions and values had become such an integral part of the highest-level civil service examination.

A National School System

Whether Kang's and Liang's reformist ideas of popular education had hit their mark or whether the Empress Dowager was influenced from elsewhere, in October 1901 she championed the establishment of a national school system. It would be structured as a hierarchy of schools located at each territorial level of government administration: county, prefecture, province, and capital. It would run alongside and feed into traditional examinations, in essence becoming another route to traditional degrees. The hope was that the new school system would supersede the examination system within perhaps a decade. But this approach did not work. There was no incentive for men to choose this new route to examination success. Private tutoring for the old examination was cheaper and more familiar than untried schools. Even more serious, there were no provisions for financing the new schools or for obtaining teachers and textbooks.

In 1904, a more detailed plan for a national school system was laid out. It specified, for example, how many kindergartens and primary schools should be established per number of families in a community, where middle schools and high schools should be established, and what should be taught. But the plan still allowed the civil service examination to continue for three more years. Therefore, even with the greater details of the 1904 plan, the new government schools died on the vine while the examination system continued to flourish.

The Most Revolutionary Act of the Century

The year 1905 was crucial in what became the program of Qing reforms. That year Japan, with a goal of bringing at least southern Manchuria into its sphere of influence, defeated Russia in war, the first victory ever of an Asian country over a European country. Japan's great success in its entrance into the modern world and its roles on the world stage, in contrast to China's pitiful performance, spurred a more widespread reform effort. Another forceful impetus was the organization of anti-Qing revolutionary groups in Japan. In Tokyo in 1905, Sun Yat-sen formed his Revolutionary Alliance with the specific goals of overthrowing the dynasty and establishing a republic. From the Manchu perspective, leading the reforms might be the only way to save the dynasty from its antagonists.

In August 1905 the most powerful provincial officials, led by Yuan Shikai, urged the abolition of the civil service examination system. In an act that should be heralded with trumpet fanfares to mark its extraordinary significance, the Empress Dowager accepted the advice and ordered the examination cast into the dustbin of history. *It was the most revolutionary act of the twentieth century.* Why? The examination had been at the heart of traditional culture: It had been the chief vehicle of orthodox state and social ideology; it had given birth to the political elites who took the posts at all levels of the imperial bureaucracy; it had given birth to the social elites, the scholar-gentry, who provided essential leadership at local levels of society.

Now, with the abolition of the examination, there was no way to convey an official ideology. Indeed, there was no longer an official ideology of state. What were left were questions without answers. From now on, what would give state and society its direction and its values? From now on, how would political and social leaders be produced? From now on, what would hold China together? Indeed, once the civil service examination was gone, there was no way to stop, divert, or even slow the tides of change.

From 1906, then, education had to succeed or fail with the new government school system. The problems—insufficient school buildings, inadequate funding, and paucity of able teachers and textbooks—had not disappeared. Likely because of the great traditional stress placed on education, local elites took it upon themselves to open and teach in schools. The school system in any particular locality was hostage to two factors—the degree of local economic development and the presence of interested elites. The system, as it developed, tended to remain weak at its base: local elites could achieve greater prestige by setting up a high school rather than an elementary school, so some communities had no elementary schools. Similarly, kindergartens and elementary schools lacked teachers because most potential instructors preferred the greater prestige (and salary) of teaching at a higher-level school. Despite the immense problems, however, the education system was quickly, if very haphazardly, revolutionized. Perhaps most revolutionary was the curriculum, with both Chinese and Western studies replacing the classics, and the social impact, as students now met daily in the classroom with other students as peers instead of studying with a personal tutor. Studies have shown that core zone counties tended to have fairly well-developed school systems, whereas poorer peripheral counties had fewer schools and students; nevertheless, even in wealthier areas, conservative traditional outlooks sometimes retarded school construction and development.[13]

THE MANCHU REFORM MOVEMENT: MILITARY CHANGE

A well-known Chinese proverb says, "Good iron is not beaten into nails; good men are not made into soldiers." Chinese civilization throughout the centuries had hailed and stressed the virtues of civilian rule and civil values. The empire could be won on horseback, the platitude went, but it had to be ruled with the writing brush. There was an imperial military examination that theoretically paralleled the civil service examination, but it had little prestige. By late imperial times, it consisted mostly of contests of strength and physical prowess and knowledge of centuries-old manuals. A man of ability and ambition simply did not route his future into the military. However, one of the major changes wrought by China's nineteenth- and twentieth-century history is, as we will see, the revaluation of the military amid the increasing militarization of Chinese politics and society.

At the opening of the twentieth century there were several types of military organizations. The oldest were the weak and useless banner and Green Standard forces. Not much better by the end of the nineteenth century were the regional armies formed during the Taiping, now mainly serving the vested interests of their leaders. In these armies there was no set number of troops; ranks were often peopled with vagrants; and officers, who had no knowledge of or interest in modern weapons, did not train their troops and embezzled the money that was to have been paid to those troops. Li Hongzhang's Anhui army had done the fighting against Japan in 1894–1895; at the time, about 60 percent of the troops had guns; the other 40 percent used swords, spears, and pikes.

There were also two "new armies," established in the mid-1890s to be used against Japan; but the war had ended before these armies, trained by German military officers and equipped with modern weapons, could be deployed. In 1895, Zhang Zhidong established the Self-Strengthening Army in Nanjing, and Yuan Shikai formed the Newly-Established Army near Tianjin. Both men tried to avoid the situations existing in the floundering provincial armies. Zhang, for example, recruited men between the ages of sixteen and twenty from peasant families in the vicinity of Nanjing; he required that their character be vouched for by neighbors and that they undergo a physical examination by a foreign doctor before being accepted. Yuan established similar procedures. Both new armies paid their men well, and Yuan insisted that part of the salary be sent to the men's families. In July 1901, the Manchus transferred control of Zhang's new army to Yuan, making him the key army builder in the country and, until his transfer to Beijing in 1907, the head of what came to be called the New Army.

In late 1903 a Commission for Army Reorganization was appointed to modernize all the country's military institutions. It mandated troop regulations like those Zhang and Yuan had initiated and ordered that each province establish a modern force manned by residents of that province. The Commission set up a system whereby New Army divisions were stationed at crucial locations across the country. Despite these reforms, central direction of the army remained fragmented. Military centralization in a real sense was made impossible because of political realities—China was fragmented into regional and provincial political interests and domains. In addition, funding for a fully modernized force was completely inadequate.

New military academies were established beginning in 1904 in Beijing and in the provinces of Shaanxi, Zhili, Jiangsu, and Hubei; they joined the ranks of the modern Baoding Academy founded by Yuan Shikai after the Boxer uprising. All the academies came to use Japanese instructors instead of the more expensive Germans. They began to produce cadets inculcated with patriotic ideas, who brought together modern military expertise with a sense of acting for the good of the country. Increasing numbers of graduates of these academies began to travel for further study at Japanese military academies, including the future leader Chiang Kai-shek. There, like students in other Japanese schools, they began to talk about the nature of China's problems. By the time they returned to China to be assigned to their posts, many of them were filled with the anti-Manchu revolutionary ideas of Sun Yat-sen and others.

More able men began to choose military careers after the abolition of the civil service examination system. The army seemed to present a new ladder that they could climb to social prestige and considerable power. Studies have shown that peripheral (but not the most peripheral) regions tended to produce the highest proportion of young men attending new military academies, like that at Baoding.[14] These were regions that traditionally did not produce many civil service degree-holders. Thus, in these areas there seemed likely a conscious awareness of the new and prestigious career possibilities in the military.

Because of the power of connections in Chinese society and the importance of the teacher–student relationship, the men at Baoding Military Academy became personally connected to Yuan Shikai through his leadership. His command came to be known as the Beiyang (Northern) Army. As a mark of the changed roles of military men in the early twentieth century, among his Beiyang officers, ten would become military provincial governors after 1912 and five would become presidents or premiers of the Republic of China. The military had become a legitimate and even determinative factor in Chinese society and politics.

THE MANCHU REFORM MOVEMENT: CONSTITUTIONALISM

The Chinese did not see the victory of Japan over Russia in 1905 as simply a triumph of Asia over Europe, but more significantly as an indicator of what its path to political modernization should be: Japan, a constitutional monarchy, had decisively defeated Russia, an authoritarian regime. In thinking about the source of Western wealth and power—and now seeing Japanese success in emulating the West—it was not farfetched to believe that somehow one of the sources might be constitutionalism.

Not only was constitutionalism politically au courant, but there were very practical reasons for turning toward constitutional structures. As it looked back over the previous half century, the court saw a country whose regions, provinces, and localities were spinning out of control from the center in centrifugal fashion. Much of the problem came from the political and military weakness and economic bankruptcy of the central government. Thus, when the Taiping war had begun to wreak its destruction, the Center had to ask civilian officials to form provincial armies to save the center. Power flowed out to the provinces—and those armies were still around almost fifty years later. Then, when it was time for reconstruction following the rebellions, the center had no money for the immense task, so it had to rely on local elites to take the lead. Studies have shown that during and after the rebellions, local elites emerged as significant leaders in establishing and managing local militia, rebuilding public works, sponsoring charitable undertakings, underwriting educational expenses, and contributing to and superintending the renovation of water control facilities. Power had devolved from the center to the local arenas. Constitutional forms might well be vehicles for strengthening the court's control over localities and their elites, tying provinces and localities more closely to the central government.

With this in mind, in 1905 the Empress Dowager decided to send missions abroad to study constitutional systems in Europe, the United States, and Japan. These missions lasted from late 1905 to late summer 1906 (one wonders whether the first "foreign" topic on the 1903–1904 civil service examination was asked with such a mission in mind). On their return, the clear choice was the Japanese model—retaining the monarchy, which itself would bestow the constitution; the court believed that this model would actually strengthen the throne's power. On September 1, 1906, the Empress Dowager proclaimed:

> The wealth and strength of other countries are due to their practice of constitutional government, in which public questions are determined by consultation with the people. The ruler and his people are as one body animated by one spirit, as a result of which comprehensive consideration is given to the general welfare and the limits of authority are clearly defined. ... Under these circumstances, we can ... adopt a constitutional polity in which the supreme authority shall be vested in the crown, but all questions of government shall be considered by a popular assembly.[15]

Celebrations broke out in cities around the country following the Empress Dowager's proclamation.

The edict of September 1 had also called for the complete revamping of the central government structures. Though this reform ignited considerable resistance among conservative officials, by November the new forms were on the books, if not yet fully implemented. The traditional Six Boards that had existed since the Tang dynasty (618–907) were to be abolished and in their place new ministries established. The Board of Revenue became the Ministry of Finance; the Board of Punishments, the Ministry of Justice; the Board of Works joined with the Board of Commerce (established in 1903) to become the Ministry of Agriculture, Industry, and Commerce—and so on. One can be skeptical about whether these were simply name changes without any substance; but it is important to understand that these name changes involved shucking off forms that had been around for over a millennium, and that in China forms can ultimately be as important as substance—forms indeed can transform into substance. The establishment of the new ministries was followed by a massive reshuffling of official posts and by a move to restructure provincial governments.

In the fall of 1907 the Empress Dowager announced that a national deliberative assembly and provincial deliberative assemblies would be established. Local assemblies were also to come into being. In August 1908 the Empress Dowager set forth a nine-year calendar of tutelage during which specific constitutional forms would be established. For example, provisional provincial assemblies would be set up in 1909, with a provisional national assembly in 1910; each year the state would take a new step toward the full realization of a constitutional system in 1917.

Had she lived, the Empress Dowager might have been able to lead China into that new system, but she died in November 1908. The Guangxu emperor, aged thirty-seven and under house arrest since the 1898 coup, died the day before she did. Though one report suggests that he suffered from Bright's disease, most historians believe that Cixi had him poisoned. She had already decided on his successor, the three-year-old grandson of her closest Manchu official (and some say her lover), Ronglu. Since the new Xuantong emperor was only three years old, his father ruled as regent. Although he and other Manchu princes, whom he allowed to have considerable power, did not undo the constitutional schedule, many of their actions in ruling were ignorant and inept. Their chief goal seemed to be maintaining and enhancing their own power. One wonders why the politically adept Empress Dowager left power in such unfit hands.

Strong officials who had served the Empress Dowager well were dismissed by Manchu princes on flimsy pretexts. The most able Manchu official, Duan Fang, was sent packing in late 1909 "for taking photographs on the way [of Cixi's state funeral], for moving about in his sedan chair with undue freedom and for making use of the trees at the Mausolea for telegraph poles."[16] This followed the dismissal early in the year of the most able Han Chinese official, Yuan Shikai, who suddenly found from the official edict dismissing him that he was ill: "Unexpectedly [Yuan] is suffering from leg disease and walks only with difficulty. He is, therefore, incapacitated for office. Let him vacate his post and return to his native place for treatment."[17] Unexpectedly indeed! With the absence of the Empress Dowager and the main officials who had propelled the reforms, the reforms seemed to languish.

Local Self-Government

The "local" in local self-government was relative; everything not national was considered local; thus, local self-government included the arenas of the province, the county, and the township. Elections for the provisional provincial assemblies were held from February to June 1909, the first Chinese elections ever for representative bodies. Many Chinese, suspicious and not completely understanding what was happening or its significance, were apathetic; bribery in the elections was common. Because of educational or economic requirements for both candidates and voters, the number of people voting relative to the entire population was very small, averaging about 0.42 percent, barely over four people per 1,000. Yet, given the fact that this was the first election in a country where elections were unknown, the elections were markedly significant events. The elected twenty-one assemblies, averaging seventy-eight representatives each, were generally bodies of provincial notables, with the vast majority being civil service degree-holders. In the fifteen provincial assemblies on which there is complete data, 89.1 percent of assemblymen held degrees.[18] But the backgrounds of the elected chairmen of the assemblies showed that the bodies were a mix of the old and the new forces in Chinese society. There were sixty-three speakers and deputy speakers in the twenty-one assemblies: fifty-one were upper degree-holders and seven held lower degrees; six had studied abroad. Indeed, of the 1,643 assemblymen, 167 (10.2 percent) had attended modern schools or gone abroad; 105, or 6.4 percent, had studied in Japan. The average age of all assemblymen was in their early forties.[19]

When the assemblies met, they discussed among other things education, local self-government, trade and industry, and police affairs. They were not cowed by provincial officials and quickly became bold and demanding. The chairman of the Jiangsu assembly called a meeting of representatives from the provincial assemblies in Shanghai in November 1909; fifty-one representatives from sixteen provinces met to draw up a petition calling for the immediate convening of the national assembly. Three times in 1910 similar petitions were presented, with the number having signed the petition increasing with each attempt—reportedly 200,000 signed the first, 300,000 the second, and 25 million the third. As one historian says, almost underplaying the stunning nature of this development, "This 'mass movement' was an unprecedented event."[20] The regent refused to grant the petition, stating that the establishment of the National Assembly should not be rushed.

The preliminary steps to establish county-level self-government bodies also began in 1909 with the setting up of offices to oversee the formation of county seat, town, and township councils. In Zhejiang province, for example, they were elected by the third lunar month of 1911 for two-year terms. County seat and town councils had twenty to fifty men; township councils, six to eight. These councils, in turn, chose the executive boards of the county seat and town (generally six members) and the township manager and his assistant. County seat, market town, and township councils and boards were meeting in the core zones and in most counties of the periphery by the late summer of 1911. On the whole, the revolutionary quality of these political changes, initiated by the Manchus, was nothing short of astonishing. If the Manchus saw these changes as a way to reestablish tighter control over the localities and their elites, local elites saw the new institutions as a way to solidify and enhance their own political leadership positions that had grown in the aftermath of the nineteenth-century rebellions.

In addition to the self-government bodies, the Qing mandated the establishment of other elite associations in counties to assist in the modernization process. Many of them were based on foreign models. In 1903 came edicts calling for the formation of chambers of commerce "to perform various managerial and mediational functions in the local economy 'in addition to the duties discharged by the chambers of commerce in foreign countries.'"[21] These were joined by mandated education associations (1906), agriculture associations (1907), lawyers' associations (1912), and bankers' associations (1915). All mandated associations were under government control. The government saw these associations, like self-government bodies, at least in part as control mechanisms over local elites. Unlike self-government bodies, the actual dates of the establishment of these associations were more dependent on local conditions and the degree of economic development. It is clear that counties in the peripheries did not have enough commercial activity to warrant the early establishment of chambers of commerce. Whereas the average date for the establishment of chambers of commerce in Zhejiang's most developed core area, the inner core, was 1906, in the outer core the average date came a year later, in 1907. In the more developed areas of the periphery the average date was 1909, but in the least developed areas they did not appear on average until 1917 or later. Similar patterns are evident with education and agriculture associations. Other less developed areas lagged behind these dates. Location and the relationship to economic development thus played a major role in a locality's timing and experience of revolutionary change.

National Self-Government

The provisional national assembly, composed of 100 elected by the provincial assemblies and 100 chosen by the Throne, met in Beijing on October 1, 1910 (thirty-nine years later to the day would see the establishment of the People's Republic of China). It was barred from discussing adoption of the constitution and limited to exchanges on the national budget, taxes, industrial development, and insurance and transportation regulations. But the assembly, like provincial assemblies a year earlier, threw caution to the winds and voted on October 24 to telescope the nine-year constitutional schedule. When the government's finance minister supported an immediate, full-fledged national assembly, the provincial assembly representatives again presented their petition for an immediate assembly, with some men showing the depth of their determination by cutting off a finger to write their petitions in blood. A sense of urgency, of the imperative of "seizing the hour, seizing the day" seemed to sweep over Chinese in the drive to realize the institutions of a modern state.[22]

The Throne caved in on November 4 and promised a full-fledged national assembly by 1913. In little more than a month, the provisional national assembly had shown itself to be the master of the court. But for them now, 1913 was not soon enough. "Now" was the cry, as over 2,000 student demonstrators marched to Tianjin government offices calling for an immediate establishment of the assembly. The appearance of court weakness encouraged more demands. The Throne was totally politically inept when in May 1911 it announced the formation of a cabinet of thirteen, comprised of eight Manchus, one Mongol bannerman, and only four Chinese. Many Chinese perceived such cabinet composition as a slap in their faces.

By the summer of 1911, many Chinese elites and students were riding a political roller coaster, with hopes for rapid realization of constitutional bodies and rights zooming high and then plummeting with the caution and ineptitude of the court. The situation was volatile and dangerous. The assemblies emerged as revolutionary organs on the provincial and national scene. From their perspective, the pace of Qing reforms was too slow.

And yet, analysis of the last decade of the Qing also suggests that the court actually reformed itself out of existence. Every reform that it initiated and oversaw hastened its own end. Ending the civil service examination opened the floodgates, leaving major ideological, political, and social questions without answers. Educational reforms sending students abroad placed the students together with their peers to question the legitimacy of Manchu rule. Military reform produced a new kind of soldier, trained in military academies and inculcated with nationalism. Administrative reform brought the reconstruction of centuries-old government institutions and raised questions about state ends. Finally, constitutionalism opened the political door to the citizens at the local, provincial, and national levels, giving the people forums in which to debate, legislate, maneuver, and vociferously demand. In these arenas it is surely not an exaggeration to call the Manchus "revolutionary."[23]

THE ANTI-MANCHU REVOLUTIONARY MOVEMENT

While the Manchus were, however haltingly, undertaking revolutionary reforms, anti-Manchu sentiment had grown both in China and among Chinese abroad who believed that the day for Manchu reforms had passed and that revolution was the only way to save China. Nationalism was emerging as a strong force in core areas and among students in Japan; in any discussions about the nation or nationalism, Manchus often ended up being lumped with foreigners as the Other.

The first decade of the twentieth century was dotted with small-scale attempts at local rebellion, with the rationale that a single spark might set off a raging conflagration. Many of these were initiated by Sun Yat-sen and his Revolutionary Alliance. The son of a poor farmer in Guangdong province, Sun (1867–1925) as a teenager had studied in Honolulu, where his brother had emigrated. Though trained in medicine in Hong Kong, he quickly tired of medical practice and began to devote his time and thought to reverse China's plight. In 1894, he formed the Revive China Society with the ostensible goal of undertaking reforms to revitalize China but with the actual aim of organizing a revolt against the Manchu government. In the fall of 1895, he attempted to launch the first of what, extending to 1911, would become ten revolts. This one, like all the others, seemed almost tragicomic—failing from various combinations of inadequate planning, confusion, bad timing, weapons not arriving, or the discovery of the plot before it could begin.

When he was not planning revolts, Sun spent his time focusing on two things. The first was raising money for the revolutionary cause in overseas Chinese communities around the world—an effort in which a major competitor was no less than the former reformer Kang Youwei, who was raising money for his Protect the Emperor Society, aimed at getting rid of the Empress Dowager. The second was putting ideological flesh on the skeleton of political aims set forth in the rationale for the founding of the Revolutionary Alliance. Sun's essential points became known as the Three Principles of the People (*Sanmin zhuyi*) and would become the guiding principles of the later incarnation of the Revolutionary Alliance, the Nationalist Party (*Guomindang*). The three principles were "nationalism," which meant ending both the rule of the Manchus and the presence of the foreign imperialists; "democracy," which, according to Sun, especially focused on elections, initiatives, referenda, and recalls; and "socialism," or, as Sun expressed it, "people's livelihood," the least fleshed-out principle, which focused primarily on equalizing land ownership and controlling capital.

Sun's Revolutionary Alliance was not the only organization established for revolution against the Manchus. In 1903, Huang Xing, a *shengyuan* degree-holder from Hunan who studied briefly in Japan, established the Society for the Revival of China (*Huaxinghui*); also strong in the organization was his fellow Hunanese, twenty-one-year-old Song Jiaoren. The next year, Zhejiang scholar Cai Yuanpei, who had attained the *jinshi* degree at the remarkably young age of twenty-two and had served in the Hanlin Academy in the 1890s, formed the Restoration Society (*Guangfuhui*). Huang's and Song's society merged with the Revolutionary Alliance at its formation in 1905, whereas the Restoration Society maintained its own integrity—though individuals did choose to become members of both groups.

In addition to the formation of revolutionary associations, individuals emerged to voice their strong protests against the Manchus in various ways. Eighteen-year-old Zou Rong, who had studied in Japan, wrote *The Revolutionary Army* in 1903. Zou argued that the Chinese were slaves to the Manchu "bandits"; that Zeng Guofan, Zuo Zongtang, and Li Hongzhang, who had helped the Qing crush the mid-nineteenth-century rebellions, were "Chinese traitors"; and that a revolution must sweep the Manchus out and usher in a republic with a constitution modeled on the American constitution.[24] Tens of thousands of copies of the tract were distributed across China and in over-seas Chinese communities; it was the most widely-circulated and influential revolutionary piece of the decade. Zou was imprisoned in Shanghai's International Settlement for distributing inflammatory literature; he died of natural causes in prison at age nineteen.

Other protests were more violent. In 1907, Qiu Jin, the revolutionary feminist, joined fellow student in Japan, Xu Xilin, with whom she also shared native place, in a plot to assassinate the Manchu governor of Anhui province. Both were members of the Restoration Society, and both had been involved in heading a school that was a front for revolutionary training and activity. Xu and two accomplices were able to assassinate the governor, though they were seized and executed immediately. When Qiu's involvement came to light, troops from the provincial capital stormed her school, seized her, and beheaded her. Today Qiu is seen as a national heroine, the earliest feminist, a great poet, and a revolutionary martyr; her most famous line was allegedly written just before her execution: "The autumn wind and the autumn rain will make me die of sorrow."

Other revolutionary efforts hit closer to the home of the Manchu national leadership. Wang Jingwei had won both the *juren* degree at age twenty and a government scholarship to study in Japan. He became a member of the Revolutionary Alliance and was a frequent contributor to the alliance's newspaper. In early 1910, he went to Beijing to assassinate the prince regent by setting off a bomb placed under a bridge on the prince regent's route. The goal? Stirring the Chinese to revolt. But a mistake by his fellow conspirators tipped the police off. Wang was arrested and imprisoned. Saved from execution by Manchu hopes that, amid their growing weakness, treating such political criminals gently might take some of the heat off themselves, Wang was released when the revolution broke out in the fall of 1911. His courage to act and to freely tell his captors what he was about made him at least temporarily, in the words of an historian, "the golden boy of Chinese nationalism."[25]

It is noteworthy how Japan served as the incubator of revolution. Not only was the key revolutionary organization formed there, but, more important, young Chinese men and women coming to Japan to study at both civilian and military schools, often on government scholarships, were turned into anti-government revolutionaries. They saw the immense difference in the degree of modernization in Japan, and it contrasted in humiliating ways with what they saw in China. Japan gave them a milieu in which their revolutionary fervor could openly grow and in which they could increase their mutual revolutionary ardor. It is little wonder that they then returned home to China to become the Zou Rongs, Qiu Jins, and Wang Jingweis.

THE 1911 REVOLUTION

The climactic act of the decade-long revolutionary drama was the revolution itself. Like many events in history that shatter the status quo, the revolution was shaped by timing and contingency as much as by planning. The setting for the beginning of the drama was the city of Wuchang on the Yangzi River in the Middle Yangzi macroregion; it was the site not only of an important New Army garrison but also of the yamen of the governor-general of Hunan-Hubei. The first contingency was that the military garrison had been weakened with the transfer of three battalions of New Army troops to deal with fighting that had erupted between military forces and citizens in Sichuan province over the issue of railroad rights recovery. If the garrison had been at full strength, the revolution might not have succeeded.

The actors in this first act were not members of the Revolutionary Alliance, but were active in two organizations that had had contact with it; they had been at work enlisting the support of New Army troops for a planned revolt. In late September, they sent messages to Huang Xing and

Song Jiaoren, asking them to participate in their planned uprising. Neither complied. Sun Yat-sen was on a fund-raising trip in the United States. He read about the revolution he had tried to ignite for so many years in a newspaper on a train outside of Denver. Thus, no recognized revolutionary leaders were present. Then, on October 9, while the revolutionaries were putting gunpowder into shells, one was careless enough to allow ashes from a lighted cigarette to fall into the powder, creating an explosion. Police came running and found revolutionary insignia and membership lists, including the names of large numbers of New Army troops. The Manchu governor-general and the commanders of the Eighth Division and the cavalry battalion (Li Yuanhong) began an intensive effort to halt any possible revolt by arresting and imprisoning the people on the lists.

Facing arrest and certain execution, the revolutionaries decided that their only choice was to proceed with the revolt. It began on the rainy and windswept evening of October 10. If the governor-general and the commander of the Eighth Division had steeled themselves to the task and not fled, it is possible that the revolt would have failed. But they did flee, along with most of the city's civil and military officials. By the morning of October 11, the revolutionaries were in charge of the city. But they had no leader. Someone mentioned the possibility of enlisting Li Yuanhong, the New Army leader. He was certainly no revolutionary or friend of one; indeed, in the first burst of fighting, he was approached by a man dispatched from the rebels asking him to throw his lot and his battalion in with the rebels. He promptly took out a knife and stabbed the man to death. When the fighting took a turn for the worse for the government, Li, fearful of what rebels might demand of him, went to hide at the home of one of his staff. Eventually found, he was asked to be their leader. When he refused, they threatened him, at least figuratively putting a gun to his head. "I am your leader," he replied. Li would go on to become the only man ever to serve twice as president of the republican government at Beijing.

The Qing responded by ordering the minister of war to plan and oversee an attack on the rebel forces at Wuchang. The logical person to lead these Beiyang forces was their old leader, Yuan Shikai, who had been rudely dismissed for a fictitious leg illness. They decided to appoint Yuan as the governor-general of Hunan-Hubei. His response: "Unfortunately my leg disease has still not healed, so I can't help you." Obviously, two could play the sorry game concocted two years earlier by the regent. Yuan was biding his time to see which way the winds would blow. The battle results showed strong anti-Qing winds, with defeat following defeat. With their backs against the wall, the Qing court was eager to learn Yuan's terms for stepping in to deal with the situation. He still did not respond when the court appointed him imperial commissioner in complete charge of the army and navy. He agreed to lead the campaign against the revolutionaries only when, on November 1, they consented to appoint him premier of the government with the right to name his own cabinet. In essence, the Manchus were steering China in the direction of a constitutional monarchy.

But that was not to be; revolutionary events were spiraling out of control. In coups in provincial and prefectural capitals and in county seats across China, mostly in cores but also in some more developed peripheries, New Army troops were joining the old scholar-gentry, rich merchants, and returned students from Japan to declare the beginning of the republic. Women, many of whom were members of the Revolutionary Alliance, also played important roles in the revolution. They oversaw secret networks among revolutionaries, raised funds, transported weapons, made bombs, and drafted banners and announcements. Women created their own militias and mini-armies, some of which saw combat. Two sisters from Zhejiang, Yin Ruizhi and Yin Weijun fought with men in the taking of Nanjing, Shanghai, and Hangzhou, in the last participating in the assault on the provincial governor's headquarters. The female director of a Shanghai hospital personally led 120 Red Cross members (fifty-four of whom were women) to Wuhan where, under gunfire, they were able to rescue many wounded fighters.[26]

By late November, fifteen provinces had seceded from the Qing dynasty. Yuan emerged as the key power broker in the struggle. As Yuan whittled down the power of the court, forcing the regent's retirement in early December, he tried to get peace talks going with the revolutionaries in order to determine what he might be able to gain from negotiations. Battles played key roles in determining the political situations. The revolutionaries would not talk with Yuan's emissaries until after he defeated them decisively at Hanyang in late November. But, in turn, the court's cause was dealt a deathblow by the defeat of its forces in Nanjing in early December after weeks of brutal fighting.

In early December the revolutionaries, in the person of Huang Xing, offered Yuan the presidency of the republic if he would support that political system and bring about the abdication of the Qing emperor. Yuan leaped at the opportunity. It was a decision that the revolutionaries would come to regret. In his career, Yuan had been a powerful and capable dynastic official serving effectively in many capacities. Yet he had had no experience with republicanism. Why did the revolutionaries hand him the republic on a silver platter? Most historians believe that the revolutionaries agreed to this in order to stop the fighting as quickly as possible to forestall the possibility that foreign powers in their treaty ports and concession areas might take advantage of the unrest to increase various kinds of imperialistic pressures and demands.

Signs of ever more threatening foreign imperialism were everywhere. In October 1911 the Chinese government defaulted on its Boxer indemnity payments. The British Foreign Office, meeting with representatives from the powerful Hong Kong and Shanghai Banking Corporation, agreed that in order to secure their loans, they would likely have to take control of crucial institutions in the Chinese government. Here was the specter of Western nations seizing part of the Chinese government. Or, perhaps even worse: "It did not seem to matter how great the Chinese interest [was] in a given case; every treaty right was once again supreme." Thus, a provincial governor could not stop the export of beans at a time of famine because a 1902 agreement had stipulated that China "had no right to interfere in the bean trade."[27] Because of such a foreign presence and threat, the Chinese were very skittish about any actions that might incur foreign wrath and retaliation. In their fighting, they were careful not to damage foreign property lest foreigners use this as a pretext to take more. Thus, fighting in the Yangzi port of Hankou had to be carefully controlled so that foreign warehouses were not hit. And in the crucial fighting in the area between Nanjing and Shanghai, revolutionary troops felt that they had to walk alongside the Shanghai and Nanjing Railroad tracks rather than ride the train or, much bolder, seize the train for their use—because Great Britain owned the line and the revolutionaries did not dare risk damaging British property. With such realities, it is not surprising that the revolutionaries turned to Yuan.

Sun Yat-sen returned to China on December 25. Though the representatives of sixteen provincial assemblies elected him provisional president of the Republic of China (an act that angered Yuan), Sun supported the earlier deal that had left Yuan in charge. The only remaining task for Yuan was bringing the dynasty to an end, a task helped in late January by a telegram sent to Yuan's cabinet from over forty commanders in the Beiyang army asking for the establishment of a republic. The abdication of the Manchus came on February 12, 1912, with the announcement that the six-year-old Xuantong emperor (Puyi) and his family could continue to live in the Forbidden City, receive a payment of 4 million dollars each year, and own the treasures of the imperial palace.

In localities, the contours and the meaning of the revolution varied according to the particular location. In most areas the revolutionary acts were like coups d'état, with local civilian leaders and/or military units seizing control. In some areas, reformist scholar-gentry and other elites who had been involved in reforms, such as recovering railroad rights or serving in chambers of commerce and local self-government bodies, simply stepped in to lead and staff temporary military governments. New Army men were often in the forefront of directing revolutionary action. In some areas revolutionary organizations, such as the Restoration Society or the Revolutionary Alliance, sometimes joined by secret societies and even underworld figures linked to criminal activity, were pivotal. In yet other areas usually more peripheral than core, political and social disorder was the order of the day. People in many areas, core and periphery, hung white flags in memory of the Ming, the last Chinese dynasty, and declared what was happening "restoration," that is, the return of rule from Manchu to Han Chinese. The date of the beginning of the revolution—the tenth day of the tenth month, or Double Ten—has since been celebrated as National Day by the Republic of China on the mainland until 1949 and afterward on Taiwan.

The thrust of events from 1905 to 1912 was extraordinarily revolutionary. The abolition of the civil service examination had begun the process of destroying traditional China by demolishing the recruitment structure for political and social elites. The move into constitutionalism was a breath-taking departure for the new state ethos. Now the abolition of the monarchy demolished the whole political structure. In place for over 2,000 years, the Son of Heaven and the empire were gone, along with all the traditional political principles, laws, customs, and morality. In their place was an untried republic, as yet only a name without substance, to be led by a man who had never supported such a system. As China entered the spring of 1912, it was beginning the process of constructing a new Chinese identity, of building a new state and nation—the new China—in a completely uncharted, unmarked future.

FIGURE 7.1   Cutting the queue became a sign of the revolution against the Manchus, but there had been talk about ending the custom even before the revolution. Some Chinese thought queues looked outlandish to foreigners and were safety risks if they might get caught in machinery.
Source: GRANGER/GRANGER, all rights reserved.

Notes

1 Cited in Maribeth E. Cameron, *The Reform Movement in China, 1898–1912* (New York: AMS Press, 1931), p. 56.

2 Sue Fawn Chung argued that the conservative bent of Cixi is a myth, that she actually favored reform. See "The Image of the Empress Dowager Tz'u-hsi," in *Reform in Nineteenth Century China*, ed. Paul A. Cohen and John E. Schrecker (Cambridge, MA: East Asian Research Center, Harvard University, 1976). I do not find the argument compelling in light of Cixi's actions: treatment of the Guangxu emperor (forbidding him to study English and then after the Hundred Days imprisoning him) and her patronage of the Boxers.

3 Mary Clabaugh Wright, "Introduction: The Rising Tide of Change," in *China in Revolution: The First Phase, 1900–1913*, ed. Mary Clabaugh Wright (New Haven, CT: Yale University Press, 1968), p. 30.

4 The report in the *Beijing xinwen huibao* (September 26, 1901) is quoted in Douglas R. Reynolds, *China, 1898–1912: The Xinzheng Revolution and Japan* (Cambridge, MA: Harvard University Press, 1993), p. 62.

5 Lu Meiyi, "The Awakening of Chinese Women and the Women's Movement in the Early Twentieth Century," in *Holding Up Half the Sky: Chinese Women Past, Present, and Future*, ed. Shirley Mow, Tao Jie, and Zheng Bijun (New York: The Feminist Press at the City University of New York, 2004), pp. 57–9.

6 Wang Zheng, *Women in the Chinese Enlightenment: Oral and Textual Histories* (Berkeley, CA: University of California Press, 1999), p. 39.

7 Lydia H. Liu, Rebecca E. Carl, and Dorothy Ko, eds., *The Birth of Chinese Feminism: Essential Texts in Transnational Theory* (New York: Columbia University Press, 2013), p. 7.

8 Wang Zheng, p. 43.

9 *Birth of Chinese Feminism*, p. 51.

10 Peter Zarrow, "He Zhen and Anarcho-Feminism in China," *Journal of Asian Studies* 47, no. 4 (November 1988), 811.

11 *Birth of Chinese Feminism*, p. 2.

12 Fan Peiwei, "Qing mo guimao jiachen ke huishi shulun" ("A Review of the Late Qing Metropolitan Examinations of 1903–1904"), *Lishi dang'an* (*History Archives* 3 [1993]: 105–10), trans. Douglas R. Reynolds in *China, 1895–1912: State-Sponsored Reforms and China's Late-Qing Revolution* (Armonk, NY: M.E. Sharpe, 1995), p. 94.

13 R. Keith Schoppa, *Chinese Elites and Political Change* (Cambridge, MA: Harvard University Press, 1982), pp. 121–2.

14 Ibid., pp. 123–4.

15 Quoted in Cameron, *Reform Movement in China*, p. 103.

16 *North China Herald*, November 27, 1909, quoted in ibid., p. 119.

17 *North China Herald*, January 9, 1909, quoted in Cameron, *Reform Movement in China*, p. 117.

18 Of these, 4.4 percent were *jinshi* degree-holders, 21.3 percent were *juren* degree-holders, and 62.5 percent held lower degrees.

19 These data come from Chang P'eng-yuan, "The Background of Constitutionalists in Late Qing China," in *China's Republican Revolution*, ed. Eto Shinkichi and Harold Z. Schiffrin (Tokyo: University of Tokyo Press, 1994), pp. 66–8.

20 Peng-yuan Chang, "The Constitutionalists," in Wright, *China in Revolution*, p. 161.

21 Schoppa, *Chinese Elites and Political Change*, p. 34.

22 The phrase comes from a poem by Mao Zedong. It is quoted, and the whole phenomenon is discussed, in Zhang Kaiyuan, "The 1911 Revolution and 'Seize the Hour, Seize the Day,'" in Eto and Schiffrin, *China's Republican Revolution*, pp. 77–88.

23 See the similar evaluation in Edward J. M. Rhoads, *Manchu & Han: Ethnic Relations and Political Power in Late Qing and Early Republican China, 1861–1928* (Seattle, WA: University of Washington Press, 2000), p. 285.

24 See the excerpt, "Zou Rong on Revolution, 1903," in *The Search for Modern China: A Documentary Collection*, ed. Pei-kai Cheng and Michael Lestz with Jonathan Spence (New York: W.W. Norton, 1999), pp. 197–202.

25 Howard L. Boorman, ed., *Biographical Dictionary of Republican China* (New York: Columbia University Press, 1970), Vol. 3, p. 370.

26 Lu, p. 59.

27 Wright, "Introduction: The Rising Tide of Change," p. 58.

Suggestions for Further Reading

Esherick, Joseph W. *Reform and Revolution in China: The 1911 Revolution in Hunan and Hubei* (Berkeley, CA: University of California Press, 1976). The author suggests that an "urban reformist elite" were the main actors in both reform and revolution.

Rankin, Mary Backus. *Early Chinese Revolutionaries: Radical Intellectuals in Shanghai and Chekiang, 1902–1911* (Cambridge, MA: Harvard University Press, 1971). This social-political study examines the secret society roots of many revolutionaries and the close links between their activity in Shanghai and the province of Chekiang (Zhejiang).

Rhoads, Edward J.M. *Manchus and Han: Ethnic Relations and Political Power in Late Qing and Early Republican China, 1861–1928* (Seattle, WA: University of Washington Press, 2000). This prize-winning book analyzes the revolution not from the perspective of revolutionaries but from that of the Manchu court; the author's interpretation of the identity of the Manchus contributes to an ongoing debate on the issue.

Schoppa, R. Keith. *Chinese Elites and Political Change* (Cambridge, MA: Harvard University Press, 1982). Using a macroregional approach, the author categorizes Zhejiang province into four zones of economic development and analyzes each zone for the nature of it social and political elites and their actions.

Zou Rong. *The Revolutionary Army: A Chinese Nationalist Tract of 1903*, trans. John Lust (The Hague: Mouton and Co., 1968) The most important revolutionary tract of the late Qing, it was written by a teenager and marked by a strong anti-Manchu fervor.

8

Selecting Identities
The Early Republic

If there is one figure from modern Chinese history that has drawn almost universal condemnation, that person is Yuan Shikai. A leading Communist spokesman, Chen Boda, in 1946 published a book, *Yuan Shikai, The Great Thief Who Stole the Nation*; a Chinese historian based in the West subtitled his study of Yuan *Brutus Assumes the Purple*. Yuan has been tarred with the charge that he betrayed the Republic, and almost universally he has been saddled with the title "father of the warlords." Yet at the time, he received considerable praise. The American ambassador to China, Paul Reinsch, reported,

> The President is very cordial and genial in his manner. He speaks fluently and to the point and loves to give a humorous turn to his thought. ... Nothing escapes his eye [;] ... he evidently has a grasp and mastery of details."[1]

No less a person than Liang Qichao said that because of his affable personality, being with Yuan was "like drinking champagne."[2] It is obvious that the problem was not Yuan's personality or ability but his policies. Whatever the historical judgment, his record should be seen in the context of the times.

LEGACIES OF THE REVOLUTION: THE POWER OF YUAN SHIKAI

Yuan assumed power at a time when almost everything in the political realm seemed up for grabs. There were no how-to manuals that could answer the difficult basic questions raised by the collapse of the two-millennia-long traditional civilization. What did republicanism mean in the Chinese context, and how was it to be implemented? In the new China, what constituted the legitimacy of a government or its elites?

In addition, the revolution and its aftermath left a serious and basic question: "Who had won?" The revolutionaries clearly did not rake in many of the spoils of victory. Their demand to have the capital relocated to Nanjing, closer to their power base and as a graphic symbol of change from the centuries-long imperial capital, was not satisfied; Yuan would not leave Beijing. The official positions meted out to revolutionaries were few and did not include crucially powerful posts like minister of finance or minister of the army. Sun Yat-sen was named national director of railroad development.

In the provinces, though there were fourteen provincial revolutionary governments, only three had military governors who were former members of the Revolutionary Alliance. In part this reflected the prerevolutionary situation when the Alliance's national leaders were not "in the know" about what was going on in the provinces. Organizationally the Alliance had been loose, lacking solidarity throughout its many geographical arenas. Further, in many areas, old elites who had been active in politics in the self-government movement or other public bodies took the political plums. Thus, though the revolutionaries came out on top in overthrowing the monarchy, a more accurate answer to the question of who won would be Yuan Shikai and the already ensconced elites.

Another legacy of the revolution and its aftermath was the rise of a potent provincialism, a development especially troubling to Yuan and his goal of a stronger centralized government. The revolution had taken the shape of individual provinces declaring their independence from the Qing dynasty. When the Republic was established, a strong sense of loyalty to the province continued. Listen to the words of Zhejiang's pro-Yuan military governor, Zhu Rui, in speaking of the province: "Protecting our local area [is] a heaven-ordained duty"; therefore, he vowed that troops from other provinces would not be allowed to enter the province.[3] It is not that this provincialism was necessarily antithetical to nationalism; they could coexist: One could show allegiance to both province and nation. But for many at a time of considerable political uncertainty and lack of clarity, one's native province, and that all-important sense of native place, was a closer-to-home way of thinking about political loyalty. In addition, some provinces were led by men who were suspicious of Yuan and were reluctant to be drawn into closer relationships with Beijing. As one historian has said, the political reality of the early Republic was a "de facto confederation of provinces."[4] Sun Yat-sen's depiction of China as a "sheet of loose sand" was an apt description of the lack of political coherence of the nation in these years.

FIGURE 8.1 Yuan Shikai strode into the presidency amid the optimism and hope of many that he was a strong leader who could help establish a republic and strengthen the nation. But he was a man still caught in traditional attitudes and approaches, and he rather quickly snuffed out the hopes of many.
Source: Topical Press Agency/Getty Images.

Yuan had built his reputation as a military reformer, though in his stints as Shandong governor and Zhili governor-general, he had also initiated reforms in education, commerce, and industry. Though he had never traveled beyond Korea (for his post as resident general) and did not know any foreign languages, he recruited men who had foreign education or experience, and he nurtured connections to foreigners. In his policies he sought to blend old and new, though in his personal life he was a thoroughly traditional Chinese man, having more than twelve wives and at least thirty children. Despite his geniality, he could be cold-bloodedly ruthless, willing to kill for political purposes almost at the drop of a hat. Thus, a Western description of his appearance at his inauguration as provisional president marks his short, plump build but not the reality of his political determination: Yuan "came in wobbling like a duck, looking fat and unhealthy, in Marshal's uniform, the loose flesh of his neck hanging over his collar."[5]

His political ideals were order, control, and rigid devotion to regulations. In his presidency, he worked continually to realize these ideals as part of his efforts to centralize in order to modernize the country. To his mind, the political world that he inherited—a republic with political parties and representative bodies at the county, provincial, and national levels—was too messy, too disorderly, too spontaneous, and so completely unpredictable that it could not in reality serve as a solid base on which to build the reforms that would make a new China. If assemblies at whatever level went off and did their own thing, there could not be the careful planning and directing that a strong head of state (assisted by focused bureaucrats) needed in order to build a modern nation-state. Yuan and those who had turned the Republic over to him were thus on a collision course from day one.

WOMEN'S SUFFRAGE AMID CONFUCIAN PARAMETERS

In the closing years of the Qing, a number of women, among them Lin Zongsu and Tan Qunying began to push women's rights strongly, especially female suffrage. The suffrage movement was launched in 1910. Lin (1878–1944), who knew Qiu Jin, founded the first suffrage organization in China, the Women's Suffrage Comrades Alliance, in November 1911. She was also one of China's first women journalists, one of whose newspapers, *Women's Times*, was dedicated to publishing information on suffrage.[6] Tang Qunying (1871–1937) was the first woman to join Sun Yat-sen's Revolutionary Alliance. Tang, also a friend of Qiu Jin, became chairwoman of the Women's Suffrage Alliance, which subsumed three other suffrage organizations, including the one established by Lin.

From the viewpoint of Confucians, women's vocations were defined by their roles in the family (as daughter, wife, and mother) and through the virtues each should play. Concerns for women's education, "rights," and suffrage were irrelevant. Some male intellectuals in the first decade of the century, however, supported these things for women. But it is clear that many women, like He Zhen, bristled at their male supporters' solicitousness: the male approach and attitudes were condescending, paternalistic, and aimed at keeping women "in their place" (that is, under the men's control). Listen to Wu Yu, who wrote many articles for the most important journal of the 1910s, *New Youth*: Chinese women must "study and improve their abilities in order to obtain their rights"; he called on Chinese women to "strive together with men in nationalism, following women in today's Britain and Germany." And even more blatant after very few women responded to Wu's admonitions, a response by a *New Youth* staff member:

> We seek women contributors who can boldly study and solve the woman problem, analyze woman's true nature, understand woman's true positions, and discuss the close relationship between women and state and society. But such women are as rare as phoenix feathers and unicorn horns.[7]

It was the "same old, same old": men defining women and thereby controlling them. Confucianism was being generally clobbered, but men, though they talked the right talk, continued to be hemmed in by a Confucian straitjacket.

Women such as Tang and Lin desperately wanted women's equality and suffrage written into the Republican state constitution. Lin received Sun Yat-sen's promise that when the National Assembly was established, women would win the right to vote. Afterwards, Lin published Sun's promise in two newspapers; but when she did so, Sun distanced himself from his own remarks. When the constitution was issued on March 11, 1912, there was no provision for either gender equality or suffrage. In men's discourse "women were asked simultaneously to wake up and to continue sleeping."[8] But some feminists would not continue sleeping. Beginning March 19, Tang and others over and over again angrily barged into the legislature, had heated debates with legislators, and broke two glass doors in a clash with security guards. To rub the men-made decisions into the open wounds of the women, when the Guomindang established its constitution and platform in April, it also contained no language on suffrage or gender equality.[9] Why not, after the men of the Revolutionary Alliance, including Sun, had previously stood firmly for that position?

Sun Yat-sen had turned the Revolutionary Alliance over to thirty-year-old Song Jiaoren, a longtime member of the Alliance, to reshape it into an open political party. Naming it the Nationalist Party (Guomindang), Song hoped that if the party could gain the majority seats in the National Assembly (to be elected in December 1912), he could emerge as prime minister. To accomplish that, he needed to merge several smaller parties with their own more conservative platforms and ideas into the Nationalist Party—an act that required political deal-making. The cost included deleting the wording for women's rights and suffrage and downplaying Sun Yat-sen's third "people's principle" on livelihood. To gain the support of the small-party conservatives, Song conceded to those who did not favor any women's public political participation and who thought Sun's "livelihood" too radical. Conservative Wu Jinglian telegraphed the conservative former Qing governor of Sichuan province that "the Revolutionary Alliance sacrificed everything."[10] The knowledge of Song's concessions to attain the party mergers ran scatter-shot throughout the party.

On August 25, 1912, the Nationalist Party held its inaugural convention. In the morning session speakers were Sun, Song, and Zhang Ji, chair of the convention who would become a leader in the right-wing of the party. While Zhang was speaking, Tang Qunying and two other feminists, Shen and Wang, took over the stage amid much yelling and commotion. Tang and Shen slapped Song's face with fans; Wang went after Song, grabbing him by the throat and threatening him with death. Tang, Shen, and Wang argued that Song's actions showed that he "had no regard for the Revolutionary Alliance and no regard for the Chinese Republic." To halt these raucous proceedings, Zhang ended the morning session. But for the feminists, the afternoon session was the bitter icing on the cake. Sun Yat-sen spoke for two hours in which he spun around 180 degrees from the position he had taken a day earlier on the issue of women's equality and suffrage. Now he advocated and supported a delay in action on the women's issue because of what he described as global resistance to woman's suffrage—even though three countries had already accepted it and at least three more would do so within five years. He "promised" that "one day" women's rights would be attained: the use of "one day" meant, of course, that this "promise" could be postponed indefinitely.

Tang stalked out of the convention in protest. She and Shen visited Sun at his residence the next day, maintaining their positions and calling Sun's attention to all the women who had risked or lost their lives for the revolution. It was said that Tang wept and sobbed so intensely that "the sound shook the room." Neither Tang nor Shen was mollified. Sun's later letter to suffragists in

Nanjing affirmed that he still favored women's equality and that the responsibility for excising the issue from the state and party constitutions was "the opinions of the majority of men" at the convention. Sun saw himself as the idealist and thinker, but he was through and through a savvy politician—passing the buck, buttering up his audiences, making up excuses why something could or could not happen, and promising things he had no way of knowing when or if they would get done. Meanwhile, women had to wait for that "one day."

In the December 1912 elections for national, provincial, and county assemblies, there were gender, age, educational, and economic qualifications for voting and serving: men, twenty-one and over, graduates of elementary school, who owned $500 in property and paid at least $2 in taxes. While National Assembly elections were marked by some corruption, they were remarkable for the relative smoothness with which they were carried out. They were the high point of electoral democracy in the twentieth and twenty-first centuries on the Chinese mainland and in Taiwan until the late 1980s. The Guomindang won approximately 43 percent of the vote, a plurality among the multiple parties; they took 269 of the 596 House of Representative seats and 123 of the 274 Senate seats: they would control 45 percent of the seats in each house.

But the euphoria was short lived. In March 1913, as he was leaving for Beijing to form the new government, party leader Song Jiaoren was shot and killed at the Shanghai train station. Yuan was implicated in the assassination: the man who hired the killer had been in communication with the secretary of Yuan's prime minister. Shock and outrage swept the country. A Wuchang newspaper offered bitter condemnation: "Yuan Shikai! The measure of your iniquity is full, and the time has come to answer for it."[11] To add insult to tragedy, Yuan on his own, without even a nod to the National Assembly's constitutional involvement, negotiated a huge loan of about $100 million from a foreign consortium. In May he proceeded to remove from their posts the major military governors who were supporters of the Nationalist Party. By the summer, an open revolt of pro-Guomindang forces began against Yuan's regime. This so-called second revolution ended in the military rout of the revolutionaries and the flight of Sun and others to Japan.

Yuan then set to work to construct what historians have seen as his dictatorship. In October, he forced the National Assembly to ratify his election as president for a five-year term. In November, he brazenly outlawed the Guomindang, evicting its members from the Assembly. In February 1914, he simply abolished all the assemblies—national, provincial, and county, making short shrift of China's democratic experiment. It is hardly surprising that Chinese have seen him as a thief and betrayer. A contemporary historian has noted: "What an affront to the educated and propertied classes who had participated in building this structure of representation!"[12] Then Yuan militarily occupied the provinces from which his troops had been kept out, attempting in the process to silence some talk of provincial autonomy by dismissing independent-minded provincial officials and reasserting Beijing's authority to make provincial appointments. He tightened general press censorship and Chamber of Commerce regulations. Police could now open the mails and search luggage at train stations. With a heavy hand, Yuan was trying to combat "the consequences of a new, participatory, radicalizing nationalism."[13]

In domestic policies under his dictatorship, Yuan carried on some of the initiatives from the last decade of Qing reforms. He called for "universal education" for all men—meaning at the time four years of free primary school; in the area of mass education he encouraged literacy campaigns using alphabetized Chinese. He appeared much the self-strengthener, adopting economic policies that would build Chinese wealth and development. He worked toward an independent judiciary to help create a legal system that the West would see as more enlightened and thus might move to end extraterritoriality. He put some government resources, for example, into agricultural experimentation in such areas as cotton growing, forestation, and livestock breeding. He was very successful in suppressing the domestic cultivation of opium.

One hallmark of Yuan's domestic reforms was his efforts to blend old and new. He restored some imperial symbols and ceremonies. He reinstituted tradition in the form of Confucianism as a state religion. In primary school textbooks, *Mencius* and the *Analects* replaced pictures and accounts of Sun Yat-sen and Huang Xing. In short, Yuan, like the self-strengtheners, was a reformer firmly rooted in traditional ways. But the context had changed from the days of Zeng Guofan, for then the traditional culture had been very much alive. With all the changes of the early years of the twentieth century, Yuan's attempts to put old wine into new bottles were simply out of step with the times.

One historian has suggested that when Yuan looked at the problems of his presidency, he diagnosed them as "imperial under-nourishment: the emperor was missing."[14] To remedy that situation, in August 1915 Yuan helped launch a campaign to have himself declared emperor; he would take the throne on the first day of 1916 as the "Grand Constitutional Emperor." In his mind must have been the thought: what better way to rebuild the centralized state and handle society's messy new forces than with the institution of the monarchy with its time-honored traditions and ethos? But it was a mistake. Even though the monarchy had been gone for barely three years, reactions showed that the Chinese political culture had already left it far behind in their memories.

A National Protection Army directed against Yuan was launched by military forces in Southwest China in late December 1915. It effectively used guerrilla attacks against Beiyang forces in Sichuan, while from the coast came attacks by Sun Yat-sen and his allies. In the meantime, many of Yuan's Beiyang forces were ambivalent at best about Yuan's imperial initiative. Foreign nations were not supportive; Japan, especially aware of the great unpopularity of Yuan's actions among Chinese elites, even helped fund the rebels. Very quickly Yuan realized that his power was collapsing. By March 22, he backpedaled to his fallback position as president, but with more provinces declaring themselves independent, he could not stanch the bleeding. His June 6 death from uremia in the midst of rebellion was undoubtedly, from a personal standpoint, a merciful ending. But for the country it was the moment of collapse into a national nightmare of bloodletting that would extend for more than a decade.

CAPITALISTS TO THE FORE

The first years of the Republic were also the beginning of what one historian has called "the golden age of the Chinese bourgeoisie," by which she meant modern-style businessmen, financiers, and industrialists—in short, capitalists.[15] Aspects of two early republican buildings suggest cardinal elements in the world of the bourgeoisie. Completed in 1917 by an entrepreneur who made millions in medicine, the Great World in Shanghai was a huge amusement palace, described as "a kind of Crystal Palace and Coney Island" rolled into one. "The third floor," for example,

> had jugglers, herb medicines, ice cream parlors, photographers, a new bevy of girls, their high-collared gowns slit to reveal their hips … and under the heading of novelty, rows of exposed toilets, their impresarios instructing the amused patrons not to squat but to assume a position more in keeping with the imported plumbing."[16]

The other building was one of the most imposing edifices in the city of Shaoxing on the southern coast of Hangzhou Bay, southwest of Shanghai. Built from 1915 to 1917, it was the headquarters of the city's Chamber of Commerce and served as the unofficial political-social-economic center for the city where municipal organizations often rented meeting rooms.

The international aspects of the Great World's exhibitions highlight its setting in the largest and most important of the treaty ports. These cities, key transit points for foreign goods to interior trade routes, had experienced increasing trade in the second half of the nineteenth century, with exports primarily of tea and silk and imports of textiles, kerosene, and sugar. By the early twentieth century that trade, as the description of the Great World shows, had even come to include Western-style toilets. Since foreigners knew neither Chinese nor local customs, Chinese merchants played key roles, managing most transactions while financing them through native Chinese banks.

Modern industrial development did not begin in Chinese cities until near the end of the nineteenth century. The Treaty of Shimonoseki (1895) gave the Japanese the right to establish factories in the treaty ports. Other foreign nations leaped at the opportunity to set up textile mills in these ports where cheap Chinese labor and local raw materials made manufacturing more profitable than in the home country. Competition from Chinese businessmen in this industry was practically nil. Despite the development of factories in cities, interior parts of the country were not affected to any appreciable degree. It is likely that the Lower Yangzi macroregion was the only region where economic changes had progressed far enough at this time to support even an incipient capitalist class.

Chinese had begun to establish their own modern firms during the early days of self-strengthening. They revealed from the beginning the close relationship between business and government that became a hallmark of economic development both under the Nationalist government of the 1920s through the 1940s and the later Communist government. In 1872 Li Hongzhang established the China Merchant Steamship Navigation Company to end the foreign domination of coastal shipping. It operated according to the formula of "government supervision, merchant management," getting much of its income from the government contract for the transport of tax grain.

In many ways, this model of business organization was similar to the centuries old imperial salt monopoly in which the government monopolized salt production and sales but farmed out

FIGURE 8.2 The Great World Pleasure Palace, with its mix of things East and West, shown here with its large "Chrysler" sign, stood as a symbol of modernizing China in Shanghai, China's capital of modernization. *Source*: National Archives, photo no. 151-FC-31A-10.

to merchants the roles of managing production and distribution. These new enterprises were not government monopolies, but in Li's company and others—the Kaiping Mining Company in Zhili province (1877) and the Shanghai Cotton Cloth Mill (1890), to name two—government support in the form of loans, tax breaks, and/or a production monopoly played a crucial role in getting the firms started. Private merchants were slow to invest in these companies, which merchants managed generally without intrusion from the government. By the end of the dynasty, the Chinese bourgeoisie was composed of merchants, bankers, compradors, a few industrialists, and overseas Chinese. Politically they played increasingly important roles as major participants in anti-foreign boycotts. In the 1911 revolutionary period their roles varied, depending on local circumstances, but they were generally not pivotal players in the local coups that made up the revolution.

World War I and the peace that followed served as catalysts for a prosperous period for Chinese business and industry. During the war from 1914 to 1918, Western eyes were temporarily averted from China to the horrors of the Western Front. That relative Western absence first gave Chinese entrepreneurs an opportunity to become involved in the flourishing wartime trade. Imports from the West dropped dramatically; the value of imports from Britain, for example, fell from 96 million taels in 1913 to 49 million in 1918. On the China side, silk exports increased by more than 50 percent. It is little wonder that China's trade deficit fell from 166 million taels in 1913 to only 16 million in 1919.

Second, the war years gave Chinese entrepreneurs the opportunity to more assertively begin to develop modern business and industry that did not use the government supervision, merchant management model. During the last years of the war and into the early 1920s, coastal cities, especially Shanghai, experienced the rapid growth of modern light industries—spinning, flour and oil mills, and cigarette factories—that was not equaled again until the 1950s. The number of textile mills grew from 22 in 1911 to 109 in 1921; the number of flour mills increased from 67 in 1916 to 86 at the end of the war. Tonnage of coal produced increased from about 13 million in 1913 to over 20 million in 1919; iron production almost doubled during the war. The development of modern Chinese banks also dates from this period; whereas there were only seven at the time of the establishment of the Republic, the number soared to 131 in 1923.

Two examples of famous industrialists point to the economic boom and the kind of men who became leaders. As in the Great World, Zhang Jian, from Jiangsu province in the Lower Yangzi, merged the old and the new. He was an old-style *jinshi* degree-holder who served as minister of industry under Yuan Shikai. In his home of Nantong, about 60 miles northwest of Shanghai, he established the Dasheng Cotton Mills in 1899. Reflecting the early republican boom, he was able to double the number of spindles at the mill from 1914 to 1922. The cotton mills were part of Zhang's efforts to make Nantong a national model that involved not only the establishment of industry but educational, philanthropic, and conservation reforms as well. The other industrialists were two brothers, Rong Zongjing and Rong Desheng, who came from a family of merchants and minor officials in the Yangzi delta city of Wuxi. In Shanghai they built the Maoxin Flour Mills and the Fuxin Flour Mills in 1901 and 1913, respectively. As a mark of the rising tide of prosperity amid China's capitalists, between 1914 and 1920 they opened eight new factories and broadened their interests into textiles, opening the Shenxin Spinning Mill.

The flurry of mostly treaty port business and industry led to a new business culture in the cities. New businessmen's associations sprang up, such as the Chinese Cotton Millowners Association (1918) and the National Bankers Association (1920). They provided arenas for joint discussions about the economic situation, industrial problems, relations with foreigners (since many businesses and industries lay within foreign settlements), and relations with the government. In addition, many of these associations began to publish their own magazines to discuss these same issues. Indeed, the claim that, at least until the 1990s, the years 1917–1923 were the "golden age of Chinese capitalism" seems well taken.[17]

The rising power of merchants was a development not only in treaty ports, but in the macroregional cores as well. Powerful entrepreneurs or groups of them were active in establishing textile and paper mills, and telephone and electric companies in core zone provincial capitals, county seats, and even larger market towns. As an example of the range of entrepreneurial undertakings, a powerful merchant named Jin in 1919 petitioned the Zhejiang Industry Ministry for the right to build an industrial complex at the market town and river port of Linpu, 15 miles southeast of Hangzhou. Included would be factories producing paper, textiles, bamboo and wood products, brushes, and tiles.[18]

Local businessmen increasingly depended on Chambers of Commerce to facilitate their business enterprises, to mediate between businesses and businessmen, and to serve as a conduit between business and government. Here the second structure symbolizing the Chinese entrée into the world of capitalism, the Shaoxing Chamber of Commerce, could take center stage. Chamber of Commerce activity became an index of the power of merchants and entrepreneurs in the locality. The government in 1917 limited the number of chambers per county to two, recognizing their potential power. But by the early 1920s, chambers had begun to get around the restrictions by establishing branch chapters. In what may be a particularly egregious example, by 1924, Jiaxing county in Zhejiang province had no fewer than thirteen branch chambers.

In localities, economic muscle was often easily translated into political clout. A foreign observer noted, "With the downfall of the Manchu regime … the government of almost every city in China was for months virtually carried on by the chambers of commerce and associated guilds."[19] On the agenda of one of the branch chambers in Jiaxing county much later, in 1924, for example, were items in regard to education, sanitation, and the town's winter defense. The fact that officials in Shaoxing saw the Chamber of Commerce building as *the* place in the city to hold their various meetings suggests the wider importance of this organization. In some cases, in the 1920s, chambers became unofficially the main local decision makers, taking power from local assemblies and other bodies. Indeed, the flexing of capitalist muscle during the early Republic puts the economic expansion of China in the 1990s and the first two decades of the twenty-first century into important historical perspective.

THE POWER OF THE GUN

If the merchant, businessman, banker, and financier were beginning to play more than bit parts on the Chinese stage during the early Republic, the stars of the show were military commanders with their supporting casts of thousands of soldiers. As long as Yuan Shikai was alive and maintained the power that he had taken, he was able to control the generals who had been trained under his command in the New Army; he had been their patron and they, his students. With his overplaying the imperial hand and the sudden erosion of his power in the spring of 1916, however, China began to collapse in confusion. Yuan's opponents were not united. There were only clusters or groupings of military men tied together by various connections. When Yuan died, the destructive genie of military competition was freed to wreak havoc over the land. The goal of this warring competition was to seize Beijing and its government institutions, for whoever took that political prize would be recognized as president of the Republic. This struggle among what became known as "warlords" produced one of the most tragic and chaotic periods in twentieth-century China.

Although it technically ended in 1928 when the country was again nominally unified, what has been called "residual warlordism" actually persisted into the 1940s.

Before the warlord situation became bleakest in the early and mid-1920s, there was one last attempt to restore the monarchy. The effort points with exclamation points to the clashing public identities on the Chinese political scene at this time of substantial change. Zhang Xun had been a senior military officer under Yuan since the formation of the New Army. Even though he served Yuan, his ultimate loyalty was to Chinese traditions and the monarchy. As for traditions, he was one of the most outspoken supporters of maintaining the official cult of Confucius. As a visible symbol of his loyalty to the monarchy, he insisted on keeping his queue and ordered that his troops maintain theirs as well. Foreigners dubbed him the "pigtailed general." (For purposes of graphically visualizing the clashing identities of the early Republic, imagine Zhang Xun at the Great World with the Rong brothers.)

In early July 1917, Zhang restored Aisin Gioro Puyi, the last Qing emperor, then eleven years old, to the Dragon Throne. He used the opportunity of being asked by the president of the Republic, Li Yuanhong, to intervene in a dispute between the current government premier, military leader Duan Qirui, on the one side, and Li and the National Assembly, which had been reestablished after Yuan's death, on the other. Zhang badly misjudged the likely reactions of the Beiyang commanders, who sent troops to storm the capital and end the less-than-two-week reign. Never again would anyone attempt to restore the monarchy, though the chaos and destruction of the period as late as 1922 led people at least in some localities to express the opinion, as Yuan had and as Zhang surely would, "that the emergence of the rightful Son of Heaven would solve local and national problems."[20] The aborted 1917 restoration episode did reveal that the governmental institutions in the capital—the bureaucracy and the National Assembly—were not really the main players on the political stage. Those roles increasingly belonged to the military. Zhang, using military forces, had restored the emperor, but opposing military forces had ousted him (and Zhang to boot). Within the less than six years since Double Ten, struggles between military forces had four times determined the identity of the Chinese government (1911–1912, 1913, and twice in 1917).

It is apparent that in the 1920s governmental institutions became pawns in the warlords' struggle for military control of the capital and by extension the country. The concerns of civilian politicians and bureaucrats focused more and more on keeping their positions and maintaining their own political power, often through cultivating connections with warlords. In this context, corruption tended to become the crucial dynamic and often decided elections and policies. In perhaps the most infamous case, Cao Kun, a Beiyang army general who led one of the major military cliques (the Zhili clique) from 1920 to 1923, won the presidency of the Republic in 1923 by spending $13,560,000 to bribe National Assemblymen to vote for him (at $5,000 per vote). As one scholar has noted about the affair, "in the act of purchase, the presidency was devalued."[21] The sorry spectacle was that from mid-1916 until the spring of 1926 China had six different presidents and twenty-five cabinets. The high hopes of a productively functioning Republic lay in shambles: the Republic had become an empty shell.

In the shaping of political culture, a republican ethos—carrying the voice of the people into the halls of government—had been aborted; in its place flourished the ethos of the military. In these years, militarization began to emerge as a major dynamic in twentieth-century China. Although all warlords were military men and held territory of varying size, the name "warlord" covered many different military types with differing goals. Some warlords perhaps actually had the abilities, character, and potential to unite the Chinese nation and become a head of state. Central China's Wu Peifu, who emerged to head the Zhili clique, one of the central warlord coalitions, for example, was a man who had received the lowest-level civil service degree. He was also a graduate of Yuan Shikai's Baoding Military Academy. A writer who had a deep love for traditional Chinese culture, he was a student of the Buddhist canon and the Confucian classics. Another example was North China's Feng Yuxiang, a self-taught Christian convert who indoctrinated his troops with Christian and traditional Chinese values and was said to baptize his troops with a fire hose. He was a committed social and educational reformer, establishing, for example, orphanages, rehabilitation centers for drug addicts, and public education facilities. Yan Xishan of Shanxi province was a third potential candidate for heading the nation. He had briefly studied the classics, graduated from a Japanese military school, joined Sun's Revolutionary Alliance, and risen to the position of military governor in the 1911 revolution. His reforms, his careful attention to rule, and his concern for promoting public morality contributed to his being called the "Model Governor."

Warlords such as Wu, Feng, and Yan vied for the top; others had lesser goals, some regional, others local. Some warlords were simply thuggish. One of the more notorious was Zhang Zongchang, the "Dog-Meat General." A famous journalist described him as having "the physique of an elephant, the brain of a pig, and the temperament of a tiger." As a measure of the man, it is said that Zhang had his "'three don't knows': he did not know how much money he had, how many troops he had, or how many women he had in his harem."[22] His Shandong military troops, which included 4,000 White Russians (dubbed "soldiers of misfortune") and a unit of several thousand boys whose average age was ten, were notorious for their practice of "opening melons," that is, splitting skulls, and for hanging strings of human heads on telegraph poles to elicit respect for their power.

Warlords striving for national power often put together coalitions in order to have greater troop strength and a broader availability of resources. Such coalitions were by nature unstable, for most often they were formed as part of a strategy to accomplish short-term or intermediate goals. Among the warlord players at the national level, coalitions did not have ideological bases. Nor were they usually based on close personal connections; a frequent pattern, in fact, was that today's ally often became tomorrow's enemy. All coalition building, as well as the shaping of policies, was driven by mercenary and power considerations. Coalitions would therefore collapse if one or more coalition member(s) were lured away for a better deal from a rival warlord; the lure of money or position to bring about the defection of a militarist or military commander was known as "silver bullets." Their use made any sort of long-range planning difficult and caused at least one militarist to predict, "We shall undoubtedly win. It is simply a matter of waiting for treason."[23] One other method to destroy coalitions was by assassinating coalition members. Reportedly a common approach was to invite the proposed victim to a banquet, where he was then murdered—a practice that one presumes would have led anyone invited to a banquet to have second thoughts about accepting.

The Beiyang militarists were separated into two main cliques that formed around Yuan Shikai's two chief lieutenants, the Anfu clique led by Duan Qirui and the Zhili clique led by Feng Guozhang. The other main player was the Manchurian warlord Zhang Zuolin. To simplify a confusing history, four major wars were fought between 1920 and 1926. The first was between the two main cliques, with Zhang joining the victorious Zhili clique. The other three wars came between victors in the first: Zhang versus the Zhili clique. Keep in mind that these were only the major wars. One historian has counted more than 140 wars fought between 1916 and 1928.

These were bloody affairs that grew bloodier over the years. Though many of the officers were graduates of military academies and could be seen as professional military men, the soldiers themselves were in many cases recruited from rural areas. Each army was tied together by the typical social bonds—linkages through family, marriage, friendship, and teacher–student and patron–protégé ties. Recruits enlisted to make a living and were in the army for an indefinite period; though national regulations specified that they were to be nineteen to twenty-six years old, commanders frequently took them at all ages, as the case of Zhang Zongchang indicates. Fatalities in battle were high, a situation made worse by the lack of medical care, where even light wounds could end in death.

Among the populace the warlord scourge included loss of life; rapes by both military victors and losers; destruction of crops, cropland, and agricultural infrastructure; and widespread economic dislocation and property destruction. Troops lived off the areas they occupied or moved through, looting and pillaging. One warlord reported,

> My men would surround a village before dawn and fire several shots to intimidate the people. We told them to come out and give up. This was the classic way of raiding a village. Sometimes we killed and carried away little pigs. ... We took corn, rice, potatoes, taro.

Peasant carts and labor were regularly commandeered. Cities were special targets for looting. A British official reported on the 1920 looting of Yuzhou in Hunan, "I have never seen more thorough work. Every shop, every house in this beautiful and prosperous city has been literally stripped. There is not a vestige of any usable commodity from one end of the city to the other."[24]

But there was more. Warlord armies needed weapons and supplies, necessities that demanded money. Two sources of money that emerged as critical to the warlord campaigns were opium and taxes. In the late Qing, the cultivation of opium had been practically eradicated in most areas. Its capacity to bring in huge profits, however, made it attractive to warlords, who forced farmers in many areas to plant opium instead of food crops. In some places, warlords forced opium cultivation by placing the land tax so high that opium was the only feasible crop to plant. Whereas the acreage of cultivated land devoted to opium production lay at 3 percent in the years from 1914 to 1919, it shot up to 20 percent in the period 1929 to 1933.

The other source of money was taxation. Extraordinarily high taxes were placed on every conceivable item, from consumer goods to licenses to lifetime situations (getting married, owning a pig, going to a brothel). Land taxes were collected far in advance (perhaps as many as ten years). Taxes on commodities in transit were exorbitant: a Hankou newspaper reported, for example, that "a shipment of paper worth $1,350 when landed at Shanghai was shipped up the Yangzi to Chengdu. It passed through eleven tax stations ... and the illegal taxation collected on it by regional authorities totaled $2,150."[25] With taxes reaching confiscatory levels and without recourse, the economy of affected communities was wrecked; the people's livelihood was, as it were, left for dead. Finally, like typhoons spawning tornadoes, warlord wars gave rise to wide-scale banditry. In many cases, what warlords did not succeed in destroying or taking, the bandits did.

One of the tragedies of the warlord struggles was that many battles were made possible and certainly more destructive because various Western nations supplied ammunition and guns, "by the gun and by the shipload," to warlords. An American suggestion in 1919 that nations join in an embargo of weapons sales to China in order to put a halt to the fighting led to an Arms Embargo Agreement, but it was so conspicuously violated that it was abrogated within ten years. Some countries, especially Japan and Russia, were interested in aiding those warlords whom they thought were most likely to seize state power. Obviously, if their pet warlord then did become president, the likelihood that they would receive privileges from his regime would be increased. The Japanese provided continual monetary and material support to Manchuria's Zhang Zuolin. Likewise, the Russians gave Feng Yuxiang money, military instructors, and arms and materiel. Great Britain maintained exceptionally close relations with Wu Peifu but did not reportedly offer government support of his rule, though British firms did offer Wu loans. In the late 1910s and early 1920s,

British and American diplomats applied some pressure on the Beijing government to bring a halt to the warlord struggles so that military disruptions of trade would cease.

Though some warlords aspired to unite the nation, warlordism was the very antithesis of nationalism. Warlord actions radically fragmented a state whose modern identity had not yet had time to develop. Their reliance on foreign arms and aid put the lie to any image of a new nation standing on its own and was in fact retrogressive when seen against the backdrop of the late Qing rights' recovery movement. Their actions and policies seriously damaged the economy and inhibited national economic progress. Warlords contributed to the growing militarization of Chinese society; and their actions gave rise to a demoralized and devastated populace, undercutting potential patriotism that might have inspired commitment to build a new China.

Finally, warlords and their actions were at odds with new forces in Chinese society, clashes that all too frequently produced bloodshed and tragedy. An example was the massacre of students near the Gate of Heavenly Peace on March 18, 1926. In the 1925–1926 warlord struggle between Feng Yuxiang and Zhang Zuolin, Feng's forces had mined the sea approaches to Tianjin to keep Zhang from landing there. The Japanese, Zhang's main patrons, who saw the Tianjin area as their sphere of influence, protested the mining because of its impact on their trade; they ordered the mines removed. Beijing students protested the Japanese ultimatum as interference in Chinese domestic affairs. Though government troops dispersed them on March 17, on the next day more students came out to demonstrate. When they tried to march to the head of state's office, police opened fire and killed forty-seven students. Sidney Gamble, an American social scientist doing social research for the YMCA, was an eyewitness:

> The shooting of the students on March 18th was a terrible tragedy. … Just how much the students threatened to use force at the Cabinet office we do not know, but once the guards started firing they kept it up for fifteen or twenty minutes. The soldiers used their bayonets on the wounded and robbed the bodies of the dead. Even glasses were snatched from one of the girls as she was getting out through a back gate.[26]

Zhu Ziqing, on the faculty at Qinghua University, participated in the march and left a much more personal description of his actions upon hearing the gunshots:

> One or two minutes later, the red-hot blood of the person on top of me streamed down the back of my hand and onto my jacket. I understood immediately that the massacre had begun. The only thing I knew was that I did not want to die; I only wanted to live. … I rolled down a hill of corpses. Later, when I realized that I had walked on corpses, I shuddered with fear for a long time.[27]

Warlord wars had thus precipitated a crisis that, because of foreign interests in China, had brought Japanese intrusion into Chinese affairs and the nationalistic student demonstration. Tragic as the loss of student lives on the Beijing streets was, their numbers paled in comparison to the deaths of the thousands of Chinese who died in the warlord struggles. Lu Xun, China's most important twentieth-century writer, summed up the despair and sense of futility created by the age of the warlords with specific reference to the March 18 tragedy:

> Time flows eternally on: the streets are peaceful again, for a few lives count for nothing in China. … As for any deeper significance, I think there is very little; for this was only an unarmed demonstration. The history of mankind's battle forward through bloodshed is like the formation of coal, where a great deal of wood is needed to produce a small amount of coal.[28]

CHINA TOTTERS ON THE WORLD STAGE

The outbreak of World War I placed China in imminent danger of becoming a battleground for European powers that had spheres of influence on Chinese soil. To forestall that possibility, China hastily declared its neutrality. That action did not stop Japan from invading the German leasehold in Shandong province in response to ally England's request to seize German properties in China. The war took imperialist Western nations out of competition with Japan in China. Japan set out to make imperial hay while the sun of World War I shone, expanding the former German holdings almost as soon as it had taken them.

Then in January 1915, as the European powers were preoccupied with the war, Japan acted to strengthen its hand in China, presenting Yuan's government with the Twenty-One Demands. This was a list of five categories of demands, mostly economic rights and privileges in Shandong, Manchuria, Inner Mongolia, the Yangzi Valley, and Fujian province. But the fifth group of demands cut more deeply into Chinese sovereignty: it required that the Chinese attach Japanese advisers to the key governmental executive, military, financial, and police bodies, making China in effect a protectorate of Japan. This group of demands also specified that China had to purchase at least half of its munitions from Japan. The spring of 1915 saw a wave of anti-Japanese protests and rallies sweep the country. When the Japanese eventually modified the demands by dropping the ominous fifth group and then issued an ultimatum to accept the rest, Yuan acceded. The day of agreement to the demands, May 7, was commemorated in subsequent years as National Humiliation Day.

In 1917, China did give up its neutrality (which had done nothing to safeguard its security) and declared war against Germany. For its part in the war effort, China sent almost 100,000 workers to northern France where they labored along the trenches, in construction, and in transport. Apart from performing valuable service near the Western front, these men went back to China with a changed worldview and (for some at least) bundles of saved cash. Their experience entitled the Chinese to participate in the Versailles Conference after the war ended.

The Shandong Issue

People all over the world had been affected by the wartime rhetoric of U.S. President Woodrow Wilson. The "war to make the world safe for democracy" and the "war to end all wars" had also been one that was supposed to bring the "self-determination" of peoples to control their own destiny inside their chosen homelands. For many colonized peoples, the message, infused with high idealism, also brought high hopes that they might once again be able to control their lives and their countries. The Chinese delegation to the 1919 Versailles Conference shared those hopes—specifically, to recover Shandong province and to eliminate the unequal treaty system. However, since the conference had convened only to deal with issues that were resulting from the war, the disposition of the unequal treaties was not included on the conference agenda.

The Chinese argued that Shandong, the home province of Confucius, and therefore a very special area for all Chinese, should be returned. They pointed to the original agreement of the German leasehold from 1898, which specified that there could be no "subletting" of the leasehold; therefore, Japan could not lay claim to the territory. They pointed out further that Chinese agreement to the Twenty-One Demands had been coerced and had not been ratified by the National Assembly. If the self-determination principle had held sway, there would have been no question that Shandong would be returned to China.

But the deck was stacked. After Japan had seized Shandong in 1914, its government proceeded to gain through secret treaty from each Allied power—Russia, Britain, France, Italy, and the United States—recognition of Japan's position and predominant interests in Shandong. When the matter would come before the Versailles Conference at the end of the war, Japan would thus be certain of Western support for its remaining in Shandong. These secret treaties underscore the flagrant nature of imperialist control and decision making: outsiders were deciding China's future without consultation with Chinese leaders. The disdain with which the imperialist powers dealt with the world's colonies and (in China's case) its semi-colonies did not bode well for the postwar world.

But there was more: the Chinese themselves contributed to the stacked deck. In 1918, Chinese leaders on their own volition signed a secret treaty with the Japanese. In exchange for a 20-million-yen loan, the Beijing government gave Japan rights in Shandong: to build two railroads, to station troops there, and to train and oversee Chinese train guards. China could thus not point to the Twenty-One Demands as being forced on them, for in this agreement the government had recognized Japan's special role in Shandong of its own free will—and all for 20 million yen.

Japan was also determined to have its way completely in Shandong. It had come to the conference with two objectives—holding on to Shandong and former German Pacific islands and getting a racial equality clause written into the Covenant of the League of Nations. The defeat of the racial equality clause was engineered mostly by countries in the British Empire, fearful of an international body's becoming involved in domestic issues of immigration and citizenship. Whatever the reason, it was a defeat for Japan, and the Japanese delegation began to make noises as if it just might walk out of the conference—as Italy had done a few days earlier. Faced with the specter of the collapse of the conference and believing that the Shandong issue could be taken up in a functioning League of Nations, Wilson caved in to Japanese pressure. But it is obvious that Japan had all the legal arguments and the political currents at the conference going its way. In China the reaction was swift and fierce, igniting a major political firestorm, which will be discussed in the next chapter.

The Washington Conference

In late 1921 and early 1922, nine world powers met in Washington, D.C.: the United States, Great Britain, France, Italy, Japan, China, the Netherlands, Belgium, and Portugal. The main goal of the Western nations, in light of predictions that war with Japan was looming in the future, was to try to limit Japan's freedom of action in military matters, specifically making efforts to halt a naval race and to limit fortifications of territory in the Pacific, East Asia, and Southeast Asia. Also included on the agenda were China and the permanent disposition of Shandong. The Chinese delegation basically called on the other nations to begin respecting China's rights, specifically its political independence and its territorial integrity; they also called for a review of the unequal treaty system.

The conference produced three treaties, the most important of which for China was the Nine-Power Treaty. It said all the right things: the nations "agreed to respect China's territorial integrity and political independence, to renounce further attempts to seek spheres of influence, to respect its neutrality in time of war, and to honor equal commercial opportunity for all."[29] But it was toothless; there was no way to enforce the agreement or to take action against a country that violated its terms. An agreement, mediated by Great Britain and the United States, was reached regarding Shandong. Japan would return Shandong but it would continue to keep economic interests, including maintaining property for use by Japanese living in the area, having Japanese serve as advisors in various businesses and industries, and having Japanese hold key leadership positions for five more years in the railroad that the Japanese had built from Qingdao to Jinan. According to the treaty, the Chinese would buy that railway from the Japanese using a Japanese loan. In short, though China received the lion's share of what it wanted, the Japanese could keep their fingers in the pie.

China did make other small, but in the historical context of its relationship with the West not insignificant, gains at the conference. Great Britain agreed to give up its leasehold of Weihaiwei, due to expire in any case in 1923. The powers allowed the Chinese to raise the customs tariff from 3.5 percent of the value of the goods to 5 percent; in addition, there was a stipulation that China would eventually gain complete control over the tariff and that extraterritoriality would be abolished. But no specifics were offered on how this would be accomplished and, even more important, when it would occur. Two years after the conference, Russia on its own gave up the right of extraterritoriality and Boxer indemnity payments even as it also allowed the return to China of its concessions in two cities.

Continuing Evidence of Imperialist Power

Despite these gains, the imperialist powers continued to appoint men to serve in Chinese governmental structures, specifically the Chinese Maritime Customs Service, the Salt Revenue, and the Chinese Postal Service. Foreign settlements in treaty ports, as well as concessions and leaseholds, still dotted the Chinese landscape, with foreigners continuing to make demands. Great Britain maintained its grip on Hong Kong, through which it had commanding control over trade throughout Southern China. Japan was becoming increasingly predominant in Manchuria, controlling the South Manchurian railway and its environs.

Three episodes point to the humiliating power that imperialists maintained, a threat that created, in the words of the inaugural address of President Xu Shichang on Double Ten in 1918, "a crisis of national existence."[30] After the 1911 revolution, foreign involvement in the Maritime Customs Service expanded from assessment and accounting to the very collection of the revenue. Furthermore, after collection, the revenue was deposited in foreign banks before it was disbursed for payment of Chinese debts; thus, foreigners were able to earn interest on what was really Chinese money. In addition, the foreign diplomatic corps in Beijing had been made "trustee" of the money before it was disbursed from foreign banks. Customs revenue was earmarked for interest payments on loans that had been secured on the basis of that customs revenue. During World War I with the growth of Chinese trade, the customs revenue collected was more than needed for the interest payments. The diplomatic corps began to control that surplus. In 1917, it let the surplus go to the Chinese government for general administrative expenses. But in 1918, it tightened the control noose around the Chinese government, telling the government specifically how the surplus could be spent. In other words, foreigners were telling the Chinese government how it must spend its own money.

In 1922 the French government, having seen the value of its Boxer indemnity decline because of depreciating French paper currency, demanded that the indemnity be paid in gold. Such a policy, if adopted, would be to the strong disadvantage of China, creating huge financial losses. In December the government referred the case to Wang Kemin, the governor of the Bank of China and former Chinese director of the Sino–French joint venture, the Banque Industrielle de Chine. After the French government tried to sweeten the deal by reopening the Banque, which had been closed a year earlier, Chinese financiers who had had deposits in the Banque lobbied the Chinese government to accept. With such pressure and with Wang's own past involvement with the bank, Wang's advice to the government—to pay the indemnity in gold—looked corrupt and antinationalistic: it was advice that was profitable for Wang and investors but harmful to China. It looked, in short, like evidence of the unholy alliance that existed between imperialist powers and the warlord governments. There was a huge public outcry. In Wang's home city of Hangzhou, a crowd attacked and destroyed his family's ancestral shrine, hacked the shrine's ancestral tablets into seven pieces, and threw them into West Lake, where they disappeared. Such was the depth of hatred for the warlord and imperialist collaboration.

In May 1923, bandits stopped an express train at Lincheng in Shandong province; they held up and kidnapped many on the train. Among the 200 taken captive were some two dozen foreigners, who were held for ransom for over a month. Foreigners and the foreign press in China reacted with outrage. A Shanghai paper noted that

> [f]ailure of the government to check banditry has made possible an occurrence which cannot but cause a feeling of deep humiliation to the people of a government that has a shadow of self-respect. That which is called a government in China … has not and is not functioning in a manner and to a degree worthy of the name.[31]

But words of condemnation were not enough for the foreign population. A note from the diplomatic corps of all the powers demanded not only penalties and indemnities, but that "Chinese railways [be put] under the powers' joint supervision in order to reform railway fiscal and management policies."[32] Such foreign oversight supposedly would prevent any future act of banditry or warlordism that would result in the seizure of money alotted to pay foreign debts. Imperialist powers saw a weak and divided China with an ineffectual government; in response, they insisted in a host of arenas that they knew what was best for China. In a frankly racist book, *What's Wrong with China?*, written in 1926, the author, Rodney Gilbert, gave his opinion: "What is really wrong with China and will continue to be wrong with her is that the Chinese are children, that their world is a child's make-believe."[33] What Gilbert and the powers did not know was that forces were underway, even as they spoke their imperialist and paternalistic platitudes, that would not only put the lie to Gilbert's opinion but would begin the eviction of imperialists from China altogether.

Notes

1 Quoted in Ernest P. Young, *The Presidency of Yuan Shih-k'ai* (Ann Arbor, MI: University of Michigan Press, 1977), p. 51.
2 Ibid., p. 243.
3 R. Keith Schoppa, "Politics and Society in [Zhejiang], 1907–1927: Elite Power, Social Control, and the Making of a Province," doctoral dissertation, University of Michigan, 1975, pp. 155–6.
4 Ernest P. Young, "Politics in the Aftermath of Revolution: The Era of Yuan Shih-k'ai, 1912–1916," in *The Cambridge History of China, Vol. 12, Part 1*, ed. John K. Fairbank (Cambridge, UK: Cambridge University Press, 1983), p. 213.
5 Quoted in Young, *The Presidency of Yuan Shih-k'ai*, p. 51.
6 https://en.wikipedia.org/Lin_Zongsu_.
7 Wang Zheng, *Women in the Chinese Enlightenment: Oral and Textual Histories* (Berkeley, CA: University of California Press, 1999), p. 49.
8 Quoted in ibid., p. 61.
9 Ibid.
10 David Strand, *The Unfinished Republic: Leading by Word and Deed in Modern China* (Berkeley, CA: University of California Press, 2011), p. 40.
11 Young, *The Presidency of Yuan Shih-k'ai*, p. 118.

12 Young, "Politics in the Aftermath of Revolution," p. 242.

13 Ibid., p. 244.

14 Ibid., p. 246.

15 See Marie-Claire Bergère, *The Golden Age of the Chinese Bourgeoisie, 1911–1937*, trans. Janet Lloyd (Cambridge, UK: Cambridge University Press, 1990).

16 Quoted in R. Keith Schoppa, *Blood Road: The Mystery of Shen Dingyi in Revolutionary China* (Berkeley, CA: University of California Press, 1995), p. 53.

17 Marie-Claire Bergère, "The Chinese Bourgeoisie," in *The Cambridge History of China, Vol. 12, Part 1*, ed. John K. Fairbank (Cambridge, UK: Cambridge University Press, 1983), p. 745.

18 R. Keith Schoppa, *Chinese Elites and Political Change* (Cambridge, MA: Harvard University Press, 1982), p. 65.

19 Quoted in Marie-Claire Bergère, "The Role of the Bourgeoisie," in *China in Revolution, The First Phase, 1900–1913*, ed. Mary Clabaugh Wright (New Haven, CT: Yale University Press, 1968), p. 268.

20 Schoppa, *Chinese Elites and Political Change*, p. 95. The opinion came from elites in Fenghua county in Zhejiang province.

21 Andrew J. Nathan, *Peking Politics, 1918–1923* (Berkeley, CA: University of California Press, 1976), p. 220.

22 Howard L. Boorman, ed., *Biographical Dictionary of Republican China* (New York: Columbia University Press, 1970), Vol. 1, p. 124.

23 Cited in James Sheridan, *Chinese Warlord* (Stanford, CA: Stanford University Press, 1966), p. 21.

24 The two quotations are in James E. Sheridan, *China in Disintegration* (New York: Free Press, 1975), p. 91.

25 Cited in Sheridan, *Chinese Warlord*, p. 26.

26 Quoted in Jonathan Spence, *Chinese Roundabout* (New York: W.W. Norton, 1992), p. 64.

27 Quoted in Vera Schwarcz, *The Chinese Enlightenment* (Berkeley, CA: University of California Press, 1986), p. 157.

28 Cited in Jonathan Spence, *The Gate of Heavenly Peace* (New York: Viking, 1981), p. 197.

29 Immanuel C.Y. Hsu, *The Rise of Modern China*, 6th ed. (New York: Oxford University Press, 2000), p. 532.

30 Nathan, *Peking Politics*, p. 129.

31 Quoted in John Fitzgerald, *Awakening China* (Berkeley, CA: University of California Press, 1996), p. 142.

32 Nathan, *Peking Politics*, p. 214, n. 54.

33 Quoted in Fitzgerald, *Awakening China*, p. 140.

Suggestions for Further Reading

Cochran. Sherman, ed. *Inventing Nanjing Road: Commercial Culture in Shanghai, 1900–1945* (Ithaca, NY: Cornell University East Asian Program, 2000). Seven essays look at a variety of aspects of commercial culture in the metropolis, including business, entertainment, industry (film and milk), advertising, and the housing market.

Koll, Elisabeth. *From Cotton Mill to Business Empire: The Emergence of Regional Enterprises in Modern China* (Cambridge, MA: Harvard University Press, 2003). This history of the Dasheng Cotton Mill in the Lower Yangzi region opens a discussion of the evolution of business practices shaping the Chinese corporation to the present.

McCord, Edward A. *The Power of the Gun: The Emergence of Modern Chinese Warlordism* (Berkeley, CA: University of California Press, 1993). A revisionist study that examines the process by which local military forces became political players in larger theaters of action as civilian politicians and bureaucrats relied on them to settle political disputes.

Schoppa, R. Keith. *Song Full of Tears* (Boulder, CO: Westview Press, 2002). This study of a lake and its surrounding society over many centuries reveals the effects of the "golden age" of capitalism from the 1910s to the late 1930s on the lake, with its plague of "developers."

Young, Ernest P. *The Presidency of Yuan Shih-k'ai: Liberalism and Dictatorship in Early Republican China* (Ann Arbor, MI: University of Michigan Press, 1977). The best biographical treatment of the frequently castigated first president of the Republic of China.

9

Constructing a New Cultural Identity
The May Fourth Movement

A story from the late Qing:

> Chaste Woman Ni ... at the age of seventeen [was] married to Ni Dechang. ... After three months she was widowed and afterwards unceasingly and with great care served her parents-in-law. After eight years, her parents-in-law, because of the family's poverty, sought to marry her. ... The day before the marriage they told Woman Ni. She pretended to agree. ... At midnight she jumped into the river and died. ... The next year, an edict of imperial praise adorned the gate of this family.[1]

A story from 1919:

> Miss Zhao of Nanyang Street in Changsha, Hunan, was unwillingly betrothed by her parents to a Mr. Wu. On her wedding day, as she was being carried to the groom's home in a sedan chair, the bride, dressed in festive red, pulled out a dagger hidden in the chair and slit her throat.

Though studies have shown that at least elite women in the mid- and late-Qing dynasty structured their own spheres of assertiveness and influence, most Chinese women labored in the centuries-old social hierarchy that placed them near its bottom. That reality and those of the others who were socially subordinated came center stage in a cultural revolution that swept over macroregional cores and into the peripheries in the late 1910s and early 1920s. Called the May Fourth Movement, it was one of the turning points in China's modern history, having cultural, social, and political dimensions. If the abolition of the civil service examination and the monarchy brought the destruction of the traditional political and social structures, the May Fourth Movement struck a paralyzing blow at traditional cultural norms and structures. In one of Lu Xun's most famous stories, "The Diary of a Madman," an official, suffering from an obsessive paranoid belief that everyone wants to kill and eat him, discovers an old history book:

> my history has no chronology and scrawled over each page are the words: "Virtue and Morality." Since I could not sleep anyway, I read intently half the night, until I began to see words between the lines, the whole book being filled with the two words—"Eat people."[2]

This was a savage indictment of traditional Chinese society—that it parroted the proper Confucian pieties, which masked the reality that Confucian values destroyed human lives by crushing them beneath a social hierarchy of superiors.

Lu desperately believed that something had to be done to awaken the Chinese to what he saw as the destructiveness of traditional culture. Personally that meant a career change for him from medicine to writing. For the Chinese people as a whole, it was something more risky. Lu captured both the danger and the opportunity in one of his strongest metaphors:

> Imagine an iron house without windows, absolutely indestructible, with many people fast asleep inside who will soon die of suffocation. But you know since they will die in their sleep, they will not feel the pain of death. Now if you cry aloud to wake a few of the lighter sleepers, making those unfortunate few suffer the agony of irrevocable death, do you think you are doing them a good turn? But if a few awake, you can't say there is no hope of destroying the iron house.[3]

DESTROYING THE CONFUCIAN STRAITJACKET: TARGETING WOMEN AND THE FAMILY

Although Confucianism as an ideology had officially ended with the abolition of the examination system, it retained its stranglehold on social relationships and ethics in Chinese society. In family life, the ancient Confucian social bonds emphasizing the importance of age and maleness retained their sway, elevating the status and power of parents over children and of men over women. Destroying the traditional system and attempting to define a new cultural base and direction was at the center of the New Culture Movement. The most influential vehicle for the expression of contempt for the old and hope for the new was the journal *New Youth*. Established in 1915, it was edited by Chen Duxiu, a traditional degree-holder, returned-student from Japan and France, and participant in the 1911 revolution. With a circulation of up to 16,000 copies, the journal provided a forum where students in all parts of the country could discuss issues.

In the lead essay of *New Youth*, "Call to Youth," Chen championed the young as China's saviors:

> The Chinese compliment others by saying, "He acts like an old man while still young." Englishmen and Americans encourage one another by saying, "Keep young while growing old." Such is one respect in which the different ways of thought of the East and West are manifested. Youth is like early spring, like the rising sun, like trees and grass in bud, like a newly sharpened blade. It is the most valuable period of life. The function of youth in society is the same as that of a fresh and vital cell in a human body. In the processes of metabolism, the old and rotten are incessantly eliminated to be replaced by the fresh and living.[4]

Those who revere mostly the past, as Chinese had done into the twentieth century, would, in Chen's estimation, "be lodged in the dark ditches fit only for slaves, cattle, and horses." In practical terms, pitting youth against age meant targeting filial piety in its various aspects. In part, it meant eliminating ancestor reverence as it had traditionally been practiced. Ancestors and the continuing roles they supposedly might play in people's lives cast a conservative shroud over the living. One did not dare act to bring shame upon the family, itself a gift of the ancestors. Thus, the Hangzhou students who destroyed banker Wang Kemin's ancestral tablets were making a strong statement not only against the marriage of imperialists and warlords but also one of considerable contempt for this Chinese tradition.

But in the present for most young Chinese, targeting filial piety meant targeting the father and mother, who had immense control over their children's lives—from career decisions to marriage to lifestyle patterns. These years saw countless rebellions of young Chinese against their fathers in particular. Sons disregarded parental wishes and even outright orders regarding various life decisions. In 1919, a young man from Zhejiang province, Shi Cuntong, wrote an article, "Against Filial Piety," attacking the coerciveness of this traditional value. In another essay, Shi described how he had personally felt the arbitrariness and domination of his father. "My family life was like hell to me. ... I suffered enormously in a home of utter darkness, abused by an ignorant father of vile temper. My father often beat me up for no good reason."[5] In "Against Filial Piety," Shi claimed that filial piety was the same as "the virtue required of a slave" and that "[t]o invoke the imperatives of filial piety these days is for the elders to demand absolute obedience from the younger generation."[6] A writer noted the widespread rebellion against the family system:

> I know a young man who abandoned his own name and substituted the title "He-you-I." Later ... I met ... a friend of mine accompanied by a young girl. ... "May I ask your family name?" I asked her. She stared at me and screamed, "I don't have any family name!" There were also people who wrote letters to their fathers, saying, "From a certain date on, I will not recognize you as my father. We are all friends, and equal."[7]

The most popular novel of the 1930s, Ba Jin's melodramatic *Family*, looked at the May Fourth generation and described the struggles of three brothers against the patriarchal extended family system and its old traditions upheld by old men.

Women were also victims in Ba Jin's novel, but in Chinese society they were in a more oppressed state than men, who, after all, could actually "call the shots." A reminder: as in the late Qing and the New Culture period, the story of "the Chinese woman and her identification with the nation mired in oppressive tradition entailed forgetting that elite women had been educated for centuries, or disregarding or trivializing their literary accomplishments."[8] Traditionally, girls in general were seen by non-elite families as burdens. Female infanticide was sometimes practiced, especially by the poor. Girls were provided for by their natal families until they were sent off to be married and then perhaps never seen again. Children were betrothed by matchmakers for the benefit of families, not to satisfy the desires of individuals; sometimes the result, as with Miss Zhao above, was devastating. If one's fiancé died before marriage or if one's husband died early, the unmarried or widowed woman should remain forever chaste, choosing death rather than risk becoming intimately involved once again. In addition to gaining praise from the emperor, parents whose daughters committed suicide might erect memorial arches for their chaste dead daughter. Some parents were known to pressure their daughters to kill themselves in order to reap praise from the community.

In one of Lu Xun's most famous short stories, "The New Year's Sacrifice," a poor widow, known only as Xiang Lin's wife, was forced to remarry against her will. She did so literally kicking and screaming because of the dominant concern about female chastity grounded deeply in Confucian culture. When her second husband died as well, Xiang Lin's wife was tortured by the fear that in the afterlife she would have to be split in two because she had had two husbands. Some young women in this period were also forbidden by their mothers-in-law to unbind their feet or even to attend school. A young woman in the distant interior of Gansu province threw herself down a well rather than deal with a mother-in-law who forbade her to unbind her feet. Suicide rates tell the tragic story: Among Chinese women, they were highest among those in their late teens and twenties; in the early twentieth century, suicide rates of women in this age group were more than double the rates in Japan and ten times more than those in Sweden. The power of "Confucius and sons" was literally that of life and death.

In the newness of greater liberation from the family system, some women were facing new choices quite openly, choices that reflected concerns of the New Culture Movement itself. An example is the title character in "Miss Sophie's Diary," the best-known story of China's most famous twentieth-century female author, Ding Ling. Sophie was a "modern girl" whose affections were divided between two men. Sophie was more attracted to the handsome, rakish Singapore playboy, but she felt guilty about her feelings. The story raised issues about the role that women were to play in the new culture (Sophie was quite sexually aggressive) and the effects that such actions had on women's psyches. Hear her out:

> I shouldn't be so open with so handsome a man and make myself look cheap. But I love him. … It seems to me no reason why I shouldn't be allowed to give him a hundred kisses provided nobody else is harmed. … Tonight I've gone completely crazy. … My heart feels as if it's being gnawed by hordes of mice, or as if a brazier were burning inside it. If only I could smash everything or rush wildly out into the night. I can't control the surges of wild emotion.[9]

FIGURE 9.1   This woodblock print of Xiang Lin's wife from Lu Xun's "The New Year's Sacrifice" expresses well in its starkness the plight of many women in traditional Chinese society.
Source: Courtesy of the Library of Congress.

With the collapse of former "established truths" and institutions and with the rise of new social and political alternatives, there should be little surprise that slogans such as "Down with Confucius and sons" began to fill newspapers and journals and to echo in street demonstrations.[10] Editor Chen of *New Youth* led the way: "Emancipation means freeing oneself from the bondage of slavery, [and it should be clear that] loyalty, filial piety, chastity, and righteousness are a slavish morality."[11] As a sign of the times, in Xiaoshan county, Zhejiang province, the characters on an arched memorial—"Respect chaste women and filial sons"—were blotted out and replaced with new ones: "Long live women's liberation." Also added was a couplet that reminds one of Lu Xun's madman:

> Beyond doubt in the Twenty-four Histories are written the ethical teachings of those who eat people.
> Beneath this memorial arch there are the ghosts of I don't know how many crushed women who have been wronged.[12]

Basically, after years of being weighted down by the crushing familial hierarchy above them, women wanted control of their lives. In 1918, Hu Shi served as the editor of a *New Youth* special edition on "Ibsenism," the thought and dramas of Norway's great realistic playwright. In focus was the character Nora in *A Doll's House*, translated into Chinese as *Nuola* (Nora). Caught in a rigidly patriarchal family system and in a situation where her husband won't forgive her for a crime she has committed in secret, Nora abandoned her family, telling her husband, "I am a human being, the same as you. No matter what, I will try my best to be a human being." The aura of Nora spread like wildfire among educated young Chinese women: Nora became a beacon for women who tried to seize control of their lives and act courageously in situations, who, in short, fought vigorously to be independent human beings.[13]

But not all women were Noras nor were they all stiflingly oppressed, even to the point of suicide. There were innumerable types of women with qualitatively different experiences in different contexts that produced neither of these extremes. A case in point is Jian Xianren, born in Cili, Hunan in April 1909 to an intelligent father who studied handicrafts, specifically mastering the art of batik, and to an illiterate mother. Her father was financially successful in opening several shops and buying farmland, while Xianren noted that her mother excelled in housework and (in a role we have seen before with literate wives) in managing the family business. The parents held education in high regard for both boys and girls and enrolled Xianren and her brother Xianwei (two years older) in a private school to study classical Chinese works by rote. In 1920 they entered a new-style single-sex upper primary school whose teachers were deeply immersed in the New Culture movement. One teacher cried when she described China's great potential gutted by imperialist depredations. A history teacher encouraged the female students: "Don't think that you will not accomplish anything because you are girls. In ancient times there were women warriors and women scientists. We have Chinese national heroines like Qiu Jin."[14] When Xianren graduated from the upper primary in 1926 and was primed to continue her education, her mother asked her to stay at home to care for her sick grandmother. Jianren did not throw a tantrum or follow Nora's lead and stalk out, but still showed her respect and filial piety by agreeing to do so. She said there was no decision because she did what she was expected to do. Xianwei, who continued his education, sent letters home to Xianren filled with progressive ideas he was imbibing, letters that excited her about the future. Xianren's story will continue in subsequent chapters.

Roughly between 1917 and 1921, intellectual discussion and emphasis on individualism and achieving individual goals reached its highest point *at any time* in modern China's history. The absence of a powerful state structure and the wide-open search for a new social, political, and ideological Way created a liberating context for the young. But most important was the rebellion of youths, both male and female, against the cultural shackles of patriarchy and family authority. Liberation from that system, when it came, promised to bring individual emancipation, the expression of individual will, and the realization of individual desires.

LANGUAGE AND LABORATORIES FOR A NEW CULTURE

The basic issue that became so politicized during the People's Republic of China—the function of art and artists in a developing state—was already significant during the New Culture Movement. It was framed as a disagreement between those who championed "art for art's sake" and those who supported "art for life's sake." These are, of course, polar views. Many artists would have opted for something in between, that is, art created with exacting artistic values but relating in some way to the context in which the artist lived. Perhaps the best example of art for art's sake during the Republic was the so-called "mandarin duck and butterfly school" in the period from 1910 to the 1930s. This was escapist and sensationalistic literature—novels and short stories—that appealed to middle- and lower-class persons in urban settings. Composed mainly of love stories, detective tales, and knight-errant novels, this huge body of work (in these years, output totaled 2,215 novels and filled 113 magazines and 49 newspapers) can best be described as lowbrow urban popular fiction.

Though most, if not all, of Lu Xun's works were powerful expressions of art for life's sake, perhaps the story providing the greatest contrast to the mandarin duck and butterfly school was his longest story, "The True Story of Ah Q." In it, Lu describes a social loser and the society he inhabits at the time of the 1911 revolution. Besides painting a scathing portrait of that revolution as empty and meaningless, Lu sketches a Chinese political culture that is unremittingly bleak and marked by self-delusion, mean-spiritedness, crassness, and a slave mentality.

Before 1917, *New Youth* was written in classical or literary Chinese, like all printed materials, whether books, newspapers, or journals. The classical style was difficult: it valued conciseness, often omitting subjects and objects; it was marked by characters that were particles, giving the sentence a tone or a particular turn; and it used no punctuation. Traditional scholars had believed that anyone intelligent enough to read the classical language should be intelligent enough to know how to punctuate it. But because of the conciseness, the particles, and the lack of punctuation, it was not only difficult but often very ambiguous. It was thus a great obstacle to increased literacy among the Chinese masses. Because the development of a modern Chinese nation-state required a more literate public, language reform was crucial. In addition, constructing a new political and social culture necessitated a new language; it was impossible to construct a new culture using a language intimately connected to and expressive of the old culture of eating people. In Lu Xun's story of the madman, the short opening segment, which tells of the madman's "recovery" and his return to a people-eating bureaucratic position, is written in classical Chinese, whereas the diary itself, which the reader comes to see is not that of a madman but of one enlightened, is written in the vernacular.

When Chen chose to use the vernacular, or *baihua*, in *New Youth* in 1917, one of its strongest proponents was Hu Shi. Hu had received his undergraduate degree at Cornell University and his doctorate from Columbia University, studying there with the famous pragmatist philosopher John Dewey. During his years at Cornell, he had written about the ability of *baihua* to bring about a literary revolution. He later wrote,

> A dead language can never produce a living literature; if a living literature is to be produced, there must be a living tool. ... We must first of all elevate this [vernacular] tool. ... Only with a new tool can we talk about such other aspects as new ideas and new spirit.[15]

This literary revolution was slowly successful. Not only did *New Youth* publish in the vernacular, but so did all new literary magazines. In 1921 the Ministry of Education announced that from that point, all texts used in primary schools would be published in the vernacular. There were some protests, but they were belated and lacked any compelling force. The literary revolution joined the anti-Confucian cultural revolution as the centerpiece of the New Culture Movement. The speed of monumental change in the first years of the twentieth century was nothing short of breathtaking: within about a dozen years, the examination system and the monarchy had been abolished, the traditional language relegated to a museum piece, and traditional culture trashed.

Chen Duxiu and Hu Shi became colleagues at Beijing University, which became one of the main laboratories of the New Culture Movement. When it was established in 1898 as Imperial University, its students were high-ranking officials and degree-holders. It was renamed the National University of Beijing in 1912. It did not have a reputation as a serious institution of study or research; rather, an education there was seen as a ticket to a governmental bureaucratic position. Professors were judged by their official rank, not their teaching ability, and were called "your excellencies." The campus lifestyles of both professors and students featured gambling and whoring; among the university's nicknames, as indications of the nature and reputation of the institution, were "the Gambling Den" and "the Fountainhead of Ribaldry and Bawdiness."

In 1916, Cai Yuanpei was appointed chancellor of the school. Cai, whom one scholar has called the "moral leader of the new intelligentsia and one of the greatest educators and liberals in modern China," held the highest degree under the traditional examination system and had spent substantial time studying in both Germany and France. He was determined to change the university's reputation and its reality. He believed that if a new language could form the basis for a new culture that was to be forged by the young, then Beijing University should be the central laboratory where that culture should be shaped.

In revamping the university, Cai insisted on three points. First, the purpose of the university was academic research, which had as its crucial goal the creation of a new culture; such research, Cai believed, should be critical of Western civilization and traditional Chinese civilization alike. Second, students should get rid of the idea that a diploma from Beijing University was their ticket to a job; the university, he argued, was not simply a replacement for the old examination system. Third, if the university was a laboratory in which to chart a new civilization, there had to be complete academic freedom. Divergent ideas had to be expressed openly and sincerely so that the new Chinese Way could be found. Deliberation, study, and debate should lead to the new Way. Cai thus brought together university scholars of all intellectual and political stripes—from reactionaries on the right to radicals on the left—to discuss possibilities for the new China, to debate ideas about the form and shape of China's modern state, and to argue and contend in an atmosphere of unfettered academic freedom. A Chinese writer noted that

> all the most ... gifted among the younger members of the Chinese intelligentsia flocked to take a place under his leadership. The result was the creation, within a few years, of an incredibly productive intellectual life, probably unparalleled in the academic history of the world.[16]

Among faculty and students trying to devise a blueprint for modern China, the excitement was electric.

Although the phrase came to be linked with a policy of Mao Zedong in the 1950s, the New Culture Movement, extending into the mid-1920s, was an era when "a hundred schools of thought" contended. It was essentially an intellectual revolution. In classrooms and debating halls, in study societies and literary organizations, in restaurants and taverns, in several hundred new newspapers and journals, men and women, old and young met and contended, their ideas set forth to battle antagonistic thoughts, to complement similar strategies, to challenge the status quo, and to propose remedies for the future. Monarchists, anarchists, socialists, Christians, atheists, Buddhists, Confucianists, anti-Confucianists, Marxists, pacifists, pragmatists, scientists, metaphysicists, poets—the list could go on—all debated the potential viability and validity of new values.

The key word was "new," the adjective that was used to modify various nouns to produce the names of many magazines: *Youth, Tide, Life, Literature and Art, Society, Epoch, Tides of Zhejiang.* The sense of having entered a new historical epoch where people had to act in new ways was pervasive among those involved in the culture debates. In an essay called "The Year 1916," Chen Duxiu rhapsodized:

> The epoch in which you are living, what epoch is this? ... To live in the present world, you must raise your head and proudly call yourself a person of the 20th century and not confine yourself to following the 19th. For the evolution of human civilization is replacing the old with the new, like a river flowing on, an arrow flying away, constantly continuing and constantly changing.[17]

During the late 1910s and early 1920s, the spirit and excitement of the intellectual quest were enhanced by lecture tours of foreigners with divergent intellectual positions. Hu Shi's Columbia University professor and adviser, John Dewey, spent 1919 and 1920 living and lecturing in China, spreading his message of pragmatism in eleven provinces; editors of newspapers and journals eagerly published his lectures. In 1921 and 1922, the British philosopher Bertrand Russell lectured widely not only on his intellectual interest in mathematical logic but also on pacifism, a subject that in the violent warlord period must have had hundreds of eager listeners. In 1922, Margaret Sanger, feminist and birth control advocate, lectured at Beijing University (with Hu Shi interpreting) on "The What and How of Birth Control"; her ideas, which fed into the period's emphasis on women's liberation, also stirred the first Chinese interest in the issue of birth control. The visit of the Indian Nobel laureate Rabindranath Tagore in 1924 touched off a heated debate because of his message praising Asian cultures and warning about importing too much Western civilization. Such foreign lectures served to validate some of the new ideas emerging in the intellectual debates and to stimulate more ideas. Perhaps most important, the lectures and their coverage in the press brought greater and greater numbers of people into the debates.

Despite the extolling of the East by Tagore and his supporters, there were louder supportive calls for two "men" whose backgrounds were clearly in the West and whose names became watchwords at the time and a siren song in China throughout much of the twentieth century. They were Mr. De and Mr. Sai. Mr. De(mocracy) became the rallying cry of those angered and humiliated by the wretched state of the Chinese state, over which warlords and their corrupt politician and bureaucratic allies had run roughshod. Even though the memory of the brief burst of democracy in 1912 and 1913 was fading, the potential for democracy seemed heightened by the victory of the "democratic" Allied powers in World War I and by the 1917 Bolshevik Revolution in Russia.

Mr. Sai (Science) was leading the march into the modern world. He dispelled the darkness of ignorance and superstition. Since whatever was "scientific" seemed progressive, the essential route to achieve the best for the future of the individual and the nation was the scientific road. A few intellectuals, such as Liang Qichao, condemned the West's use of science for the construction of sophisticated weapons of destruction during World War I. But the vast majority of Chinese saw science as a panacea for the country's ills. The emphasis on science was less on pure research as an academic discipline than on its impact on popular thinking—science was the very essence of the meaning of "modern." Thus, when Shanghai's Commercial Press published a four-volume collection of "scientific" subjects, the table of contents read like a blend of serious scientific topics and Ripley's Believe It or Not: "The Structure of the Atom," "Einstein's Theory of Light and Energy," "The Unimaginable New Discoveries in Astrology," "Strange Reptiles," "Four-Legged Birds," "New Cures for Tuberculosis," and "Bicycles on Water." Science at this stage, in short, often took the form of undisciplined knowledge.

THE MAY FOURTH INCIDENT AND ITS AFTERMATH

The New Culture Movement is part of what is generally known as the May Fourth Movement, an amorphous range of political and cultural activities that can be dated from the founding of *New Youth* in 1915 to roughly 1923 or 1924 and that, taken together, can be considered a cultural revolution. It takes its name from a primarily student demonstration in Beijing on May 4, 1919, an incident fueled by nationalistic fervor that substantially changed the direction of the whole cultural revolution movement. Prompted by the Allied decision to allow the Japanese to retain control of Shandong, the incident was the beginning of a marked increase in the politicization and political involvement of students.

A year before, on May 21, 1918, about 2,000 students from a number of Beijing colleges had joined in a protest demonstration against a series of agreements that China was signing with Japan—the contents of which were largely kept secret because of what Chinese leaders were willing to give up to Japan (like the right to station troops in northern Manchuria and Inner Mongolia). They marched to the office of China's president to ask for both the content and the annulment of the treaties. President Feng received thirteen students, who trustingly accepted his word that nothing would be done to harm China's interests. Similar demonstrations took place in Shanghai, Fuzhou, and Tianjin. Although the protests died down quickly, they were, in effect, rehearsals for the May Fourth incident.

By May 1919, of the 2,228 students at Beijing University, an estimated 20 percent, or about 450, were politically active. When word came about the decision at Versailles, the activists, who were members of a number of student organizations, met to plan a demonstration for May 7, the anniversary of the signing of the Twenty-One Demands. However, rumors and bitter anger about the turn of events led students to move the demonstration up to May 4. Some students were so outraged that they were moved to write anti-Japanese denunciations in blood on the walls of university dormitories and lunchrooms. Supported by faculty, about 3,000 students from thirteen universities and colleges massed at the Gate of Heavenly Peace in front of the Forbidden City. Government representatives tried to end the protest, but to no avail. A manifesto "of all the students of Beijing," distributed at the demonstration, read in part,

> This is the last chance for China in her life and death struggle. Today we swear two solemn oaths with all our countrymen: (1) China's territory may be conquered, but it cannot be given away; (2) the Chinese people may be massacred, but they will not surrender.[18]

Once the students left the square to march to the home of one of three Chinese officials who were seen as Japanese collaborators, the orderliness of the protest broke down. Shouting "The traitors! The traitors!" they invaded his house and, before torching it, smashed all the furniture. One of the other suspected collaborators was seized and beaten. Fighting lasted for several hours, at the end of which thirty-two students were arrested. After the arrests, the driving goal of the other students was to get the release of their fellow demonstrators. To accomplish this, students went on strike; protest telegrams poured in from around the nation. On May 5, Beijing students established a citywide Student Union bringing together students from middle and high schools with those from colleges and universities; female students were for the first time specifically included.

Ironically, after the arrested students were released on May 7 and the student strike was canceled, tensions steadily escalated. The government issued new restrictions on all further student meetings and protests; in addition, Cai Yuanpei was forced to resign as Beijing University's chancellor. Almost immediately, more students were arrested. Professors and teachers formed their own alliance. Word came that a pro-warlord official had been named to head the Ministry of Education and that the government was determined to crack down on student organizations. Then on May 19, the Student Union declared a general strike, demanding, among other things, that China's president refuse to sign the Versailles Treaty, punish the allegedly pro-Japanese traitor-officials, and restore Cai to his position.

The next two weeks saw the government policy toward the students waver from harsh to lenient; the harsh periods were due mostly to Japanese pressure on the government to crush anti-Japanese demonstrations. Students continued their strike and set out in clusters all over Beijing to give impromptu anti-Japanese lectures on street corners. John Dewey reported on June 4, "We saw students making speeches this morning about eleven, ... and heard later they had been arrested. ... There are about ten thousand striking in Beijing alone."[19] By June 4 (a date that seventy years later would feature a bloody massacre of citizens on these same streets), over 1,100 students had been arrested. On June 5, more than 1,000 female students from the Beijing area, in unprecedented action, marched to the presidential palace demanding the release of the prisoners and freedom of speech.

FIGURE 9.2   These demonstrators at the Gate of Heavenly Peace on May 4, 1919, carry placards denouncing Chinese officials who were seen as collaborating with the Japanese.
Source: Courtesy of the Kautz family and YMCA Archives.

By this time, what was going on in Beijing was simply part of a larger nationwide protest movement. The Beijing Student Union served as a prototype for similar organizations in cities such as Shanghai, Wuhan, and Tianjin and ultimately for a Student Union of the Republic of China, established in June. Students served as the yeast, as it were, for a rising nationalistic ferment. At Shanghai especially, patriotic sentiment was strong. The Shanghai Student Union issued the following rationale for their actions:

> Throughout the world, like the voice of a prophet, has gone the word of Woodrow Wilson, strengthening the weak and giving courage to the struggling. And the Chinese have listened, and they too have heard. … They have been told that in the dispensation which is to be made after the war, unmilitaristic nations like China would have an opportunity to develop their culture, their industry, their civilization unhampered. They have been told that secret covenants and forced agreements would not be recognized. They looked for the dawn of this new era; but no sun rose for China. Even the cradle of the nation was stolen.[20]

Ten thousand attempted to march in a demonstration in the city on May 7. The Shanghai Student Union launched a boycott against Japanese goods. Students sent from Beijing reported on government repression in the capital and further fired up the anger of Shanghainese. Whereas the Beijing unrest had continued to center on teachers and students, in Shanghai by late May the nationalistic fever had spread to businessmen, merchants, and laborers. The demonstrations and boycott culminated in a general strike that began on June 5. Its goal: to try to force the Chinese delegation at Versailles to refuse to sign the peace treaty. The trump card of the Shanghai general strike was that the city was the economic heart of the Republic of China and that a long general strike could bring an already weak economy to its knees. Bankers warned the government that "the financial market cannot be maintained tomorrow if the problem is not solved today."

On June 6, industrial workers joined the strike, first printers, then textile workers, and, most important, streetcar workers, whose participation paralyzed the city. The extent of the rising tide of nationalism can be seen in the fact that even the notorious underworld organizations, the Green and Red gangs, ordered their members not to disrupt the strike. The strike continued until June 12, when it was learned that the three offending pro-Japanese officials had been dismissed. Demonstrations continued to punctuate city life until the announcement came on July 2 that the delegation at Versailles had refused to sign the treaty.

Significant as that point was—that the Chinese delegation was asserting that China was a nation in a forceful way—even more important on the domestic front was that political victory had gone to the people through the efforts of the student unions and those involved in the general strike. In cities, the movement was really a mass protest by students, the urban professional class (journalists, teachers, doctors, lawyers, and engineers), leaders and managers of business and industry, shopkeepers, and the urban working class. Acting together, they had forced the government to change its positions, not only to oust the officials whom it had in the beginning strongly supported but also to refuse to sign the Versailles Treaty.

POLITICAL CHANGE FIRST: CULTURAL CHANGE WILL FOLLOW

Such a positive result of direct, in-your-face political action, from the perspective of patriotic Chinese, had crucial implications for the direction of the May Fourth Movement. Two main camps began to emerge in what would become a struggle over the direction of the movement and of

China itself. Some began to point to the events in the spring and summer of 1919 as evidence of what could be accomplished through direct political action. In order to change China, they argued, why not continue this kind of political action? How, they asked, can we build a modern Chinese culture (a task that, even if possible, would have to take generations) at a time when the people who hold political power have the power to jail and even shoot down those who are offering alternatives to present policies? First, they asserted, we must alter the political system to make it more conducive to other modern changes. Direct, even violent, political action must become the central focus of activity, the main tool for revolutionary change. A leading spokesman for this view was Chen Duxiu, *New Youth* editor and dean of the School of Letters at Beijing University.

Political tools that received increasing attention for their potential to deal with China's problems were Marxism and, after the success of the Bolsheviks in 1917, Leninism. One of the early converts to Marxist-Leninist thought was Li Dazhao. Brought to Beijing University by Cai Yuanpei to serve as head of the university library, Li eventually taught history, political science, and economics. On the editorial board of *New Youth*, he became one of the most influential and popular faculty figures at the university; he was always ready to talk with students about everything from personal problems to politics. Li's first attraction to Marxism-Leninism may have been a case of "nothing succeeds like success," in this case the success of Marxism-Leninism in the Russian Revolution. A year after the Bolshevik success, he commemorated the anniversary in *New Youth* with an essay, "The Victory of Bolshevism." Six months later, in May 1919, he devoted a complete issue of the journal to articles on Marxism.

By late 1919, he had become not only a supporter of its aims but also a true believer in its main doctrines. The summer of 1920 began to see the formation of study societies that would become the building blocks for political organizations. In Beijing, Li established the Society for the Study of Marxism, at whose meetings he and other faculty lectured on Marxism. Mao Zedong, a student whom Li had befriended at Beijing University by finding him a job in the library, returned to his home in Hunan province to form such a study group. Chen Duxiu, who had been imprisoned briefly in the aftermath of the May Fourth incident and who had moved to Shanghai in 1919, was one of eleven intellectuals and journalists who formed a Marxist Study Society in that city to discuss socialism and Marxism. In their meetings, punctuated by personal animosity and ideological disagreements, they discussed news that they exchanged with the Beijing study group and a new one in Guangzhou, prepared for the expansion of propaganda work, and talked about the development of a more permanent organization. These organizations were the forerunners of the Chinese Communist Party.

In the twenty-first century, when Communism in most areas of the world had collapsed following its miserable record throughout the twentieth century, it may seem hard to understand the appeals of Marxism-Leninism to the Chinese of the early 1920s. On the most basic level, the adage that nothing succeeds like success provides one answer: this ideology had been tried and was successful in providing the base for overthrowing autocratic rule in Russia. Chinese intellectuals also felt strongly inclined to the Soviet model after the apparently generous 1919 offer by the Soviet government in the Karakhan Declaration. This declaration promised to return all the privileges that the czars had won in unequal treaties as well as to renounce Russia's share of the Boxer indemnity. These acts clearly marked the Soviet Union as a cut above the other imperialists who at the Versailles Conference had so recently thumbed their noses at China and its plight.

Then there was the intellectual attractiveness of Marxism for the May Fourth generation: above all, it was scientific. Marx's idea of historical materialism explained history and the chief dynamic of historical development: history moves through stages—from slave to feudal to capitalist to socialist to Communist, propelled from stage to stage by classes struggling for control of the means of production. Such an explanation offered a vision of where a particular society was in its march forward in revolutionary progress toward the Communist utopia. Leninism explained China's plight as a semi-colony of the imperialist powers, arguing that for Western capitalism to survive, Western nations had to develop empires with raw materials and cheap labor. Lenin claimed that, cut off from the support of their colonies, Western capitalism would wither. Leninism further provided the all-important revolutionary vehicle, a tightly organized and controlled party; in addition, it offered an individual revolutionary ideal shaped by patriotism and self-sacrifice. The most important appeal of Marxism-Leninism was that it seemed to offer a sweeping systemic solution to China's myriad problems.

> [I]t provided a self-consistent, universalistic, and "scientific" view of the world's history which enabled one to reject the imperialist West in the name of Western "scientific thought" and explain China's humiliating backwardness as due to her bondage to "capitalist imperialism."[21]

CULTURAL CHANGE FIRST: POLITICAL CHANGE WILL FOLLOW

If Chen, Li, and others were moving quickly toward the establishment of a political party that might become an important revolutionary tool, the other camp that developed in the aftermath of the May Fourth incident staked out a very different approach. They contended that any meaningful political change had to be preceded by and therefore built upon cultural change. By the nature of things, cultural change cannot be engineered rapidly by tools like violence; it is a slow effort based on evolutionary rather than revolutionary dynamics. One of the most important advocates of this path to change was Hu Shi, whose personal tendencies and education under Dewey must certainly have inspired this solution. Pragmatists saw a world of problems that needed solving and searched for solutions to each problem. Since problems diverged in different areas, among different kinds of people, in different arenas of life, careful study should reveal the solution to each problem, which would then serve as the "truth" in each circumstance. Solving that problem through reform was the key. Hu argued that "[t]here is no liberation *in toto* or reconstruction *in toto*. Liberation means liberation from this or that institution, from this or that belief, for this or that individual; it is liberation bit by bit, drop by drop."[22] For this reason, Hu attacked what he called "isms"—such as Marxism and Leninism—as overarching creeds, blueprints, systems, or "fundamental solutions" that seemed to offer a way out of China's predicament.

Many Chinese had difficulties with this approach. For a civilization in crisis, this "bit by bit, drop by drop" solution focusing on education and evolutionary change was not in the least intellectually satisfying. But more important, this approach would take many years, perhaps decades, even a century or more; even then, its adoption would bring no guarantee that it could remake China before China might indeed disintegrate and fall completely into Western hands. As one May Fourth intellectual, Shen Dingyi, put it,

> Under the present circumstances, part of the Chinese people and their land has become fish and pork on the cutting board. … [P]owers … hold their knives [in readiness]. … We should take over the knife, kick away the cutting board, and refuse to be fish and pork."[23]

For many Chinese intellectuals and students, so recently enamored of individual liberation, the emerging priority came to be the fate of the nation, the thinking being that without national liberation individual liberation would ultimately be meaningless.

Thus, from 1919 on, and picking up steam into the early 1920s, the direction of the May Fourth Movement changed. Its focus on enlightenment and individual liberation through the shattering of traditional cultural hierarchical bonds was swallowed up by an emphasis on national salvation, that is, on liberating the nation from imperialist and warlord control. For this reason, one Chinese historian has called the movement "an abortive revolution because its intellectual goal of enlightenment was unrealized" when the "revolutionary imperative of national salvation eclipsed demands for enlightenment."[24] It is also significant that, as in traditional times, during the New Culture Movement intellectuals were in charge. Initially in the switch to direct political action at the time of the May Fourth incident and afterward, intellectuals remained in the forefront. But by the late 1920s they would begin to lose their leadership positions. Once the Nationalists and Communists were ensconced in power, intellectuals were no longer in the historical forefront; instead they became a distrusted social group that was continually subject to all sorts of repression and mistreatment. The revolution, as it developed, had many major implications for Chinese society and social groups.

NEOTRADITIONALISMS

Both those who favored big system solutions and those who preferred pragmatic approaches nevertheless agreed that traditional culture was at the heart of China's problems and that a new China had to be created. For those wanting to build a Chinese nation, this position presented a problem in itself. From the late eighteenth century on, when nations were constructed, they were usually based on the history, traditional myths, and culture of the society building the nation. Both the big system proponents and the pragmatists were rejecting those traditional myths and culture. Upon what foundation, then, was the new nation to be built? At the time, there was not much agreement on the nation's new building blocks.

In contrast to the advocates of isms and problems, there were scholars who adamantly opposed rejecting traditional Chinese culture. They argued that Chinese culture could, indeed *must*, be the basis for the nation. There were three such neo-traditional schools of thought. All of them shared several positions. They were all suspicious and distrustful of Western values—individualism, materialism, and utilitarianism—and their validity for China's development. They all believed that traditional Chinese values that came to constitute a "core of truth" were in fact antithetical to Western values. The anti-Western slant of these views fit well the anti-imperialist thrust beginning to emerge in the early 1920s and contrasted with the Western-oriented solutions that were offered by the advocates of systemic solutions and pragmatism. These three schools actually predated the May Fourth Movement, having emerged out of the radical rethinking of Confucianism and Chinese culture in the late 1890s reform movement.

The "national essence" school sought to find elements in traditional culture other than Confucianism that might serve as ideas or practices that could be used in building a nation. There were, for example, different philosophical and religious traditions: non-Confucian schools of thought, most of which had risen with Confucianism in the middle and late Zhou dynasty (1122–221 B.C.E.) and the important religious import from India, Buddhism. On a somewhat different level, there were knight errant tales with their tradition of action and "heroic violence"—popular ideas that had penetrated among the Chinese masses. There thus came to be a populist thrust in this school that broke through the elite-controlled images and practices of standard Confucianism. In essence this school gutted the authority of the Confucian classics, making them simply a part of the larger body of Chinese literature. If this school was against the old Confucian orthodoxy, it was also strongly anti-Western; its arguments struck deep into Western assumptions and practices. For example, national essence adherents contended that the basic idea that had inspired Western attitudes and approaches since the Enlightenment—the idea of progress—was a delusion, little more than a "modern superstition."[25] The Western drive for power and wealth was destructive of the "inner life" of a culture and its inhabitants. China, they contended, must build a nation using its own "internal spiritual powers of renewal."

Cai Yuanpei brought a number of these national essence scholars to Beijing University in his effort to have open debates over divergent ideas that could potentially be used in creating the new China. During this time, these scholars were most vocal in opposing the replacement of classical Chinese with the vernacular. One, in answer to the argument that the vernacular would benefit China because it would facilitate literacy, responded that

> the language most popularly used was not necessarily a better one. More bread and jam were consumed than roast turkey throughout the world; yet could we say that the latter was less delicious and nutritious than the former only because it was rarer and that we should all eat "only" bread and jam?[26]

Charitably, it could be said that most national essence arguments were not so lacking in depth.

The 1898 reformer Liang Qichao was the leading advocate and thinker in the "national character" school. Unlike the national essence thinkers who searched the past for a non-Confucian basis for a new China, Liang sought to uncover a living national character of the Chinese people. He argued, "nations have a nature like people and that their fate depends upon this intangible quality, visible in religion, customs, and language."[27] The key for Liang was the strengths of the family system—the very system under so much attack in the May Fourth Movement. In it Liang found elements that he claimed were crucial for building a new China. Respect for rank and concern for future generations were important aspects of the system that Liang stressed as especially important for the formation of a modern nationalism. Further, he claimed that the ideal of reciprocity—that the claims of authority on the part of men and elders were balanced by the moral claims of subordinates on those in authority—should undercut the vehement May Fourth attack on familism. Like the national essence school, Liang attacked the West and its values. Liang had gone to France as an observer at the 1919 Versailles Conference. He had come away with a completely negative impression of the West as morally bankrupt and degenerate. He saw Western life dominated by an emphasis on science and technology, a focus that he claimed helped produce economic and social systems that led directly to hedonism, corruption, and greed. His was the voice of a Cassandra, prophesying disaster for China if it followed the Western path into the modern world.

The third neo-traditionalist approach sought to set forth the modern relevance of Confucianism. From the 1898 reform movement until the death of Yuan Shikai, this effort focused on attempting to make Confucianism a state religion. But by the May Fourth period, this attempt seemed no longer credible amid arguments by secularists that, in the context of scientific progress, religion for society at large would soon become obsolete. Confucianism's great champion and the most influential neo-traditionalist thinker in the May Fourth period was Liang Shuming, invited by Cai to join the Beijing University faculty in 1917. He set forth his major ideas in his book *Eastern and Western Civilizations and Their Philosophies*. He argued that Western civilization was based on two legs: One was rational calculation focusing on the external world, a process that gave rise to the development of science and to attempts to master the environment; the other was rational calculation focusing on individual self-interest, an effort that led to democracy and, in its communal arena, Communism. Throughout, Western thought had stressed skepticism and utilitarianism.

China's culture, Liang asserted, was far superior. It was shaped by the living force of the cardinal Confucian virtue of *ren*, a word that is difficult to translate but means something like "human empathy" or "human heartedness." Under its umbrella, Chinese society had been "tolerant and flexible, frugal and agrarian, cooperative and nourishing of human sentiments."[28] In short, Liang argued that Confucian values were superior because they recognized that reality was fluid and experience was often intuitive; thus, the Western emphasis on rational analysis was faulty and misleading. Of all the neo-traditionalists, Liang was probably the most conservative. Whereas the national essence and national character thinkers set forth their ideas as the foundation for the Chinese nation, Liang's ideas hearkened back to the traditional pre-nationalist views of the primacy of culture, or what has been called "culturalism." It is also important to note that none of the neo-traditionalist schools concentrated on the individual, the focus of the initial phase of the May Fourth Movement.

THE HISTORICAL SIGNIFICANCE OF THE MAY FOURTH MOVEMENT

Historians have generally ranked the May Fourth Movement with the abolition of the civil service examination and the overthrow of the monarchy and the imperial regime as one of the most significant revolutionary milestones in China's twentieth-century revolution. Whereas the first two cast off the old and made necessary the still unknown new, the third, although also discarding the old, initiated an earnest search for the new. The May Fourth Movement is an important demarcation in the intellectual and cultural history of China. Scholars have called it China's Renaissance, in part because the vernacular first came to be used then. It was in the Western Renaissance that writing in the Western vernaculars—French, Spanish, Italian, and so on, as opposed to Latin—first came into practice. Scholars have also called it the Chinese Enlightenment, a term recalling the important role of science and experimentation and the casting out of tradition. It may also be called an intellectual and cultural revolution, in which the old and traditional were discarded—even trashed—and various kinds of bold experimentation with new ideas and methods were attempted. It was the first of a series of attempts to dismantle traditional culture.

Because it discarded traditional Chinese culture, the May Fourth Movement has drawn strong reactions from various Chinese political forces. The identities of these forces almost necessarily reflect their stand on the meaning of the traditional culture for a modern Chinese nation-state. For the Nationalist regime of Chiang Kai-shek and his successors the movement seemed too radical, destroying much good that lay in Chinese tradition; further, with its increased emphasis on direct political, often violent, action, it was linked too closely with the rise of Chinese Communism. The Nationalists viewed the movement with considerable distrust and suspicion. The Communists, whose party grew out of the intellectual ferment and issues of the time, looked more kindly on the May Fourth period but looked with a jaundiced eye at the first phase, which emphasized the role of intellectuals in enlightening society so as to realize individual aspirations. Condemning the emphasis on the individual as "bourgeois," the Communists throughout their history have attacked those who maintained such a mentality and intellectuals in general, who seemed by their very nature to be tainted with the toxin of individualism. Thus, the reaction of both major political parties was colored with negativism toward this crucial modern movement.

Finally, any postmortem must stress that the time given to these cultural revolutionaries to make major social and cultural changes was absurdly short. Their efforts were largely aborted—overtaken as they were by the sweep of revolutionary political events. The movement for cultural criticism and renewal was swallowed whole by the movement for national salvation.

Notes

1 Pei-kai Cheng and Michael Lestz with Jonathan Spence, eds., *The Search for Modern China: A Documentary Collection* (New York: W.W. Norton, 1999), p. 235.
2 Lu Hsun, "A Madman's Diary," in *Selected Stories of Lu Hsun* (Beijing: Foreign Languages Press, 1972), p. 10.
3 Lu Hsun, "Preface to the First Collection of Short Stories, 'Call to Arms,'" in *Selected Stories of Lu Hsun*, p. 5.
4 Ssu-yu Teng and John K. Fairbank, eds., *China's Response to the West* (Cambridge, MA: Harvard University Press, 1954), p. 240.
5 Quoted in Yeh Wen-hsin, *Provincial Passages* (Berkeley, CA: University of California Press, 1996), p. 111.
6 Ibid., p. 181.
7 Quoted in Chow Tse-tsung, *The May Fourth Movement* (Stanford, CA: Stanford University Press, 1960), p. 184.
8 Gail Hershatter, *Women in China's Long Twentieth Century* (Berkeley, CA: University of California Press, 2007), p. 82.
9 Ding Ling, "Miss Sophie's Diary," in *Miss Sophie's Diary and Other Stories* (Beijing: Panda Books, 1985), pp. 59–60.
10 Any subtlety and complexity in Confucianism was lost as students and most intellectuals treated Confucianism as the enemy and as monolithic.
11 Teng and Fairbank, *China's Response to the West*, p. 241.
12 R. Keith Schoppa, *Blood Road: The Mystery of Shen Dingyi in Revolutionary China* (Berkeley, CA: University of California Press, 1995), p. 108.
13 Wang Zheng, *Women in the Chinese Enlightenment: Oral and Textual Histories* (Berkeley, CA: University of California Press, 1999), p. 50.
14 Helen Praeger Young, *Choosing Revolution: Chinese Women Soldiers on the Long March* (Champaign, IL: University of Illinois Press, 2001), pp. 19–20.
15 Leo Ou-fan Lee, "Literary Trends I: The Quest for Modernity, 1895–1927," in *The Cambridge History of China, Vol. 12, Republican China, 1912–1949, Part 1*, ed. John K. Fairbank (Cambridge, UK: Cambridge University Press, 1983), p. 467.
16 Quoted in Chow, *The May Fourth Movement*, p. 52.
17 Quoted in Leo Ou-fan Lee, "Modernity and Its Discontents: The Cultural Agenda of the May Fourth Movement," in *Perspectives on Modern China, Four Anniversaries*, ed. Kenneth Leiberthal et al. (Armonk, NY: M.E. Sharpe, 1991), pp. 161–2.
18 Quoted in Chow, *The May Fourth Movement*, pp. 106–7.
19 Ibid., pp. 149–50.
20 Quoted in Joanna Waley-Cohen, *The Sextants of Beijing* (New York: W.W. Norton, 1999), p. 207.
21 John K. Fairbank, Edwin O. Reischauer, and Albert M. Craig, *East Asia, the Modern Transformation* (Boston, MA: Houghton Mifflin, 1965), p. 670.
22 Cited in ibid., p. 669.
23 Schoppa, *Blood Road*, p. 65.
24 Quoted in Leo Ou-fan Lee, "Modernity and Its Discontents," p. 173.
25 The phrase and many of these arguments come from Charlotte Furth, "Intellectual Change: From the Reform Movement to the May Fourth Movement, 1895–1920," in Fairbank, *The Cambridge History of China, Vol. 12, Republican China, 1912–1949, Part 1*, p. 361.
26 Quoted in Chow, *The May Fourth Movement*, p. 281.
27 Furth, "Intellectual Change," p. 362.
28 Ibid., p. 370.

Suggestions for Further Reading

Ding Ling. *Miss Sophie's Diary and Other Stories* (Beijing: Panda Books, 1985). In addition to the title story, this volume contains other stories on Shanghai life in the 1930s and on the bitter realities of life in the countryside.

Fitzgerald, John. *Awakening China: Politics, Culture, and Class in the National Revolution* (Stanford, CA: Stanford University Press, 1998). This award-winning book analyzes the processes of China's being awakened and provides a rich depiction of the "politics of mass awakening."

Greider, Jerome B. *Hu Shih and the Chinese Renaissance: Liberalism in the Chinese Revolution, 1917–1937* (Cambridge, MA: Harvard University Press, 1970). The standard biography of this pragmatic liberal. In the vanguard of the language revolution, his career included important educational and diplomatic roles.

Lu Xun. *Selected Stories of Lu Xun* (Beijing: Foreign Languages Press, 2000). This anthology of Lu's most famous stories includes the preface of his collection *Call to Arms.*

Schwarcz, Vera. *The Chinese Enlightenment: Intellectuals and the Legacy of the May Fourth Movement of 1919* (Berkeley, CA: University of California Press, 1986). A study of the May Fourth generation and the legacies of the movement in the lives of its participants.

10

Drawing the Sword of Opposition
Identity Increasingly Politicized

For Chinese early in the twentieth century, nationalism was a new lens through which to see their identity. In imperial times there had been China the central country, with that centrality situated clearly in its culture. But the nineteenth-century nightmare of foreign invasion and military defeat had effectively made a shambles of China's assumed cultural superiority. Events had forced Chinese political, social, economic, and intellectual leaders by the early twentieth century to see China simply as one of many nations and as one of the weakest. In their view, the most outstanding characteristic of the Chinese nation in the context of continuing imperialist pressure was a thorough and humiliating impotence. That view was drummed into the population at large through such annual public commemorations as National Humiliation Day, the anniversary of China's 1915 acceptance of the Twenty-One Demands. The question of the early twentieth century thus became how to build national power as quickly as possible so as to prevent not only continuing national humiliation but even dismemberment.

THE BIRTH OF THE CHINESE COMMUNIST PARTY

A strong government was essential; to establish such a government meant building political parties to serve as the engine and military forces to serve as the vehicle by which to defeat the warlords and their supporters and then expel or, at the least, deal more effectively with the imperialists. Since this is the story of the seeds of revolution, a blow-by-blow account highlights the relative slowness of developments and the complex, often intricate and usually tense, dance between the Chinese Communist Party (CCP), Sun Yat-sen's Guomindang, and advisors sent from the Communist International in Moscow. This chapter might be entitled "How to Make a Revolution," but the story it tells does not adhere to the neat outline that historians often structure to show the macro-trajectory, or large course, of revolution. Instead it was a messy, often unclear, and always muddled process. For a revolution is made by people who, in the process of revolution, do not know the end results; therefore, their choices and decisions are often shaped by personalities, emotions, and reactions to contingencies and day-to-day realities.

The CCP was established first. As the previous chapter showed, a number of things—the intellectual attractiveness of Marxism-Leninism, the success of the Bolshevik Revolution, and the apparent generosity of the Karakhan Declaration—predisposed some Chinese intellectuals and journalists to favor the Soviet model. Another essential element in moves to form a Communist Party was the initiative of the Communist International, or Comintern, an organization that Lenin established to incite and direct world revolution. A mission led by the twenty-seven-year-old laborer-turned-Comintern agent Gregory Voitinsky arrived in Beijing in April 1920; he had what has been called a "winning personality," which facilitated his work with Chinese students and intellectuals. In the capital, he met intellectuals including Li Dazhao; Li gave Voitinsky a letter of introduction to Chen Duxiu, then living in Shanghai. The Comintern delegation traveled to Shanghai to meet Chen and others in the Marxist Study Society. In September 1920, Chen Duxiu turned *New Youth* into a Communist journal subsidized by the Comintern.

By summer 1920 a Communist cell group was functioning in Shanghai, overseeing the establishment of a Russian language school, the beginning efforts to organize labor unions, and the formation of a Socialist Youth Corps, later to be known as the Communist Youth Corps. By January 1921, eight Socialist Youth Corps organizations with about 300 members were reportedly established in a number of cities. Other Communist cell groups were formed in Beijing, Canton, Hankou, Jinan, and Changsha (established by Mao Zedong) and by Chinese students in Japan and France. Each was initially composed of only a handful of men and women. The revolution started bit by bit, drop by drop.

In the years 1919 and 1920, over a thousand Chinese male and female students participated in work-study programs in France. Their goal was to join study with manual labor. This was a pointed break with past traditions in which Chinese scholars grew their fingernails long to underline the fact that they did not work with their hands. In a practical sense, working in factories ranging from the production of bean curd to automobiles paid the costs of studies and of daily life. Ultimately, the goal of work-study was to offer training and some knowledge of technology that could be of use upon their return to China. For many students, however, life in France above all further politicized them, introducing them to socialist doctrine and Marxism-Leninism, as well as labor strikes. It was this context that led to the founding of Chinese Communist cells in Europe. Two of the most important Communist leaders in the middle and late twentieth century—Zhou Enlai and Deng Xiaoping—participated in the work-study program.

Back in China, in November 1920 Voitinsky met with Sun Yat-sen. Sun had fled to Japan after the brief second revolution against Yuan Shikai in 1913. In the next few years he came to see that establishing the strong government of a full-fledged republic would require a strong party and some effective military apparatus. In Japan he had experimented with setting up a more tightly organized party, with party members swearing personal loyalty to him; this demand alienated too many people, so Sun dropped the idea. When he returned to China in 1916, he spent most of his time in Canton, reorganizing his parliamentary-style Guomindang still as an open party and trying to link himself to the warlord in the area whose forces might assist in executing Sun's goals. But his party reorganization had little import, and various attempted military arrangements did not work. During these years, Sun was clearly spinning his wheels; he was thus ready to make contact with the Comintern agent to see whether there might be anything to gain.

Meeting Sun was an important development for the Comintern. In summer 1920 at the Second Comintern Congress, policies regarding Communist movements in colonial and underdeveloped countries were on the agenda. Given the very small number of Communists in any of these countries (many did not yet even have Communist parties) and the reality that they had insufficient power to accomplish much, should Communists adopt the short-term tactic of joining bourgeois parties for national ends in a united front against common enemies? Lenin said yes: a temporary united front made tactical sense; once the common enemies were defeated, the united front would end and the former allies would then become enemies. Others in the Comintern (the Indian M. N. Roy and the Soviet Union's Leon Trotsky) argued that national ends should play no role because the real struggle was the class struggle of workers and peasants around the world against the forces of feudalism and capitalism. Lenin's position, however, carried the day. Voitinsky's meeting with Sun was thus in line with the recently decided Comintern policy initiative.

Twelve delegates attended the founding congress of the CCP, which met in the Shanghai French Concession in July 1921; the party had only fifty to sixty members. At the congress, the delegates elected the central executive committee and chose Chen Duxiu as secretary-general. They came down very firmly on what seemed to be an uncompromising decision that they could have no relationships with other parties. Attending the congress as a Comintern representative was a Dutch Communist, Hendricus Sneevliet (also known as Maring), every bit as aggressive and stubborn as Voitinsky was mild and unassuming. Since Comintern agents had to tutor and work closely with the Chinese, their personalities and approaches were significant for the success of their work. From the perspective of the still small group of committed Communists, both Comintern revolutionary expertise and financial assistance were crucial. Following Moscow's policy, Sneevliet began to urge the Communists to join Sun Yat-sen's Guomindang, still an open parliamentary-style party. The young CCP did not initially support such a move, but Comintern influence on the infant Chinese party was understandably strong.

Pressure from Moscow in this regard became stronger with the meeting of the Congress of the Toilers of the East in January and February 1922. There the focus was East Asian countries and their "revolutionary liberation … and solidarity with proletarian Russia."[1] To bring about this liberation, speakers argued, required both the development of strong proletarian movements of workers and peasants and cooperation with "bourgeois nationalists." The Guomindang was singled out as the Chinese party that might be crucial for the development of the revolutionary effort in China.

In December 1921 Sneevliet had journeyed to South China to meet Sun Yat-sen to discuss China's situation and its relationship to Russia. Whether they discussed cooperation between the CCP and the Guomindang is uncertain, but since Sneevliet had become one of cooperation's biggest supporters, it is probable that it was at least mentioned. Sun reportedly had many positive things to say about Russia and its new system. In April 1922 Sneevliet opened a hornet's nest with his advice to Socialist Youth Corps and CCP members to join the Guomindang. CCP leader Chen Duxiu said, in essence, "No way!" CCP members even questioned the idea of a united front. But by June the party, mindful of the discussions at the earlier Congress of the Toilers of the East, and coming to see that the Guomindang was "relatively revolutionary and democratic," issued a manifesto that it was ready to join with the Guomindang. The decision to participate in a united front was confirmed at the Second Party Congress in July 1922. The united front took dead aim at two opponents—the warlords and the imperialists: defeat the warlords once and for all and kick out the imperialists, ending the reign of the unequal treaty system.

Most Chinese Communists favored an outright alliance between the parties, but Comintern agents' talks with Sun about some sort of united front had made it clear that he opposed an alliance of separate parties because he ultimately did not want two major parties vying with each other. Sun favored letting individual CCP members join his party, forming what came to be called a "bloc within" system. CCP members adamantly opposed that possibility, arguing that a bloc within would blur class organization and reduce the CCP's independence. In essence, CCP members were contending that the political identity of the party and of themselves was at stake in such a decision. But when push came to shove, Sneevliet weighed in: "The Comintern has already decided on the 'bloc within'; will you obey the decision?" Given its dependence on the Comintern, the CCP had no choice but to obey. Thus, from the very beginning, the key decision for the united front was made primarily by Sun and the Comintern, with the CCP forced into a decision by its Comintern adviser. The bloc within was ratified at the Third Party Congress in the summer of 1923.

GIVING THE GUOMINDANG A NEW IDENTITY

In August 1922, Sun met Adolf Joffe, a top Russian diplomat, who had been sent to China for high-level governmental discussions but who quickly made arrangements to see Sun. The two talked at length in late January 1923 and apparently set down basic approaches for greater cooperation between Russia and the Guomindang. Sun asked for financial aid and for advisers on "military and political problems." He announced his intention of sending a military mission to Moscow to study governmental and party organs. The talks did produce a joint statement noting that although the Communist system could not be introduced into China, Russia would support China's national independence and reunification. Sun followed up his talks with Joffe by sending one of his most trusted aides, Liao Zhongkai, to Japan for extended discussions with Joffe, who was in Japan on assignment.

The main thrust of Russian support was tutorial: Russia would provide advice and training for Sun to restructure his party and to form a party army. In autumn 1923, the Comintern dispatched Michael Borodin to help reorganize the Guomindang. A Russian Jew, Borodin had lived in the United States from 1905 to 1917, had returned to Russia at the time of the revolution, and had since served as Comintern agent in Mexico and several European countries. Many sources describe him as almost larger than life—a big, husky man with a magnetic personality and great intelligence. In China, Borodin used his ability to build substantial power quickly.

As a political party, the Guomindang was open, often factionalized, frequently unruly, and with nothing to keep it directed and coherent. In short, it was not the kind of organization that could pull off a revolution. Thus, Borodin drafted a new Guomindang constitution, translated into Chinese by Liao Zhongkai. It restructured the party in Leninist fashion according to the concept of "democratic centralism," which envisions a hierarchical party structure. Debate and discussion ("democracy") occur at each level of the hierarchy, with recommendations passed up the chain of command. Once the top level (in the party, the Central Executive Committee) reaches a decision, there is no more discussion and the decision must be carried out ("centralism"). In short, it is a structure with a façade of democratic-style discussion, but in substance, at the end of the process, it is really centralized autocracy. Further, because of the presence of surveillance operatives at every hierarchical level and in every arena of party activity, such a party is extraordinarily difficult to subvert. By early 1924, then, China's two parties were both Leninist-style organs.

There is evidence that the reorganization was not popular with many Guomindang members. In the late fall, many meetings were held at which Borodin and Liao explained the reasons for the restructuring. Borodin even had to defend the changes in meetings with members of the CCP and the Socialist Youth Corps. From men connected with the Guangdong party office, Sun received a petition claiming that the revised party constitution had really been drafted by Borodin and CCP leader Chen Duxiu; they argued that the bloc within was a plot for the CCP to take over the Guomindang. Sun rejected the petition, saying that the constitution had been "prepared by Borodin at my request and checked by myself. ... Chen Duxiu had no part in this." He went on to explain, "the capitalist countries will never be sympathetic to our Party. Sympathy can only be expected from Russia, the oppressed nations, and the oppressed peoples."[2] Thus, the united front proceeded with constant backbiting, fear, suspicion, and distrust.

The Guomindang's ideology, in contrast to its structure, was more homegrown. In 1923 and 1924 Sun had set down his own thinking about the direction and goals of the party and state; he had spoken about many of these ideas since the days of the Revolutionary Alliance. Known as the Three Principles of the People, they championed nationalism, democracy, and socialism (vaguely described as "people's livelihood"). For Sun, the realization of nationalism had more meaning than simply asserting China's national rights.

He argued that the thing blocking peace for all the world was imperialism and that its elimination had to be a priority. The first step in doing so for China was to reinvigorate the country's sense of nationhood and to rebuild, indeed reconstitute China's status as an independent, autonomous state. Then China's whole foreign policy outlook and approach had to be reconstructed to be focused on peace and a general sense of international morality. In that way, China could help lead the world to a greater sense of unity (and, in words recalling the Confucian past) of the brotherhood of all mankind. Sun thus transformed Chinese nationalism into an internationalism that was markedly morally transformed.

Sun's description of democracy uses many of the distinctions used by Communist leaders in the late twentieth century regarding the issues of human rights. He argued that the idea of freedom in China and the West was extraordinarily different. Western cultures had at least in modern times focused on freedom for the individual, while China in its present state had to focus on freedom for the nation. Chinese would argue that individual freedom in any case should never be inordinate. Indeed, if China was ever going to establish its sovereignty as a nation, Chinese must be willing to give up individual freedoms.[3] Democracy for Sun meant "that all people ... should enjoy the same political rights," and he enumerated those rights as the right to vote, to recall officials, to undertake initiatives, and to hold referendums. Whereas the people had four major political rights, the government held five powers—executive, legislative, judicial, examination, and censorship.

In his discussion of people's livelihood, Sun took on the Marxists, who argued that China's central social and economic problem was uneven distribution of wealth; Sun asserted that the real problem was the "grinding poverty of the Chinese people." He called for socialist solutions—the equalization of land ownership and the development of government-owned enterprises. But he also called for other reforms, including rent reductions for farmers and gaining control of the tariff in order to protect native Chinese industry. A centerpiece of his economic package was an idea he borrowed from the American economist Henry George: a tax on the increase in the value of landed property, in Sun's term the "unearned increment"—since whoever held the land had done nothing to earn the amount that increased in value over time.

In addition to a restructured party and an ideology that gave the polity direction, the other essential prerequisite for building a strong government and nation was a capable military force. That would be important for any seizure of power, but even more so at a time when the nation was ruled by an array of warlords and when society had become increasingly used to political decisions made by force of arms. With a view toward beginning the building of an army, Sun sent a delegation led by Chiang Kai-shek (Mandarin pronunciation, Jiang Jieshi) to Russia from August to November 1923. Chiang had attended military schools in both China and Japan before the establishment of the Republic. A member of the Revolutionary Alliance, he participated in the 1911 revolution in Shanghai and was involved in anti-Yuan Shikai activities until 1916. After that time he lingered in Shanghai, working as a stockbroker and forming close ties with the Green Gang, Shanghai's and the Lower Yangzi's underworld secret society. It was not until 1921 that Chiang began to work for Sun Yat-sen; it is little wonder that he was, in the words of one historian, "a somewhat irregular member of Sun's entourage." Many others were much closer to Sun than Chiang. The purpose of Chiang's mission to Moscow was to study Soviet government and party institutions and to inspect military academies with a view to understanding military organization and training. A more general goal of the mission was developing closer relations between the Guomindang and Russian leaders. However, the longer he remained in Moscow, the more disillusioned Chiang became about any long-term alliance between Russia and China.

The cornerstone of a modern army, *loyal above all to the party*, was a military academy. In 1924, under Borodin's and Liao Zhongkai's leadership, one was established at Huangpu (usually called Whampoa), 10 miles downstream from Canton. Reportedly the Soviet government contributed 3 million rubles to set up the school and pay its initial running expenses; in addition, Borodin subsidized it on the order of 100,000 Canton dollars every month. Though he was not Sun's first choice, Chiang Kai-shek was appointed commandant in May. Almost 500 cadets formed the first class, beginning in June 1924; between seventeen and twenty-four years old, those who were admitted had to pass an entrance examination. The academy's course of study was six months. Upon graduation, the cadets had to serve in the army one year for every two months they were students at the academy. In his address at the opening ceremonies on June 16, 1924, Sun set forth the goals of the academy:

> What is our hope in starting this school today? Our hope is that from today on we will be able to remake our revolutionary enterprise and use students of this school as the foundation of a revolutionary army. ... Without a good revolutionary army, the Chinese revolution is doomed to failure. Therefore ... our sole hope is to create a revolutionary army to save China from extinction.[4]

FIGURE 10.1   Though Chiang Kai-shek (standing) succeeded Sun Yat-sen (seated), they were not especially close comrades. It was Sun's naming Chiang to head the Whampoa Military Academy that propelled Chiang to the party's and country's top leadership posts.
Source: AFP/Getty Images.

Sun's Three Principles of the People were the ideological core of their training. Sun appointed Liao Zhongkai as the senior political officer in control of political training and indoctrination. "The curriculum … was meant to promote a moral and political sense of direction to youths, often of rural middle-income backgrounds, who were disillusioned and discontented; it was designed to form a foundation for an indoctrinated, disciplined officer cadre."[5] Faculty and administrative staff were balanced between Communists and Nationalists, with many of the former being part of the bloc within. Zhou Enlai, for example, who would become a pivotal member of the leadership of the People's Republic after 1949, was a political instructor at Whampoa. Despite the conspicuous presence of Communists and Comintern advisers (there were about a thousand Soviet military advisors in China by early 1925), the cadets became fiercely loyal to Chiang, who supervised the training of the first three classes. Many would come to play roles as his generals in the 1930s and 1940s, and almost all would become his avid backers as members of his strongest supporting faction, the Whampoa clique.

THINGS FALL APART: SUN'S DEATH AND THE MAY 30TH MOVEMENT

The realities of Chinese social and political culture tended to produce political parties that were composed of factions based on personal connections. The glue of connections that held personal networks together—based on kinship, native place, alumni connections, friendship, teacher–student ties, and political patron–client ties—was the strongest political binding agent. Sometimes the political landscape saw factions or personal networks come together as coalitions. Such coalitions tended to be much less cohesive than personal-connection factions; they tended to be tenuous, held together perhaps by ideology or strategy or long- or short-term goals. Sun Yat-sen, named Guomindang leader for life and the most prominent national figure in China, headed a party with many factions and networks even though it had been restructured in the Leninist mode. Party members owed personal loyalty and support to him; many had followed him since the Revolutionary Alliance days in the early years of the century. But among the factions and networks, there was considerable competition, even bitter disagreement, about policy and ideology.

There were party members all along the political spectrum from right to left, but for our purposes, seeing the basic split between right (conservative) and left (liberal) clarifies the general elements of disagreement. On the political right were those who believed that the Soviet Union had too much power in shaping the Chinese revolution, that Borodin had become a much too powerful decision maker, and that the bloc within was basically a bad policy that had to be eliminated. These were people such as Dai Jitao, Sun Yat-sen's personal secretary from 1916 on. Graduate of a Japanese university, Dai had become one of the most active popularizers of Sun's ideas and had been part of the Shanghai Marxist Study Society. But the course of events convinced him that the Soviet Union and the CCP were becoming the chief beneficiaries of CCP–Guomindang cooperation in the united front. Especially irritating to the rightists was the tendency of Communists who had joined the Guomindang as individuals to cohere in separate groups, almost as if they were a party within the larger party.

On the political left were those whose political positions were similar to those of the Communists, offering some support for social and economic as well as political revolution, though they may have had doubts about the extent of the power of Soviet advisers. These were men such as Liao Zhongkai and Wang Jingwei, both extremely close associates of Sun Yat-sen. American born and Japanese educated, Liao had been with Sun since 1903, had with his wife been a member of the Revolutionary Alliance, and had played an important role in shaping the cooperation between the Comintern and the Guomindang. He worked with Borodin closely on a number of projects and, as we have seen, Sun sent him to Japan for further talks with Joffe about the Communist system. Wang, once known as the "golden boy of Chinese nationalism" for his 1910 attempt to assassinate the Manchu prince regent, had been one of the most active members of the Revolutionary Alliance. From 1917 on, he was a member of Sun's entourage, renowned for his handsomeness, "a humbler of female hearts."[6]

In the center were those such as Chiang Kai-shek, who was not as close to Sun as Dai, Liao, and Wang. The centrists made their own way, supporting Sun and his working with the Soviets but capable of going to the right or left, depending on contingencies. The continual presence and important roles of the Communists within the party kept the issues regarding the pros and cons of the united front alive and usually, but not always, just below the surface of day-to-day activities. Although the political right carped about superficial issues such as the power of Borodin in day-to-day decisions, the basic difference in outlook over what the revolution was to be was not broached.

In June 1924, a group of conservatives took the case of Communists in the Guomindang co-alescing into units to Sun and the Central Executive Committee. They pointed out that they did not object to individual CCP members joining the Guomindang, but that it was not proper for there to be a party within the party. They pointed to the relatively large number of Communists who held positions on the Guomindang Central Executive Committee and to the successful efforts of Communist units within the party to place Communist ideas at the forefront of party publications. The Central Committee decided in late summer to leave things as they were. In a sense, Sun added insult to the conservatives' injury, so to speak: when he established a new party organ, the Political Council, to advise on political issues, he named none other than Borodin as its head. Although superficial calm remained, conservatives were rankled by Borodin's and the CCP's seeming domination of Sun and the Guomindang left. For their part, CCP members were nervous and irritated by the continual rumblings of Guomindang discontent. The united front was clearly ill, but Sun was still holding it together.

But then he died. On a trip to Beijing in late 1924 and early 1925 to discuss the national situation with Zhang Zuolin, the Manchurian warlord currently controlling the capital, he became ill. Surgery showed incurable liver cancer, and he died on March 12. On the day before he died, Sun signed two documents, one a testament drafted by Wang Jingwei and the other a statement to the Soviet Union. The latter read in part:

> I leave behind me a party which, as I always hoped, will be allied with you in its historical task of liberating China and other suppressed peoples from the yoke of imperialism. ... I therefore charge my party to maintain permanent contact with you. I cherish the firm belief that your support of my country will remain unaltered.[7]

His hope for continued support from the Soviet Union certainly did not indicate that Sun was aware at the time of his death of the desperate seriousness of the united front's ill health.

Death transformed Sun; he became a potent symbol of patriotism and unfinished revolution. But, for all its power, a symbol cannot hold parties together. The situation was worsened by what became known as the May 30th Movement. At a Japanese-owned textile mill in Shanghai, a Chinese worker was killed by a Japanese guard after he and other workers broke into the factory during a strike lockout and wrecked some machines. Demonstrations of public outrage led to the arrest of several students. On May 30, thousands of demonstrators massed before the police station to demand their release. With little warning, a British inspector gave orders to fire on the crowd; eleven were killed and at least twenty wounded. Furor erupted in cities and towns around the country in the form of street demonstrations, incendiary articles in newspapers, and strikes. The humiliation of having foreign troops on Chinese soil who could kill Chinese with impunity led to an unprecedented anti-imperialist explosion that considerably increased the visibility of the CCP and the Guomindang. The number of CCP members reportedly rose from 1,000 in May to around 10,000 near the end of the year. In the aftermath, the CCP was able to organize the Shanghai General Labor Union during its leadership of a Shanghai protest strike in early June. The May Shanghai killings, moreover, were compounded by more bloodshed. On June 23, British troops in Canton opened fire on demonstrators protesting the May 30 deaths, killing 52 and wounding over 100 more. These shootings increased the deepening sense of national peril; demonstrations of rage and revolutionary fervor swept the country. In Canton and Hong Kong, anti-British outrage produced a sixteen-month strike and a boycott of British goods.

The contingencies of Sun's death and the May 30th Movement put great pressure on the parties. The May 30th Movement especially increased the likelihood that the military phase of the revolution itself was near and that revolutionary goals (which might safely remain vague or substantially undiscussed if the revolution was still in the distant future) now had to be sharpened. But such honing of goals necessarily drove greater wedges between the factions and networks that already existed. The remainder of the year saw an increasingly malevolent polarization. As identities were politicized into right or left, conservative or radical, revolutionaries began drawing the sword. In August, Liao Zhongkai, so instrumental in the united front, was assassinated in Canton on his way to attend a meeting of the Central Committee; though the identity of the killers was never certain, party members from the right wing were implicated. Liao's murder ironically had the effect of turning the revolution more to the left, since key right wingers, who had ties to those apparently involved in the killing, left the province.

From November 1925 to January 1926, a group from the right wing met in the Western Hills section of Beijing before Sun's coffin to demand that Borodin be dismissed and that the bloc within, indeed any relationship with the CCP, be dropped. But at the Second Guomindang Congress in January 1926, 60 percent of the 278 delegates were leftists or Communists, 23 percent might be termed centrists, and only 16 percent were rightists. In reaction to the domination of the congress by the left wing, and further indicative of the politicized polarization, in March the rightists held their own party congress in Shanghai, charting their own direction for the future. In the Guomindang itself within a year of Sun's death, politically things had fallen apart.

THE BEGINNING OF MASS MOBILIZATION

In the face of bitter competition in the united front, one thing that kept the CCP cooperating was the opportunity that the front gave them to mobilize workers and farmers under Guomindang cover. Marx had argued that the motive force for revolution would be the urban working class (the proletariat). This was still the basic outlook and approach of the CCP, though since at least the Congress of the Toilers of the East, there had been a strong conviction that the peasantry would have to become important players in the revolutionary game.

First, the workers. The first major effort of the Communists to organize unions was a tragic disaster. In the fall of 1922, workers, demanding better pay and the recognition of unions, struck various railroads and mines in North China. Various associations approximating unions sprang up throughout the region. Communists, having formed labor clubs along the Beijing–Hankou railway route, wanted to unite them into a national federation under the logic of "strength in numbers." Representatives of these clubs met in the city of Zhengzhou in Henan province to finalize a constitution drafted earlier. Even though the warlord of the area, Wu Peifu, forbade the meeting, they came to the city and essentially found themselves locked out by troops and police. They re-acted by calling a general strike on February 4, in effect shutting the railway down. Wu Peifu, an-gry at this action that was costing him $50,000 per day from railroad revenues, brutally broke the strike, killing thirty-five workers and injuring many more. Among the laborers, the CCP received failing marks for its leadership.

The main geographical focus for sustained organizing of both workers and farmers was, as might be expected, in Canton, where the party and army were headquartered, as well as its sur-rounding areas and its province of Guangdong. In the spring of 1924 the Guomindang leader Liao Zhongkai, in an effort to begin to unite separate labor organizations in the city, had arranged a May Day rally to which all unions were invited and at which there was a large turnout. Sun Yat-sen's address pointed to tensions in the united front as he tried to shift the CCP's emphasis from class struggle to the hurtful economic privileges of foreigners. Despite the turnout, when confer-ences were later slated to discuss larger unions, workers initially gave the cold shoulder to the initiative. Workers were embedded in their local organizations, could not see the advantages of being grouped in organizations they did not know; and even more they distrusted the organizers. Organizing unions was not easy work.

In May 1925, the CCP called a National Labor Congress in Canton in another attempt to unite unions into a single labor federation. They succeeded in forming the National General Labor Union. Though its membership nationwide had risen to 1.2 million by May 1926, the most important branch in Shanghai had to go underground by the fall of 1925. Unionization was not on the whole working successfully. In the aftermath of the 1923 tragedy on the Beijing–Hankou railroad line, only one railway in Northern China as of late 1926, the Beijing–Suiyuan line, had a union. The sea-men's union operated only on ocean liners. The Anyuan miners' union, in which organizers such as Communists Liu Shaoqi and Li Lisan had done earlier work, had been totally suppressed. Thus, the record of Communists in organizing labor unions during the years 1923–1926 was quite bleak.

The earliest attempt to organize farmers came in Zhejiang province in the fall of 1921. There the local political activist Shen Dingyi, a member of both the CCP and the Guomindang, orga-nized a rent-resistance movement, which local authorities easily crushed. In 1922 and 1923 the Socialist Youth Corps organizer Peng Pai set up active farmers' associations in several counties east of Canton along the South China Sea. The Guomindang took the first steps toward actively organizing farmers into associations in summer 1924, establishing a Farmers Bureau to train spe-cial deputies to be sent to the countryside to investigate conditions and propagandize about and establish farmers' associations. The CCP moved quickly to take over this effort when the Farmers Bureau was replaced by a more permanent Farmers' Movement Training Institute. It was also not easy work. Without connections, it was hard to enter villages for the work of organizing; farmers were distrustful and uncooperative. The attitude of village elites was especially hostile because farmers' associations were their potential enemies; thus, elites attacked potential organizers using local militia units or local toughs.

Borodin believed that progress in the establishment of farmers' associations was the key to a successful military campaign north through northern Guangdong and Hunan provinces. The presence of large numbers of associations would facilitate the march of troops through the area by creating a more supportive population. Thus, he began to subsidize the Farmers' Movement Training Institute with about $1,500 per month to help pay salaries and the costs of printing pam-phlets and posters. The first five classes at the Training Institute produced 545 men who were trained to do the work of rural organizing. They were sent to Guangdong and Hunan (targeted for

TABLE 10.1 Membership in Farm Associations

Province	May 1925	June 1926	December 1926
Guangdong	210,000	647,766	n.a.
Henan	n.a.	270,000	n.a.
Hunan	n.a.	38,000	1,200,000
Hubei	n.a.	7,200	287,000

military purposes), with a few dispatched to the provinces of Guangxi, Fujian, Anhui, Henan, and Shandong. Once established, the associations focused on reducing rents paid by tenant farmers to landlords and lowering various taxes that hit some localities very hard.

Even if associations were established (and it was sometimes over the dead bodies of local power holders), problems with their functioning were continual. There was not much discipline to keep associations in line; they often did what they wanted and did not report to the center. Their local actions were dogged by poor local leadership and by the refusal of members to pay their local dues. Elites, who stood to suffer financially from the efforts of farmers' associations, sometimes joined them in order to subvert them. The number of farmers brought into the associations increased dramatically in 1926, the first year of the military Northern Expedition, as the table above shows. But the huge increase in some areas meant large-scale fighting between farmers and landlords. In most cases, county governments usually sided with landlords.

The role of the Northern Expedition itself in the organizing that accompanied and followed it is remarkable. In June 1926, one month before the beginning of the Northern Expedition, 66 percent of all farmers in associations (647,766 out of 981,442) were in Guangdong province. The number of farmers organized in Hunan and Hubei during and immediately after the military campaign soared (see Table 10.1). Two interesting sidelights of the organizing were (1) that the relatively large number organized in Henan province (where CCP membership also rose swiftly) represented work among the secret society Red Spears (whole Red Spear organizations were brought into farmers' associations at one time) and (2) that Mao Zedong served as principal of the Farmers' Movement Training Institute from May to October 1926.

THE EMERGENCE OF CHIANG KAI-SHEK AND THE NORTHERN EXPEDITION

In the meantime, Commandant Chiang at Whampoa was becoming more suspicious of the aims of the Communists. In his diary, criticisms of Soviet advisers became more numerous in early 1926; he wrote, "I treat them with sincerity but they reciprocate with deceit. It is impossible to work with them."[8] The Guomindang and the Soviet advisers disagreed over when the military campaign to defeat the warlords should begin, with the Guomindang ready to go but the Soviets urging caution. In early March, Chiang became aware that an orchestrated campaign to get rid of him seemed to be developing, with Wang Jingwei most often named as his successor. In that context of considerable distrust and even paranoia on Chiang's part, on March 20 a gunboat commanded by a Communist officer mysteriously neared Whampoa Island. Chiang, reportedly fearful that a coup against him was underway, undertook his own coup against Communists in the area. Although Borodin was not in Canton, Chiang arrested over thirty Soviet advisers and declared martial law. As a result of these actions, Borodin later agreed to a substantial decrease of Communist power and prerogative in the party, allegedly because of pressures from Stalin, leader of the Soviet Union, who evidently did not perceive the growing dangers to the Communist effort. With the immediate presumed political threat under control, Chiang continued his plans for the military campaign to unite the country. The episode revealed Chiang's active suspicion of Communist intentions, although he still favored cooperation in the united front; it also pointed clearly to the intraparty feuding that repeatedly saw drawn swords.

In July 1926, as the head of the National Revolutionary Army (NRA), Chiang began the Northern Expedition, a two-pronged campaign to reach the Yangzi River and gain South and South Central China for the Guomindang. The armies on the western route moved up through Hunan province, which had been "softened" by the mass mobilization, quickly reaching their goal. They were already fighting in the Yangzi area in late August, and they took the key metropolis of Wuhan on October 10. Units from this western route then turned to Jiangxi province, capturing its capital by November 8. Despite some serious problems—summer floods, cholera, and transport difficulties—the success of the NRA was remarkably rapid. There were a number of reasons. The nature of the army itself was crucial. Trained solidly for two years and filled with national spirit, this new military force was strictly forbidden to prey upon the population by looting and raping, the usual way warlord armies operated. Soviet advisers played key positive roles. Credit for the general strategy has been given to the Soviet general Vasily Blyukher; further, each corps and even some divisions had Soviet advisers. Rivalries among four warlords in Hunan province also allowed the NRA to hasten their conquest. In addition, success seemed to breed success, as the early military victories brought competent troops from Guizhou warlords into the Nationalist effort.

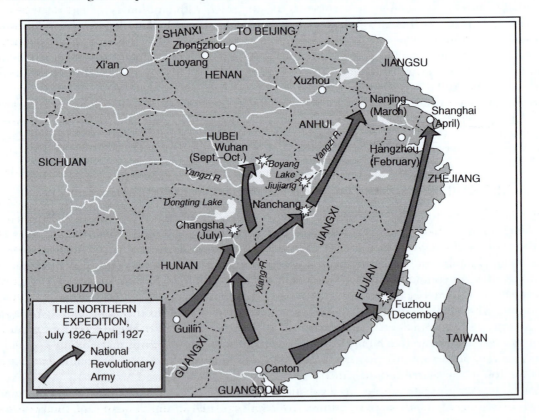

MAP 10.1 The Northern Expedition, 1926–1927.

But perhaps the most important reason for the rapid military victory in the area, as I have stated, was the political work that preceded and accompanied the campaign. Mao Zedong, active in the mass mobilization in Hunan, his home province, reported that from January to June 1926 the organizational activity was underground, but that it became open with the arrival of the NRA.[9] In addition to the army's good treatment of the people and their property, this activity helped to win over the local population to the Nationalist cause. Farmers' association members served as scouts, guides, and porters for the army; people along the campaign route offered baked sweet potatoes and other foodstuffs and water to the troops; farmers assisted by harassing the enemy's rear.

Coinciding with and following the successful campaign was a frenzy of mass mobilization of farmers and laborers. Before the Northern Expedition in Hunan, Hubei, and Jiangxi, farmers' association membership numbered less than 50,000, but Communist leaders claimed by the end of 1926 that there were 1.5 million organized farmers in ninety-one counties of Hunan and Hubei alone. Although likely exaggerated, this figure nevertheless points to a gigantic increase in the number of farmers now politically mobilized, even if for some it was in name only. The organizers toned down the rhetoric of class struggle, focusing instead on lowering rents and taxes, reducing food prices, and opening grain storage facilities at times of shortages. But this agenda naturally stirred up the hostility of landlords, who took retaliatory and often violent actions against tenants, responses that, in turn, elicited violent tenant reactions in an ever-escalating struggle between the classes. Violent outbursts also marked the spread of labor mobilization. In the wake of the military victory, mostly Communist organizers formed dozens of unions. Agitation for higher wages and better working conditions led to a wave of strikes in November 1926. By spring 1927, an estimated 400,000 workers were in unions, 90,000 of them in industry. Participating with unions and the farmers' associations in rambunctious public demonstrations were women and students, who took to the streets to denounce imperialism and to march for the coming of a new Chinese nation.

Such mass activity raised the crucial question of where the revolution was headed: should it take on social and economic goals, as the Communists desired, or should it remain primarily political in its call for ousting warlords and imperialists? Increasingly, in the fall of 1926, those two ideological stances became associated with particular places. Wuhan, to which Borodin, CCP members, and adherents to the Guomindang left had traveled, became the center of the mass mobilization and leftist activity. The city of Nanchang in Jiangxi province, which Chiang Kai-shek had made his military capital, also became the capital of sorts of the Guomindang right, an ideological position toward which Chiang himself was rapidly heading. In late 1926, relations between Borodin and Chiang became icily hostile.

Borodin later pointed to the Chiang-inspired Central Committee decision in early January 1927—to keep party headquarters and the governmental capital in Nanchang and away from the radicalism of Wuhan—as the first sign that a break with Chiang was inevitable. The impasse over the location of the capital caused the already tense relationship to deteriorate rapidly. It even strained relations between Comintern agents. When Voitinsky traveled to Nanchang to try to save the united front and work things out with Chiang, Borodin attacked him as an "anti-revolutionary compromiser," and Voitinsky charged that Borodin was "harming the Chinese revolution and the position of Soviet Russia."[10] In March 1927, Borodin and the Guomindang left named Wang Jingwei as Guomindang leader in a direct challenge to Chiang. In response, Chiang struck out at Communists and leftists in several Jiangxi cities.

Disagreements over military strategy only worsened what had become an unbridgeable rift. In the spring of 1927, the immediate goal of the NRA was the capture of Shanghai, then controlled by the warlord Sun Chuanfang. Powerful warlords—Feng Yuxiang and Zhang Zuolin—remained in the North, and there were concerns about whether they might ally themselves with Sun Chuanfang. Soviet advisers advocated pushing north toward the city of Zhengzhou to link up with Feng Yuxiang's forces before heading toward Shanghai. Chiang, in contrast, was negotiating with Zhang Zuolin and preferred a move directly toward Shanghai.

As Chiang's forces made their way to Shanghai from the Southwest, Communists and Guomindang leftists, who had organized and now led Shanghai labor unions, initiated an uprising against Sun Chuanfang. In late February, as the NRA took the city of Hangzhou, workers staged a general strike to undercut Sun's power and thereby make NRA seizure of the city easier, action that might be likened to the softening up of the Hunan route by precampaign organizing. Though the six-day strike was broken brutally by Sun's men (swordsmen were sent into the streets to perform summary executions), it politically mobilized hundreds of thousands of workers and revealed the strength of Communist power. It also increased the conviction among Shanghai businessmen and adherents of the Guomindang right wing that the Communists had to be stopped. Then on March 21, as the NRA was nearing the southern edge of the city, the Communist-led General Labor Union called another general strike, involving over 600,000 workers. Heavy fighting erupted as workers cut electrical and telephone lines and occupied railway and police stations. The workers' strategy seemed to be not only to make the NRA takeover easier but also to seize and hold Chinese areas of the city. The commander of the NRA, Bai Chongxi, ended the strike when he took the city on March 24.

Chiang, already suspicious and worried over the import of the actions of leftists in Wuhan, was now faced with a potentially explosive situation of leftist and labor power in Shanghai. The General Labor Union was attempting to turn the situation against the imperialists by demonstrating for the seizure of the city's foreign concession areas, action that would most certainly have brought a strong Western response. Western nerves were already on edge, for on March 24 the American, British, and Japanese consulates in Nanjing had been looted, and there had been attacks on foreigners resulting in at least six deaths. After discussions with city business elites, Guomindang veterans who still had ties to the left wing of the party, and the underworld Green Gang, with which he had had ties since the 1910s, Chiang moved to attack those who had made it easier for him to seize the city.

On the night of April 11, the Communist head of the General Labor Union was invited for dinner at the home of Green Gang leader Du Yuesheng; there he was murdered. Early the next morning, Green Gang members and forces loyal to Chiang attacked all union headquarters; protests about these attacks led to NRA soldiers opening fire on civilians. In this Red Purge, hundreds were mowed down by machine guns in the bloody attacks; survivors described how, on that day heavy with rain, the streets ran red with blood. The American Vice-Counsel in Shanghai reported that

> Execution squads patrolled the streets and on finding a suspect, they questioned him, examined him for the tell-tale red [at this point, [the] Communist's trademark was to wear a red necktie]. If found, they ordered the victim to open his mouth, thrust a revolver into it, and another coolie came to the end of his Communist venture. I myself saw a rickshaw stopped, the coolie grabbed by the police, his shirt jerked from his neck, disclosing the red stain. He was rushed to the side of the road, compelled to kneel down, and unceremoniously shot while the crowd of people on the street applauded.[11]

An estimated 5,000 were killed; thousands more fled the city in panic. The Shanghai slaughter, for some, came to signify Chiang's treachery—turning brutally on those who had helped him take the city. This tragedy was the beginning of what, from the perspective of the left, is called the White Terror: an effort to destroy the power of the left and especially the Communists, who had attained so much power through their bloc within party membership. The rationale of Chiang and the Guomindang conservatives was set forth right after the events in Shanghai:

> [S]ince the beginning of the Northern Expedition, while members of the Guomindang have been laboring faithfully either on the field of battle or elsewhere, and while the militarists of the country have been gradually eliminated, the Communists, taking advantage of our success, have seized important cities as their centers for propaganda and usurped the power of the Party. ... For the welfare of the Revolution as well as that of the Guomindang, we are forced to adopt this strong measure to purge the Party of all undesirable elements.[12]

The terror spread over the country in almost all the major cities and continued well into 1928. In Zhejiang province alone, almost 1,000 people were executed in April 1927; though the number of victims dropped during the summer, another wave of terror swept the province late in the year and into the next. The revolution was destroying its own; millions of young, idealistic Chinese were losing their heads. The battle over ideology and the direction of the Chinese revolution was being fought with executioners' weapons.

Both sister and brother (Jian Xianren and Jian Xianwei) were waiting to see how the Northern Expedition would turn out, though when Xianwei returned for their grandmother's funeral, both decided that they would begin to work with the Communist Youth League. Both traveled to Hunan's provincial capital, Changsha, where Xianwei entered the Workers' Movement Institute (WMI) for leadership training for labor unions and Xianren attended a preparatory middle school for teacher training. Both vigorously participated in the Communist student movement. Soon after their arrival in Changsha, they met the most famous Communist leaders in Hunan: Mao Zedong, Guo Liang, Li Weihan, and Xia Xi. Xianwei was working at the WMI on Horse Day (May 20, 1927) when Nationalist troops surrounded and seized both the WMI and the Peasant Movement Institute. Somehow Xianwei made it to see Xianren at her school and informed her that the CCP had recruited him to run messages for the party. In that role, he moved to a hostel, passing himself off as a student preparing for examinations. The White Terror of the Nationalist party confirmed for Xianren that her activities as a Communist were the right thing to do. When she heard that, routinely, when the Nationalists killed girl students, they cut off their hands and breasts and displayed their mutilated bodies as an object lesson for women supporting the CCP, Xianren's response was: "I knew I must carry out the work I was assigned to do."[13]

Xianren left Changsha in late 1927 or 1928 to work as an apprentice in a handicraft factory producing stockings. But her main work was for the Communist Party: "I was doing work for the CCP, burying roots and sowing seeds. I was a CCP root, burying myself among the workers, sowing propaganda seeds and recruiting for the Organization."[14] When the manager of the stocking factory discovered her Communist work, she slipped away to a contiguous county, made contact with the local party organization, which found her a teaching job at a local middle school. Provided with her own housing, she could offer other CCP workers cover in dicey situations. Her name appeared on a list of Communists wanted by the Nationalist government; she reacted by seeking out relatives living in the mountains and disguised herself as a peasant to ride out the time.

The purge and its disarray forced choices on the Communists and the Guomindang left in Wuhan. Stalin argued that the purge had clarified the China situation by having Chiang show his true colors. Almost as if he were blind to what was happening, he continued to call for the

Communists to work with the Guomindang left and to strike out at those allied with Chiang. Given the political realities of the purge, CCP General Secretary Chen Duxiu cynically said that these orders were "like taking a bath in a toilet."[15] For its part, the left began to doubt the intentions of the Communists, especially after one agent showed leftist leaders one of Stalin's telegrams. When these leftists began discussions with Chiang early in the summer, the Communist effort was doomed. Soviet advisers and some of Borodin's staff began to leave in late June. The final split between the CCP and the Guomindang left came in mid-July. Borodin himself, after four years of substantial power on the Chinese scene, left at the end of July. Hated by Chiang, who had put a price on his head, Borodin did not dare go down the Yangzi toward Nanjing and Shanghai; he went overland to the north and then across the Gobi Desert to the Soviet Union. Later Borodin described the Guomindang as a "toilet, which, however, after you flush it, still stinks."[16] He would end up dying as a political prisoner in one of Stalin's Siberian gulags in 1948.

The last months of 1927 saw several Communist efforts to rise up and establish CCP-led regimes, but they were all short lived and ineffective. The Nanchang (Jiangxi) uprising began on August 1 (celebrated today as the founding of the Red Army). It was initially a quick military success as they seized the city. But then the new "regime" seemed not to know what to do next. Its armies marched south toward Guangdong in devastatingly oppressive heat and quickly became plagued by desertion and disease; equipment was lost; the populace offered no support; and the whole effort simply disintegrated. There were several so-called Autumn Harvest Uprisings slated to begin on September 10 in Hunan and Hubei. The Hubei uprising collapsed almost as soon as it began. Mao Zedong was in charge of the Hunan uprising, where the participants were an army of farmers, miners, soldiers, and bandits. But the effort petered out when he could get only about 2,000 "troops" to attack the city of Changsha and when even these began fighting among themselves. Mao prevailed upon many of his "soldiers" to travel with him to the famous bandit lair and stronghold of Jinggangshan on the Hunan–Jiangxi border. In all these late summer–early fall uprisings, there was simply insufficient planning, leadership, and manpower.

By far the most tragic of the Communist attempts to stage rebellions during the White Terror was the "Canton commune," founded by Communists and workers in that southern city. The decision to stage the uprising was made by the Communist provincial committee, who planned to recruit about 2,000 workers and some Communist cadets from Whampoa; the difficulty was their shortage of arms. But the date of the uprising had to be moved up when police found the rebels' cache of bombs. Even so, the effort started out fairly effectively with the seizure of most police stations, the railroad station, telegraph and post offices, government offices, and Guomindang headquarters. There was much looting and burning of property (police later reported that 900 buildings had been gutted). But there was not much popular support: only about 3,000 workers out of an estimated 290,000 in the city area participated. Between 3,000 and 4,000 were killed in the two-day Canton commune, many by execution squads that roamed the streets, often nabbing completely innocent people in an "orgy of revenge." Historians often point to this disaster as the low point of Communist fortunes; the CCP itself has called it (ridiculously) euphemistically the "heroic battle in the retreat of a revolutionary high tide."[17] It was the last CCP urban uprising for the next twenty years.

Two other noteworthy casualties in 1927 were Li Dazhao and Chen Duxiu, the co-founders of the CCP. On April 6, Beijing city police raided a building in the Soviet embassy compound on a tip that Chinese Communists were using it to plan an uprising. The thirty-six Chinese found there were arrested; among them was Li, who had taken residence there in December 1926 when the rabidly anti-Communist warlord Zhang Zuolin seized the capital. Despite the appeals of prominent North Chinese citizens, he was executed by strangling at the age of thirty-eight. In the summer of 1927, Chen was deposed as secretary-general of the CCP by Comintern agents—ultimately by Stalin—and blamed for everything that had happened to the CCP. He was guilty, they declared, of "opportunism," even though he had only been following their orders. He was formally expelled from the party in 1930. In 1932, he was arrested by Chiang's Nationalist government, tried, and sentenced to fifteen years in prison. He was paroled at the start of the war with Japan in 1937 and died in obscurity in a small town in Sichuan province in 1942.

By August 1928, Chiang and the NRA reached Beijing. The Nationalist Revolution had grown out of the uneasy united front collaboration of the two Leninist-style parties, the CCP and the Guomindang. After Sun's death and the May 30th Movement, political positions (and therefore identities) had tended to become more inflexible. Political polarization between left and right inhibited revolutionary progress as the CCP and the Guomindang left and right tended to turn in on themselves, drawing swords to strike out against their perceived foes and, they would have said, the foes of revolution. Now, in the success of the Northern Expedition, the CCP was vanquished, seemingly dead after a short life of six years, one of its founders dead, the other deposed. Stalin's policy of trying to call the shots from Moscow had been a tragic mistake, but Communists and especially Stalin had difficulty accepting any personal responsibility for mistakes. Chinese Communist history is thus littered with scapegoats. Yet in many ways the important role of Soviet aid and advisers was a harbinger of other foreign aid that would come to China later, from the United States in the 1940s and the Soviet Union again in the 1950s. The CCP would rise again, but its leaders would be of a different sort than the May Fourth intellectuals who had formed and given life to the party in this, its first incarnation.

Finally, at least on the map, China was unified for the first time since the death of Yuan Shikai had given birth to the warlords. The Nationalist Revolution had been the springboard for Chiang Kai-shek's rise to power: now he was faced with the immense tasks of reconstruction after years of war and of the construction of a new, viable Chinese state.

FIGURE 10.2 This particularly gory beheading in the streets of Canton in December 1927 was typical of the bloody street violence that ended the ill-fated Canton commune.
Source: Pictures from History/Bridgeman Images.

Notes

1 C. Martin Wilbur and Julie Lien-ying How, *Missionaries of Revolution* (Cambridge, MA: Harvard University Press, 1989), p. 31.
2 Ibid., p. 92.
3 Sun Yat-sen, "The Three Principles of the People," in *The Road to Communism: China since 1912*, ed. Dun J. Li (New York: Van Nostrand Reinhold, 1969), p. 118. The quotations below are from the same source.
4 Quoted in Pei-kai Cheng and Michael Lestz with Jonathan Spence, eds., *The Search for Modern China: A Documentary Collection* (New York: W.W. Norton, 1999), pp. 253–4.
5 Frederic E. Wakeman, Jr., *Spymaster: Dai Li and the Chinese Secret Service* (Berkeley, CA: University of California Press, 2003), p. 26.
6 Quoted in Wilbur and How, *Missionaries of Revolution*, p. 219.
7 Ibid., p. 124.
8 Ibid., p. 250.
9 Mao Zedong, "Report on an Investigation of the Peasant Movement in Hunan," in *Selected Readings from the Works of Mao Tsetung* (Beijing: Foreign Languages Press, 1971), pp. 24–5.
10 Wilbur and How, *Missionaries of Revolution*, p. 387.
11 Robert C. North, *Chinese Communism* (N.P., World University Library, 1971), p. 104.
12 Quoted in Cheng and Lestz with Spence, *The Search for Modern China*, p. 264.
13 Helen Praeger Young, *Choosing Revolution: Chinese Women Soldiers on the Long March* (Urbana, IL: University of Illinois Press, 2001), p. 26.
14 Ibid.
15 Quoted in C. Martin Wilbur, *The Nationalist Revolution in China, 1923–1928* (Cambridge, MA: Harvard University Press, 1983), p. 131.
16 Jonathan Fenby, *Generalissimo: Chiang Kai-shek and the China He Lost* (Collingdale, PA: Diane Publishing, 2005), p. 158.
17 Howard L. Boorman, ed., *Biographical Dictionary of Republican China* (New York: Columbia University Press, 1970), Vol. 1, p. 112.

Suggestions for Further Reading

Jordan, Donald. *The Northern Expedition: China's National Revolution of 1926–1928* (Honolulu: University of Hawaii Press, 1976). A narrative analysis of the military campaign of the Nationalist Party to unite China, destroy the warlords, and push out the imperialist powers.

Schoppa, R. Keith. *Blood Road: The Mystery of Shen Dingyi in Revolutionary China* (Berkeley, CA: University of California Press, 1995). Written as a murder mystery, this prize-winning book suggests new ways of approaching and understanding the Chinese revolution of the 1920s.

Strand, David. *Rickshaw Beijing: City People and Politics in the 1920s* (Berkeley, CA: University of California Press, 1989). This book suggests that new political forces and styles were at play in the capital, giving rise to an expanded public sphere.

Taylor, Jay. *The Generalissimo: Chiang Kai-shek and the Struggle for Modern China* (Cambridge, MA: The Belknap Press of Harvard University Press, 2009). This lively and highly readable biography of Chiang is controversial in its revisionism, but important nevertheless.

Wilbur, C. Martin and Julie Lien-ying How. *Missionaries of Revolution: Soviet Advisers and Nationalist China, 1920–1927* (Cambridge, MA: Harvard University Press, 1989). Encyclopedic in scope, with fascinating documents, narrative, and analysis of the Nationalist revolution.

Part 3

Revolution and Identity

Social Revolution and the Power of
Tradition, 1928–1960

11

Revolution in Retreat
The Nanjing Decade

After the Northern Expedition, Wen Yiduo became professor of English and American literature at Nanjing University. Having studied at the Art Institute of Chicago and Colorado College, he had developed ambivalent views about the West. But his poetry also revealed considerable ambiguity about China. One of his most famous poems, "Dead Water," set forth one startling vision of China at the opening of what has become known as the "Nanjing Decade" (1928–1937), when the Chinese capital was located in Nanjing:

Here is a ditch of hopelessly dead water.
No breeze can raise a single ripple on it.
Might as well throw in rusty metal scraps
or even pour left-over food and soup in it.

Perhaps the green on copper will become emeralds.
Perhaps on tin cans peach blossoms will bloom.
Then, let grease weave a layer of silky gauze,
and germs brew patches of colorful spume.

Let the dead water ferment into jade wine
covered with floating pearls of white scum.
Small pearls chuckle and become big pearls,
only to burst as gnats come to steal this rum.

And so this ditch of hopelessly dead water
may still claim a touch of something bright.
And if the frogs cannot bear the silence—
the dead water will croak its song of delight.

Here is a ditch of hopelessly dead water—
a region where beauty can never reside.
Might as well let the devil cultivate it—
and see what sort of world it can provide.[1]

Wen described a China left for dead after twelve years of warlord and revolutionary destruction as "hopelessly dead water"—littered with scraps of rusty metal, scum, and germs. Cleaning up the mess—the gargantuan task of reconstruction and transformation—might require a superhuman (here Wen says "the devil"), and it is possible that beauty can never again reside there; but there is at least the element of hope that Wen shared with many Chinese that China could be transformed from dead water to the better day of emeralds, jade wine, and songs of delight.

CHIANG KAI-SHEK (JIANG JIESHI): THE MAN AND HIS POWER

The man upon whom the task fell was Chiang Kai-shek. He had been tried in the arenas of military leadership, warlord politics, and factional party struggle and emerged at the top. Now the question was, could he lead the country on to construct a modern nation-state that could keep at bay foreign threats and enemies as it bettered the lives of its own citizens? Chiang was a cold, aloof, and distant man. He was determined, even single-minded, intolerant, and afflicted with a fierce temper. As one historian suggested, "People did not love Chiang Kai-shek, but they were impressed by him."[2] He saw himself as selfless and moral. As time passed, he came to identify himself more and more with China and to see anyone who opposed him as betraying China in clearly treasonable fashion. There could, in short, be no loyal opposition. In terms of his rule, such qualities meant that he did not know how to delegate, he often paid little attention to chains of command, and, perhaps the worst tendency of a military figure, he thought force could triumph over every obstruction.

In December 1927 Chiang married Soong Meiling, daughter of a Chinese businessman who had been a longtime financial supporter of Sun Yat-sen. Indeed, Meiling's next older sister had married Sun, and her oldest sister was married to the financier H. H. Kung, soon to become an important player in Chiang's government. Moreover, the three sisters' brother, T. V. Soong, would also become an important government figure. The marriages of two Soong sisters to the key leaders of the Guomindang, Sun and Chiang, and the close-knit family group at the top of the government were quite remarkable. Soong Meiling was a good match for Chiang. A graduate of Wellesley College, she spoke fluent English. She was attractive and urbane; and she was able to some degree to conceal or, at the least, to soften some of Chiang's hard edges.

The marriage was controversial because Chiang was still married to his second wife, Chen Jieru. His relationships with his first two wives were in some ways a measure of the man, but in the larger sense, perhaps a measure of how many Chinese husbands dealt with their wives. He had gotten her to marry him by claiming his twenty-year-old arranged first marriage was unhappy and celibate (despite his fathering Chiang Ching-kuo). It is said that on their wedding night in 1921, Chiang passed his syphilis onto his new wife; her treatment for the disease left her infertile. When he decided to marry Soong Meiling, he told Chen that he was marrying Meiling only for political convenience, that he had arranged for Chen a five-year "study" tour of the United States, after which she could return and their marriage would continue. In the United States, Chen learned via the press that Chiang in reality had denied their marriage, dismissing Chen as a concubine. Lies, manipulation, controlling women's lives, passing on a deadly disease—all signs of an egoistic and non-empathetic man. In addition, to get approval for the marriage, especially since the Soong family was Christian, Chiang had to promise that he would "investigate Christianity." Following that pledge, he was baptized in Shanghai in October 1930. "Soong Meiling stood beside her husband at that ceremony and repeated vows with him to dramatize their joint dedication to Christian principles and to the rejuvenation of China."[3]

It could be said that Chiang's power lay in three positions that he held. As head of state (his specific title was chair of the State Council), he had the power to set domestic policy and to deal with foreign powers. As chair of the party's Central Executive Committee, he controlled the organ that, in line with the thought of Sun Yat-sen, was to serve as tutor for the people until they eventually could develop a full-fledged republic. Significantly, the length of this party tutelage was not spelled out. As commander-in-chief of the party army, Chiang held military power, his most important resource. Holding these three posts made Chiang look supreme, but as time went on, it was the man himself who seemed to emerge supreme as the institutions of party and state shrank before his apparent indispensability. But in the beginning, he seemed anything but indispensable.

MILITARY POWER, PARTY FACTIONALISM, AND RESIDUAL WARLORDISM

The influence of the military in Chinese politics and society had seemingly grown exponentially since the 1911 revolution. Whereas the army at the end of the Qing had numbered about 400,000, by 1922 there were 1,200,000 men under arms; by 1929 that number had shot up to 2,000,000. In 1929 over half of the 630,000 Guomindang members were soldiers; even more crucial, in terms of party rule, in 1935, 43 percent of the Central Executive Committee were soldiers. On the provincial leadership level during the Nanjing decade, 25 of the 33 men who served as provincial chairs were generals. Revealing Chiang's commitment to the military was the fact that during the period, fully 66.7 percent of national government expenditures were funneled to the military and to payment on debts.

Although the Northern Expedition had technically united the country and ended the warlord scourge, "residual warlordism" remained a dangerous political and military challenge. That danger was compounded by the reality that Chiang did not achieve firm control of the party apparatus until near the end of the Nanjing decade. Before surveying the civil wars that continued to rake China in the 1920s and 1930s, it is important to understand the party challenges Chiang faced. When he rose to power, Chiang had faced the party's left-wing challenge of the government at Wuhan, led by Wang Jingwei. Indeed, from late 1927 to mid-1928, leftists controlled many provincial and local regimes. In Zhejiang, for example, the government sponsored a rent-reduction campaign; in Jiangsu, in the name of eliminating superstitions, temples were confiscated and turned into welfare centers.

While Wang was in Europe in 1928–1929, others of the left, specifically the journalist and former Communist Chen Gongbo, continued to call for mass organizations that could give the new regime a popular base. In late 1928 Chen founded the Society of Comrades for Guomindang Reorganization. It and its leftist members came to be called the Reorganizationist Clique, with its own constitution, its own party headquarters in Shanghai, and branches around the country. Its formation came at a time when Chiang and the party were cracking down on local and provincial leftist power. The established approach to rid the party of "undesirables" was to order party reregistration, during which the unwanted simply would not be allowed to register as party members. But violence was also a tactic to get rid of perceived threats to Chiang's party control: the assassination of the maverick Zhejiang party leader Shen Dingyi in August 1928 is only one example. Chiang played his trump card against the left at the party's Third Congress in March 1929, when he changed the rules to prevent a strong presence of the left by appointing 75 percent of the delegates. At the congress, left-wing leaders were expelled from the party, some (like Chen Gongbo), forever, and others for a specified number of years; because of his stature, Wang Jingwei was simply reprimanded for "straddling parties." Chiang's efforts to defeat the left could weaken and humble the once-strong faction, but as events would show, the left would not disappear.

Warlords were still around, waiting for opportunities, because Chiang had coopted them into the Northern Expeditionary armies instead of defeating them. During the Northern Expedition, the important warlords had been named heads of branch political councils as a way of gaining their support. Chiang and his advisers had determined that these councils had to be abolished and the bloated armies demobilized. Chiang's own army had to be reduced from its 240,000-man size, for the cost of supplying it and keeping it in the field was 60 million yuan more than Chiang's government revenues. But a demobilization meeting of the chief warlords that Chiang called in early 1929 was a fiasco. When Chiang appeared to be asking for a sacrifice from the militarists but not from himself, the conference disintegrated and in effect led to a series of costly civil wars. These were no small affairs. Since there were so many similarities to the mammoth warlord wars of the early and mid-1920s, one can legitimately ask whether the warlord period was over and, alternatively, whether in fact, during this stage of his career, Chiang Kai-shek was simply the biggest (and ultimately, the last) warlord.

The very first war in this new series of struggles began the month (March 1929) that Chiang set for abolishing the branch political councils. What follows is a catalogue-like descriptive outline of these wars, set down in this fashion to underline the ongoing nature of the challenges Chiang faced. Added also are the five military campaigns Chiang launched against a revived Communist threat in Southeast China and the campaign against the Japanese in Manchuria; both of these will be discussed at length in the next two chapters. As you read this list, do not become concerned about remembering the complex details; the important point is to give you some understanding of the instability, even chaos, that occupied the attention of the Nanjing government; of the challenges to Chiang from a wide array of enemies; and of the fragility with which Chiang held power.

1. March to May 1929—Militarists of the Guangxi clique (in Southern China) rebelled against Chiang's control. With 230,000 men, they seemed by themselves a formidable force. But there were rumors that they were going to ally with the northern warlord Feng Yuxiang. Chiang, using the typical warlord ploy of the "silver bullet," bought Feng off with a bribe of 2 million yuan and a promise that Feng could take charge of Shandong province. Chiang won the war in two months.
2. May 1929—When Chiang reneged on his Shandong promise to Feng, Feng challenged him. Chiang seemed the master warlord tactician, offering key outfits in Feng's army massive silver bullets. Over 100,000 of Feng's army defected to Chiang. The war was thus mercifully short.
3. October to November 1929—Feng's army fought Chiang's forces in Henan province.
4. February to September 1930—A longtime master strategist, the warlord Yan Xishan announced that he would side with Feng against Chiang in a Northern Coalition. Not only did the Guangxi clique say that it would coordinate its activities with this coalition, but two Guomindang factions, Wang's Reorganizationist clique and the extreme right Western Hills faction, supported this serious challenge. Fighting raged from May to September, with a new national government formed at Beiping (the new name, "northern peace," given to the city of Beijing, or "northern capital," when Nanjing became the capital) with Yan as head of state. The final success of this campaign against Chiang would have been determined by whether the Manchurian warlord Zhang Xueliang joined the coalition. Continuing his brilliant silver bullet campaign, Chiang bought Zhang off with a 10-million-yuan bribe. The coalition thus failed. Zhang, emboldened, immediately led 100,000 of his men into North China to dominate that region.
5. December 1930—The first extermination campaign against a revived Communist movement in Jiangxi province failed.
6. February 1931 to January 1932—Almost a year of cold war threatened to erupt into a hot war. It began with Chiang's arrest of Hu Hanmin, head of the main legislative body in the government. In support of Hu, militarists in Guangxi and Guangdong, backed by Wang Jingwei, the Western Hills group, and others, established a breakaway government in Canton on June 1.

A civil war would likely have broken out if Japanese aggression in Manchuria had not exploded into a war. As it was, Chiang resigned his posts, and a new government under Sun Yat-sen's son Sun Fo lasted for twenty-five days in January 1932 before Chiang returned to power.

7. May to June 1931—The second extermination campaign against the Jiangxi Communists failed.
8. September to December 1931—The Manchurian campaign against the Japanese aggressors was waged.
9. July to October 1931—The third extermination campaign against the Communists failed.
10. January to March 1932—A campaign in the Shanghai metropolitan region against the Japanese invasion occurred.
11. January to March 1933—The fourth extermination campaign against the Communists failed.
12. March 1933—Japan seized the Inner Mongolian province of Rehe.
13. August 1933—Japan took the eastern part of the Inner Mongolian province of Chahar.
14. October 1933 to October 1934—The fifth extermination campaign against the Communists succeeded.

This is an appalling list. It shows that from October 1928, when Chiang first became head of state, until the end of the successful campaign against the Communists in October 1934, Chiang's forces were involved in actual warfare or on the brink of potential warfare for forty-five of the seventy-two months—roughly 62.5 percent of the time. Further, at some times, as in 1931, Chiang faced up to three struggles concurrently. In trying to understand the Nanjing decade and Chiang's role in it, this context of hot war and cold war upon which Chiang had to focus is extraordinarily important. Finally, it should be stressed that although party factions did not appear as military opponents after the 1931–1932 "cold war," party factions continued to thrive in challenges to Chiang. He began to consolidate his power at the Fifth Party Congress in 1935. But he did not firmly establish his power over party factions until the Extraordinary Congress in Wuhan in March 1938, eight months after the beginning of the war against Japan. Even though some of the internecine warfare and factional struggle may have been to some degree his responsibility, its reality meant that the needed tasks of transforming the dead water, of reconstructing Chinese society, had to wait another day.

SECRETS OF CHIANG'S ABILITY TO RETAIN POWER

Military Sources

Given the immense political and military opposition he had to face and the obstacles he had to overcome, it was more than just a minor miracle that Chiang was able to keep the reins of power. What were his sources of power? Most basic was that he was a military man at a time when military force was the sole arbiter of power. He was also a master of warlord politics, flexibly linking himself to different factions at different times and freely using silver bullets to shatter warlord coalitions. In practical terms, the teacher–student bonds he had built up at the Whampoa Military Academy were crucial; he had served as hands-on commandant for four Whampoa classes that produced about 5,000 soldiers—all of whom shared special master–disciple *guanxi*, or connections. Chiang would come to depend on the Whampoa clique in many ways, as we will see.

Victory in the Northern Expedition had swelled party ranks from 150,000 in 1926 to 630,000 in 1929, with a third of those members under twenty-five years old—people without much historical memory of major revolutionary changes: they would have been only seven or eight at the time of the 1911 revolution and about fifteen at the time of the May Fourth incident. Party victory understandably attracted thousands of opportunists ready to seize whatever prize they could. Chiang's chief of staff, He Yingqin, already in early 1928, had worried about what a huge influx might do to the party: "Party headquarters at all levels are concerned only about the quantity, and pay no attention to the quality [of the new members]. The spirit of the party becomes more rotten by the day."[4]

Another complaint, of a similar nature, focused on the governmental bureaucracy, men charged with executing crucial policies. Many had served old-style warlord regimes and now crowded into Nanjing to grab the spoils of victory—new official posts. Though some may have been motivated by a desire to serve, most seemed to be mainly concerned with making money and seeking power. The upshot was an administration that featured two of the three bêtes noires of sound and effective government—an ineffectual, unresponsive bureaucracy and uncontrolled, open corruption. (The third bête noire, political repression, will be discussed momentarily.)

The problems with bureaucracy were certainly known in China prior to this regime, but bureaucratic delay and obstacles seemed to have become even more egregious. One observer noted,

> a document arriving at a provincial government office was transmitted through thirty-seven steps, each of which consumed from a few hours to a few days. … A reply after a half year's time was a surprise to no one. Not a few documents perished on their long and dreary journey, buried alive in someone's desk drawer.[5]

As for corruption, it was omnipresent. In 1935 the author Lin Yutang aptly noted that "The commonest conjugation in Chinese grammar is that of the verb 'to squeeze' [to be corrupt]: '*I squeeze, you squeeze, he squeezes, we squeeze, you squeeze, they squeeze.*' It is a regular verb."[6] There was a penetrating sense in many circles that the existing structures were no longer revolutionary. Indeed, Chiang himself admitted in 1932: "The Chinese revolution has failed." His hope was "to restore the revolutionary spirit that the [party] had in 1924."[7] In that vein, Chiang welcomed the establishment of the Blue Shirts, the active core of the Whampoa Clique.

The Blue Shirts was formed at the prompting of young officers upset about the health of the nation, particularly the ills of the party and the state. They argued that the party, which had been the vehicle of revolution, "now seem[ed] to have dissipated the hopes of the masses."[8] The Blue Shirts saw fascism as the way to restore China. Many had become familiar with German Nazism from contact with the German military advisory mission that Chiang brought to China to manage and advise on military academy education. In addition, hundreds of Chinese soldiers went to Germany and Italy to study military science. Hitler's rise seemed to signal to many that fascism was in the vanguard of historical progress. Chiang himself argued, "Can fascism save China? We answer: yes. Fascism is now what China most needs … fascism is a wonderful medicine exactly suited to China, and the only spirit that can save it."[9] In a very real way, the Blue Shirts were the political institutional reaction against the May Fourth Movement. Chiang again made the point: "In the last several decades we have in vain become drunk with democracy and the advocacy of free thought. And what has been the result? We have fallen into a chaotic and irretrievable situation."[10] The remedy: fascism with its emphasis on the "total exaltation of the nation," the "total abnegation of the individual," and "obedience to the supreme leader."

The Blue Shirts were a dominant force in many of Chiang's programs. They were in charge of political training in the army, government, and schools and active in setting up people's militia units. In addition, the Blue Shirts were closely involved with two major programs. One was "Special Services," the public security government organ charged with intelligence gathering and responding to perceived enemies of state. Headed by the notorious Dai Li, the Military Commission's Bureau of Investigation and Statistics became infamous for its active involvement in spying, sabotage, kidnapping, assassination, and terror. Dai was something of an honorary member of the Whampoa clique; although he never graduated from the academy, he was held in such esteem by Chiang that he received a diploma "through special dispensation." A measure of the perceived importance of Dai's work for the regime and of its increasing political repression—the third bête noire of sound and effective government—was the ballooning size of Dai's bureau. In 1932, when it began, it had 145 operatives; three years later, it had over 1,700; and at the end of World War II, there were between 40,000 and 50,000. The Blue Shirts themselves were disbanded in 1938, but they quickly reappeared under a new name, the Three People's Principles Youth Corps.

A second major effort of the Blue Shirts involved Chiang's New Life Movement, a campaign that began in 1934 in order to spread the fascist spirit and challenge the anti-traditionalism of the May Fourth period. Chiang apparently hoped that New Life's ideological appeal to a resuscitated Confucianism might prove a potent alternative to Communism. It is hard to imagine how Chiang could have ever seriously believed that appeals to a "sloganized Confucianism"—calling for the upholding of "propriety, justice, honesty, and sense of self-respect"—would have been able to catch the attention of and engage most Chinese. Chiang also restored Confucianism as a state religion and made Confucius's birthday a national holiday.

The discourse of gender equality and women's rights of the 1910s and 1920s seemed to be swallowed up in the 1930s by the demands of nationalism. Arranged marriage remained the norm through the 1940s. Educated male reformers on the "woman's problem" saw the nuclear family as the unit to further nationalism. To be successful, there had to be a gendered division of labor in the family. There was no space, no place for "Noras." This meant that women's traditional "domestic roles were written into modernity." The nuclear family was "the place where women contributed to the nation by creating a comfortable and nurturing environment for husband and children."[11]

The import of the Confucian virtues for day-to-day life was clarified somewhat by the issuance of ninety-five rules by which people were to live their lives, rules like these:

Everyone should keep himself clean all the time.
Do not spit in the streets.
Shoes should be worn correctly.
Walk and sit with correct posture.
Do not write on walls.
Say "good morning" to others every morning.
Do not make noise while eating and drinking.
Do not urinate as you please.
Do not laugh while others have funerals.
Keep to the left when walking on the street.

To be sure, some of these things—maybe all—were not bad; but, given the seriousness of China's problems, these slogans, perhaps appropriate for a military academy, were laughable. But Chiang contended, perhaps not too compellingly, that they were central to the New Life Movement. He claimed,

> If we are to have a new life that accords with [propriety, justice, honesty, and a sense of self-respect], then we must start by not spitting heedlessly. If we are to restore the nation and gain revenge for our humiliations, then we need not talk about guns and cannon, but must first talk about washing our faces in cold water.[12]

Chiang's vision of the movement's goals showed how far he had traveled on the road to fascism. The purpose of the New Life Movement, he stated, was

> to thoroughly militarize the lives of the citizens of the entire nation so that they will culti-
> vate courage and swiftness, the endurance of suffering and a tolerance for hard work, and
> especially the habit and ability of unified action, so that they will at any time sacrifice for the
> nation.[13]

Financial Base

Another important reason for Chiang's ability to dominate potential rivals was his superior financial base in Shanghai. During the 1910s, when he worked as a stockbroker in that city, he had developed very close ties with bankers and financiers, on the one hand, and with the underworld Green Gang, on the other. For putting down the labor unrest in his bloody coup of April 12, 1927, he received 3 million yuan from Shanghai business interests; their contributions continued. Since Chiang's military expenses were at least 20 million yuan each month and since his Shanghai supporters were not committed enough to come up with the money voluntarily, Chiang had to resort to forced contributions. His agents, for example, demanded 500,000 yuan from the Nanyang Tobacco Company and 250,000 yuan from the Sincere Company Department Store. When businesses and industries refused, they were threatened, they faced extortion, or their leaders were abducted. A Western observer noted that "[w]ealthy Chinese would be arrested in their homes or mysteriously disappear from the streets. … Under no previous regime in modern times had Shanghai known such a reign of terror."[14] Many of the legitimate taxes also reached government coffers through Shanghai: during the decade, taxes on trade and industry produced up to 85 percent of total revenue.

Political Skills and Authoritarianism

We have already seen how skilled Chiang was in navigating the tricky and dangerous waters of warlord politics. Those same skills stood him in good stead in the equally tricky factional politics of the Guomindang. Not only did the Reorganizationists, the Western Hills faction, and the Whampoa clique exist, but two other factions also maintained substantial power. The CC (Central Club) clique was built by two brothers, Chen Guofu and Chen Lifu, who were nephews of the 1911 revolutionary Chen Qimei, a close associate of Chiang. The government bureaucracy was their base; they controlled many bureaucratic organs and agencies, youth organs, and labor unions. In contrast, the power of the Political Study clique lay not in positions but in its relationship to Chiang. Its two central members were sworn brothers of Chiang; as a result, this clique wielded great power. It stressed "technical expertise and bureaucratic professionalism." Tensions between cliques were great, for there was continual jockeying for power among them. For example, the Blue Shirts thought all the civilian cliques were corrupt; they especially opposed the CC clique, for many of the functions performed by both cliques overlapped; the CC clique, in turn, was especially resentful of the Political Study clique because of its close relationship with Chiang.

By the mid-1930s, Chiang had become the indispensable man, and both party and government became increasingly enfeebled. There were the five branches of government envisioned by Sun Yat-sen: the Executive Yuan, the most powerful, made up of ten ministries and overseeing the bureaucracy; the Legislative Yuan, a law-making body, but not in the mode of a Western-style parliamentary body; the Judicial Yuan, the highest judicial body; the Control Yuan, serving as

FIGURE 11.1 The state designed this mass wedding ceremony during the New Life Movement to link it to pledges of loyalty to the Guomindang and the legacy of Sun Yat-sen. Note the marriage of East and West, with men wearing traditional Chinese gowns and women, Western bridal gowns.
Source: Pictures from History/Bridgeman Images.

censorate; and the Examination Yuan, dealing with civil service examinations. But as a measure of the languishing of government, only 8 to 13 percent of the budget in the 1930s went toward the functions of the bureaucracy. Chiang's hands were everywhere; as one commentator put it, "In terms of authority, he was the head of everything."[15]

With such a centralized government structure, the relationship between the center at Nanjing and localities across the country was complicated both by elements of culture and by recent history. With cultural emphasis on family, personal networks, native place, and local gods, the natural focus of Chinese civilization was still local. But in addition, historical developments since the late Qing had only enhanced the power of the locality and its elites. The weakened central regime during the late nineteenth century, and the politically and socially fragmented period between 1911 and 1927, had given local elites in institutions such as self-government bodies and Chambers of Commerce increasingly important political roles in their communities. Crucially, they had been undirected and undeterred by the central government (when it existed).

Chiang shared the view of Yuan Shikai that considerable local autonomy and local elite initiative were not conducive to rapid nation building and could potentially lead to further social and political fragmentation. Thus, Nanjing was determined to penetrate society more deeply than the imperial state had done. In the imperial state, the lowest level of government penetration, that is, where a state bureaucrat served in his official capacity, had been the county. Townships that made up counties had local leaders. Under Chiang's government, the county once again became the lowest level at which a state official ruled. But below the county level, the Center established a system of wards composed of townships, which were made up, in turn, of rural villages and urban neighborhoods. The heads of each of these units were appointed by the magistrate in bureaucratic fashion, not chosen by the people in the units. The whole structure was undergirded by the traditional *baojia* system of group mutual surveillance in which groups of families were made responsible for the actions of others in their group. Despite repeated tinkering with local administration and despite claims that the ward-township-village-neighborhood apparatus could serve as the framework for democracy, this regime's vision of nation building remained top-down.

Chiang's authoritarianism is evident not only in his public roles but even more so in his reaction to dissent. Individual dissenters often kept unwanted appointments with Dai Li's assassins. In 1933 Yang Quan, secretary-general of Academia Sinica, China's highest study and research organization supported and controlled by the government, was ambushed. The reason came from the other hat that Yang wore, as secretary-general of the China League for Civil Rights, a role that brought him in conflict with Chiang's policies. In reaction to the killing, Cai Yuanpei, the former chancellor of Beijing University during the May Fourth period and now president of Academia Sinica, resigned all his posts and left China for Hong Kong, but not before he denounced Chiang's government publicly. In 1934, Shi Liangcai, Shanghai civic leader and editor of the important newspaper *Shenbao*, was gunned down; he had been critical of Chiang's policy toward Japanese aggression.

If the dissenters were plural, such as students, Chiang did not send assassins but police. There was enough fear of possible student disruptions that in 1930 all campus nonacademic organizations were forbidden unless they were tightly controlled by the Guomindang. Beginning in 1931, students began to protest Chiang's acquiescence to the Japanese seizure of territory and their nonstop demands. In the repression that followed, some students were killed. But Chiang generally reacted to student demonstrations by sending forces in predawn raids on student dormitories, making arrests, and/or forcing students' expulsion. Political repression became Chiang's seemingly inevitable reaction to any challenge. Journalists were frequently arrested, and newspapers and magazines censored. In 1930, a Western newspaper reported that "[c]ontrasted with the enthusiasm of less than eighteen months ago, the sense of hopelessness … among all Chinese today is perhaps the worst feature of all."[16]

This period of dissent saw a great outpouring of creatively impressive work, especially in the novel, poetry, and drama. The giants in the world of the novel in this period were Mao Dun and Lao She. Mao's masterpiece, *Midnight*, was published in 1933; it depicted the crisis of Shanghai's commerce and industry caused by the forces of international capitalism. Lao She, an ethnic Manchu, parodied the wretched state of China in his 1932 novel *Cat Country*, where even an invasion by "small people" cannot get the cat people to agree on what should be done. His greatest work was *Camel Xiangzi* (1936), translated into English as *Rickshaw*. The unhappy story of a young Beijing rickshaw puller, it takes a biting look at poverty-stricken lower-class life in the northern capital. In the genre of poetry, Wen Yiduo of *Dead Water* fame was a major figure.

The major new genre of literature was the spoken drama. Traditional Chinese theater was opera, a dramatic form incorporating singing, dance, and balletic gymnastics. Spoken drama began only in the twentieth century, inspired by the West and by a turn against tradition. The foremost dramatist of the day was Cao Yu, who, in his last year as an undergraduate at Qinghua University, wrote *Thunderstorm*, probably the play performed most often in the twentieth-century Chinese theatre. Its themes include the May Fourth struggle for emancipation from the constraints of family and the brutal effects of capitalism on labor, but it is at once made darker, more powerful, and more modern by Cao's exploration of the theme of incest.

CHIANG'S RECORD

Given the gigantic tasks of reconstruction that China faced, the large number of political and military enemies that continued to dog Chiang, and the limitations, miscalculations, and failures of his government, any progress toward the establishment of a modern nation-state during the Nanjing decade may seem remarkable. There were, however, positive aspects to Chiang's record, though each accomplishment had a downside.

Chiang had risen to power under the banner of nationalism, the goals of his revolution having been, on the one hand, to eliminate warlords and unite the nation and, on the other, to expel the imperialists and liberate the nation. With his victory against the warlords, Chiang thus had the opportunity to begin to negotiate the end of the almost century-old unequal treaty system. One of the most continually irritating aspects of China's semi-colonial position under the system was its loss of ability to set and collect its own tariffs. This meant that it could not protect its own nascent industry by raising tariff rates to keep out cheaper Western-made products. Between July 1928 and May 1929, China successfully negotiated its tariff autonomy with seven major powers and gained control of the Maritime Customs Service. Through negotiations it was also able by 1931 to reduce the number of foreign concessions from thirty-three to thirteen. Because it set forth new law codes (as demanded by the West), it was able to begin to negotiate the issue of extraterritoriality for the first time. The downside of these negotiations was that not until 1943 was extraterritoriality finally abolished, and then not so much because of negotiations but rather as a gesture from the United States and Great Britain to a wartime ally.

Despite the continued political and military challenges, Chiang was able to stop the warlord period's trend toward territorial fragmentation. But it was a slow and not completely successful process. In 1934, Chiang firmly controlled only seven of eighteen provinces (Henan, Hubei, Jiangxi, Anhui, Jiangsu, Zhejiang, and Fujian). He was able to seize the opportunity of his campaigns against the Communists on the Long March (see the next chapter) to solidify his control over four others (Hunan, Guizhou, Sichuan, and Yunnan). When war broke out with Japan in the summer of 1937, however, one-third of the Chinese provinces (six) were still beyond Chiang's control (Guangdong having been corraled in late 1936).

Economic Development

To build a modern nation-state required not only reconstruction after years of war but also large-scale development in industry, utilities, and mining. In 1933 these sectors of the economy accounted for less than 4 percent of the net domestic product. Even though the modern sectors of the economy grew from 1931 to 1936 at a rate that compared well with that of other countries, the problem was the very small base from which China began its development. At the time of Chiang's victory in 1928, China had only about 1,220 miles of railroad. Its output of electric power was just 0.88 million megawatts, only 1 percent of the output in the United States and less than 18 percent of that produced in Russia. With such small bases, even moderate rates of industrial growth would appear large. Thus, by the end of the decade, China's railroad mileage had grown by what sounds like a whopping 80 percent—all the way up to 2,300 miles.

In many ways, Chiang could be seen as the heir to the long line of self-strengtheners stretching from nineteenth-century leaders such as Li Hongzhang and Zhang Zhidong through Yuan Shikai in the early Republic. Though two Western commentators called him "an economic ignoramus," he knew generally what he wanted to do: to modernize China's economy, often using Western models, in order to preserve a state that he increasingly envisioned as based on traditional values.[17] Like Yuan, he believed that central control and decision making were keys for modernizing the economy and the state. Chiang focused most of his plans for modernization on the areas of communications, transportation, and manufacturing because development in these areas would provide crucial infrastructure for defense and a significant base for further modernization.

Unfortunately, progress in industrial development was minuscule. Blueprints for a large-scale four-year plan to industrialize the Yangzi Valley had to be shelved because the state could not fund the prescribed construction of communications and factories. State plans to build four new steel mills shriveled into the construction of only one small plant. By 1937, China with its 400 to 500 million population had less industrial production than Belgium, with 8 million people. Even with attention focused on construction of highways, railroads, and telegraphs, the little that was accomplished is rather shocking: by 1937, China had the same mileage of modern highways as Spain, one-third of the telegraph lines of France, and less railroad mileage than the state of Illinois.

Why such drop-in-the-bucket accomplishments? The political and military challenges were, of course, significant, but other serious challenges also curtailed significant reconstruction and development. Economic and fiscal difficulties were debilitating. The worldwide depression was anything but a stable context for economic development and expansion. From 1929 to 1931, because of the currency situation, China actually experienced an economic boom. China was the only large country in the world that had a currency based on silver. When the stock market crashed in 1929, the world price of silver dropped, reducing the worth of China's currency. This depreciation meant that other countries' goods were too expensive for Chinese to purchase, so that, for the time being, foreign competition in China was no problem. Silver also flowed into the country with foreign investments in the low-priced Chinese economy. With huge silver reserves, Chinese banks offered Chinese entrepreneurs loans for business expansion at low interest rates. But in 1931 Great Britain and Japan went off the gold standard in order to make their goods more marketable, setting up direct competition with the Chinese. The depression then hit China. Even worse was to follow. The bottom fell out of the economy following the 1934 U.S. Congress' passage of the Silver Purchase Act in 1934: it had the effect of draining China precipitously of its silver reserves and sending the economy tailspinning into deeper depression.

Even more serious for China's economic reconstruction and development was its insufficient and poorly structured tax base. Traditionally, the crucial tax for the Chinese central government was the land tax. But collecting it after so many years of war and turmoil was problematic. With considerable disruption of local economies and the upheaval caused by population flight and resettlement over the previous decades, land ownership in many areas was unclear. The situation necessitated a census before taxes could be collected, but a census was both too time-consuming and too expensive. Because of this, Chiang and the government decided simply to write off the land tax: if provinces wanted to collect it, they could do so.

The national government thus became dependent on tariffs, excise taxes, and borrowing. The taxes were counterproductive. Fully 50 percent of the government's revenue came from customs duties (as opposed to 1 percent at the time in the United States). The tariffs handicapped trade and industry, the modern sectors that the government wanted to develop, by making it more expensive to purchase machinery or items needed for manufacturing (during the decade, total purchased manufacturing equipment reached 500 million Chinese dollars). The government in Nanjing also levied a salt tax, a tobacco tax, a stamp tax, and "consolidated taxes," which were collected at the time of manufacture on about fifteen items such as flour, kerosene, matches, rolled tobacco, cotton yarn, and cement. In the main, these taxes were regressive, hitting hardest those least able to pay. With such a tax base, it is hardly surprising that much industrial development was stillborn. Other than these taxes, the government was dependent on borrowing. The pitfall here was that to attract capital, the government had to offer a high rate of return on bonds and loans; and when they offered attractive rates, these government options attracted 70 percent of the nation's available investment capital. Thus, there was so little capital to invest in nongovernmental industrial and commercial enterprises that these entities had to pay up to 20 percent interest in order to attract capital. Like the tax structure, borrowing was also counterproductive to the larger goal of economic development.

One other strategy that the government used to garner funds for development was to become directly involved in setting up and managing economic enterprises. A private stock company, the China Development Finance Corporation, was established by T. V. Soong in 1933 to marshal funds from Chinese and foreign investors in order to foster economic development. This corporation offered loans and jointly managed utilities, water control, and mining enterprises. In addition, the Bank of China, headed by Soong, and the Ministry of Industries, became involved in commercial and light industrial enterprises—all in a quest for governmental revenue and, most assuredly, for their own enrichment as well.

Apart from puny comparisons with development in other nations, the most successful areas of development were communications and transportation. There was construction on two major railroad trunk lines. In 1935, the east–west Longhai line that ran from the seacoast in northern Jiangsu to near the Gansu–Shaanxi border was extended west of Xi'an. The north–south Canton–Hankou line was completed in 1936. The construction of an iron bridge over the Qiantang River just south of Hangzhou linked two other rail lines, the Zhejiang–Jiangxi and the Shanghai–Hangzhou–Ningbo. Highway construction produced over 115,000 kilometers of paved roads by 1936. Modern airlines with regular air routes were established. Telegraph lines went up after undergoing much destruction in the warlord period; long-distance telephone communication expanded.

To sum up, given the immense structural and contingent problems facing the processes of modernization and state-building in the Nanjing period, any progress that was made can generally be seen as a glass half-empty. Recent scholarly research has suggested that this is too bleak a view, that in reality—at least in state-building—the glass was perhaps closer to half-full. The formation of various state institutions focusing on national civil service, taxation, and foreign affairs survived into the People's Republic; in other words, the PRC did not have to start out with a blank slate. Further, the state enterprise system with its key *danwei* (unit) organization (see Chapter 16) took on some of its main attributes during the 1930s and 1940s, not during the 1950s.[18]

AGRICULTURE: THE WORLD OF THE CHINESE FARMER AND HIS WIFE

One scholar has posited that by 1850 in late imperial China, the population "had already come close to occupying and using most of the accessible economic space, particularly permanently cultivable land."[19] A British economic historian reporting on the Chinese agricultural situation in the early 1930s noted that "[t]here are districts in which the position of the rural population is that of a man standing permanently up to the neck in water so that even a ripple is sufficient to drown him."[20] Although historians debate whether Chinese farmers were becoming more deeply mired in poverty or, to use another word, "immiserized," the fact of life for Chinese farmers, who made up at least 80 percent of the population, was a numbing poverty that could only give rise to a brutalized existence. Two examples are given, the first from the core zone of the Lower Yangzi macroregion, the richest area of China. The place is a village in Xiaoshan county across the river from Hangzhou; the time, the 1920s:

The inside of all thatched roof farm homes ... were the same: black rafters, gray walls, a dirt floor, a kitchen table, a bench, farm implements, and amulets from the local temple. There was generally nothing on the walls. ... The floors were covered with chicken shit; and people walked through it with their bare feet. Amid such conditions, the popular saying in the area: "Nothing to eat, nothing to wear—those things still go to the little king [the landlord]."[21]

The second comes from far western China, a peripheral region on the border between Sichuan and Shaanxi provinces; the time, the early 1940s:

The peasants up and down the valley lived and died in their special fashion. ... The father of one family died. Since his wife had been failing and the family was very poor, they decided not to bury him right away. Perhaps the old woman would die, too, before really warm weather came and the old man began to smell. Then they could save by burying both with one funeral. The old lady agreed, so they stored the coffin in their darkest, coldest room, the old woman's sickroom, and piled stones on its lid to keep the dogs out.[22]

It is perhaps not surprising that the death rate in China in 1930 was 250 percent higher than in the United States and even substantially higher than in India. What were the likely causes? In part it resulted from the appallingly bleak poverty and its consequences, malnutrition and starvation. It also stemmed from the use of night soil, human and animal excrement, for fertilizer; night soil carried many often-lethal parasites—hookworm, liver fluke, and blood fluke. If night soil was not properly fermented to kill these worms, they became a great danger. If, for example, fecal-borne hookworm eggs hatch, the worm can pass through the skin of a farmer's leg as he, wearing only shorts, slogs through a rice paddy. The half-inch worm eventually finds its way to the farmer's intestinal wall, where it lives sucking blood; if joined by hundreds of its blood-sucking kin, they can devour a half-pint of the farmer's blood daily, causing anemia and eventually death. Indeed, it is estimated that close to a quarter of all deaths in China resulted from infection by these parasites.

The most difficult reality farmers faced was nature; against it there was no protection. Will it ever rain? Will it ever stop raining? How do we deal with the rice driven into the mud by the high winds? What about the cotton destroyed by hail? In pre-insecticide days, how do we deal

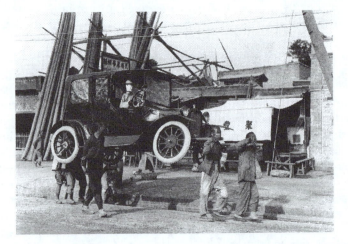

FIGURE 11.2   This elaborate paper Model A Ford and its chauffeur were designed to be burnt at a graveside for use in the deceased's afterlife.
Source: Sidney D. Gamble Photographs, Archive of Documentary Arts, Duke University.

with pests like rice borers and grasshoppers? A pertinent example were the Yangzi River floods in 1931, when days of torrential rain raised the river an unprecedented 15 feet above its normal level. Dikes broke, flooding "an area the size of New York state," with water at "an average depth ... of nine feet. ... And over twenty-five million people—a population approximately equivalent to the entire farm population of the United States—were displaced and suffered losses from the flood."[23]

The problem is that 1931 was not anomalous. Rain, wind, hail, and drought in 1934 and 1935 made those years nightmares as well. As a result, the rice harvest was down by a third from 1931, soybeans by 36 percent, and wheat by 7 percent. A farmer planted his crop, having borrowed money for the seeds; he worked from dawn to dusk. When natural disaster struck and his crop was wiped out, the bills for the seeds and other expenses still had to be paid. This meant a trip to the pawnbroker—if there was indeed anything to pawn. If natural disasters came in twos or in groups, the farmer could very easily lose everything. His and his family's only choice might be to abandon their village and emigrate elsewhere—a chilling possibility given the fact that all their connections were in their home area and they would be moving to an area peopled only by the Other.

Even if his crop was harvested, if he was a tenant farmer he had not only outstanding bills to pay, but rent to the landlord as well. It is estimated that about 50 percent of all farmers rented all or some of their land, though the extent of tenancy varied throughout China. In the North, tenancy was less and many farmers were small landholders. In Central and South China, as well as in Sichuan, tenancy was more widespread (though less so than in countries such as France, Ireland, and Denmark). Since the Chinese practiced partible inheritance, in which the land was divided equally among the sons of the family, each succeeding generation would have less and less land to farm, making its livelihood ever more precarious.

For its part, Chiang's government established regulations in the Land Law of 1930 that limited rents to 37.5 percent of the harvest. For tenants who had been paying 60 to 70 percent, this change was obviously helpful. Unfortunately, like so many plans and laws set forth by the Nanjing government, the law—which even stipulated that tenants could buy the land from an absentee landlord if they farmed it for a decade—was never implemented. Reports indicate that rents thus remained in the 50 to 70 percent range. Beyond this stillborn law the government was afraid to go, for its fear of social unrest and its desire to maintain generally good relations with rural elites prevented further action. Some have said that the decision not to collect the land tax for the national government was a clear indication that Chiang was unwilling to tackle the mammoth problems of farmers and the countryside or to do something to rein in local elites whose power had also risen during the government-weak warlord period.

The government did develop certain programs to try to increase agricultural productivity, funding and sponsoring research on new varieties of seed and on fertilizers and pesticides. Attention was paid as well to developing disease-resistant silkworms, as well as tea and cotton plants, and marketing their products more effectively. The infrastructure of agricultural production began to be renovated as some rivers were dredged and some irrigation systems constructed. In dealing with agricultural issues, the government continually faced an immense country whose localities and conditions were incredibly varied. Agricultural problems differed from locality to locality, and methods of dealing with them of necessity had to vary.

Rural Reconstruction Efforts

Another approach used in trying to come to grips with agricultural problems was promoting projects of rural reconstruction. These efforts were designed to promote various rural reforms in specific areas; in essence, they were holistic attempts to develop an area. Interestingly, in light of the government's inability and unwillingness to engage the rural populace in basic change, these were initially begun by private citizens. The first to be undertaken, although not well known, was the East Township Self-Government Association in Zhejiang province. There in 1928, the reformer Shen Dingyi inaugurated the economic, educational, and political development of the township through, among other things, the establishment of mass organizations and self-government bodies, the setting up of cooperatives and schools, and the initiation of programs of conservation, medical care, and sericulture reform.

Two more well-known efforts at rural reconstruction focused on education as the key to remaking China. James Yen's Mass Education Association, established in over sixty market towns and villages in Ding county (Hebei province), set up "people's schools" to offer some practical education for the masses with an emphasis on public ethics. Yen expanded his work in the creation of a "model village," with an emphasis not only on education but also on public health, agricultural reform, and economic development. The Nanjing regime gave considerable latitude to the noted Confucian scholar Liang Shuming in his management of the Shandong Rural Reconstruction Institute. This body oversaw development efforts in two counties, with a focus on education and particularly on bringing about good class relations between elites and masses; Liang's program developed out of his hatred of the Marxist idea of class struggle. The Nanjing government itself also became involved in setting up two short-lived experimental counties as models of bureaucratic reform. The creators of all these rural reconstruction efforts envisioned them as models of local development and potential models for the nation. Liang, for example, believed that his Shandong experiment would catch fire and spread across the nation. In the end, all these efforts at model building for the nation were, like so many plans during the Nanjing decade, stillborn. It remained for them to be destroyed completely in the fires of war with Japan.

The Cooperative Movement

One effort to deal with rural economic problems, especially the lack of available credit, was the establishment of cooperative associations. The first cooperatives in China dated from 1918, established mostly in Hebei province under the auspices of the China International Famine Relief Commission. The commission had been formed after the North China famine of 1920–1921 and was involved, with heavy missionary participation, in spearheading various rural improvement efforts such as building roads and dikes and digging wells. Other cooperatives were begun by individuals: Zhejiang's first cooperatives, for example, appeared in 1928 with the rural reconstruction experiment of Shen Dingyi. After 1928 provincial governments encouraged the establishment of cooperatives; Nanjing got behind them only beginning in 1934. Official patronage caused the number of cooperatives nationwide to shoot up 1,181 percent to 46,983 (with 1.5 million members) on the eve of war with Japan. Though there were various types of cooperatives—production, retailing, and credit—the last were the most numerous: in Zhejiang, for example, 91.2 percent in 1932 were credit cooperatives. There was an urgent rural need for institutions to provide loans at reasonable rates of interest; in 1931 the annual rate of interest on loans in rice-producing areas was 28 percent; in wheat-producing areas, 38 percent. Local residents, mostly elites, created a fund whose monies could be loaned out at lower interest rates than those of the standard creditors—pawnbrokers, merchants, and rich farmers and landlords.

Despite their increasing number, several aspects of the Chinese cooperatives suggest that they are misleading in terms of producing meaningful change in the countryside. Studies have shown that during the 1930s, when cooperatives might have been significant institutions meeting urgent rural credit needs, the increase in cooperatives did not stem from a groundswell of local enthusiasm over their potential. Their surge in numbers came rather from government stimulus; in other words, this is another example of the Nanjing decade's top-down governance. Certainly it seemed, from the case of the East Township cooperatives, that such local bodies needed outside impetus, even patronage, to be organized and to function effectively; various cooperatives flourished under Shen Dingyi's leadership, but all of them collapsed within a few years after his death.

Another problem was that cooperatives were dominated by elites, often for the benefit primarily of elites. Local farmers did not necessarily perceive that buying shares in the cooperative would greatly benefit them. But the most negative aspect of the cooperative was that at the height of the cooperative fever under the Nanjing government, less than 3 percent of the total money loaned out to farmers came from cooperatives; over 97 percent came from traditional usurious sources. The cooperative effort even became a bureaucratic boondoggle, as each county with cooperatives got a new county official, the director of cooperatives.

By the end of the Nanjing decade, Wen Yiduo was writing no more poetry. It was clear that the "dead water" of his 1928 vision had simply become filled with more debris and that the world had not been transformed into a better place. During the decade, Wen had become politically passive, calling on his students at Qinghua University to shun involvement in politics. As if trying to avoid looking at the turmoil around him, he turned his attention ever further back to the Chinese past, to serious study of early Daoist writings and to explications of Tang dynasty poetry. When war broke out against Japan in 1937, he joined his family, whom he had sent on ahead to far Southwest China to avoid the conflagration. He could not have known then that he would soon regain his interest in current affairs and that eventually it would cost him his life.

Notes

1 Quoted in Leo Ou-fan Lee, "Literary Trends: The Road to Revolution, 1927–1949," in *The Cambridge History of China, Vol. 13, Republican China 1912–1949, Part 2*, ed. John K. Fairbank and Albert Feuerwerker (Cambridge, UK: Cambridge University Press, 1986), pp. 457–8.
2 Lloyd E. Eastman, *The Abortive Revolution* (Cambridge, MA: Harvard University Press, 1974), p. 279.
3 Howard L. Boorman, ed., *Biographical Dictionary of Republican China* (New York: Columbia University Press, 1970), Vol. 3, p. 139.
4 Lloyd E. Eastman, "Nationalist China during the Nanking Decade, 1928–1937," in Fairbank and Feuerwerker, *The Cambridge History of China*, p. 118.
5 Eastman, *The Abortive Revolution*, p. 12.
6 Ibid., p. 14.
7 Ibid., p. 1.
8 Ibid., p. 32.
9 Quoted in ibid., p. 40.
10 Ibid., p. 42.
11 Gail Hershatter, W*omen in China's Long Twentieth Century* (Berkeley, CA: University of California Press, 2007), p. 21.
12 Eastman, T*he Abortive Revolution*, p. 67.
13 Ibid., p. 68.
14 Eastman, "Nationalist China during the Nanking Decade, 1928–1937," p. 132.
15 Eastman, *The Abortive Revolution*, p. 280.
16 Eastman, "Nationalist China during the Nanking Decade, 1928–1937," p. 138.

17 Quoted in Eastman, *The Abortive Revolution*, p. 281.
18 See, for example, Julia Strauss, *Strong Institutions in Weak Polities: State Building in Republican China, 1927–1940* (New York: Oxford University Press, 1998) and Morris L. Bian, *The Making of the State Enterprise System in Modern China: The Dynamics of Institutional Change* (Cambridge, MA: Harvard University Press, 2005).
19 Mark Elvin, "The Environmental Legacy of Imperial China," in *Managing the Chinese Environment*, ed. R. Edmonds (Oxford: Oxford University Press, 1998).
20 R.H. Tawney, *Land and Labor in China* (Boston, MA: Beacon Press, 1966), p. 77.
21 R. Keith Schoppa, *Blood Road: The Mystery of Shen Dingyi in Revolutionary China* (Berkeley, CA: University of California Press, 1995), pp. 100–01.
22 Graham Peck, *Two Kinds of Time* (Boston, MA: Houghton Mifflin, 1967), p. 208.
23 Eastman, *The Abortive Revolution*, p. 188.

Suggestions for Further Reading

Bian, Morris. *The Making of the State Enterprise System in Modern China: The Dynamics of Institutional Change* (Cambridge, MA: Harvard University Press, 2005). This revisionist work shows that state-building efforts during the Nanjing decade were effectively positive in some areas, leaving a legacy for the state leaders of the People's Republic.

Chu, Samuel, ed. *Madame Chiang Kai-shek and Her China* (White Plains, NY: EastBridge, 2005). Brief essays that capture varied aspects of Madame Chiang's life and throw light on her China.

Coble, Parks. *The Shanghai Capitalists and the Nationalist Government, 1927–1937* (Cambridge, MA: Harvard University Press, 1980). This book shows that the Nationalist government did not represent or derive great support from capitalists and entrepreneurs, but that it worked to control and exploit them.

Eastman, Lloyd. *The Abortive Revolution: China under Nationalist Rule, 1927–1937* (Cambridge, MA: Harvard University Press, 1974). A discussion of the mostly failed policies of the Nationalist government, which acted as if its revolution was over and its only goal was to remain in power.

Wakeman, Frederic E., Jr. *Spymaster: Dai Li and the Chinese Secret Service* (Berkeley, CA: University of California Press, 2003). This well-written biography of the brutal chief of the Chinese secret police sheds light on the nature of Chiang Kai-shek's regime and on the Republic of China in general.

12

Revolution Reborn
The Communists in the 1930s

A study of the Communist movement in the 1930s points to at least two unfortunate elements of history. First, the trouble with the history of a revolution (actually, of any history) is that we see the finished product, but we don't see the roads not taken. The lives of people, parties, governments, and nations have many crossroads, some as on superhighways, others as on small rutted trails, which, if taken, would have produced a very different history. Going back to look at those crossroads and their nature allows us to see that *nothing* about the finished product was inevitable. The CCP's efforts to resuscitate itself following Chiang Kai-shek's White Terror in 1927 and 1928 were marked by many possible different paths, as we will see. A second unfortunate fact about the history of revolution is that the winner gets to decide on and shape the revolution's past and thus create the standard way of seeing that past. In the Communist revolution of the 1930s, Mao Zedong emerged by mid-decade as the first among his peers; by the end of the decade, he was writing the canonical works for the party. It is little wonder that for much of the rest of the twentieth century, the history of the Communist movement in the 1930s was seen either as one with Mao at center stage or as one that bore Mao's imprimatur. This phase of the revolution was, however, considerably more complex than a simple Mao Story.

THE PARTY: "SO WIDELY SCATTERED AND SO BADLY MAULED"[1]

The policy choices that the CCP had made in the 1920s had left it dying on the side of the revolutionary road. The bloc within, which had originally seemed like a Trojan horse from which to destroy the Guomindang, had stirred up rightist Guomindang fears that grew into an unimagined tidal wave. Repeatedly, specifically after Chiang's March 1926 coup against the Soviet advisers and his April 1927 massacre of leftists and CCP members in Shanghai, Stalin had chosen to have the CCP continue the united front—each time with very negative consequences. The party's Autumn Harvest uprisings and Canton commune in the second half of 1927 were total disasters. Party membership, which had reached about 60,000 in April 1927, had collapsed to less than 10,000 by year's end. The party seemed to be in free fall.

Ironically, the Comintern, largely responsible for the CCP's bitter fate, would until 1935 wield even greater power than it had during the united front period. It helped reconstruct the CCP, burdened by its shattered leadership and scattered membership, with key shifts in both party leadership and in party membership. Each man who emerged as a party leader was a generation or more younger than the now discredited CCP general secretary Chen Duxiu, who had been born in 1879: Mao Zedong, the oldest, born in 1893; Qu Qiubai (b. 1899), Li Lisan (b. 1900), Chen Shaoyu (a.k.a. Wang Ming, b. 1907), and Qin Bangxian (a.k.a. Bo Gu, b. 1907). Less grounded in traditional China, all except Mao had studied abroad, Qu, Chen, and Qin in the Soviet Union and Li in France. The major shift in party membership was a large influx of peasants and a decline in the number of intellectuals and urban workers; it was a shift that gave rise to considerable anxiety among established party members, for it portended definite changes in policies and styles. One scholar has asserted that

> [h]istory might have been very different if the original leaders of the Chinese Communist party [had not been killed or later expelled]. They were civilized and sophisticated urban intellectuals, holding humanistic values, with cosmopolitan and open minds, attuned to the modern world. … Their sudden elimination marked an abrupt turn in the Chinese revolution."[2]

A word about the word "peasants." To this point in this book, I have refrained from using this word as a synonym for "farmers" or for the "farming population." Both of the latter, I would argue, are more neutral terms. "Peasant" has more primitive overtones. A peasant somehow seems cruder, less developed, more elemental than a farmer. Although "peasant" has been used in other geographical contexts, it is used most often by the developed world to describe a social type in the undeveloped world. The use of the word seems patronizing on the part of the modern West. Why didn't the United States, even in its undeveloped days, have peasants? They were, it seems, always farmers. In any event, I prefer to continue to use "farmers." But, almost ironically, the Communists have translated the term *nongmin* as "peasant" and have used it in dividing the farm population into groupings (rich peasant, middle peasant, and poor peasant). To substitute "farmer" in this case would seem inappropriate.

The problems of direction for the party and of its organizational difficulties were staggering. To make matters even more difficult, the party was now outlawed: It could not operate in the open as it did before 1927. With many peasants now joining the party, what direction should the party take? How could the scattered membership be reconstituted while the White Terror was still going on? How could the party put the lid on the factionalism that bedeviled it especially at times of defeat, when many were thrashing about for scapegoats? How could the party bind itself together as it concurrently rebuilt when the wide geographical dispersal of its members alone made communications difficult? It took six to nine months for communications to reach certain remote areas. It is said, for example, that Commander He Long, based in western Hunan and Hubei provinces (called the Xiang-exi base area), did not hear about decisions made at the July 1928 Sixth Party Congress until the spring of 1929.

He Long was one of the military figures who, with other CCP members, had retreated far from the cities to remote regions that they could use as so-called base areas, where they could organize and mobilize people, living off the land and building their strength. Mao put it this way: "The base area is our home from which we carry on revolutionary struggles against the enemy. If he does not come, we train soldiers and mobilize the masses here; if he comes, we fight him from our home." Zhang Guotao became the head of the Eyuwan base area on the borders of Hubei, Henan, and Anhui. Mao himself retreated to Jinggangshan on the border between Hunan and Jiangxi, where in early 1928 he and Zhu De established a rural base area. Base areas, like bandit lairs in traditional times, were established on the borders of different provinces. They all began with little power. Mao, contrary to the others, was already able to take two county seats in mid-1928. Zhang did not take his first county seat until the winter of 1929, an indication of the remoteness and poverty of his base.

When He Long established his base, he had only twenty men armed with eight rifles. Jian Xianren's brother, Xianwei, on the Nationalists' "wanted list," joined He Long's growing army that same year. In 1929, Xianren herself joined He's army; assigned to a training unit, she taught reading and writing to illiterate soldiers. He Long, born in 1896 to a poor peasant family in a minority ethnic group (the Tujia) in Hunan, received no formal education. At the age of 20, he beheaded a tax collector with a butcher cleaver, thus avenging his uncle who had been killed by that tax collector for defaulting on his taxes. He had to flee as an outlaw, became in turn a bandit and, likely in part because of his charismatic and outgoing style, was able to cobble together a small army as he morphed into a small warlord. He and his army sided with the Nationalists in the beginning of the Northern Expedition but joined the CCP in late 1926.

When she began teaching in the army in 1929, Xianren was almost an immediate success; she was still among only a handful of women in the army, and word had spread that she was an excellent teacher, patient and commiserating with the illiterate soldiers whenever they had learning difficulties. But she was emotionally overwhelmed when He Long asked her to teach him to read and write; he said that he recognized only three characters. Xianren complied. We do not know how long it was before the 33-year old He asked the 20-year-old Xianren to marry him. She hesitated, but her colleagues persuaded her it was the right thing to do. At the time of the marriage, the base area was encircled by the Nationalists; and two days after the wedding, they were in battle.

Mao Zedong, who would become one of the giants of the twentieth century, was born in Hunan province, the eldest son of a wealthy peasant with whom Mao did not get along. Educated at the village primary school, he went on to study at several higher-level schools, where he was introduced to some Western political and philosophical works. In 1913 he began to study at the Hunan First Normal School in Changsha, the provincial capital. Turned on by *New Youth*, the radical journal edited by Chen Duxiu, he had an essay on physical fitness and its relation to the nation published in the journal's April 1917 issue. Mao served as director of the Changsha Student Association in 1917 and 1918 and graduated from the First Normal School in June 1918. Three months later he was in Beijing, working in the Beijing University library under the founding CCP member Li Dazhao and auditing some courses. Though in the capital city only about six months, he reportedly was deeply influenced by Li's vision of a new China.

He returned to Changsha, where he was active in May Fourth activities, founding his own journal, the *Xiang River Review*, in the summer of 1919. Forced to leave because he had antagonized the provincial warlord by organizing a student strike against him, Mao went back to Beijing for discussions with Li Dazhao and then to Shanghai for conversations with Chen Duxiu. He read the *Communist Manifesto* and wrote that "I considered myself a Marxist" by September 1920. In early 1921, he organized a branch of the Socialist Youth Corps. He was one of the two Hunan representatives at the CCP's First Party Congress in July 1921. In the next several years he worked to organize party activities and labor strikes in Hunan. Under the bloc within option, Mao joined the Guomindang and at its First Party Congress was elected as an alternate member of the Central Executive Committee. In 1925 and 1926 he threw himself into organizing peasants into associations, serving in Canton as the director of the important Peasant Movement Training Institute. In 1927 he went to Hunan to assess the revolutionary potential of the peasant situation. He predicted that

[w]ithin a short time, hundreds of millions of peasants will rise in central, south, and north China with the fury of a hurricane; no force, no matter how strong, can restrain them. They will break all the shackles that bind them and rush to the road of liberation. All imperialists, warlords, corrupt officials, and bad gentry will meet their doom at the hands of the peasants. All revolutionary parties and comrades will be judged by them.[3]

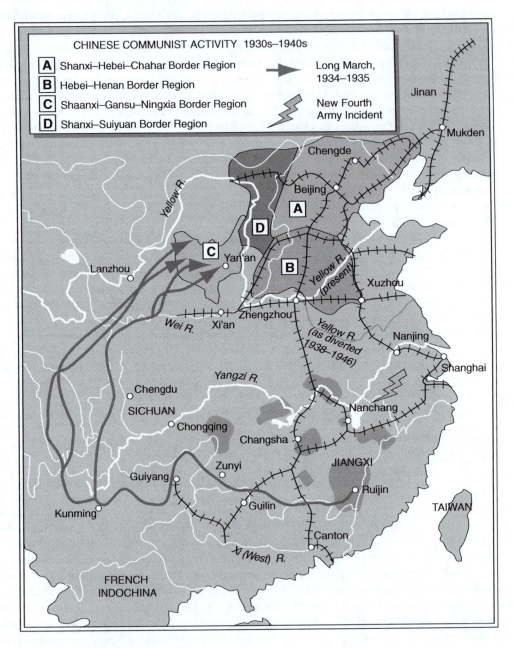

MAP 12.1   Chinese Communist Activity, 1930s and 1940s.

At the base at Jinggangshan to which Mao fled in late 1927, he worked closely with Zhu De, so closely in fact that among Jiangxi peasants, Zhu Mao "was an all-powerful personage who wanted to make the people happy."[4] Zhu had studied at a number of modern schools in his native Sichuan and graduated from the Yunnan Military Academy in 1911, where he later became an instructor. He participated in the 1911 revolution, in the campaign against Yuan Shikai in 1916, and in warlord struggles in Sichuan until 1921. He was in Germany from 1922 until 1926, studying intermittently and building a police record through political agitation—ending up expelled from the country. Having joined the Guomindang in 1912, he became an officer in Chiang's Guomindang army in 1926; but he left it in summer 1927, making known his membership in the CCP, which he had joined in Germany.

He met Mao for the first time in 1928, when he became commander of the Fourth Red Army and charged with its expansion. Composed mostly of illiterate peasants and workers, the Red Army gave priority to political training. To do so, the army was structured with parallel organizations, one to direct political work and the other to command the military. In late 1928, Guomindang military pressure forced evacuation of the Jinggangshan base and led to the Red Army's seizure of Ruijin in Jiangxi. There, on the Jiangxi-Fujian border, Mao and Zhu began to organize and expand their control.

FINDING ITS WAY: THE PARTY'S FACTIONS

Despite the slowly growing base areas in rural and mostly mountainous areas, the Comintern and the CCP central leadership, still located in Shanghai, continued to stress the necessity of party leadership by the urban proletariat. At the Sixth Party Congress held in Moscow in mid-1928, leaders declared that the new instrument of CCP political power would be the "soviet," or council, a decision-making and control body. The congress called for CCP members to "proletarianize" the party by making workers the bulk of the membership and leadership. Indeed, the nominal general secretary of the party from 1928 to 1931 was the onetime coolie-turned-labor organizer Xiang Zhongfa, the only urban worker to lead the party before the establishment of the People's Republic. But he was overshadowed immediately by the longtime labor organizer Li Lisan and then, from late 1930, by the so-called 28 Bolsheviks.

Li Lisan is mostly known for his "line," or policy plan, for the party: national revolution, he posited, could be ignited if he could mobilize urban workers to rise up in key cities and support them with the Red Army. He argued that the proletariat, not the peasantry, was the key to revolution, receiving support for this line from the CCP Central Committee in Shanghai. He therefore had Mao, Zhu, and their army attack Jiangxi's capital, Nanchang; but they were forced to withdraw without success. In late August 1930, Communist forces led by Commander Peng Dehuai seized Hunan's capital, Changsha, but held it for only seven days; another attempt to take the city in September also failed. With these humiliating defeats, the Li Lisan line, essentially the line of the Comintern, collapsed. Li was sent packing in the fall of 1930 to Moscow, where he remained for the next fifteen years.

Quickly stepping into the party's leadership vacuum was a group with the unlikely nickname "28 Bolsheviks." These men had been chosen by the CCP in the mid-1920s to attend the newly formed Sun Yat-sen University in Moscow for training as party cadres. Most remained in Moscow for four years, becoming known for their staunch support of Stalin's China policy. They also became the favorite students of the university head Pavel Mif. In mid-1930, when Mif traveled to China as Comintern representative, the 28 Bolsheviks returned with him and became actively involved in efforts to oust Li Lisan. When they succeeded, leaders of the group were catapulted into power with the support of Mif. In January 1931, twenty-four-year-old Wang Ming (Chen Shaoyu) became CCP general secretary and proceeded to pack the CCP Politburo with more of the 28 Bolsheviks. When he left in 1932 to become CCP representative to the Comintern, his close ally Bo Gu (Qin Bangxian) became general secretary; he served in that capacity until 1935. In 1931 the Shanghai-based Bolsheviks, in an effort to solidify their control over the party, set out to establish firmer control over the rural base areas than had been exercised by Li Lisan. The base areas, or rural soviets, had been governed to that point by "front committees"; from this point on, they were to be controlled by a central bureau that was responsible directly to the Politburo in the hands of the 28 Bolsheviks.

From his Jiangxi or Central Soviet, Mao Zedong warily watched first the leadership of Li Lisan and then that of the 28 Bolsheviks at the Shanghai Party Center. He shared Li's sense that revolution was imminent. In a famous letter to military commander Lin Biao in January 1930, he argued,

> China is in such a state of constant trouble and anarchy that the anti-imperialist, anti-warlord, and anti-landlord revolutionary high tide is inevitable and will come very soon. China is littered with dry firewood that can quickly turn into a raging fire. The phrase "A single spark can start a prairie fire" is an apt description of the current situation.[5]

But Mao greatly opposed Li's efforts to get him to put his army under more central control in order to carry out Li's line. Twice in mid-1930 he essentially sat on his hands, not carrying out military orders, and twice he received stinging rebukes from the Party Center in Shanghai. Mao's power and that of his soviet was growing strongly as the 28 Bolsheviks tried to assert more control over the rural soviets. Political realities were rapidly undercutting the power of the Shanghai Party Center and the Comintern. "The constant shift in the Comintern line, and ... the imposition of the [28] Bolsheviks as leaders of the party had simply undermined the faith of party members."[6] By early 1931, the Shanghai Party Central Committee, in the words of one scholar, "was reduced to little more than a liaison organization relaying instructions from the Comintern to the soviets."[7] But it was not until 1933 that the Shanghai leaders finally moved out to the Jiangxi Soviet, a signal at last that the revolution's focus had shifted away from the cities and to the rural soviets.

THE JIANGXI SOVIET

Chiang Kai-shek, too, was especially worried about the rising strength of Mao Zedong's Jiangxi Soviet. He launched his first extermination campaign against it in December 1930; it ended the same month, a failure. That same month Mao had his own crisis to deal with. In his drive for power and in his capacity as general political commissar of the Jiangxi Soviet Red Army, he had angered some local Communists (native to Jiangxi province) by ousting them from military posts and replacing them with his own men. When they formed an anti-Mao group, Mao moved against them, arresting about seventy and imprisoning them at the town of Futian. An infuriated local commander and several hundred troops stormed the prison and freed about twenty; they then rebelled against Mao. Mao's Red Army subsequently captured and massacred hundreds.

This conflict clearly revealed the tensions between locals and outsiders (even though political allies, they were still the Other); it was a problem that the Communists would face repeatedly in the years before 1949. The Futian incident also showed that Mao's rise to power from the very beginning was marked by "harsh and bloody conflict." It is also noteworthy that at this early stage Mao turned a basic political struggle into an ideological crusade of sorts. He asserted that his opponents were members of "a nationalist secret organization known as the 'A.B. League' (Anti-Bolshevik League)," whose existence threatened the revolution. He would use this tactic many times in his career, charging political opponents with treason.[8] In reaction to this bloody Futian incident, Mao was criticized at the Jiangxi Soviet's First Party Congress in early November 1931 for his unduly violent handling of the affair; he lost his position as the army's political commissar but was given a position in the soviet government.

By 1931 over a dozen soviets were located in parts of some 300 Chinese counties. Most were located in the foothill regions of Central China, between the plains to the north and east and the higher mountains to the south and west. In November 1931 came the landmark meeting of the First All-China Soviet Congress, held at Ruijin in Mao's Jiangxi Soviet. The congress established a national regime, the Chinese Soviet Republic. Mao was appointed chair of the new government, with Zhang Guotao, head of the Eyuwan soviet, and Xiang Ying, a former Li Lisan supporter, appointed vice-chairs. Mao did not, however, control the party; that power still lay in the hands of the Shanghai-based 28 Bolsheviks.

The Chinese Soviet Republic was a state within the state. It called itself "the democratic dictatorship of the proletariat and peasantry"—even though, of course, there were no urban workers in the soviets that comprised the Soviet Republic: The Comintern fiction and that of the Party Center still in Shanghai had to be kept ideologically alive. Most important, for the first time the CCP had its own "state" where it could begin to experiment with social revolution. It adopted a constitution; in the area of its rule, it issued laws and maintained political and military control. By early 1932 that area, containing about 3 million people, was about 15,000 square miles in seventeen counties (the more than a dozen smaller soviets scattered throughout central China had a population of about 6 million).

LAND REFORM (ACTUALLY, LAND "REVOLUTION")

Mao's Jiangxi Soviet had issued a land law in February 1930; that law now became the Land Law of the Soviet Republic, issued in November 1931. It was at the heart of the revolution, for it provided the guidelines for the confiscation and redistribution of land that would result from and constitute class struggle. The law was based on a hierarchical rural society stretching from wealthy elites to hired hands. It called for the confiscation of the land of "feudal landlords, village bosses, gentry, militarists, and other big private landowners" and for its redistribution to poor and middle peasants and to "hired farmhands, coolies, and toiling laborers."[9] This prescription for rural revolution seems quietly objective, but it masked a fluid indeterminacy and a screaming and bloody violence that ripped apart communities and shattered lives—for it meant the seizure of private property and wealth without compensation, a process that destroyed people's livelihoods and forever changed their lives. In addition to these confiscations, the lands of counterrevolutionaries and of religious institutions or temples were to be confiscated. "Rich peasants" were a special category that will be discussed later.

What was the configuration of Jiangxi society that would be affected by such radical change? In the period between December 1929 and May 1930, Mao himself conducted a detailed investigation of the economics, society, and culture of Xunwu county to the south of the Jiangxi Soviet's main city of Ruijin. Through this investigation, Mao "wanted to understand both how a revolution could be won through the efforts of peasants and how a mass-based party composed primarily of peasants could be built."[10] The configuration of Xunwu society does not, of course, necessarily fit that of other counties in the province, but it gives us some clue to the possible percentages of people in the categories constructed for land confiscation and redistribution in this area. As Table 12.1 shows, rents were paid in kind, that is, in rice or other grains.[11]

As the table indicates, over 92 percent of the population of Xunwu county were to receive land, taken from just over 7 percent of the population, if all the rich peasants had their land confiscated, and from less than 4 percent if rich peasants kept their land. As for landholding, peasants owned 30 percent of the land in the county, landlords owned 30 percent, and 40 percent was held by corporate owners such as temples and lineages.

Land revolution or, as it is more commonly called, "land reform," was a time-consuming process. At least one estimate suggests that it would take up to half a year for land reform managers to break through peasant passivity and suspicion and make the village population amenable to

TABLE 12.1   Rural Population in Xunwu County, Jiangxi Province, 1930

Large landlords (receive rent of more than 33.25 tons of rice)	0.045%
Middle landlords (receive rent of between 13.3 and 33.25 tons of rice)	0.4%
Small landlords (receive rent of less than 13.3 tons of rice)	3.0%
Rich peasants (have surplus grain and capital to make loans)	4.0%
Middle peasants (have enough to eat and do not receive loans)	18.255%
Poor peasants (have insufficient grain and receive loans)	70.0%
Manual workers (craftsmen, boatmen, porters)	3.0%
Loafers (no occupation or property)	1.0%
Hired hands (permanent and day laborers)	0.3%

revolutionary activity. Implicit in the whole land reform process was that power would flow from the people in what would later be called the "mass line." In a late 1929 meeting, Mao had drafted resolutions relating to the masses and the Red Army, setting down the principle that the masses had the right to criticize errors and faults in the Red Army and that the masses would have the power to carry out party resolutions. Mao believed that in the past, too many errors had resulted from top-down decisions by arrogant official elites who paid scant heed to the situation of local populations. Populist that he was, Mao deeply believed that the masses had both more practical expertise and more moral authority than even party cadres. He believed that party cadres and local soviet leaders had "to be willing pupils of the masses, not just their leaders, and not to regard the masses as clumsy and stupid country bumpkins but as people who deserved trust and must be involved in administration and political campaigns."[12] Thus, every step of the land reform process had to be decided on by mass meetings of the people being affected. Given the vast range of human personalities and idiosyncrasies, it is easy to see how the land reform process would stretch into months or longer.

The process, which for the first time brought the rural wretched poor into political participation, went as follows. Once an area was designated for land reform, three committees were formed. Poor peasants and landless laborers served on all three. The first, a confiscation committee, conducted a census, categorized the population (more on this shortly), and charted the amount and quality of the landholdings. The second, a land committee, made up of the obligatory poor peasants and laborers, party cadres, and representatives of families who had sons in the Red Army, managed the distribution of land. They first called a mass meeting to decide the method of land division—either in equal portions, according to the number of consumers, or using a mixed method, with some in a family, say children under the age of four or those over fifty-five, receiving less than a full share. From the land law:

the local soviet governments shall on no account carry out this measure [redistribution] by force or by an order issued by higher authorities, but shall explain this procedure to the peasantry from every angle. This measure may be put into operation only with the direct support and at the desire of the basic masses of the peasantry. Thus, if the majority of the middle peasants so desire, they may [be allowed] not to participate in the redistribution [of land].[13]

Further, since the quality of the soil was to be taken into account in the land redistribution, the land reform leaders had to adjust the amount redistributed so that those receiving poorer-quality land would receive proportionately more. When redistribution was complete, a third committee came into operation, functioning as an inspection team that investigated complaints and worked to solve attendant problems.

Difficult as these matters were, the trickiest problem was categorizing the peasants into their most appropriate social groupings. If a person was fortunate enough to be placed in the rich peasant category rather than the landlord classification, he could look forward at least temporarily to less trauma in his economic and personal life. Even better was placement in the middle peasant group, for land reform often brought rich peasants severe difficulties as well. One can imagine the way landlords tried to use any method—connections, bribes, threats—to be placed in the rich peasant rather than the landlord category. One can also imagine the ways that the process stirred up old bitternesses and animosities that existed in the village and how these tensions flared up into wars of words or fists.

Category boundaries, especially between landlord and rich peasant and between rich and middle peasant, varied, of course, according to local conditions. In some counties, for example, rich peasants were better off, and in others worse off, than rich peasants in Xunwu; in the former counties they might approximate a small Xunwu landlord; in the latter, they might be closer to the Xunwu middle peasant. No objective standards existed for land reform categories; they were all and always relative—to the locality, its economic situation, and the attitudes and approaches of those managing the whole process. Even more unsettling, they could also be reevaluated at any time, with a person being moved from one category to another.

The rich peasant category was especially ambiguous and, for that reason, became a major issue and something of a hot potato. Although the earlier Jiangxi Soviet land law of February 1930 had called for the confiscation of rich peasant land, in practice in 1930 and early 1931 Mao held back. He took only the rich peasants' land that exceeded the amount of a share of land redistributed to lower categories; and in later redistributions, he took only their good land. This more lenient policy partially stemmed from Mao's desire not to antagonize large numbers of powerful people at the beginning of his revolutionary effort. This social stratum could throw all sorts of monkey wrenches into land redistribution.

For this approach, Mao was roundly attacked by the 28 Bolsheviks, who were influenced by Stalin's paranoia and his treatment of the kulaks, the small stratum of relatively well-to-do peasants, whom Stalin targeted in the late 1920s for no less than physical liquidation. The 28 Bolsheviks argued that since the rich peasants had in the past made loans at usurious interest rates, even a hint of a lenient policy toward them would mean watering down the class struggle and blurring class lines. Thus, the land law of the Soviet Republic read:

It is a peculiar feature of the Chinese rich peasant that he is at one and the same time a landowner and a usurer; therefore, his land shall also be subject to confiscation. If a rich peasant, after his land has been confiscated, does not participate in any counterrevolutionary activities and works his land by the use of his own labor power, he may be assigned land, but not of the best quality.

Thus, sometimes a rich peasant was dispossessed and then partly repossessed. But in light of the thinking of the 28 Bolsheviks, from this time on, rich peasants received only poor land.

From June 1933 to October 1934, the Jiangxi Soviet launched a massive land investigation campaign to reclassify peasants. In ordering the investigation, Mao wrote,

> We should take the working class in the countryside as the leaders, rely on the poor peasants, firmly ally with the middle peasants, and resolutely attack the feudal and semifeudal forces. Weed out all landlords and rich peasants who falsely call themselves "middle peasants" or "poor peasants."[14]

This campaign was really intended to mobilize peasants and bring them closer to the party; Chiang Kai-shek's fourth extermination campaign had failed in early 1933, but there was every likelihood that he would launch another such campaign against the Soviet soon. At such a precarious time, this campaign verged on the ridiculous in its policies, that lurched first one way and then the opposite, revealing not only the slipperiness of class categories but also an anchorless party.

A major issue here was once again the rich peasant, specifically the demarcation between rich peasant and rich middle peasant. Mao's definition of a rich peasant was too complex, filled with a range of possible factors that might conceivably constitute a rich peasant classification. The result was mass confusion when investigators attempted to use the definition to make policy. From June to October 1933, many middle peasants were reclassified as landlords. In this context, the People's Commissariat stepped in to redefine the rich peasant, specifying that he was one whose total income included no more than 15 percent from exploitation. This definition necessitated yet another investigation (from October to December) and still yet another categorization. This time, many of the landlords were reclassified as middle peasants. In one county, for example, out of 3,125 households, 1,512 (48 percent) were reclassified from landlords or rich peasants to middle and even (incomprehensible as it seems) poor peasants![15] Then suddenly in early 1934, a new, more bitter attack was aimed at the rich peasants. With such rapid changes, one might be a middle peasant in June, a landlord in October, and a poor peasant in December—all without any change in economic status whatsoever! The whole land reform process began to antagonize the very people whom the party hoped to attract. The obvious fluidity and continual reassessments of class rankings and the utilization of class struggle, which often led to violence, confused and alienated too many people. At a time when the movement needed the support of larger numbers, it was turning too many of the most powerful people in the communities into enemies. For that reason, the land reform experiment was discontinued and Mao put into effect the Guomindang land law, which specified a rent ceiling for tenants of 37.5 percent.

The Marriage Law of 1931

Mao addressed gender as well as class issues in the Soviet Republic. A purpose of the CCP government, as specified in the "Outline of the Constitution of the Chinese Soviet Republic" in November 1931, was "to guarantee the thorough emancipation of women." Announced in December 1931, the new marriage law outlawed arranged marriage, forbade marriage through purchase and sale, stated a minimum marriage age, and generally made divorce easy. If one's husband was in military service, however, no divorce could be granted. Putting into effect all these changes regarding marriage-related procedures in the base areas met considerable peasant resistance. For example, peasant men protested resentfully over the Communist divorce policy (which, indeed, was also opposed by most local cadres). To smooth over opposition when peasants sharply disagreed with aspects of the Communists' marriage agenda, the party set aside the offending aspect. The chief marriage goal of the May Fourth Movement—freedom of marriage choice—seemed too revolutionary, as "[a]rranged marriage remained near-universal in the rural areas and was the dominant form throughout China during the Republican period."[16]

In 1928, the party had noted that one of its main tasks was "to recognize peasant women as extremely active participants in the revolution."[17] In Jiangxi, it should be noted, the motive for the "emancipation" of women was not gender equity but, in line with the 1928 statement, to gain their support and help in order to mobilize them for the national revolution. Unfortunately, Red Army soldiers and party cadres often took advantage of women against their will. For example, women were coerced into marrying soldiers whose poverty would have prevented a traditional arranged marriage. Widows were forcibly married to party cadres just after their husbands' deaths. CCP authorities even cooperated secretly in fostering prostitution, sending "teams of laundresses" to Red Army units.

THE OTHER SOVIETS

As we have seen, although the Jiangxi Soviet was the CCP center of power and governance, it was not the only base area and its policies were not necessarily executed in other bases. These soviets and their experiences are the roads that in the end were not taken in the Chinese revolution, but it is still important to remember that at the time, no one knew the eventual route and that many Chinese lives were in any case affected by them. The Eyuwan (Hubei-Henan-Anhui) soviet, led by Zhang Guotao, paid less attention to economic work than did Jiangxi; it also placed more emphasis on the emancipation of women. Zhang Guotao pushed the anti-rich peasant line more wholeheartedly than Mao. In instituting the mass line, Zhang again departed from the Jiangxi Soviet model, relying on the Red Army to coerce cooperation rather than mobilizing the masses through land reform. The result of this approach was that when there were military losses of territory to Chiang Kai-shek's forces and the coercing military was out of the picture, the mass organization and reform efforts that did exist simply collapsed.

Chiang's third extermination campaign against the Jiangxi Soviet (July to October 1931) gave the Eyuwan soviet the opportunity to expand its territory, but like the Jiangxi Soviet, it was dogged by factional disputes that exploded into a major opposition movement that in turn gave rise to mass arrests and a wide-scale purge. In the end, although Chiang's campaign was shortened by the Japanese aggression in Manchuria, the Eyuwan's Fourth Red Army helped the Jiangxi Soviet combat Guomindang attacks. As a prelude to Chiang's fourth campaign against the Jiangxi Soviet, he first undertook action against the Eyuwan and Xiang-exi soviets. Moving against Eyuwan from July to September 1932, Chiang's army forced the abandonment of the base area. As Zhang Guotao and others fled to northern Sichuan, their military losses decreased their active forces by half, from 30,000 to 15,000.

In December 1932, Zhang established the new Sichuan–Shaanxi base area, where, over the next two years, policies more radical than those in the Jiangxi Soviet were set in place. Policies dealing with land confiscation and redistribution were harsher; a military draft of peasants was instituted; and, as in the Jiangxi Soviet, youth were mobilized in organizations called Red Guards that provided support for the Red Army—all policies formulated for survival against attacks by Sichuan warlords. By the spring of 1935, Zhang and his comrades had been forced to move again to the border of Sichuan and Xikang, where they rendezvoused with the evacuees from the Jiangxi Soviet on the Long March (see below).

The Xiang-exi soviet (west Hubei and Hunan) was even more peripatetic than the original Eyuwan soviet. Controlled by He Long, it developed more rapidly and in different arenas of action from the Jiangxi base. Using better-developed mass associations, the base leadership mobilized the population in campaigns for land reclamation and production and against social evils such as opium, gambling, and superstition.[18] In an effort to achieve the widest support possible, it did not pursue a strong policy against rich peasants. Forced to abandon the base in October 1932, He fled with his 3,000 troops to northeastern Guizhou province, but they found it difficult to establish a new base and kept on the move. During this period, they gave up their open advocacy of revolution and appealed to peasant rebels and Miao tribesmen. Late in 1934, they did establish a base area in the border region of Guizhou, Sichuan, Hunan, and Hubei. But in the fall of 1935, they abandoned it to move on their Long March to the new Communist base in Shaanxi.

THE LONG MARCH

The Extermination Campaigns

Chiang Kai-shek was extraordinarily fearful of the expansion of Communist power, but there is evidence that he underestimated their fighting ability. In the first two campaigns that Chiang launched against the Jiangxi base (December 1930 and May to June 1931), he used former warlord troops to try to wear down the Red Army. The Red Army's advantages lay in their speed and expertise as guerrilla fighters, in their knowledge of the base area, and in their support by the masses, mobilized by land reform and the threat of war. In both of these campaigns, the Communists lured Guomindang armies into the base area. Overextended and without proper defensive preparations, the Guomindang forces were then denied intelligence by the base's mobilized masses, who, even worse, destroyed bridges to prevent them from retreating and harassed and attacked them from behind. In the third campaign from July to October 1931, Guomindang forces penetrated deeply into the base area, but the Japanese war in Manchuria forced Chiang to retreat. The fourth campaign in early 1933 once again failed, falling victim to the Red Army's speed (which "tired the government troops out in chasing them") and to the mass mobilization (which meant that Chiang's army "had no one to use, thus making [them] both blind and deaf").[19]

The fifth and finally successful campaign was launched in October 1933, with Chiang's forces totaling a million men. This time Guomindang forces moved slowly, building networks of roads to facilitate supply lines, constructing blockhouses (some built only two-thirds of a mile apart), and undertaking political mobilizational work with masses along the campaign routes. These strategies gradually tightened the noose around the soviet. The Red Army tried to counter by building their own version of blockhouses and by "short, swift [military] thrusts" that would disrupt National Army troops before reinforcements could be brought, but these tactics were to no avail. Mao was chair of the Soviet Republic's government but was not in the party's military decision-making hierarchy. Thus, at an August meeting CCP General Secretary Bo Gu, Red Army political commissar Zhou Enlai, and Comintern agent Otto Braun began to plan the evacuation. At the same time, Commander Xiao Ke was sent west out of the Jiangxi Soviet with his 9,000 strong Sixth Army Group to be the "pathfinders" for what would be the Long March route and destination. Xiao, who had been with Mao since 1928 and played a pivotal role in the Futian Incident, was, like Mao and He Long, from Hunan. His pathfinding goals were aborted by a disastrous military defeat in Ganxi, Guizhou where two-thirds of his troops were killed. As a result, the lack of a set destination created party factional issues.

In mid-October 1934, about 86,000 (including thirty-five women) broke out of the base to the southwest and began a 368-day forced march of about 6,000 miles. This was the fabled Long March, in the words of Edgar Snow "an Odyssey unequaled in modern times."[20] The marchers faced bombing attacks from Chiang's air force and harassment from Tibetan troops. Snow totes up the statistics and, in doing so, points to the almost superhuman quality of the trek:

> Out of a total of 368 days *en route*, 235 were consumed in marches by day, and 18 in marches by night. Of the 100 days of halts—many of which were devoted to skirmishes—56 days were spent in northwestern [Sichuan], leaving only 44 days of rest over a distance of about 5,000 miles, or an average of one halt for every 114 miles of marching. The mean daily stage covered was … nearly 24 miles—a phenomenal pace for a great army and its transport to *average* over some of the most hazardous terrain on earth.
>
> Altogether [they] crossed 18 mountain ranges, five of which were perennially snow-capped, and they crossed 24 rivers. They passed through 12 different provinces, occupied 62 cities, and broke through enveloping armies often different provincial warlords, besides defeating, eluding, or outmaneuvering the [Nationalist forces]. They entered and successfully crossed six different aboriginal districts.[21]

In the mountains they suffered from altitude sickness and frostbite. In the even worse marshlands, quicksand-like bogs swallowed people alive. Hunger, exhaustion, and illness were their continual companions. It is not surprising that only 8,000 reached their eventual destination.

One of the most famous military incidents along the march was the crossing of the Dadu River, a raging torrent in western Sichuan province. It had been the site of the 1863 defeat of the army of Taiping leader Shi Dakai. "On moonless nights, local legends ran, 'you can still hear the spirits of our Taiping dead wailing at the Dadu river crossing and over the town where they were slaughtered.'"[22] Crossing the river at any one of the three heavily guarded crossings would have been difficult without other obstacles. But crossing the Luding Bridge was made almost impossible because the planking had been ripped off the chain suspension bridge and because the bridge was targeted by enemy machine guns on the other side. To make the task even more treacherous, as Red Army shock troops began to make it across, Chiang's forces set the bridgehead on fire. But twenty soldiers made it across the 300-foot span high over the turbulent water below, crawling across from chain to chain and at the end racing through the flames that burned their clothing and singed their hair. With reinforcements, they were able to defeat two regiments defending the bridge.

WOMEN ON THE LONG MARCH

The Long March was not a single march from the Jiangxi Soviet to Yan'an, but a series of marches from the other base areas and other Communist armies. Xiao's Sixth Army Group joined forces with He Long in the Xiang-exi base area becoming the Second Front Army. Xiao was married to Xianren's younger sister, Xianfo in December 1934. The two brothers-in-law were then political and military allies as well. Twenty days after Xianren gave birth to their first child on November 1, 1935, He and Xiao started their armies on the Long March, thirteen months after Mao's forces had reached Yan'an. He Long decided that his daughter, He Jiesheng, would not be left behind with relatives but would be taken on the Long March—the youngest "Long Marcher" on the famous trek. He Long made the decision, but Xianren paid the physical price of carrying her during the 11-month march: pain and exhaustion. Both mother and daughter became extremely ill at least once, with the baby almost dying.

The marchers scaled snow-covered mountains, always keeping to the winding more perilous paths, and avoiding main roads. Crossing rivers was always difficult—without piers or even ropes to pull boats close to the riverbank. Yet, Xianren reported that

[t]he people treated us very well. When people, especially women, saw me carrying the baby, they gathered all around. I did some propaganda work. I told them why we came here and why we wanted to go to Xikang. Of course, it was to fight Chiang Kai-shek and the Japanese. They were very sympathetic to me."[23]

All along the way Xianren and her sister did propaganda work.

Men did it too. The women had the advantage because it was easier for them to get into contact with the ordinary people … if you are a young man and try to talk with a young girl or a young wife, it wouldn't be accepted. If you are a woman, you can talk with men or women, old or young. Other work which both men and women did was recruiting soldiers, expanding the army. Women comrades were good at that work."[24]

Perhaps the most surprising perils of the trek were not the steep mountain ranges, but the grasslands, "stinking swamps and bogs near the Tibetan border." Xie Fei, a Long March soldier, commented:

That damn place was really strange. Just grass, no trees. It wasn't mountainous, just flat land. It rained every day and the sun came out every day. The ground was all wet. At first the vanguard troops sank into the bog. If you tried to pull them out, you would sink too. They couldn't climb out and they couldn't be rescued either. You could only watch them die. Once we learned this lesson we let the animals walk first. If the animal sank then the people wouldn't die.

The marchers had to sleep standing up lest they sink into the saturated ground. Xianren also commented on the area: "If you had wounds on your feet, they would get infected and the skin would rot because the water was poisonous."[25] It was in these grasslands that Jian Xianfo gave birth to Xiao Ke's son.

WHICH POLITICAL ROADS TO TAKE?

Along the Long March, beyond the personal perils and dangers, momentous political happenings occurred. In January 1935, a crucial meeting took place in Zunyi in Guizhou province; by this time, less than half—only about 40,000—of the original Long March troops remained alive. That high casualty rate, added to the initial fact of the forced evacuation, put military policy under the spotlight. Speeches and discussions at the meeting offered a postmortem of the Jiangxi Soviet. Mao, who had not taken part in the military decision making, attacked the losing military strategy of Otto Braun and Bo Gu as too static, as focusing on a "pure positional defense." That line was approved by party resolution. Mao's performance at Zunyi and the party's criticism of his factional rivals pointed to the fact that Mao's star was rising. He became one of the five-man Secretariat, thus emerging as one of the party's five most important party leaders. Perhaps even more important, given the party's factionalism, he was also named to the CCP Central Military Leadership Group, thereby bringing to an end the domination of military affairs by Bo and Braun. Thus, for the first time, Mao defeated the 28 Bolsheviks, now officially blamed for the Soviet's military defeat; and he would lead in taking a new or at least different revolutionary road. As one writer has summed up:

The Zunyi [m]eeting marked the end of the soviet movement in central China. Obsessed with ideological doctrines and basking in revolutionary enthusiasm, Bo Gu and his supporters lacked a profound insight into political relationships within which the CCP found itself enmeshed. Neither could they balance this deficiency with an adequate experience in military command.[26]

Immediately after the Zunyi meeting, the party asked Zhang Guotao, still based in northern Sichuan, to use his Fourth Front Army to begin offensive actions against Guomindang forces south of his base in order to relieve pressure on the Long March's First Front Army. But instead of complying, Zhang moved north to fight provincial forces in Shaanxi. In part as a consequence, in the late winter and spring of 1935, Mao's First Front Army experienced one defeat after another at the hands of Guomindang forces. By that spring, Mao's troops numbered only 15,000 compared to Zhang Guotao's 80,000. Mao and Zhang met in June in the new base area that Zhang had set up on the Sichuan–Xikang border, and almost immediately a bitter factional struggle erupted between them. Later that month, He Long's and Xiao Ke's forces united with Zhang's Fourth Red Army. Having almost split with Mao, Zhang, it seems, believed that with He's and Xiao's assistance he might be able to take control of the CCP from Mao. Though He Long vowed to shoot Zhang for being a traitor, Xiao was more easily swayed and Zhang assigned him the command of a division. The future was in the balance: it was time for another decision on which revolutionary road to take.

Though there was an important policy question at issue—where would they all head?—the real problem was political power. Zhang had over five times as many men, but Mao had the political power as a member of the party Secretariat. Meetings during the summer did involve some give-and-take on both sides, but in the end the friction and animosity were too great. In September the two groups completely split; Zhang was not even present at the Politburo meeting when Mao criticized him for his "opportunism" and for "splitting the Red Army, thus displaying his 'warlord' tendency."[27] Mao then promptly took his Long Marchers north to Yan'an in Shaanxi province with a view to establishing a new base area on the borders of Shaanxi, Gansu, and Ningxia. Zhang, talking about establishing a base area in the far northwest from which it might be easier to make contact with the Soviet Union, moved his forces first west toward Xinjiang before he too eventually turned back to Yan'an, where He and Xiao had already gone. But his going to Yan'an was not out of friendship. Indeed, he pointedly repudiated Mao's leadership. In 1938 he made his break official by defecting to Chiang Kai-shek's side. Although he served the Guomindang in minor roles, he never again played a major political role, moving to Hong Kong in 1949 and eventually to Canada, where he died in 1979.

The Meaning of the Long March

In the accounts of party history, the Long March is hailed as a victory; indeed, until the late 1990s, the political leadership of the CCP and the government of the People's Republic was dominated by veterans of this extraordinary military trek. It must, however, be emphasized that the Long March actually occurred because of a great defeat, one probably even proportionately greater than the Communist defeat of 1927. Listen to Mao, writing in late 1936:

> Except for the Shaanxi-Gansu border area, all revolutionary bases were lost, the Red Army was reduced from 300,000 to a few tens of thousands, the membership of the Chinese Communist Party was reduced [by disastrously huge numbers] and the Party organizations in Guomindang areas were almost entirely wiped out. In short, we received an extremely great historical punishment.[28]

Identifying the Long March as a victory, then, surely comes in part from the survival, if only of less than 10 percent, from such brutal natural and human forces. It is an uplifting tale of the defiance of superhuman odds, of dedication and sacrifice. Most important, it produced among the survivors an unquestionable sense of mission and dedication: whereas others had died, they had survived. Therefore, to atone for the deaths of their comrades, they had to commit their all to the revolution to assure victory. For Mao, who emerged as the leader on the march, the experience strengthened his "already deeply ingrained voluntaristic faith that men with the proper will, spirit, and revolutionary consciousness could conquer all material obstacles and mold historical reality."[29] And it gave him a further sense of destiny: he and he alone would be the one to lead China out of its miserable past into a future bright with hope. It was thus Mao and his leadership that profited most from the development and perpetuation of the Long March legend, for he was able to make it his story and the story of modern China.

The Three-Year War

When the Long Marchers broke out of the Jiangxi base, they left about 42,000 troops to make raids on and tie down Chiang's troops and, in the process, to keep a foothold and networks of support in the region. For the next three years they continued sporadic guerrilla activity in eighteen bases, primarily along the borders of eight provinces; it is called today the Three-Year War. For many, the hardships of living a primitive existence in rugged mountains brought a bonding almost as intense as the trials along the Long March brought its veterans.

The strategies were local. Since each locale was different, the logical approach demanded sensitivity to local realities and willingness to learn from the locals. "Living on society's margins, stretching out tendrils into it, learning its ways, and studying its social arrangements not to change it but to strike deals with it" was the strategy of these guerrilla bands—a sharp contrast to the often bureaucratic-centralist style of the Jiangxi Soviet and later policies at Yan'an. Ultimately, tailoring the revolutionary approach to the locality proved to be a more successful revolutionary strategy.[30] In localities, then, manipulating individuals through local organizations or kinship ties, not mass mobilization, was the key strategy.

Guerrillas' political and social policies toward the people in areas they controlled ranged from trying to carry out land reform to working for reductions in rents and interest, from resisting the government's military and labor drafts to confiscating grain and distributing it to peasants. With the exodus of so many men in the Long March, East Central China experienced what one historian has called the "feminization of the party."[31] That meant that women played important roles as intelligence gatherers, fighters, quartermasters, and nurses. In many ways, they provided Communist continuity in the area after the Long March. Although there are no direct lines between the Three-Year War and the success of the Communist revolution, the war contributed to the revolution by tying down forces that Chiang could otherwise have used against the main Red Army, by making true the Communist claim that it was a nationwide movement, and by providing bases that the party could use to move into all parts of Eastern China during the war against Japan.

BUILDING THE BASE AT YAN'AN

Twice in its fourteen-year history up to 1935, the CCP had been almost wiped out; the bloodletting purge by Chiang in 1927 and 1928 and the military shellacking by Guomindang forces in 1934 and 1935 probably would have led any betting person to predict that it would completely disappear. This would be the case especially if one considered where the Long Marchers wound up and where they would try to resuscitate the moribund party: northern Shaanxi province—a remote, barren, backward region marked by miserable poverty. Listen to Zhou Enlai's evaluation:

> Peasants in Shaanxi are extremely poor, their land very unproductive. ... The population of the Jiangxi Soviet numbered 3,000,000 where here it is at most 600,000. ... In Jiangxi and Fujian people brought bundles with them when they joined the Red Army; here they do not even bring chopsticks; they are utterly destitute."[32]

So much land in the province was given over to growing opium that when drought hit this already arid region, there was not enough cultivation of food grains to feed the population. Poverty and malnutrition, even starvation, went hand in hand.

Yan'an, to which the CCP moved in late 1936–early 1937 was an impoverished market town with a population of perhaps 10,000 when it became the Shaan-Gan-Ning base area capital. There was nothing much to distinguish the town; throughout much of its history, it had been a military outpost guarding against invasion from regions to the west and north. Life there was hard. Many Long Marchers lived in caves hewn out of the rocky mountains. Yet Yan'an would one day become almost as legendary as the Long March.

In addition to the physical demands of life in Shaanxi, political challenges abounded. When the Long Marchers arrived in northern Shaanxi, they were met by local Communists who had already been active in party mobilization since the early 1930s. In the spring of 1935, Liu Zhidan and Gao Gang had established a Shaanxi-Gansu soviet and were directing a vigorous land reform program in the twenty-two counties they controlled. Then the outsider Long Marchers marched into the area as if in invasion. The outsider–local situation must have seemed reminiscent of the dynamics of the Futian incident of 1930. In the beginning, Mao did not seem to handle this situation any more intelligently than he had at Futian. Advance Red Army units in August 1935 arrested Liu, Gao, and other local Communist leaders and imprisoned them for deviating from the party line. But when Mao arrived in late October, the men were released. The arrests were later blamed on party "sectarianism" and personal ambitions. Neither Liu, who was killed in battle in 1936, nor Gao had apparently resisted arrest; and most of those who were involved were absorbed into the party. Over the next decade, tensions and conflicts between the newcomers and the locals continued. In the words of one historian, "[i]ndependent local leadership preoccupied with development of the border region as a revolutionary base was frequently at odds with a party hierarchy dominated by southerners whose concerns were primarily national."[33]

The many revolutionary roads not taken are in the land of history's "might have beens": If the party had continued to focus on the urban proletariat instead of the peasantry, then ... If the 28 Bolsheviks had remained in control, then ... If the Red Army had adopted a different military strategy during the fifth extermination campaign, then ... If the strategies and policies of soviets beyond the Jiangxi Soviet had prevailed, then ... If Zhang Guotao had defeated Mao, then ... If Zhang had won out in his desire to have the Long Marchers turn west, then ... The list is endless, and we can never answer the questions. What we do know is the many roads taken: the focus of the party was now clearly on the peasantry; Mao Zedong was on his way to the top; the experiments of the Jiangxi Soviet, not those of other soviets, were harbingers of the future; the work of fashioning the Jiangxi Soviet went for naught in the disastrous military defeat by Chiang; and the Long March ended in the barren northwest. There the party would be rebuilt and fashioned into an organization that within little more than a decade would take over the country.

FIGURE 12.1   Mao Zedong at Yan'an with Zhou Enlai, whose support of Mao at the Xunyi conference on the Long March was the first close alliance of the two major Communist leaders.
Source: Keystone/Getty Images.

Notes

1 The phrase is from Jerome Ch'en, "The Communist Movement, 1927–1937," in *The Cambridge History of China, Vol. 13, Republican China, 1912–1949, Part 2*, ed. John K. Fairbank and Albert Feuerwerker (Cambridge, UK: Cambridge University Press, 1986), p. 173.

2 Simon Leys, "The Art of Interpreting Nonexistent Inscriptions Written in Invisible Ink on a Blank Page," *The New York Review of Books* (October 11, 1990), 12.

3 Mao Zedong, "Report on an Investigation of the Peasant Movement," in *The Rise to Power of the Chinese Communist Party*, ed. Tony Saich (Armonk, NY: M.E. Sharpe, 1996), p. 198.

4 Lucien Bianco, *The Origins of the Chinese Revolution, 1915–1949* (Stanford, CA: Stanford University Press, 1971), p. 64, fn. 10.

5 Mao Zedong, "Letter to Lin Biao (January 5, 1930)," in Saich, *Rise to Power*, p. 485.

6 Benjamin I. Schwartz, *Chinese Communism and the Rise of Mao* (Cambridge, MA: Harvard University Press, 1951), p. 166.

7 Saich, *Rise to Power*, p. 511.

8 The phrase is Saich's, *Rise to Power*, p. 510.

9 "Land Law of the Soviet Republic (November 1931)," in Saich, *Rise to Power*, p. 556. All subsequent quotations from this law come from this source.

10 Mao Zedong, *Report from Xunwu*, trans., Roger R. Thompson (Stanford, CA: Stanford University Press, 1990), p. 11.

11 The table is from Mao, *Report from Xunwu*, p. 122. Copyright (c) 1990 by the Board of Trustees of the Leland Stanford Jr. University. All rights reserved. Used by permission of the publisher, Stanford University Press, sup.org.

12 Ch'en, "The Communist Movement," p. 178.

13 Saich, *Rise to Power*, p. 557.

14 Ibid., p. 604.

15 Ch'en, "The Communist Movement," p. 195.

16 Gail Hershatter, *Women in China's Long Twentieth Century* (Berkeley, CA: University of California Press, 2007), p. 16.

17 Saich, *Rise to Power,* p. 372.

18 See, for example, Gregor Benton, *Mountain Fires: The Red Army's Three-Year War in South China, 1934–1938* (Berkeley, CA: University of California Press, 1992), pp. 360–5; Odoric Y.K. Wou, *Mobilizing the Masses: Building Revolution in Henan* (Stanford, CA: Stanford University Press, 1994).

19 Quoted in Ch'en, "The Communist Movement," p. 205.

20 Edgar Snow, *Red Star over China* (New York: Modern Library, 1938), p. 177.
21 Ibid., p. 216.
22 William G. Rosenberg and Marilyn B. Young, *Transforming Russia and China* (New York: Oxford University Press, 1982), p. 144.
23 Helen Praeger Young, *Choosing Revolution: Chinese Women Soldiers on the Long March* (Urbana, IL: University of Illinois Press, 2001), p. 42.
24 Ibid., p. 35.
25 Ibid., p. 50.
26 Saich, *Rise to Power,* p. 524.
27 Ibid., p. 658.
28 Mao Zedong, "Strategic Problems of China's Revolutionary War," in *Selected Works of Mao Tse-tung* (New York: International Publishers, 1954), Vol. 1, p. 193, cited in Maurice Meisner, "Yenan Communism and the Rise of the Chinese People's Republic," in *Modern East Asia: Essays in Interpretation*, ed. James B. Crowley (New York: Harcourt, Brace & World, 1970), p. 274.
29 Meisner, "Yenan Communism," p. 271.
30 This information on the Three Years War comes from Gregor Benton, "Under Arms and Umbrellas: Perspectives on Chinese Communism in Defeat," in *New Perspectives on the Chinese Communist Revolution*, ed. Tony Saich and Hans van de Ven (Armonk, NY: M.E. Sharpe, 1995), pp. 124–6. See also his *Mountain Fires*.
31 Benton, "Under Arms and Umbrellas," p. 126.
32 Quoted in Maurice Meisner, *Mao's China and After* (New York: Free Press, 1999), p. 37.
33 Mark Selden, *The Yenan Way in Revolutionary China* (Cambridge, MA: Harvard University Press, 1971), p. 72.

Suggestions for Further Reading

Averill, Stephen C. *Revolution in the Highlands: China's Jinggangshan Base Area* (Lanham, MD: Rowman & Littlefield, 2006). This study gets beyond the "class analysis and Western social theories" explanation for the origins of the Communist revolution by revealing the complexity of the socioeconomic landscape that was that revolution's base.

Saich, Tony. *The Rise to Power of the Chinese Communist Party* (Armonk, NY: M.E. Sharpe, 1996). This is a masterful analysis containing documents of the CCP from its founding until 1949; in its breadth and coverage it is unsurpassed.

Snow, Edgar. *Red Star over China* (New York: Random House, 1937). The journalistic classic, reporting on the rise of the Communists in the 1930s and on their clashes with the forces of Chiang Kai-shek.

Thompson, Roger, tr. and ed. *Mao Zedong: Report from Xunwu* (Stanford, CA: Stanford University Press, 1990). Mao wrote this report after an on-site examination and investigation in Xunwu county, Jiangxi province in the spring of 1930; it covers aspects of daily life and presents crucial information on social and economic relationships.

Young, Helen Praeger. *Choosing Revolution: Chinese Women Soldiers on the Long March* (Urbana, IL: University of Illinois Press, 2001). Composed of personal narratives from twenty-two female soldiers in the Red Army, these accounts provide not only a different perspective but also, in their description of daily life on the Long March, a more realistic picture than the standard heroic tale.

13

A Rising Clash of National Identities

China and Japan, the 1920s and 1930s

"China is a society, but she is not a nation. Or rather, it would be fair to say that China is a society of bandits. ... The Chinese people are bacteria infesting world civilization."[1] The speaker was Major General Sakai Ryu, chief of staff of the Japanese forces in North China. The date was 1938, when Japan and China were at war. The judgments expressed reveal several things, the most obvious being a contemptuous attempt to dehumanize the Chinese. Japanese attitudes like this were the foundation of their role in China in the 1930s, years in which modern imperialism reached its height. The first phase of imperialism had been the treaty port system, with its various stipulations about foreign rights. It had been followed, more ominously, by the seizure of Chinese tributary states and, in the scramble for concessions in the late 1890s, the seizure and use of Chinese territory for a specified period of time. The economic imperialism embodied in the Boxer Protocol and the foreign support of warlords was insidious but dangerous in its impact. In all these phases of imperialism, China seemed almost a limp and passive victim.

But, in the words of one historian, "Japanese imperialism [was one of] the midwives of modern Chinese nationalism."[2] In the 1930s, when Japan undertook its most flagrant phase of imperialism, China, or at least the Chinese people, had begun to stiffen their resistance. In the end, it was the often brutal imperialism of the Japanese that stimulated nationalist feelings in areas of active warfare.

A CASE OF MISTAKEN IDENTITY

One of the most striking aspects of Sakai's assertion is his claim that China was not a nation, but only a society of bandits. For the Japanese at least, such a belief might be a rationale for Japan, risen to modern nationhood with astounding speed, to whip China into shape and for Japan to take its proper place in the world as the East Asian regional leader. But Sakai's statement completely misread Chinese realities. Nationalism had been a force in Chinese core areas for thirty years and in some peripheral areas for less time. Hundreds of thousands had fought a revolution in the 1920s to establish China's national identity. Sakai's misreading points to a more serious reality that dogged Japan's understanding of China: Japan *thought* it knew China better than it really did.

The pattern of Chinese–Japanese relationships in the modern period had been checkered, to say the least. Japan had defeated China in war in 1895, had sent troops in with the Allied expedition to quell the Boxers in 1900, had insisted on its Twenty-One Demands in 1915, and had held on to Shandong for three years following the end of World War I. This had been Japan's imperialistic identity. Yet for China, Japan had other identities as well. It also became China's teacher, in that role turning on its head the tributary relationship of long ago, when China had been elder brother to Japan's younger brother. In the early years of the century, young Chinese flocked to Japan's schools to learn the secrets of Japan's rapid modernization. Kang Youwei talked of Japan as a model. Sun Yat-sen lived in Japan from 1897 to 1898, 1900 to 1903, 1905, 1906, 1910, and 1913 to 1916; he became close friends of many Japanese, who offered him financial and moral support in his revolutionary undertakings. Even Mao Zedong had contacted one of these, Miyazaki Toten, to visit his school in Changsha; Miyazaki complied. Chiang Kai-shek had attended military school in Japan from 1908 to 1911 and, as we will see, strived mightily and foolhardily for some agreement with Japan in the 1930s. Similarly, many Chinese warlords of the 1920s and 1930s had attended schools in Japan, and a number had Japanese advisers on their staffs. So, for many Chinese, Japan's identity was certainly not all negative.

Japan's Reading of Contemporary China

From Japan's perspective, it shared many things with China. Japanese had borrowed heavily from China's traditional culture, and though they had amended and shaped many of these cultural traditions to Japanese realities, they continued to share many cultural values and roots. Their historical relationship for more than a millennium led some Japanese to assume, at least in the face of a possible threat from the West, that cooperation, if not friendship, was a likely scenario. In comparison to the West or any other nation, Japan knew most about China: it had more experts and research on China than any country in the world.

Take, for example, the East Asia Common Culture Academy (Tōa Dōbun Shoin), established with Japanese government support in Shanghai in 1901, primarily to train young Japanese in studies of the Chinese language and contemporary China and to prepare young Chinese to enter regular schools in Japan. Graduates of the school were often hired by the Japanese Foreign Ministry for detailed investigations in areas the ministry deemed important. For example, five graduates were assigned from 1905 to 1907 "to major outposts across [Xinjiang] and Mongolia, to report on Russian activities in the wake of the Russo-Japanese War." In terms of Chinese domestic developments, in 1909 and 1910 the Foreign Ministry wanted an "[i]nvestigation in thirteen provinces of North, Central and South China, of the workings of China's new provincial assemblies, official/non-official relations at the local level, provincial educational systems, [and] the campaign to suppress opium."[3] A requirement for graduation from the Common Culture Academy was an extensive investigative fieldwork project on an area of contemporary China. Three- to nine-man teams spent the summer before graduation intensively investigating political, social, and economic aspects of every province in China. Guidelines and instructions for the investigations were drawn up carefully. Confidential reports went to the government, but three series of encyclopedic studies were published: a twelve-volume survey of the Chinese economy (1907–1908), an eighteen-volume gazetteer of the provinces of China (1917–1920), and an eight-volume revised gazetteer of the provinces (1941–1944). The information published in these works was generally dependable. Certainly, no other country had studied China in such depth.

But knowledge must be processed by persons who have their own biases and assumptions about life, others, and the world. Despite the fact that many Chinese had studied and lived in Japan and that many Japanese had lived, worked, and journeyed throughout all areas of China, the knowledge thereby gained somehow was not established. In the words of one historian:

How much of this "knowledge" … penetrated very deeply into the Japanese psyche? Did not the psychological antibodies of bullying and insensitivity powerfully counteract most cases of possible infection [by knowledge]? Knowledge—in the form of scholarly books and reports and learned specialists—thus coexisted in tension with dark ignorance.[4]

In addition to this psychological predisposition not to see what existed, there was a language problem that clouded the vision of China among Japan's specialists and contributed to Japan's drawing wrong conclusions about China's identity. Although the Japanese graduates of the Common Culture Academy had to be able to converse in Chinese in order to accomplish their fieldwork, most Japanese experts on China and certainly most Japanese politicians did not know Chinese. The problem stems from the nature of the Japanese language. It is a combination of Japanese phonetic symbols that stand for syllables (called a "syllabary"), on the one hand, and Chinese characters (called *kanji* in Japanese), on the other. Whereas today most contemporary Japanese is written predominantly in the Japanese syllabary, before the 1950s formal Japanese was written mostly in Chinese characters. Thus, Japanese assumed they could read Chinese newspapers and other publications and understand the Chinese situation, what the Chinese were thinking, and the nature of Chinese attitudes and goals. But this was a faulty assumption for several reasons. First, many Japanese *kanji*, though they looked the same, had different meanings or shades of meaning from Chinese characters. Second, to understand the psyche of a contemporary society, the key is knowing the spoken colloquial language; the Japanese experts did not know how to speak Chinese. Third, until the 1920s and in some cases into the 1930s, most Chinese publications were written in classical Chinese, not the vernacular; so when Japanese experts on China read Chinese, they were reading the traditional classical prose.

Dependence on the classical prose sources that they read caused Japanese views of China to be "innocent of the social science approaches of the twentieth century and anchored to the classical tradition in which the Chinese elites had been steeped."[5] This meant that the dominant way Japan's experts conceived of contemporary China was as "unchanging." Listen to Naitō Konan, one of Japan's most important scholars of China: "We no longer need to ask when China will collapse. It is already dead, only its corpse is wriggling."[6] Japan's China experts generally knew or understood little about the head-spinning changes and transformations in early-twentieth-century Chinese society. Warlords? Just like traditional Chinese generals in the interregnum between dynasties. Republican government? Just a surface blip in the ongoing stream of Chinese politics. Since traditional China lay just beneath the surface, information that suggested otherwise was either not analyzed or, more likely, not even perceived or processed. Such faulty assumptions, perhaps epitomized in Sakai's ignorant evaluations, were the foundation for policies that could not succeed because they were not based on reality.

Contextual Problems

Two other contemporary contextual situations also contributed to Japan's misreading China's identity and being unable to react to realities. The first was related to Japan's perceived national interests in China. Japanese strategists had located Japan's sphere of interest in North China. Japan had swallowed Korea whole in 1910. The Russo–Japanese War had brought it control of the strategically important 650-mile-long South Manchurian Railroad, which ran from Harbin in central Manchuria to Port Arthur on the tip of the Liaodong peninsula. Japan's role on the continent was based on its predominance in Manchuria, with its raw materials, farmland, and living space.

Thus, in the early Chinese Republic, Japan had given special support to "its" warlord in Manchuria, Zhang Zuolin. Japanese had relied on Zhang to work with them to protect their interests. Since Zhang had become involved in the major warlord wars over control of Beijing, Japan's relationship to Zhang as direct patron had great potential benefit if he emerged as the Chinese head of state. In the 1920s, Japan was excessively focused on warlords, and it was financially burned in several cases when loans given to warlords were insufficiently secured. The focus on warlords and the North drew Japan's vision away from the growing Nationalist revolution in the South. Though some Japanese merchant capitalists had begun to talk of the strategic importance of greater involvement with markets in Central and South China, the fixation on the North continued. Lack of flexibility in Japan's policy approach to China (part of which stemmed from the knowledge problem) made it difficult for policymakers to change their course.

A second problem was the changing nature of the Japanese political system. Although political parties had emerged in the 1920s as the main power brokers, the downsides of a more open political system also became visible. Both in election campaigns and in making policy, political gamesmanship that toyed with popular emotions came to play a role. If, for example, a policy needed changing but such change would reflect negatively on Japan's image or past policy or the image of a particular party, politicians sat on their hands and changed nothing. Given these circumstances, in the late 1920s and early 1930s increasing military aggressiveness in Japanese political culture made the support of more moderate approaches less and less possible. Political parties and the civilian government itself came under a surging domestic attack in the late 1920s before a 1932 coup effectively ended party and civilian rule and the military emerged as the key governmental force.

Troubles Emerge

As long as warlords continued to posture and battle, Japan could continue to muddle through on the continent without having to make substantial changes in policy. But relations between Japan and China were far from cordial. Talks over trade and tariffs in 1925 and 1927, though conducted on Japan's side under Foreign Minister Shidehara Kijūrō, who was known for his emphasis on international cooperation, were tense and inconclusive. Then several serious factors disrupted the business-as-usual situation and began to markedly destabilize the relationship.

Out of South China in the mid-1920s came a vibrant and aggressive Chinese nationalism aimed at warlords (such as Zhang Zuolin) and imperialists (such as Japan). This expansion of a strong nationalism came at about the same time that difficulties began to shake the Japanese economy and as Japanese began to question the effectiveness and wisdom of civilian party rule. Waiting in the wings was the Japanese military, which had watched political parties slash its budgets and reduce its numbers. The initial military activities were prompted by civilian politics, with the party in charge playing on general fears of Communism and trying to appear hard-nosed in its policies toward revolutionary forces that included Communists. In May 1927, well before Chiang Kai-shek began the northern campaigns of his Northern Expedition, the Japanese government transferred Japanese troops from Manchuria to Shandong, the goal being to protect Japanese living there. Among the Chinese in general, the brief occupation of these troops was hardly noticed amid the crack-up of the united front and the growing White Terror under Chiang Kai-shek.

But then, in April 1928, 2,000 Japanese troops were again sent to Shandong to protect Japanese lives. Objective observers noted that at this time there was no valid reason to do so; there were no threats to Japanese civilians, and Communists were no longer involved. Though sent to the port of Qingdao, the Japanese troops were moved to Jinan to try to deflect Chinese forces from Japanese interests there. Serious fighting broke out between Japanese and Chinese troops.

The Japanese seized that city and held it under martial law until April 1929. This "Jinan incident," in which several thousand Chinese were killed, led to substantial bitterness, a variety of protests, and a nationwide boycott against the Japanese. Anger and distrust were being ratcheted up.

JAPANESE AGGRESSION TURNS MANCHURIA INTO MANCHUKUO

During the Qing dynasty, the reigning Manchus had wanted to maintain Manchuria as the Manchu homeland, so they kept Manchuria closed to Chinese immigration. Because of this policy, in the early twentieth century it was still relatively sparsely settled. For Japan, Manchuria offered space for emigration but, even more, a source for industrial raw materials, an abundance of arable land, and a base for further actions on the mainland. After 1912, Japan encouraged Koreans, now Japanese subjects, to move there as a way of making Japan's presence more secure. With a population of about 30 million in 1930, Manchuria was home to 1 million Japanese subjects, about 80 percent of them Korean; foreign investment there was 75 percent Japanese, and of all of Japan's trade with China, 40 percent was with Manchuria.

As Chiang Kai-shek's Northern Expedition moved north to Beijing in 1928, his actions seemed more and more threatening to Japan's position on the continent. On May 18, about a week after the end of the fighting in the Jinan incident, the Japanese government sent identical notes to Chiang in Nanjing and Zhang Zuolin in Beijing warning that Japan might have to act if the situation in the North became destabilized. The message read in part, "the Japanese government ... may possibly be constrained to take appropriate and effective steps for the maintenance of peace and order in Manchuria."[7] The Japanese warned Zhang to return to Manchuria while his army was still intact and stated explicitly that they would not let defeated armies or those pursuing them cross the border into Manchuria. It is obvious that the Japanese were becoming increasingly wary of what Zhang might do. Since 1925 Zhang had been installed in Beijing, sometimes as part of a military coalition, at other times as the lone de facto head of the government. Now, with the Japanese warning, Zhang decided to return to Manchuria. On the way home on June 4, a faction in the Japanese army blew up his train and killed him; in the challenging new world of Chinese nationalism, they simply did not trust him. He was succeeded by his son, Zhang Xueliang, a reputed opium addict, who in negotiations with the Japanese over the course of the next few months agreed to continue to work with the Japanese in friendly fashion. When Zhang raised the flag of the Nanjing government at Shenyang (Mukden) in December 1928, the Japanese issued a mild warning but did nothing to back it up. Japan formally recognized Chiang's government in June 1929.

Once Zhang gave his allegiance to Chiang, he was named commander of the Northeastern Frontier Army. Nanjing then set out to establish a greater Chinese presence in Manchuria. Guomindang branches were organized everywhere; party publications trumpeting anti-imperialist rhetoric sprang up. The Nanjing government loudly demanded the return of treaty rights claimed by Japan, including extraterritoriality. It also tried to undercut the Japanese economic position. For example, it set up competing railroads, which, using techniques such as rebates and rate wars, began to eat into Japanese railroad profits. Zhang Xueliang refused to negotiate the railroad disputes that resulted. The Nanjing regime constructed port facilities at Yingkou on the eastern coast of the Gulf of Liaodong and planned to do so at Huludao, on the gulf's western coast, to challenge Japanese facilities at Dairen.

The years from 1928 to 1931 saw increasing tensions over seemingly small things—railroad "wars" and violent incidents between Korean settlers and Chinese over mundane disputes involving property boundaries and irrigation rights. At the beginning of July 1931, in the so-called

Wanbaoshan incident, Japanese consular police, using machine guns, fired over the heads of Chinese farmers to disperse them after a confrontation with Korean farmers over the construction of an irrigation ditch. Like other incidents, this was a pinprick—no serious casualties occurred. Yet Japanese extremists used the right-wing press in both Japan and Korea to intensify the increasingly bitter feelings against China, giving rise to anti-Chinese riots in both Korea and Japan. In Korea, Chinese residents were attacked, their shops and homes looted; 127 Chinese were killed and several hundred wounded. Then, in August 1931, there came to light the killing two months earlier of one Captain Nakamura, who, traveling as an agricultural expert, was arrested near the Manchurian–Mongolian border. Apparently involved in a secret mission, he was carrying heroin, probably to use in transactions with the Mongols. After seizing him, the Chinese shot him as a spy. The Japanese press had a field day with the story, demanding that the murder of an officer of the Imperial Army be avenged and, above all, that Japan put in place a stronger policy with regard to Manchuria.

The Japanese military in the field saw these things close at hand and magnified them into a towering threat to Japan's position. There are no inevitabilities in history, yet one must say that the almost palpable tension that had developed between the two countries had to find some form of release and that it would likely be violent. Thus, field officers in Manchuria, without the agreement or even knowledge of the military authorities or the government in Tokyo, plotted to make Japan's position secure by taking over Manchuria. On September 18, 1931, they blew up a length of track on the South Manchurian Railroad, just to the north of Mukden near a large barracks housing Chinese troops. The destruction was not even bad enough to prevent the next train from passing the point successfully. Be that as it may, the Japanese army blamed the bombing on the Chinese and used it as a pretext to begin a military campaign. Tokyo repeatedly declared that the military action would be halted, only to find that it had to eat its words as the military action continued. Japanese military policy was being made autonomously in the field; it had no controls.

The Guomindang military's "resistance" against Japan in the Manchurian fighting amounted in reality to nonresistance; military commanders in some cases ordered men about to go into battle to lay down their arms and simply surrender. The outrage for patriotic Chinese was that Chiang had established his government under the banner of nationalism, but his military decisions seemed cowardly and almost treasonous. Even after all of Manchuria had fallen, Chiang refused to break off relations with Japan, much less to respond with a strong military reaction. What is the explanation for such a seemingly treacherous anti-nationalistic tack? Partly it was timing. When the Manchurian incident occurred, Chiang's military was in the middle of its third extermination campaign against the Jiangxi Soviet. In fact, the "Manchurian incident" (the euphemism the Japanese used to cloak their bloody war) led to Chiang's ending the third campaign.

But Chiang's appeasement of the Japanese was more than contextual timing. Chiang believed that his army was not strong enough to fight two wars at one time—taking on both Japan and the Chinese Communists. Chiang was relying on German military advisers to help him strengthen his armies. His response to the ever more virulent Japanese aggression in North China was that the Communists had to be dealt with before the Japanese: the Japanese he compared to a skin disease, whereas the Communists were a disease of the heart. Obviously, a more serious heart problem needed to be treated first—unless, of course, the skin disease was melanoma, not a bad comparison given Japan's malevolent actions.

By early 1932, the Japanese conquest of Manchuria was complete. Instead of seizing it outright, as they had done with Korea in 1910, the Japanese decided that setting up a puppet state under Manchu leadership might tone down excessively negative foreign reaction. In the fall, the

Japanese renamed it and recognized the independent state of Manchukuo (meaning "land of the Manchus") under the leadership of the last Qing emperor, Henry Puyi. In the years before 1937, Japanese leaders and Chinese Manchurian subjects worked to construct a unique independent Manchukuo national identity. But when war erupted in China in 1937 and especially after the beginning of the Pacific war in 1941, the independence of Manchukuo became a complete sham.[8] In the meantime, the League of Nations' Lytton Commission reported in autumn 1932 that Japan was guilty of military aggression in Manchuria; the League itself adopted the report in early 1933. Japan, thumbing its nose at the world, walked out of the League. International condemnation united Japanese public opinion, creating an even more dangerous chauvinistically charged situation.

For China the turn of events was ominous. In general,

> Japan's determination to take Chinese territory as a direct colonial possession, in contrast to the indirect colonial penetration of an earlier era, created a new type of foreign danger for China, one which pressed Chinese leaders to assume national ... responsibility.[9]

Chiang's reaction of nonresistance stimulated many outraged citizens to protest through demonstrations and boycotts; it is no exaggeration to say that the Manchurian incident and the months afterward transformed China's political environment. No small result of the loss of Manchuria was that China lost 15 percent of its revenue that had come into that area through its tariffs. Given the fact that 50 percent of Nanjing's total revenue came from customs duties, this was a substantial reduction.

JAPANESE AGGRESSION ON THE MARCH

The Shanghai Incident

The Chinese people struck back at Japan through a very effective boycott in the autumn of 1931. It slashed the sale of Japanese products in China by two-thirds. Tensions were especially high in Shanghai, with its population of 30,000 Japanese citizens; many of them called for the military to come in and end the boycott. The Japanese Manchurian army (the Guandong army) funneled money to Shanghai to start an incident that would take Manchuria out of the spotlight. The military declared the boycott an act of aggression. Skirmishes broke out at the end of January 1932. With the cries of Japanese ultranationalists ringing in military ears—"Teach the Chinese a lesson"—the Japanese navy (wanting to get in on some of the patriotic glory with the Guandong army) bombed the Zhabei sector of northern Shanghai. The Chinese Nineteenth Route Army, against the will of Chiang Kai-shek, resisted forcefully. Fighting was brutal, with the Japanese eventually sending 70,000 troops to Shanghai and utilizing planes to drop fire bombs and advanced tanks and artillery to shell civilian areas. Over 4,000 Chinese soldiers were killed; the Japanese lost not quite 800.

This undeclared war raged around Shanghai for six weeks (January to March 1932); the fighting stopped when both countries agreed to an armistice. Clearly, Japan had decided that it would not push the matter at this time. On the Chinese side, recriminations abounded. Chiang was furious that the Nineteenth Route Army had put up any resistance; he feared that it might ignite a full-scale war with Japan that would endanger his own position. So he transferred the army, composed largely of men from Guangdong, to out-of-the-way Fujian province. Many supporters of the army contended that Chiang had contributed to the army's incomplete success by withholding both funds and reinforcements. For many Chinese, the Nineteenth Route Army became instant heroes, the names of its leaders appearing as brand names for cigarettes and other goods. The reason? As one historian put it, "The Chinese people, who had been gagging on never-ending humiliations

FIGURE 13.1 Triumphant Japanese soldiers almost literally crow about their military victories in great bravado from the rooftops.
Source: Bettmann/Getty Images.

and pusillanimous compromises, took the Nineteenth Route Army to their hearts."[10] The Shanghai incident only increased the polarization that was developing between those who called for resistance against this flagrant imperialist threat and the government. Chiang's response was to suppress the protests and protesters, a policy that only ratcheted up the level of animosity.

Gobbling Up the North

The years from 1933 to 1937 saw the patterns repeated again and again: Japanese aggression, Chiang's appeasement, mass Chinese reaction, and Chiang's brutal suppression of the demonstrating population. During the U.S. war in Vietnam later in the century, American leaders talked of a domino theory: that if one Southeast Asian country fell to Communism, all would topple like lined-up dominoes; in that war, this theory was not applicable. But the concept might apply here, for what one sees in looking at the years 1933 through 1935 is the toppling of Chinese property and rights before the Japanese onslaught.

What follows is a summary of the eight major Japanese aggressions in these three years. Japan won every contest but one. But also important in this catalogue of tragedy is the import of each of China's defeats, the reaction of China's people to the defeats, and Chiang's reaction to the people's reaction.

1. January 1–3, 1933

LOSS OF SHANHAIGUAN

Import: The name Shanhaiguan literally means the "pass between the mountains and the sea," the site where the Great Wall ends at the Gulf of Liaodong. The Jinzhou (Manchuria)–Tianjin Railroad ran through the pass, linking now Japan-held Manchuria with China within the Wall. Its fall was of great symbolic significance, because it was through this pass almost 289 years earlier that the Manchus had come on their way to taking over China. A shock wave washed over thinking Chinese: could this be déjà vu? Might this be the start of another conquest of China? Many in Chinese society were unnerved.

Chiang's response: No reinforcements were sent to assist the Ninth Brigade, which fought well but was no match for the Japanese. Chiang did not act in part because he was in the beginning phase of his fourth extermination campaign against the Jiangxi Soviet.

Popular reaction: There was fear that Chiang would now be willing to abandon Hebei province, where Beiping was located. This perception arose in part because the priceless collection of traditional art masterpieces of the National Palace Museum as well as Foreign Affairs Ministry archives began to be sent south. There was considerable clamor for resistance. The Chinese delegation at the League of Nations cabled that Shanhaiguan should be retaken.

Chiang's reaction: Chiang struck a pose of resistance, cabling the League of Nations delegation about Japan's rumored move into the Inner Mongolian province of Rehe, "[Rehe's] territory is the door to north China. If the Japanese invade it, we must resist with all our might."[11]

2. February 23–March 4, 1933

LOSS OF REHE PROVINCE, INNER MONGOLIA

Chiang's response: Whatever Chiang had meant by his cable to the League of Nations delegation, he did not resist with "all-out might." He ordered the poorest and most politically unreliable troops to fight the battles; they mostly just melted away before the Japanese attacks. He dispatched no planes; he sent no guns. Troops from the national army did not arrive until the battle was over, even though the Japanese invasion had been expected for months. Chiang pursued his anti-Communist campaign in Jiangxi.

Import: In addition to the loss of territory the size of the states of Virginia, Maryland, and West Virginia in just over a week, the conundrum of Chiang's motives grew ever larger.

Popular reaction: Disbelief and chagrin. Longtime party leader Hu Hanmin:

> When Shanhaiguan fell and at the time of the Rehe crisis, he used the pretext that the Jiangxi Communists were rampaging. ... I do not argue that the Communists should not be eliminated, but in today's situation ... resisting Japan is more important than eliminating Communists.

Madame Sun Yat-sen: "The Chinese people want resistance against Japanese ... imperialism. ... The time has come when [Chiang's government's] phrases about 'prolonged resistance' can no longer hide the facts of betrayal, cowardice, and nonresistance."[12]

Chiang's reaction: To reiterate his "first internal pacification, then external resistance" policy.

3. May 1933

TANGGU TRUCE

Import: This negotiated settlement created a demilitarized zone (DMZ) between the Great Wall and Beiping the size of the state of Connecticut. Chiang negotiated it to stop the Japanese advance and the certain takeover of the cities of Beiping (Japanese troops were only 13 miles from the city) and Tianjin. Chinese troops had to be out of the DMZ, but Japanese troops could remain in

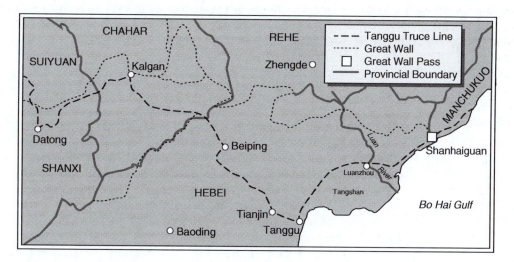

MAP 13.1   North China, Mid-1930s.

the area because of their right under the Boxer Protocol. There were a number of secret provisions, one of which allowed the Japanese to have dominant police powers in the DMZ.

Popular reaction: All the most important newspapers used words like "surrender" and "defeat" to describe the truce. Chiang and others in the government were called "traitors." Chiang was compared to Yuan Shikai, as someone "willing to cave into Japanese demands in exchange for their support for his dictatorship."[13] Journalist Zou Taofen in his *Life Weekly* vigorously attacked the agreement.

Chiang's reaction: After the Tanggu Truce, Chiang struck out at his opponents. In June, Yang Quan, the secretary for the League for the Protection of Civil Rights—organized in reaction to Chiang's suppression of the anti-Japanese activity—was assassinated. Zou Taofen, warned that his life was in danger, left China for Europe and the United States; it was a way of silencing him without ambushing him, as with Yang. While Zou was away, Nanjing closed his journal. On Chiang's government, Jiang Tingfu, history professor at Qinghua University, wrote:

> Assassination is not politics, it is not party struggle, it is killing people, vilely killing people, savagely killing people. Whatever party, whatever faction, uses assassination to overthrow an enemy party or faction exposes its own weakness. It only proclaims to the world, "if we depend on what we advocate, our policies, our achievements, our organization, we cannot support our position. Therefore, we must use murder."[14]

4. August 1933

LOSS OF EASTERN CHAHAR, INNER MONGOLIA

Import: The lost territory was slightly larger than the state of Connecticut. Even more significant was what had led up to the Japanese seizure. The Japanese had held on to this area before, but it had been won back from them with relative ease, not by Chiang but by the warlord Feng Yuxiang.

The Japanese were able to retake it because Chiang applied all sorts of pressure, including a blockade, to weaken Feng. Two disturbing questions: why would Chiang not fight the Japanese when Feng showed that it could be done effectively, and why did Chiang and his generals in essence help the Japanese retake territory that they had earlier lost?

5. April 1934

JAPANESE ASSERTION OF THE AMŌ DOCTRINE

Import: Although not a formal declaration by the government, the Foreign Ministry asserted this doctrine. Its import was ominous, for, if carried out, it virtually set up a Japanese protectorate over China. Japan would control all aid and development programs that China established with Western nations. The statement read in part, "Any joint operations undertaken by foreign powers even in the name of technical or financial assistance … are bound to acquire political significance. … Japan therefore must object to such undertakings as a matter of principle."[15]

Popular reaction: While Western governments protested, the Chinese press stridently denounced Japan. Articles asked whether this was the first move toward the establishment of a Japanese protectorate. There was general agreement that this policy drastically worsened Sino–Japanese relations.

6. June 1935

HE-UMEZU AGREEMENT

Import: This agreement substantially eroded the power of the Nanjing government in the North. Accompanied by an order that all anti-Japanese activities must stop, it removed all Guomindang and Nanjing government bodies and all army troops from Hebei province. It also removed the mayor of Tianjin and the governor of Hebei. In addition, the agreement threatened to bring Beiping and Tianjin into the earlier-established DMZ if anti-Japanese actions did not cease.

QIN-DOIHARA AGREEMENT

Import: This agreement basically gave Japan a free hand in the Inner Mongolian province of Chahar. It stipulated that the Chinese could not interfere with activities undertaken by Japan or Manchukuo there.

Popular reaction: Though the Nanjing government's censorship of the press grew ever more restrictive, the press response to this agreement generally echoed the ideas of a Tianjin paper that blasted the "traitorous Kuomintang [Guomindang]." "It clears the way for Japanese imperialism, selling the nation's territory and the people's rights. Whatever Japan wants the Kuomintang gives them."[16]

Chiang's reaction: Chiang, constantly pressured by the Japanese, stiffened measures to stifle anti-Japanese activity.

7. September 1935

DEMAND FOR AUTONOMY FOR FIVE NORTHERN PROVINCES

Import: This was the only one of the eight dominoes that did not fall. If Chiang had acceded to this demand, the five northern provinces of China (Hebei, Shandong, Shanxi, Chahar, and Suiyuan) would have been made independent, with the Chinese government removed. Japan's motives in

North China were military, political, and economic as well. Japan desired to join this area with Manchukuo and itself to become a powerful economic bloc.

Popular reaction: This demand shocked even Chiang and other government leaders.

8. December 1935

ESTABLISHMENT OF THE HEBEI-CHAHAR COUNCIL

Import: This development spelled the loss of eastern Hebei province (with its cities of Beiping and Tianjin) to the Japanese.

Popular reaction: This change helped stimulate an anti-Japanese student campaign called the December Ninth Movement. It began in Beiping on December 9 to protest Japan's demands for North China's autonomy. Marked by protest demonstrations and rallies, the movement spread to the nation's cities. Students carried the word to rural areas as well. National Salvation Associations, headquartered in Shanghai, were established across the nation; they called for the removal of Japanese troops and the puppet regimes in Manchukuo and East Hebei.

Chiang's reaction: Raids on schools, the arrest of student leaders, and the closing of campuses were Chiang's responses to China's fervently nationalistic students. Chiang and the right wing of the Guomindang attacked them as "tools of the Communists." By March 1936, most students had been silenced, but their ideas would bear some fruit in the months ahead.

Appeasement Begins to Fade

Chiang had initially tried to defuse the December Ninth Movement by coopting students, inviting student leaders to come to Nanjing for discussions. Some did, but others saw little purpose in the meeting. The Beiping Student Union, for example, noted that Chiang had called a similar meeting after Manchuria fell; then he had vowed to win back the territory within three years. The students wrote, "Four years have already elapsed. Not only has no effort been made to recover the lost provinces, but Rehe, and East Hebei, and six counties in northern Chahar have also gone under Japanese control."[17]

By summer 1936, Chiang was well aware of the nation's restiveness. The National Salvation movement, far from being nipped in the bud, was expanding. Chiang also had to deal with a short-lived rebellion of generals from Guangxi and Guangdong provinces who were demanding to fight the Japanese in the North. Following its suppression, Chiang gave the first indication that he might consider some resistance to the Japanese in the future. Specifically, he set forth the idea that appeasement had its limits. Although he still hoped that any future trouble might be handled without recourse to war, he was at least countenancing that possibility. This hint did not mean that Chiang was reacting to nationalistic pressure. In November he had seven leaders of the National Salvation Association arrested, to the outrage of millions of people across the country. It was a harbinger of what would become known late in the century as "human rights" problems. Even Western intellectuals—Albert Einstein and John Dewey, for example—cabled Chiang's government asking for the leaders' release. At home the arrests only stimulated anti-Japanese activity.

THE XI'AN INCIDENT

Out of this context came one of the most sensational and still mysterious episodes in twentieth-century China. Since the Long Marchers had reached Yan'an in late 1935, Chiang had used large numbers of troops to blockade the Communist base. By late 1936 the troop count stood at about 170,000. Its main commander was Zhang Xueliang, the former military leader of Manchuria, who, with many of his troops native to Manchuria, was none too happy to be in Northwest China fighting other Chinese. It was the victory of Japan in Manchuria that had ousted Zhang and his fellow Manchurian troops. In part because of their own loss of their homeland, they were very sympathetic to the ideas of the National Salvation movement. In April 1936, Zhang had met with Zhou Enlai to discuss a possible united front—between the CCP and the Guomindang to fight the Japanese.

Many Chinese, including Zhang, simply could not understand why Chinese should be fighting Chinese at a time when the Japanese were eating them alive. Chiang's record was a dogged, continuous struggle against the Communists: his troops fought five extermination campaigns against the Jiangxi Soviet; they fought the Long Marchers; then, once they reached Yan'an, Chiang used his best troops to blockade and quarantine the Communists.

In October, Chiang ordered Zhang to begin a campaign against the Communists. Zhang and his fellow commanders just sat on their hands. In early December, Chiang flew to Xi'an to determine what was going on. After days of "fruitless exhortations and harangues," he had finally had enough. He relieved Zhang of his command, placed a more malleable general at the head of his forces, and ordered that the army begin an anti-Communist campaign on December 12.

In the predawn hours of December 12, a unit of Zhang's troops, under the direction of Zhang and his fellow officers, attacked Chiang's resort headquarters. Although many of Chiang's bodyguards were killed in the attack, Chiang was able to escape to a cave on a nearby mountain. Zhang's men found him still in his pajamas, without his false teeth, cold, and scratched up. They put him in detention—the general having kidnapped his president—and presented him with a group of demands, all dealing with the national crisis with Japan. They included reorganizing the government to include all groups working for national salvation; halting all civil struggle among Chinese; releasing the seven leaders of the National Salvation Association and all political prisoners; guaranteeing people's right to assemble and to organize to achieve patriotic goals; working to carry out the will of Sun Yat-sen; and convening a National Salvation Conference.

The Nanjing government faced a difficult decision. Should they launch a military effort to free the president, now held against his will? Would it be less dangerous for Zhang to try to work things out diplomatically? Action proceeded on both fronts. Nanjing mobilized the air force and army at Luoyang, some 200 miles east of Xi'an, for a possible strike. On the negotiating front, Nanjing dispatched Chiang's Australian advisor, W.H. Donald, the government's intelligence czar and Blue Shirt leader Dai Li, and Chiang's brother-in-law, T.V. Soong. Madame Chiang Kai-shek also flew in, dramatically announcing to Chiang, "I am here to share your fate and to die with you, if God so wills it."[18] Negotiations dragged on, as Chiang seemed his usual obstinate self.

Having much earlier opened discussions with Zhang about anti-Japanese resistance, the Communists, headquartered little more than a hundred miles away at Yan'an, also had choices to make. Their chief enemy was now practically in their hands; should he be seized and killed? Or would Chiang be more valuable alive in the present crisis with Japan if he could be persuaded to join a united front? Despite Mao's rise to power apart from help from Moscow, there was still contact between Yan'an and the Soviet capital. When Stalin weighed in on the side of keeping Chiang alive, arguing that his prestige was still a valuable asset of great potential use in a nationwide united front, the Communist leadership in Yan'an were either confirmed in or swayed to that position. With this decision, Zhou Enlai on December 16 flew to Xi'an to join the negotiations and push Chiang to accept the leadership of a new united front of the CCP and Guomindang against the Japanese.

Negotiations continued until December 25, when Chiang's captors released him after he reportedly gave verbal assurances that he would support a united front. He put nothing in writing and later declared that he had not agreed to anything. The big question was, why would his captors have been satisfied with mere verbal assurances? Was Chiang, with a considerable record of betraying people who had helped him (as at Shanghai in 1927), now deemed trustworthy? In any event, Chiang flew back to Nanjing, now holding Zhang Xueliang captive. Zhang was court-martialed and then kept in custody under Chiang's control. Moved to Taiwan when the Guomindang lost the civil war in the late 1940s, Zhang remained under house arrest at least until 1991 and possibly longer. He left Taiwan in December 1993 and settled in Hawaii, where he died in October 2001. For his part, Chiang emerged from the affair as a national hero. Approximately 400,000 people watched his motorcade from the Nanjing airport on his return; spontaneous celebrations of joy and relief erupted in cities around the country, with many people apparently willing to forget Chiang's extended period of appeasement and the harsh repression of many Chinese civilians.

What really happened in Xi'an is unclear. In any postmortem on the episode, many issues are still mysterious. Chiang claimed that he did not agree to anything; he wrote in his diary, "I must maintain the same spirit which led Jesus Christ to the cross." He was released, he claimed, when Zhang Xueliang read Chiang's diary and was converted to "the greatness of your personality. Your loyalty to the revolutionary cause and your determination to bear the responsibility of saving the country far exceed anything we could have imagined." Though Zhang never spoke about the event, the language describing this personal "revelation" seems too stilted and hagiographic. Yet that was Chiang's line—"the resolute leader, the conversion of the captors, the unconditional release."[19] But his actions told a different story. Almost immediately, the title of Zhang's command, the "Bandit Suppression Headquarters," was dropped; there was a cease-fire between Nanjing's forces and the Red Army; and within little more than eight months, a united front was established. It does, in short, seem as though Chiang gave assurances; it is still a mystery why his captors were so willing simply to accept his word without gaining more substantial corroboration of his decision—even holding hostages until he transformed his words into action.

The Communists would have us believe that it was the superior negotiating power of Zhou Enlai that brought Chiang's conversion. Zhou's December 25 telegram to Yan'an noted that the negotiations had produced a real change in his attitude. Zhou thus became the hero in the affair, described as having undertaken a dangerous and heroic venture in coming to Xi'an. The language and almost superhuman quality of Zhou's contribution seem once again more hagiographic than real.

There are two other significant points in an analysis of the Xi'an incident. Guomindang historians, in addition to hewing to Chiang's line about his refusal to negotiate, often point to the incident as the reason Chiang was unable to succeed in eliminating the Communists. They argue that "at the time of the [Xi'an] coup, they [only] held four small [counties] in northern [Shaanxi], an area of roughly about 70 sq. kilometers."[20] Once Zhang's army was sent elsewhere, they were able to expand and thrive. The implication is that the perfidy of Zhang Xueliang prevented Chiang from succeeding in his longtime goal of exterminating the Communists. Finally, a recent interpretation sees the whole episode as primarily a "military rebellion" of Zhang and his forces against the central government. Since this scholar believes Chiang was moving away from appeasement in any circumstance, the main import of the episode was military. Just as Chiang was able to defeat the southwestern warlords over the issue of resistance against Japan before the Xi'an incident, the Xi'an incident allowed him to deal with a northwestern military threat by pulling Zhang's military away and breaking up its forces.[21]

MARCO POLO BRIDGE

During night maneuvers of Japanese troops near the Marco Polo Bridge 15 kilometers west-southwest of Beiping on July 7, 1937, shots were fired at the Japanese soldiers. When one soldier turned up missing, the Japanese demanded the right to search a nearby town. Although the missing soldier returned less than half an hour after he disappeared, his commanders did not realize that he had returned. In the meantime, when Chinese troops refused to allow the Japanese to search the town, Japanese troops opened fire, and a battle ensued. Though negotiations brought a settlement by July 11, tensions remained high. Fighting broke out again near the end of July, this time with thousands of Chinese casualties. Within days, the Japanese gained control of the whole region of Beiping and Tianjin.

It was not only in the field that tensions were high: the positions of the two governments were hardening. On July 27, Japanese Prime Minister Konoe Fumimaro announced that he would seek a "fundamental solution of Sino–Japanese relations." Three days later, Chiang Kai-shek asserted, "the only course open to us now is to lead the masses of the nation, under a single national plan, to struggle to the last."[22]

Was full-scale war inevitable? Though nothing in history is inevitable, by late summer 1937 neither country would compromise. National identities had hardened. In Japan's view, it had given too much to the continental struggle to back down. Even though the story of the relationship between the two nations during the 1930s was one long string of Chinese capitulations to Japanese demands, appeasement never satisfied Japan's territorial and political appetites. Japan's attitude was almost that capitulation at every turn was not enough: China also had to show respect to Japan, and cheerfully as well—with a smiling countenance, kowtow and be kicked while they were down. Otherwise, China should be taught a lesson. In the summer of 1936, a Japanese merchant was murdered in Shanghai. The Japanese press read a conspiracy into the killing. One newspaper wrote that

> the latest incident is a clear instance of China's lack of sincerity and its attitude against Japan and the Japanese. … Anti-Japanese feeling in China is spreading like wildfire … [and] drastic steps must be taken by Japan in the present situation."[23]

In the summer of 1937, a Japanese commander in North China stated that he was going to lead "a punitive expedition against Chinese troops, who have been taking acts derogatory to the prestige of the Empire of Japan."[24] It was almost as if Japan wanted the Chinese to thank the Japanese for invading them. With such attitudes and with Japan's long history of involvement, Japan would not likely back down or compromise.

On the Chinese side, there could also be no compromise. The tension and drama of the Xi'an incident and Chiang's mysterious "escape" had brought him popularity. The perception, whether it matched the reality or not, was that he had committed himself to resistance against the Japanese. It would have been politically suicidal for Chiang to return to a policy of appeasement. He could not backtrack. Thus, in any crisis, he had to avoid even the appearance of caving in to Japanese threats or attacks. This meant, as Chiang himself said, that China had only one choice if Japan persisted: "to struggle to the last."

Notes

1 Quoted in John Hunter Boyle, *Modern Japan, The American Nexus* (Fort Worth, TX: Harcourt Brace Jovanovich, 1993), p. 185.
2 Albert Feuerwerker, "Japanese Imperialism in China: A Commentary," in *The Japanese Informal Empire in China, 1895–1937*, ed. Peter Duus, Ramon H. Myers, and Mark R. Peattie (Princeton, NJ: Princeton University Press, 1989), p. 435.
3 These assignments are listed in Douglas R. Reynolds, "Training Young China Hands: Tōa Dōbun Shoin and Its Precursors, 1886–1945," in Duus et al., *Japanese Informal Empire*, pp. 236–7.

4 Feuerwerker, "Japanese Imperialism in China," p. 437.

5 Marius Jansen, *Japan and China: From War to Peace, 1894–1972* (Chicago, IL: Rand McNally College Publishing, 1975), p. 366.

6 Quoted in Shumpei Okamoto, "Japanese Response to Chinese Nationalism: Naitō (Konan) Torajirō's Image of China in the 1920s," in *China in the 1920s*, ed. F. Gilbert Chan and Thomas H. Etzold (New York: New Viewpoints, 1976), p. 164.

7 The quotations come from Howard L. Boorman, ed., *Biographical Dictionary of Republican China* (New York: Columbia University Press, 1970), Vol. 1, p. 121.

8 Prasenjit Duara, *Sovereignty and Authenticity: Manchukuo and the East Asian Modern* (Lanham, MD: Rowman & Littlefield, 2003), pp. 66–7.

9 Parks Coble, *Facing Japan* (Cambridge, MA: Harvard University Press, 1991), p. 31.

10 Lloyd E. Eastman, *The Abortive Revolution* (Cambridge, MA: Harvard University Press, 1974), p. 91.

11 Coble, *Facing Japan*, p. 93.

12 Quoted in Coble, *Facing Japan*, pp. 98–9.

13 Ibid., p. 114.

14 Ibid., p. 87.

15 Ibid., p. 154.

16 Ibid., p. 212.

17 Ibid., p. 288.

18 Ibid., p. 347.

19 Ibid., pp. 346–7.

20 *Chiang Kai-shek, His Life and Times*, trans. Chun-ming Chang (New York: St. John's University Press, 1981), p. 523, quoted in Coble, *Facing Japan*, p. 348.

21 Coble, *Facing Japan*, pp. 355–6.

22 James B. Crowley, *Japan's Quest for Autonomy* (Princeton, NJ: Princeton University Press, 1966), pp. 338–9.

23 Coble, *Facing Japan*, p. 309.

24 Quoted in Lyman Van Slyke, "Nationalist China During the Sino-Japanese War, 1937–1945," in *Cambridge History of China, Vol. 13, Republican China 1912–1949, Part 2*, ed. John K. Fairbank and Albert Feuerwerker (Cambridge, UK: Cambridge University Press, 1986), p. 550.

Suggestions for Further Reading

Carter, James H. *Creating a Chinese Harbin: Nationalism in an International City, 1916–1932* (Ithaca, NY: Cornell University Press, 2002). This fascinating study probes the meaning of nationalism in a city that went from Russian to Chinese to Japanese control; the focus here is on the processes of nationalism.

Coble, Parks. *Facing Japan: Chinese Politics and Japanese Imperialism, 1931–1937* (Cambridge, MA: Harvard University Press, 1991). This important study sees the rise of public opinion as crucial in Chinese politics in the face of Japanese imperialism; it argues that both Chiang Kai-shek and the Japanese "placed the Communists in a favorable position."

Duara, Prasenjit. *Sovereignty and Authenticity: Manchukuo and the East Asian Modern* (Lanham, MD: Rowman & Littlefield, 2003). This "illuminating and provocative book," in the words of a reviewer, explores Japanese and Chinese nationalism in Manchukuo, their interactions, and efforts to create an "authentic national identity" for the people of the new state.

Duus, Peter, Ramon H. Myers, and Mark R. Peattie. *The Japanese Informal Empire in China, 1895–1937* (Princeton, NJ: Princeton University Press, 1989). This important collection of essays looks at three areas: trade and investment, culture and community, and experts and sub-imperialists.

Mitter, Rana. *The Manchurian Myth: Nationalism, Resistance, and Collaboration in Modern China* (Berkeley, CA: University of California Press, 2000). This analysis, which focuses on the period 1931–1933, is masterful in depicting the complexity of resistance and collaboration and in showing the weakness of Chinese nationalism even in the face of Japanese occupation.

14

The Sino–Japanese War, 1937–1945

Items published in the *Japan Advertiser*, a Tokyo English-language newspaper, on December 7 and 14, 1937:

> Sub-lieutenant[s] Toshiaki Mukai and … Takeshi Noda, … in a friendly contest to see which of them will first fell 100 Chinese in individual sword combat before the Japanese forces completely occupy Nanjing, are running neck and neck. On Sunday when their unit was fighting outside Kuyung, the "score" … was … Mukai, 89 and Noda, 78.
>
> The winner of the competition [over] who would be the first to kill 100 Chinese with his Yamato sword has not been decided. … Mukai has a score of 106 and his rival has dispatched 105, but the two … found it impossible to determine which passed the 100 mark first. Instead of settling it with a discussion, they are going to extend the goal by 50.
>
> Mukai's blade was slightly damaged in the competition. He explained that this was the result of cutting a Chinese in half, helmet and all. The contest was "fun," he declared. … Early Saturday morning when [he was interviewed] at a point overlooking Dr. Sun Yat-sen's tomb, another Japanese unit set fire to the slopes of Purple Mountain in an attempt to drive out the Chinese troops.[1]

These events were reportedly part of the atrocity now known as the Rape of Nanjing at the beginning of the eight-year-long Sino–Japanese War. An estimated 20 million Chinese died in that war. Many more were wounded; more yet became homeless refugees. The war, coming at the end of a century-long trauma of imperialist depredations, was China's worst nightmare. In the end, it paved the way for the CCP to triumph at last and put in motion the revolution that they hoped would establish a modern socialist state. But first, the Chinese holocaust.

THE WAR'S GENERAL COURSE: AN OVERVIEW

Central China: The Japanese Go for the Jugular, 1937–1938

Though the fighting had begun in the North and continued there (see below), the main battle-ground for the first sixteen months of the war developed along the Yangzi River, from Shanghai to Yichang at the mouth of the Yangzi gorges. Chiang initiated things by stationing three divisions in

Shanghai, an act that brought Japanese reinforcements and the outbreak of fighting in mid-August. The destruction in the struggle for the city—at least its Chinese and Japanese sectors—was horrific, with Japanese gunships killing civilians and military alike with their point-blank barrage. Chiang lost 60 percent (270,000) of the modernized core of his army in the three months of fighting; the Japanese, more than 40,000. In early November the Japanese actually put forward an initiative to settle things, but Chiang did not respond until early December, at which point his forces were in full retreat and the Japanese, sensing a rout and a victory, retracted their proposal.

After the defeat at Shanghai, Chiang's policy seemed to be to trade space for time, that is, to retreat and give up territory to the advancing Japanese, pulling them farther inland, away from their resources. Chiang believed that preindustrial Western China, to which he was retreating, would be able to hold out indefinitely against the Japanese, and that time would ultimately be on his side.

The Japanese reached Chiang's capital, Nanjing, in December and unleashed one of twentieth century's most terrifying war crimes. From the Tokyo War Crimes trials come accounts of one atrocity after another. Examples: on December 15 the Japanese armies captured up to 2,000 of Nanjing's police officers who were corralled into a small area and gunned down. After the machine-gunning ceased, any of those who were found still breathing were buried alive. On the next day, a similar event occurred with about 5,000 refugees who had fearfully sought refuge in the Overseas Chinese Reception Center: the Japanese rounded them up, machine-gunned them and tossed their bodies into the icy Yangzi River.

Individual experiences seem all the more gruesome and disturbing. On December 14, one Yao Jialong, a lifelong resident of Nanjing, was forced to watch Japanese soldiers gang-rape his wife. Also watching were his young son and daughter, who witnessing the sexual penetrations and hearing the screams of their mother, cried out for the Japanese to stop. The Japanese soldiers' response: they skewered the eight and three-year-old on their bayonets and roasted them black over a hot fire.

Sometime between December 13 and 17 in a street near the city wall's Zhonghua Gate, many Japanese soldiers gang-raped a young Chinese girl. As it was continuing, several Buddhist monks walked past. Acting out of contempt, the Japanese stopped their raping and ordered the monks to rape the girl as well. When the monks refused to do so, the Japanese soldiers tore off their clothes and with their bayonets cut off the monks' penises, leaving them to bleed to death on the street.[2]

To their families, troops sent photographs of beaming soldiers alongside naked women they were about to rape or had raped and of smiling soldiers holding up severed heads.

> Foreign observers at the time estimated the number of dead at around 40,000, later histories revised the figure upward to 200,000, and the memorial to the massacre in today's Nanjing speaks of tens of thousands of rapes and a total of 300,000 dead.[3]

Whatever the number (and that issue is still sharply politicized in the early twenty-first century), even the lower estimates are shocking, "a scene of mass murder run viciously amok."[4] This terror likely had a constellation of reasons, foremost of which was Japanese embitterment about and desire for vengeance over Chinese resistance. When the war began, the Japanese predicted a few months' war, with the despised Chinese practically rolling over and playing dead. The bloody battle at Shanghai mocked those predictions. The attitude of Japanese officers going into Nanjing was that the Chinese would pay. Scholars also point to the fact that most Japanese troops were "poor farmers, industrial workers, and criminals" who were physically abused by their officers and filled with propaganda laced with racial slurs about the moral depravity of the Chinese.[5] In other words, many soldiers may have been in a sense primed to act. Once they were in Nanjing and their officers

FIGURE 14.1   Amid their watching fellow-soldiers, Japanese soldiers are shown bayoneting Chinese in what has become known as the Rape of Nanjing in December 1937. The rape and slaughter in the Chinese capital rank as one of the worst war crimes in World War II.
Source: Keystone/Getty Images.

gave them orders to revel in crimes against the Chinese, there was little to check their atrocities. Japanese commanders believed that the fall of Nanjing and the subsequent horrors there would bring the collapse of further Chinese resistance. They were wrong.

Chiang's forces moved upriver, first to Wuhan until it fell in October 1938, then to Chongqing on the Yangzi River in Sichuan province. Wuhan fell to Japanese forces, clearly superior in artillery, tanks, and planes, four days after Canton met a similar fate. Thus, by late 1938, most of the major industrialized cities had been taken by Japan; from that point on, though there would be other campaigns, the war in East, Central, and South China generally reached a stalemate. New Japanese forecasts after taking Wuhan—that they would win within three years—went the way of earlier wrong predictions. Throughout the stalemated war, Japanese atrocities seemed simply a part of their military repertoire. In east central Zhejiang province in 1940, the Japanese used biological warfare against three cities, dropping bubonic plague-infected material and starting epidemics, and used poison gas against at least one other city. Less well known than the infamous activities of Unit 731, which conducted bacterial warfare research on people in Manchuria, this terrorist strategy seems one that the Japanese were very willing to use.[6]

IN THE NORTH: THE TRANSPORTATION WAR

In Northern China after the Marco Polo Bridge action, the Japanese quickly built their army up to 200,000. They took Beiping and Tianjin and then moved out along railroad lines heading south. Their dependence on train transportation for moving troops and supplies meant that seizing and protecting 3,000 miles of rail lines and occupying urban centers along those lines became a Japanese focus. Maps of Japanese occupation in the North by mid-1938 show not large chunks of territory held but rather a "network of points and lines."[7] Japan's first major defeat came in April 1938 at Taierzhuang near the Shandong–Jiangsu border as Japan was moving to take the important railroad center of Xuzhou; Chinese sources assert that 30,000 Japanese were killed. China's failure to coordinate its military units, however, prevented it from following up on the victory.

In June 1938, in an effort to slow Japan's march, the Nationalists blasted open the Yellow River dikes. This drastic action stopped the Japanese advance for only three months. But the Chinese people in the flooded area—who were not warned—could probably have raised the question "With friends like these, who needs enemies?" It is estimated that at least 300,000 people, and perhaps up to 800,000, were drowned; with the inundation of 4,000 to 5,000 villages, over 2 million were left homeless. Even at the end of the war in 1945, "all that could be seen of some villages was the curving roof of a temple and top branches of leafless trees that poked through many feet of river silt."[8] Remarkably, Chiang did not even note this monumental tragedy in his diary.[9] The flood changed the course of the Yellow River so that now it entered the sea south rather than north of the Shandong peninsula.

The Communists spent the early years of the war establishing base areas across the North. United front or not, by 1939, Chiang, using 150,000 to 500,000 of his best troops, had already re-instituted a military and economic blockade of the Shaan-Gan-Ning base led by Mao Zedong, in effect halting its possible expansion. Beginning late that same year, the Japanese set out to consolidate their control by clearing areas of anti-Japanese guerrillas, establishing large numbers of linked strong points (similar to the blockhouses in the fifth Guomindang campaign against the Jiangxi Soviet), and forming puppet governments. These policies began to reverse the successes that the CCP had brought about in organizing peasants. In addition, one of the prime Japanese concerns remained keeping railway and road networks open and protected: the Japanese even had to construct rail lines in Shanxi province to make them consistent with the gauge (the distance between the rails) of surrounding provinces. With its control of the rails, Japan could more effectively exploit economic resources and limit some of the mobility of the Communists.

Because of these policies, in August 1940 the Communists' 8th Route Army launched its largest campaign of the war, the Hundred Regiments Campaign. Eventually 104 regiments of about 190,000 men militarily challenged the policies of consolidation that the Japanese were attempting. In the first three weeks of the campaign, Communist forces attacked all major rail lines and roads, cutting them in many places; they destroyed bridges, bombed switching yards, and made inoperative the facilities at important coal mines. The second phase of the campaign focused on attacking the blockhouse-like strong points, the goal being to get the Japanese to pull back to city garrisons and leave the countryside to the Communists. By December 1940 the campaign came to an end without any strategic success.

The viciousness of the Japanese response led some Communist leaders to second-guess the campaign, which came to seem a huge mistake. Responding with furious revenge, the Japanese launched the "kill all, burn all, loot all" campaign in July 1941; it would continue for almost three and a half years to November 1944. In effect, the Japanese declared open season on any and all Chinese. All of North China became like the later free-fire zones in the U.S. war in Vietnam, where anything alive was fair game: simply put, it was the adoption of indiscriminate violence applied to the Chinese population in general. Most small towns and villages in the path of the Japanese troops had their atrocity tales. These mopping-up campaigns were accompanied by other "pacification" policies, specifically the construction of blockade lines and fortified outposts. By 1942, almost 7,500 miles of blockade lines had been set and almost 8,000 fortified outposts built. In addition, the Japanese attempted to restrict the mobility of Communist guerrillas by digging ditches and moats and setting up palisades. With the exception of the Shaan-Gan-Ning base area, all other Communist base areas were so disrupted that they were reduced essentially to guerrilla bases.

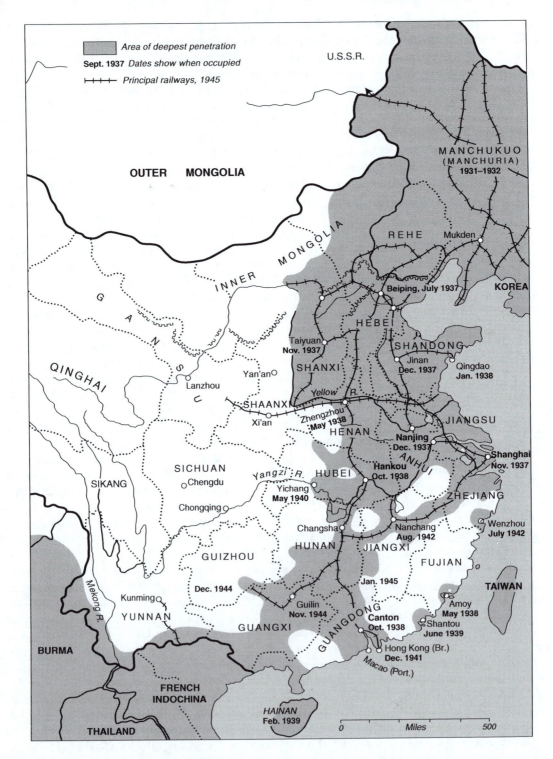

Legend:
- Area of deepest penetration
- **Sept. 1937** Dates show when occupied
- Principal railways, 1945

U.S.S.R.

OUTER MONGOLIA

MANCHUKUO
(MANCHURIA)
1931–1932

INNER MONGOLIA

REHE

Mukden

GANSU

KOREA

Beiping, July 1937

QINGHAI

HEBEI

SHANDONG

Lanzhou

Taiyuan
Nov. 1937

SHANXI

Jinan
Dec. 1937

Qingdao
Jan. 1938

Yan'an

SHAANXI

Yellow R.

Xi'an

Zhengzhou
May 1938

HENAN

JIANGSU

Nanjing
Dec. 1937

Shanghai
Nov. 1937

SICHUAN

Chengdu

Yangzi R.

HUBEI

Hankou
Oct. 1938

ANHUI

ZHEJIANG

Chongqing

Yichang
May 1940

Changsha

Nanchang
Aug. 1942

Wenzhou
July 1942

HUNAN

JIANGXI

FUJIAN

GUIZHOU

Dec. 1944

Jan. 1945

TAIWAN

Mekong R.

Kunming

YUNNAN

Guilin
Nov. 1944

GUANGXI

GUANGDONG

Canton
Oct. 1938

Amoy
May 1938

Shantou
June 1939

Hong Kong (Br.)
Dec. 1941

Macao (Port.)

BURMA

FRENCH
INDOCHINA

HAINAN
Feb. 1939

THAILAND

0   Miles   500

MAP 14.1   The Sino–Japanese War, 1937–1945.

FIGURE 14.2 Japanese troops enter a city in northern China on their invasion in 1937.
Source: Photo 12/Alamy Stock Photo.

PUTTING THE HEAT ON CHIANG: THE SITUATION IN CENTRAL CHINA, 1939–1942

When the war in Central China stalemated after the fall of Canton and Wuhan in late 1938, the Japanese worked to consolidate their control over the territory they held. (Overall in both North and Central China, it was only about 10 percent of the land area—mostly cities and rail lines.) The army in Central China did not emphasize pacification to the degree that the northern army did; pacification was consistently utilized as a policy only in the Lower Yangzi region and particularly in the triangle formed by connecting the cities of Shanghai, Hangzhou, and Nanjing. The main Japanese strategy was to apply enough pressure on Chiang's government in Chongqing so that it would eventually collapse.

Pressure came from bombing attacks. Though part of the reason for choosing Chongqing as the wartime capital was that it was frequently fog-enshrouded in fall and winter and thus provided some degree of protection from bombers, many raids were successful. From 1939 to 1941, Chongqing suffered through 268 bombing raids that destroyed much of the city and killed thousands. The air war was an effort to demoralize not only the residents of Chongqing but those of other cities—Xi'an, Kunming, and Guilin—as well.

In addition, pressure came from an economic blockade that the Japanese tried to institute throughout Central China—but that in most areas leaked like a sieve. The most effective pressure came from various Japanese victories that deprived Chiang's "Free China" (as the territory the Guomindang controlled was called) of the supplies, arms, and ammunition that it needed to carry on any sort of sustained military action. Canton's fall with the Japanese control of the Canton-Hankou Railroad meant that supplies could not reach Sichuan and Yunnan provinces from Hong Kong or Canton. Another route for getting those needed supplies was by rail from Hanoi in northern Vietnam to Kunming in Yunnan. But that route was closed as well when the Japanese took northern Vietnam in September 1940. Then the only route left open to Chiang's China was the Burma Road, completed in late 1938, a 715-mile mud-surface route connecting Mandalay in

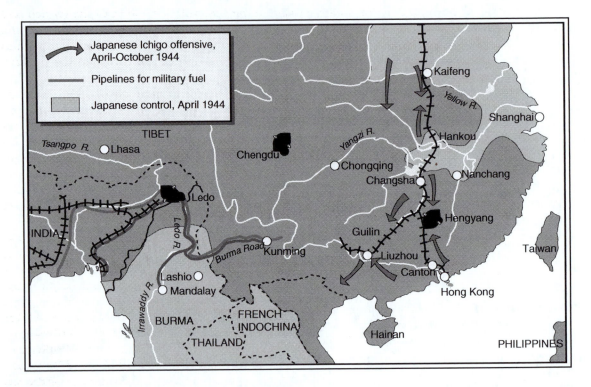

MAP 14.2   Japanese-occupied Areas of China, 1937–1945.

Burma with Kunming. Despite the fact that a truck convoy might be considered a thrill-a-minute ride, what with slippery roads over high mountain passes, one-lane sections, rickety bridges, and landslides, it was a crucial lifeline for Chiang until it, too, was closed when the Japanese seized Burma in early 1942. Then the only alternative left was an airlift of supplies, a method that would bring in only a fraction of what had come over the Burma Road.

During the stalemate in Central China through 1942, the Japanese undertook several campaigns that had limited objectives. As part of an effort to make the economic blockade more effective, in June 1940 the Japanese seized Yichang at the mouth of the Yangzi gorges to stop the hemorrhaging of trade up through the gorges to Chongqing. In the late spring and summer of 1942, the Japanese launched an offensive in Zhejiang and Jiangxi provinces aimed at destroying air bases that might be used to bomb the Japanese islands. These bases had been the intended landing sites for planes involved in the (James) Doolittle Raid over Tokyo in April 1942, an act that enraged the Japanese military leadership.

THE ICHIGO OFFENSIVE (APRIL–DECEMBER 1944)

Though most areas in China could not see the impact, the war's face changed dramatically with the Japanese attack on Pearl Harbor on December 7, 1941. Japan's troops had to be stretched thinner, since from then on it had to deploy troops to Southeast Asia and the Pacific in larger numbers—likely part of the reason for the continuation of the military stalemate. The United States (along with the other Allied powers) became an ally of China; the U.S. military role in China (which will be treated in more detail below) changed the contours of the China war. A good example is the post-Doolittle campaign of 1942: if U.S. planes had not been involved in the raid and intended to land at bases in Southeast China, it is likely that Japan would never have launched the military campaign through Zhejiang and Jiangxi.

Japan's 1944 Ichigo ("Number One") offensive had goals similar to those of the 1942 Zhejiang–Jiangxi offensive—to destroy air bases in South Central China. These bases were being used by American pilots under the leadership of General Claire Chennault. In late 1943, Chennault's pilots began to launch punishingly effective bombing attacks on Japanese bases in China and on Japanese shipping along the coast. The U.S. chief of Chiang Kai-shek's allied staff, General Joseph Stilwell, had warned that such action might bring Japanese retaliation; it came in the form of the Ichigo offensive. But the offensive was not only aimed at the South Central air bases. It actually began in the North, and an additional aim was to create a north–south route from Mukden in Manchuria to Hanoi that could be an alternative to sea routes.

The offensive was a rout; in only one battle, for the city of Hengyang in Hunan province, did the Chinese put up any sustained resistance. The Japanese seized major cities that had to that point been untaken, and they destroyed all the bases that Chennault's men had used. Having created a military gash slicing the country apart from north to south through Central China, the Japanese turned west toward Chongqing. The threat seemed so dire that British and U.S. civilians were evacuated from Chiang's capital. But then the Japanese suddenly stopped. Analysts argue that for Japan at this point, fighting a losing battle against American forces in the Pacific island campaigns, simple survival was their main goal, not delivering a deathblow to Chiang. The Ichigo offensive, in the words of one historian, "pushed [Chiang's] regime almost to the edge":[10] Almost half a million soldiers were killed or wounded; property damage was immense; fully one-quarter of the factories contributing to Free China's economy were destroyed; and almost the complete grain crop of 1944 (from the province of Henan and large parts of Hunan, Jiangxi, and Guangxi) was lost, making the problem of the rice supply for the population nothing short of desperate.

THE EXODUS

When the fighting erupted in and around Shanghai in August 1937, millions of Chinese fled. Leaving one's native place with no specific place to go to (except out of the way of the enemy) would be frightening in any culture. But for the Chinese, for whom personal connections were the defining feature of one's identity and one's life in society, becoming a refugee meant giving up that known and comfortable world of connections for a new identity in sojourning with strangers. Travel itself could be undependable and dangerous, and life would now be lived in a dangerously unpredictable world. It was not a decision to take lightly, but it was often taken out of the sheer panic of being caught in the brutal grip and bloody warfare of the enemy.

There were many different kinds of refugees in the exodus out of the Yangzi valley. Millions were individuals and their families. Though most went west, following the government as it moved up the Yangzi in phases, not all went in that direction. Some from the Lower Yangzi went south into Zhejiang or Fujian; others fled to Jiangxi and points southwest. But the greatest number—several million—went up the Yangzi gorges into Sichuan. There they experienced what would best be called "culture shock." Many of those accompanying the government were used to prosperity and a modern lifestyle. They were moving into an area that the modern world had scarcely touched; it was like moving from the late 1930s back into the Qing dynasty. Sichuan and Yunnan

FIGURE 14.3   Carrying household furnishings and bags of all shapes and sizes, this crush of refugees fled Shanghai in panic to escape the Japanese onslaught. Their destination depended largely on their economic
resources.
Source: Keystone/Getty Images.

had never even been under Chiang Kai-shek's control. Many refugees tended to look askance at the
locals, with sneers and condescension; locals reacted with resentment and charged refugees more
for the same items bought for lower prices by locals. Thus, it was not only the refugees who were
disconcerted by having to reside in a world of strangers, the local residents also were put off by
these outsiders with their continual pretension and demands.

There were also institutional refugees. Whole factories were moved. Workers dismantled
machines and equipment and packed them up on barges to be sent upstream and reconstructed.
After the Marco Polo Bridge incident, military-related facilities such as arsenals and airplane plants
were moved. The government, desperate for wartime necessities, offered incentives for private
companies to move as well, offering low-interest loans, free factory sites, and a guaranteed profit
of between 5 and 10 percent for five to seven years. In the end, 639 private companies moved,
75 percent of which were able to return to production. Though this seems a sizable number, it was
only a small portion of the current industrial plant, and they were unable to provide the needed
wartime items. Most companies chose to relocate not in China, at risk for wartime damage, but in
Hong Kong or the International Settlement in Shanghai. After Pearl Harbor, when the International
Settlement fell to Japan, that site was also no longer desirable.

In addition to companies, schools and colleges were moved. Laboratory equipment and
libraries were, like factory parts, packed up, placed on barges, and transported inland. Since
educators and students had been in the forefront of the National Salvation Association and anti-
Japanese activities during the 1930s, Japanese lashed out especially at them during their military
onslaughts. For example, Nankai University in Tianjin was bombed, shelled with artillery, and
then set afire with kerosene. Universities in cities such as Shanghai, Wuhan, and Nanjing were
bombed repeatedly. The staffs of over fifty educational institutions fled into the interior, with
those of twenty-five retreating to Hong Kong or the foreign concession area in a treaty port. To
strengthen their resources in areas where conditions were often miserable, some universities

joined together with others in their wartime exile. The most famous was Southwest Associated University in Kunming, an amalgam of the three famous universities of Beijing, Qinghua (China's equivalent of MIT), and Nankai.

SOLDIERS AND THE MILITARY

The Nationalist army was a coalition of armies numbering around 3.5 million; the soldiers in most of its units were descendants of warlord armies. The core or Central Army numbered about 300,000 in 1941 and rose to 650,000 by the end of the war. Most of its officers had been trained by German instructors in the 1930s at the Central Military Academy in Nanjing. The Central Army had the best training, equipment, and military expertise of any of the units in the coalition of armies. The military capability, the quality of leadership, and even the loyalty of many of the armies to Chiang's regime varied widely. Some armies, which had been warlord armies, remained more loyal to their former warlord leader than to Chiang Kai-shek. It is probably not surprising that a good number of non–Central Army commanders defected with their troops to the Japanese; between 1941 and 1943, sixty-nine generals defected. Nor is it particularly shocking to learn that in 1944 a coalition of militarists plotted a coup against Chiang's government.

Rank-and-file armies in the early twentieth century were composed of volunteers and those who had been forced to join. Conscription, or building an army through a draft, was first tried in 1933; the system established then was made universal at the outbreak of the war with Japan, but it had for all practical purposes collapsed by 1941. Reorganized that year, the draft system remained, but it was seriously flawed. Chongqing determined how many men, ages eighteen to forty-five, it needed and assigned a quota to each province, which, in turn, generally assigned quotas to counties, where party cadres were to manage the actual draft. Though theoretically there was to have been one to two months of training for conscription management, barely 3,000 men had any training in the decade from 1936 to 1946. This situation created a scandalous administration of this important system. Local officials made up or falsified records, sold exemptions, stole money provided by the government to support families of draftees, and drafted those officially exempt: underage children and sole sons of families. The rich were not drafted but the poor were taken, men who had no money to buy their way out. If local draftees were not enough to fill the quota, passersby were snatched up. An American GI reported that streets in one city were roped off and that all men of draft age who were caught there were simply sent to the front.

Even the sick were drafted; in fact, in 1942, only 28.9 percent of the draftees from Sichuan province came up to Chinese health standards. Most then were in no shape to face the trials of induction. Draftees were forced to march many, perhaps hundreds, of miles to reach their units. They were, in the words of the American journalists Theodore White and Annalee Jacoby, "doomed men."[11]

> Frequently the recruits were tied together with ropes around their necks. At night they might be stripped of their clothing to prevent them from slipping away. For food, they received only small quantities of rice. … For water, they might have to drink from puddles by the roadside—a common cause of diarrhoea. … Medical treatment was unavailable, however, because the recruits were not regarded as part of the army until they had joined their assigned units.[12]

It is estimated that more than a million men died on their way to their units. Once with their units, the men were poorly and lightly fed, mostly rice with a few beans or turnips. White and Jacoby noted that

American soldiers used to laugh when they saw Chinese troops carrying dead dogs slung from poles; they cursed when a pet puppy disappeared from their barracks. The Chinese troops stole dogs and ate them because they were starving and because the fat pets the Americans kept ate more meat in a week than a Chinese soldier saw in a month.[13]

Partly because of diet but also because of appallingly wretched sanitation conditions, contagious diseases—dysentery, tuberculosis, influenza, and typhus—frequently raced through units, joining malaria and a host of vitamin-deficiency diseases as killers.

Wounds received in battle would not bring automatic death, but that was a good possibility. If soldiers were lucky, they might make it to a primitive hospital four days to a week after being shot or otherwise injured. "An abdominal or head wound meant certain death; an infected gash meant gangrene."[14] Large numbers, of course, were killed on the battlefield. Even though a military stalemate had generally been reached by 1939, many Chinese soldiers continued to die in battle. According to Chinese statistics, in 1940, 340,000 men were killed; in 1941, 145,000; in 1942, 88,000; and in 1943, 43,000. Altogether in the war, Chinese figures show wartime casualties at 3,211,419 and deaths at 1,319,958.

COLLABORATION

With such horrific statistics as a result of actions by the Japanese, it is not surprising that any Chinese who worked with the Japanese would have been viewed as traitors. Millions of people, however, lived in areas controlled by Japan; and Japan, not wanting the burden of governing directly, used Chinese who collaborated with them. Collaboration may be defined as actions that had the effect of maintaining Japanese power, attaining Japanese ends, or making Japanese control tolerable. Most subsequent Chinese, carrying the torch of Chinese nationalism, have condemned collaborators as morally reprehensible traitors. But a host of reasons can be offered to explain why someone would have chosen to collaborate. Among them may have been a sincere belief that collaboration was the best way to protect the area and its people; previous experience in Japan or connections to the Japanese; previous experience in governing and a desire to serve the people; being forced to do so; a desire to profit economically, politically, or socially from collaboration; or a combination of reasons.

The type and extent of collaboration varied markedly across the occupied territory. A collaborator might have acted under Japanese direction, with Japanese participation, or with tacit Japanese approval. The range of collaborative actions was thus broad. Some collaborators worked directly in Japanese institutions; others worked at the command of the occupiers; some worked for the Japanese for a time and then resisted; others simply assented to Japanese rule by not actively resisting. One writer has noted the types of collaborators seen in Europe during World War II; China had all these types. Unconditional collaborators supported the occupying power in every way; their slogan might have been "Our enemy is my friend." In occupied areas, these were men who served as spies and in different capacities in Japanese military police organs. There were also neutral collaborators—"I conform": those who decided that life must continue, who were determined to survive the war, and who would conform in whatever way was necessary. In occupied zones, these were the largest number of citizens and groups, like principals and teachers at schools set up under Japanese-controlled regimes; they often promoted Japanese propaganda.

The actions of two other collaborator types point to the reality that collaboration and resistance, "far from being irreconcilable opposites, were as close as two sides of the same coin."[15] There were the conditional collaborators ("I collaborate to a point"). Many collaborationist regimes at the provincial and county levels were of this type. They worked with the Japanese but kept their own institutions, appointed their own subordinates, and occasionally opposed the Japanese in support of a Chinese interest. Finally, there were the tactical collaborators ("I do but I don't"), those who performed public service acts that facilitated the workings of the society or economy under the regime.[16]

In essence, whatever the brand, all collaborators adopted a new identity. Since motive and intent were crucial aspects of choosing an identity as a collaborator, the choice was a complex, even ambiguous phenomenon involving individual histories, social circumstances, economic self-interest, personal and family safety, and individual inclination. Individual motive and intent generally cannot be gauged, given the nature of the sources; further, even if collaborators had set down their reasons, the issue in retrospect is so emotionally charged that those public reasons would be highly suspect.

There were two main collaborative governments. A "provisional government" in Beiping was established in December 1937, headed by Wang Kemin. We have met Wang before: it was his recommendation in 1923 that the Boxer indemnity to France be paid in gold, thus linking the warlord government to the imperialists directly. Wang did this in part because he himself stood to profit. The action led to destruction of his ancestral tablets by protesters in Hangzhou. Wang had collaborated with the Japanese from 1935 on, serving on a council that oversaw the demilitarized zone established in the Tanggu Truce. The provisional government oversaw the five northern provinces of Hebei, Chahar, Suiyuan, Henan, and Shandong. It issued its own currency, starting in early 1938, to finance its operations. In Nanjing in March 1938, the Japanese established the "Reformed Government," headed by Liang Hongzhi, a scholar and longtime fixture in warlord governments. Wang and Liang met in late 1938 in Manchuria, where they established a joint committee for the government of China and promised to coordinate and control the postal service, customs, transportation, education, and foreign affairs.

The Japanese were well aware at the time these regimes were being established that former warlord associates did not rank high on the prestige lists of most Chinese. Ideally, Japan would have liked to find someone with sufficient name recognition and prestige to rival even Chiang Kai-shek and thereby possibly compel Chiang to enter negotiations. In 1939, they hit the jackpot—Wang Jingwei, longtime Guomindang leader, former close ally of Sun Yat-sen, and rival to Chiang Kai-shek. Negotiations in 1939 led to the March 30, 1940 establishment of a new government in Nanjing, recognized by both Wang Kemin and Liang Hongzhi. It was ironic: Wang Jingwei, who had been the golden boy of nationalism following his 1910 attempt to assassinate the Qing regime's prince regent, thirty years later became the betrayer of Chinese nationalism to a foreign power. But Wang had his reasons. He apparently sincerely believed that peaceful accommodation with Japan was the only realistic way to maintain China's national interests and unity. He contended that it was his government, not Chiang's, that was the legitimate national government; further, he argued that he was Sun Yat-sen's rightful heir.

Chiang did not bat an eye over Wang's decision, though the Japanese waited until it was clear that he would not react before they formally recognized Wang's regime. The Japanese tried to invest Wang's government with the appearance of some independence and equality. In early 1943, the Japanese gave up their concession areas in China and their right of extraterritoriality; Nanjing responded by following Japanese bidding and declaring war on the United States and Great Britain. Nanjing also took over the International Settlement and the French concession in Shanghai. A treaty in October 1943 stipulated that Tokyo and Nanjing would cooperate "as equal and independent neighbors in the establishment of Greater East Asia." Wang thus seemed to have bought into the Japanese idea of a pan-Asian and anti-Western bloc. From this point on, the Japanese made various overtures to Chiang, some through his security and intelligence chief, Dai Li, arguing that

Chiang's main interest lay in collaborating with Nanjing in order to finally break the back of the Communist movement and that he should thereby break off his relationships with the United States and Great Britain. This idea swayed a number of Chiang's conservative supporters but did not have sufficient appeal for Chiang.

However later Chinese have seen Wang, it is clear that for millions of Chinese in the Nanjing-Shanghai-Hangzhou triangle, Wang was the accepted head of state and his government, patterned administratively on the Guomindang government in Chongqing, provided some protection for the people. As it turned out, of course, Wang's reason for collaborating—that it was the only way to save China—was incorrect. Wang did not live to see the end, however, dying of illness in Japan, where he had gone for treatment in late 1944. The other two main collaborators, and, indeed, those who had worked in Wang's government, were brought to trial as traitors after the war ended. Wang Kemin died in prison in late 1945; Liang Hongzhi was executed in November 1946; and a number of high-ranking officials in Wang Jingwei's administration were executed as well.

WARTIME PROPAGANDA

Those who did not collaborate at all but resisted the Japanese advance were urged on in their actions by propaganda. The Chinese word for "propaganda" (*xuanchuan*) does not carry with it the negative sense of manipulation that the English word contains. It means to inform and to advocate, and it was the word used in Chinese materials for popularizing the war so as to build commitment from the masses for victory.

The war had the effect of driving the artists and writers out of the eastern cities, most of them captured by the Japanese, into the rural hinterland. The goals: to reach the people where they were and to promote the cause of the war. "Literature must go to the countryside; literature must join the army" was the slogan of the All-China Resistance Association of Writers and Artists. Not only did the slogan point to the arena of action, it also propelled intellectuals to examine their own roles in the nation's current crisis. Despite their recognition of the horrors of war, many were positive about the role the war could play in helping to remake China. For example, in his poem "Ode to the War of Resistance," written in 1937, Guo Moruo exclaimed (and the context must be Chiang Kai-shek's long record of appeasement):

> When I heard the rumble of guns above Shanghai,
> I felt nothing but happiness.
> They are the auspicious cannons announcing the revival of our people.
> And our nation has determined to resist till the end.[17]

Intellectuals and artists were motivated by the hope of national revival, by a spirit of individual responsibility for the nation, and by outrage at the foreign oppression of Chinese society and culture.

Their tools? Cartoons and newspapers were at the heart of things. Cartoons could summon up bitter, ironic, even sardonic truths and attitudes about the war; they could provide impressions about the human side of often horrifying events. Japanese troops were commonly depicted as snakes and beasts. Cartoonists made much of their bestiality. Feng Zikai, the most famous of the political cartoonists, for example, drew a graphic picture of a nursing mother in Zhejiang province being killed in a bombing attack. He accompanied the sketch with a short explanatory poem:

> In this aerial raid,
> On whom do the bombs drop?

A baby is sucking at its mother's breast
But the loving mother's head has suddenly been severed.
Blood and milk flow together.

Newspapers offered descriptions of Japanese war atrocities and of the courses of battles, interviews with military commanders and government spokesmen, and advocacy pieces and editorials. Political language in newspapers, tracts, and flyers has been described as "simple, emotionally charged, and laced with gritty imagery."[18]

The cultural form that likely had the largest impact was spoken drama. These productions ranged from those of well-organized civilian and military traveling drama troupes to more impromptu and improvisational newspaper plays and street plays. Newspaper plays were primarily informational, recounting in improvisational ways accounts in the news, dealing, among other things, with battles, Japanese atrocities, and heroic Chinese resistance. Street plays, commonly performed by four or five actors and lasting less than half an hour, had more complex plots and stressed audience participation. They were "improvised piece[s] grounded in simplicity, flexibility,

FIGURE 14.4 In this cartoon, artist Feng Zikai shows a woman decapitated by Japanese bombs. Feng pioneered using traditional brush drawings to depict episodes of daily life that he observed.
Source: Feng Zikai: A mother's head severed. From *China Weekly Review* 88.6 (April 8, 1939): 177.

and interaction, unified by the theme of war, and serving as a rallying cry for resistance."[19] For a rural populace accustomed to traveling opera troupes as a part of village festivals, the news and propaganda conveyed in street plays and other dramatic forms would have swept them up in the issues of the day more easily than newspapers and cartoons. The CCP was adept at using all these cultural forms to promote ideas of socialism and the making of a new China.

THE UNITED STATES AND CHINA IN WARTIME: ROUGH SLEDDING

Early in the war, the Soviet Union, driven by the common aim of defeating Japan, was Chiang Kai-shek's biggest supplier of foreign assistance. From 1937 to 1939, it sent 1,000 airplanes plus substantial amounts of artillery, munitions, and gasoline. It provided low-interest loans, volunteer pilots, and about 500 military advisers. It is noteworthy that almost no aid was sent to the Communists. Decreased after 1939, when World War II erupted, the aid was stopped with the German invasion of the Soviet Union in 1941.

In contrast, at the Sino–Japanese War's beginning, Great Britain and the United States did very little to assist China out of fear of angering Japan, though the United States, at least, was sympathetic to China's plight. By 1940, the United States began to supply more aid; in 1941, China, like other allies, began to receive lend-lease, assistance that essentially provided free arms and materiel to those fighting the Axis aggressors. That same year, the air force's American Volunteer Group (the "Flying Tigers") under General Claire Chennault became active in Burma.

After Pearl Harbor made them allies, the U.S. goal in China was to build Chiang's forces until they were strong enough to take back Eastern China, which could then be used as an air base to attack the Japanese islands. Sufficient arms and supplies were necessary for such a rebuilding program, but, as we have seen, after the Burma Road was cut in 1942, the only way to get the necessary items to Chiang and his forces was the airlift over northern Burma's mountainous "Hump." The tonnage that the United States airlifted into China equaled the Burma Road's 1941 tonnage only in 1944. Only a pittance reached Chiang when what was needed was a profusion of aid. The situation was compounded by the fact that China, as part of the China–Burma–India (CBI) theater of the war, was low on the totem pole in receiving aid from the United States and other allies. The policy was Europe first; and that priority meant that of the total lend–lease aid given by the United States, China received a paltry 1.5 percent in 1941 and 1942, 0.5 percent in 1943 and 1944, and only 4 percent in 1945. U.S. strategic policy and the constraints of the airlift created a situation in which the United States had in reality little chance of achieving its policy objective of building Chiang's army.

Other problems also bedeviled the relationship between China and the United States. The commander of the CBI theater and the chief of Chiang Kai-shek's allied staff was General Joseph Stilwell. On paper, Stilwell looked like the perfect man for the job. He spoke Chinese, having studied it in Beijing during the May Fourth period; he therefore had some knowledge of Chinese society and culture. But he did not get along with Chiang at all; their personalities clashed bitterly. Stilwell, whose appropriate nickname was "Vinegar Joe," was direct, frank, tactless, and unwilling to put up with bureaucratic hassles and ritualistic procedures. He was not a man to stroke other men's egos. Chiang, who often needed stroking, was indirect, proud, a man of few words, and deeply aware of status and its import. Stilwell did not hide his disdain for Chiang. "The trouble in China," he asserted, "is simple: we are allied to an ignorant, illiterate, superstitious peasant son of a bitch." Stilwell's code name for Chiang in communications was "Peanut." He once mused on Chiang: "Why can't sudden death for once strike in the proper place?"

They also had substantive policy differences. Most basic was that Stilwell saw Japan as the enemy against which all military strategy and strength should be brought to bear. In Chiang's estimation, the Communists were a more crucial enemy than the Japanese, hence his continuing blockade of the Communist areas using some of his best troops. Given such a basic disagreement, it is not surprising that in looking at particular military strategies, Chiang and Stilwell did not see eye to eye. Part of Stilwell's goal was to increase the rate and effectiveness of U.S. supplies and equipment headed to Chiang's army so that the army could be built up to retake Eastern China. As long as he had to rely solely on the airlift, this was hardly possible. Stilwell thus wanted to take Burma from the Japanese and reopen the Burma Road. Chiang thought this was asinine: why send Chinese soldiers to Burma when they could be fighting to take Eastern China? Instead, Chiang argued, why not use the Flying Tigers (reorganized after 1941 as the China Air Task Force) to bomb Japanese bases and shipping? Claire Chennault had clearly gotten Chiang's ear.

In the bloody days of early fall 1944, President Franklin Roosevelt, in order to stanch the bleeding, sent Chiang a demand that he put Stilwell "in unrestricted command of all your forces." Whatever the reality and however Roosevelt perceived his demand, given the long history of China's subordination to foreign imperialism, the demand that Chiang turn his army over to a foreigner was flagrantly imperialistic. Stilwell gleefully described the moment when he turned the demand over to Chiang:

> I handed this bundle of paprika to the Peanut and then sat back with a sigh. The harpoon hit the little bugger right in the solar plexus, and went right through him. It was a clean hit, but beyond turning green and losing the power of speech, he did not bat an eye.[20]

In the end, instead of getting to run Chiang's army, because of Chiang's uncompromising insistence, Stilwell was recalled from China.

By that time, the original goal of using Eastern China to bomb Japan had been shelved; given the circumstances, that goal seemed impossible. Instead, the United States utilized an "island-hopping" campaign—fighting up from the South Pacific in blood-drenched island confrontations. Once they reached the island of Saipan in the Marianas Islands in July 1944, the Japanese islands were within bombing range. The war would last another year, a period in which both Chiang and Mao positioned themselves for the war that was to follow the war. When the war suddenly ended in August 1945 after the dropping of the atomic bombs in Japan, the race was on to see who would emerge as the ruler of a new China.

THE COMMUNISTS IN YAN'AN, 1942–1945

The united front established by the two political parties after Chiang's sensational kidnapping in late 1936 had not worked effectively. Though nominally under Guomindang control, the main Red Army, the 8th Route Army in the North, was able to maneuver for its own goals. Though it lost tens of thousands of men in bitter fighting with the Japanese, it was able to use the warfare to expand its own power in North China. Chiang reacted to the expansion with the reinstitution of the military and economic blockade of Mao's base. That might be said to have effectively ended cooperation. But a bloodier event ended the united front in reality if not in name.

The New 4th Army was composed of both Guomindang and Communist detachments, the latter formed from old units involved in the Three-Year War in Southeast and Central China. Relations between Guomindang and Communist detachments in this army were not good. Communists resented having to take orders from Nationalist leaders, and in late 1939 Communist units clashed with Nationalists. Guomindang leaders, seeing the Communists roving across North China, wanted to keep Central China off limits against any possible Communist expansion there. Since the New 4th Army was based in Anhui province, south of the Yangzi River, the Guomindang ordered its Communist detachments to relocate north of the Yangzi. All except the Headquarters detachment did so. In October 1940, bitter fighting between Communist units and Guomindang units ended in the destruction of the Guomindang detachments; this battle put the lie to the existence of any kind of united front.

After this confrontation, negotiations between the Guomindang and the Headquarters detachment went from bad to worse. In early December, Chiang gave the Communists a New Year's Eve deadline to move all New 4th Army units north of the Yangzi and all 8th Route units north of the Yellow River. Once the Headquarters detachment finally started to move, it was harassed by Guomindang units. Attempting to regroup, the Headquarters detachment was encircled by Nationalist troops who conducted a turkey shoot, massacring 3,000 and wounding many more, who were taken to prison camps. Many of those killed were noncombat staff, the high command, and those linked to them. Although bad blood had been increasing in this army and both sides had been guilty of military infractions against the united front, Nationalist actions here were denounced as perfidious. Though the various Communist detachments of this army regrouped once again south of the Yangzi, the incident was, in the words of Theodore White, "one of the major turning points in China's wartime politics."[21]

The war years were also important for the Communists in shaping their party strategy and in developing approaches that would become useful following 1949. The party became more focused on its identity, coherence, and even purity. Wartime immigrants who poured into Yan'an created these concerns: an estimated 100,000—likely up to 50 percent of them students, teachers, journalists, and intellectuals—from 1937 to 1940. Party membership swelled rapidly, from 40,000 in 1937 to some 800,000 by 1940.[22] The need for quality control and party cohesion and direction caused the party to draw a firm party "line" and use it to screen out dissenters. Such greater party central control allowed more administrative oversight of the huge population variety among and within regions that the party controlled. Its downside, however, was a burgeoning civil and military bureaucracy, with its inevitable emphasis on routinization and hierarchy. To deal with that problem, the party devised the "to the villages" (*xiaxiang*) program—which would remain an important element in its repertoire of state policies. Higher-level party cadres were sent to the countryside to live with and learn from peasants and to help begin to decentralize various party and government functions. Intellectuals were also sent later to break down the barriers between urban elites and peasants. Like the Guomindang regime's dilemma, one of the party's most intractable problems remained deciding what was the most appropriate relationship between the central regime and the localities, between the role of the state and local initiative.

The motive force of the revolution during the anti-Japanese war was mass mobilization undertaken by the party. The most important strategy of mass mobilization, class struggle, was used both in base areas and in guerrilla zones—not to carry out radical land reform but to reduce rents, taxes, and interest. Because of the relative paucity of landlords in the North, there were few problems with tenancy and rent; the key resentment among the masses there was over heavy taxes. The party sent work teams to villages to mobilize peasant associations to directly challenge village elites. It is no exaggeration to argue that the "rise of the peasant associations fundamentally changed rural power relations."[23] A second wave of mass organizing focused on setting up women's and workers' associations as part of mobilizing the population for war.

The timing of mobilizational efforts varied from place to place. In some bases of North China, these efforts were well under way by 1939 and 1940; in others, they were not started until

1943 and 1944. Reforms began in Central China bases only in 1941. Rich landlords were more of a problem in Central and South China, but they were not generally demonized until 1943. Class struggle became almost tangible in the struggle meeting, the "most intense, condensed form of peasant mobilization."[24] These intense, often violent episodes were launched in the North against local despots by 1942 but did not occur in Central China until autumn 1943. Party cadres chose the targets and encouraged the expression of latent peasant anger against village bosses and landlords. These staged events became pivotal in shattering mass apathy and passivity and disrupting what former solidarity had existed among targets and community. There were also additional strategies of base-specific mass mobilization.[25]

The secret of Communist revolutionary success varied from place to place, from time to time, and from tactic to tactic. Communist cadres had to understand all aspects of the locale—the natural environment; the social, economic, and political structures; and particular needs and grievances—then build networks and coalitions with local leaders, mobilize local inhabitants, and carry out pragmatic and flexible policies. These efforts were frequently unsuccessful; leftist excesses and rightist betrayal were common; and many times contingencies, not strategies, gave the Communists their success. In Henan's Rivereast base, for example, the Communists succeeded only when the Japanese withdrew their troops from the area after the beginning of the war in the Pacific in late 1941.

In contrast to these initiatives, two other party efforts emphasized unbending party control. An extraordinarily important strategy to attain party cohesion was the rectification campaign, the first of many in the history of the CCP and its political regime. By late 1940 and early 1941 the situation at Yan'an had become tense and troubled. The developing military situation provided the greatest threat and seems to have heightened the lack of party coherence. The Nationalists had 400,000 soldiers blockading Shaan-Gan-Ning to its south and east. The New 4th Army incident and Guomindang pressure on its remnant units and on the 8th Route Army as well put the Communist military on the defensive. In this context, Mao launched the rectification campaign in February 1942. It had several goals. One was to inculcate a uniformity of spirit and a focus on the party's mission into the party's tens of thousands of new members, many of them intellectuals and students who had come from coastal cities.

A second goal was to challenge Wang Ming, the party's general secretary in 1931 and 1932, and his other returned students from Russia. Though Wang did not have any organizational base in the party, a number of the 28 Bolsheviks did, and they continued to try to speak as the authoritative Marxist–Leninist theoreticians. By this time, Mao's party position was strong and secure enough that he wanted to assert his own theoretical vision as the new party orthodoxy, one that emphasized Chinese particularities, not the standard Russian orthodoxy. One such particularity was to make the peasants equal partners with the proletariat in the vanguard of the revolution. Railing against the dogmatic application of Marxist–Leninist thought by Wang Ming and his cohorts, Mao argued that "the arrow of Marxism–Leninism must be used to hit the target of the Chinese revolution." He continued:

> We must tell [those who regard Marxism–Leninism as religious dogma] openly, "Your dogma is of no use," or to use an impolite phrase, "Your dogma is less useful than excrement." We see that dog excrement can fertilize the fields, and man's can feed the dog. And dogmas? They can't fertilize fields; nor can they feed a dog. Of what use are they?[26]

To rectify or reform their thoughts, cadres were to participate in small-group sessions studying documents Mao selected; they had to write out detailed self-criticisms; they were often criticized in mass meetings; and they had to confess their errors. If this last step was difficult or impossible for the cadres being rectified, they might be isolated and various psychological pressures used against them. In the end, they were often sent to the countryside for menial work and ostracism. Mao believed in the power of human beings to change their thoughts and their lives. At least theoretically, such a position meant that, unlike Stalin, with his great and bloody purges in which many died, Mao would not resort to murderous terror. He once remarked that if you cut off men's heads, they do not grow back like cabbages. The goal should be to change men's minds. Even so, there is a spectrum of names for what Mao wanted to do, ranging from innocuous to frightening, reflecting the controversy that such a process can engender. From rectification (changing one's ways) to reeducation (a goal firmly in line with traditional Chinese moral training) to thought reform (implied authoritarianism) to brainwashing (inhuman destroyer of individuality)—whatever view one takes of the process colors its meaning. In the end, the process grew out of the radical logic of those who were certain that they possessed the Truth.

For intellectuals, the other target of rectification, Mao expanded his thoughts on the functions of art and literature in a socialist society in May 1942. Art and literature were "powerful weapons for uniting and educating the people ..., as well as [helping] the people wage the struggle against the enemy with one heart and one mind."[27] Mao's points in this speech and in party decisions in spring 1942 foreshadowed the future relationships of state to society, here specifically to intellectuals and artists. Art and literature served the "people"—defined as workers, peasants, and soldiers, not the petty bourgeoisie, students, or intellectuals. Above all, they served the revolutionary cause.

> In the world today all culture, all art and literature belong to definite classes and follow definite political lines. There is in fact no such thing as art for art's sake, art which stands above classes or art which runs parallel to or remains independent of politics. Proletarian art and literature are part of the whole cause of the proletarian revolution. ... Therefore, the Party's artistic and literary activity occupies a definite and assigned position in the Party's total revolutionary work and is subordinated to the prescribed revolutionary task of the Party in any given revolutionary period.[28]

The phrase most destructive to writers and artists came at the end: "subordinated to the prescribed revolutionary task of the Party in any given revolutionary period." It meant that they would have to tailor their work to be politically correct by changing with every shift in the party's policies; it meant that their creativity had to be straitjacketed. They would have to give up their own consciousness and take on the consciousness of the masses. This was worse than the old eight-legged essay prescribed for the traditional civil service examination.

When the author Ding Ling criticized Yan'an culture for its sexism and male dominance, she was sent to the countryside. Many writers who had criticized aspects of Yan'an society recanted their criticisms in the rectification effort. But the writer Wang Shiwei did not. He had written two essays that drew attention to the culture of the "new elites" in Yan'an. One, "Wild Lilies," pointed out the inequalities in lifestyle between the ruling Yan'an elite and non-elites and called for a common lifestyle for both groups. For this the party made him an object lesson, putting him on trial, as it were, in struggle meetings from May 27 to June 11, 1942. The author Ai Qing, who earlier had said that he had to include the negative realities at Yan'an (in his words, he could not depict "ringworms as flowers"), attacked Wang vigorously:

> [Wang] depicts Yan'an as dark and sinister; he pits artists against statesmen, old cadres against the young and stirs them up. His viewpoint is reactionary, and his remedies are poisonous. This "individual" does not deserve to be described as "human" let alone as a "comrade."[29]

Forgetting the adage about cabbage heads, the party executed him in 1947 as they evacuated Yan'an. Historians have noted that Wang was "one of the 'last speakers for the cosmopolitan strain of May Fourth intellectual experimentation'" in the CCP.[30] In addition, they have seen the virulence of the campaign against him as a prototype of the style of denunciation that became the rage during the later Cultural Revolution (1966–1976), when "[i]t was not enough just to attack a person's ideas; it was necessary to show that the person concerned was thoroughly evil and had always been so."[31]

At the end of the war, there were nineteen Communist base areas spread across Northern China in the provinces of Shaanxi, Shanxi, Shandong, Hebei, Rehe, and Liaoning, with Communist units in Anhui and Jiangsu. Communist regimes stretched over a roughly 250,000-square-mile area. Mao claimed that there were 1.2 million CCP members by the close of the war. Communist military forces had increased almost tenfold from the opening of the war, from 92,000 in the 8th Route and New 4th Route armies in 1937 to 910,000 in 1945.

The Communist movement benefited enormously from the war against Japan. One might even suggest that the war saved the Communist movement. We cannot obviously replay history. But if we could, it would be interesting, as in the sciences, to conduct a "CCP viability" experiment. In that historical experiment we would eliminate the variable of Japan—take Japan out of the picture altogether. It seems likely that in that scenario Chiang would have smashed the Communist movement, if not during the Jiangxi Soviet period, then most certainly when the bedraggled and decimated Long Marchers reached Yan'an. The war against Japan gave the Communist movement breathing room and time to expand its support through its nationalistic appeal in fighting the Japanese, its policies of mass mobilization, and the military etiquette ("respect the masses") that it inculcated in and enforced on the 8th Route Army.

WARTIME GUOMINDANG CHINA

Whereas things were looking red and rosy for the CCP, in Guomindang China there were various cancers eating at the innards of the state. From about 1942, much of the Nationalist army seemed to give up. Though it and the Communist troops tied down a million Japanese troops for eight years, its effectiveness in the last three to four years of the war was practically nil. This was an ominous development for a state whose political power was built on the army. What did that portend for the state? One thing that increased the military tragedy of the war was that many of the accomplishments of Chiang Kai-shek's Nanjing decade, specifically building the infrastructure of a modern state, were destroyed in the war—highways, railroads, industry, bridges, and roads.

The tragedy was ironically intensified by the scorched-earth strategies used by Chiang's forces to deny the Japanese use of these facilities. These strategies substantially increased the suffering of the Chinese people and ruined the Chinese countryside. The blowing up of the Yellow River dikes is one example, but others are depressingly numerous. Two will suffice. In 1933 a bilevel bridge across the wide Qiantang River that flows into Hangzhou Bay began to be constructed; it was a great engineering feat and linked, for the first time, the two sides of the river by both rail and car. It was finished with great fanfare in late September 1937, four years after it began. Three months later, in late December, the Chinese blew it up to keep the Japanese from using it.

Later, in the post-Doolittle campaign through Zhejiang and Jiangxi provinces, 62,000 workers were requisitioned to destroy railroad tracks, highways, and even small mountain and village roads in a frantic and futile effort to stop the Japanese.[32] The logic of such scorched-earth efforts seems indeed farfetched. The Japanese had already made the Zhe-Gan railroad inoperable when they blew up its bridges; what was the logic that called for using forced labor to add to the destruction by pulling up the tracks? The governor of the province passed off the highway destruction rather lightly, noting that of the 3,717 kilometers of provincial highways before the war, *only* 759 were destroyed by Chinese government order. That figure represents over 20 percent purposefully destroyed. Such questionable imposed self-destruction seems to suggest not only panic but, more important, a tragic loss of perspective and sense of reality on the part of military and perhaps civil authorities.

The most virulent cancer attacking the body politic was inflation. Whereas prices rose approximately 40 percent during the war's first year, from the time of Pearl Harbor in 1941, they increased more than 100 percent each year. Table 14.1 reveals the gory details. Thus, a trinket that cost 1.04 yuan at the start of the war would have cost 2,647 yuan at war's end. Nothing erodes the political support of a people for its government faster than inflation, even of the slowly rising kind, much less the marauding strain of inflation seen here. It was produced by simply printing more money when there was an insufficient supply. Its results included hoarding of commodities, creating scarcities and even higher prices; corruption that spiraled out of control; and ravaged standards of living among officials, soldiers, intellectuals, people on fixed incomes, and students. Some, if not all of these, were groups that were dangerous to offend. For sowing the wind of inflation by printing money, Chiang would reap the whirlwind.

Perhaps the most critical effect of the eight-year-long war and military ineffectiveness, the destruction caused by the scorched-earth policy, and the inflation was rampant demoralization. Did the government of Chiang Kai-shek really care about the needs of the Chinese people under its control? One answer might be its response to a natural disaster of immense proportions, a famine that ravaged Henan province in 1942 and 1943. Though reports of the serious famine reached Chongqing by October 1942, the government did not send any government representatives there until November. They returned to say that the situation was desperate. The government responded by sending 200 million dollars (paper money, the value of which had been deeply eroded by inflation) for famine relief, instead of relief grain itself. By March 1943, fully half a year after the situation had already become tragic, only 80 million dollars had arrived. But worse:

It was left to lie in provincial bank accounts, drawing interest, while government officials debated and bickered as to how it might best be used. In some places, when money was distributed to starving farmsteads, the amount of current taxes the peasants owed was deducted by local authorities from the sums they received; even the national banks took a cut of the relief funds as profit.

TABLE 14.1   Value of Note Issue in Terms of Prewar Prices, 1937–1945[33]

(amount and value in millions of yuan)			
End of Period	**Amt. of Note Issue of Gov't Banks**	**Average Price Index**	**Value of Issue in Terms of Prewar Notes**
1937 (July)	1,455	1.04	1,390
1938	2,305	1.76	1,310
1939	4,287	3.23	1,325
1940	7,867	7.24	1,085
1941	15,133	19.77	765
1942	34,360	66.2	520
1943	75,379	228.0	330
1944	189,461	755.0	250
1945 (August)	556,907	2,647.0	210

Up to the beginning of March 1943, the government had provided money for the equivalent of a pound of rice per person for the "10,000,000 people who had been starving since autumn."[34] Eyewitness accounts by Theodore White told the horrific story:

> There were corpses on the road. A girl no more than seventeen, slim and pretty, lay on the damp earth, her lips blue with death; her eyes were open and the rain fell on them. People chipped at bark, pounded it by the roadside for food; vendors sold leaves for a dollar a bundle. A dog digging at a mound was exposing a human body. Ghostlike men were skimming the stagnant pools to eat the green slime of the waters. … The people … were tearing up the roots of the new wheat; in other villages people were living on pounded peanut husks or refuse. Refugees on the road had been seen madly cramming soil into their mouths to fill their bellies, and the missionary hospitals were stuffed with people suffering from terrible intestinal obstructions due to the filth they were eating. … In a fit of frenzy the parents of two little children had murdered them rather than hear them beg for something to eat. Some families sold all they had for one last big meal, then committed suicide.
>
> By spring … the missionaries now reported something worse—cannibalism. A doctor told us of a woman caught boiling her baby: she was not molested, because she insisted that the child had died before she started to cook it. Another woman had been caught cutting off the legs of her dead husband for meat; this, too, was justified on the ground that he was already dead. In the mountain districts there were uglier tales of refugees caught on lonely roads and killed for their flesh … we heard the same tales too frequently, in too widely scattered places, to ignore the fact that in Henan human beings were eating their own kind.[35]

An estimated 2 to 3 million died of starvation. White perceived "a fury, as cold and relentless as death itself, in the bosom of the peasants of Henan [and] that their loyalty had been hollowed out to nothingness by the [inactions] of their government."[36]

Notes

1 Quoted in Pei-kai Cheng and Michael Lestz with Jonathan Spence, eds., *The Search for Modern China: A Documentary Collection* (New York: W.W. Norton, 1999), pp. 329–30. There is some question today about whether this killing contest actually occurred or whether it may have happened but not as described in the newspaper. It arises as an issue because of Japan's continuing inability to confront the actions of its military during the war. See Bob Tadashi Wakabayashi, "The Nanking 100-Man Killing Contest Debate: War Guilt Amid Fabricated Illusions, 1971–1975," *Journal of Japanese Studies* 26, no. 2 (Summer 2002): 307–40.

2 Quoted in Dun J. Li, *The Road to Communism: China since 1912* (New York: Van Nostrand Reinhold, 1969), pp. 208–09.

3 James L. McClain, *Japan, A Modern History* (New York: W.W. Norton, 2002), p. 449.

4 The phrase is Joshua Fogel's in "The Nanking Atrocity and Chinese Historical Memory," in *The Nanking Atrocity, 1937–38: Complicating the Picture*, ed. Bob Tadashi Wakabayashi (New York: Berghahn Books, 2007), p. 278.

5 Mark Eykholt, "Aggression, Victimization, and Chinese Historiography of the Nanjing Massacre," in *The Nanjing Massacre in History and Historiography*, ed. Joshua Fogel (Berkeley, CA: University of California Press, 2000), p. 16.

6 For the activities of Unit 731, see Sheldon H. Harris, *Factories of Death: Japanese Biological Warfare, 1932–1945, and the American Cover-Up* (London: Routledge, 1994).

7 Lyman Van Slyke, "The Chinese Communist Movement during the Sino–Japanese War, 1937–1945," in *Cambridge History of China, Vol. 13, Republican China 1912–1949, Part 2*, ed. John K. Fairbank and Albert Feuerwerker (Cambridge, UK: Cambridge University Press, 1986), p. 627.

8 Ibid., p. 555.
9 Jay Taylor, *The Generalissimo: Chiang Kai-shek and the Struggle for Modern China* (Cambridge, MA: The Belknap Press of Harvard University Press, 2009), p. 155.
10 Odd Arne Westad, *Decisive Encounters: The Chinese Civil War, 1946–1950* (Stanford, CA: Stanford University Press, 2003), p. 29.
11 Theodore H. White and Annalee Jacoby, *Thunder out of China* (New York: William Sloane Associates, 1946), p. 132.
12 Lloyd E. Eastman, "Nationalist China during the Sino–Japanese War, 1937–1945," in Fairbank and Feuerwerker, *Cambridge History of China, Vol. 13, Republican China 1912–1949, Part 2*, p. 572.
13 White and Jacoby, *Thunder out of China*, p. 133.
14 Ibid., p. 138.
15 Werner Rings, *Life with the Enemy: Collaboration and Resistance in Hitler's Europe* (Garden City, NY: Doubleday, 1982), p. 128.
16 It should be noted, of course, that such acts also underscore the shortcomings of the regime in not providing those services.
17 Chang-tai Hung, *War and Popular Culture: Resistance in Modern China, 1937–1945* (Berkeley, CA: University of California Press, 1994), p. 272. © 1994 by the Regents of the University of California. Published by the University of California Press.
18 Ibid., p. 276.
19 Ibid., p. 57.
20 Cited in Eastman, "Nationalist China," p. 580.
21 Based on White and Jacoby, *Thunder out of China*, p. 75.
22 John Wilson Lewis, *Leadership in Communist China* (Ithaca, NY: Cornell University Press, 1963), p. 110, cited in Van Slyke, "Chinese Communist Movement," p. 620.
23 Ch'en Yung-fa, *Making Revolution: The Communist Movement in Eastern and Central China, 1937–1945* (Berkeley, CA: University of California Press, 1986), p. 221.
24 The phrase is Ch'en Yung-fa's, *Making Revolution*, p. 220.
25 The examples from Henan are in Odoric Wou's magisterial study *Mobilizing the Masses* (Stanford, CA: Stanford University Press, 1994).
26 Tony Saich, ed., *The Rise to Power of the Chinese Communist Party* (Armonk, NY: M.E. Sharpe, 1996), pp. 1066–7.
27 Ibid., p. 1123.
28 Quoted in J. Mason Gentzler, *Changing China* (New York: Praeger, 1977), p. 232.
29 Saich, *Rise to Power*, pp. 983, 1120.
30 Timothy C. Cheek, "The Fading of the Wild Lilies: Wang Shiwei and Mao Zedong's Yan'an Talks in the First CPC Rectification Movement," *The Australian Journal of Chinese Affairs*, no. 11 (January 1984): 26, cited in Saich, *Rise to Power*, pp. 983–4.
31 Saich, *Rise to Power*, p. 984.
32 Huang Shaohong, *Huang Shaohong huiyilu [Remembrances of Huang Shaohong]* (Nanning: Guangxi renmin chubanshe, 1991), p. 402, and *Qu xianzhi [A gazetteer of Qu county]* (Hangzhou: Zhejiang renmin chubanshe, 1992), p. 403.
33 Taken from Eastman, "Nationalist China," p. 585.
34 White and Jacoby, *Thunder out of China*, pp. 173–4.
35 Ibid., pp. 169–72.
36 Ibid., p. 177.

Suggestions for Further Reading

Brook, Timothy. *Collaboration: Japanese Agents and Local Elites in Wartime China* (Cambridge, MA: Harvard University Press, 2005). An important study of the controversial phenomenon of collaboration at ground level.
Coble, Parks. *Chinese Capitalists in Japan's New Order: The Occupied Lower Yangzi, 1937–1945* (Berkeley, CA: University of California Press, 2003). This significant study discusses the range of reactions of the Chinese bourgeoisie to Japanese control in the Lower Yangzi region.

Cohen, Paul. *Speaking to History: The Story of King Goujian in Twentieth Century China* (Berkeley, CA: University of California Press, 2008). In a tour-de-force, Cohen shows the uses to which fifth century B.C.E. King Goujian were put as a model in China's Sino-Japanese War.

Fogel, Joshua, ed. *The Nanjing Massacre in History and Historiography* (Berkeley, CA: University of California Press, 2000). Essays in this important book look at what happened in Nanjing in late 1937 and early 1938, how Chinese and Japanese historians see it, and the interpretive challenges posed by the event.

White, Theodore H., and Annalee Jacoby. *Thunder Out of China* (New York: William Sloane, 1946). The authors create a vivid picture of wartime China; it well deserves its reputation as a classic.

15

Toward Daybreak
Struggling for China's Identity, 1945–1949

On July 15, 1946, in Kunming a memorial service was held for Li Gongpu, a leading member of the Democratic League, a liberal group opposing the government of Chiang Kai-shek. Li had been assassinated six days earlier by Chiang's secret police. Speaking at the service was Wen Yiduo, whose poem "Dead Water" had been marked by hope for a new China on Chiang's ascension to power in 1928. After eschewing political involvement during the Nanjing decade, Wen had become involved in reform politics during the Sino–Japanese War. He was outraged by Li's murder, chalking the killing up to the government's great fear of any opposition:

> The reactionaries believe that they can reduce the number of people participating in the democratic movement and destroy its power through the terror of assassination. But let me tell you, our power is great. … The power of the people will win and truth will live forever! Throughout history, all who have opposed the people have been destroyed by the people! Didn't Hitler and Mussolini fall before the people? Chiang Kai-shek, you are so rabid, so reactionary, turn the pages of history, how many days do you think you have left? You're finished! It is over for you! Bright days are coming for us. Look, the light is before us. Just as Mr. Li said as he was dying: "Daybreak is coming!" Now is that darkest moment before dawn. We have the power to break through this darkness and attain the light! To attain democracy and peace, we must pay a price. We are not afraid of making sacrifices. Each of us should be like Mr. Li. When we step through the door, we must be prepared never to return.[1]

That afternoon, as he was walking home, Wen was gunned down on a Kunming street, a victim of the terrorist assassins that he had castigated earlier in the day. His murder became a rallying cry for people across China to stand up against the homicidally repressive regime of Chiang Kai-shek.

A year later, as we have seen, Wang Shiwei was executed by the Communists at Yan'an. It is clear that neither side in the coming civil war would let anybody stand in its way. The nation, not individuals, was what mattered, unless, of course, those individuals were the decision-making elites of each party.

FIGURE 15.1 Poet, devotee of classical studies, and professor at Qinghua University, Wen Yiduo gave up his scholarly career to face the social and political problems he saw in Chiang Kai-shek's China. For that he paid with his life.
Source: ChinaStock/Beijing Office.

THE SITUATION AT WAR'S END

In the last months of the world war, the United States was becoming increasingly concerned about postwar East Asia. A destroyed Japan and a China in civil war seemed open invitations to the Soviet Union to try to take advantage of the situation for its own benefit. Since a united China would be a deterrent, the United States hoped to broker an agreement between the Communists and Nationalists before the end of the war. Franklin Roosevelt appointed the Oklahoma Republican Patrick Hurley, a man with no previous knowledge of or acquaintance with China, first to be his personal representative to Chiang and then the U.S. ambassador to China. Hurley, who stepped off the plane in Chongqing and startled the Chinese with a Choctaw war whoop, was hardly the diplomat to bring the two sides together. He did escort Mao from Yan'an to Chongqing after the war ended. Face-to-face talks between Chiang and Mao lasted until October 10, when an agreement on principles was reached. Photographs captured a smiling Chiang and Mao toasting each other. Mao left for Yan'an the next day, but Zhou Enlai remained in Chongqing to try to work out the details. Major principles established in the agreement included democratization and recognition that all political parties were legally equal; the unification of military forces; and the convocation of a political consultative conference that would plan the reorganization of the government and ratify a new constitution. Ominously, there was no agreement on the legality of the ten remaining Communist base areas and their governments.

While Mao and Chiang were negotiating and agreeing on rather grandiose political principles, a frantic race was on between Communists and Nationalists to reach Japanese-occupied territory as quickly as possible. Whoever could be present to accept the Japanese surrender would have a leg up in controlling that particular territory. The United States, not surprisingly, threw its weight in this race behind wartime ally Chiang Kai-shek. American planes ferried half a million Guomindang soldiers into North China, Taiwan, and Manchuria to try to get them there before the Communist troops

FIGURE 15.2   Despite the smiles and the openly hearty toasts on Double Ten (National Day) in 1945, the six-week meeting of Mao and Chiang ultimately failed in attaining lasting agreement between the Communists and Nationalists.
Source: Jack Wilkes/The LIFE Picture Collection/Getty Images.

arrived. Since the CCP had expanded over North China throughout the war, they had a huge advantage in that region and in reaching Manchuria, where 700,000 Japanese troops waited to surrender.

Complicating the situation in Manchuria was the presence of the army of the Soviet Union. Stalin had promised at the wartime conference at Yalta in February 1945 that the Soviet Union would enter the war against Japan within three months after the war in Europe ended. They did so on August 8, three months to the day after VE Day, promising Chiang's government that they would withdraw three months after Japan's surrender. Though the Soviet Union did not provide direct military aid to the Chinese Communists, the Soviet army did prevent the United States from landing Nationalist troops at some of the northeastern ports. The Eighth Route and New Fourth Route armies did exploit the Soviet hold on Manchuria by moving there quickly by foot and by junk from Shandong and by seizing substantial amounts of arms and equipment from the surrendering Japanese. When Chiang determined that the Soviets' withdrawal by November 15 would in reality leave the Communists holding Manchuria, he persuaded them to delay their pullout. When they left in May 1946, they dismantled many of the former Japanese factories and stole their modern industrial equipment.

In November 1945, Patrick Hurley resigned as U.S. ambassador, attacking the State Department and its Foreign Service officers for undercutting his work and for playing into the hands of the Communists. In December, President Harry Truman appointed the highly respected General George Marshall as his special envoy to China, charged with working out a cease-fire and convening the political consultative conference. In the beginning, it seemed as though he would make things happen. A cease-fire was announced on January 10, with a general truce and a halt to North China troop movements put in place on January 13. The Political Consultative Conference (PCC), composed of thirty-eight delegates (eight from the Guomindang and seven from the CCP), met from January 11 to 31. There were agreements on almost all substantial civilian and military issues. But from that point on, things began to deteriorate. The problem was that there was no one to enforce the agreements.

The rapidity and sweeping nature of the agreements and then the immediate difficulty in getting them enforced raised questions about the motives of both the Guomindang and the CCP. One possibility was that neither party was of one mind on the issues, that some in each party may have wanted the accords and others did not, and that the latter sabotaged the effort. Another possibility was that the accords were simply window dressing for the benefit of the United States, which, from the Guomindang perspective, would continue its aid program. Another possibility, given the rapid turn to military action, was that the accords were simply a way to buy time for working up to military readiness.

The parties shared the blame for the failure of the Marshall mission. The Guomindang reneged on some of its PCC political pledges, and the Communists refused to carry out some military pledges. In Manchuria, where things got militarily hot very quickly, both sides were guilty of breaking the cease-fire. Fighting there spread slowly, beginning in late January; truce teams sent by Marshall did not get permission to land until April. Marshall was able to engineer a truce in June, but that also fell apart.

But ultimately, the Marshall mission failed because its goal was an impossibility. That the United States could step into a rivalry to the death that had been festering for twenty years and settle it with a few agreements that depended on the good faith of the rivals was idealism with hardly a trace of reality. Further, Marshall was supposed to be an even-handed mediator. Yet the United States continued to funnel huge amounts of aid to the Nationalists while Marshall was trying to get the Communists to agree to a settlement. A huge supply program of arms and equipment was in the works for the Nationalists. In February 1946 the United States established a military advisory group to help Chiang further develop his military; it gave 500 million dollars to the China aid program of the United Nations Relief and Recovery Administration, most of it to go to Chiang; and in June and August 1946, it gave the Nationalists credits to purchase additional equipment that would be useful in combat. Not surprisingly, the Communists began to attack this relationship in summer 1946. When Marshall tried some even-handedness by pressuring Chiang to undertake major economic and political reforms to strengthen his regime, his government reacted with bitterness, Prime Minister T.V. Soong saying that "in the old days 'for one government to tell another it should do these things would mean war.'"[2] When Marshall left China in January 1947, he offered his evaluation of the problem:

> Sincere efforts to achieve settlement have been frustrated time and again by extremist elements of both sides. The agreements reached by the Political Consultative Conference a year ago were a liberal and forward-looking charter which then offered China a basis for peace and reconstruction. However, irreconcilable groups within the Guomindang, interested in the preservation of their own feudal control of China, evidently had no real intention of implementing them. ... The reactionaries in the Government have evidently counted on substantial American support regardless of their actions. The Communists by their unwillingness to compromise in the national interest are evidently counting on an economic collapse to bring about the fall of the Government, accelerated by extensive guerrilla action against the long lines of communication—regardless of the cost of suffering to the Chinese people.[3]

ECONOMIC SUICIDE

China turned quickly to large-scale civil war, one of the largest wars of modern times. The actual struggle between the Guomindang and CCP was ultimately decided on the battlefield, but there were underlying problems with Chiang's rule that were probably more significant in understanding the cause of his defeat. Marshall in the statement above pointed to a crucial reality when he noted that the Communists "are evidently counting on an economic collapse" to bring down the Guomindang.

FIGURE 15.3   As inflation became ever more virulent during the civil war, people were overcome with fear. Here, in December 1948, panic-stricken Chinese make a run on a Shanghai bank.
Source: Henry Cartier-Bresson/Magnum Photos.

It was, in the end, Chiang's inability to deal with wrenching economic problems that likely defeated him. We saw in the previous chapter how rampant inflation during the Sino–Japanese War eroded people's buying power. By 1945 the government's revenue was covering only one-third of its expenditures; to make up what was needed, it simply printed more money, apparently an easy solution. But the demoralizing outcome was "a government with neither the will nor the ability to do anything but watch over the deterioration of the nation's urban economy."[4] Growing inflation was fueled by shortages of consumer goods, business restrictions, corruption, speculation, and hoarding. The exchange rate for Chinese dollars to U.S. dollars stood at 7,000 to 1 in January 1947 and 45,000 to 1 in August 1947. Prices in July 1948 were *three million* times higher than in July 1937. And into 1949 the situation deteriorated even further. Chiang's government made two major fiscal efforts to stem the disastrous tide. Wage and price controls, introduced in 1947, were not enforced across China in uniform fashion, but mostly in the Lower Yangzi region. Then in 1948 the government introduced a new currency. Neither policy worked.

What did this mean to the consumer? In the county of Xiaoshan in Zhejiang province, on the eve of the Communist takeover in April 1949, a picul of rice (about 133 pounds) cost more than 8 billion Chinese dollars, 785,400,000 times more than in 1937. At this rate, each *grain* of rice cost about 2,500 Chinese dollars.[5] At such a rate of inflation, Chiang had lost the city dwellers—businessmen, salaried classes, intellectuals, workers—and those in the countryside as well. The economic collapse was total.

By late 1947 and 1948, the very fabric of rural society seemed to be unraveling. Banditry, the traditional sign of feeble political control and deteriorating economic conditions, was pervasive. The inflated currency inspired so little confidence that exchange payments—such as land sales, bride prices, purchases of oxen or furniture, workers' wages, and loans—were being conducted by barter … landlords fled the countryside for the relative security of walled towns. … Ordinary peasants, too, abandoned the farms, becoming recruits to the growing ranks of the hungry and destitute, many of whom died in the streets and alleyways of cities. … 10 million people were threatened with starvation in 1948; 48 million—about one of every ten Chinese—were refugees. … The most desperate reportedly sold their wives and daughters—in 1946, the price of fifteen- and sixteen-year-old girls in [Zhejiang] was said to be 4,000 yuan.[6]

POLITICAL DISASTER

If two words were worn out by their continual use to describe Chiang Kai-shek's government, they were "corrupt" and "incompetent." Corruption had been the watchword during the war against Japan, when Chongqing government officials, especially family members and hangers-on in Chiang's circle, lived high on the hog. Rumors spread about the extravagant banquets frequented by officials and their women, dressed to the nines, about the luxury items (oranges, butter, perfumes) smuggled in from abroad, and about items carried over the Hump on the airlift for Chiang's favorites. Bitterness among the nonelites, who had to put up with shortages and austerity during the war, only increased as the end of the war turned into another war. An article in a popular political journal in the spring of 1947 evaluated the political situation in Chiang's China:

> The basis of the present regime's support has been the urban population: government employees and teachers, intellectuals, and business and industrial circles. At present, no one among these people has any positive feelings toward the Nanjing regime. The [Guomindang's] tyrannical style is causing deep hatred among liberal elements …; the government officials by indulging in corrupt practices and creating every kind of obstruction have caused extreme dissatisfaction in business and industrial circles; and the violent rise in prices … and the continuation of civil war is causing sounds of resentment to be heard everywhere.[7]

Repeatedly there had been calls for political liberalization, specifically reforms that might open up the political arena to non-Communist groups to share power to some degree with the Guomindang. In 1941 a number of minor political parties joined in a Federation of Democratic Parties, all opposed to the Guomindang monopoly of government power. A suspicious development in Chiang's eyes, this federation became involved in 1944 with a group of militarists considering a coup against Chiang. This mix of Western-style political liberals and old-line militarists was a coming together of strange bedfellows, but nothing came of the affair except to heighten Chiang's suspicion and distrust of the federation. In October 1944 the federation became the Democratic League, sometimes referred to as the Third Force, that is, neither Guomindang nor CCP. Chiang might have tried to join with the Democratic League to build a stronger political base, but he never did. The League itself was divided over which main party to support. In the end Chiang turned to his Guomindang secret police, who arrested many and assassinated key League figures such as Li Gongpu and Wen Yiduo. Finally, in October 1947, the Nanjing government outlawed the League, with most of its members fleeing to Hong Kong.

As a prime example of its ineffectiveness, Chiang's government was never able to win public support for its war against the CCP. Chiang further antagonized political dissenters by branding them as Communist tools or dupes. CCP cadres did work undercover to influence the student movement and to recruit students for propaganda and education networks, as well as intelligence sources. But protests went beyond Communist manipulation. From the end of World War II into 1948, the political landscape was marked by almost constant protest even as Chiang's secret police continued to use terror against protesters. Four students were killed in protests in Kunming in December 1945. In December 1946 and January 1947, Beijing exploded in anti-American demonstrations when news spread of an alleged rape of a Beijing University coed by a U.S. marine. In May and June 1947, by the time the civil war was openly raging, high schools and universities in major cities were swept up in an Anti-Hunger, Anti-Civil War movement. From April to June 1948, a Movement to Protest American Support of Japan sprang up at a time when the United States was moving toward a more conciliatory phase of the occupation of Japan. Then in July 1948, students who had been flown out of Manchuria as a publicity ploy and then not given enough assistance to survive demonstrated against the government. Authorities machine-gunned the marchers, killing fourteen and wounding over 100. Basically all these protests were aimed at ending the civil war, ending the close involvement of the United States with the Guomindang, and changing government priorities from military to civilian. Protestors were consistently met by government reactions ranging from disregard to disdain to violent attack.

MILITARY STRUGGLE

In the beginning, the Guomindang had a huge advantage in numbers of men and amount of war materiel. Its forces numbered roughly 3 million men, with an estimated 6,000 artillery pieces, compared to about 1 million Communist troops having about 600 artillery pieces. Guomindang forces won the initial battles in 1946; they won all the major cities in Manchuria except Harbin and regained control of much of Rehe and Hebei provinces, key northern railroads, and many towns in northern Jiangsu, and even—to the humiliation of the Communists—took Yan'an. In the midst of these losses, a number of Communist military units defected to the Guomindang.

Initially pushed north of the Sungari River in Manchuria, Communist forces, now called the People's Liberation Army (PLA), under the leadership of Lin Biao in late 1946, began hit-and-run raids into southern Manchuria that were the beginning of the turning of the tide. It was not all smooth sailing for the PLA; in early 1947, Lin lost a major battle for a railway junction against Chiang's forces supported by air power. But Lin quickly regrouped and launched a campaign that began to isolate cities held by Nationalist forces. Neither Chiang nor his American advisers foresaw how fast the Communists were able to transform their anti-Japanese guerrilla units into large regular armies. In the areas they controlled, they recruited soldiers and mobilized support among the local population.

It is likely that only a small percentage of the peasantry actually participated as soldiers in the fighting. But the key was their mobilization to play important support roles in the transport and organization of supplies. Peasant support for the Communists rose dramatically with the mobilization fostered by land reform and local political change. Once the military tide shifted to the Communists in 1948, military victories also attracted more peasant support and participation.

Chiang had made a major strategic blunder when he committed half a million of his best men to Manchuria before he had solidified his control south of the Great Wall. With the Communists in control of the countryside, Lin Biao's campaign quickly turned Nationalist-controlled cities into islands in a Communist sea. To prevent them from being completely cut off and forced to surrender, Chiang began costly airlifts to these cities. It was a self-destructive economic blunder: for example, Chiang used his whole military budget for the second half of 1948 to supply only one city for two months and four days. That necessitated printing more money, causing another surge in inflation. When his American advisers suggested that he move his troops in Manchuria south of the Wall to try to better his position in North China, he refused.

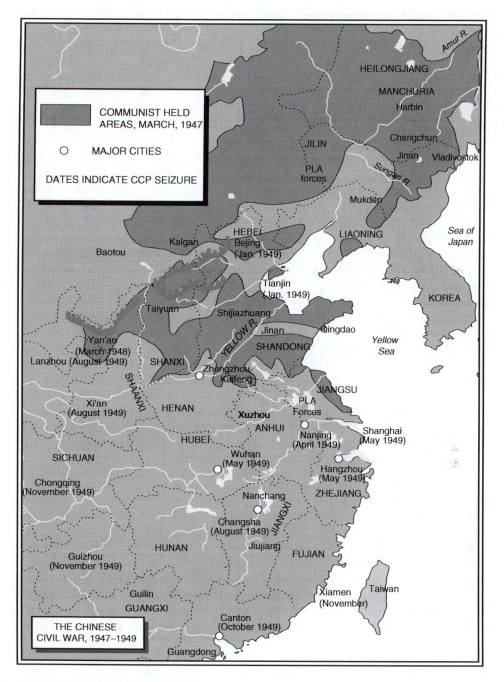

MAP 15.1 The Chinese Civil War, 1947–1949.

By mid-1948, the Communists were about equal to the Guomindang in numbers of well-armed troops and ahead in numbers of artillery pieces. In the end, the Manchurian campaign ended in a smashing Communist victory in November 1948; it cost Chiang 470,000 of his best troops and countless weapons and pieces of equipment. An American adviser noted that it "spelled the beginning of the end" for the Guomindang war effort.[8] In essence, Chiang lost the civil war even before the battlefields shifted into China proper.

The battle for Central China broke out almost at the same time that the Manchurian campaign was ending. Each battle now saw huge numbers of Guomindang soldiers defecting, taking with them more and more materiel. Forsaking their longtime guerrilla action in North China, the Communists now used their Manchurian strategy of deploying large armies against Chiang's troops. Committing 600,000 troops to the battle of Huai-Hai, which focused on the railway center of Xuzhou, the Communists faced the same number of Nationalist troops. The over-two-month-long battle began in October 1948 with the prompt defection of two Guomindang divisions. Chiang's army still had superiority in equipment and was supported by an air force. But the Communist military leaders were clearly better strategists than the former Whampoa commandant. Chiang, biased in favor of the officers who had graduated from his academy, refused to listen to superior strategists (former warlords) who wanted to make a stand at a more favorable position along the Huai River. He chose instead to stand at Xuzhou, where his forces were exposed on three sides. Communist forces simply smashed the Guomindang troops. Chiang lost almost half a million men and almost all of his mechanized troops.

Beiping fell on January 31, 1949. By early 1949, Chiang had lost most of China north of the Yangzi; although fighting continued throughout the year, Chiang and his Guomindang national army had been defeated. The capital, Nanjing, fell in April; Shanghai and Wuhan in May; Xi'an in August; Canton in October; and Chongqing in November. Seeking a site to which to retreat and perhaps regroup, Chiang looked toward his wartime base of Sichuan, but the military commander there refused. Thus, in December the Guomindang government fled to Taiwan.

DID CHIANG LOSE THE WAR OR DID MAO WIN THE WAR?

The question of whether the Communists won the civil war or whether the Guomindang lost it has frequently been raised. Obviously, both conclusions are correct. But on balance, which one carried more historical weight? On the winning Communists: in the civil war, as in the Sino–Japanese War, the secret of Communist success was understanding the particular local situation and acting pragmatically and flexibly. They made mistakes in various localities and, as a result, lost support, but "[i]t was the Communists' increasing skills in fitting in locally that gave them the edge in the competition with their enemies, and that saved them when they were squeezed between superior military forces."[9] In the military struggle, commanders of the PLA "appl[ied] a strategy that elevated flexibility in the field to the highest art of defensive warfare."[10] The Communists emerged as the superior military strategists in both offensive and defensive warfare; Lin Biao's record of success is noteworthy.

Chiang must be found wanting in the arena of military strategy and execution. Military decision making was supposedly Chiang's strong suit, but his record is filled with copious blunders: his unwise troop commitment to the Manchurian campaign; his disastrous decision to airlift supplies to maintain control of the cities; his blind and narrow primary trust in officers who were personally connected to him in the Whampoa clique; and his ridiculously weak strategy at Xuzhou, a battle that he personally insisted on directing even though he was 200 miles from the fighting.

But only part of the struggle was military. And when one looks at other crucial arenas, it seems clear that Chiang blew it. His political approaches and reactions were counterproductive to his goal of winning the support of the Chinese elites and masses. The Communist Eighth Route Army went out to win the hearts and minds of the Chinese peasants and, in many cases, they did; in contrast, the Guomindang secret police goons who assassinated and terrorized those who dissented from the Guomindang line alienated tens of thousands for every victim they shot. A corrupt Guomindang elite, living the good life while those around them were suffering from the depredations of war, seemed as incongruous and scandalous as a banquet given during the Henan famine.

Finally, it was the economy that gutted support for Chiang's government. People watched, incredulous that the government could do nothing but worsen the inflation scenario—a scenario that made the government seem not only inept but, worse, uncaring. Since people went to the market daily, they constantly confronted the demoralizing reality of inflation: from morning to night, prices might rise two or three or more times. When four grains of rice cost 10,000 cash, the Chinese were, indeed, as the Chinese idiom put it, "eating bitterness," that is, suffering. It had been little more than three decades since Chinese political culture had had an active sense of the Mandate of Heaven. Though no one perhaps spoke of it, the collective conclusion must surely have been, if only in passing, that for Chiang Kai-shek and his government the mandate was at an end.

JAPAN'S COLONY, TAIWAN

The victory over Japan had returned Taiwan and the Penghu Islands (Pescadores) to Chinese control. The island had become part of the Japanese empire through the Treaty of Shimonoseki that ended the first Sino–Japanese War in 1895. Because the Chinese now had to deal with an island whose twentieth-century life had been shaped and led by Japanese, a brief historical overview provides essential information. Originally inhabited by Malayo-Polynesian aborigines, Taiwan saw Han Chinese settlement begin in the late Ming dynasty. It was brought under Chinese control in 1683, when the Manchus finally ended the last Ming resistance. It was ruled as a prefecture of Fujian province from that time until 1887, when it became a separate Chinese province.

Resistance and Suppression

Eight years later, Taiwanese found themselves Japanese subjects. For many Taiwanese it was an unhappy reality. Initial panic at the exodus of Qing officials was followed by armed resistance across the island, five months of sustained fighting, and seven more years of sporadic attacks. Resisters raided Japanese military installations, police stations, and other public sites. The Japanese reacted brutally, killing 6,000 Taiwanese in the June 1896 Yunlin massacre and slaying 12,000 more between 1898 and 1902. In the fear and panic of the time, many fled to the central mountainous area, inhabited mostly by the aboriginal peoples, or across the Taiwan Strait to the Chinese mainland; it is said that most of the upper-degreed gentry sailed the 90 miles to China.

From the beginning, there was much Japanese discussion and disagreement about the status of Taiwan. Assimilation became a key issue: should the people of Taiwan be integrated into the Japanese empire, equal to the residents of the Japanese islands themselves; should they remain subordinate islander inhabitants; or should there be some relationship in between these poles? The answer to the assimilation question varied according to the time period and the nature of the rule from Tokyo and of the particular governor-general, the supreme power in the colony. Whatever the stance on assimilation, there was always a strong overlay of the idea that the Japanese were "bearers of a superior culture to be imparted" to the Taiwanese.[11]

The Beginnings of Modernization

From 1898 to 1915 the Japanese moderated their rule: the power of the military was lessened, and the governor-general allowed domestic affairs to be carried out by his chief of civil administration, from 1898 to 1906 the rather enlightened Goto Shimpei. During this time, he established the base for substantial economic development. A railroad was built connecting Taipei in the north to the seaport of Kaohsiung in the south. An important harbor was dredged and opened at the northern port of Keelung. The number of miles of primary and secondary roads was tripled; postal and tele-graph facilities were expanded; telephone service, began; a hydroelectric-generating plant, a public hospital, and a medical college, constructed; the first modern newspaper, published; a banking sys-tem, established; and attention paid to public health and sanitation. During this modernizing pro-cess, Taiwan became economically tightly connected to Japan, sending exports of rice, sugar, and camphor to the "mother country" and, after 1902, importing the majority of its goods from Japan.

There were six more armed insurrections from 1907 to 1915. Further, a particularly nasty ep-isode occurred when the Japanese decided to open the mountains, home of the aborigines, to log-ging. This effort necessitated a subjugation campaign against the aborigines that included attacks from the air and naval bombardment from off the island's east coast. After this spate of revolts and violence abated, the domestic situation calmed down.

A More Liberal Colonialism

From 1915 through the 1920s, the Japanese seemed to tone down their colonial harshness. In part this reflected changes in Japan. The idealism of President Wilson, which resonated in many countries around the world, did so in Japan as well. The success of democracy, or at least party government in Japan from 1918 to the late 1920s, suggested a more tolerant attitude from Tokyo. In 1918 and 1919, the Japanese government adopted an assimilation policy that treated Taiwan "as an extension of Japan proper," a change that "moved from high-handed police control and differential treatment of the Taiwanese to a more enlightened self-governance, emphasis on education, and cultivation of a more congenial relationship between Japanese and Taiwanese."[12] Thus, the direct involvement of police in local administrations was decreased; law codes were rewritten to make them less draconian; governmental reorganization produced considerable decentralization so that local communities had more control; and elements of self-government were introduced.

Perhaps most important, there was a more liberal public climate, a tolerance of ideas that might earlier have been considered subversive. A Taiwanese New Culture movement that paralleled the May Fourth Movement in China began in 1920, when Taiwanese students in Tokyo organized the New People Association and the Taiwanese Youth Association. That same year they began to publish *Taiwan Youth*, like *New Youth* an effort to stir progressive thinking and to discuss the state of affairs on the island; by 1927, its publication site had been relocated to Taiwan. In 1921, a Taipei doctor organized the Taiwan Cultural Association "to advance Taiwanese culture"; though he claimed it had no political goals, it eventually supported such political movements as the establishment of a Taiwan parliament and home rule. The 1920s saw the development of a feminist movement, the organiza-tion of the Taiwan Communist Party, and the establishment of a Taiwan Farmers' Union.

Probably most interesting in light of early-twenty-first-century talk of "Taiwan's indepen-dence" were efforts in the 1920s and 1930s to assert Taiwan's separateness. The New People Asso-ciation rejected both integration with Japan and restoration to China, calling for home rule and a Taiwan parliament. A new organization, the League for the Establishment of a Taiwan Parliament, carried the ball on the latter from its founding in 1923 until its demise in 1934. Throughout those years, it sent a number of petitions to the Japanese Diet asking for a parliament. The 1926 petition had 2,000 signatures, indicating no small support, but the Diet heard none of the petitions. In 1931 and 1932 Taiwan consciousness appeared in debates to create a more Taiwan-centered literature written in Taiwanese. In the words of one scholar, this debate "revealed the anxieties and ambivalent feelings of a colonized people in their attempts to develop a national language. [It also] functioned to sever the Taiwanese intellectuals' emotional ties to China."[13]

Finally, in the first half of the 1930s, some island Taiwanese leaders established the Taiwan League for Local Self-Government to work for greater power and influence on the island. These men argued that Taiwanese leaders were best prepared to deal with internal developments and problems, that they had the education and experience to do so, and that it was proper that they lead. This effort at home rule was suppressed during the war, but it reemerged after 1945.

Colonial Policies during the War (1937–1945)

As war with China neared, Japan's governor-general instituted policies of industrialization and "imperialization" to place Taiwan on a war footing—militarily able and with an industrial base that would help Japan's cause. Japan indeed helped lay modern Taiwan's industrial base. By the late 1930s, in addition to agriculture-related industries such as chemical fertilizers, food processing, and canning, Taiwan was producing steel, aluminum, cement, chemicals, and petroleum. The number of factory workers rose almost 600 percent from 1914 to 1941—from 21,800 to 127,700; the number of miners soared over 800 percent—from 6,500 to 53,700. A hydroelectric power plant on the west coast supplied 100,000 megawatts. Several industrial complexes were built, such as the Japan Aluminum Company plants in Hualien on the east coast and Kaohsiung on the southwest, which by 1940 were supplying Japan with a sixth of the aluminum it imported.

Imperialization was an ominous development, however, when viewed in the context of the more liberal period of the 1920s and early 1930s. It was an effort to mold Taiwan into the model of Japan as the empire moved to war. In April 1937, for example, newspapers were ordered to stop publishing Chinese-language sections, and elementary schools were ordered to stop teaching classical Chinese. Later that year, colonial authorities began to discourage the use of Chinese at all. In the early 1940s, the Japanese overlords ordered all Chinese, including those of aboriginal stock, to change their family and personal names to Japanese names. Given the importance of surnames for cultural identity, this effort was nothing less than an attempt to destroy traditional identity and replace it with a new subordinate colonial identity. Records indicate that only about 7 percent of the Han Chinese had complied with this order by the end of the war. Other attempts were also made to destroy elements of Chinese culture and replace them with Japanese culture. The Japanese banned traditional Chinese operas and puppet plays, likely because they could become subversive. Chinese marriage and funeral ceremonies were forbidden, to be replaced by the respective Japanese ceremonies. The Japanese attempted to force Shintoism on the Taiwanese, building public shrines and decreeing that each home should have its own Shinto shrine for household worship. Scholars have judged that on the whole the policy of imperialization was not very effective, but the effort itself was something akin to cultural terrorism.

During the war itself, Taiwanese were recruited for military service, a change in Japanese policy, which before 1937 did not allow colonial subjects to serve. Over 200,000 Taiwanese served in the Japanese army or navy during the war, and over 30,000 died. Many more were drafted to labor in military-related industries. Significantly, there were no major Taiwanese resistance or sabotage efforts during the war.

Taiwan itself became an important staging and supply area for the attack on Canton in the fall of 1938 and for the naval seizure of the island of Hainan in late winter 1939. By 1940 the Japanese navy controlled the Taiwan Strait and the coastline of Fujian province. The sudden end of the war surprised all on the island. Controlled a half century by a now totally defeated Japan, Taiwan had to face a new world. Reportedly enthusiastic crowds welcomed Nationalist troops coming over in the aftermath of the surrender. Taiwan and the Penghu Islands reverted to Chinese control on October 25, celebrated from that time on as Restoration Day.

GUOMINDANG RELATIONS WITH THE TAIWANESE: FEBRUARY 1947 AND ITS IMPACT

The crowds did not remain enthusiastic for long. Over the next year and a half, many Taiwanese came to believe that Japanese rule, police state though it was, was preferable to control by Chiang Kai-shek's Guomindang. The problems were deep; certainly it was the case, as one scholar explained, that both Taiwan and China had changed so much since 1895 "that the retrocession was less the restoration of historical ties than the attempt to forge an entirely new relationship."[14] In large part, the root of the problems lay in the legacy of the colonial era.

Despite the colonial political controls, Japanese economic and educational policies had helped create a Taiwanese elite who had worked with the Japanese in carrying out day-to-day administration. The level of education had become quite high. In 1917, 21 percent of Taiwanese boys had attended primary school, but by 1943, 81 percent did; for girls in the same period, the percentage had increased from 4 to 61. There were few in Taiwan who could not read Japanese. For education beyond high school, young Taiwanese went to Japan. In 1922, 2,400 Taiwanese were studying in Japan; in 1942 that number had risen to 7,000. As part of their educational agenda, the Japanese had set up Taiwan Normal School, which trained most of the island's teachers, and Taipei Imperial University. Many Taiwanese also profited from Japanese industrialization policies, emerging as economic elites in industry and business.

On the whole, after years under Japanese control, Taiwan enjoyed a higher standard of living and a higher level of education, better public health and sanitation, and more economic advancement than the mainland. The downside was that the Taiwanese were no better than second-class citizens under the Japanese—discriminated against systematically, working always for the benefit of Japan, and frustrated in their political aspirations. Part of the problem that developed under the Nationalists stemmed from the hope of many among the Taiwanese elite that they could transform their educational and economic credentials into greater political participation and control.

From the perspective of the Nationalists, the crucial goal in governing Taiwan was establishing tight central control that would facilitate the reintegration of the island with the mainland as quickly as possible and expunge Japan's influence. Chiang appointed Chen Yi, a former governor of Fujian province, as commander of the Taiwan Garrison as well as the main administrator of the Taiwan Provincial Administrative Executive Office. In that capacity, he was in charge of all the governmental organs. In many ways the governmental situation was, then, quite similar to the system of the Japanese governor-general.

In almost all major policy areas, Chen's administration clashed with the Taiwanese elites. His effort to control every aspect of the economy ran head-on into the attempts by wealthy Taiwanese to open or expand businesses in areas that had been dominated by Japanese companies or the colonial regime. What the Taiwanese saw instead was that mainlanders moved into these areas with the connivance of the government. The disposition of Japanese property was also controversial. The Taiwanese, arguing that Japanese property had originally been taken from them, claimed that they should rightfully receive it; the Chen administration's position was that all Japanese property must revert to the government. More and more, it seemed to many Taiwanese that the Nationalist government was just like the Japanese colonial regime in its exploitation of the Taiwanese—except that the Nationalists, they noted, added a few negative qualities: dishonesty, incompetence, inefficiency, and unpredictability. For most Taiwanese, inflation, unemployment, and a decline in public sanitation meant a decline in living conditions. In central Taiwan, it is said that the masses talked of three "hopes"—the hope after Japan's surrender and before the coming of Nationalist troops that things would improve; the "lost hope" on seeing what the government of Chen Yi was doing; and the hopelessness that things would never improve.

Part of that despair stemmed from the mainlanders' receiving the lion's share of government posts and positions in the state enterprises and monopoly bureaus; the situation in fact was almost a monopoly. Only three of the first twenty-three county magistrate positions went to Taiwanese. Only one of the twenty-one highest provincial government positions went to a Taiwanese. As many as 36,000 Taiwanese lost the posts that they had held in the bureaucracy. Far from having a greater say and role in politics, the Taiwanese were doing far worse than they had done under the Japanese.

Could they protest? No. Chen, like Chiang in the past, interpreted any dissent from his policies as unpatriotic and as tinged with treason. The Nationalists tended to see and treat Taiwan as a conquered territory rather than as a part of the motherland being returned after many years. Many Nationalists treated the Taiwanese as disloyal to start with because of their having worked with the Japanese. In response, the Taiwanese were quick to point out that they were also involved in many years of resistance and that if they did work with the Japanese, it was because they had no choice since the Qing government had signed them over to the Japanese. Because most Taiwanese spoke Japanese, language became an issue of loyalty to the Nationalist regime: use of Japanese created political problems. Conversely, the speed with which the populace learned the Mandarin dialect, the "national tongue" (which the government promoted beginning in 1946) was a mark of their commitment to Chineseness. The colonial period had indeed created huge identity problems for both the Taiwanese and mainland Chinese alike: in the context of the colonial era, how did each side identify itself in relation to the other?

Each side viewed the other with disdain. The Nationalist mainlanders talked endlessly about the "Japanization" or, even worse, the "slavization" of the Taiwanese, a condition that left the Taiwanese ignorant of the mainland and its culture. Their lack of fluent Chinese, the Nationalists claimed, made them unready to participate in political decision making as a part of China. Nationalist hostility and scorn of the Taiwanese would not die quickly; when asked in 1967 how she could tell the difference between mainlanders and Taiwanese, one mainland woman declared that she could smell the difference. The Taiwanese, on the other hand, joked of the five things that all Nationalist officials wanted from their leadership in Taiwan: gold, rank, cars, homes, and women. Rampant corruption, Taiwanese contended, was "part of the mainland's defective political culture." Some Taiwanese said that "the dogs (Japanese) had left, but the [greedy and uncultured] pigs (mainland Chinese) had come."[15]

In this context, the Taiwanese began to press for a greater political role, pleading for self-government that would make Taiwan into a model province for the mainland. Representative assemblies were established in 1946, but they had very little power and only proved frustrating to the aspirations of the Taiwanese elites. Men such as Wang Tiandeng, a newspaper publisher, spoke out about political issues; Wang served on the Provincial Consultative Assembly that was set up in 1946. That same year, he was jailed for "undermining public confidence in authority," but the case was dismissed for insufficient evidence.

FIGURE 15.4   Squid porridge. The depth of negative feelings about the Guomindang massacres of native Taiwanese in the February 28, 1947 (the 228) "incident" are shown in one family by a 70-year-old ritual. Since the arrest and disappearance of Mr. Lee Eng-chong's father and uncle on March 10, 1947, when they had sat down to eat their dinner of squid porridge, the Lee family continues to "eat bitterness" in remembrance of the tragic time by eating squid porridge annually on March 10.

Source: Aflo Co. Ltd./Alamy Stock Photo.

On February 27, 1947, in the context of rising inflation, open civil war on the mainland, and deteriorating relationships between mainlanders and Taiwanese, an incident occurred that would freeze relationships between the two sides for forty years. A policeman from the Monopoly Bureau struck a woman who was being arrested for selling cigarettes illegally; a crowd gathered and another officer fired into the crowd, killing one person.

This incident brought to a head all the bad feelings that had festered. All over the island, Taiwanese began fighting Nationalist forces for control of railroad and police stations and government buildings. In the turmoil there were cases of outright murder of mainlanders by Taiwanese. A February 28 Settlement Committee was hurriedly formed by the Taipei City Council to end the escalating crisis.

At this point, the deteriorating situation merged with the desire of Taiwanese elites for greater self-government, already apparent in the Japanese colonial era. Although these elites had played little or no role in the initial uprising, the Settlement Committee was composed of many prominent Taiwanese leaders. The committee met with Chen Yi a number of times during the first days of March, moving closer and closer to urging Chen to enact political reforms in some form of self-government. For whatever reason, the committee was emboldened. On March 6, it drew up the Thirty-Two Demands, a list of political reforms and requests. The next day, three leaders including Wang Tiandeng presented Chen with the list, which included

> the election of mayors and [county] magistrates, greater Taiwanese representation in the provincial administration (including government bureaus, courts, and police), abolition of the trade and monopoly bureaus, and that Taiwanese not be drafted to fight in the mainland's civil war. … [And finally] the abolition of the Administrator's Office and Garrison Command and greater Taiwanese control over the military forces on the island.[16]

Chen was furious. The committee, realizing that it had overreacted, retracted the next day most of the demands that it had made, especially the last two.

But it was too late. Chiang and Chen would not let such a challenge go unanswered. Martial law was declared as more Nationalist troops from the mainland poured ashore in ports north and south. There was little resistance; this had not been planned by the Taiwanese as a military action, but rather as an attempt at reform. The Settlement Committee was declared illegal since it was "part of a revolt." When quiet was restored by March 13, the government announced a campaign to "exterminate traitors"—that is, prominent Taiwanese elites who, in the words of one scholar, "may have offended anyone in the government."[17] Part of the campaign was to sweep through villages to find those leaders who might have fled the cities. Japanese-language materials and other items—flags, uniforms, phonograph records—were confiscated. Terror spread over the island. An estimated 10,000 Taiwanese were killed. Among them was Wang Tiandeng, who was burned alive after being doused with gasoline by the policemen who captured him. Another 30,000 were wounded. In essence, the aftermath of the February 28 incident was the wiping out of a whole generation of potential Taiwanese leaders.

There were a few carrots to go along with the bludgeoning stick. A regular government was established in April 1947, with Chen Yi called back to the mainland. A Provincial Committee was set up to offer the new governor advice on ruling the island; seven of its fifteen members were Taiwanese. But the committee had no power. The government announced its plans to put its own self-government program into practice, but when it was finally announced in 1950 and 1951, it was restricted to city, town, and county—not extended to the provincial level—and the bodies had no say or control over local governments or budgets.

In the meantime, things only got worse for Taiwan and the Taiwanese. Chiang's impending loss on the mainland stimulated the flow of huge numbers of refugees to Taiwan. In November 1948, for example, 31,000 came each week. This influx made unemployment, housing and food shortages, and crime worse. Then, as Chiang made his decision to retreat to Taiwan, authoritarian control grew ever more severe. Reprising his tragic act of twenty-two years earlier, Chiang in 1949 launched another White Terror. Tens of thousands of people, Taiwanese and mainlander alike, were killed or arrested because they had some sort of alleged link to the Communists. Internecine struggle, like a bacterial contagion, had at last spread to Taiwan.

Wen Yiduo ... Wang Shiwei ... Wang Tiandeng. ... Would the day never break?

Notes

1 "Wen Yiduo: The Poet's Farewell, 1946," in *The Search for Modern China: A Documentary Collection*, ed. Pei-kai Cheng and Michael Lestz with Jonathan Spence (New York: W.W. Norton, 1999), p. 338.

2 Suzanne Pepper, "The KMT [GMD]–CCP Conflict 1945–1949," in *Cambridge History of China, Vol. 13, Republican China 1912–1949, Part 2*, ed. John King Fairbank and Albert Feuerwerker (Cambridge, UK: Cambridge University Press, 1986), p. 735.

3 "General Marshall: The Mediator's View, 1947," in Cheng and Lestz with Spence, *The Search for Modern China*, p. 341.

4 Pepper, "The KMT [GMD]–CCP Conflict," p. 742.

5 R. Keith Schoppa, *Xiang Lake: Nine Centuries of Chinese Life* (New Haven, CT: Yale University Press, 1989), p. 225.

6 Lloyd E. Eastman, *Seeds of Destruction* (Stanford, CA: Stanford University Press, 1984), pp. 81–2.

7 Quoted in Pepper, "The KMT [GMD]–CCP Conflict," p. 738.

8 Immanuel C.Y. Hsu, *The Rise of Modern China* (New York: Oxford University Press, 1970), p. 730.

9 Odd Arne Westad, *Decisive Encounters: The Chinese Civil War, 1946–1950* (Stanford, CA: Stanford University Press, 2003), p. 107. Pepper, "The KMT [GMD]–CCP Conflict," p. 781.

10 Pepper, "The KMT [GMD]–CCP Conflict," p. 781.
11 The phrase is in Harry J. Lamley, "Taiwan Under Japanese Rule, 1895–1945: The Vicissitudes of Colonialism," in *Taiwan: A New History*, ed. Murray A. Rubinstein (Armonk, NY: M.E. Sharpe, 1999), p. 204.
12 Sung-sheng Yvonne Chang, "Taiwanese New Literature and the Colonial Context," in Rubinstein, *Taiwan*, pp. 262–3.
13 Ibid., p. 267.
14 Steven Phillips, "Between Assimilation and Independence: Taiwanese Political Aspirations under Nationalist Chinese Rule, 1945–1948," in Rubinstein, *Taiwan*, p. 276.
15 Ibid., p. 291.
16 Ibid., p. 294.
17 Ibid., p. 295.

Suggestions for Further Reading

Ch'en Yungfa. *Making Revolution: The Communist Movement in Eastern and Central China, 1937–1945* (Berkeley, CA: University of California Press, 1986). This book is indispensable in revealing the diversity and complexity of the Communist revolution.

The China White Paper, August 1949. Originally issued as United States Relations with China, with Special Reference to the Period, 1944–1949 (Stanford, CA: Stanford University Press, 1967). This is an eye-opening summary with documents on U.S. policy and actions regarding China during the civil war from the point of view of the U.S. Department of State.

Peck, Graham. *Two Kinds of Time* (Boston, MA: Houghton Mifflin, 1950). This book by an American journalist is an account based on his travels in China that, in the words of a reviewer, is a "superbly written mixture of comic adventure, travel description, battle reporting, and caustic social analysis of old China."

Westad, Odd Arne. *Decisive Encounter: The Chinese Civil War, 1946–1950* (Stanford, CA: Stanford University Press, 2003). This insightful book revisits the civil war with a view to underscoring the reasons for the Communist victory and the Guomindang defeat.

Wou, Odoric. *Mobilizing the Masses: Building Revolution in Henan* (Stanford, CA: Stanford University Press, 1994). The empirical richness and analytical care of this study underscore the complex and diverse possibilities of revolutionary change.

16

Paths to the Future

Mao Zedong stood in triumph at the Gate of Heavenly Peace to announce the establishment of the People's Republic of China (PRC) on October 1, 1949: "We, the 450 million Chinese people, have stood up and our future is infinitely bright." Mao spoke of a sense of Chinese identity far removed from the China subjected to foreign powers. Moreover, the Chinese people shared Mao's enthusiasm. Here is the memory of that day by Li Zhisui, the man who later became Mao's personal physician:

> The crowd went wild, thundering in applause, shouting over and over, "Long live the People's Republic of China!" "Long live the People's Republic of China!" I was so full of joy my heart nearly burst out of my throat, and tears welled up in my eyes. I was so proud of China, so full of hope, so happy that the exploitation and suffering, the aggression from foreigners would be gone forever.[1]

The civil war was not yet over: Chiang Kai-shek's flight across the Taiwan Strait had prolonged it. But surely the end was near. The battlefield defeats had been clear and decisive; the Guomindang was beaten and demoralized; states around the world were recognizing Mao's regime as the legitimate government of China. The "liberation" of Taiwan was the priority on the PLA's docket for 1950.

But then, into this likely historical scenario, was thrust a wrenching contingency: North Korea's June 1950 invasion of South Korea. When that happened, the United States ordered the U.S. Seventh Fleet to enter the Taiwan Strait between the PRC and Taiwan to prevent either Mao or Chiang from taking advantage of the crisis to continue the civil war. That U.S. action meant that, well seven decades later, the civil war was still essentially unfinished. There thus developed two paths, with different directions and configurations, to the Chinese future.

THE STRUCTURE OF THE COMMUNIST PARTY-STATE

Because a revolution is action and movement, tragic and melodramatic, it seems ironic to begin a discussion of the Chinese Communist revolution with a sketch of institutional structures plunked down in their stark immovability. But it is necessary to ready the stage for the high drama.

Mao and CCP leaders structured three huge bureaucracies to carry out crucial ruling functions: party, state (or government), and military. At each territorial-administrative level (Center [or nation], province, prefecture, city, county, and township) there was a full range of both party and state organs. A small party committee generally held power at each level. At the Center, the committee was called the Politburo, chaired by the chair of the party and composed of generally fourteen to twenty-four members. Its support staff was the Secretariat. When the Politburo was not meeting, its Standing Committee, made up of five or six of the most powerful leaders in the country, held power. The party had a Central Committee as well (ranging in size from about 100 until 1966 to almost 300 in the 1980s and 1990s and stabilizing at about 200 in the twenty-first century). It did not always exercise much power, mainly ratifying Politburo decisions. The Central Committee's full meetings were called "plenums," and they were numbered in the order in which they met following meetings of the Party Congress, a body composed of as many as 1,500 people. For example, the Eighth Party Congress met in 1956; but the Eleventh Plenum of the Eighth Party Congress met in 1966 and inaugurated the tragedy known as the Cultural Revolution. Finally, the party had departments, called "Central Committee departments," which, unlike the Central Committee, wielded considerable power. These included the Propaganda Department and the Organization Department, the latter charged with making staff appointments.

The state or government, like the party, had organs at each territorial-administrative level. The most important government body after 1954 was the State Council. Headed by the premier, it was composed of vice-premiers in charge of specific arenas of responsibility and of those in charge of commissions and ministries. Two very important commissions were the State Planning Commission and the State Economic Commission. Theoretically, the party made policy and the state executed it. Because of the complementary nature of party and state, the ruling structure in the PRC was often referred to as the "party-state."

The military (the PLA) had bureaucratic rank just like the State Council. It was *outside* the jurisdiction of the state and answered to a *party* body, the Military Affairs Commission. The military's highest priority was protecting the party, not the state. It was the party that propelled the revolution. The party used the military just as it used the state to try to achieve its goals.

To these institutions were brought "an operational set of principles and practices ... [that might be] labeled the 'Yan'an complex'" because they were developed during the years at Yan'an.[2] For the first decades of the PRC these included the essential nature of ideology in keeping cadres in line with the aims of the party leaders; the importance of the mass line, and, in the same vein, decentralized rule; a disdain for specialists and a preference for officials who could serve in a variety of areas; and, remembering the case of Wang Shiwei, witch hunts, false accusations, and confessions extracted in any way possible from those considered enemies within the Communist movement.

Because Mao Zedong dominated the PRC from its founding until his death in 1976, it is important to survey his thought for those ideas and approaches that seemed to have special significance. One of his most significant emphases was voluntarism—"that properly motivated people could overcome virtually any material odds to accomplish their goals."[3] It was a strong conviction that the people could exercise willpower to change their world. Traditional Chinese social thought, in contrast, had emphasized that fate was a major force in all lives. One was fated to be born male or female, rich or poor, to be married to this or that individual, to live in this place or that, to be subject to this natural disaster or that physical illness. One must then accept that fate with resignation. It was a world where forces of nature, society, and birth reality dominated humans. Mao's revolutionary romanticism and strong populist faith trumpeted that humans did not have to stand cowed by fate, that they could transcend their fate with willpower and determination. A poem called "Swimming," which he wrote in 1956, puts it this way:

> Standing at a ford, the Master once said:
> "Thus life flows into the past!"
> Breeze shakes the masts
> While Tortoise and Snake Hills are motionless.
> A grand project is being conceived—
> A bridge will fly across
> And turn a barrier into a path.
> To the west, new cliffs will arise;
> Mount Wu's clouds and rains will be kept from the countryside.
> Calm lakes will spring up in the gorges.
> Were the goddess still alive
> She would be amazed by the changes on this earth.[4]

Through a number of large-scale construction projects and by a wide variety of forceful and positive changes brought about by the Communist regime in its first eight years, Mao had brought this new view of human capabilities into the Chinese social, political, and natural worlds. In terms of practical policies, Mao looked to the mass line and mass campaigns as structures through which to mobilize the willpower of the people. The problem, as will become apparent, is that sometimes Mao's "revolutionary romanticism" had a way of soaring out of control, with insufficient grounding in reality.

FIGURE 16.1 In the early PRC, mammoth projects of both reconstruction and development were undertaken. Here workers labor to build the first bridge across the Yangzi at Nanjing.
Source: Marc Riboud/Magnum Photos.

If Mao placed great faith in the "people," he had nothing but hatred and loathing for intellectuals. Mao's strong anti-intellectualism was directed not only against scholars, writers, and journalists but against scientists, engineers, and doctors as well. He chalked up the problems of late imperial China to intellectuals who were products of the civil service examination system and who were in charge of state and society. Further, intellectuals were usually city-based elites who in many cases had been enemies during the revolution. They had none of the practical sense of the people, yet they gloried in their presumed superiority, putting on airs and demeaning the masses. Mao also thought that they constantly raised nit-picking objections to his programs and policies. His opposition to intellectuals seriously and negatively affected developments in the PRC. Although the First Five-Year Plan (see p. 303), shaped and executed with Soviet support, did follow the Soviet model and emphasized technical expertise, Mao subsequently moved away from that practice. In the twenty years from 1957 to 1976, he frequently demonized intellectuals, attacking them viciously and creating, as it were, an intellectual scorched-earth policy that undercut China's situation more devastatingly than even China's military scorched-earth policy had during World War II. Listen to Mao in early 1958 comparing himself to the anti-intellectual first Chinese emperor in the Qin dynasty (221–207 B.C.E.): "He buried only 460 scholars alive; we have buried 46,000 scholars alive. You [intellectuals] revile us for being Qin Shi Huang. You are wrong. We have surpassed Qin Shi Huang a hundredfold."[5]

Another of Mao's preeminent concerns was the crucial nature of ideology. To be ideologically correct (or, in the slang of the time, properly "red" or Communist) was absolutely essential. Only ideological correctness could carry the revolution to a successful conclusion. What was ideological correctness? From the years at Yan'an, it was "Mao Zedong Thought," an evolving body of thought, often emphasizing practice, not simply theoretical ideas. During his life, Mao was not only the producer but also the interpreter and the keeper of the ideological canon.

Mao's thinking on class contributed greatly to Mao Zedong Thought. For many reasons, it was quite remarkable for class to become a focus. As one scholar notes:

It is hard to imagine a society less subject to class analysis than was China in the 1910s and 1920s [when Marxism-Leninism began to flourish]. Capitalism had barely penetrated the country, and feudalism in its traditional European form had long ceased to exist. Among the key players were regional warlords who had no place in the Marxist analytical scheme. Even Chiang Kai-shek seems to have acted primarily for himself and the GMD rather than in the interests of any of the classes … at the time. Members of China's urban proletariat were, in most cases, the first generation off the farm and retained strong personal ties to the countryside. In the rural villages, strong ties of kinship cut across supposed class divisions, and clan associations managed the rural rituals.[6]

Be that as it may, Marxism–Leninism seemed to many intellectuals to answer so many questions about China's plight that class automatically became part of the formula of revolution. The core value regarding class was class struggle, which Mao believed would mark society until Communism was attained. Mao further taught, in what might be called "ideo-biology," that class status could be determined by political attitudes and that then, unless there were changes in attitude, class status was passed on almost genetically to succeeding generations. Once a landlord, always a landlord; once a capitalist, always a capitalist. As one scholar suggests, Mao really had created castes—"social orders with permanent, hereditary status that sharply [shaped] one's life experiences and prospects."[7] Even marriage prospects hinged on class status. A person of bad class became a public enemy of the people, defined primarily as the working class and the peasantry.

THE EAST IS RED: HALLMARKS OF THE COMMUNIST REVOLUTION

The first eight years of the PRC are generally viewed as the most successful period of Communist rule under Mao's control. The debilitating inflationary cycle was broken with government policies on price controls, balanced budgets, austerity measures, and currency reform. The new regime began the rigorous task of reconstruction following the years of war and turmoil. The government expelled most foreigners and confiscated their property. The PLA in a fashion was able to atone for the wars China had lost in the preceding century by fighting the U.S. army to a standoff in Korea. Most important, Communists were able to launch aspects of their revolution across China.

Land Reform

The heart of the Chinese revolution—land reform—had already begun in the late 1940s, before the Communist military victory. According to Liu Shaoqi, the second-ranking Chinese leader in 1949, the objectives of land reform were "to free the rural productive forces from the shackles of the landlords' feudal land-ownership system, so as to develop agricultural production and open the way for new China's industrialization."[8] The process involved destruction of the old agricultural system through class struggle and construction of a new system based on collective rural production. Applying the concept of class struggle across the board was problematic, given the ecological and social variety of the Chinese countryside. In the North, as we have seen, landlordism was not a major problem, as the peasant often tilled the land that he owned; tenancy rates in the 1930s ranged from about 10 to 15 percent. In the South and Southwest, however, tenancy rates were much higher (56 percent in Sichuan), and absentee landlords exploited tenants. The social and political culture of different regions also differed sharply: for example, lineage groups dominated localities in the South, whereas secret organizations like the Red Spears were important in the North and the Elder Brothers' Society often held sway in the West. Within regions themselves, there were also stark differences: for example, in the Shaan-Gan-Ning base area, the Yan'an subregion was "sparsely populated, bandit-ridden badlands," whereas in the subregion directly to its north, the population was dense, farming was intensive, tenancy rates were high, and commerce was more developed.[9] To apply one formula for revolution generally, therefore, proved to be impossible.

The multiplicity of regional wartime experiences also created marked differences in people's attitudes and expectations. The long, brutal warfare of much of the North contrasted with the relatively peaceful Shaan-Gan-Ning base, separated as it was by the Guomindang blockade. Some parts of Central and South China had been controlled by the Japanese for varying lengths of time and other parts not at all. Manchuria had experienced a long period of Japanese colonial rule. The Southwest had been the Guomindang base, subject to Japanese bombing but not ground invasion. The CCP had taken control in the North in the midst of war, but in East, Central, South, and Southwest China the Communist armies seized large amounts of territory with relatively little military action. Land reform in the North thus took place mostly before and during the civil war, whereas in the South it happened after the establishment of the new national government. Therefore, the party's approach to land reform varied according to the time when it occurred; it was time- and space-specific.

Mobilizing peasants in rural villages by setting up mass organizations, which was far easier than land reform, was still usually slow and difficult. The task of organizing peasants was, in the words of the Henan province wartime propaganda chief, "difficult and protracted work. It requires a great deal of patience. One can never organize the peasants by simply issuing a manifesto, holding a meeting, or giving a theatrical performance." The first task in this society, built as it was on personal connections, was to gain access to a village. If organizers and mobilizers were from the village or had close ties to a resident of the village, the effort would be easier. Cadres from outside the local community had tougher problems. They had to possess networking skills, and they had to begin their work by cultivating social ties in the community. Only by first winning the trust of people in the locality could they begin to build grassroots networks; and only after they had constructed those networks could they begin to undertake various programs of action.

The other cultural hurdle was breaking down the social-psychological barrier that existed between peasants and local elites. In that traditional relationship, peasants knew their place and were extraordinarily careful not to offend or upset their landlords or others in positions of power. They were masters at knowing how to play their social role as subordinates. But now the Communists were mobilizing peasants to be aggressive in attacking those who had held power over them. Peasant Lin in Long Branch village would have felt very leery about attacking Landlord Wu. Though Wu might be under attack now, what would happen if the Communist cadres were ousted or if the Communist cause went down to defeat and Wu and other landlords returned? Allaying such fears was a formidable task.

Land reform in North China was often characterized by a violent settling of old scores against local elites. In the last months of 1945, the scores being settled were often those against elites and even middle and poor peasants who had collaborated with the Japanese. The violence associated with land reform followed a directive of May 1946 that gave free rein to poor peasant leagues and peasant associations to expropriate and redistribute land and property, telling cadres to keep their hands off, a policy that encouraged extremism among the masses. This more radical phase of the land reform effort coincided with the Guomindang's unexpectedly strong 1946 military offensive. Party leaders claimed that land reform was important for mobilizing the populace against attacks by Guomindang forces. County men formed militia units; local self-defense units transported supplies and ammunition; women's associations managed surveillance posts; youth associations worked in rear areas; cultural teams did propaganda work; and peasant associations spearheaded army recruiting. The connection between land reform, recruitment, and military mobilization was continually stressed.

The years 1948 to 1950 saw a moderation in the land reform effort to turn away from such leftist excesses as misclassifying villagers' class status, killing landlords and rich peasants, taking land from middle peasants, and attacking commercial and industrial enterprises. After the party came to power in 1949 and with the promulgation of the agrarian reform law in June 1950, land reform began in all areas. The Communist regime faced gigantic challenges; in most areas no advance work had been done, and there was therefore little, if any, structural readiness for great social change. There was generally no sense of class sentiments. In many areas of the South and East, tenants rented land from a landlord in their own lineage. Given the all-important kin and native place networks, villagers could not easily understand what "feudal" class structures were or what exploitation meant. The pattern of mobilization used in the North was copied elsewhere: target local tyrants, initiate the struggle meeting, and inaugurate a rent reduction campaign. Work teams played a much larger role in land reform after 1949 than in the North in the 1940s. Despite their involvement, there were violent social outbursts, and an estimated 1 to 2 million landlords were killed—either in the heat of struggle or by execution. An estimated 88 percent of households in the countryside had completed the land to the tiller movement by summer 1952. In the end, almost 43 percent of China's arable land was redistributed to about 60 percent of the population in the countryside.

Economists debate what impact land reform had·on agricultural productivity. But the main impact was political. Land reform had revolutionized ways of thinking. Ding Ling's novel *The Sun Shines over the Sanggan River* (1948), accorded a 1951 Stalin Prize in literature, revealed the changes in the peasant population. In this scene, a local bully called Schemer Qian is being attacked in a struggle meeting:

> Peasants surged up to the stage shouting wildly: "Kill him!" "A life for our lives!" A group of villagers rushed to beat him. It was not clear who started, but one struck the first blow and others fought to get at him. ... One feeling animated them all—vengeance! They wanted vengeance. They wanted to give vent to their hatred, the sufferings of the oppressed since their ancestors' times, the hatred of thousands of years; all this resentment they directed against him. They would have liked to tear him with their teeth. ...
>
> "Bah! Killing's too good for him. Let's make him beg for death. Let's humble him for a few days, how about it?" Old Dong's face was red with excitement. He had started life as a hired laborer. Now that he saw peasants just like himself daring to speak out and act boldly, his heart was racing wildly with happiness.[10]

The social and political horizons of countless poor and middle peasants "had been broadened by the class-oriented perspective of the CCP."[11] Land reform had created new functional associations and social groupings that tended to displace old kinship, religious, and voluntary associations. The common experiences of class struggle gave rise to a stronger social cohesion among those struggling against landlords and village despots and also created a new demarcation of "us" from "them." In the old society, the "them" for any community was most likely the outsider, the person from a different native place; now the Other, the enemy, was inside the community itself, and his status as a class alien could be resurrected and used at will.

FIGURE 16.2 Surrounded by tenants and villagers, the landlord in the center is under attack at a struggle meeting during land reform in the early 1950s. Many such meetings turned deadly when long-term rage exploded into violence.
Source: Sovfoto/UIG via Getty Images.

Revolution in the Family

One month before the agrarian reform law was announced, the state issued the Marriage Law of 1950. One stipulation of that law allowed single women, divorcees, and widows to own land in their own names; land reform thus benefited one group in Chinese society that had never been able to hold land. But the law went well beyond economic rights; it struck at the very heart of the traditional family system and might be seen as a culmination of efforts to change a system stretching back thirty years to the May Fourth period. The Marriage Law abolished the traditional family system "based on arbitrary and compulsory arrangements and the superiority of man over woman." The new system was based "on equal rights for both sexes, and on the protection of the lawful interests of women and children."[12] Arranged marriages, child betrothals, polygamy, and the selling of women into marriage were forbidden. Women, as well as men, could initiate divorce proceedings. Infanticide was prohibited. Equal rights for both sexes was revolutionary indeed in the context of traditional Chinese gender relationships and practices such as footbinding.

And yet, as with the Marriage Law announced during the Jiangxi Soviet, the law was on the books but was not always put into practice. The right to divorce created considerable confusion and disorder when hundreds of thousands of women in unhappy marriages tried to divorce. Husbands and their mothers, who stood to lose wives and daughters-in-law, were angry. The local party cadre whose job it was to execute the law was caught in the middle.

> If the cadre (usually a man) carried out his duties under the marriage law, he might find himself faced with an angry village and a serious handicap in the "important" work to come. If he did not, he was returning women illegally to families who would undoubtedly make them feel their anger for the loss of face they had suffered.[13]

In most cases, the local cadres became the major problem that undercut the Marriage Law; it was not strictly enforced in the countryside. The number of murders and suicides stemming from the issue of divorce soared into the tens of thousands. A recent study has argued that rural women were much more ready to divorce under the new law and be open about it than were urban women; further, in divorces, male peasants suffered most as a result.[14]

Urban Revolution

As in land reform, the urban phase of the revolution targeted class enemies. In 1951 and 1952, the party attacked purveyors of what it called "non-Communist bourgeois values." Targets of the Three-Anti Campaign were party cadres, government bureaucrats, and factory managers; the goal was to eliminate waste, corruption, and mismanagement. Targets of the Five-Anti Campaign were the national bourgeoisie—industrialists and big businessmen—for corruption, including bribery and tax evasion. Like the land reform campaigns, this gave rise to the sense of an enemy presence and a distrust that both mangled old connections and created new commonalities, identities, and networks.

These campaigns had a number of important impacts. They destroyed the self-confidence of the targeted groups and discredited them in the eyes of those, like workers, who had been their traditional subordinates. They removed personnel who had been retained since before liberation and new cadres whose ideals were not orthodox, and thus allowed for the recruitment of new mid- and lower-level personnel in business enterprises and the government. Economically, the campaigns brought money from fines and back taxes from large firms to be used for investment in new government enterprises. Heavy fines could be handled by having businesses sell stock to the state, thus creating public–private enterprises. Such arrangements would allow the state to appoint a cadre to take a leading role in management; that would often result in the establishment of party branches in large- and medium-size businesses. Thus, economic involvement led to greater political control.

Like the Guomindang regime in the late 1920s and early 1930s, the Communist regime sought to sink its roots deeply into Chinese society. Whereas the Guomindang attempt had not been successful, the *danwei* (unit), precursors of which existed under the Guomindang, was a very effective arm of the Communist party-state. By the early 1960s, every person had been assigned to a unit: if he was employed, the unit was at his or her place of work; for students, the unit was at the school; for unemployed or retired people, it was in the neighborhood. The Communist government then used these *danwei* to enforce control, political conformity, surveillance, and ideological correctness at the lowest level of the polity. One had to get permission from one's *danwei* to get married, to have a child, to get a divorce, or to change a job. The *danwei* controlled housing, gave out ration coupons, oversaw the birth-control program, mediated disputes, and supplied burial funds. They were also the basic building blocks of mass campaigns.

Providing the balancing social framework for these local units were state-sponsored mass organizations based on shared interests or specific objectives. They attempted to enlarge the masses' horizons as they joined together the whole country across provincial and regional lines. By 1953, for example, trade union membership had risen to 12 million; 9 million were in the New Democratic Youth League (the pre-1957 name of the Communist Youth League); and as many as 76 million women had joined the Women's Federation. These organizations were especially significant forces in the campaigns that became so central a part of the early years of the PRC. Both the mass organizations and the mass campaigns provided frameworks for carrying out the party's directives and vehicles for mass mobilization.

AT WAR WITH THE UNITED NATIONS: THE KOREAN WAR

Six months after declaring the Marriage Law and five months after announcing the Agrarian Reform Law—that is, generally well before many of the revolutionary programs and campaigns could even get started—China was at war in Korea. It was extraordinarily horrific timing; the PRC was less than fourteen months old, struggling with basic tasks of reconstruction and hardly able to commit itself thoroughly. But it did so, convinced that its actions were necessary. From the beginning Mao had decided that in foreign affairs, China should "lean to one side," that of the Soviet Union. He had traveled to Moscow in early 1950 to sign a Valentine's Day accord with Stalin, though Stalin's treatment of Mao was worse than rude. From the perspective of the United States at the time, such an agreement carried the simple (if wrong) message that the perceived Communist threat was monolithic.

Then in late June 1950, the Cold War suddenly became hot when the Democratic Republic of Korea (North Korea) invaded the Republic of Korea (South Korea). After World War II, the Soviet Union had accepted the surrender of the Japanese north of the 38th parallel, a task that the United States performed south of that parallel. The Soviet and U.S. occupation of those respective areas had eventually produced regimes that favored the former occupiers. The Soviet-linked regime of Kim Il-sung and the U.S.-connected regime of Syngman Rhee faced each other with great hostility. After the North's invasion of the South, the United States and other nations fighting under the flag of the United Nations entered the Korean peninsula at a time when the defeat of the South seemed imminent. North Korean forces, seemingly unstoppable, had driven down the full length of the peninsula to a small perimeter around the southeastern port of Pusan. It was UN Commander Douglas MacArthur's decision to execute an amphibious landing at Inchon on the west coast in September that saved the day, turning a North Korean rout of the South into a panicky North Korean retreat. Whereas the original UN goal had been to contain Communism by pushing North Korean forces north of the 38th parallel, thus restoring this line as the boundary between the two Koreas, the UN (with the United States calling the shots) changed its policy and decided to "liberate" the North. In the fall, UN forces invaded North Korea.

By the end of June, the United States had already given evidence of its hostility to the PRC when it sent the U.S. Seventh Fleet into the Taiwan Strait. China saw the United States as the world's foremost imperialist nation, once more intervening in the Chinese civil war; Zhou Enlai called it "armed aggression." By the fall of 1950, that imperialist power was now leading the charge up the Korean peninsula toward Chinese territory. Even before the Inchon landing, China had warned that it would intervene if UN forces invaded North Korea. The United States passed it off as a meaningless bluff. MacArthur had made increasingly belligerent statements about the artificiality of the border between China and North Korea ("they are all Communists"), about bombing sites in China ("take out all the industrial cities"), and about "unleashing" Chiang Kai-shek against the mainland. The PRC felt that its own security was threatened by UN actions. Mao explained China's entrance into the war in late November as follows:

> Historical facts teach us that a crisis in Korea has much to do with the security of China. With the lips gone, the teeth would be exposed to the cold; with the door broken, the house itself would be in danger. For the people of China to aid the people of Korea in their struggle against the U.S. is *not merely a moral responsibility but also a matter closely related to the vital interests of our own people, a decision necessitated by a need for self-defense.* Saving our neighbors at once means saving ourselves. To protect our own country, we must help the people of Korea.[15]

Chinese troops in large numbers entered the war, totaling 700,000 very quickly. The Chinese commitment was huge. China used 66 percent of its entire field army (the equivalent of twenty-five field corps), 62 percent of its artillery (seventy divisions), 70 percent of its air force (twelve divisions), all three of its tank divisions, ten railway engineering divisions, and two public security divisions. Commanded by Marshal Peng Dehuai, Chinese forces were noted for their speed and stealth. The early Chinese campaigns were extraordinarily successful, with UN forces being driven far south of the 38th parallel in late January 1951. As fighting continued, however, China's primitive logistical supply system and lack of aircraft and anti-aircraft guns made China's situation desperate. In the end, it was for China a brutally costly war. An armistice was not reached until mid-1953, and many Chinese were killed in the last year of the war by withering UN firepower. About 1 million Chinese soldiers were killed.

At home, the Chinese government rallied the masses to the war's support; communities, for example, contributed money for the construction of planes and other war materiel. From February 1951 to 1953, the party whipped up hatred for the United States through the campaign of "Resist America, Aid Korea" and its targeting of "counterrevolutionaries." Especially at risk were former Guomindang members or Guomindang military personnel, who were now suspected of sabotage. Execution of suspects was the rule rather than the exception. In Guangdong province alone in the period from October 1950 to August 1951, over 28,000 people were executed. Estimates of those

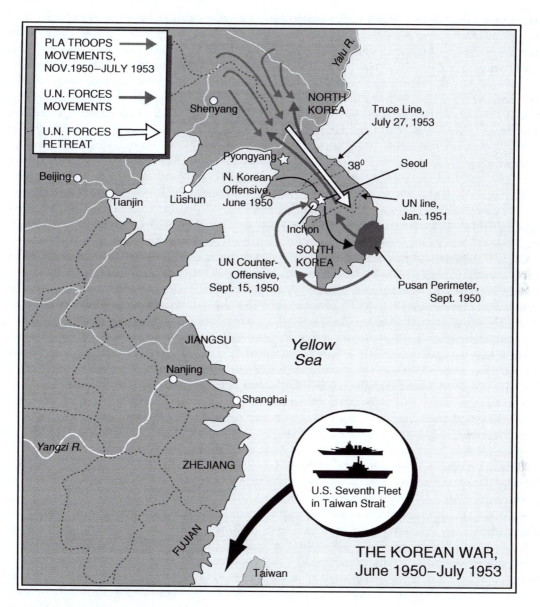

MAP 16.1 The Korean War.

killed nationwide have reached over 500,000, with perhaps the same number committing suicide. The exact number will never be known.

THE FIRST FIVE-YEAR PLAN (1953–1957)

In 1953, the year the Korean armistice was reached, the government announced its First Five-Year Plan, to be structured on the Soviet model of state-controlled economic development. The focus was on heavy industry, the goal being to lay a foundation for subsequent industrial and economic development. Manchuria was a main laboratory for the developing plan: it had many industrial plants that had been held for years by the government (under Japan, then the Nationalists, now the Communists); they were mostly in heavy industry, and the area was close to the Soviet Union. Thousands of Soviet engineers and technical advisers came to China to teach Soviet methods during these years. The Chinese followed their Soviet patrons to the letter, and the advances were remarkable: most of the goals set forth in the plan were substantially exceeded. For example, the production of coal by 1957 had reached 115 percent of the plan's goal, as had almost 130 percent of the steel, 220 percent of units of machine tools, and 188 percent of truck units. Economic growth was a high 8.9 percent annual increase, with agricultural output rising 3.8 percent annually and industrial growth climbing an impressive 18.7 percent per year. These solid and impressive statistics are underscored by other data showing how the lives of Chinese were being substantially bettered. Life expectancy, a good measure of the health and economic conditions of a country, rose from thirty-six years in 1950 to fifty-seven years in 1957—an amazing increase. Wages for workers were up by a third; for peasants, income was up by a fifth. It was indeed a stellar beginning.

China's industrialization was to be built on the back of increased agricultural production; land reform was to lead to that higher production. But land reform could not stop at the land to the tiller stage, where land was broken up into small parcels. What was needed for higher production was large-scale farms on which the resources of many farmers could be pooled, making possible the use of machines—tractors, seeders, combines, bailers—to bring more efficiency to farming. Policymakers thus saw collectivization—bringing farmers together in cooperative units—as a key to modernizing agriculture and as a way to make collecting tax grain easier. To ease the difficulties of moving into collectives, the government plan set forth a gradual phased process. The first step was mutual aid teams (MATs) where traditional practices of peasant cooperation in sharing labor and farm animals and tools were formalized; in this phase, peasants continued to own their own land, implements, and farm animals. In a typical MAT, there were generally ten or fewer cooperating households. In many areas, they were members of the same lineage. Whereas an estimated 40 percent of all peasant households were MAT members by the end of 1952, the number reached 92 percent in 1956. The date of establishment of these MATs varied greatly according to the area of the country, a reality that had serious impacts on subsequent phases of collectivization.

The next stage of collectivization was the establishment of lower-level agricultural producers' cooperatives (APCs). These were made up of approximately three to five MATs or about thirty to fifty households. In the semi-socialist lower-level APC, the principle of "central management but private ownership" was operative. Members gave land, draft animals, and equipment as capital shares to the cooperative and received a dividend, after wages were deducted, for what they had contributed. The pace of establishment of lower-level APCs was highly variable. In some areas organized in 1951, the lower-level APC did not appear in Southeast China until 1954 and 1955. By that time, considerable local resistance had begun against the effort; this was especially the case where the land to the tiller phase had taken longer than anticipated and MATs had not been developed. In these areas, cadres, in order to keep up the timetable of collectivization, had moved directly from private ownership to the lower-level APC. In Zhejiang province, for example, because of the lateness of the end of the land to the tiller phase, by 1953 only 3,300 APCs had been formed; but by 1954, cadres had established 53,000. This huge increase in so short a time suggests that cadres were forcing the formation of APCs, a clear violation of the government's rule that the process should be voluntary. It was clear that farmers, many landless for so many years, deeply resented having to contribute their recently acquired land to a cooperative.

Even though it seems commonsensical that if collectivization were to become solidly rooted in the countryside it would take substantial time, the party-state repeatedly showed a "great leap" mentality and a tendency for this mentality to become ever grander. In part, that can be laid at Mao's feet, for, as noted earlier, he had a grand, almost romantic belief in the power of people to overcome all odds. In the context of a perceived general success of collectivization at the lower-level APC stage, with Mao forging the path, the leadership decided to push full steam ahead to the establishment of upper-level APCs. This was done, somewhat incredibly, at a time when only 15 percent of peasant households were members of *lower-level* APCs. Frantic organizing in the last months of 1955 led to the skyrocketing membership in lower-level APCs of over 80 percent of peasant households in January 1956. A tragic aspect of these decisions and efforts is that the party leaders abandoned the strategy of pragmatism and flexibility that had brought them political and military victory. As a result, they began to undercut what they had tried to build.

Higher-level APCs were far more revolutionary than their lower-level predecessors. They comprised 200 to 300 households. Land was owned by the collective; private ownership was ended. Payments for contributions of land and other assets were ended; payment was strictly for labor. By the end of 1956, almost 88 percent of peasant households had become at least nominal members of higher-level APCs. At least one scholar has seen this completion of collectivization as one of the most important developments in the First Five-Year Plan: "it was an enormous achievement of social and institutional transformation to bring the great bulk of the Chinese people under socialist forms of organization."[16]

Many peasants may have had a different view of the impact of collectivization. Some considered the establishment of the higher-level APC as a negative turning point in their relationship to the party-state and in their day-to-day relationships with the rural cadres who, in many cases, had forced this formation on the people. Further, after the higher-level APC formation, the state attempted to institute direct planning in agriculture. Though they backtracked on this effort, the farmers were still hit with a flurry of marketing restraints, quotas, and rations that increasingly constrained and shaped their actions. As the state daily became more central in decision making about farming, peasants lost control over their lives to the rural cadres serving as agents of the party-state.

THE TAIWAN MODEL: AUTHORITARIANISM AND REFORM

Development in the Republic of China (ROC) on Taiwan offers interesting comparisons to development in the PRC. Supposedly in the throes of death in 1950 and on the verge of total extinction, the Guomindang regime on Taiwan in the following two decades experienced a miracle of economic resurrection.

The Iron Fist

When Chiang Kai-shek was re-inaugurated as president of the ROC on May 1, 1950, he admitted that he was personally responsible for the loss of the mainland to the Communists. All his important bases had failed—the army disintegrated, the party in shambles, and the state shrunk to one province. Under the circumstances, he had to get what was left of his house in order, aware, as he continually reminded his listeners, that they were still involved in a civil war and that everyone's goal must be to retake the mainland. In a first step to overhaul the party, he appointed a Central Reform Committee composed of former students and confidantes. They developed plans to restructure the party's systems of ideological training, organization, and discipline. As had been the practice in the party since the 1920s, another process of party reregistration weeded out undesirables, whether they were politically suspect, corrupt, or just incompetent. These tasks were completed by the Seventh Party Congress in October 1952, a meeting that accepted the principle that opposition to Communism and resistance against the Soviet Union were basic to all other party missions. It was recognized, however, that in this period of opposition to Communism and the Soviet Union, party goals should also include making Taiwan a model province of Sun Yat-sen's Three Principles of the People.

Chiang used the ongoing civil war (now the Cold War) as the justification for stringent authoritarian controls. Martial law continued. No one could challenge the Guomindang—which meant no new political parties. Only newspapers sanctioned by the government could be published. The security system was reorganized. A National Security Bureau under the leadership of Chiang's son, Chiang Ching-kuo, was formed to coordinate all security bureaus in the Guomindang; the ministries of defense, foreign affairs, and the interior; the Taiwan Garrison Command; the military police; and the local police. These were tight networks, stringently controlled, and were instrumental in cracking down on any dissent, almost always labeled Communist conspiracies or subversion. The White Terror that Chiang had begun in 1949 continued throughout the 1950s and beyond.

In these years, the government "arrested, imprisoned, and executed thousands on insufficient or circumstantial evidence."[17] Those targeted were sometimes the very famous. The governor of Taiwan province, Wu Kuo-chen, was forced to leave the island in 1953 after he criticized Chiang for his strong-arm tactics against dissenters; once he was off the island, he condemned Chiang's regime as a "police state." In 1955, Sun Li-jen, commander of the army and personal chief of staff to Chiang, was obliquely implicated in a plot to overthrow the government; he spent the rest of his life under house arrest. And these had been Chiang's friends. Being based in Taiwan had not changed Chiang's longtime policy of brutally crushing dissent, whether student or otherwise. With the memory of wartime anti-student protests, Chiang appointed his security chief son to head the Chinese Anti-Communist National Salvation Youth Corps; it was the only legal intercollegiate organization.

In politics, the Guomindang under Chiang maintained an iron grip. Since the government was still theoretically the government of all China, Chiang and the party declared that the life of representative bodies in the government—the National Assembly, the Legislative Yuan, and the Control Yuan—would be extended indefinitely since nationwide elections obviously could not be held. Eventually, in 1969, as men in these bodies began to die, the party allowed supplementary elections. In any case, in these bodies, Taiwan had only a very small representation. For many Taiwanese, the absurdity of having little say in the determination of policies that affected only them was more than a little disturbing. In addition to controlling the political situation in Taipei, the Guomindang manipulated local politics. They handed out economic privileges—for example, licenses in lucrative businesses and industries—to cooperative politicians. They also made certain that one group of people did not hold on to local power for a long time by encouraging factions and then playing them off against each other.

Any suggestion of serious opposition or proposals of political alternatives brought a rapid and heavy-handed response. A liberal journal, *Free China Fortnightly*, supported by men such as the May Fourth period leader Hu Shih, was shut down when in 1960 its editor, Lei Chen, and a Taiwanese politician organized a China Democratic Party. Lei was arrested and imprisoned for ten years. Four years later, P'eng Meng-min, chair of the Political Science Department at National Taiwan University, and two students issued a "Self-Rescue Declaration of Taiwan," appealing to both Taiwanese and mainlanders "to work together to establish a democratic country because Taiwan was in reality already independent of China."[18] P'eng received an amnesty after the announcement of an eight-year prison sentence, largely because of pressure from the United States, but the two students spent at least eight years in prison. The government kept very strict control of literature and the arts as well as popular culture, handing out prison sentences as if they were going out of style. Authoritarianism ruled the day.

THE TAIWAN "MIRACLE"

Through currency reform and various measures to take surplus money out of circulation, Chiang's government reduced the 3,000 percent inflation in the first half of 1949 to 300 percent in 1950, to 8.8 percent in 1952. Then it turned to more long-term reform.

Rural Reforms

Although Chiang had essentially written off the peasants in his Nanjing decade decision to allow land taxes to revert to provinces, one of the first initiatives of his Taiwan government dealt with peasants. Perhaps Chiang had seen the error of his ways. A more likely explanation was that the Guomindang government in Taiwan could act forthrightly in this regard because they had no connections to and thus were unconstrained by local landlords. In 1949, the government ordered the reduction of rent to 37.5 percent, the same limit it had set in the Nanjing period. A second step in what should be called land reform—though of a sharply different type than on the mainland— was the sale of public lands to tenant farmers. This land, which had come into government hands from the Japanese colonial administration and from Japanese residents of the island, totaled almost 20 percent of all the arable land in Taiwan. Farmers could buy 1.2 to 4.8 acres of paddy land and 2.4 to 9.6 acres of dry land at a cost of 2.5 times the harvest of the annual main crop per 2.4 acres (known in Taiwan as a *jia*).

In early 1953, the government took the reform one step further with a land to the tiller program. Each landlord could keep up to 7.2 acres (3 *jia*) of paddy land and 14.4 acres (6 *jia*) of dry land. If the landlord owned more, the government would buy it and then sell it to tenants for 2.5 times the yield of the main annual crop. The government gave 70 percent of the payments to landlords in land bonds and 30 percent in the form of stock shares from four government businesses. The latter substantially boosted the government's efforts to spur business. If the landlord was not interested in investment in business and industry, he could sell these stocks to those who were; many became wealthy with such stock from Taiwan Cement, Taiwan Pulp and Paper, Taiwan Industry and Mining, and Taiwan Agricultural and Forestry. In the land reform effort, mostly completed by the end of 1953, 194,823 tenant families received 345,800 acres (140,000 hectares) of land previously held by landlords. It was a remarkable bloodless effort, obviously helped in part by the relative small number of people and small amount of acreage involved. Historians also have noted the important contributions in financial assistance and technical expertise from the Sino–American Joint Commission on Rural Reconstruction, which was established under an act by the U.S. Congress to set up and oversee Taiwanese rural projects. After land reform, farmers' associations were established to provide credit, assistance with marketing and sale of farm commodities, advice and assistance on setting up industries in predominantly rural areas, and aid for the rural establishment of services such as clinics and transportation facilities.

The Keys to General Economic Development

From 1960 to 1970, Taiwan was the fastest-growing economy in the world, with an annual GNP (gross national product, or the total value of all the goods and services produced by a nation in a year) of 9.7 percent. There are a number of reasons for such rapid economic growth. Certainly the relatively developed economic infrastructure inherited from the Japanese colonial period was important. Political stability (no major disruptive episodes followed the February 1947 tragedy) was crucial to sustained and rising growth. But in the discussion that follows, the focus is on the role played by the many experienced and well-educated experts in business, industry, and government; on the important contributions of the United States from the early 1950s to the mid-1960s; on the pragmatic responses of the Taiwan government to challenges; and on the importance placed upon education in the development of human resources.

Whereas the Maoist vision emphasized for its leaders ideological correctness and (in the process of destroying those who had expertise—see Chapters 17 and 18) placed its hopes in the common sense of the masses, the Taiwan model exalted the experts. Highly trained and committed professionals, many of whom had been educated abroad, drove the economic juggernaut. Many had majored in economics and engineering. Two of the most famous were Yin Chung-yung (K.Y. Yin), trained as an electrical engineer, and Li Kuo-ting (K.T. Li), a physicist. Yin has been called the "moving spirit" behind the industrial reform of the 1950s: "His goal of an industrialized, independent, and self-sustaining Taiwanese economy combined elements of the *laissez-faire* approach and state planning." Li was the dynamo and "Taiwan's chief economic planner" from 1963 to the late 1980s.[19] Both men cooperated with U.S. aid officials, adapting a variety of Western economic theories to Taiwanese realities. A number of men who worked with them in economic planning later became extraordinarily important politically: for example, Tsiang Yen-shih emerged as Guomindang secretary-general in the 1980s; Yen Chia-kan became premier in 1969, vice-president of the ROC in 1973, and president of the ROC from Chiang Kai-shek's death in 1975 until 1978; and Lee Teng-hui served as vice-president (1984–1988) and then president (1988–2000) of the ROC.

The role of the United States in the Taiwan miracle was crucial. The United States first freed up Taiwan to focus on domestic reform by underwriting Taiwan's military security with the Taiwan–U.S. Mutual Defense Treaty of 1954 and by providing military aid. In the arena of economic development, 100 million dollars of U.S. nonmilitary aid from 1951 to 1965 went to infrastructure-building and -strengthening projects (especially in areas such as communications, transportation, and electricity) and to undertakings that fostered human resources. Not only did U.S. economic aid provide about half of the capital formation in Taiwan in these years, but U.S. specialists also played important roles in advising Taiwan policymakers and in training technicians. The United States was Taiwan's chief cheerleader, in the early 1960s urging Taiwan to expand its economy aggressively and promising more economic aid. From the perspective of the Cold War, of course, it was to the advantage of the United States to show how well a "free" Taiwan was doing in contrast to the PRC.

The United States could provide economic aid and advice, but it was the government in Taipei that had to devise and execute policy, and it was generally both pragmatic and creative. In the early 1950s, Taiwan had a huge trade imbalance, exporting primarily sugar and rice and importing almost everything else. To expand business and industry so as to produce manufactured goods for export, the government embarked on a program of tax incentives and rebates. Once industries became productive, high tariffs (a nominal rate of over 40 percent, but rising as high as 160 percent) were set in place to protect infant industries. The First Four-Year Plan (1953–1956) focused not on heavy industry, as did the PRC's First Five-Year Plan, but on light industry in order to produce goods for export and for domestic use. The configuration of the plans in both Chinas developed out of perceived needs and economic realities. In Taiwan, the government provided funds for those establishing textile mills and fertilizer plants. The textile industry developed especially rapidly, and many new jobs were created. By 1956, as the industrial production index soared to about 155 percent, per capita income leaped by 40 percent. The Second Four-Year Plan (1957–1960) continued the important goal of expanding production of electricity, but turned the focus more to heavy industry and national defense industries.

In the late 1950s and early 1960s, the government focused increasingly on strategies to raise exports; above all, that meant expanding industrial production. Setting tax limits, offering tax exemptions, and providing government services in finding industrial plant sites were all part of the strategy to stimulate the establishment of labor-intensive industries in textiles, paper and paper products, chemicals, plastics, and rubber products. More attention to the financial infrastructure—reactivating important banks to assist in promoting industrial production, establishing machinery for investment banking, and setting up a stock market—involved efforts to "accelerate economic development," the announced goal of the Third Four-Year Plan (1961–1964). On the whole, the 1950s and 1960s saw Taiwan's economy change from an agricultural base to an industrial one, as Table 16.1 shows.

One institutional development that points to the creativity and pragmatism of the government with regards to economic development was the establishment of export processing zones. The first one was formed at the southern port of Kaohsiung in late 1966; two more were established near Taichung in 1970. They were the "first tax and duty free industrial processing zones" in Asia, set up to encourage exports and attract foreign investments. For the latter, the zones "provided smooth entry, established factory sites, cheap power and utilities, various tax concessions, preferential customs treatment, tariff protection against competition, guarantees against expropriation, easy access to ports, and other incentives."[20] Cheap labor, especially by a skilled female labor force, was one of the big draws that attracted such U.S. firms as General Electric and Singer Sewing Machine Company and such Japanese firms as Hitachi and Canon. Electronics and electrical machinery became the most important exports of these zones. Because of these zones, exports from 1960 to 1970 shot up from U.S.$174 million to U.S.$1.56 billion.

One other significant contextual element for Taiwan's meteoric economic rise was its emphasis on education, which tended to raise the quality of its workforce and the literacy of its citizenry. From 1952 to 1960, the number of colleges and universities rose from 4 to 15, secondary schools from 148 to 299, and primary schools from 1,248 to 1,982. The percentage of six-year-olds attending school increased from 57.9 percent in 1952 to 72.9 percent in 1960 to 85.3 percent in 1970. Between 1954 and 1968, 13 percent of Taiwan's budget was spent on education. In 1968, as further evidence of the government's ongoing commitment to education, compulsory school attendance was raised from six years to nine.

TABLE 16.1 Growth of the Net Domestic Market

	Agriculture (%)	Industry (%)
1952	35.9	18.0
1959	30.4	25.7
1970	19.2	32.5

The paths to the future for the two Chinas could not have been more different. They shared only one thing: the authoritarianism of their governments. The White Terror in the ROC and the Red Terror in the PRC under governments of what were essentially police states left no room for dissenters. But on the development road, Taiwan emphasized scientific and economic expertise, a literate and educated populace, land reform where landlords were reimbursed for the land they lost, openness to the international community for investment and trade, and a strong relationship to the United States, which helped reduce some of the military expenditures that otherwise would have slowed domestic economic development. In contrast, the PRC leadership stressed the innate moral power of the people (downplaying expertise), the power of ideology to shape human lives, the importance of struggle in moving forward, self-reliance (remaining relatively closed to the outside world), land reform that featured violence and the deaths of hundreds of thousands of people, and a relationship, rocky from the start, with the Soviet Union. Despite these differences, both the PRC (1949–1957) and the ROC (1949–1970) had made relatively good beginnings on the road to development. Unfortunately for the PRC, the situation would soon begin to go very, very bad.

Notes

1 Li Zhisui, *The Private Life of Chairman Mao* (New York: Random House, 1994), p. 52.

2 Kenneth Lieberthal, *Governing China* (New York: W.W. Norton, 1995), p. 51.

3 Ibid., p. 63.

4 Cited in Jerome Chen, *Mao and the Chinese Revolution* (London: Oxford University Press, 1965), p. 346. By permission of Oxford University Press. The reference to Tortoise and Snake Hills refers to Wuhan. Tortoise Hill in Hanyang and Snake Hill in Wuchang were joined by a bridge across the Yangzi. The cliff in the west refers to the coming building of the Three Gorges Dam.

5 Lieberthal, *Governing China*, p. 71.

6 Ibid., p. 74.

7 Ibid., p. 75.

8 Quoted in Edwin E. Moise, *Land Reform in China and North Vietnam* (Chapel Hill, NC: University of North Carolina Press, 1983), p. 106.

9 Pauline Keating, "The Yan'an Way of Co-operativization," *China Quarterly* 104 (December 1994): 1029–31.

10 Ding Ling, *The Sun Shines over the Sanggan River*, selection cited in *The Search for Modern China: A Documentary Collection*, ed. Pei-kai Cheng and Michael Lestz with Jonathan Spence (New York: W.W. Norton, 1999), pp. 369–71. Used by permission of W. W. Norton & Company.

11 The phrase is from Frederick C. Teiwes, "Establishment and Consolidation of the New Regime," in *The Cambridge History of China, Vol. 14, The People's Republic, Part 1: The Emergence of Revolutionary China, 1949–1965*, ed. Roderick MacFarquhar and John K. Fairbank (Cambridge, UK: Cambridge University Press, 1987), p. 87.

12 "The Marriage Law of the People's Republic of China, May 1, 1950," reprinted in J. Mason Gentzler, *Changing China* (New York: Praeger, 1977), p. 268.

13 Margery Wolf, *Revolution Postponed: Women in Contemporary China* (Stanford, CA: Stanford University Press, 1985), p. 18.

14 Neil Diamant, *Revolutionizing the Family: Politics, Love, and Divorce in Urban and Rural China, 1949–1968* (Berkeley, CA: University of California Press, 2000), pp. 317–27.

15 Quoted in Mineo Nakajima, "Foreign Relations: From the Korean War to the Bandung Line," in MacFarquhar and Fairbank, *The Cambridge History of China, Vol. 14, The People's Republic, Part 1: The Emergence of Revolutionary China, 1949–1965*, p. 275.

16 Teiwes, "Establishment and Consolidation," p. 110.

17 Peter Chen-main Wang, "A Bastion Created, a Regime Reformed, an Economy Reengineered, 1949–1970," in *Taiwan: A New History*, ed. Murray A. Rubinstein (Armonk, NY: M.E. Sharpe, 1999), p. 330.

18 Ibid., p. 335.

19 Gary Klintworth, *New Taiwan, New China: Taiwan's Changing Role in the Asia-Pacific Region* (New York: St. Martin's Press, 1995), p. 117.

20 Ibid., p. 123.

Suggestions for Further Reading

Chen Jian. *China's Road to War: The Making of the Sino–American Confrontation* (New York: Columbia University Press, 1994). This book reexamines the source of China's decision to go to war and finds several contributing ideological and practical factors, none of which includes a threat to its national security.

Diamant, Neil J. *Revolutionizing the Family: Politics, Love, and Divorce in Urban and Rural China, 1949–1968* (Berkeley, CA: University of California Press, 2000). This revisionist study, based on archival research, focuses on divorce as a way to understand more fully gender and ethnic relationships as well as urban–rural and state–society relations.

Ding Ling. *The Sun Shines over the Sanggan River*, trans. Yang Hsien-yi and Gladys Yang (Beijing: Foreign Languages Press, 1954). This Stalin Prize-winning novel focuses on land reform in North China.

Lieberthal, Kenneth. *Governing China: From Revolution through Reform* (New York: W.W. Norton, 1995). Rich in insight and detail, this is a comprehensive analysis of Communist China's government and politics.

Siu, Helen F. *Agents and Victims: Accomplices in Rural Revolution* (New Haven, CT: Yale University Press, 1989). This rich study puts the land reform campaign in historical context as it explores the relations between local elites and national power in Xinhui county, Guangdong province.

17

Coming Unglued

mid the considerable economic success it experienced in the first years of the 1950s stood two harbingers of the bad times ahead for the Communist leadership. Harbinger One was the purge in early 1954 of Gao Gang, Politburo member, head of the State Planning Commission, and key party-state-military figure in Manchuria; and of Rao Shushi, key party and state leader in Eastern China as well as head of the Central Committee's Organization Department. The reason: an apparent power play to replace Liu Shaoqi and Zhou Enlai among the top leadership. Although the dynamics here were apparently strictly politically personal, the episode was an indicator that the leadership at the top, a ruling coalition put together during the Yan'an years (and Gao had helped build the Shaan-Gan-Ning base), was not necessarily permanent. Factionalism, so much a part of the early CCP years, would rear its increasingly disruptive head in the years ahead.

Harbinger Two was the 1955 campaign against intellectual-author Hu Feng. A professional editor and writer, Hu had struggled since the 1930s with orthodox Communist literary critics who contended that politics and ideology, not artistic values, should dominate art and literature. Hu's position was that artistic standards and the autonomy of the artist were crucial. For orthodox Maoists, this position was anathema; the Yan'an legacy of party control of thought, art, and literature had to be maintained. Therefore, in mid-1955, the party launched a vitriolic nationwide campaign against Hu Feng and "Hu Fengism." Hu was arrested and imprisoned, and one of his closest disciples was committed to a mental hospital. The hysteria of the campaign further intimidated intellectuals, writers, and artists and even led to some suicides in these circles. The relationship between the state and its intellectuals, long demoralized and generally cowed into silence, deteriorated even further and set the stage for greater tragedies.

"LET A HUNDRED FLOWERS BLOOM!" (THEN CUT THEM DOWN)

In apparently sharp contrast to the anti-Hu Feng campaign, Mao and a rather reluctant party began to make overtures to those very intellectuals they had mired in alienation. Perhaps the motive was a keen awareness that the anti–Hu Feng campaign's excess had so browbeaten intellectuals that, if things continued as they were, they would never again contribute to or facilitate China's national progress. Perhaps the motive was a sense that developments under their leadership had gone so swimmingly that this was the opportune time for overtures to those intellectuals they had helped to alienate. Indeed, some historians detected by early 1956 what might be called a "relaxed moderation" in party-state policies regarding the outside world.

In foreign policy, the watchword—after war in Korea and assistance in the anti-French struggle in Vietnam—became "peaceful coexistence." It was a policy facilitated by Zhou Enlai, who emerged as foreign minister and who played an important role at the April 1955 meeting of the representatives of twenty-nine independent Asian and African states in Bandung, Indonesia. In what might be called the "Bandung line," Zhou argued, "What our nations in Africa and Asia need is ... to establish peaceful, cooperative relations with [developing] countries of other regions as well."[1] Zhou's leadership in Bandung helped pave the way for his successful tour of Asian countries a year and a half later and for visits of Asian leaders to Beijing. It was this moderate policy that allowed the beginning of ambassadorial talks with U.S. diplomats, first in Geneva in late 1955, then later in Warsaw. Beijing's stature in the Communist world was also raised by the general loss of face the Soviet Union experienced in that world from Premier Nikita Khrushchev's criticism of Stalin (dead in 1953) and from the Soviet Union's invasion of Hungary in October 1956.

The international initiatives perhaps raised the confidence of the leadership that they could deal constructively with Chinese intellectuals. In a policy first set forth by Zhou Enlai in January 1956, confirmed by Mao in May, and announced in late May by Lu Dingyi, director of the Propaganda Department of the Central Committee, the party called for the input, suggestions, and reactions of intellectuals to current conditions in state and society. Lu said:

> If we want our country to be prosperous and strong, we must, besides consolidating the people's state power, developing our economy and education and strengthening our national defense, have a flourishing art, literature, and science. That is essential. Let a hundred flowers bloom; let a hundred schools of thought contend."[2]

Perhaps what was most striking in Lu's speech, which on its face seemed to be a call for tolerance, or at least openness, was the frequent intimations of Mao's restrictions on art and literature presented at the 1942 Yan'an forum. One wonders how many of the hundred flowers heard these lines?

> [I]n the case of art and literature ... we can see things that are obviously pernicious. The stuff written by Hu Feng is one such example. Pornographic and gutter literature that debauches people and turns them into gangsters is another. Still another example is the so-called literature summed up in phrases like "let's play mah-jongg and to hell with state affairs" and "the moon in America is rounder than the moon in China," etc. It is perfectly right and proper for us to look on literature of this pernicious kind as a par with flies, mosquitoes, rats, and sparrows and rid ourselves of it all.[3]

It is probably not surprising that writers at first hesitated to speak out after the calls for blooming and contending. Scientists and engineers first came forward with calls for less interference in their work by generally ignorant party cadres, for fewer time-consuming political sessions, and for more accessibility to Western as opposed to Soviet publications. When writers, many of them members of the May Fourth generation of intellectuals, did begin to speak out, their criticisms were leveled against party and bureaucratic dogmatism and against areas where the party had failed to live up to its principles. There was obviously immense dissatisfaction with an increasingly bureaucratized party-state.

Two journals, *People's Literature* and *Literary Studies*, became the vehicles for critiques by intellectuals. They published short stories by the journalist Liu Binyan, who wrote of the discrepancy between Communist ideals and PRC reality. In the fall of 1956, a new literary voice, Wang Meng, published a short novel, *The Young Man Who Has Just Arrived at the Organization Department*, which pointed to the unresponsive and arbitrary nature of party leaders. But on the whole, though there were sporadic criticisms of the party-state, the campaign seemed in late 1956 and early 1957 quite moribund. Intellectuals were still somewhat afraid to put themselves on the line, and party leaders seemed uncertain about whether they wanted this campaign and how to handle the criticism they received.

Then, in February 1957, Mao tried to breathe new life into the effort, seeming to praise those who had criticized the bureaucracy; the goal was to achieve greater unity to meet the challenges ahead. For five weeks in May and June the flowers bloomed, intellectuals apparently convinced that the Yan'an restrictiveness had been lifted. Criticisms of basic party policy and of the party itself were brutally frank. Moreover, the criticism spread quickly to other groups, including farmers and urban workers. By mid-May, students on campuses around the country were putting up critical wall posters. At Beijing University they were attached to what became known as the Democracy Wall. The criticism was sharp. Lines from a poster at Qinghua University in Beijing read:

What does it mean when the Communists say ... they let the people enjoy things before they do the same? ... In Yan'an was Chairman Mao, who had two dishes plus soup for every meal, having a hard time? Were the peasants who had nothing to eat but bitter vegetables, enjoying the good life? Everyone was told that Chairman Mao was leading a hard and simple life. That son of a bitch! A million shames on him! ... Our pens can never defeat Mao Zedong's Party guards and his imperial army. When he wants to kill you, he doesn't have to do it himself. He can mobilize your wife and children to denounce you and then kill you with their own hands! Is this a rational society? This is class struggle, Mao Zedong style! This is the spiritual side of our age.[4]

By June 8 the party moved to tear out the blooming flowers by their roots, stopping the movement it had started. Noisily proclaiming a nationwide "anti-Communist plot," it announced a campaign against "rightists." This was a bitter harvest for intellectuals and artists. The execution of the campaign was itself an object lesson in party arbitrariness: a statement by the party center that at least 5 percent of the leaders in any area were likely rightists was taken to mean that local party branches had to find a quota of 5 percent who would be so tagged. Many were attacked; sometimes the primary objective of denouncers was to take the positions of those they denounced. Within the next few months, between 400,000 and 700,000 intellectuals lost careers and titles and were jailed, sent to labor camps, or to do heavy labor in the countryside. Some committed suicide. Most were not rehabilitated until 1979, many of them posthumously. These experiences—ostracism, imprisonment, forced labor, and exile—made it less and less likely that creators would want to create. It is not surprising that in the following Great Leap Forward period, the published literature hewed to the political line. Common themes of stories and poems were the bad old days and the wonderful present, Joe Peasant learning the value of cooperation with his fellow peasants, and utilizing wartime fervor for carrying out party-state policies. Mao in a real sense had burned his bridges to China's intellectuals, in effect discarding them as of no use in the development of a modern socialist China; the chasm between the party and intellectuals was both deep and gaping.

FIGURE 17.1 This is an object lesson in revising history. In the photograph on the right, Peng Zhen, who is holding a shovel with Mao on the left, has been airbrushed out of the 1958 photograph. This revision was done when Peng lost his official position in 1966.

Sources: left: China Photo Service/Sovfoto; right: Sovfoto/UIG via Getty Images.

THE GREAT LEAP FORWARD (AND BACKWARD)

Mao's disdain for the intellectual elites pointed all the more to his infatuation with people power, specifically the power of the mobilized masses to remake China. A mobilized populace was the key both to leaping over the mistakes that other developing states had made and leaping forward into the developed future. We have seen that by late 1956 almost 90 percent of the rural populace were members (some quite unwillingly) of higher-level APCs. The relative ease with which this had been accomplished gave PRC leaders—especially Mao—a sense that collectivization could now be carried to its logical conclusion. Attempting to turn what was a fairly consistent twentieth-century "great leap" mindset into a reality, in 1958 the party launched the Great Leap Forward, a utopian campaign, part of which was to establish communes on which Chinese life and labor would be militarized. A Politburo resolution in August 1958 called the people's communes "the basic social units of Communist society" and called for "actively us[ing] the form of people's communes to explore the practical ... transition to communism."[5] Mao and the party-state hierarchy assumed that larger agricultural production units would bring more efficiency and productivity. The commune on average was made up of about 5,500 households—approximately twenty-five times bigger than the higher-level APC. It became the locality's main governmental unit and socioeconomic organization, charged with agricultural production; the development and fostering of industry and commerce; the provision of health care, police and social services, and education; and the collection of taxes. With astonishing speed, by the end of December 1958, 99.1 percent of all rural families had become members of communes. On communes, private garden plots and private ownership of livestock were forbidden; the number of rural periodic markets where peasants had in the past sold vegetables, eggs, and perhaps pigs was consequently cut back. Authorities adopted a Communist distribution system whereby earnings were paid on a per capita basis—not on the basis of labor contributions. Thus, differences between incomes on communes were greatly reduced.

Perhaps two commune structures best epitomized the Great Leap: the backyard steel furnace and the commune mess hall. Rooted in Mao's idealistic populism was the sense that if the people had a participatory stake in production, their energies would be released and production would increase dramatically. Although industry had generally not been located in the countryside,

FIGURE 17.2 It is easy to understand how backyard smelters in the Great Leap Forward brought deforestation. With so many located in areas all over China, the task of finding fuel to keep fires hot enough was immense—all in the end, a futile and disastrously wasteful effort.
Source: Sovfoto/UIG via Getty Images.

Mao believed that communes should develop local industries in which people could participate and thereby contribute their productive capacities.

Steel-making was one such area. Communes built their own steel furnaces—at least 1 million dotted the Chinese landscape. Fueling them led to large-scale deforestation; any wood, including that of used coffins, was gathered to stoke the flames to keep them as hot as possible. All over China, furnace fires studded the black nights. For the cause, people contributed iron tools and implements, window frames, pots and pans—all to go into the making of pig iron. But because the manufacturing techniques were faulty, what was produced cracked easily. Useful iron implements, tools, and utensils, in many cases necessary for daily tasks, had been turned into something totally useless. Not only that, but in its useless state, this material filled railroad car after railroad car, which then clogged train yards and snarled train traffic throughout the country. In terms of economic development, it was ridiculous: the expense of setting up the furnaces and the use of huge numbers of people to operate them surpassed by far any contribution to China's steel industry. Yet the primary and ultimate goal was political: to marshal the people's energy and give them a stake in the making of the new China. For example, there is this view of steel making in Hunan province:

> Iron and steel production is not simply a technical job; it is also a political task that has an important bearing on all other activities. ... [After the introduction of the idea of commune steel making], more than half a million written pledges were sent to the party [in the Shaoyang region] in support of the campaign. The people felt elated and stimulated; millions of hearts had only one wish—to fight hard to achieve and surpass the goal of producing 300,000 tons of iron in 1958. ... The people composed a song describing [the construction of large numbers of furnaces]:
>
> The Communist Party is really wonderful.
> In three days, more than a thousand furnaces were built.

The masses' strength is really tremendous.
The American imperialists will run off, tails between legs.
The Chinese people will now surpass Britain.
The East wind will always prevail over the West wind.[6]

Perhaps no change made a starker difference in people's daily lives than commune mess halls. A traditional centerpiece of farm life—the daily coming together of the family for shared meals—was now gone. Though not meant to be a direct blow to family cohesion, it probably undermined to a degree the closeness of the family unit. From the standpoint of agricultural production, mess halls "meant that each commune member had three extra hours for work or study, labor productivity had been raised by about 30 percent, and six million units of female labor power had been released from domestic chores."[7] The construction of mess halls was a major undertaking. In the average-sized county of Xiaoshan in Zhejiang province, 2,726 mess halls were constructed between 1958 and 1962. In a zero-sum situation, massive mess hall construction meant massive deforestation.

Other commune institutions such as nurseries and kindergartens also tended to erode familial cohesion. Grandparents, freed from the responsibility of babysitting their grandchildren, could spend their time at "happiness homes" for the elderly. Some children boarded at primary schools and even kindergartens away from home, thus removing them from their parents' control at an early age. The state thus impinged far more deeply on people's lives than ever before, for the first time ever penetrating directly into family life by beginning to replace traditional family practices with governmental services.

From one viewpoint, these revolutionary changes advanced the social and economic position of women. Changes in commune living freed women from the daily responsibilities of cooking and child care; now they were available to labor on the land with the men, a reality that helped equalize the status of men and women. More significant, for the first time rural women achieved their own economic identity; an estimated 90 percent performed farm labor in 1958 and 1959. From another perspective, however, this shift simply redefined women primarily as workers who labored with men outside the home. The sense of the CCP was that *proper* women served the state, not simply the family. This policy perpetuated the Yan'an period's talk of the "national woman," identified as a new unit for purposes of the party-state, but certainly not for purposes of gender equity.[8]

Life in the people's communes also saw the culmination of the militarization of Chinese society, a trend that had been gradually developing since the first years of the twentieth century. The commune workforce was organized into military units named "brigades" (sometimes "companies") and was further divided into "production teams" or "platoons." Overseeing brigades were management districts, usually denoted as "battalions." The use of military terminology points to the militarization of labor even as it suggests the degree of regimentation imposed on the people by the party-state. In some areas at least, the military ethos was conveyed by the rhetoric of competition in the massive production campaigns. Cadres in one Guangdong commune, for example, asserted that in their competition with other areas, "Our soldiers and horses are strong, our generals brave and numerous. ... Clad in our armor and ready in our formations, we await the battle cry."[9] Peasants were referred to as "fighters" on the "agricultural front"; the countryside became the "battlefield"; and nature itself became an "enemy" to be overcome.[10]

The establishment of the commune militia further enhanced militarization on the commune. Able-bodied citizens between the ages of fifteen and fifty were in the ordinary militia, and sixteen- to thirty-year-olds were in the so-called hard-core militia. By January 1959, 220 million men and women were serving as militia members. Most members of the hard-core militia never fired a gun, but they trained two to three hours each day and were thus "psychologically mobilized." Militia members were required to adhere to "rising, eating, sleeping, setting out to work, and returning from work" at the same times: such "togetherness" strengthened one's sense of identity with the collective and spurred group discipline.

In some areas, the Great Leap Forward was marked by the massive mobilization of labor for water control and irrigation projects undertaken with the goal of increasing agricultural production. Upward of a million workers might be mobilized for a particular project: images of Chinese workers as countless numbers of "blue ants" were conjured up in the Communist-paranoid and racist West. By early 1958, some 100 million peasants had worked on projects that enabled over 19 million acres to be irrigated for the first time. In Xiaoshan county, Zhejiang, for a specific example, from February to May 1952, 840,000 workers from six counties widened a river southeast of the provincial capital of Hangzhou.

Despite the ability of the authorities to mobilize hundreds of thousands of workers on worthwhile public projects, it was clear by the end of 1958 that the Great Leap had fallen flat on its face. The utter failure of the steel-making experiment and its ripple effect on the economy at large were compounded by a deepening agricultural tragedy. Though the 1958 harvest was dismal, grain production estimates had been extremely overinflated. In large measure, such exaggeration of production grew directly out of the dynamics of the Great Leap campaign; the battle rhetoric often associated with the competition between communes to produce more than others created a mentality that the sky was the limit in terms of production. Inflated statistics were passed up the chain of command and inflated even more; more crucial, few attempts, if any, were made to verify the validity of the reports. In August 1958 projections had posited a minimal harvest of 240 million metric tons of grain, with a maximum perhaps up to 300 million tons. But by December the reported harvest had soared, according to the party, to 375 million metric tons—double the harvest of 1957 and clearly an impossibility. And yet the State Statistical Bureau confirmed that figure in the spring of 1959. The figures were very satisfying to Mao because they confirmed his own assessment of the production benefits of the commune system.

The tragic problem developed when the taxes assessed by the state, collected in the form of grain, were based on the estimates of the harvest. Since the estimates were so high compared to how much was really produced, the state ended up taking most of the grain that was produced. The upshot was that little grain was left for the masses. People in the countryside were beginning to go hungry. The situation was compounded by widespread mismanagement of communes that had been so hastily put together that there was insufficient time for effective organization. Some crops were not harvested, or harvested incompletely, or harvested too late because too many people had been assigned to backyard steel furnaces or had left for cities. Party leaders touring the provinces in the fall saw evidence of serious problems. Even Mao saw that communization, as it had been attempted, was going too far too fast, and that adjustments in the Great Leap had to come. For example, the steel production goal for 1959 had been set at 30 million tons, a nearly 600 percent increase over 1957—clearly another impossibility. Mao, in his infinite irrationality, wanted the goal to be dropped to 20 million tons so that the increase would be only about 400 percent! Some leaders, fearful that a disaster might be approaching, compelled Mao to relinquish the post of president of the PRC to Liu Shaoqi at a party central committee meeting in December 1958.

At first glance, studying the decision making of the Chinese leadership during the Great Leap causes one to ask whether they had all taken leave of their senses. Projections of and reports on harvests all had little relation to reality. For example, on the basis of the reported huge

1958 harvests, leaders decided that since so much grain had allegedly been produced, the amount of land to be sown in grain in 1959 should be reduced, with more land devoted to cotton and non-grain crops. Thus, in 1959, with a worsening problem of insufficient grain in the country as a whole, government decisions made almost certain that the grain harvest would fall by at least another 25 million metric tons. Further, some areas experienced the failure or malfunctioning of water control and irrigation projects that had been constructed so rapidly by so many workers that the work could not possibly have been overseen properly; especially in North China, these flawed projects harmed rather than helped production.

The answer to what was going on was not, of course, that people had lost their senses. Instead, people, including those in leadership circles, were paranoid about questioning the Maoist "line" even when that line made no sense. Comrade Li asked whether production projections are too high. Reaction: He must be a rightist! Mr. Zhang questioned the validity of impossibly high harvest reports. He is surely a class enemy! Comrade Shen asked whether water projects carried out so swiftly and constructed with untrained workers would function properly. He dares to question the will and power of the people? He is obviously a counterrevolutionary! In other words, building on a series of political campaigns and terror related to those campaigns, Mao had created an ongoing situation that saw honest questioning and honest disagreement as evidence that questioners and those who disagreed were the enemy, traitors to the revolution. Only Mao understood and could properly interpret what was revolutionary and what was not. Even before the formal Mao cult of the 1960s developed, Mao had so traumatized the Chinese polity that few people would even dare to raise questions about his positions.

The Lushan Conference

In July 1959, in a month-long conference of Chinese leaders at the resort of Lushan in Jiangxi province, rancor over the Great Leap began to tear apart the "political consensus" of the leadership group that had formed at Yan'an.[11] Called "one of the most fateful in the history of the PRC," this meeting set the stage for the national tragedy of the so-called Cultural Revolution that would dominate the 1960s and 1970s.[12] The major clash pitted Mao against his defense minister, Peng Dehuai. Undoubtedly, personal issues and motives, such as ambition, animus, and jealousy, were involved in this confrontation. But the policy issues were crucial. In a letter to Mao that the chairman made public, Peng charged that the Leap was not working, that the huge grain harvest figures were not credible, and that he was concerned about the direction of policies. In an earlier writing he had set forth concerns. Because too many of the male population, especially the young, strong, and stalwart, had gone off to stoke the first of the communes' iron-smelting projects, the important and essential harvest of grain and vegetables had been left in the hands of women (many of them old) and children. Because of their inexperience and lack of stamina, much grain and many vegetables simply did not get harvested. Peng wondered how with no (or insufficient) food people were going to be able to survive. But he vowed to become an advocate for the people's interests.[13]

On July 23, in response to Peng's criticism, Mao went for the jugular. He was visibly agitated. "Now that you have said so much, let me say something, will you? I have taken sleeping-pills three times, but I can't get to sleep." He then proceeded to attack Peng for going beyond the pale of permissible criticism. Peng's position amounted to what Mao called his "right opportunism." There it was: Peng was a counterrevolutionary rightist! Only one leader at the meeting, attended by luminaries such as Liu Shaoqi and Zhou Enlai, stood up for Peng and obliquely challenged Mao. That was Zhu De, founder of the Red Army in the late 1920s and chess partner of Peng. But no one followed up, and for his audacity Zhu had to write his own self-criticism. But Mao was not finished: he accused Peng of complaining to Khrushchev about Great Leap policies on a June trip to Warsaw Pact countries. He made that accusation based on Khrushchev's July 18 open criticism of the Chinese communes and Great Leap policies in a speech in Eastern Europe. Then Mao made a threat. If criticisms continued, "I will go to the countryside to lead the peasants to overthrow the government. If those of you in the Liberation Army won't follow me, then I will go and find a Red Army, and organize another Liberation Army."[14] After this confrontation, Peng, the heroic Chinese commander during the Korean War, was dismissed at a September meeting of the Enlarged Military Affairs Committee. Lin Biao, a strong supporter of Mao, was named new defense minister.

There were other, more long-lasting consequences of the Lushan showdown. Mao had poisoned the air among China's leaders. Labeling Peng's critique an "unprincipled factional activity," Mao made it less likely than ever for oppositional viewpoints to be taken as anything but treachery and, worse, counterrevolutionary activity. How could free discussion ever occur again among the handful of decision makers in the Politburo? More tragic for the nation, the confrontation seemed to make Mao more obstinate in supporting and even expanding the Great Leap. Before Lushan, Mao, both in late 1958 and early 1959, had spoken of slowing down the Leap and adjusting policies to fit changing circumstances. But after Lushan, as if in a defensive response to criticism, Mao's attitude changed to one of full steam ahead. In early 1960 Mao led the charge for a new Great Leap, advocating establishing urban communes, sending party cadres to the countryside to learn from the peasants, and maintaining the impossible agricultural goals and the far too high tax levies. As another indication of Mao's turn further to the left was his support of a revised "constitution" for the major Manchurian Anshan Iron and Steel Works that would do away with the management approach modeled on the Soviet system and replace it with one emphasizing political orthodoxy and correctness.

This second Great Leap failed spectacularly. Output of heavy industry in 1961 dropped precipitously by about 47 percent compared to 1960, and in 1962 it dropped another 22 percent. Light industry production in 1960 fell about 10 percent from 1959, another 22 percent in 1961, and another 8 percent or more in 1962. But it was in agriculture that the bottom fell out and helped produce one of the world's worst twentieth-century tragedies. Grain output had been at 200 million tons in 1958; it dropped to 170 million tons in 1959 and to 144 million in 1960—a 28 percent decline from two years earlier.

THE WORST FAMINE IN HISTORY

The crisis of declining grain harvests was exacerbated in 1960 by natural disasters. Typhoons caused devastating flooding in parts of South China and in Manchuria; drought was so severe along the Yellow River that its water level was decreased by two-thirds; insect pests affected vast areas. Over 60 percent of farmed land was affected, resulting in paltry harvests. The depth of the tragedy is revealed by the fact that per capita food production would not reach its pre-1957 level until the early 1970s.

Rural areas were more affected than cities, though all suffered. Overall Chinese mortality rates, averaging 11.1 per thousand in 1956 and 1957, climbed to 14.6 per thousand in 1959 and shot up to 25.4 per thousand in 1960. Some regions suffered more than others. Table 17.1 shows the number of deaths in particularly hard-hit provinces, using 1957 as the pre-famine baseline.[15]

Best estimates are that 30 million people died because of the famine, which was worsened by nature but stemmed basically from human policies that bordered on sheer lunacy. Such statistics

TABLE 17.1 Numbers of Deaths in Particular Provinces, 1957 and 1960

Province	1957	1960
Anhui	c. 250,000	2,200,000
Gansu	142,041	538,479
Guangxi	261,785	644,700
Henan	572,000	1,908,000
Hubei	290,600	670,300
Hunan	370,059	1,068,118
Jiangsu	424,500	785,900

can only suggest the nightmare of these years for the masses. People were not allowed to become refugees and move to other areas in search of food. Most knew only what was happening in their areas and did not know the extent of the famine. Starving people ate rice husks, corncobs, weeds, grass, tree bark, even earth itself in an effort to remain alive. The situation was so severe in Anhui province that in at least one county "boiled water was a luxury because fuel was scarce"—until as late as 1969![16] Malnutrition was rampant.

In Chengdu [the capital of Sichuan province], the monthly food ration was reduced to 19 pounds of rice, a third of an ounce of cooking oil, and 3.5 ounces of meat when there was any. Scarcely anything else was available, not even cabbage. Many people were afflicted by edema, a condition in which fluid accumulates under the skin because of malnutrition. The patient turns yellow and swells up. The most popular remedy was eating chlorella, which was supposed to be rich in protein. Chlorella fed on human urine, so people stopped going to the toilet and peed into spittoons instead, then dropped the chlorella seed in; they grew into something looking like green fish roe in a couple of days, and were scooped out of the urine, washed, and cooked with rice. They were truly disgusting to eat, but did reduce the swelling.[17] It is little wonder that the per capita consumption of food items in these years fell to shockingly low levels, as Table 17.2 shows.[18]

Even in provinces like Hebei, where the famine was less severe, social problems stemming from the tragic conditions abounded. Wives were sold. Wives left their families and, in a survival strategy, started living with better-off men. The number of divorces shot up. Bandits attacked trains and grain storage facilities. And as with the great Henan famine during World War II and other famines in the Chinese past, cannibalism reared its ugly head. A Sichuan official reported that

> one day a peasant burst into his room and threw himself on the floor, screaming that he had committed a terrible crime and begging to be punished. Eventually it came out that he had killed his own baby and eaten it. … With tears rolling down his cheeks, the official ordered the peasant to be arrested. Later he was shot as a warning to baby killers.[19]

But there were greater criminals. Though it is said that Mao *even* denied himself meat for seven months in 1960, he was not in the least contrite for his role in the catastrophe. In early 1961, he denied categorically to future French President François Mitterand that there was any famine at all in the country. The truth, as a Chinese economist noted, was that "the Great Leap exacted a 'high price in blood.'"[20]

Just as scandalous as leading the country into such a state was the fact that the government did very little to respond to the crisis, called by one scholar "the most severe challenge the Party had faced since coming to power in 1949."[21] The party seemed paralyzed. The state gave out almost

TABLE 17.2   Per Capita Consumption of Major Food Items, 1957 and 1960

(in catties, with a catty approximately equivalent to a pound)		
	1957	1960
Grain	406.0	327.0
Urban	392.0	385.0
Rural	409.0	312.0
Vegetable oil	4.8	3.7
Urban	10.3	7.1
Rural	3.7	2.9
Pork	10.2	3.1
Urban	18.0	5.4
Rural	8.7	2.4

no relief funds. From 1958 to 1962, years that included the height of the famine, relief for rural areas totaled about 450 million yuan per year—or about 0.8 yuan per person on the communes. This was at a time when a kilogram of rice cost between 2 and 4 yuan! In 1960 bandages were applied to try to stanch the massive bleeding: the assessed tax was scaled back slightly, grain exports were cut back, and wheat imports were arranged—though mainly for urban consumption. If this had been imperial China, people would certainly have been asserting that the Mandate of Heaven was sliding away from the regime in power.

THE SINO–SOVIET SPLIT

Even though Mao had risen to power more in opposition to Moscow than with its support, Mao and the Communist leadership had decided in the first months of the PRC to lean to the side of the Soviet Union in foreign relations. The Sino–Soviet security treaty of 1950 and the presence of thousands of Soviet technical and industrial advisers coming to assist in the Soviet-modeled First Five-Year Plan underscored this foreign policy choice. China continued to see the United States as the chief imperialist power in the world, and the reality was that the Soviet Union was the sole Chinese shield against any possible U.S. nuclear missile attack. That uncomfortable reality hit home in 1957, when the United States announced that it would be sending Taiwan Matador missiles that were capable of carrying nuclear warheads. In light of such a threat, that fall, when Mao traveled to Moscow for the fortieth anniversary celebration of the Bolshevik Revolution, Khrushchev promised Mao "a sample of an atomic bomb" and the information needed to complete its manufacture. In 1958 and 1959, the Soviet Union did help China develop, among other nuclear-related facilities, uranium mines and a nuclear testing site. China thus looked to the Soviet Union for protection, guidance, training, and aid.

But even so, from the beginning, this had not been the rosiest of relationships. Stalin had been downright rude to Mao when he had traveled to Moscow in early 1950. One might have thought, given the rocky relationship between Mao and Stalin since the late 1920s, that Mao would have taken a certain glee over Khrushchev's de-Stalinization campaign in 1956. But instead, for the Chinese leadership, the Soviet premier's criticism of Stalin stirred up considerable consternation about what the campaign meant in terms of trends in the Soviet Union and the leadership situation in China.

Then came the Great Leap. In it the Chinese had chosen to break with the Soviet model that it had adopted so thoroughly earlier in the decade. The bad blood that became evident developed in different arenas, including practical policy and ideology. From the Soviet perspective, they had spent much and given huge amounts of development aid and assistance to the Chinese; they had tutored the Chinese in their technocratic model of development; they had done what they could to help protect and nurture Chinese progress. To witness the Chinese embark now on the radically different developmental route of mass mobilization was upsetting, especially because things in China seemed to be going so drastically wrong. Furthermore, the Soviet Union saw itself as the world's Communist leader and the patron for developing Communist states. The Chinese actions were like a slap in the face. From the perspective of the Soviet Union, Khrushchev's criticism in the summer of 1959 was understandable. From the Chinese perspective, it was unjustifiable intervention in China's domestic affairs.

The Taiwan Strait Crisis

There were other sources of the uneasy, almost queasy relationship between the Soviet Union and China. Most came from the reality that the two countries had their own national perspectives in mind and their own national interests to protect and nurture; two Communist states they were, but when national push came to national shove, ideology played a markedly subsidiary role. Mao and the Chinese leadership were often put off by what they considered Khrushchev's weakness in the face of the actions of Western states. In 1956, he had announced that the policy of the Soviet Union was "peaceful coexistence" with the non-Communist world.

The summer of 1958 presented several object lessons in this regard. When a pro-Western regime in Iraq was overthrown, the United States sent forces to Lebanon and Great Britain sent forces to Jordan to prop up those Western-leaning regimes. Khrushchev did not respond strongly, insisting on trying to work out the issues diplomatically. The Chinese considered him overly cautious. As a sign of Mao's displeasure with and disdain for the Soviet premier's action, when Khrushchev flew to Beijing for a summit with Mao (July 31 to August 3), Mao greeted him in not very diplomatically correct circumstances—at a swimming pool, where "the two leaders [sunned] themselves on their towels 'like seals on the warm sand.'"[22] At this meeting, Mao was offended by three requests from Khrushchev that had military overtones: that the Soviet Union be allowed to build a radio station on Chinese territory to be able to communicate with Soviet submarines in the Pacific; that Soviet submarines be allowed to refuel at Chinese ports and that their crews be allowed short leaves at the ports; and that for China's protection the Soviets be allowed to station interceptor planes in China. Mao considered them all encroachments on Chinese sovereignty. The meeting ended without Mao telling Khrushchev that he had plans up his sleeve to try to change the current stalemate with Taiwan through the use of force, an action that would challenge the United States.

The United States, as we saw in the previous chapter, quickly became a close supporter of the Taipei regime. In mid-1954 Beijing declared that it was about to "liberate" Taiwan. In September the PRC began to bombard two small islands very close to the coast but still held by the Nationalists on Taiwan—Quemoy, off the coast at Amoy, and Matsu, near Fuzhou. In December the United States and Taiwan, in a clear response to Beijing's challenge, signed a mutual security treaty. In 1955, with hardly any dissent in the U.S. Congress (the vote in the Senate was 83–3; in the House, 410–3), President Dwight Eisenhower was given the authorization to use American combat forces to defend Taiwan and the islands it controlled in the Taiwan Strait. Step by step, the United States was being drawn militarily into the Chinese civil war. The Eisenhower administration opted to take such a stance as a clear symbol of its ability to be tough in the face of Communist threats. Vice-President Richard Nixon laid it on the line, demonstrating the U.S. belief at the time that there was a monolithic Communist threat endangering the world:

> If we let them know that we will defend freedom when the stakes are small, the Soviets are not encouraged to threaten freedom where the stakes are higher ... that is why the two small islands ... are so important in the poker game of world politics."[23]

China, without assurance of Soviet support, pulled back and agreed to the ambassadorial talks that began with the United States in 1955. These talks, however, came to a sudden end in December 1957 as relations between the two countries deteriorated.

On August 23, 1958, the PRC launched a massive bombardment of Quemoy less than three weeks after the Mao–Khrushchev summit. At least one scholar thinks that among Mao's motives was to show Khrushchev that if a nation stood up to the United States, the United States would back down. But Mao clearly miscalculated the U.S. response, which was quick and extensive. President Eisenhower ordered the U.S. Seventh Fleet to convoy Nationalist supply ships to the island and for U.S. planes to airlift Nationalist troops to the island, announcing in a World War II mentality that to abandon the offshore islands would be a "Western Pacific Munich." It was not until September 5 that Soviet Foreign Minister Andrei Gromyko made it to Beijing for consultations; Soviet support for the PRC's position did not come until September 7, fully fifteen days after the crisis had begun. The day before, Zhou Enlai had called on the United States to reopen the ambassadorial-level talks that had been halted nine months earlier. The U.S. government suggested to the PRC that "mutual de-escalation" would be best for all concerned. Beijing responded by stopping the shelling for a week; and when they resumed it, they shelled the island only on even-numbered days.

The best evidence suggests that the PRC was trying to force a Nationalist withdrawal from the island, not that this was preliminary to an invasion. Whatever the case, the episode was a disaster for Sino–Soviet relations. Khrushchev was bitter that he had not been informed of Mao's plans; under the 1950 security treaty, Mao had that obligation. More important, Mao's actions might have precipitated a war between China and the United States into which the Soviet Union would have been pulled—at a time when it was trying to maneuver its own summit with the United States. By late 1959, in the eyes of Moscow, in initiating the Taiwan Strait crisis and undertaking the Great Leap Forward, Mao had been guilty of huge miscalculations; indeed, the "magnitude of miscalculation in both instances suggested megalomania."[24] As a direct result of the Taiwan Strait crisis, Khrushchev decided to cancel the nuclear weapons technology offer that he had made to Mao in the fall of 1957 in Moscow—a cancellation that in turn embittered Mao and the Chinese government.

China in Tibet

China's relationship with the Soviet Union was also affected by Chinese actions in Tibet, specifically as they related to India. To understand the situation, a brief look at China's history in Tibet is important. The protectorate that China had established over Tibet in the eighteenth century remained into the twentieth century. By the late nineteenth century, however, given the weight of China's domestic and foreign-related burdens, Chinese hegemony over Tibet remained in theory but in actuality was a dead letter. In the 1880s and 1890s Great Britain, strongly entrenched on the Indian subcontinent and intent on seizing small principalities in the Himalayas, was beginning to knock on Tibet's door. In 1893, the British got trading rights at a post just inside the Tibetan border with the stipulation that a British official could be stationed there to oversee the trade. When the Tibetan religious and political leader, the Dalai Lama, refused to answer British requests for the further opening up of relations, the British invaded to force negotiations. In August 1904, British troops led by the British viceroy in India, Lord Curzon, seized the Tibetan capital, Lhasa. In the Anglo–Tibet convention of 1904, Britain opened up three Tibetan towns for trading, levied a huge indemnity, and sent forces to occupy Tibetan territory contiguous to Sikkim (which Britain held) until the indemnity could be paid. In a real sense, the British were making Tibet their protectorate. China had not been a party to the convention; its Manchu official in Lhasa had refused to participate.

The situation was complicated by the fact that the British government had not given Curzon orders to invade Tibet. They were aware of the historical relationship between China and Tibet and also did not want to have the Tibetan situation damage their relationship with China. Therefore, in 1906, the Anglo–Chinese convention modified the 1904 convention by recognizing "China's legitimate authority over its dependency Tibet."[25] British actions in Tibet were a wake-up call for the Chinese, who, though they could hardly afford to act as they were inching toward revolution, decided that they had to act more aggressively in their Tibetan protectorate. In 1910, Chinese troops entered Lhasa, deposed the Dalai Lama (a practice begun already in the eighteenth century), and moved to take more direct control of day-to-day rule. But then the Qing dynasty was overthrown in 1912. Given the political and military weakness of the early Republic, the Dalai Lama, in exile in India, returned to Lhasa in 1913 and ruled until his death in 1933. British efforts to resolve the question of Tibet's political status at a conference in Simla, India, in 1913–1914 ended in fuzziness: Tibet, the Simla Convention said, would maintain its autonomy from China, but it would also have to recognize Chinese suzerainty. All Chinese leaders from Sun Yat-sen to Chiang Kai-shek to Mao Zedong claimed that Tibet was part of the Chinese nation. Even though Chiang Kai-shek's regime did not control the government in Lhasa, it still interfered in Tibetan affairs—in 1937, for example, throwing its support behind a young boy as the tenth Panchen Lama, the second in authority after the Dalai Lama.

By the time that the PRC was established in 1949, India had been independent from Britain for two years, and Britain no longer had a particular interest in Tibet's political status. Thus, in 1950, when it seemed as if the PRC would move to establish direct control, Great Britain and the United States, when contacted by Lhasa, did not respond with any support. Though the Chinese government tried to negotiate a "peaceful liberation," the Tibetan government put them off. As a consequence, in October 1950, PLA forces invaded Tibet and quickly captured the weak Tibetan army. Tibetan appeals to the UN were turned aside mainly at the urging of India, which was backed by Great Britain. Tibet had no choice but to negotiate with Beijing; an agreement, the "Seventeen-Point Agreement for the Peaceful Liberation of Tibet," was signed in May 1951. Point One states in no uncertain terms: "the Tibet people shall return to the big family of the Motherland—the People's Republic of China."[26] In this formal agreement, Tibet thus recognized China's sovereignty—in exchange for which China agreed to maintain the traditional political and economic system, including the Dalai Lama. The Dalai Lama telegraphed Mao his acceptance of the arrangement in October 1951.

Scholars point out that the period 1951 to 1959 saw a moderate Chinese policy in Tibet. Mao's policy was one of gradual change, believing that the cooperation of the Dalai Lama was the key. Mao's "Tibet strategy sought to create cordial relations between Han (ethnic Chinese) and Tibetans, and allay Tibetan anxieties so that Tibet's elite would over time genuinely accept 'reintegration' with China and agree to a social transformation."[27] The Indian representative in Lhasa noted indeed that there is everywhere a keenness to imitate the Chinese ... and this is particularly noticeable among the respectable bunch of official families in Lhasa. ... The inroad of neo-Chinese culture into Tibetan society ... is truly remarkable for what was static in this land has become alive and dynamic. There is not a home in Lhasa where portraits of Mao and his colleagues have not found a place in the domestic shrine.[28]

But by the mid-1950s, things had begun to deteriorate. Although Mao had been willing in Tibet to slow the social revolution that was remaking China, others in the Chinese leadership saw no reason to make Tibet an exception. The United States, fueling the unstable situation, had by 1957 actually started to train and arm anti-Chinese Tibetan guerrillas. Further, there were many dissatisfied ethnic Tibetans living in China proper, especially in Sichuan, Qinghai, and Xikang. When authorities in Sichuan tried to move toward agricultural collectivization, riots erupted among ethnic Tibetans and quickly turned into outright rebellion. In 1959, rebels and refugees moved toward the political unit of Tibet, crossing its borders and spreading rebellion toward Lhasa. In the wake of a mass demonstration in Lhasa, the PLA opened fire and bloody fighting erupted; the Dalai Lama fled to India, which welcomed him with open arms—a welcome the Chinese bitterly denounced as "interference in China's internal affairs."

China's relations with India were yet another sore point in the relationship between China and the Soviet Union. The year before the Dalai Lama's flight, relations between India and China had turned sour, a reality that played into the Tibetan crisis. The initial disputes concerned borders. China had constructed a road to link Xinjiang and Tibet, but the road ran across the Aksai Chin plateau, an area claimed by India. When India sent patrols to ascertain the situation, the Chinese detained them for several weeks. When India protested this action, Zhou Enlai argued that the borders had never been firmly set and that the road ran through Chinese territory. Prime Minister Jawaharlal Nehru was firm in his demand that China pull back behind its borders. Then came the Tibet crisis. India was openly sympathetic to Tibet, granting asylum to the Dalai Lama and thousands of Tibetan refugees. Clashes between Chinese and Indian troops occurred in high Himalaya mountain passes that the Chinese tried to occupy in order to stop the flow of Tibetan refugees. In clashes in August and October 1959, over ten Indian soldiers were killed and more were taken prisoner.

The Soviet Union, which saw India as an ally, never took China's side in any of these affairs. Indeed, the Soviets explicitly rejected the Chinese claims that India was at fault both in the Xinjiang–Tibet road controversy and later in the bloody clashes in the passes. Their rejection on September 10 was followed three days later with the announcement that Moscow was extending aid to New Delhi in the form of $375 million for India's current Five-Year Plan. From the Chinese perspective, this was adding insult to injury.

With the deterioration of relations between China and India and between China and the Soviet Union came the end of Mao's period of moderation in dealing with Tibet. In the view of the PRC, government efforts to nurse Tibet along to the Chinese point of view had failed. Beijing believed that the only alternative remaining was brute force. One scholar has described the years for Tibetans after 1959 succinctly and with a sense of the incredible Tibetan loss:

Buddhism was destroyed and Tibetans were forced to abandon deeply held values and customs that went to the core of their cultural identity. The class struggle sessions and the constant barrage of propaganda contradicting and ridiculing everything they understood and felt, sought to destroy the social and cultural fabric of the Tibetans' traditional way of life. These were terrible times for Tibetans in Tibet.[29]

CRACK-UP

Everywhere China and the Soviet Union turned, they found more to distrust about each other. Mao and his colleagues could not abide Khrushchev's criticism of Stalin, his support of peaceful coexistence, his apparent cozying up to the Eisenhower administration, his silence and anger about the Taiwan Strait crisis, his support of India and outspokenness about Chinese blame in that crisis, and his military requests of the Chinese that seemed, from their perspective, to smack of old-time imperialist demands. Khrushchev could not abide the apparent blitheness with which the Chinese leaders played with war in a nuclear age—whether in the Taiwan Strait or the Himalayan passes. Even more, he could not tolerate Mao's cavalier attitude toward nuclear war, stated in May 1958 at the Eighth Party Congress:

> If [nuclear] war breaks out it is unavoidable that people will die. We have seen wars kill people. Many times in China's past half of the population has been wiped out. ... We have at present no experience with atomic war. We do not know how many must die. It is better if one-half are left, the second best is one-third. ... After several five-year plans [China] will then develop and rise up. In place of the totally destroyed capitalism we will obtain perpetual peace. This will not be a bad thing.[30]

Khrushchev found the Great Leap Forward abhorrent; not only was it a radical departure from the Soviet model, but it was leading to chaos and confusion, to economic loss and deprivation, not to development. All the Soviet expense and work in trying to help build China was going up in the smoke of backyard steel furnaces. Khrushchev looked at Mao and saw, if not a dangerous madman, then a dangerous megalomaniac.

Khrushchev and other Soviet leaders flew to Beijing in October 1959, one month after the Soviets had sided so strongly with India. The meetings were cold and hostile: Khrushchev did not change his position. In the months that followed into February 1960, the Chinese sent a string of protest notes to the Soviet Union about its foreign policy "neutralism" in the Sino–Indian dispute. Chinese leaders celebrated the ninetieth anniversary of Lenin's birth in April 1960 by lambasting Soviet foreign policy. For the first time, Beijing stated openly that the Soviet Union had lost the qualities that the leader of the Communist world must display and argued that China was now the center of Leninist orthodoxy, which could lead the world Communist movement. It was, in the words of one scholar, "a public declaration of independence from the Soviet Union."[31]

In mid-July 1960, as starvation was spreading in China, Khrushchev suddenly called back to the Soviet Union all the scientists, engineers, and industrial advisers who had been working in several hundred Chinese firms. In a June meeting in Bucharest, the Sino–Soviet split had erupted into the open, with Khrushchev and Peng Zhen, the Chinese delegate, attacking each other in scathing personal, national, and ideological denunciations. This must have been the proverbial straw that broke the camel's back. When Soviet advisers were called back, they took with them all their blueprints and materials; no fewer than 257 scientific and technical projects were cancelled. By early September, no Russian technical and scientific advisers were left. The short-term effects on China were severe, especially in light of the economic crisis and the institutional turmoil into which the Great Leap had thrown party and state.

The abruptness of the withdrawal meant that construction stopped at the sites of scores of new plants and factories while work at many existing ones was thrown into confusion. Spare parts were no longer available for plants built according to Russian design and mines and electric power stations developed with Russian help were closed down. Planning on new undertakings was abandoned because the Russians simultaneously canceled contracts for the delivery of plans and equipment.[32]

As divorces go, this was a particularly hostile and bitter crack-up. No reconciliation would take place for almost thirty years, and when it did come, the world would be completely changed. For the time being, China had to cope with the largest famine in history, the economic shambles of the Great Leap Forward, an alienated intelligentsia, a splintering leadership, and humiliation in foreign affairs. China was entering a new dark age.

Notes

1 Mineo Nakajima, "Foreign Relations: From the Korean War to the Bandung Line," in *The Cambridge History of China, Vol. 14, The People's Republic, Part 1: The Emergence of Revolutionary China, 1949–1965*, ed. Roderick MacFarquhar and John K. Fairbank (Cambridge: Cambridge University Press, 1987), p. 283.

2 Lu Dingyi, "Let Flowers of Many Kinds Blossom, Diverse Schools of Thought Contend," in *The Search for Modern China: A Documentary Collection*, ed. Pei-kai Cheng and Michael Lestz with Jonathan Spence (New York: W.W. Norton, 1999), p. 387.

3 Ibid., pp. 387–8.

4 Gregor Benton and Alan Hunter, eds., *Wild Lily, Prairie Fire* (Princeton, NJ: Princeton University Press, 1995), pp. 100–01.

5 Quoted in Allen S. Whiting, "The Sino–Soviet Split," in MacFarquhar and Fairbank, *The Cambridge History of China, Vol. 14, The People's Republic, Part 1: The Emergence of Revolutionary China, 1949–1965*, p. 500.

6 Yin Zeming, "The Strength of the Masses is Limitless," in Cheng and Lestz with Spence, *The Search for Modern China*, pp. 405–06.

7 Issue of October 25, 1958, cited in Roderick MacFarquhar, *The Origins of the Cultural Revolution, Vol. 2: The Great Leap Forward, 1958–1960* (New York: Columbia University Press, 1983), p. 103. This was the situation specifically in Henan province.

8 See the discussions in Christina K. Gilmartin, Gail Hershatter, Lisa Rofel, and Tyrene White, eds., *Engendering China* (Cambridge, MA: Harvard University Press, 1994). Especially helpful are Gao Xiaoxian, "China's Modernization and Changes in the Social Status of Rural Women," and Lisa Rofel, "Liberation, Nostalgia, and a Yearning for Modernity." The term "national woman" is Tani Barlow's.

9 Helen F. Siu, *Agents and Victims* (New Haven, CT: Yale University Press), p. 176.

10 Quoted in MacFarquhar, *Origins of the Cultural Revolution, Vol. 2*, pp. 101–02.

11 Kenneth Lieberthal, "The Great Leap Forward and the Split in the Yan'an Leadership, 1958–1965," in *The Politics of China, 1949–1989*, ed. Roderick MacFarquhar (Cambridge, UK: Cambridge University Press, 1993), p. 111.

12 The phrase is from Lieberthal, "The Great Leap Forward and the Split in the Yan'an Leadership, 1958–1965," in MacFarquhar and Fairbank, *The Cambridge History of China, Vol. 14, The People's Republic, Part 1: The Emergence of Revolutionary China, 1949–1965*, p. 311.

13 Cited in MacFarquhar, *Origins of the Cultural Revolution, Vol. 2*, p. 200.

14 Mao Zedong, "Speech at the Lushan Conference, July 23, 1959," in *Chairman Mao Talks to the People*, ed. Stuart Schram (New York: Pantheon Books, 1974), p. 139. The earlier quotation is on p. 131.

15 Roderick MacFarquhar, *The Origins of the Cultural Revolution, Vol. 3: The Coming of the Cataclysm, 1961–1966* (New York: Columbia University Press, 1997), pp. 2–3.

16 Ibid., p. 1.

17 Jung Chang, *Wild Swans* (New York: Simon & Schuster, 1991), pp. 231–2. Copyright © 1991 by Globalflair Ltd. Reprinted with the permission of Touchstone, a division of Simon & Schuster, Inc. All rights reserved.

18 MacFarquhar, *Origins of the Cultural Revolution, Vol. 3*, p. 14.
19 Ibid., p. 234.
20 The economist was Sun Yefang. Cited in Thomas P. Bernstein, "Stalinism, Famine, and Chinese Peasants," *Theory and Society* 13, no. 3 (May 1984): 343.
21 Nicholas R. Lardy, "The Chinese Economy under Stress, 1958–1965," in MacFarquhar and Fairbank, *The Cambridge History of China, Vol. 14, The People's Republic, Part 1: The Emergence of Revolutionary China, 1949–1965*, p. 378.
22 MacFarquhar, *Origins of the Cultural Revolution, Vol. 3*, p. 95.
23 Cited in Thomas G. Paterson, J. Garry Clifford, and Kenneth J. Hagan, *American Foreign Policy: A History* (Lexington, MA: D.C. Heath, 1977), p. 501.
24 Whiting, "The Sino–Soviet Split," p. 501.
25 Melvyn C. Goldstein, *The Snow Lion and the Dragon* (Berkeley, CA: University of California Press, 1997), p. 25.
26 Melvyn C. Goldstein, *A History of Modern Tibet, 1913–1951* (Berkeley, CA: University of California Press, 1989), p. 765.
27 Goldstein, *The Snow Lion and the Dragon*, p. 52.
28 Quoted in Tsering Shakya, *The Dragon in the Land of Snows* (New York: Columbia University Press, 1999), p. 117.
29 Goldstein, *The Snow Lion and the Dragon*, p. 60.
30 Cited in Whiting, "The Sino–Soviet Split," pp. 488–9.
31 Maurice Meisner, *Mao's China and After* (New York: The Free Press, 1999), p. 235.
32 "The Sino–Soviet Split—The Withdrawal of the Specialists," *International Journal* (Toronto) 26, no. 3 (Summer 1971): 556, cited in Meisner, *Mao's China and After*, p. 236.

Suggestions for Further Reading

Becker, Jasper. *Hungry Ghosts: Mao's Secret Famine* (New York: Free Press, 1996). This is a graphic account of the famine produced in the wake of the Great Leap Forward; here Mao receives the full blame.
Li Zhisui. *The Private Life of Chairman Mao* (New York: Random House, 1994). Controversial and fascinating, this is a thoroughly critical view of the public and private life of Mao by the doctor who treated him and eventually embalmed him.
McFarquhar, Roderick. *The Origins of the Cultural Revolution, Vol. 2: The Great Leap Forward, 1958–1960* (New York: Columbia University Press, 1983). This standard work is insightfully analytical and compelling in its presentation.
———. *The Origins of the Cultural Revolution, Vol. 3: The Coming of the Cataclysm, 1961–1966* (New York: Columbia University Press, 1997). The author's conclusion to his three-volume series on the roots of the Cultural Revolution; it is compelling history.
Schram, Stuart. *Chairman Mao Talks to the People: Talks and Letters, 1956–1971* (New York: Pantheon Books, 1974). Among other things, this documentary collection reveals Mao's approaches to problems and difficulties with all of his soaring idealism, his sneering at conventional practices and at opponents, and his frequent earthiness and frankness of speech.

Part 4

From "Politics in Command" to the Glory of Getting Rich

Contemporary Change and Identity, 1961–2018

18

Death Dance

The Great Proletarian Cultural Revolution

They lured her from her home, telling her that her child had been injured in an accident. They dressed her as a whore and dragged her before tens of thousands of people at Qinghua University, where she was taunted and jeered and humiliated. Afterward, under the orders of Chairman Mao, they threw her into prison, where she lived in solitary confinement for over a decade. With the express permission of Chairman Mao, they publicly tortured and beat her husband. In the end, mortally ill and the target of frequent beatings, he was put in a darkened room, naked and untreated; there in 1969, he died alone. The man? He was, until late 1967, the president of the PRC, Liu Shaoqi. His wife, Wang Guangmei, had been an important political figure in her own right. Both had allegedly become enemies of the revolution—like countless "cows, ghosts, snakes, and monsters" who would be attacked during this phase of the Chinese revolution, the last insane act of Mao Zedong's career, the Great Proletarian Cultural Revolution.

During the height of the Cultural Revolution, the adulation of Mao, whose cult had transmuted him almost into a deity, reached such a point that at certain times every day people had to perform a "loyalty dance" to Mao, "the Reddest Sun that Shines in our Hearts." Flight attendants on airplanes reported that in flight they had to do the loyalty dance. In places around the country, villagers began meetings performing the loyalty dance to tunes like "Sailing the Seas Depends on the Great Helmsman, Making Revolution Depends on Mao Zedong's Thoughts." In truth, what was being performed in China during these years was a death dance. In this macabre performance each step led to higher and higher human costs, to deeper and deeper chaos, to greater and greater destruction. Once begun, the dizzying tempo of this dance inexorably picked up speed until the relentless pace threatened to spin China apart and once again toward civil war. Insanity might indeed be an understatement.

WHY?

The cataclysm of the Great Leap Forward had created a bitter split in the party leadership. Following Mao's ouster of Peng Dehuai at Lushan and the Great Leap with its deadly aftermath, a number of leaders, including President Liu Shaoqi and CCP General Secretary Deng Xiaoping, began to see Mao's whole approach as antithetical to the goal of building a modern socialist state. As the state began a slow recovery from the disasters of the late 1950s, a dispute between the Maoist line with its fundamentalist approach and the Liu-Deng line with its pragmatic approach began to fester.

Scholars have suggested that the two-line approach is simplistic and covers a more complex reality; for our purposes here, however, drawing the line starkly highlights the most essential differences in understanding subsequent developments.[1]

Though Mao clearly saw that the Great Leap had failed, he was not particularly upset. He still trusted his Communist goals and believed in motivating people through moral incentives. If people were properly motivated by revolutionary goals, he did not doubt that they would use all their energies unstintingly and give their all to achieve those goals. Peasants, whom Mao had called "blank sheets," would build a strong China simply because Mao would write on them the words to inspire them to superhuman effort if need be. Mao obviously thought that people (as opposed to "enemies of the people") were by nature good. They also had more innate abilities, more common sense, than did intellectuals. Thus, Mao was ready to rely completely on them. He was, as we have seen, hostile to the established, bureaucratized party cadres and to experts of any variety. It was much better to be ideologically correct than to have the correct factual knowledge, better, in other words, to be red than expert. Perpetual revolution through perpetual class struggle was a necessity because enemies of the people—intellectuals, capitalists, former Guomindang adherents, and reactionaries—would rear their ugly class heads to challenge the people. Indeed, Mao had called his clash with Peng Dehuai at Lushan a "class struggle"—with Peng, the longtime Communist military hero, tagged a "bourgeois element."

In contrast, Liu Shaoqi and Deng Xiaoping believed that the failure of the Great Leap was an unmitigated disaster that simply could not be repeated. They argued that people were most motivated by material incentives, that is, by rewards, bonuses, and higher wages when they excelled or when they worked harder than others. Human nature being what it is, they were convinced that these incentives would be stronger than moral encouragement, suasion, and propaganda. Mao reviled such policies because they had the smell of "revisionism," a revising of Marxism by sneaking in capitalistic elements and methods—a practice Mao associated with the despised Khrushchev. In the debate over redness versus expertise, Liu and Deng championed expertise. Getting the job done right was the main criterion in deciding whether the method of doing it was right or wrong. If a person was ideologically correct, that is, properly red, but did not know the first thing about a crucial manufacturing procedure, then, this line would argue, he should not attempt the job because he would likely mess it up. Get someone instead who knew how to do the job. Deng put it simply: "It doesn't matter if the cat is white or black, so long as it catches mice."[2] More pragmatic than Mao's approach, the Liu–Deng line valued knowledge of technology and science as well as organizational and procedural approaches that emphasized logical and efficient routines. In the same vein, it also valued political stability, which was a prerequisite for the successful building of a modern socialist nation.

In the late 1950s, Mao had shown an increasing tendency to manage and control the party in what might be called "guerrilla" fashion; that is, he depended on small, informal, usually ad hoc meetings for major decision making. Sometimes that meant making decisions himself and then bouncing them off several of his closest supporters. After the Great Leap, Mao's comrades restored collective decision making in an effort to restrain him, relying on larger, more formal central work conferences to which experts were invited. Both Liu and Deng spoke of serious shortcomings in the party leadership. Mao resented their approach; as party chairman, he still had a commanding presence in the party and thus still had the power to intervene directly in any situation. He was especially annoyed by Deng, who in his role as party general-secretary tended to ignore Mao and make decisions on his own.

In 1962 Mao began a "Socialist Education Campaign" to deal with the quality of local cadres and to refocus the party on the value of class struggle. Only about 2 percent of the rural population belonged to the party in 1960; local party cadres thus had no choice other than to work effectively with local officials and their communities. Since many had become local party leaders in the halcyon days of the early 1950s, the turmoil of the Leap and the famine might have made them less eager to do the party's bidding; they could indeed become obstructionist, hence the need for the Socialist Education Campaign. But the campaign almost immediately became an issue in the struggle between the two lines. The party decided that the campaign work was to be undertaken by large work teams made up of party cadres; as we have seen, Mao distrusted party cadres and would have preferred to use the masses more directly.

The campaign reintroduced class struggle into local communities once again. Class labels that either had been ascribed at the time of land reform or were inherited had become fixed by this time. There was no way to escape one's label; the families of the four bad types—landlords, rich peasants, counterrevolutionaries, and bad elements—would always remain the four bad types. As might be expected, these class labels could quickly become deadly weapons in local political struggles. For this reason, Liu and Deng rewrote directives for the work teams that deemphasized class struggle. Mao was scandalized: he saw his program for rectification changing into a tool for revisionists to reassert party control in the countryside. He became convinced that the Chinese revolution was in danger. Seeing himself and the revolution as one and the same, he felt compelled to destroy the party that he had spent his life building but that now, in his estimation, had gone completely wrong. The statement "one divides into two" was heard increasingly in the years after 1962. Though originally meant to describe the Sino–Soviet split, it came to signify the necessity of struggling against "capitalist roaders" within the CCP.

THE VIOLENTLY RADICAL RED GUARD PHASE, 1966–1969

Between 1964 and 1966, Mao set out to forge a coalition that would help him take on the party. It was composed ultimately of three components. Most important was the PLA under the strong Mao supporter Lin Biao; the PLA probably did more than any other group or institution to build the Mao cult. Second was a group of what has been called "radical intellectuals." Key here was Mao's wife, Jiang Qing. In the 1930s Jiang had been a second-rate Shanghai actress; she had journeyed to Yan'an, where she linked up with Mao; until the early 1960s she stayed out of the political arena. Beginning in 1963, she emerged as leader of an effort to reform the world of culture and the performing arts. Her associates were men from the Chinese Academy of Sciences in Beijing and the Municipal Propaganda Department in Shanghai. The third component in Mao's base was groups of the mass population mostly from cities who saw themselves as increasingly disadvantaged. One such group was high school and college students who faced shrinking opportunities for upward mobility. Another group was workers who were negatively affected by a system of employment that brought workers in on a temporary or part-time basis so that enterprises could pay them lower wages and no pension or medical benefits. Mao cultivated these groups and bided his time.

In late 1965, Mao took the first step toward beginning his battle against revisionism. He became very upset about a play, *Hai Rui Dismissed from Office*, written by the deputy mayor of Beijing, Wu Han. Hai Rui was a morally upright and caring Ming dynasty official who was wrongly dismissed from office by the emperor. Mao chose to believe that Wu Han really meant the play to be an allegorical critique of Mao's dismissal of Peng Dehuai at Lushan. He asked the Five-Man Group on cultural revolution, formed in 1964, to look into the matter. The Group was headed by Peng Zhen, mayor of Beijing, who made it clear very quickly that the Group would take the play at its historical face value and not as an allegory. Suspecting such a reply, Mao had also asked one of Jiang Qing's Shanghai colleagues, Yao Wenyuan, to write a harshly critical piece on the play; it was published in early November 1965 and is often considered the opening salvo of the Cultural

Revolution. When Peng Zhen and the Five-Man Group persisted in their defense of Wu Han, Mao and his allies pilloried them at an April meeting; at a Politburo meeting in May, the Five-Man Group was abolished, and Peng and others lost their official positions. Mao then established a new Cultural Revolution Group composed of his strong personal supporters, headed by his longtime personal secretary, Chen Boda, and including Jiang Qing; her ally, the sinister security apparatchik Kang Sheng; and two men from among Jiang's Shanghai allies, Yao Wenyuan and Zhang Chunqiao, director of the Shanghai Propaganda Department.

Between mid-May and mid-July, Mao stayed out of sight, leaving it up to Liu Shaoqi to carry out the Politburo's May decision to continue the war against revisionism and the "people of the Khrushchev brand still nestling in our midst."[3] By late May, unrest had broken out at several Beijing colleges, stirred up by allies of the new Cultural Revolution Group. A big-character wall poster by a teaching assistant in the philosophy department at Beijing University drew much attention when Mao had it broadcast and published all over the nation; it attacked the university's administration for having supported the original Five-Man Group on the *Hai Rui* issue. Liu's answer to handling the increasingly restive college campuses where students were beginning to challenge the authority of those in power was to send large work teams made up of party cadres. These work teams attempted to restore the authority of university officials and rein in the more fire-eating radical students. Mao and his allies were furious; they saw Liu Shaoqi as doing the same thing he had done in the Socialist Education Campaign—undercutting the effort to achieve class struggle. More and more they saw Liu as a person "of the Khrushchev brand."

In mid-July, on his way to Beijing, Mao stopped for a swim in the Yangzi. Designed to show that he was fit for battle (after years of rumored illness and even death), the swim garnered huge media coverage. The tone of the articles was like a political weather vane: Mao was going to take Beijing like a typhoon.

FIGURE 18.1 Mao swims the Yangzi as a sign that he's a force to be reckoned with at the beginning of the Cultural Revolution in the summer of 1966. His swim was emulated by people all over the country.
Source: Sovfoto/UIG via Getty Images.

The official report ... carried by the New China News Agency began. ... "The water of the river seemed to be smiling that day" and went on to tell of a militiaman ... who "became so excited when he saw Chairman Mao that he forgot he was in the water. Raising both hands, he shouted: 'Long live Chairman Mao! Long live Chairman Mao!' He leapt into the air. But soon sank into the river again. He gulped several mouthfuls, but the water tasted especially sweet."[4]

Though we must wonder what kind of pollutant tasted sweet, the fact was that all over China, people began to throw themselves into rivers to emulate Mao's swim. It was doubtful, however, that they could outdo the seventy-two-year-old chairman: His speed, reported by official sources, turned out to be "four times the world record"!

On August 5, 1966, during a Central Committee meeting attended by only about half of the members, Mao wrote a big-character poster of his own. Its title says it all: "Bombard the Headquarters," by which he meant the CCP itself. Thus, he launched a ten-year experiment in madness, one of the most bizarre and spectacular events of the twentieth century. It was a struggle over the direction of the revolution—pragmatic reform undertaken gradually by experts and regularized bureaucrats or revolutionary turmoil brought by young Red Guards in a never-ending revolution fueled by class struggle. It was also in part a personal power struggle: Mao had reportedly felt so out of power, so ignored by other leaders of the party-state, that he had to restructure his own power base and claw his way back to power. It was, in addition, Mao's quest for revolutionary immortality.

In August, rebellious student groups reorganized themselves as Red Guards; soon most colleges and middle schools had their own Red Guard units. Shouting slogans like "It is justified to rebel," a million young people assembled on August 18 in Tiananmen Square to see Mao at sunrise on top of the Gate of Heavenly Peace. Eight such rallies were held between then and November 26; a total of 13 million students came as if on a pilgrimage (or, as it was more commonly said, on their own "Long March") to see their "Great Helmsman," their "Red Sun," their "Supreme Commander." Mao directed them to destroy the four "olds": old ideas, habits, customs, and culture. They were to be the soldiers in the war against party and state leadership; they were to be the vanguard in the class struggle. Mao announced that his successor would be Lin Biao. He made no secret of the fact that the two targets of the Cultural Revolution artillery were Liu Shaoqi and Deng Xiaoping.

The last months of 1966 saw utter confusion. Red Guard units rampaged throughout China, seeking and destroying anything representative of the feudal past and the bourgeois present. Their actions ranged from somewhat amusing to criminal. Shop names and street names were changed to make them more revolutionary. People with long hair were seized and had it cut off. "Women wearing tight slacks were subjected to the 'ink bottle test': If a bottle of ink placed inside the waistband could not slip freely to the ground, the pants would be slashed to shreds."[5] More destructively, Red Guards ransacked homes and pillaged museums and libraries. They indiscriminately trashed books and newspapers, the notes and writings of scholars, religious art, and recordings of Western music.

But their "revolutionary action" went well beyond destroying things. As the tempo of the death dance sped up, mindless violence and brutality became the beat. Red Guard youths tortured and beat people, especially teachers, principals, intellectuals, and those with bourgeois backgrounds—sometimes to death. A female Red Guard reported how her middle-school classmates participated in the beating to death of an elderly former businessman—and one of those who joined in the murder was the victim's own granddaughter. The humiliation and degradation that Red Guards inflicted drove many to suicide. The most well-known likely such victim was Lao She, author of the important novels *Rickshaw* and *Cat Country* and a number of important plays. Middle-school Red Guards repeatedly ordered him to attend struggle meetings; they ransacked his house and burned his books. His body was discovered in a lake in late August, a victim of suicide by drowning or perhaps even of murder.

In the face of the aimless violence in the fall of 1966, Mao and the Cultural Revolution Group further radicalized the movement. They informed Red Guard organizations that Liu Shaoqi and Deng Xiaoping had to be struggled against. In speaking of Liu and Deng, one of the Cultural Revolution Group ordered demonstrators to "flog the curs which have fallen in the water" and to "make their very names stink."[6] Liu and Deng began to be strongly criticized and subjected to humiliating and often physically painful struggle meetings. In the summer of 1967 they were put under house arrest.

As this drama played itself out at the capital, Red Guard units around the country often engaged in violent fighting, not always with conservatives but with rival groups of Red Guards. Factionalism was a serious problem. Sometimes the source was strategy; as time wore on, the source increasingly became disputes over who were more grandly red, over who were the most committed and vigorous supporters of Chairman Mao. Fighting also erupted between Red Guards and groups of farmers and workers who resented the youths inserting themselves forcibly into local situations they knew nothing about. Local cadres began to form conservative mass organizations among workers ("Scarlet Guards") to fend off attacks of Red Guards. The situation in many places was becoming dangerously polarized. One of the most polarized cities by the end of the year was Shanghai, where the government became immobilized by the demands and struggles of Red Guards and Scarlet Guards. All over the country, in provinces and in cities in similar situations, governments were collapsing; China was descending into chaos.

Destruction of many of these institutions had been Mao's purpose; the question was what would replace them. The Shanghai political and economic paralysis ended only when the PLA was brought into the city to maintain order and when Zhang Chunqiao of the Cultural Revolution Group went to the city in January 1967 and with the support of radical organizations destroyed the existing party and government structures. In February he announced the establishment of the Shanghai People's Commune, a name reminiscent of the Paris Commune of 1871, a model to which the Chinese radicals had been attracted. But the institution of this model promised complete and immediate democracy, and Mao feared that attempting to follow that model would only lead to more chaos. What emerged instead out of the Shanghai experience and developments in several provinces was the revolutionary committee. Composed of revolutionary masses (Red Guards and the workers' "Revolutionary Rebels"), party cadres, and the PLA, the revolutionary committee became the new governmental structure promoted by Mao and his colleagues. The presence of the army in the local and provincial leadership structures was important. Because regular party structures were weak, if functioning at all, and because often-violent factionalism made any constructive action impossible, the army emerged as the key power broker and dominant player in both political and economic matters. Mao increasingly depended on the military for maintaining some degree of stability.

The most dangerous situations in the months that followed developed when mass organizations formed factional ties with military commanders. The Wuhan Incident of July 20, 1967, is a case in point. In Wuhan, as in many areas, the PLA had a natural predisposition to side with conservative mass organizations, first because many of the organizations' leaders were party officials whom the PLA commanders knew before the chaos had started and, second, because conservative bodies like the PLA favored order and stability. In many areas, then, the PLA had moved to quash radical organizations. In early 1967, to halt such actions, the Maoists decreed that in the future only the central government could decide what organizations could be suppressed. The upshot of this decision was that conflicts between conservative and radical mass organizations increased because the PLA was unable to intervene. As radicals seized trains loaded with arms intended for export to North Vietnam, the PLA supplied conservative groups with arms for defense against the radicals. Because of the increasingly dangerous situation, the commander of the Wuhan Military Region had two meetings with Zhou Enlai and two representatives of the Cultural Revolution Group. After the second, a large conservative organization known as the Million Heroes stormed the hotel where the representatives of the Cultural Revolution Group were staying, detained them, and probably beat one of them. Zhou Enlai, who had already returned to Beijing, had to come back to Wuhan to gain the release of the detained man. Beijing then sent air and naval forces to seize Wuhan and restore order.

Bloody and destructive battles erupted all over the country between the PLA and revolutionary rebel groups who were seizing weapons from military bases. By late summer 1967, China tottered on the edge of anarchy. The domestic turmoil spread briefly into the international arena when rebels took over the Foreign Ministry in Beijing for two weeks. The "proletarian internationalism" that they attempted to put into practice was perhaps best symbolized by their seizure and burning of the British diplomatic compound in the capital. By early September even Mao saw that if the anarchy continued, China's political and economic systems might simply collapse. He thus gave the PLA orders to restore order. It was not quickly accomplished.

In the spring and summer of 1968 another wave of violence erupted between competing rebel groups, purportedly encouraged by Mao's wife, Jiang Qing, who had emerged as the cultural

FIGURE 18.2 In the late twentieth century, Zhou Enlai was the most admired PRC leader. Despite his always siding in the end with Mao, he continued to be viewed as more moderate and humane.
Source: © Marc Riboud/Magnum Photos.

dictator of the revolution. Struggles were especially bitter in Shanxi, Shandong, Hebei, Guangdong, and Guangxi provinces. It was the battles at Qinghua University in Beijing, however, that led finally to the end of the radical mass organizations that had wreaked such havoc. There, struggles between Red Guard groups, each claiming to be more Maoist than the other, had begun a campus war with "cold" weapons—stones, bricks, and concrete chunks catapulted by each side—but had quickly escalated to "hot" weapons—rockets and projectile missiles carrying fire bomb warheads—launched against rivals' dormitories. In this "war," a number of students were burned alive. In the summer of 1968, workers from the area were sent to the campus to try to restore order; five of them were killed in the continuing fighting. The conflict finally was extinguished when Mao visited the campus in late July and scolded the student radicals. To the more moderate faction he presented mangos, which, being a gift from the Red Sun, were put under glass for people to file past and admire in adoration.

This violent phase of the Cultural Revolution came to an end with the meeting of the Ninth Party Congress in April 1969. Fought to destroy the party, the revolution ended up reasserting party power. But there was a significant change: military officers were represented in important positions as never before. In many ways, the twentieth-century trend toward the militarization of Chinese politics and society was seen in this new face of the party. Of the 279 members and alternates of the new party Central Committee, 45 percent were from the PLA, 28 percent from revolutionary party cadres, and 27 percent from revolutionary masses. With the rise of the military, the commander of the PLA and Defense Minister Lin Biao, often linked with the Cultural Revolution radicals, gained considerable stature.

A postmortem of this phase of the Cultural Revolution would need to consider both the short-term and long-term results. Those intellectuals and writers who survived suffered harassment, persecution, and torture. They faced a dictatorial leadership that went so far as to impose a formula for "artistic creation": always emphasize the positive, always emphasize the heroic character, and always emphasize the primary character. In her role as cultural czarina, Jiang Qing was immovable: she condemned traditional operas as feudal. She led the way in developing a politically and ideologically correct repertoire of five "revolutionary model operas"—all but one military in theme. Set during the war against Japan were *Red Lantern* and *Shajiabang*, each focusing on a war hero, in the first a railroad worker and in the second a teahouse owner. *Taking Tiger Mountain by Strategy* dealt with the successful seizure of a bandit hideout by the PLA in 1946. *Raid on the White Tiger Regiment* was set in the Korean War. The nonmilitary opera, which was also the only one with a contemporary theme, was *On the Docks*; it told the story of a battle against a saboteur. Reportedly, these revolutionary operas were popular and at times spectacular in music, dance, and presentation, but with such a small repertoire, they had a stultifying impact on the art world.

An estimated 400,000 to 500,000 Chinese were killed in these three years. The indictment against the Gang of Four (the extreme leftists in control during much of the Cultural Revolution, that is, Jiang Qing and cronies) at their trial in 1980–1981 specified that "2,600 people in literary and art circles, 142,000 cadres and teachers in units under the Ministry of Education, 53,000 scientists and technicians in research institutes, and 500 professors and associate professors in medical colleges and institutes" were persecuted and that "an unspecified number" of them died.[7] Mistreatment of party cadres and government officials was widespread. The purge rate of provincial and regional officials was 70 to 80 percent; altogether about 3 million people were purged, with most rehabilitated only in the late 1970s. Others endured beatings, torture, and even death. The best known was Liu Shaoqi, the former president of the government and leader in the CCP since 1923. He was denounced as a "renegade, traitor, and scab hiding in the Party, a lackey of imperialism,

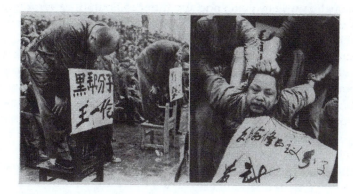

FIGURE 18.3 Victims of the Cultural Revolution were paraded through the streets, forced to don dunce caps, and became the target of struggle meetings.
Source: Walter Oleksy/Alamy Stock Photo.

modern revisionism, and the Guomindang reactionaries."[8] Expelled from the party in October 1968, he was tortured and beaten by Red Guards; he died of pneumonia without medicine or medical care in a remote prison. Deng Xiaoping, Mao's other main target, fared somewhat better. Like Liu, humiliated at struggle meetings, he was sent to Jiangxi province in an exile of sorts, where he remained under house arrest and worked part-time as a fitter in a tractor plant. His son, Deng Pufang, was permanently paralyzed below the waist when he fell from a building at Beijing University after being pursued by Red Guards.

Among the long-term consequences of the Cultural Revolution was a weakening of the party-state; these years shattered the party, fragmented its leadership, and in its place established weak and untried institutions. Further, the struggle between the two lines had not in the end been decisive. Mao and the radicals had to pull back in order to stop the Cultural Revolution's death dance from ending in death for the national polity. So the struggle would continue, though not against a backdrop of national anarchy. With the conclusion of this violent phase, the nation as a whole saw a substantial migration of people from cities to the countryside. Over 4 million high school and university students (many former Red Guards) were sent to the countryside to live with farmers and undergo a period of reeducation, an experience that left many without college opportunities and that helped create a "lost generation" of disillusioned, cynical, and even antisocial adults. They had lost faith in the moralistic rhetoric of Mao and above all in the value and validity of the Communist political system; it is not surprising that they were open to the rampant materialism that would shape the 1980s and 1990s.

Two other groups finding their way to the greater poverty and inconvenience of farm life were party cadres and bureaucrats, sent for productive labor and political study—more realistically, hard labor and indoctrination—at so-called May Seventh Cadre Schools. Up to 3 million bureaucrats and party cadres spent varying lengths of time in the countryside.

THE MYSTERY OF LIN BIAO

The first phase of the Cultural Revolution stimulated the rise of a kind of malignant factionalism. The second phase (1969–1976) was marked by continual factional disunity, tension, and struggle. At least four factions tried to take the leadership of the Cultural Revolution in particular ideological directions: Lin Biao, ultraleft military; Mao and the Gang of Four, ultraleft; Zhou Enlai, centrist; and Deng Xiaoping, pragmatist. Rumbling beneath the surface as an increasingly pressing concern was the question of Mao's successor.

The most mysterious of the factional struggles concerned Lin Biao, the hero of the Manchurian campaign in the civil war, who had been named defense minister after the ouster of Peng Dehuai in 1959. He had been one of Mao's strongest supporters during the Cultural Revolution and perhaps the central figure in building up the cult of Mao. With the military dominance at the Ninth Party Congress in 1969, his power had increased substantially. It is at this point that the story of Lin becomes murky: historical sources go all over the map in describing the man and his motives. The original source of tension between Lin and Mao, who in 1966 had named him his successor, remains unclear to this day. Lin may well have thought that Mao's pulling back from the radicalism of the Cultural Revolution meant giving up any gains that had been made in the movement. With this in mind, some have contended that Lin in his radicalism was pushing a new Great Leap to get the Cultural Revolution back on track, but others have pointed out that Lin had never taken any interest in economic matters and would not have pushed a policy like this one. One scholar contends that "[w]here broad issues of domestic and foreign policy were concerned, e.g., economic strategy or diplomatic initiatives, he was basically passive to the point of being virtually invisible; the attitude was truly one of 'Do whatever the Chairman says.'"[9]

Some contend that ill feelings sprang up over issues of foreign policy, specifically on how to deal with the Soviet Union and the United States. Fighting with the Soviet Union had erupted on an island in the Ussuri River in March 1969, and in late summer there was a serious outbreak of fighting in Xinjiang. Ominously, word had also gotten out from Eastern Europe that the Soviet Union was talking "about a 'surgical strike' against Chinese nuclear weapons installations."[10] The announcement of the Brezhnev Doctrine—that the Soviet Union's role was to make sure that a country once Communist would stay that way—only made the Chinese more apprehensive about Soviet intentions.

The tense relationship with the Soviet Union had stimulated some Chinese leaders to think about a possible rapprochement with the United States. Bringing the U.S. "card" into play might make the Soviet Union a little less aggressive and thereby help attain greater national security. In this context, Beijing began rethinking its relationship with the United States. In late 1968, Beijing had suggested to Washington that they resume the sporadically held ambassador-level talks in Warsaw. The talks did not resume until January 1970 primarily because of a lukewarm U.S. response. The United States was still deeply mired in its war in Vietnam, and only slowly did Washington become aware of the depth of the Beijing–Moscow split. After an exchange of letters between Zhou Enlai and President Richard Nixon in late 1970 and early 1971, Zhou invited Nixon's national security adviser, Henry Kissinger, for a secret visit to Beijing to plan a visit by the president. Kissinger went in July and again in October. In the midst of the planning, China won a huge victory: on October 25, 1971, it was admitted to the UN, replacing Taiwan in that body and taking its place as one of the five permanent Security Council members. China was stepping out on the world stage more visibly than at any time since World War II. Four months later, in February 1972, Nixon made his historic visit. Some sources indicate that ideologically Lin opposed the rapprochement with the United States. Others contend that such opposition was fictional, that Lin took no position, indeed had no interest in foreign policy directions apart from specific military issues.

Much has been made of Lin's personal ambition. Beginning in mid-1970, Lin pressed Mao to have the post of the presidency of the PRC written into the new constitution; he repeatedly urged Mao to reassume that post. Mao resisted these demands and was irritated at Lin's persistence.

He believed that Lin wanted the post himself and that he was trying to manipulate the political situation to his own ends. At another ill-starred meeting at Lushan in August and September 1970, Mao turned quite hostile over the issue and had Chen Boda, who had taken Lin's line, purged from the party. Relations between Lin and Mao, scholars have generally agreed, were all downhill after this time.

Some scholars, however, have challenged the thesis of Lin's ambition. Lin, they claim, did not want the chairmanship himself. He was a shy man who was bothered by a sometimes-incapacitating chronic illness. The heavy public duties of the position were not attractive to him, especially meeting foreign visitors—a duty he hated. These scholars do admit that Lin's wife, Ye Qun, was ambitious and pushed him in directions in which he might not normally have gone; he was reportedly quite dependent on her, even to the point of asking her "whether he should swallow or spit out phlegm in his throat."[11] These scholars contend that Lin's continual bringing up of the chairmanship to Mao stemmed from the general desire on the part of all the leadership to constantly bring to the fore the genius of Mao and how this position would only underscore further his greatness and brilliance. This version points to the way the Mao cult had changed Chinese politics. Mao now expected that he would be treated as indispensable: "Now there was an extreme concern with slogans and the Mao cult, a game that was de rigueur for all actors, not just Lin Biao and the [radical intellectuals]."[12]

Whatever the reasons, after Lushan, Mao and Lin were on a collision course. Mao verbally targeted those closest to Lin, almost goading him to act. The official story of what happened was first supplied by Zhou Enlai. Lin began planning a coup attempt in early 1971. The objective of the so-called Plot 571 was to arrest two men from the Gang of Four and precipitate a crisis that Lin could use the military to handle. In the end, the plot was changed to an attempt to assassinate Mao by blowing up his train. When it did not evolve as planned, Mao escaped. On September 13, Lin and his entourage attempted to flee, apparently to the Soviet Union, but their plane crashed in Mongolia, killing all on board, including Lin's wife, Ye Qun, and his son, Lin Liguo.

Many today believe that the chief conspirator was twenty-four-year-old Lin Liguo, who, with the obvious help of his father, had been made the deputy director of the General Office and the deputy chief of operations for the Chinese Air Force. Some scholars even question whether Lin Biao knew about the plot before it went awry. Whatever the case, in this extraordinary, still-mysterious episode, Mao's chosen successor or those closest to him had attempted to assassinate the Great Helmsman. Questions about Mao's judgment of his comrades-in-arms arise from Lin's actions, but Mao's treatment of Liu Shaoqi had already raised them. Even more, the in-house machinations and treachery in this episode raise questions about any supposedly salutary impacts of the Cultural Revolution on political culture; it appears instead to have created a climate where palace intrigues as bizarre as any in imperial days seemed the norm.

The Gang of Four

The years after Lin's demise saw an increasing focus on who would emerge as Mao's successor. There was an even greater sense of urgency in doing so because Premier Zhou Enlai had cancer and because the health of Mao, ill with amyotrophic lateral sclerosis ("Lou Gehrig's disease"), was failing rapidly. In this context, the manipulation of the political scene by the so-called radical intellectuals to try to establish their position as Mao's successor became intense. Until the fall of 1972, the core of the group was Jiang Qing and her two Shanghai-based allies, Zhang Chunqiao and Yao Wenyuan. That fall, Mao brought to Beijing a handsome young (thirty-seven years old) Shanghai radical, Wang Hongwen, to be groomed for top leadership. Wang, a former factory security chief who had risen since January 1967 to become Shanghai's leader and political commissar of Shanghai's PLA garrison, became the fourth radical in the Jiang Qing group, subsequently known as the Gang of Four. Wang's unusual rise stemmed from the fact that when Mao surveyed the political scene, he saw no one who looked like a potential successor. Zhou was ill, and he was bitterly opposed by the Gang of Four in any case. The Gang of Four and the PLA were bitter enemies; choosing someone from either camp would bring the other out screaming in opposition. Even if Mao had wanted to name a radical who had been on the scene during the first phase of the Cultural Revolution, there was no one he would choose. Given the traditional Chinese views of female rulers, Mao could not consider grooming his wife for the job. He also felt that Zhang Chunqiao, the most accomplished of the radicals, would create such a backlash with his insistence on radical policies that all the gains (?) of the Cultural Revolution would be lost. Thus, he decided to give Wang a shot; Wang's personable presence might also help give the image of the radicals a boost.

It was the radicals who in early 1974 promoted the rather mysterious "Anti-Lin [Biao], Anti-Confucius campaign." This movement coupled as targets the radical Lin and the reactionary Confucius, but it was actually aimed at Zhou Enlai in an attempt to discredit the man who was most often seen as a moderating and pragmatic influence on policymaking. Though linking the two seemed farfetched, the Gang explained that though Lin had appeared far left, he was actually far right. Any results of the campaign are hard to determine; its importance rests in its revelation of the Gang of Four's determination to beat back anyone who might emerge as Mao's successor. Then in mid-1974, Zhou's permanent move to the hospital made it essential that Mao choose someone to serve for Zhou in running the daily business of the country. In the less than two years since his presence in Beijing on the Politburo, Wang Hongwen had not distinguished himself and had become mostly a pawn of Jiang Qing. So Mao looked elsewhere. His surprise choice, and an outrage to the Gang of Four, was Deng Xiaoping, the number two target during the Cultural Revolution. He was pulled from his Jiangxi exile and brought back to Beijing as first vice-premier. Mao made this astonishing decision because of his considerable uncertainty about the military and the role that it might play in politics; the taste of the Lin Biao affair was still strong in his mouth. He wanted a reliable and respected old comrade whom key generals could trust and who could take over the Military Affairs Commission and maneuver military leaders out of constant participation in politics.

Policy documents produced under Deng's direction during his year in power foreshadowed the direction in which he would take China during the 1980s and 1990s; they are a good indication of why the Gang of Four opposed him. Deng called for speeded-up industrialization by introducing foreign technology, putting quality first, and restoring material incentives. Deng also called for more expert leadership based on an education with higher standards. At Politburo meetings Deng criticized the Gang of Four; Jiang Qing, the main spokesperson for the Gang, repeatedly battled with him. Mao seemed ambivalent; he publicly backed Deng, but he also encouraged the radicals to set forth their own views. For whatever reasons, Jiang had apparently become estranged from Mao, having moved away from the government compound of Zhongnanhai. Mao's health was deteriorating quickly. By 1975,

> [h]aving trouble speaking, he could only utter some mumbled words and phrases. ... When his speech was at its worst, he could only write down his thoughts with a pen. Later ... he could not walk on his own; he could not even move a step without help.[13]

Jiang was increasingly strident in her determination either to succeed Mao herself or at least to have someone from the Gang do so.

THE YEAR OF THE DRAGON

The year 1976 was traumatic for the Chinese nation. When Zhou Enlai died on January 8, the logical choice to replace him was Deng Xiaoping. But Mao, perhaps fearing that ensconcing him in power would lead to the inevitable undoing of Cultural Revolution values, replaced him with a dark horse, Hua Guofeng. During the Cultural Revolution, Hua had been secretary of the CCP provincial committee in Hunan and had been a member of the Politburo since the Tenth Party Congress in 1973; now he became acting premier. The Gang of Four was infuriated by this appointment; the early months of 1976 saw them increasingly hell-bent in their drive to seize power. In their obsession and with a good deal of hubris about their closeness to power (Mao *was* Jiang's husband, estranged or not; and Mao generally shared *their* radical views, not those of others), the Gang made no allies among other groups that might have enlarged their potential. It seems apparent that public policies and the country as a whole were at most in the peripheral vision of the Beijing players in 1976: the Cultural Revolution had come down to one thing and one thing only—seizing the helm from the Great Helmsman.

In mid-March small groups began to leave wreaths in memory of Zhou Enlai at the Heroes Monument in Tiananmen Square. This happened at a time when the Gang of Four was continuing to work to discredit Zhou—and by extension that other pragmatist, Deng Xiaoping. On March 25, a Shanghai newspaper controlled by the Gang called Zhou a capitalist roader; students in Nanjing demonstrated in protest, writing anti–Gang of Four slogans in tar on railroad cars. In Beijing the parade of wreath bearers continued to come to Tiananmen Square, with the number escalating daily. On April 4, on the eve of the Qing Ming festival, the day Chinese traditionally tend the graves of their family dead, an estimated 2 million flocked to the square with wreaths. Some eulogies praised Zhou:

> He left no inheritance, he had no children, he has no grave, he left no remains. His ashes were scattered over the mountains and rivers of our land. It seems he left us nothing, but he will live forever in our hearts.

Others attacked the Gang of Four; here specifically Jiang Qing:

> You must be mad
> To want to be an empress!
> Here's a mirror to look at yourself
> And see what you really are.
> You've got together a little gang
> To stir up trouble all the time,
> Hoodwinking the people, capering about.
> But your days are numbered.[14]

The Gang was convinced that the masses, in remembering Zhou, were really saying that Deng should be his legitimate successor. Obviously fearing the people (whom they always claimed they championed), they worked with other like-minded government leaders to declare what was happening a counterrevolutionary incident. The next day, when many people returned to the square, they found that police had already taken away all the wreaths. Violence broke out; outraged citizens burned police vehicles and a police command post. Eventually, public security and Beijing garrison forces appeared; they attacked and beat people who remained on the square. This Tiananmen incident was a new breed of demonstration in the PRC, an apparently spontaneous outpouring of grief and admiration for a man truly revered and a public action undirected by the government or any other authority. Perhaps the Gang had reason to fear. In any case, two days later, Mao ordered that Deng Xiaoping be stripped of all his posts and that Hua Guofeng be named premier and first deputy chairman of the CCP. Mao had named yet another successor.

But there were more shocks to come. On July 6, Zhu De, the founder of the Red Army during the days of the Jiangxi Soviet and one of Mao's earliest allies after Chiang Kai-shek's White Terror of 1927, died. Then, in the predawn hours of July 28, a devastating earthquake with a magnitude of 7.8 on the Richter scale leveled the city of Tangshan near Tianjin. At least 250,000 people were killed with some estimates going as high as 660,000.

> Nature's evil drama had changed the face of Tangshan beyond recognition. Scattered concrete beams and pillars, ... tilting utility poles, water towers cut in half. ... Floorslabs hanging in mid-air, twisted reinforcing bars. ... In that dismal fog, the most heart-rending of all were the corpses hanging from tall buildings. Some were pinned only at the hands by floorslabs, their split skulls flopped to one side; some had their feet smashed as they tried to jump, and they hung upside down in mid-air. They were the victims with the quickest reflexes; they had already been startled awake from their dreams, they had already jumped out of bed, and run to the porch or window, but their escapes were cut short by death. There was a young mother, with half her body already out a third-storey window, but a heavy floorslab had fallen and crushed her there on the windowsill. She died in mid-air, with a child in her arms. Rocking with the building in the aftershock, her hanging hair swung in the fog.[15]

Horrifying as the experience was, the life of the survivors was also tragic. About 10,000 people lost their spouses in the earthquake; over 4,000 children were orphaned; at least 3,800 were made paraplegics or amputees. In traditional China such disasters were interpreted as the natural world's reflection of similar traumas in the world of humans. The Gang of Four in Beijing, not wanting people to think about what kind of portent this might be, ordered a movement to criticize the Mandate of Heaven idea and associated superstitions—and to continue the attacks on Deng Xiaoping, the unrepentant capitalist roader.

Then on September 9, Mao himself died. He had had major heart attacks on May 11, June 26, and September 2. The national mourning period continued into early October. People, especially party officials, had to take great care in how they mourned. The Cultural Revolution had so politicized every action that mourning that was in some way out of the ordinary—that is, with too much grief (which might raise questions about sincerity) or too little (which might evidence anti-Mao feelings)—could be suspect and therefore dangerous. The Central Committee's obituary of Mao read in part:

> The passing away of Chairman Mao Zedong is an inestimable loss to our Party, our army and the people of all nationalities in our country. ... His passing away is bound to evoke immense grief in the hearts of the people of our country and the revolutionary people of all countries. The Central Committee of the Communist Party of China calls on the whole Party, the whole army, and the people of all nationalities in the country to resolutely turn their grief to strength: We must carry on the cause left behind by Chairman Mao.

The statement also noted as an accomplishment Mao's many factional victories over party rivals: "during the Great Proletarian Cultural Revolution [he triumphed] over the counter-revolutionary revisionist line of Liu Shaoqi, Lin Biao, and Deng Xiaoping."[16] Little, of course, did the writers of this document know that within less than two years, Deng would be resurrected and forthrightly set out to bury Mao and Mao's form of revolution.

But Mao's corpse was not buried. Although Mao had pledged in the 1950s to be cremated, the Politburo after his death decided that Mao's body, like Lenin's in the Kremlin, must be preserved and maintained in a mausoleum built on the axis running through the center of Tiananmen Square to the Gate of Heavenly Peace to the Forbidden City. It was as if Mao's commemorators envisioned him as equivalent to an emperor from days long gone. But the preservation of the corpse did not properly fit the dignity of a departed emperor, for attending doctors did not know exactly how to do the heavy-duty embalming. When they injected too much formaldehyde into his body,

> The results were shocking. Mao's face was bloated, as round as a ball, and his neck was now the width of his head. His skin was shiny, and the formaldehyde oozed from his pores like perspiration. His ears were swollen, too, sticking out from his head at right angles. The corpse was grotesque.[17]

Though they were able to right the damage, the scene points to a reality that Mao appears to have forgotten amid the adulation in his last decades as the Great Helmsman—that he too was one of the people, not a god, and that he too would die, like so many who died because of his policies.

For those who survived Mao, the moment for which all the maneuvering in the last years of the Cultural Revolution had taken place had now come. The Gang of Four was too sure of themselves and not as prepared for eventualities as their opponents. With word being bandied about that the Gang was prepared for a military coup and that it had 100,000 armed Shanghai militia ready to take up its cause, others in the government, including Hua Guofeng, were increasingly on guard. In early October, after some fire-eating speeches by Jiang Qing and Wang Hongwen and word that the Gang had told their followers that good news would be coming by October 9, Hua and his allies decided that they had to act. They arrested the Gang of Four on October 6. A Chinese scholar put it tersely: "When Jiang Qing was arrested at her residence, her servant spat on her. The Cultural Revolution was over."[18]

There were two codas to the story of the Cultural Revolution. The first was the political trial of the Gang of Four (November 1980 to January 1981). This trial followed the years of the late 1970s, when every conceivable difficulty and problem in Chinese society—from weak schools to bad harvests to infertility—was blamed on the Gang of Four, often referred to with five fingers, not four, held up; the fifth, of course, represented Mao. Among charges at the trial were that the Gang had persecuted 729,511 party cadres and citizens and killed 34,800 of them. All were found guilty; everyone but Jiang Qing confessed. Jiang and Zhang Chunqiao were sentenced to death, but after the trial, their sentences were commuted to life imprisonment; the others received prison terms of varying length. In May 1991, Jiang committed suicide in prison.

The four were blamed; they were found guilty, and the slate was apparently wiped clean. But no one asked the million-dollar question: why did hundreds of millions of Chinese permit themselves to be so led astray into such disastrous policies by a mere handful of plotters? Was there something about Chinese political culture or national personality that would allow a response that seems so unthinking, so lemming-like? On this level, the more likely answer is the same as that of the earlier question regarding why no one questioned the policies of the Great Leap Forward—fear of those in authority, quaking before the infallibility of Chairman Mao and the power of his minions.

But, more troubling, for many it was not simply a passive following of authority. Many joined willingly in violence, engaging in wanton destruction, rape, murder, and allegedly even cannibalism.

The historical record of the Cultural Revolution is filled with voluntary criminal acts on the part of many civilians—like the earlier-described school-age granddaughter who willingly participated in the murder of her grandfather or the writer Ma Bo, who described how much he enjoyed beating people. Some suggest that such acts and antisocial outbursts were an explosion of anger against party and state bureaucrats that had been building since 1949. A Shanghai journalist explained,

> Once the labels were available, once you could attack someone by calling him a "revisionist" or a "capitalist-roader," the labels were used like cannon, just to attack anyone against whom you felt any grievance of any kind, whether public or private.

A young Chinese writer suggested, "It is more plausible to say, but difficult to admit, that almost everyone was at fault. We might better say we all turned abnormal for a while. But then, how do we explain *that?*" He concluded soberly, "We won't be done with the history of the Cultural Revolution until we can answer that question. The trouble is, few want to try. It requires self-dissection of a painful kind."[19]

MAO IN RETROSPECT

The second coda to the Cultural Revolution was the summer 1981 adoption of the "Resolution on Certain Questions in the History of Our Party since the Founding of the PRC." Before looking at the party's official handling of Mao's record, it is interesting to note what Mao himself thought. At a meeting with Politburo colleagues less than three months before his death, in June 1976, Mao mentioned two things that he had accomplished of great consequence: his defeat of Chiang Kai-shek and his fighting to defeat the Japanese. Curiously, he did not mention any of his record after the establishment of the PRC. When asked about the Cultural Revolution, he replied that "[t]hat revolution remained unfinished ... and all he could do was pass the task on to the next generation. If he could not pass it on peacefully, then he would have to pass it on in turmoil."[20]

Reportedly, 4,000 party leaders participated in some fashion in drawing up the 1981 party resolution. Deng Xiaoping played a key role; like most other party leaders who had been purged during the Cultural Revolution, he was "eager to avenge [himself] on Mao's ghost, [but he] appreciated the political need to preserve Mao as a symbol of both revolutionary and nationalist legitimacy."[21] The resolution noted that Mao's contributions far transcended his mistakes. Specifically, it pointed to his success in the revolutionary struggle against the Guomindang (as Mao also had noted) and in the economic successes in the socialist transformation in the first years of the PRC. But it criticized Mao strongly for the extent of the 1957 anti-rightist campaign (interestingly enough, a campaign headed by Deng Xiaoping); for his leftist proclivities and mistakes in the Great Leap Forward; for his disregard for Leninist principles in sponsoring a personality cult and his "personal arbitrariness," and for his leftist error in planning and conducting the Cultural Revolution. In the end, it said that the "chief responsibility for the grave left error of the Cultural Revolution, an error comprehensive in magnitude and protracted in duration, does indeed lie with Comrade Mao Zedong."[22]

Perhaps it was the economic expert Chen Yun who best captured Mao's historical role:

> Had Chairman Mao died in 1956, there would have been no doubt that he was a great leader of the Chinese people. ... Had he died in 1966, his meritorious achievements would have been somewhat tarnished, but his overall record was still very good. Since he actually died in 1976, there is nothing we can do about it.[23]

Notes

1 Kenneth Lieberthal, *Governing China* (New York: W.W. Norton, 1995), p. 125.
2 Richard Baum, *Burying Mao: Chinese Politics in the Age of Deng Xiaoping* (Princeton, NJ: Princeton University Press, 1994), p. 29.
3 Cited in Harry Harding, "The Chinese State in Crisis," in *The Cambridge History of China, Vol. 15, The People's Republic, Part 2: Revolutions within the Chinese Revolution*, ed. Roderick MacFarquhar and John K. Fairbank (Cambridge, UK: Cambridge University Press, 1991), p. 133.
4 Ibid., p. 138.
5 Ibid., p. 144.
6 Cited in Richard Evans, *Deng Xiaoping and the Making of Modern China* (London: Hamish Hamilton, 1993), p. 183.
7 Harding, "The Chinese State in Crisis," pp. 211–12.
8 Ibid., p. 226.
9 Frederick C. Teiwes and Warren Sun, *The Tragedy of Lin Biao* (Honolulu: University of Hawaii Press, 1996), p. 161.
10 Roderick MacFarquhar, "The Succession to Mao and the End of Maoism," in *The Politics of China, 1949–1989*, ed. Roderick MacFarquhar (Cambridge, UK: Cambridge University Press, 1993), p. 263.
11 Teiwes and Sun, *The Tragedy of Lin Biao*, p. 14.
12 Ibid., p. 163.
13 Cited in MacFarquhar, "The Succession to Mao," pp. 295–6.
14 Both of these are cited in MacFarquhar, "The Succession to Mao," p. 302.
15 Qian Gang, *The Great China Earthquake* (Beijing: Foreign Languages Press, 1989), pp. 41–2.
16 "Central Committee 'Obituary' on the Death of Mao Zedong, October 1976," in *The Search for Modern China: A Documentary Collection*, ed. Pei-kai Cheng and Michael Lestz with Jonathan Spence (New York: W.W. Norton, 1999), pp. 444–5.
17 Li Zhisui, *The Private Life of Chairman Mao* (New York: Random House, 1994), p. 20.
18 MacFarquhar, "The Succession to Mao," p. 370.
19 Perry Link, *Evening Chats in Beijing* (New York: W.W. Norton, 1992), p. 153.
20 Jonathan D. Spence, *Mao Zedong* (New York: Lipper/Viking, 1999), p. 178.
21 Maurice Meisner, *Mao's China and After* (New York: Free Press, 1999), p. 444.
22 Ibid., pp. 463–4.
23 *Ming Bao*, January 15, 1979, p. 1, cited in Roger Garside, *Coming Alive: China After Mao* (New York: McGraw-Hill, 1982), p. 190.

Suggestions for Further Reading

Chang Jung. *Wild Swans: Three Daughters of China* (New York: Doubleday, 1991). A fascinating story of three generations of Chinese women from 1909 to 1978; the Cultural Revolution is of central focus.

Huang Shu-min. *The Spiral Road: Change in a Chinese Village through the Eyes of a Communist Party Leader* (Boulder, CO: Westview Press, 1989). This lively and absorbing story of a party cadre in Lin Village in Southeast China looks at his experiences from the time of land reform into the 1980s.

Ma Bo. *Blood Red Sunset: A Memoir of the Chinese Cultural Revolution*, trans. Howard Goldblatt (New York: Viking, 1995). This is a harrowing and horrifying memoir of a young man sent into the Mongolian grasslands during the Cultural Revolution; the dust jacket calls it "potent" and "unbridled."

Perry, Elizabeth J., and Li Xun. *Proletarian Power: Shanghai in the Cultural Revolution* (Boulder, CO: Westview Press, 1997). This careful and well-written analysis has a revisionist force in showing the far more prominent role played in the Cultural Revolution by workers in Shanghai than elsewhere; it shows how ordinary citizens played important roles in this mass campaign.

Yang Rae. *Spider Eaters: A Memoir* (Berkeley, CA: University of California Press, 1997). Yang's memoir, like Ma's (above), draws its power from her descriptions of her life in Manchuria's Heilongjiang province tending hogs during the last portion of the Cultural Revolution.

19

Reforms and Reactions, 1978–1995

I n the last year of his life, Mao chose as his successor Hua Guofeng, secretary of the Hunan CCP committee, a newcomer to national leadership, weak on credentials, burdened by his bland personality, and surrounded by vigorous veterans of the Long March. But his chief diffi-culty in continuing as Mao's successor was Deng Xiaoping. In the aftermath of the April 1976 Tian-anmen incident, Deng had been summarily dismissed from all his posts in the party-state. He had gone into hiding immediately after the Politburo made his case an "antagonistic contradiction"—transforming him into an enemy. By mid-1977, however, with the avid support of PLA command-ers and high-level party-state bureaucrats, Deng was reappointed to his old governmental posts. In 1978 the party reassessed the 1976 incident as "revolutionary," overturning Hua's continued support of the Gang of Four's judgment that it was "counterrevolutionary." Hua was ousted in December 1978, when Deng reached the leadership position he sought.

OPENING THE WINDOW TO THE WORLD

Deng had a little over eighteen years to remake China according to his vision—and remake it he powerfully did. Deng's policies were based on two tracks, economic reform and political authoritarianism—or, more directly put, open the door to market capitalism but slam it shut on any effort to liberalize the political system. Despite much discussion and debate among officials and intellectuals over the years, these tracks remained the basic framework of reform of the economy and non-reform of the political system until the present (2019).

At the Third Plenum in December 1978, he clarified how to realize what he dubbed the Four Modernizations (in agriculture, industry, national defense, and science and technology).

> Carrying out the Four Modernizations requires great growth in the
> productive forces and … changes in all methods of management,
> actions, and thinking that stand in the way of such growth. Socialist
> modernization is therefore a profound and extensive revolution.[1]

In sum, nothing less than a revolution—in economic structures, methods, actions, and thought—was needed to bring about China's modernization. Such a revolution had to be concerned about both the nation's relationship to the outside world and its internal or domestic situation.

During the 1970s and 1980s China opened many windows to the world. The number of countries that established diplomatic relations with China rose from 57 in 1970 to 119 in 1979 to 171 in 2017. One of the most important diplomatic relationships was with the United States. The Taiwan question had loomed over this relationship since the United States had fostered close ties in the 1950s and 1960s. The February 28, 1972, Shanghai Communiqué, negotiated during Nixon's visit, set down the general framework for relations between China and the United States. From the Chinese perspective, most important were the general foreign policy pledges and the U.S. statement on Taiwan. Both countries pledged not to seek hegemony in the region and to oppose other countries' attempts to do so. They agreed that trade, cultural, and scientific exchanges should be increased and that they should work to establish full diplomatic relations. The crucial statement on Taiwan dealt with the conception of "one-China":

> The United States acknowledges that all Chinese on either side of the Taiwan Strait maintain [that] there is but one China and that Taiwan is a part of China. The United States does not challenge that position. It reaffirms its interest in a peaceful settlement of the Taiwan question by the Chinese themselves. With this prospect in mind, it affirms the ultimate objective of the withdrawal of all U.S. forces and military installations from Taiwan. In the meantime, it will progressively reduce its forces and military installations on Taiwan as the tension in the area diminishes.[2]

Domestic problems in both countries delayed the opening of full diplomatic relations until January 1979. To nurture the burgeoning U.S.–China relationship, Deng visited the United States that winter. The diminutive (4 feet 9 inches) leader was serenaded at the Kennedy Center in Washington, DC, with the strains of "Getting to Know You." He donned a ten-gallon hat and ate barbecue at a Texas rodeo. At the Johnson Space Center in Houston, he took the controls of a space-shuttle simulator. It was a public relations coup. After the first corporate agreements in late 1978 with Coca-Cola and Boeing, U.S.-based firms greatly expanded their operations in Chinese investments and trade.

As China stepped ever more firmly into the international arena, people-to-people contact increased. In the 1980s large numbers of foreign tourists brought rapid growth in the tourist industry, and ever greater numbers of Chinese also traveled abroad. The number of students studying overseas rapidly increased, as did the number of foreign students coming to China. From 1979 to 1989, approximately 80,000 students and scholars went to the United States alone, and the total number of student visas from 1983 to 1988 reached 150,000. The government sent students abroad to acquire advanced training in order to help achieve the Four Modernizations on their return. Even though some students stayed longer in their programs than the government had expected and some students chose to remain in the United States, the government was undeterred. As evidence of this "brain drain," by 1989, 11,000 students had become permanent residents in the United States.

"Opening" also referred to expanding foreign trade and encouraging foreign investment. Beginning with a handful of loans, credits, and joint ventures, "opening" eventually led to full foreign ownership and operation of enterprises. In many ways this was a shocking development for it seemed a déjà vu of the pre-1949 domination of Chinese cities, businesses, and industries by Westerners. But now China was calling the shots, and its leaders believed that foreign investment and know-how were the engines to rev up that drive. In 1979, four special economic zones (SEZs) were opened on the Southeast Coast to offer special concessions to foreign investors. They were Shenzhen, across the border from Hong Kong; Zhuhai, near Macao; and Shantou and Xiamen, across the Taiwan Strait from Taiwan. Fourteen more were added in 1986; in that year, Hainan Island was also so designated. To lure foreign investments, the Chinese provided many incentives: low tax rates, convenient transportation networks, new industrial plants, and a well-trained, cheap labor force. In many ways, the SEZs were reminiscent of the old treaty ports. They provided the foreigners with amenities for a privileged lifestyle that featured Chinese servants. They created a world that was, in the words of one critic, "savagely capitalist." But the SEZs brought enormous economic benefits:

> the influx of foreign capital to finance industrial enterprises and various modernization projects, the alleviation of chronic shortages of foreign exchange, greater access to the advanced scientific and industrial technology of Japan and the Western countries, and employment for Chinese workers who would otherwise be unemployed.[3]

Joint ventures in these and other cities also helped create a flourishing private sector.

The SEZs and the desire to attract foreign investors had a cascading effect that went far beyond the delimited zones. If foreigners expected to do business in China, they needed predictable and regularized economic conditions in which to work. Predictability came with laws that protected property, specified taxes, and governed contracts. But China essentially had no such laws as of 1977. It was "governed by decrees, by bureaucratic regulations, and by personal orders of various officials."[4] In the 1980s, China began to develop a legal system that included laws, a court system, and lawyers knowledgeable about the new laws and procedures. In 1980 China had only about 3,000 lawyers. Goals announced in 1993 had called for the training and establishment of 150,000 lawyers by 2000; China reached that goal in mid-2009.[5]

Becoming part of the international economic system meant that China wanted to join international economic organizations such as the World Bank, the International Monetary Fund, and the Asian Development Bank. These provided low interest loans and various kinds of technical and economic advice. In 1980 China replaced Taiwan in the World Bank and the International Monetary Fund. Membership was a two-way street: it could greatly benefit China, but it also meant that China had to follow international guidelines and be more forthright about the details of its economic realities.

Finally, "opening" meant more porous borders with Chinese returning from overseas with new outlooks and information; foreigners traveling in China talking with Chinese about ideas and concerns (in 1987–1988 alone there were 6,000 foreign students and 36,000 foreign experts and staff in the country); increasing numbers of foreign books and journals available; the presence of computers and electronic media. What about Western bourgeois ideas? Policymakers understood that an opened window might let in some mosquitoes and flies, but self-assuredly noted that they could be quickly swatted down and killed.

ECONOMIC REFORMS ON THE HOME FRONT

The important first step in this economic revolution was to deal with China's population problem. By the late 1970s, China had 25 percent of the world's population (with two-thirds under the age of 30) but held only 7 percent of the world's tillable land. Although the important issue of limiting population growth was mentioned in passing in the 1950s, no restrictive policy was developed until the late 1970s. Indeed, in the 1960s and early 1970s, families often had five or six children. In 1973, discussions began about the feasibility of a policy of limiting the number of children in a family to one. In the mid-1970s the government began to disperse birth control devices and ratchet up population control propaganda. Population had to be controlled to allow China to modernize and raise its people's living standards. In June 1979, the government decided to institute the one-child-per-family policy except among ethnic minorities. This call prompted a new marriage law that raised the marriage age for men to twenty-two (up from twenty) and for women to twenty (from eighteen).

When 1981 statistics revealed that about 6 million "one-child" families had another baby and that over 1.5 million families with five children or more had another baby, the government passed a more draconian population control law. If a woman had one child, she had to have an intrauterine device implanted; and if a couple had more than one child, the wife or husband had to be sterilized. Birth-control cadres had to fill sterilization quotas and, if necessary, force even late-term abortions. Families who had more than one child lost various welfare and medical benefits and might be fined; in the rural areas, they might even lose their land. Such policies enforced the international image of a totalitarian state intruding into the most intimate decisions.

With such negative impacts, did the policy work to stimulate economic reforms? Susan Green-halgh has reported that Chinese officials claim that from 1979 to 2003, the one-child policy prevented 300 million births or about 13 million births a year.[6] If 13 million children had been added to the population each year, China's working age population relative to its dependent population would have been reduced by 0.75 percent for years between 1980 and 1995. Since economists have noted that when the working-age population grows at a more rapid rate than its dependent population (as it did in China in the 1980s), the per capita productive economic capacity expands. If 13 million children had been added per year, it would, according to economic scholars, have reduced by 0.78 percent the annual growth rate of the per capita GDP. That means that without the one-child policy, China's GDP per capita would have been 13.2 percent lower in 1995 than it was.[7] Indeed the one-child policy helped stimulate China's economic miracle. The policy's social and cultural impacts will be discussed in Chapter 20.

The economic liberalization in the 1980s began with the grassroots level "household responsibility system." Poor Anhui farmers on their own initiative removed their land from commune control and began to farm it as families. Deng learned of this action and allowed it to stand, when this return to pre-Communist farming practice increased production. The party-state's decision to institutionalize it indicated that pragmatism rather than ideology formed the new path of the 1980s and 1990s. Individual households leased land for fifty years; even though this was not private ownership, the land could be bought, sold, and inherited. Farmers could decide on their own how to farm. Once they paid their state grain quota, they could sell their produce/commodities and keep the profits. The people's communes, in place for a quarter of a century were gone; by 1983, 98 percent of farm households were participating in the responsibility system. Indeed, reform of the domestic economy using capitalist techniques (or, in Chinese governmental euphemism, "socialism with Chinese characteristics") became the most important economic feature shaping Chinese life.

Being able to keep profits was the crucial incentive that prompted the rapid development of family farming and stimulated a surge in agricultural production. In the period from 1978 to 1984 the annual average gross value of agricultural output was an impressive 9 percent. The new possibility of attaining some wealth motivated farmers to move resources into cash crops that would bring higher prices; some farmers invested in or established food processing and other small-scale township and village enterprises (TVEs). After the mid-1980s, prosperity in the countryside was indeed maintained because of the expansion of such TVEs, which by 1995 employed over 125 million workers.

With these changes, per capita income in rural areas almost doubled from 1978 to 1984. Improved living standards for many farmers meant new homes, better diets, and purchase of consumer goods. Stories spread of newly affluent farmers buying not only modern conveniences and luxuries, but even their own airplanes. Generally, not surprisingly, local CCP cadres fared very well, using their political power to select the best land for their families and to buy into the most profitable businesses. The new system allowed farmers to rent out their land and to hire wage laborers for help on the farm. Those who worked essentially as subtenants and hired hands were among the poor. Most towns and villages in the countryside were marked by greater inequality. The reappearance of class divisions was usually rationalized by Deng's saying, "some must get rich first."

In urban business and industry, the "market model"—allowing the production and distribution of goods to be determined by the market rather than by central government planners—was adopted in late 1979. An industrial responsibility system replaced the old system where the state had received all the profits. Now an autonomously operating for-profit enterprise paid the state a 55 percent tax on its revenues and could keep half of the profits after production costs were deducted (the state received the other half). Decisions were to be made by factory managers, who could also hire and *fire* their employees. The key word here is "fire," for up to this point in the PRC, workers in state enterprises (i.e., all enterprises) could never be fired. They held "the iron rice bowl," the term that described lifetime job security. The late 1980s saw booming industrial production. As the private sector grew, the urban economies of many cities were invigorated. Urban workers saw their average real wages more than double in the decade from 1979 to 1989. Controls on the prices of small consumer items were lifted, and prices were allowed to float according to the market level.

With improving living standards, consumer items that became all the rage included colored televisions, stereos, electric fans, refrigerators, and sewing machines. In the 1990s the list expanded to include air conditioners, high-tech sound systems, and motorcycles. Table 19.1 reveals the depth of the consumer revolution in selected cities; the statistics reflect the fact that per capita income doubled between 1978 and 1990 and went up another 50 percent from 1990 to 1994.

The beginning and acceleration of Deng's economic reforms in the late 1970s through 2000 caused a surge in demand in the industrial labor market. An estimated 100 to 130 million farmers, freed by the government from restrictions binding them to their land, traveled to urban centers with the purpose of joining the industrializing workforce. This so-called floating population was composed of workers attached to neither their former registered and certified rural household (hukou) nor to urban hukou in work or neighborhood units. They were joined by migrant day laborers who came into towns and cities from surrounding areas. Many in the floating population had no jobs and quickly became the wretched poor. The lucky found lodging in bleak shantytowns that grew up at the city's edge; others lived on the streets, in parks, under highway overpasses, and in train stations. If they found jobs, floaters usually took low-paying ones that other workers

TABLE 19.1   Consumer Items Owned per 100 Households in Selected Cities, 1986 and 1995[8]

	Refrigerators		Washing Machines		Color TVs	
	1986	**1995**	**1986**	**1995**	**1986**	**1995**
National Average	18	66	65	89	29	90
Beijing	62	98	76	100	51	102
Guangzhou	52	102	68	105	46	111
Shanghai	47	98	39	78	36	109
Shenzhen	77	102	73	97	83	125
Wuhan	29	96	24	91	17	94
Xi'an	14	83	72	96	33	101

FIGURE 19.1 Here Chinese Communist Secretary General Zhao Ziyang (r) gestures on conferring with Chinese paramount leader Deng Xiaoping during a session of the 13th Party National Congress in October 1987. Though Deng would sack Zhao after the 1989 Tiananmen crackdown, these two were in the vanguard of charting and leading the domestic progressive economic reforms featuring a market economy and a larger emphasis on business and industry privatization. Deng and Zhao laid the groundwork that led to China's economic miracle and a growing world power less than a quarter century later.
Source: John Giannini/AFP/Getty Images.

refused to do: street vendors, prostitutes, hawkers. The number of floaters grew to 70 million by 1993, doubled by 2003; hit 251 million at the end of 2014; and predicted to be 291 million in 2020, which will be one-sixth of the country's population. Statistics showed that 65 percent of the floaters "floated" in their native provinces; they were youthful: an estimated 80 percent were between the ages of fifteen and thirty-five. Commentators pointed to a substantial rise in street crime, especially petty theft. Government authorities, police, and permanent city residents generally viewed the floating population with disgust and repugnance. In sum, just as in the countryside, where the reforms had brought rapidly increasing economic and social inequality, so it was also in the cities, where shantytowns and luxury boutiques existed side by side.

In the relationships between the city-dweller and rural migrants, the critical issue was the two-tier household registration system (the hukou), based on urban and rural location, which privileged those in urban sites. When rural residents left their homes, they were without the support of hukou-based government social programs. The household registration (*hukou*) system had traumatic effects upon this floating population in the 1980s when hundreds of millions were "let go" from state corporations and cooperatives. Since then, an estimated 200 million Chinese lived outside their officially registered areas and thus were mostly ineligible, unlike urban hukou recipients, to receive basic government support services. Urban residents received priority over migrants when it came to employment opportunities, and when migrant workers did find jobs, they tended to be dead-end positions. While urban workers were supported by unemployment benefits and laws that favored them over their employers in case of disputes, rural hukou holders had no such protections. In 2008, the central government promulgated laws that guaranteed equal access to jobs, established a minimum wage, and required employers to provide contracts to full-time employees that included unemployment benefits. However, a 2010 study revealed that rural workers earned 40 percent less than urban workers, and only 16 percent received unemployment benefits.

Urban areas profited from the work of rural migrants and from the local taxes they paid, in the end leading to a wealth transfer to the wealthier urban regions from the poorer rural regions.

FIGURE 19.2   A common sight in China during the reform era were groups of people—migrant workers and the floating population—camping out in train stations or on the streets. Here migrant workers sleep in the Guangzhou train station.
Source: Julio Etchart/Alamy Stock Photo,

However, many rural residents were hesitant to give up their agricultural hukou status. As rural hukou holders, they held property rights not afforded to their urban counterparts, which allowed them to use land both for agricultural production and for personal use.

Children of rural workers faced difficult challenges. They were initially not allowed to enroll in city schools; to attend school, they had to live in their rural hometowns at their hukou registration sites with their grandparents or other relatives. Commonly called "home-staying children," (about 130 million strong in the 1980s), they lived by necessity away from their parents, who had generally moved to urban areas without being able to change their household registration. Later, when the government emphasized the construction of public schools and because the central government subsidized those schools based on enrollment rates of *children with local hukous*, migrant children were required to pay much higher fees. Students with rural hukou had to pay inflated admission fees of 3,000–5,000 yuan—coming out of an average annual household income of close to only 10,000 yuan—and were required to take their college entrance exams at their hukou locality, from which it was often harder to get into college. The difficulties migrant children faced caused many to drop out; during the middle school years, only about 30 percent remained.

In 1979, Beijing began largely unsuccessful attempts to reform the hukou system. All suggested relaxations of hukou regulations from the 1980s until 1999 were undone, or at the very least interrupted, by laws promulgated in 2003. Then in 2014 came the most drastic change, at least on paper: the policy line between rural and urban hukou was eliminated. Experts were uncertain about what this change would actually mean; they argued that previous "reforms" did not change the hukou system in any basic way, but simply decentralized hukou decision making to the local governmental level. To no one's satisfaction, they suggested no change in the hukou system, thus unfortunately continuing to contribute substantially to China's urban and rural disparity.

POLITICAL AUTHORITARIANISM

If, after 1978, greater economic freedom and various ripple effects arose from the policy of "opening" and the impacts of reforms, the political realm in its repressiveness remained as bitterly cold as an Arctic night. There was an occasional thaw, but it was followed by a return to even more frigid conditions. It is important to see, however, that the government leadership was not monolithic in its attitude toward political liberalization; some favored greater political tolerance, whereas others championed repression to keep order and stability. Factional struggle was as much a reality as struggle between the government and those in society pushing for greater political change.

Democracy Wall (1978–1979)

In November 1978, posters went up on a stretch of wall along Chang'an Boulevard, which runs across the north end of Tiananmen Square. Featuring essays and poetry, they offered general support for Deng and criticism of Hua Guofeng and Mao Zedong; they were soon joined by papers, pamphlets, and mimeographed magazines with titles such as *Explorations, April 5 Forum*, and *Beijing Spring*. At the wall itself, debates sprang up about a host of political and social issues. Many of the participants were blue-collar workers with a high school education or less. Deng first gave the wall his blessing ("The masses should be allowed to vent their grievances").

But many leaders perceived the combustible potential of the situation. At the moment that the Democracy Wall began to flourish, hundreds of thousands who had been sent to the countryside during the Cultural Revolution were returning to the cities with petitions of grievance about their unjust sufferings. The party's General Secretary Hu Yaobang called for the reexamination of cases of "unjust persecution." Over 100,000 people came to Beijing and Shanghai alone. In Beijing, rural petitioners sat down in front of the residence compound of the Chinese leaders, Zhongnanhai, and refused to leave until their petitions were received. Given the potential for social turmoil from this source, the Democracy Wall's widening criticism of existing conditions became yet another potentially disruptive element beyond the party's control. The memory of Cultural Revolution violence was all too fresh; unleashing a new round, some leaders thought, would undercut any hope of achieving the Four Modernizations.

Then a poster entitled "The Fifth Modernization" was placed on the Wall by Wei Jingsheng, a twenty-eight-year-old electrician who had served four years with the PLA. The Fifth Modernization was, he said, democracy, the "holding of power by the laboring masses themselves. ... [In democracy] the people must also have the power to replace their representatives any time so that these representatives cannot go on deceiving others in the name of the people."[9] Hu's faction, including the editor and associate editor of *People's Daily* and leaders at the Chinese Academy of Social Sciences, supported political toleration and moves toward democratic reform. It, however, was clearly in the minority; most party leaders opposed any political liberalization. Deng was still open to the minority. In a speech to senior leaders on March 16, he stated that if "the old road of suppressing differing opinion and not listening to criticism" were followed, "the result will ... make the trust and support of the masses disappear."[10] Yet he was increasingly ready to go with the majority.

In essays published in the journal *Explorations* on March 25, editor Wei Jingsheng challenged Deng with blistering criticism:

Does Deng Xiaoping want democracy? No, he does not. He is unwilling to comprehend the misery of the common people. He is unwilling to allow the people to regain those powers usurped by ambitious careerists. He describes the struggle for democratic rights—a

FIGURE 19.3   Wei Jingsheng emerged as China's most famous late-twentieth-century political dissident. Imprisoned in the Democracy Wall episode in 1979 after his calls for a Fifth Modernization (democracy), he was allowed to leave China in the late 1990s for the United States.
Source: Patrick Durand/Sygma via Getty Images.

movement launched spontaneously by the people—as the actions of troublemakers who must be repressed. … If his idea of democracy is one that does not allow others to criticize those in power, then how is such a democracy different from Mao Zedong's tyranny concealed behind the slogan "The Democracy of the Dictatorship of the Proletariat"?[11]

With the movement beginning to spread across China, Deng was convinced by the majority that it must be stopped. Thus, on March 29, the Beijing municipal government issued strict new regulations limiting mass meetings and demonstrations. On that day the "four cardinal principles" were issued, shoving out of sight the "four big freedoms" that had been set down in 1978 in the revised constitution (the freedoms to "speak out freely, air views fully, engage in great debates, and write big-character posters"). The four cardinal principles set the boundaries of the four big freedoms: "All activities in opposition to socialism, in opposition to the proletarian dictatorship, in opposition to leadership by the party, or in opposition to Marxism–Leninism–Mao Zedong Thought … are prohibited by law and will be prosecuted."[12] In January 1980, Deng proposed the permanent elimination of the four big freedoms from the constitution.

Democracy Wall under Deng was apparently no more viable than the Hundred Flowers were under Mao. It should not, of course, have been surprising, given the fact that Deng over two decades earlier had been in charge of trampling the flowers. The upshot was that Wei Jingsheng, along with other activists and journal editors, was arrested. Wei was charged with "counterrevolutionary incitement" and spying—specifically, turning over information to a foreign journalist about the just-finished debacle of China's invasion of Vietnam. Tried in October 1979, Wei was sentenced to fifteen years in prison; most of his arrested colleagues received from ten to fifteen years, often in solitary confinement. By the end of 1979, the Democracy Wall was moved to an out-of-the-way place two miles from its former location. The closing of the Wall at the beginning of the economic reforms was symbolically indicative of the repressive political policies that continually won out over more progressive policies in later "reform" regimes.

The key figure among those who were primarily economic reformers was Zhao Ziyang, provincial reformer in Sichuan and protégé of Deng Xiaoping, who became premier in the early 1980s. The second of Deng's protégés, Hu Yaobang, was a political liberal. He had served for many years

MAP 19.1 The PRC, 2018.

as head of the Communist Youth League and the Chinese Academy of Social Sciences; he became party general secretary in the early 1980s. Both were opposed by more conservative figures. In the reform context of the 1980s, those opposed to capitalistic reform were the old Maoists, who in the 1960s and 1970s would have been tagged leftists or radicals. In the 1980s and 1990s, however, holding their same positions, they became conservatives or reactionaries, political labels being completely relative to their context.

Conservatives Lash Out: the Early 1980s

From the 1942 Yan'an Forum on Arts and Literature into the 1980s, intellectuals and writers had been the political and ideological lightning rods for the party-state. Angry and belligerent attacks on individual artists had repeatedly kicked off mass campaigns. In 1981 and 1983, conservatives, intensely threatened by the economic reforms, "opening," and their impacts on party ideology and Chinese society, lashed out in two campaigns, in 1981 against "bourgeois liberalization" and in 1983 against "spiritual pollution." Both were indicative primarily of the intense struggle between reformers and conservatives. In the first, the party targeted several writers, criticizing them for forsaking the four cardinal principles and glorifying bourgeois values. Their scapegoats were the snakes and monsters of Western liberal political thought and the continually-talked-about bugaboo of pornography. They were most afraid of intellectuals challenging the party-state. Deng and even the liberal Hu Yaobang denounced the works of some writers.

In the 1983 anti-spiritual pollution campaign the target was those with an "attitude of doing anything for money." In a speech at the Second Plenum of the Twelfth Party Congress, Deng decried writers and artists who used "low and vulgar form and content to turn an easy profit."[13] His remarks presented conservatives with a weapon to attack reformers. Mao's heirs, they railed: "the reforms are leading to pornography and box office values in literature and art. This must be stopped. The people must be trained in the four cardinal principles." As an upshot, several minor figures in the reform faction lost their jobs. Editorial rantings, haranguing speeches, and sporadic searches focused mostly on specific elements of "pollution": Western-style individualism, clothing, hairdos, and facial hair; pornographic (called "yellow" in Chinese) films and videotapes; "decadent" music; and the reappearance of "feudal" superstitions and religion. All of these evils were allegedly a spin-off of capitalism, about which ultraconservative Deng Liqun screeched in surveying the biggest SEZ of them all: "Nothing in Shenzhen is socialist except for its five-starred flag. [It is] practically like Hong Kong."[14]

The campaign ended abruptly when Hu and Zhao, backed by Deng, fought back. When, at a party meeting, Deng Liqun charged that "spiritual pollution threatens the life of the party," Zhao retorted that foreign countries wanting to invest in China were beginning to have second thoughts because of the spiritual pollution campaign and that, if China was going to continue to modernize, it had better stop this sideshow. As if to taunt the conservatives, Hu and Zhao both began wearing Western-style suits and ties for public functions rather than the old Mao jacket.

Exit Hu Yaobang (1986–1987)

More serious practical problems for the reformers erupted in late 1986. The year before there had been a flurry of student unrest across the country over a wide range of issues: poor campus living conditions, racial tensions and relations, party-state corruption, and outrage at the Japanese prime minister's visit to a Shinto shrine where some war criminals were buried. In addition, inflation was rising, and many people were experiencing malaise from a sense of unequal opportunity in the new economy. In the summer party leaders had begun to debate the advisability of instituting greater political reforms. The debate only sharpened the antagonism between the factions.

Several liberal social theorists and critics began to call for basic political change, including a multiparty parliamentary system. The most influential, the astrophysicist Fang Lizhi, one of China's leading scientists, was no shrinking violet when it came to speaking about politics. In an open session with students in November 1986, he declared, "I am here to tell you that the socialist movement, from Marx and Lenin to Stalin and Mao Zedong, has been a failure. I think that complete Westernization is the only way to modernize."[15] Speaking on various campuses, he encouraged students to take the struggle for democracy into their own hands. In December students took to the streets in Fang Lizhi's home city of Hefei in Anhui province to protest the fact that slates of candidates for the provincial People's Congress were put up solely by the party. Within the month, demonstrators on 150 campuses in seventeen cities and numbering in the tens of thousands, called for greater freedom, an end to party nepotism, and better university dormitories and cafeterias. They were met by a stone wall. In Shanghai, Mayor Jiang Zemin reminded the students that the four big freedoms were no longer in the constitution. He then sent police to forcibly remove students camped around city hall. Demonstrations quickly died down. In Beijing, Deng ordered students to get back to class; they did.

The major casualty of the affair was Party General Secretary Hu, one of Deng's chosen successors. Following his more liberal political views, he had called for conciliation with the students. Faced with a barrage of panicked shrieks from the conservatives about the dangers of bourgeois democracy, Deng decided that Hu had to go. The party line: Hu had not been tough enough in his efforts against spiritual pollution and had not provided proper leadership for the party. Hu resigned in January 1987. Several prominent intellectuals, including Fang Lizhi, were expelled from the party, and in the wave of anti-"bourgeois liberalization" that swept over the country in 1987, other liberal intellectuals were asked to resign from the CCP.

THE DEMOCRACY MOVEMENT ("BEIJING SPRING," 1989)

The late 1986–early 1987 demonstrations were the precursors of the so-called Democracy Movement in the spring of 1989. Between the two movements, the liberal reformers had held sway, with many of the older conservative members of the Politburo retiring at the Thirteenth Party Congress in the fall of 1987; at the congress, Zhao Ziyang was confirmed as Hu's successor as general secretary. In 1988 the economy started overheating, with rising inflation, declining wages, and rising unemployment. To complicate the economic picture, that spring the government began to deregulate prices of specific retail items—eggs, meat, vegetables, and sugar; in July, cigarettes and alcoholic beverages were added to the list. Before each deregulation occurred, consumers tended to panic, going on buying sprees out of fear that once price controls were gone, inflation would go through the roof. People began to use all their savings and regular checking accounts to buy up items rumored to be next. For example, in the Manchurian city of Harbin in July 1988, the main department store sold 200 times its usual monthly average of electrical appliances; in a three-day period later that month, account holders withdrew 12 million yuan from their bank accounts. Both Zhao and Deng had supported price deregulation, but Deng abandoned that position, leaving Zhao suddenly high and dry.

Coupled with the economic woes were social problems. Some grew out of the economic difficulties. Between 20 and 30 million workers in state enterprises were laid off; urban unemployment in August 1988 was over 4 million. The situation was not helped by the ever greater influx of the floating population, which reached 1.1 million in Beijing alone. Crime was increasing, especially the white-collar corruption of party bigwigs and cadres. Several racial incidents unsettled college campuses. There were calls for demonstrations against party cadre corruption and nepotism and for human rights. The party took it on the chin in public opinion polls as cynicism and rhetorical defiance of the party became common. Just 7 percent of 600,000 workers thought that the party had changed for the better in the last three years. Among students, the party fared especially poorly. In one poll, 62 percent of undergraduates and 92 percent of graduate students contended that the main causes of student unrest were party cadres who were dishonest and venal and who were blind to the realities of democracy.

Among the party leadership was a growing dissatisfaction with Zhao's economic policies. Premier Li Peng, for one, wanted to pour ice water on the overheated economy by slowing down the pace of development. Li and others seemed to be winning: At the end of the year, price controls were reinstituted on items ranging from eggs to shoes to washing machines. Zhao began to be hammered by some of the older conservatives who had left the Politburo but stood carping in the wings that Zhao favored bourgeois ideologies. Many began pressing Deng to get rid of Zhao. In the midst of troubles all around, liberal intellectuals, including Fang Lizhi, continued to write and speak about the necessity of democratic reforms. On January 6, 1989, Fang sent an open letter to Deng, asking for the release of all political prisoners, including Democracy Wall victim/hero Wei Jingsheng. Within two months, letters supporting Fang had been sent by seventy-five scholars.

A contingent event brought together many of the strands in the increasingly uneasy national situation: on April 15, Hu Yaobang died. He had been the students' supporter in 1986 and the strongest voice in the government for political reform. As in the case of Zhou Enlai in 1976, commemoration of Hu became a pretext for action. Students flocked to Tiananmen Square and took to the streets of cities across the country, organizing autonomous student organizations. They called for the same reforms as two years earlier—democracy, an end to party nepotism and corruption, increased budgets for education, plus three new demands: a reevaluation of the role of Hu Yaobang, rehabilitation of victims of the campaigns of the early 1980s, and publication of the incomes of top leaders and their children.

Party leaders immediately denounced the demonstrations with harsh language. Deng and the party condemned student actions as "turmoil," a particularly combative judgment. Zhao, already in serious trouble among party leaders because of the economy, further alienated conservatives by his efforts to deal with the students in a more conciliatory way. The party's condemnation only stiffened the backs of student leaders, who organized huge demonstrations, one of the largest on the seventieth anniversary of the May Fourth Incident. Between May 4 and 19, over 1.5 million students in 500 colleges and universities across the country demonstrated in support of student actions in Beijing; by the end of May that number soared to 3 million. Some flagging of student commitment in early May was revived by a hunger strike staged at Tiananmen Square, the destination of the demonstration marches. The hunger strike changed the situation dramatically. It turned the student effort into a moral crusade against an evil government, a crusade that posed the possibility of martyrdom. In that vein, for hunger strikers, compromise was less possible; the rhetoric of moral superiority and outrage was heightened.

The new reality created by the hunger strike split student demonstrators into two camps, mirroring the division in the government leadership. Student leaders such as Wu'er Kaixi and Wang Dan were willing to seek a compromise, but others such as the female student Chai Ling were moral zealots unwilling to budge an inch. Chai best states the zealot position:

> [H]ow can I tell them [my fellow students] that what we are actually hoping for is bloodshed, the moment when the government is ready to butcher the people brazenly? Only when the square is awash with blood will the people of China open their eyes. Only then will they really be united.[16]

Several government initiatives failed because student radicals refused to participate. A second change brought by the hunger strike was that, more than any other strategy or tactic, it stimulated support from Beijing society at large. By mid-May demonstrators were being supported and joined by workers, teachers, police, doctors, nurses, and journalists.

Student occupation of the square, which was increasingly awash in trash and festering with unsanitary conditions, was a huge embarrassment to the Chinese government when Mikhail Gorbachev arrived on May 15 to normalize relations between China and the Soviet Union. What was to have been a crowning glory for the aged Deng turned into bitter humiliation. After Gorbachev's departure on May 18, party hard-liners led by Premier Li on May 20 announced the imposition of martial law, arguing that what was at stake was "The nation's reform and opening to the outside world, and the fate and future of the People's Republic."[17] Units of the PLA were ordered to clear the streets of demonstrators. But an estimated 1 to 2 million people in Beijing took to the streets to block the advancing soldiers and to dissuade them from taking action against the demonstrators. The government ordered the troops pulled back temporarily. On May 24 Party General Secretary Zhao was ousted and placed under house arrest. In a remarkable book, *Prisoner of State: The Secret Journal of Premier Zhao Ziyang*, published in the spring of 2009, Zhao, who died in 2005, argued that the key dynamic of the whole episode was not to suppress a student rebellion but "to settle a power struggle between conservative and liberal factions."[18]

This massive and unprecedented display of people power in stopping the PLA advance brought industrial workers into the demonstrations. On April 20 the Beijing Workers Autonomous Federation had been formed. Concerned more with bread-and-butter issues ("The bureaucratic cats get fat, while the people starve") than abstract issues of democracy, the federation nevertheless had thrown its support behind the students. Its membership shot up from 2,000 in early May to 20,000 after the declaration of martial law. Students in the square had little contact with the federation until, with student ranks beginning to thin at the end of May, they invited the federation to set up their headquarters at the square.

FIGURE 19.4   Constructed from Styrofoam and plaster in the closing days of the democracy movement in late May 1989, the "Goddess of Democracy" was a potent symbol of the effort which was, in the end, doomed.
Source: Peter Turnley/Corbis/VCG via Getty Images.

For two weeks the stalemate between the people and the PLA continued. On May 30 the demonstrators unveiled a Styrofoam and plaster statue, the "Goddess of Democracy," the last major effort of the movement. In the early morning hours of June 4 came the crackdown. The PLA moved into the city from the west. Many citizens died along their route on Chang'an Boulevard and its western reaches; in the square itself there were few, if any, casualties. Estimates of those killed have ranged from the hundreds to the thousands. The PLA also had losses. On one stretch of the boulevard, sixty-five PLA trucks and forty-seven armored personnel carriers were reportedly totally destroyed, and another 485 damaged; government sources reported that in this battle alone, six PLA soldiers were killed and 1,114 wounded.

The government's rationale for the crackdown was fear of anarchy and counterrevolution. Conservatives in the leadership, epitomized most clearly by Premier Li, were certain that the movement had to be stopped. Most threatening to the leadership was the formation of independent workers' unions, the large numbers of citizens from many walks of life who had supported the movement, the actions of the people of Beijing in immobilizing the PLA, and the rhetoric of the students. From the perspective of the people, the *People's* Liberation Army had been mobilized for the first time *against* the people. Around the world there was shock, dismay, and condemnation that the government had not been willing to seek a compromise and had resorted instead to brute force. Only later did it come to light that the students also had to share the blame, that the tragic stalemate was kept alive in part because a handful of student radicals refused to consider compromise. Protest demonstrations over the government's bloody handling of the crisis erupted in at least a dozen places around the country. The bloodiest was in Chengdu, the capital of Sichuan province, where rioting led to martial law, which led, in turn, to the killing of thirty to 300 people. In Shanghai six people were killed and as many injured when a train plowed into a group of demonstrators; protestors, in turn, torched the train.

With mass arrests, the government once again enforced at least outward conformity to its rule. The aftermath of Beijing Spring was harsh repression. The number of cadres expelled from

FIGURE 19.5   In an act of incredible bravery (and perhaps foolhardiness), this young man stepped into the path of a column of tanks on June 5, 1989. He succeeded in stopping the tanks before a group of friends hustled him away. His identity and subsequent experiences are unknown.
Source: AP Photos/Shutterstock.

the party for participating in or sympathizing with the Democracy Movement numbered in the thousands. Along with newspapers and journals, intellectuals became government targets as political dissenters were caught and imprisoned. In the end, after trials for counter-revolutionary crimes in early 1991, thirty-one dissidents were convicted and sentenced to two to thirteen years in prison. Fang Lizhi and his wife, who had taken refuge in the U.S. embassy following the episode, were allowed to leave the country in June 1990.

The political crisis in the spring of 1989 did not end the wrangling between avid reformers and embittered conservatives. In the 1980s, Deng had adopted a policy of "two steps forward, one step back" in a pragmatic move to market socialism rather than taking the big plunge in one bold move, a policy which had led to much dislocation in Russia, for example. In 1989, Deng chose centrist Jiang Zemin, the former mayor of Shanghai, to be the party general secretary. Jiang supported reforms and in April 1991, he selected another former mayor of Shanghai, reformer Zhu Rongji, to head economic restructuring efforts as governor of the People's Bank of China. Cries of conservatives became ever more strident, asserting that the "'reformist road' was actually the 'capitalist road.'"[19] Deng, eighty-seven years old, who now walked and talked with difficulty, grew increasingly angry. When a group of retired conservatives called on the Central Committee in late 1991 to restructure the SEZs because they were in reality capitalist and had become quicksands of peaceful evolution (rather than revolution through class struggle).[20] Deng knew he had to act dramatically to save his reform program.

From January 18 to February 21, 1992, Deng traveled to the South to inspect two SEZs, Shenzhen and Zhuhai, and visit several cities. His goal was to highlight the progress brought by reform and "opening," thereby justifying his policies. On the tour he called for even faster progress:

> We should be bolder in carrying out reforms and opening up to the outside world and in making experimentations; we should not act like a woman with bound feet. For what we regard as correct, just try it and go ahead daringly.[21]

The Fourteenth Party Congress, which met in October 1992, confirmed Deng's directions for rapid economic market reforms. It also swept into the Politburo seven strong supporters of Deng's program.

After Deng's southern tour, state enterprises were given greater autonomy to deal with capitalist markets at home and abroad and to issue stocks that could be bought and sold on stock exchanges that were set up in Shenzhen and Shanghai. In the middle of the decade, economic czar Zhu Rongji was able to slow a soaring inflation—24 percent in 1994—to a respectable 6 percent in 1996 and still maintain the charging economic growth. Whereas at the beginning of the 1990s most of the foreign investment had come from overseas Chinese via Hong Kong and Taiwan, by late in the decade multinational groups, including Japanese and U.S. corporations, had begun to surpass the earlier investors. In the 1990s China experienced an economic boom unprecedented in that country or perhaps in the world. From 1991 to 1997 the gross domestic product (GDP) rose at an annual average rate of 11 percent. Between 1980 and 2000, the size of the Chinese economy quadrupled. Indeed, as one journalist put it, "The explosion of wealth in China may prove to be the most important trend in the world during this age."[22]

Deng himself died on February 19, 1997. Perhaps an American scholar said it best: "Although Deng Xiaoping could claim a long revolutionary lineage, he will best be remembered as the father of Chinese capitalism."[23] Indeed, one of the hallmarks of the reform period was the exaltation of material incentives over ideology. Deng's pragmatic openness to capitalistic innovations in order to build a modern socialist state is undoubtedly best symbolized by his statement that "It doesn't matter if the cat is white or black, so long as it catches mice." Deng's second most famous dictum—"To get rich is glorious"—carried the day. Even his lingering death (his last public appearance came in February 1994) helped perpetuate his program, for it allowed Jiang Zemin and the reformers time to gain firm control of the policymaking apparatus. The Fifteenth Party Congress, held seven months after his death, in September 1997, reconfirmed the party's commitment to Deng's vision.

GOVERNMENT ACTION IN DEALING WITH THE IMPACTS OF REFORMS

Apart from the political rivalry and factionalism over reform, there were both positive and negative changes that reforms brought the consumer. In the 1990s, the party-state began to address the social, economic, and political challenges created by reforms. Problems with corruption, the environment, and population issues are discussed in Chapter 20.

Income Disparity: Growing Economic Inequality

Personal income and opportunities to make money seemed paramount concerns for individuals looking at themselves and at society in general. The amassing of money and material goods seemed to have become an increasingly legitimate value in itself, along with the thought that the end (making money) justified any means. The attitude seemed to be "I'll take whatever I can get; everyone else be damned." In Beijing, the slang expression *sha ci* ("to kill the closest") became common in the mid-1990s among money-hungry men and women.

> To *sha ci* was to take advantage of those close at hand, one's confidants and friends, to get a foot in the door of the marketplace and steal a march on the competition. If in the process, a former comrade-in-arms, a childhood friend, or long-term associate had to be sacrificed for the sale of a business deal, then so be it.[24]

A crucial issue in the drive for wealth was the growing income inequality among people within cities, between cities and rural areas, between coastal regions and the interior, and between state and private workers. There were reports of an embittered jealousy ("red-eye" disease) among city dwellers of other city dwellers who were outpacing them in the race for riches.[25] It was common for workers in state sector enterprises to complain about their less lucrative situation than that of private sector workers. All people tended to rail against the advantages of party cadres, who were often (and with just cause) accused of corruption and greed. Personal discontent with one's economic plight was not helped by the escalation in conspicuous consumption; the wealthy bought not only one car but three or four, among them often a Lexus or a BMW. Two of the most discontented and embittered groups among the new social and economic have-nots were intellectuals and educators. Some professors were paid half as much as waitresses in joint venture hotels; some moonlighted by setting up noodle stands or shoe stalls.

There was not only jealousy about others' success relative to one's own; the income gap and the consequent difference in living standards were upsetting for other reasons. Still-believing CCP members saw the return of capitalism and its evils as anathema; that is why the party continued to try to cover it up by calling it "socialism with a Chinese face." Among authorities and the masses alike, there were concerns that the widening income disparity had the potential for unleashing social disruption and chaos. Those who saw their incomes and living standards as lower than those of other groups tended to believe that better-off groups had unfair advantages. Social perceptions produced various social rifts that had the potential to undermine social harmony.

Income Disparity: City versus Countryside

Early in the reform period, urban workers watched enviously as farmers became entrepreneurs in the countryside. The average annual savings of a farm household in 1979 was little more than 10 yuan, but by 1994 it was almost 600 yuan. But in the 1990s, cities became the far more advantageous location than the countryside. In the mid-1990s, the average annual income for city dwellers was 3,855 yuan, while in the countryside it was less than 1,550 yuan, a per capita income ratio of 2.49 to 1.

In the past, a rural–urban split may not have been so noticed when there was far less mobility in China. But in the 1990s, farmers could see urban realities and lifestyles on television and thus be reminded of just how great the gap was. Many rural families also had members who joined the floating population; they sent or brought back news of the vastly different situation in cities. In the 1980s and 1990s, many cities helped perpetuate this split by establishing discriminatory laws against rural migrants. The tensions between urban and rural areas revived the clash that had long marked Chinese society; authorities had generally taken the side of the cities. In severe floods in the summers of 1990 and 1998, for example, the state blew up dikes and levees protecting farmland along the Yangzi River in order to save cities downstream. Farmers lost their homes, their crops, their farm animals—all to save the cities, a stark example of what seemed an obvious second-class citizenship. Another example of the pro-city bias was found in the system of state subsidies. In the late 1980s, for example, city dwellers received average overall subsidies (like grain subsidies) that came to almost 40 percent of their total income, whereas taxes in the countryside were so high that they exceeded state subsidies by 2 percent.

FIGURE 19.6   Symbols of the growing gap between rich and poor: a Shenzhou shantytown (in the foreground) has the backdrop of a castle at an amusement park.
Source: kpzfoto/Alamy Stock Photo.

High taxes remained a major problem in the countryside. Though the national government's tax on rural household income was set at 5 percent, local government officials collected other special levies, tolls, and fees that jacked up the total tax bill for the rural dweller from 15 to even 50 percent of a household's income. When much of the added tax money ended up in local officials' pockets and reappeared in luxurious lifestyles, farmers became embittered, a feeling that asserted itself in violent outbursts. In January 1993, for example, about 10,000 farmers in Renshou county, Sichuan province, reacted to their crushing burden of about 115 separate taxes. They attacked township government offices, burned a police car, and destroyed the homes of township elites. Temporarily soothed by government promises, the farmers exploded again in late spring, when the county government persisted in demanding new taxes. Thousands launched attacks on office buildings, set fires, burned vehicles, and took a policeman hostage. Eventually the government backed down. In August 2000 in the area of the old Jiangxi Soviet, 20,000 farmers, armed with sticks and clubs, revolted against harsh taxes; hundreds of farmers were arrested.

Income Disparity: Regional China

Deng's economic reform strategy was for Guangdong, the Southeast Coast, and Shanghai and Pudong (the territory of Shanghai east of the Huangpu River) to be the engines driving the national economy. Indeed, this region where the SEZs were established from 1979 to 1986 saw rapid growth. From 1990 to 1995, though making up only 15 percent of Chinese territory, the coastal areas received 67.4 percent of foreign investments. That helped produce such prosperity that farm homes in Zhejiang province, for example, were attractive, modern, two-story structures with garages, satellite dishes, and all the modern conveniences, quite similar in appearance inside and out to homes that might be found in any U.S. suburb.

The interior areas lagged far behind in economic development. Whereas Central and Western China were about equal in per capita GDP (the total value of goods and services produced solely within the domestic economy), the Central provinces attracted substantially more foreign investment—a fact that would likely put this region on a faster track to development. In the first half of the 1990s, the GNP (GDP plus earned income from investment or work abroad) of Eastern China increased by 16 percent each year, compared to 9 percent in Central and Western China; there was a predictably large gap in per capita wealth. Of the Chinese people who lived in absolute poverty, 90 percent lived in the Western areas. Amid such poverty, consumption expenditures were understandably very low. Table 19.2 highlights the regional disparity through the regional percentages of per capita GDP and population from 1980 to 2005.[26]

TABLE 19.2 Regional Population and Gross Domestic Product Data

	1980		1990		2000		2005	
	GDP	**Pop.**	**GDP**	**Pop.**	**GDP**	**Pop.**	**GDP**	**Pop.**
Eastern	43.8. T	33.9	45.9	34.1	53.5	35.1	55.6	35.8
Central	22.3	28.3	21.8	28.5	19.2	28.1	18.8	27.5
Western	20.2	28.7	20.3	28.5	17.3	28.5	16.9	28.2
Northeastern	13.7	9.1	11.9	8.8	9.9	8.6	8.7	8.4
Total	100	100	100	100	100	100	100	100

Over the years, the disparity gave rise to considerable bitterness in the Central and Western regions over policies that favored the coast. Aware of the situation, the National People's Congress in the spring of 2000 voted to shift the national development focus to the nine provinces and autonomous zones of Central and Western China. The policy shift came for crucial reasons: the relative poverty in the Central and Western regions brought reduced consumer demand; fears of social unrest were acute in a region with many ethnic minorities; increasingly high crime rates spiraled up from the brutal poverty; and there was an increasingly rapid degradation of the region's environment. Premier Zhu Rongji (1998–2003), who oversaw the planning for the development of the Western region stated in his government report that the development effort was "a systematic project and long-term task which may take the efforts of several generations."[27] The government undertook ten major projects including railroad construction, water-control projects, the construction of eleven new airports and the renovation of nine more, and the construction of a 4,200-kilometer natural gas pipeline from Xinjiang province to Shanghai.

Notes

1 "Quarterly Documentation," *China Quarterly* 77 (March 1979): 168.
2 Jonathan D. Pollack, "The Opening to America," in *The Cambridge History of China, Vol. 15, The People's Republic, Part 2: Revolutions within the Chinese Revolution, 1966–1982*, ed. Roderick MacFarquhar and John K. Fairbank (Cambridge, UK: Cambridge University Press, 1991), pp. 423–4.
3 Maurice Meisner, *Mao's China and After* (New York: Free Press, 1999), pp. 457–8.
4 Kenneth Lieberthal, *Governing China* (New York: W.W. Norton, 1995), p. 151.
5 Michael Sainsbury, "Squeeze Put on China's 150,000 Lawyers," *The Australian* (June 19, 2009): www.theaustralian.news.com.au/business/stormy/0.25656688-17044.00.html
6 Susan Greenhalgh, "Science, Modernity, and the Making of the One-Child Policy," in *Population and Development Review* from the Wiley Online Library (June 2003), p. 1.
7 Zhihao Yu, "Demographic Dynamics and Economic Take-Off—the Economic Impact of China's Population-Control Policies" (2008): www.tandfonline.com/doi/abs/10.2753/CES1097-1475440105, pp.1–4, 6.
8 Taken from Deborah S. Davis, "Introduction: A Revolution in Consumption," in *The Consumer Revolution in Urban China* (Berkeley, CA: University of California Press, 1999), p. 4.
9 Quoted in Jonathan Spence, *The Search for Modern China* (New York: W.W. Norton, 1990), pp. 626–7.
10 Quoted in Richard Baum, *Burying Mao: Chinese Politics in the Age of Deng Xiaoping* (Princeton, NJ: Princeton University Press, 1994), p. 78.
11 Wei Jingsheng, "Democracy or a New Dictatorship?" *Explorations* (March 1979), reprinted in *Wild Lily, Prairie Fire*, ed. Gregor Benton and Alan Hunter (Princeton, NJ: Princeton University Press, 1995), p. 182.
12 Quoted in Baum, *Burying Mao*, p. 79.
13 Ibid., pp. 157–8.
14 Ibid., p. 160.
15 Ibid., p. 201.
16 Quoted in Geremie Barmé, *In the Red: On Contemporary Chinese Culture* (New York: Columbia University Press, 1999), p. 329.
17 "Li Peng's Announcement of Martial Law, May 20, 1989," in *The Search for Modern China: A Documentary Collection*, ed. Pei-kai Cheng and Michael Lestz with Jonathan Spence (New York: W.W. Norton, 1999), p. 497.
18 Adi Ignatius, "Tiananmen Ghosts," *Time* 173, no. 20 (May 25, 2009): 28.
19 Richard Baum, *Burying Mao*, p. 339.
20 These ideas are set forth clearly in Damien Ma, "After 20 years of 'Peaceful Evolution' China Faces Another Historic Moment," *The Atlantic* (January 22, 2012).
21 "Main Points of Deng Xiaoping's Talks in Wuchang, Shenzhen, Zhuhai, and Shanghai from January 18 to February 21, 1992," in *China Since Tiananmen*, ed. Lawrence R. Sullivan (Armonk, NY: M.E. Sharpe, 1995), p. 151.

22 Nicholas D. Kristof and Sheryl Wudunn, *China Wakes* (New York: Random House, 1994), p. 14.
23 Meisner, *Mao's China and After*, p. 521.
24 Geremie R. Barmé, *In the Red: On Contemporary Chinese Culture* (New York: Columbia University Press, 1999), p. 98.
25 Lieberthal, *Governing China*, p. 308.
26 Shantong Li and Zhaoyuan Xu, "The Trend of Regional Income Disparity in the People's Republic of China" (January 2008), www.adbi.org/files/dp85.regional.income.disparity.prc.pdf
27 Li Cheng, "China in 2000: A Year of Strategic Rethinking," *Asian Survey* 41, no. 1 (January–February 2001): p. 83.

Suggestions for Further Reading

Baum, Richard. *Burying Mao: Chinese Politics in the Age of Deng Xiaoping* (Princeton, NJ: Princeton University Press, 1996). This analysis of Chinese politics in the reform years of Deng Xiaoping is insightful and readable. Baum carries his study up to the spring of 1989.

Liang, Zhang. comp. *The Tiananmen Papers*, ed. Andrew Nathan and Perry Link (New York: Public Affairs, 2001). Purported to be government documents and records of government meetings during the crisis of 1989, this, in the words of a reviewer, is "an absolute must read for anyone interested in the politics" of the episode.

Liu, Xin. *In One's Own Shadow: An Ethnographic Account of the Conditions of Post-Reform Rural China* (Berkeley, CA: University of California Press, 2000). This eye-opening study focuses on a rural community in contemporary Shaanxi province where the reforms have brought poverty and loss of dignity and power.

Liu, Xinwu R. *"Jumping into the Sea": From Academics to Entrepreneurs in South China* (Lanham, MD: Rowman & Littlefield, 2001). A nuanced case study of a group of academics who developed and attempted to manufacture and market a new kind of alarm system.

Solinger, Dorothy. *Contesting Citizenship in Urban China: Peasant Migrants, the State, and the Logic of the Market* (Berkeley, CA: University of California Press, 1999). This insightful study (and award-winning book) appeals to historians and social scientists; Solinger explores the world of the floating population, its motivations, and its experiences.

20

The Economic Miracle and Its Shadows, 1992–2018

The administrations of party general secretaries Jiang Zemin (1989–2002) and Hu Jintao (2002–2012) were thoroughly committed to the continuation of economic reforms. For the nation, the economic success was spectacular as China became the world's second largest economy in 2010 and the largest trading nation in the world in 2013. Its Gross Domestic Product in 2016 made up 14.9 percent ($11.2 trillion) of the global output, which was second only to that of the United States (25 percent, 18.6 trillion). China became the world's largest exporter of goods in the world in 2009. Data from 2011–2013 show that in the world economy China produced 90.6 percent of all personal computers; 80 percent of all air conditioners; 70.6 percent of all mobile phones; 63 percent of all shoes; 60 percent of all cement; 50 percent of all DVDs; 49.8 percent of all pork products; 48.2 percent of coal; and 43.1 percent of clothing.[1]

During the 28-year period 1989 to 2017, the annual growth GDP rate averaged a remarkable 9.69 percent. Statistics from the World Bank show this stunning economic progress through GDP per capita from 1978, the inauguration of the reforms, to 2016 and projected to 2022.

China, GDP Per Capita, Selected Years
1978—185.4   2010—4,560.5
1992—366.5   2016—8,123.2
2000—959.4   2022—12,834.7 (projected)[2]

THE JIANG AND HU YEARS: ECONOMIC REFORMS AND POLITICAL CHANGE

The most daring of Jiang Zemin's economic proposals was partially privatizing state-owned enterprises (SOEs). Privatization had immense economic, social, and political implications for the Chinese people and the Chinese state, as well as for personal and national identity. SOEs made up 40 percent of industrial output in 1997 and were critical in the areas of high technology and heavy industry (steel, mining, machine building, and petrochemicals). Almost 70 percent of these SOEs were losing money and had to be subsidized by the state, a policy that depleted the state budget and did nothing to spur development and modernization. The effort was daring for two reasons. First, by conventional definition, "socialism" (which all the reformers still claimed was the Chinese system) is a system where the state owns and controls industry. If the state was now giving most industry (key industries were to be excepted) over to private hands, where was the socialism that was allegedly the hallmark of the system? Second, the SOEs employed over 120 million workers. When enterprises were privatized and profit became the bottom line, many of these workers were let go. Despite worries about the potential for serious social unrest in such a case, the Fifteenth Party Congress in September 1997 gave the go-ahead to privatization.

That policy change entailed a drastic restructuring of the social and economic landscape. After three years of this restructuring, directed by Zhu, the financial condition of 52.5 percent of the SOEs had been reversed: they were out of financial trouble. Despite the resulting unemployment and rising urban poverty rates, privatization continued. In 2002, the government approved dismantling the State Power Corporation, breaking it up into a number of private power companies. In 2003, plans were announced for the privatization of television production. In 2004, the State-Owned Asset Supervision and Administrative Commission (SASAC) turned over 300,000 small SOEs to provincial and local governments; many of these were sold to private firms.[3] In 2005 the pace of privatization slowed somewhat as the government became increasingly focused on growing economic inequality.

Changes in the Communist Party

At the beginning of the twenty-first century, the party-state redefined the party. In February 2000, Jiang Zemin publicly discussed what became known as the "Three Represents." The CCP, he argued, should continue to lead China as long as it represented the "advanced forces of production, advanced culture, and the interests of the people."[4] In essence, with the first two "represents," he opened the party membership up to capitalists and technocrats (advanced forces of production in the reformist agenda) and intellectuals (advanced culture). It was an historic break with Marxist doctrine and the Maoist past. Jiang promoted these ideas because of problems and challenges facing the CCP. There was nothing to suggest that the party-state would necessarily liberalize politically, but the public announcement of the "Three Represents" suggested that it was reacting to challenges pragmatically. There were indications that such a pragmatic face—and the fact that the party stood no longer for Marxist–Maoist dogma, but mainly for economic reform and nationalism—helped to rehabilitate the party, at least in the minds of the younger generation.

From 2000 to 2009, party membership in the country rose from 61.0 million to 75.9 million (5.8 percent of the population). While only 1 percent of university students were party members in 1990, by 2003, the number had risen to 8 percent; in mid-2009, the number of CCP members who were university students had soared to 20 percent. While in 2000, 18 percent of party members were college graduates, in mid-2009 that number had reached 34 percent. In 2016, no fewer than 41 million (46 percent) had college degrees from junior colleges or above. The face of the party was changing markedly.

A New Generation of Leaders: Changing to Hu

At the Sixteenth National Party Congress in November 2002, Jiang retired as party general secretary, having served in the post for thirteen years; he retained his position as head of the Military Affairs Commission until September 2004. The new general secretary was Hu Jintao, handpicked by Deng and groomed by Jiang. Hu, head of the Communist Youth League in the 1980s and member of the Politburo Standing Committee since 1992, was an activist reformer, seventeen years younger than Jiang, who also took the position as head of the Central Military Commission on Jiang's retirement. A new generation of leadership emerged, containing more experts in economics and finance than any in the past. The continuation of the reformist line was underscored by the naming of Wen Jiabao, a former aide of deposed reformer Zhao Ziyang, to the post of premier.

In the first years of the century, while countries around the world entered hard economic times, China's torrid economy continued apace. President Hu and Premier Wen strongly reaffirmed the reforms at the 2006 meeting of the National People's Congress. Wen stated, "We should unswervingly push forward the reform and the opening. ... Although there will be difficulties on our way ahead, we cannot stop; retrogression offers no way out."[5] One major challenge of the time was to move the economy from an investment driven track to a consumption driven track, all the while maintaining high growth but keeping in check the bugaboo of inflation. A second challenge was that the public sector had begun to expand with a slowdown of the private sector. One aspect of this problem was the work of Jiang Zemin and Zhu Rongji in partially privatizing SOEs, still enterprises owned by the state and thus remaining in the public sector. Seven years after joining the WTO, assets of the SOEs had tripled. Partially as a result, the central government's revenue in the first nine months of 2010 soared by 22.4 percent. Inflation, though not severe, slowed any momentum to an emphasis on consumer spending. It was yet another reversal in the thirty-year reform of decentralizing China's control of property and economic activity.[6]

Both Jiang and Hu believed that the party had to remain paramount in the economic and political systems. In contrast to Jiang, Hu was much more people centered. The slogan that Hu coined to symbolize his approach was the "harmonious society," an approach that put people first. In the harmonious society, the emphases were on democracy, the rule of law, a prosperous society, a cleaner environment, good living standards without huge gaps of wealth, and improved morals and education. He spoke of "scientific development," "a development model that placed people's livelihood and the protection of the environment first."[7] Hu's "scientific development" and "harmonious society" were included in an amendment to the constitution at the Seventeenth National Party Congress in 2007, just as Deng's "socialism with Chinese characteristics" was enshrined there in 1992 and Jiang's "Three Represents" was added in 2002.

Whither Democracy?

There was, however, yet another political component in the mix. In 2006 and 2007 Hu and Premier Wen Jiabao made strong positive statements about democracy. In a February 2007 article published in the *People's Daily*, Wen argued that it is "entirely possible for us to build a democratic country with the rule of law under socialist conditions."[8] What was the context for his remarks?

Like the household responsibility system, elected villager committees began as an initiative by villagers in two counties in Guangxi province in late 1980 and early 1981. Village elders, former cadres, and community-minded villagers formed them, without the knowledge of local authorities, to address political problems that were growing out of the household responsibility system. County administrators reported this development to their prefectural superiors, who recommended that villager committees be established throughout the regions. In December 1982, villager committees to manage neighborhood issues were written into the national constitution as elected mass organizations of self-government. In November 1987, the provisional local self-government law allowed villagers to elect villager committees and village heads in multicandidate elections. In some places, county and township officials on their own introduced voting. In others, villagers who had heard about the law pressured townships to let them nominate and vote for committee members.

From the beginning, local administrators harbored doubts about the role of villager committees, fearing that they might become uncontrollable. Many local officials thus did all they could to delay or rig elections. Tactics included conducting elections with very little warning, demanding that party members vote for handpicked nominees, banning unapproved candidates from making speeches, annulling elections if the "wrong" candidates won, and insisting that voting be conducted by a show of hands. By the late 1990s, the use of elections had spread to 60 percent of China's villages in almost every province. Rural people were quick to recognize that elections were a tool to target corrupt, arrogant, and incompetent cadres. When they were deprived of their vote, they fought back, lodging complaints at higher levels.

With the passage of a revised local self-government law in November 1998, self-government shed its trial status and reached a new level. It named two groups to be the formal decision-making body of a village: the villager committee and the villager assembly (the supreme organ in village government). Since as many as 400 to 600 persons might attend villager assemblies, the government established a representative assembly of roughly twenty-five to forty members to serve as the permanent organ when the villager assembly was not in session.

The self-government law clarified many election procedures. All villager committee candidates had to be directly nominated by villagers (in the villager assemblies), more candidates than positions were required, and voting had to be done in secret. At least fifteen days before the election, an appointed election committee had to register village residents who were at least eighteen years old. Voting was done in three ways: mass voting, where voters went to a central polling place in the early morning, voted, and remained there until the end of the count; individual voting throughout the day; and voting via the roving ballot box, carried around the village to people who could not get to the polling station. One of the most democratically advanced provinces by 2000 was coastal Fujian, advanced in the sense that it had nomination by villagers in general, and its candidates for the representative assembly were selected by direct primary; a secret ballot and a voting booth were required; and there was an open public count of the votes.

In his speech to the National People's Congress in October 2007, Hu mentioned democracy over sixty times and called for township-level elections in all of China's townships. In July 2009, he called for democracy in the party, so that members could participate, vote, and supervise in all of the party's internal matters. Hu was definitely talking the democratic talk. The problem is that the democratic walk was unsteady and uncertain. In 2000, a committee of the party Central Committee set down a projected calendar for democratic achievements (reminiscent of the Empress Dowager's constitutional calendar a century earlier): direct elections of township heads, mayors, provincial governors, and certain national-level positions were projected. In fact, even before the 1989 Tiananmen crisis, the direct election of village heads and local committees had been initiated, but there had been no significant success at implementing direct elections at any higher level of the administrative hierarchy, even the town or township. The reasons? First, according to the Chinese constitution, local assemblies ("people's congresses") were to be directly elected; but from the town, township, and county up to the central government, officials were indirectly elected by people's congresses at the administrative level directly below. Second, town and township heads were basic-level cadres; if they were directly elected, the process would undermine the central principle that cadres are appointed by the Party, which indeed was critical to the processes and power of Party leadership.

The reality of the lack of democratization was shown by numerous episodes around the country. Probably most famous is what happened in July to October 2005 in Taishi village in Guangdong province. Villagers wanted to recall (in effect, oust) the head of the Taishi village committee for corruption and to elect another. When regional officials and police refused to permit new elections, there were peaceful demonstrations. Police reacted violently, using billy clubs and fire hoses against old women. Officials then intimidated recall signers to withdraw their names.

The sordid episode, the duplicity of government and party, and the extraordinarily shoddy treatment of people trying to exercise their democratic prerogatives seemed to make the democratic talk totally empty.[9]

But while Hu's sloganeering thrust populism to the fore, in political reality he emerged "as a strong Leninist leader who … sought to clamp down on dissent and to limit the range of ideas expressed in the public sphere."[10] Hu's speeches toughened the rhetoric regarding dissent; he resurrected the attack on "bourgeois liberalization" that Deng had laid to rest almost two decades before. In June 2005, he moved to control the Internet, requiring "all Chinese websites and bloggers … to register their real names with authorities or risk being closed down by the end of the month."[11] Hu, then, was a curious mix, emphasizing people but limiting their political rights; one writer called Hu's political approach, "populist authoritarianism."[12]

BROAD RAMIFICATIONS OF THE REFORMS

The Realities of Economic Inequality

The income and wealth inequality noted in Chapter 19 only worsened in the period from 2005 to 2016. A study by Chinese economists revealed in June 2005 that the richest 10 percent of Chinese held 45 percent of the wealth while the poorest 10 percent controlled only 1.4 percent.[13] In that year, The World Bank declared that there were 150 million Chinese living in acute poverty. In 2016, a Peking University study reported that China had one of the world's highest levels of income inequality, with the richest 1 per cent of households owning a third of the country's wealth and the poorest 25 per cent of Chinese households owning just 1 per cent of the country's total wealth.[14]

In 2016, the per capita disposable income (money left for spending or saving after payment of taxes and other mandatory charges) of urban households was 33,616 yuan (4,881 USD) at the exchange rate in December 2016 of 6.887 yuan per USD. In contrast, the per capita disposable income of rural households was 12,363 yuan (1,795 USD). Or, even more out of economic kilter, was the per capita disposable income of rural households in impoverished areas: 8,452 yuan (1,227 USD). Urban households made 2.72 times as much disposal income as rural households.[15]

Decentralization

The economic reforms brought decentralization, a shift in economic decision making to the lower levels of the Chinese state. A continuing feature of the Chinese state from imperial times into the twenty-first century has been "the central government's perennial struggle to ensure local compliance with national policy."[16] The context for this struggle is the country's immense diversity—regional, cultural, and economic: "China cannot be understood as a monolith."[17] From the beginning of reforms, central policymakers decided that local communities had to have the capability to use local resources to spur economic growth and stability. Beijing and localities cut an implicit deal that localities could initiate economic policies different from those promoted in Beijing so long as they maintained the desired stability. During the 1980s and through the mid-1990s, authority in the political system fragmented. Governing bodies at the provincial, city, county, and township levels gained substantial political and economic initiative and became powerful in the economy. They did so at the expense of the central state bureaucracies stretching from Beijing to those same localities.

The Center retained crucial powers. It continued to appoint all provincial leaders (city, county, and township leaders were appointed by the next higher level). It maintained substantial coercive powers, controlling, for example, crack units of the PLA and civilian security agencies.

FIGURE 20.1   Modern advertising underscores the economic inequality (cute, well-fed babies and a young urban woman undressing), clearly in the "realm" of a developed China, pointedly counterposed to the wizened old man and the poverty of the streets in the special economic zone of Shenzhen in 1993.
Source: Marc Riboud/Magnum Photos.

It maintained considerable economic power, continuing to allocate scarce resources such as petroleum and electric power and controlling the money supply. Its degree of authority varied according to issues, population control being one where it was especially strong.

Given the risky political nature of such a decentralized system, where more and more power tended to slip away, in the late 1990s CCP Chairman Jiang Zemin and Premier Zhu Rongji initiated a recentralization effort. The central government's power of appointment was an important weapon against provincial leaders who were seen as becoming too powerful; they were transferred to other posts or forced to retire. In 1996 the government announced that local cadres were duty-bound to "remain in unison with the central authorities with Jiang Zemin as their core" and that they "must resolutely counter and suppress opinions that are opposed to the party's basic lines."[18] Beijing also asserted greater control of localities by setting quotas that local officials had to meet—from grain production to the number of corrupt officials who had to be arrested. Most significant in the recentralization effort was the central government's announcement that the Center would now take a larger share of the income tax revenue. Whereas the central government's share had fallen in 1993 to 22 percent (with the rest going to local governments), the major tax reforms initiated in 1994 brought a doubling of the Center's share by 1995. Since then, through 2016, the Center's take has averaged about 50 percent of total revenue.[19]

From 1995 to 1998 the Beijing regime also reined in some of localities' freewheeling economic activity. They forbade deficit budgets in an effort to stop provinces and localities from overspending. As part of national bank restructuring in 1998 and 1999, they took away the power that provincial governors and city mayors had over banks located in their areas. They checked what appeared in the mid-1990s as mindless overbuilding and overdevelopment in some cities—such as Pudong, where the occupancy rate of 250 skyscrapers in 1997 was less than 50 percent. As throughout much of China's history, the relationship between the Center and the localities remained problematic. But the past thirty years of reform had shown that "the current political structure, with its high degree of formal central control and informal local autonomy, inherently limit[ed] the central bureaucracy's ability to monitor local activities."[20]

Increasing Individual Responsibility: Expansion of the Social Safety Net

For individuals and other units in Chinese society, decentralization also had a profound impact. The agricultural and industrial responsibility systems gave the individual farm family and the individual factory or firm much choice in what and how to produce, how much to produce, and what to do with that produce. It thus took away control and decision-making power from higher levels in the system. As the state reduced its central economic planning and decentralized its administrative powers, it in turn helped increase the power of factory managers and directors. When the government cut back on the financial support that it once gave to institutions like schools and the media, they were forced to raise the money they needed. That meant a new world for some, with implications far beyond finance. The print and broadcast media, for example, raised funds primarily by selling advertising. But advertisers could pressure the media about what they published or broadcast, so the new funding requirements had an impact on what was printed and broadcast.

At the level of the individual, in pre-reform days, workers did not have to contribute to their pensions or for their medical care. But given the growing number of persons receiving pensions and the escalating per capita costs of health care, decentralizing the social welfare system was the only fiscally sound option from the state's perspective. Beginning in the mid-1990s, copayments began to be required for insurance coverage, and contributions to pension funds also became standard. One result was that many people could not afford payments to retain comparable benefits. Even more serious was that the vast majority of the Chinese population had no social security support. A 1998 study showed that 100 million retirees received "only a partial pension or none at all" and that "only 34 percent of the Chinese population [was] covered by any sort of social safety net." In the total Chinese population at the end of 2007, 201.1 million people were covered by life insurance (15 percent of the population) while 220.5 million had medical insurance (17 percent of the population).[21] Nine hundred million rural Chinese, however, had no pension. The proportion of elderly was rising faster in China "than in any other major country."[22]

Between 2005 and 2016, the economic social safety net expanded considerably, though for many Chinese it was still inadequate to cover required expenses. By December 2016, almost 379 million people were enrolled in a basic pension program for urban workers and staff, 25 million more than in 2015. More than 508 million urban and rural residents participated in a basic pension insurance program. Almost 750 million were part of a basic health insurance program (58 percent of the population). Health care expenditure as a percentage of China's total GDP rose from a low in 1994 of 3.7 percent to 5.6 percent in 2013, "one of the most dramatic increases in health care spending in modern history."[23] Premiums for life insurance (which included health and accident insurance) more than quintupled from 52 billion USD in 2006 to 262 billion USD in 2015.

"The extraordinary growth of life insurance in China was primarily driven by demand for savings/investment instruments by an increasingly urbanized and well-educated population, with rising available household incomes and personal financial assets."[24]

In 1999 the government established a minimum living standard assistance for all urban residents. Funds for this payment came from local governments, which determined the amount for their area. People receiving this aid numbered 4 million in 2000, 22.4 million in 2003 and 60.6 million in 2016.[25] All in all, the statistics underline the government's growing support for social security in general.

Unemployment

If workers liked the reforms in part because they gave them the opportunity to choose their jobs and their locations, the other side of the coin was that the state no longer guaranteed a job. Given the realities of population, the problem of unemployment reached staggering proportions. In the mid-1990s there were approximately 580 million people in the workforce: 160 million in urban areas and the rest, about 420 million, in the countryside. It was estimated that fewer than 200 million were actually needed in the rural workforce; of the remaining 200 million, an estimated 100 million found work in the 1980s in Township and Village Enterprises (TVEs). That still left a surplus of 100 million people without employment who became the floating population. But that was not even the whole picture, because the population in the countryside was growing by roughly 15 million a year.

Unemployment, with its possible social and political ramifications, became a serious problem. The *urban* unemployment figures (not even counting the floaters) at the end of 1998 had risen from 8 to 8.5 percent (16.4 million). Exacerbating these demographic realities was the closing of SOEs that were operating in the red, thereby increasing the number of unemployed. Forty million people were added to the ranks of the unemployed between 1995 and 2002 because of this restructuring. As if that were not bad enough, at century's beginning, 4 million new unemployed were added because of the government's policy of downsizing the bureaucracy, and 10 million new unemployed were added after being displaced by technology in rural industries. The worst news of all was that finding new jobs for laid-off workers became increasingly difficult. In 1998, 50 percent found reemployment; but in 2001, only 30 percent did so; and in the first half of 2002, the number had dropped to only 9 percent. Given these hard, cold realities, the government began to set up the rudimentary welfare safety net system that covered some workers with unemployment insurance, a minimum wage, pensions, health insurance, and disability payments. But it was projected to take years, if not decades, to cover most workers.

Under these circumstances, increasing labor agitation and turmoil in the 1990s was not surprising. As an example, take Sichuan in the second half of 1997, when there were 500,000 unemployed in the province. In July, 10,000 workers marched in the city of Mianyang after losing their jobs when textile factories closed; the police arrested the leaders of the protest. In August, 500 retirees rallied outside government offices in another town to protest declining pension payments, and over 1,000 unemployed pedicab drivers fought with police. In October in the city of Zigong, 300 workers who had not been paid by their radio factory employer for over a year found themselves confronted by riot police when they marched in protest. In the 2010s labor discontent resulting in strikes and protests seemed to grow. The numbers of strikes and protests from wages in arrears, insurance payments, and other causes skyrocketed from 656 in 2013 to 1,379 in 2014 to 2,774 in 2015.[26]

After the ballooning unemployment in the late 1990s and the first years of the 2000s, unemployment began to ease. Reaching 10.1 percent in 2004, it retreated to 9 percent in 2006. In 2007, 12.04 million Chinese found jobs—a six-year high in urban areas—and the unemployment rate dropped to 4.2 percent. From 2008 to early 2017, the rate hovered at about 4 percent each year. Yet with a huge aging population, unemployment issues could spring up at any time. In October 2016, retired soldiers came together in Beijing to protest the insufficient lump sum payment they received at their retirement, the local government's inadequate support, and their inability to find new jobs. In light of the reforms, the blueprint of which called for the mustering out of 300,000 additional soldiers, the government had much work to do to bring these retirees back into the workforce. Retirement age was set in 1978: 60 for men, 55 for women who are civil servants or employees of state enterprises; and 50 for all other women.

CORRUPTION

The reforms stimulated corruption, which was present almost everywhere, and in all shapes and varieties. Clearly, corruption long predated the reforms, but, in a social system based on personal connections, reforms opened up new possibilities for corruption that were too enticing for many to resist. If the goal was getting rich, the thinking went, do whatever it takes.

Criminal corruption included theft, murder, robbery, kidnapping, gang crimes, crimes with the marks of the Mafia—violent threats to public security. The government hit this corruption head-on with its series of "Strike Hard" campaigns in spasms under all four post-Mao leaders: under Deng in 1983–1987; under Jiang in 1996–1997 and in 2001; under Hu in 2002–2003, 2007, and 2009–2010; and under Xi in 2014–2015. While initially these campaigns were focused on outright crimes, their mission came to include political dissenters, "ethnic splittists" especially in Tibet and Xinjiang (often simply called "terrorists"), and suspect religious movements (like the Falun Gong). Provincial and local Strike Hard campaigns were held almost every year after 1983. Local authorities often targeted underground churches, unregistered Internet cafes, and farmers resisting high taxes.

These crackdowns were known for their speedy trials and harsh penalties, especially executions. Though the government called the number of executed a "state secret," Amnesty International, Human Rights in China, Human Rights Watch and news agencies such as the Inter Press Service have estimated the number killed in these campaigns: 24,000 in 1983–1987; 15,000 per year in the 1990s; 12,000 in 2001; 6,500 in 2007; 3,000 in 2012; and 2,400 in 2014–2015.[27] The organization Human Rights in China estimated that China executed 8,000 people each year, almost twenty times the number of people executed in all other countries combined. If that estimate is on target, since the first Strike Hard campaign in 1983, 272,000 Chinese would have been executed. On January 1, 2007, China's Supreme People's Court regained the right to review all death penalty cases. In effect, that decision transferred the power over life and death back to the central government from local courts which had held that awesome power since 1984.[28]

Widespread corruption in the reform years was mainly in the realm of "white collar" crime, which included bribery, embezzlement, nepotism, smuggling, extortion, cronyism, kickbacks, deception, fraud, squandering public monies, illegal business transactions, stock manipulation, and real estate fraud. The historical context itself promoted corruption. Five decades of socialist rule had brought into power party leaders, cadres, and managers of state enterprises who monopolized the means of production, resources, education, and recruitment into the system. They often used their position and its resources for their own betterment, and they manipulated recruitment so that family members and connections could profit as well.

Nepotism

Given the Chinese family system, nepotism was often egregious. The son of the senior ultra-conservative party leader Hu Qiaomu, who directed an anticorruption campaign in 1986, Hu Shiying by name, was reportedly involved in "illicit activities, including providing pornographic videotapes for PLA sex parties and skimming off 3 million [yuan] in tuition fees to his privately operated correspondence law school."[29] When he was arrested, his father tearfully appealed to Deng to show mercy to his son; Hu Shiying got off with a slap on the wrist—all charges against him were dropped. In order to get and maintain support for the reforms, Deng allowed party figures (and their families), whose support he needed for the reform efforts, to profit from opportunities provided by the reforms. Children of these men took positions from which they gained spectacular windfalls. Utilizing their personal and family connections, they were able to manipulate lucrative stock and real estate deals, gain inside information, receive hard-to-get licenses, and avoid prosecution—all in an effort to become fabulously wealthy. Ethically gray areas existed because of the blurred lines between public and private, an issue in Chinese culture for centuries.

One of the infamous examples of official corruption was the Beijing municipal government's involvement in the 1990s in taking bribes for the issuance of construction permits. Mayor (and Politburo member) Chen Xitong and many others made huge fortunes. Chen's fate points to a major problem in getting corruption under control. After a brief secret trial in July 1998, he was sentenced to sixteen years in prison; but authorities took no further action against a large number of other officials who were rumored to have been involved in the huge corruption scheme. The reason for the inaction? Fear on the part of Chairman Jiang Zemin about loss of support in the government if Chen implicated many officials in the scandal. The words of Chen on his arrest must have echoed menacingly in the halls of party-state power: "It is true that I may have to take moral responsibility in the Beijing municipality. But who is to take responsibility for corruption in the entire CCP?"[30]

To help control corruption, Beijing sent down hundreds of regulations; anticorruption bureaus were set up; hotlines were established so that people could report corruption; and cadres in official positions were regularly rotated. But these mechanisms could not do the job because they were all under the control of the party, and the party itself was rife with corruption. Any strong, continuous action against corrupt party members could have had serious political consequences for those in power. Thus, early in his leadership, Jiang decided that he would not touch the families of "first-generation revolutionaries," no matter how much they were involved in corrupt activities. Clearly politics, neither morality nor civic pride, was in command.

In the late 1980s and 1990s, the public became increasingly indignant over the situation even as they joined in. Whereas a government official might earn 300 yuan per month, a waitress in a joint venture hotel could earn 900 or 1,000 yuan. Communist party cadres and *danwei* heads who gave permission for marriage, renting an apartment, and even having a baby frequently demanded bribes. Petty graft and bribery became common inside and outside the party and the government. By the end of the 1990s, however, there were signs that the party leaders were at last beginning to deal seriously with the issue. From 1998 to 2000, fifty-one high-ranking ministerial and provincial-level officials were tried and publicly humiliated for various types of corruption. Some were imprisoned, and some were even executed. In 2006, Liu Zhihua, the vice-mayor of Beijing, who had been charged with oversight in the construction of Olympic venues, was cashiered when it was discovered that he was receiving kickbacks from land sales.

ANTI-CORRUPTION POLICIES AS TOOLS AGAINST OPPOSING FACTIONS

Corruption charges often went hand in hand with manipulating and weakening rival political factions; indeed, such charges became the main attack vehicle in political struggles. Hu Jintao in March 2006 began a new anticorruption campaign called "eight honors, eight disgraces," a reflection of his sense (and others as well) that a money-crazed China had lost its moral bearings. The eight honors, eight disgraces were to be a new moral measure for the conduct of party officials. First published officially in an English translation in October 2006 by Xinhua News Agency, it was printed widely in the Chinese press.

Love the country; do it no harm.
Serve the people; do no disservice.
Follow science; discard ignorance.
Be diligent, not indolent.
Be united; help each other; make no gains at others' expense.
Be honest and trustworthy; do not sacrifice ethics for profits.
Be disciplined and law-abiding, not chaotic and lawless.
Live plainly; struggle hard; do not wallow in luxuries and pleasures.

In September 2006, Hu had Chen Liangyu, Politburo and Central Committee member as well as chair of the Shanghai Municipal Council, dismissed for corruption, for siphoning off money from the Social Security Fund in Shanghai. He was eventually given an eighteen-year prison sentence. Chen had been important in Jiang's faction; Chen's dismissal was not only a way for Hu and Wen Jiabao to put teeth behind new anticorruption efforts but a way to weaken his party opponents.

But it was in the administration of President and Party Chair Xi Jinping (2012–) that anticorruption purges netted their most significant catches. Xi, the nature of whose rule is discussed further in Chapter 21, made a vow from the beginning that in moving to crush corruption, he would "catch high-ranking 'tigers' as well as lowly 'flies.'"[31] As Jiang and Hu before him, Xi had the exclusive authority to decide who was corrupt and who was not. In other words, in a world awash in corruption with many possibilities of whom to pursue, he chose his actual or potential political opponents. The pursuit of corruption in essence masked an elite power struggle.

With Jiang Zemin as his patron, Bo Xilai, a "princeling" (offspring of Bo Yibo, longtime political and military leader, one of the so-called "Eight Immortals"), was a go-getter, a high flyer, a political star.[32] In 2010 *Time* named him one of the World's 100 Most Influential People. He modernized and transformed the city of Dalian where he served as mayor; he was provincial governor of Liaoning; he served as Minister of Commerce in Wen Jiabao's cabinet; he gained a seat on the 25-member Politburo in 2007; he was appointed party chief of Chongqing, where he moved to deal with corruption and handled that municipality's problems effectively. He developed the so-called Chongqing model, which increased state control and was driven by a neo-leftist ideology. He was clearly one of the most important and powerful men in China.

His career was cut short by his wife's involvement in the 2011 murder of an Englishman, by his own corruption and ruthlessness, and by blackmailing and torturing Chinese in Chongqing's "strike hard" campaign in 2009–2010. In what became a "show-trial," Bo was charged with bribery, embezzlement, and abuse of power, was found guilty, and sentenced in 2013 to life imprisonment with confiscation of all his personal assets. But the real issue was likely not corruption but rather the threat he posed to Xi Jinping.

FIGURE 20.2   In a star-studded career, Bo served as mayor of Dalian, governor of Liaoning province, member of the Politburo from 2007 to 2012, and Communist Party Secretary of Chongqing. A hero of the "New Left," he was charismatic and casual, completely unlike the usual Communist leaders; here he warmly welcomes U.S. Secretary of Commerce Gutierrez in May 2007. In 2012, he was found guilty of corruption, stripped of all his assets, and sentenced to life imprisonment.
Source: www.commerce.gov via Wikimedia Commons.

But the highest-ranking "tiger" was an ally of Bo, Zhou Yongkang, who, at the beginning of 2012, was "arguably the most powerful man in China," controlling China's huge domestic security apparatus and a 100 billion USD budget.[33] He was also one of the nine members of the standing committee of the politburo of the CCP. The Forbes 2011 list of the World's Most Powerful People placed Zhou at twenty-ninth out of seventy. Like Bo, he was linked to Jiang Zemin's network. Zhou was an avid supporter of Bo's Chongqing model, traveling to that city in 2010 to praise Bo for his tactics in rooting out corruption. Zhou was the only member of the standing committee of the Politburo who voted against sacking Bo. Rumors swirled around Bo and Zhou, that they were plotting a coup against or an assassination of Xi in order to seize power, and that Zhou had tried to assassinate Xi twice. Xi was careful to get Jiang Zemin's agreement that Xi could go after these men in his network. In the end, Zhou was expelled from the Communist party and in 2015 sentenced to life in prison; over three hundred people in his network came under investigation. Zhou was the most senior official found guilty of corruption since the 1949 founding of the PRC.

Xi Jinping was extremely disturbed about widespread corruption among the PLA leadership. He said that the PLA was totally corrupt and announced a complete restructuring of the armed forces; details were announced at the Third Plenum of the Central Committee in November 2013. Two generals, Xu Caihou and Guo Boxiang, were expelled from the party in 2014. They and other senior officers had accepted bribes and sold promotions at a time when the PLA was striving to build a competent officer corps. Investigators also audited 4,000 officers (including eighty-two generals) and inflicted penalties on over 200 in the form of reprimands, demotions, and dismissals.

The key question for leaders regarding the handling of corruption is what steps could be taken to weaken the systemic nature of corruption without completely eroding the power of the Communist Party. In the Chinese system it seemed that nearly all officials were more or less liable to corruption and if the CCP tried to take action against all corrupt officials and cadres, the party in the end would do away with itself. Living in a political culture saturated with corruption gave rise to a culture of distrust, anxiety, and uncertainty as seen in this blog from the party secretary in Maoming City, Guangdong: "If you say that I am a corrupt official, I say that all officials are corrupt. Why have you specifically selected me? Today you caught me; tomorrow your own people will catch you too."[34] It is telling that this official notes that it will be "your own people" who will undo one's work and/or one's life.

ENVIRONMENTAL CRISES

Environmental concerns, such as corruption, predated the reforms. In part they stemmed from the huge population increase from the eighteenth century on. They came also with the general industrialization of the country, mostly in the twentieth century. But as one commentator noted, part of the environmental degradation came because industrialization occurred under a socialist regime:

> with the land and its resources publicly owned, no one [took] responsibility for the land or represent[ed] its interests. For another, water and energy [were] supplied to consumers at no cost or at a heavily subsidized cost, and there [was] no incentive to conserve their use.[35]

The consequences of reforms and the emerging consumer society had a devastating impact on the crucial environmental triumvirate—air, water, and land. Before 2009, even though the Chinese government was beset by both international criticism and domestic protest, the central government did not begin to focus on environmental issues; in the context of the times, local government resistance, buoyed by their alliance with business, was strikingly powerful.

The burgeoning number of cars, motorcycles, and trucks intensified both air and noise pollution. Industrial smokestack and vehicle emissions and the pollution caused by the major source of cheap fuel, soft coal, choked cities. As rural industries proliferated, the noxious pollution of rural chemical and fertilizer factories obscured the sky in many areas of the country with its yellow-brown haze. The air in Beijing was sixteen times more polluted than that in New York City, a worrisome problem at the 2008 Beijing Olympics. Much talked about before the Games was how the ever-serious pollution might affect the athletes themselves. To lessen the brown-gray smog, the government closed factories, halted most construction work, and set up a system where cars with odd-numbered license plates and those with even-numbered plates alternated in driving days. The United Nations Environment Programme gave the government much praise: "From reducing air pollution to big investments in public transport and renewable energies, the organizers made major efforts to insure that the Games marked a step forward in terms of an eco-friendly mass spectacular sporting event."[36] The Chinese leadership seemed to have begun to lead the way; Hu's ideas of "scientific development" envisioned an "eco-friendly" world and lifestyle. But when some environmental studies of the Games were completed, scientists called the Beijing Games "the most polluted ever." Soot particles blotted out the sun on some days: the soot was double that in Athens in 2004, triple that in Atlanta in 1996, and 3.5 times that in Sydney in 2000.[37] It was a reminder that unless environmental problems were taken with the utmost seriousness, China's environmental future looked grim.

China's government mandated clean air standards, but the air quality in 90 percent of China's cities did not meet them. The government's decision to make the automobile industry a central feature of the next stage of development promised to have a disastrous environmental impact. A 2015 prediction: "A quarter of a billion of automobiles would pollute the air, require paving over still more acres of scarce farmland, exhaust the country's oil reserves, and render China's already congested cities unnavigable."[38] Whereas in 2007 there were 59 million vehicles, in 2016 the number had more than tripled to 194 million.

The water situation was dire. Almost a third of industrial waste water and over 90 percent of household sewage poured into waterways without being treated. Almost 80 percent of China's 278 cities did not have sewage treatment facilities.[39] The amount of sewage and industrial wastes flushed into the country's streams and coastal waters in 1995 totaled 37.3 billion tons, in 2000, 41.5 billion tons, and from 2000 to 2012, wastewater increased 65 percent to 68.5 billion tons, in volume comparable to the annual flow of the Yellow River (58 billion cubic meters) per year. Ninety percent of the water flowing through cities was not drinkable. Analyzed in terms of five grades, water rated in grades one to three was not polluted. In north China in 2013, only 21 percent of shallow water (from shallow wells and surface water) was rated in the first three grades and only 23 percent of deep water (in deep aquifers). Guidelines about usage of water state that grade five water should not only not be drunk but should not even touch human skin; 57 percent of shallow water and 50 percent of deep water fell into this fifth category.[40]

In 2014, Premier Li Keqiang declared a "war on pollution." The "10-Point Water Plan," announced in April 2015 was the government's most comprehensive policy to that date and seriously began to treat dangerous ground- and surface-water pollution. It was estimated in 2015 that more than 300 million Chinese were using polluted water sources and that since 1995 11,000 water quality-related emergencies occurred. As an example, in April 2014, water in the city of Lanzhou in Gansu province was contaminated by benzene from a nearby factory; the city temporarily shut down its water supply when examinations showed that a liter of tap water contained 200 micrograms of benzene when the national safe limit was just 10 per liter.[41]

Pollution was not the only water problem: there was simply not enough available water. In 1997 half of all of China's cities had a water shortage; indeed, the volume of tap water consumed in China's urban centers increased five times from 1982 to 1997. One basic problem was the distribution of the water supply. Southern China had 75 percent of the water supply for about a third of the land; Northern China had comparatively little water. The brutal facts were that China supported 20 percent of the *world's population* with only 7 percent of its water, or in more China-centered terms, the North China Plain was home to roughly 42 percent of China's population, but it contained only 8 percent of the country's water resources.

The South-to-North Water Transport Project was undertaken to provide water to the North with three routes of canals and pipelines from the South, "a lifeline for water in the short term." Two of the three routes, the central and the east, have provided about 25 billion cubic meters of fresh water from the Yangzi River. The central route from the Han River, the Yangzi's longest tributary, proceeded from the Danjiangkou Dam in Hubei province to Beijing where it provided a third of the city's water; construction on this route was completed in November 2013. The eastern route uses the upgraded Grand Canal in part, moving through Jiangsu, Anhui, Shandong, Hebei, and the city of Tianjin; completed in December 2014, it carried a greater volume of water than the central route. The ultimate goal is to provide 44.8 billion cubic meters of water. The western route was still under discussion; if it was built, it would carry water from three western Yangzi tributaries, but the route through rugged mountains makes the engineering for this route even trickier than for the other two.

In reconfiguring the Danjiangkou Dam as part of the new system, water in the reservoir rose 13 meters. This unfortunate development plus the construction of canals and tunnels along the route plus the desire to reduce pollution resulted in the forced relocation of 345,000 Chinese, who faced the physical and psychological trauma of the move and of lives being uprooted and

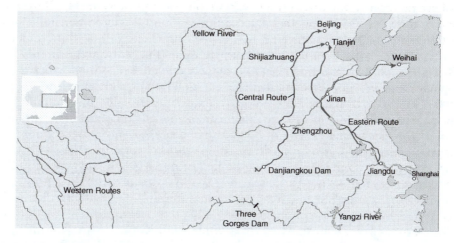

MAP 20.1 South to North Water Transport Project. Water available for each Chinese is one-fourth of the global average and is expected to shrink to one-fifth. North China's water deficit has created difficult problems. It is feasible, experts say, that the comprehensive operation of the water transport project may begin to eliminate some difficulty by 2020.

turned upside down. Critics have called this ramification of the project "authoritarian environmentalism."[42] They also noted that the system could not possibly provide all the water that the North needed, and they especially rued the cost. Originally budgeted at 62 billion USD, the construction costs reportedly soared to over 80 billion USD even without any work being done on the western route. Critics also feared that the fresh water sent from the Yangzi would become polluted during the lengthy routes, the two totaling 2,700 miles. To help to prevent water contamination, industries were prohibited from locating on reservoirs or their watersheds. The relocation of farmers away from the project's waterway was also taken to make contamination by sewage less possible.

Soil erosion increased at a dangerous rate, especially in the Western region as it began to undergo government-directed economic development. Blamed were the fast rate of industrialization and urbanization and the lack of money to deal with environmental problems. The land around both the Yellow and Yangzi rivers had serious erosion that contributed to an upstream reduction in their flow. As deforestation, destruction of vegetation in general, and desertification increased, Beijing and areas in North and Northeastern China experienced increasing numbers of sandstorms.

Another environmental area of concern was land usage. In the era of economic reforms, some farmers began abandoning their land for what they considered more profitable pursuits. The conversion of cropland into various uses that might bring more money led to a significant decline in cultivated land and raised a deadly serious question: from where in the twenty-first century would the supply of grain to feed China's billions come? Fish ponds, forests, grazing lands, rural enterprise sites, and even golf courses appeared where there was once productive cropland. In late 2016, there were 683 golf courses in China, with sixty in water-starved Beijing alone. In January 2017, the government closed down 111 of those courses, in order to turn them back to arable land and to conserve water. Golf courses posed an environmental threat because they were 43 percent larger than courses in, say, the United States; golf courses also took inordinate amounts of water to keep the greens green and to provide "hazards" on the courses.[43] In north China where the lack of water for daily usage was itself a concern, the lavish use of water for a sport and hobby mainly for the wealthy seemed reprehensible.

In recent years there have been many episodes of rioting by farmers over the confiscation of their land by authorities without adequate compensation. In December 2005, in Dongzhou, Guangdong, farmers rioted when their land was taken as the site for a coal-fired factory; their reaction came not only for the loss of land, but because the pollution from the factory would kill off the fishing that was their livelihood. At least twenty people were killed there when a local paramilitary force opened fire. In April 2008, on Hainan Island 6,000 farmers rioted when a huge parcel of land—7,000 hectares (17,290 acres or 3.3 square miles)—was confiscated to build a golf course without sufficient compensation; more than 300 farmers and several policemen were injured in the melee. The shocking fact is that during the past thirty years, the net loss of arable land equaled almost a million acres each year, cutting China's already tiny total by almost 10 percent.[44] This meant that whereas in 1973 arable land per capita had been 1.6 mu, it had fallen to 1.2 mu by 1993 and was projected to fall to 0.83 mu by 2030 (a mu is about one-sixth of an acre).

There were many regulations and agencies to monitor and deal with all these problems. But at the root of trying to solve these problems lay perhaps the most difficult matter in preserving and controlling the environment. Many environmental issues touched on the interests of many people, groups, and institutions: decision making became highly political. Negotiations over the construction of the controversial Three Gorges Dam on the Yangzi River revealed the kind of deal making that became a central attribute of environmental decision making, as well as under the reforms in general.

The dam is the largest in the world, 1.5 miles wide and more than 600 feet high. The massive project was completed in autumn 2008, creating a reservoir named Emerald Drop Lake, 525 feet deep stretching for 410 miles. The dam provides flood protection and electricity for Middle Yangzi provinces like Hubei and Hunan. Severe floods in 1990 and 1998 gave credence to the arguments of dam supporters. But 1.4 million people who lived west of the dam site—mostly in Sichuan province—had their homes, cities, and cropland inundated and were forced to resettle. From the dam, Sichuan obviously received no flood benefits and would not even get much of the generated electrical power.

Deal making became necessary because the main political actors—the provinces of Sichuan, Hunan, and Hubei and the pertinent central government ministries—had no decision-making authority over each other. Thus, the chief institutional proponent of the dam, the Ministry of Water Resources, was compelled to lead negotiations among parties who for various reasons were opposed. Among the deals was an agreement to reduce the height of the dam from the original design, which, had it been implemented, would have flooded the city of Chongqing. The height limit also made the city a major port since the reservoir behind the dam ended at the city. Oceangoing ships of up to 10,000 tons displacement were able to sail to the city. This was possible because the dam was built with an intricate system of locks and ship lifts. To help pay the cost of resettling the displaced residents, Sichuan received special funds from the State Planning Commission. But resettlement was very expensive. When the city of Wanxian submitted its $2.9 billion estimate of the cost of resettlement for its people, the figure shocked Beijing decision makers, who had budgeted only $3.5 billion for all provincial resettlement expenditures.

Environmentalists, who had generally been opposed to the dam's construction, watched troubling signs with some alarm, though the government initially discounted them as serious. Pollution of the reservoir's water was a given almost from the beginning. But cracks were reported in the dam. Then, beginning in the fall of 2007 and continuing to at least the spring of 2009, landslides became a problem. As the lake filled, the sheer weight of the water created pressure on surrounding mountainsides causing them to cave in; erosion of the shore also contributed. Landslides of up to 50,000 cubic feet of rocks and mud crashed into the lake, creating waves as high as 165 feet. Though the lake reached its planned depth of 525 feet in September 2008, it was lowered to 480 feet in order to lessen the chances of landslides. Since the dam's becoming fully functional in the fall of 2008, two major facilities were added. In July 2012, the last of the water turbines in the underground plant began production. In December 2015, the ship lift, which was essentially a kind of elevator for ships (and an engineering marvel) was completed. It lifted vessels plus the water the ship floated on (up to seven million pounds) some 370 feet. Larger vessels had to use the five-stage lock system, which took up to three hours, whereas the ship lift option took only forty minutes. The elevator annually allowed six million more tons to cross over the dam.

Notes

1 "Made in China?" www.economist.com/.../21646204-asias-dominance-manufacturing-will-endure … See also Matt Schiavenza, "China's Dominance in Manufacturing—in One Chart," *The Atlantic* (August 5, 2013). www.theatlantic.com/china/archives/2013/08/chinas-dominance-in-manufacturing-in-one-chart/278366

2 GDP by country, World Bank. knoema.com

3 Mary E. Gallagher, "China in 2004: Stability Above All," *Asian Survey* 41, no.1 (January–February, 2005): 25.

4 Li Cheng, "China in 2000: A Year of Strategic Rethinking," *Asian Survey* 41, no. 1 (January–February, 2001): 84.

5 Joseph Fewsmith, "China in 2007: The Politics of Leadership Transition," *Asian Survey* 48, no. 1 (January–February, 2008): 84–5.

6 Guoguang Wu, "China in 2010: Dilemmas of 'Scientific Development,'" *Asian Survey* 51, no. 1 (January–February, 2010): 20 and 22.

7 M.E. Gallagher, "China in 2004: Stability above All," *Asian Survey* 45, no. 1 (January–February, 2005): 26.

8 Joseph Fewsmith, "China in 2007: The Politics of Leadership Transition," *Asian Survey* 48, no. 1 (January–February, 2008): 86–7.

9 Hu Ping, "Tianshi Village: A Sign of the Times," *China Rights Forum*, no. 4 (2005). www.hrichina.org/sites/default/files/PDFs/CRF.4.2005/CRF-2005-4_Taishi.pdf

10 Tony Saich, "China in 2005: Hu's in Charge," *Asian Survey* 46, no. 1 (January–February, 2006): 37–8.

11 Ibid., p. 39.

12 Ibid., p. 37.

13 Tony Saich, "China in 2006: Focus on Social Development," *Asian Survey* 47, no. 1 (January–February, 2006): 42.

14 While China's income inequality is more severe than other large countries, in comparison wealth inequality is worse in the U.S. where the wealthiest 1 per cent of U.S. households owned 42 per cent of all U.S. wealth in 2012.

15 www.stats.gov.cn/english/pressrelease/201702/t20170228_1467503.html

16 https://worldview.stratfor.com/.../bridging-gap-between-chinas-central-and-local-governments

17 Ibid.

18 Quoted in Willy Wo-lap Lam, *The Era of Jiang Zemin* (Singapore: Prentice Hall, 1999), p. 218.

19 John Brondolo and Zhiyang Zhang, IMF Working Paper: "Tax Administration Reform in China: Achievements, Challenges, and Reform Priorities" (March 2016), p. 7. www.imf.org/external/pubs/ft/wp/2016/wp1668.pdf

20 See endnote 7.

21 Li Cheng, "China in 1999: Seeking Common Ground at a Time of Tension and Conflict," *Asian Survey* 40, no. 1 (January–February, 2000): 122.

22 Howard French, "Pension Crisis Looms in China," *The New York Times* (March 20, 2007).

23 www.ey.com/Publication/vwbuAssets/EY-the-rise-of-private-health-insurance-in-china/$FILE/EY-the-rise-of-private-health-insurance-in-china.pdf

24 www.aon.com/inpoint/bin/pdfs/white-papers/ChinaWhitepaper2016.pdf

25 See endnote 6.

26 Murray Scot Tanner, "China in 2015: China's Dreams, Xi's Party," *Asian Survey* (January–February, 2016): 25.

27 See the Inter Press Service News Agency report: www.ipsnews.net/.../china-crime-strikes-hard-sees-1000-executions-in-three-months. See also www.amnesty.org/download/Documents/128000/asa170472002en.pdfandfrom*TheEconomist*www.economist.com/.../china/21582557-most-worlds-sharp-decline-executions

28 Wang Guangze, "The Mystery of China's Death Penalty Figures": www.hrichina.org/sites/default/files/PDFs/CRF.2.2007/CRF-2007-2_

29 Richard Baum, *Burying Mao: Chinese Politics in the Age of Deng Xiaoping* (Princeton, NJ: Princeton University Press, 1994), p. 176.

30 Lam, *The Era of Jiang Zemin*, p. 77.

31 Jamil Anderlini, "Captured in a Chinese Tiger Hunt," *The Financial Times* (March 31, 2014). www.ft.com/content/5a324b-b0e5-11e3-bbd4-00144feab7de

32 The "Eight Immortals" (sometimes known as the "Eight Elders") were a group of longtime elderly members of the Communist Party of China who held substantial power during the 1980s and 1990s.

33 www.ft.com/content/5a324b-b0e5-11e3-bbd4-00144feab7de

34 Thomas Heberer, "China in 2014: Creating a New Power and Security Architecture in Domestic and Foreign Policies," *Asian Survey* 55, no. 1 (January–February, 2015): 88.

35 John Bryan Starr, *Understanding China: A Guide to China's Economy, History, and Political Structure* (New York: Hill & Wang, 1997), pp. 168–9.

36 http://unep.org/Documents.Multilingual/Default.asp?DocumentID=562&ArticleID=6086&I=en

37 www.telegraph.co.uk/sport/othersports/olympics/london2012/5597277/Beijing-olympics-were-the-most-polluted-games-ever-researchers-say.html

38 Heberer, p. 170.

39 "Water Pollution in China": factsanddetails.com/china/cat10/sub66/item391.html

40 China.waterrrisk.org/resources/analysis-revews/8-facts-on-china-wastewater/

41 Dongmei Han, Matthew J. Currell, and Guoliang Cao, "Deep Challenges for China's War on Water Pollution," *Environmental Pollution* 218 (November 2016):
    www.sciencedirect.com/science/article/pii/S0269749116310363

42 Michael Webber, Britt Crow-Miller, and Sarah Rogers. "The South–North Water-Transfer Project: Remaking the Geography of China," *Journal of Regional Studies* 5, no. 3 (2017): https://doi.org/10.1080/0034340 4.2016.1265647

43 "China Shuts Down 111 Golf Courses as it Continues its Assault on 'Sport for Millionaires,'" *Independent* (January 23, 2017).

44 Starr, p. 170.

Suggestions for Further Reading

Barmé, Geremie and Linda Jaivin. *New Ghosts, Old Dreams: Chinese Rebel Voices* (New York: Times Books, 1992). This book, using selections from the visual and literary arts, examines the world of dissent in the days after the 1989 suppression.

Chetham, Dierdre. *Before the Deluge: The Vanishing World of the Yangtze's Three Gorges* (New York: Palgrave Macmillan, 2004). Vivid descriptions of towns and their people along the Yangzi before they were submerged in the Emerald Drop Lake; the book gives "slice-of-life" pictures of Chinese society.

Dutton, Michael. *Streetlife China* (Cambridge, UK: Cambridge University Press, 1998). Described as a "guided tour of the cultural landscape of contemporary China," this intriguing collection includes newspaper articles, interviews, an exploration of slang terms, social analysis, and sections on Mao memorabilia.

Perry, Elizabeth J. and Mark Selden, eds., *Chinese Society: Change, Conflict, and Resistance*, 2nd edition (London: RoutledgeCurzon, 2003). This collection of essays on many realities in contemporary Chinese society is well written and insightful; its theme, indicated in the subtitle, gives it cohesion.

21

Whither China?

2008–2018

The date was auspicious: August 8, 2008 (08/08/08), since eight is the luckiest number in Chinese culture. Pronounced "ba," which sounds similar to "fa," it means "to make a fortune," "wealth," "prosperity," and "success." The event: the opening of the Beijing Summer Olympics. Four billion people around the world watched its opening ceremony, a more-than-three-hour performance with 15,000 dancers, drummers, and performers. The ceremonies, showcasing the artistic genius of famed film director Zhang Yimou, highlighted China's traditional Confucian culture. It was a watershed event, manifesting to the world China's remarkable economic development, creative power, and national pride—a major step toward winning international respect and admiration. The Games were a triumph for a nation so often humiliated in its weakness by foreign nations; China won more gold medals (48) than any other country and won a total of 100 medals, second only to the United States' 112 medals. The games' theme, "One World, One Dream," captured the international goals of the Olympics succinctly. But the question in this chapter is how much China in the first two decades of the twenty-first century is itself "one world"; how much are China's state and its citizens "one world"?

HUMAN RIGHTS

Continually in its treatment of its citizens, the PRC has differentiated some Chinese from others, never seeing the country as "one world." From the very beginning in the 1950s, the constitution guaranteed the "people" certain rights but then specified who the people were and noted that some of them (capitalists, intellectuals, and Guomindang supporters) were not really people. During the Cultural Revolution, some people were denoted by the color red (obviously good), others (were they people or not?) by the color black (obviously bad). The many ethnic minorities have been consistently handled differently from the Han Chinese. And it has been repeatedly made clear that those opting to dissent politically have their own place in China— house-arrest, prisons, or labor camps.

The issue of human rights was not only a domestic Chinese issue, but one that was increasingly raised in the context of global interdependence and citizenship. As one scholar has stated, "China's compliance or noncompliance with the norms of the human rights regime constitute[d]

389

the most rigorous test of international citizenship, for human rights present[ed] an immediate challenge to the principle of state sovereignty."[1]

Human rights have been defined as "claims" upon the society in which a person lives—"which … every individual has, or should have."[2] To this way of thinking, it applies, or should, to all human beings in every society. This sense grew out of the Western concept of an individual's natural rights and has been set down in various UN covenants, the most basic being the Universal Declaration of Human Rights, adopted in December 1948. Rights guaranteed there include

> every person's right to life, free from arbitrary killing, and to physical and psychological integrity, free from torture or mistreatment; to freedom from slavery, and from arbitrary arrest, detention, or other physical restraint; to fair trial in the criminal process; to freedom of residence and movement within one's country, including the right to leave any country, as well as the right to return to one's own country; to freedom of conscience and religion, expression, and association; to participation in government; to the equal protection of the law; as well as, and not least, a claim to have basic human needs satisfied—food, shelter, health care, an adequate standard of living for oneself and one's family, education, work, and leisure.[3]

As a UN member since 1971, China was required to respect these principles. The PRC has had four constitutions (1954, 1975, 1978, and 1982). All four guaranteed economic, social, cultural, political, and civil rights: freedom "of speech, correspondence, press, assembly, association, demonstration, and for freedom of person, freedom of religious belief, the right of appeal against state functionaries, and the autonomy of national minorities."[4] Other civil rights included in the Universal Declaration, however, were not included in the Chinese constitutions: "freedom of residence or movement, the right to choose one's work, freedom from forced labor, freedom from torture, and the right to the presumption of innocence." Although the right to strike was included in the two 1970s constitutions, that right was eliminated in the 1982 document. The "crucial limitation" about rights enunciated in the Chinese constitutions was that law in China was based on the "will of the state … [and] [s]ince the Constitution was not judicially actionable, the state was not obliged to put the guaranteed right into action."[5]

The Falun Gong

Over the years, in its treatment of dissidents and Tibetans, for example, the PRC was accused of violating many of the rights specified in the Universal Declaration by countenancing torture, arbitrary arrest, unfair trials, the selective use of the law, and trampling on freedom of religion, expression, and association. A recent object lesson in China's treatment of dissenters involved the religious sect Falun Gong (Buddhist Law Sect). On April 25, 1999, outside the CCP compound Zhongnanhai in Beijing, over 10,000 members of the Falun Gong silently gathered and held a sit-in to protest derogatory treatment of the sect's founder by local magazines. The demonstration alarmed Communist leaders; this sort of spontaneous happening had not occurred since 1989. But they were even more apprehensive because Falun Gong had grown dramatically since its formation in 1992. The government itself credited it with having 2 million members, and the sect claimed tens of millions of adherents. Even worse, during its years of existence, the identity of its founder had gone from recognized master of *qigong* (defined by one scholar as Chinese yoga—a routine emphasizing a form of calisthenics and breathing exercises) to comparison to great religious figures in world history. Shades of Hong Xiuquan and the Taipings!

Also shocking to the government leadership was the extent to which the sect had penetrated the party and government. Three of the five Falun Gong members who were selected to negotiate with Premier Zhu Rongji were high-ranking officials. In addition, one of the most vocal supporters of the movement was the former chief administrator of the hospital that treated top government leaders; he had the audacity to send Jiang Zemin a note suggesting that Falun Gong could accomplish things that Marxism could not. From the government's perspective, the movement had to be suppressed. At a time when the moral center of society was not clear, the consequences of allowing the sect to continue and perhaps mushroom out of control were unthinkable.

Thus, the government set out to publicize widely the faults of the movement, pointing to how many people had died because they relied on the sect's teachings rather than seeking proper medical care. They lambasted the sect's founder, then residing in New York. They jailed sect members, many of whom continued periodically to protest the government persecution. The year 2000 brought coordinated waves of protest by sect members in the capital, and the government continued the crackdown. Then on January 23, 2001, five Falun Gong practitioners set themselves on fire in Tiananmen Square; two died. Suddenly the government's statements about the danger of the sect did not seem to be so outrageous. If there had been sympathy among the populace for the sect to that point, many now began to see it in a different light. The government was determined to snuff it out, making it known that "followers could either disavow their beliefs or be taken in for re-education."[6] On the whole, however, it seemed that the self-immolations had taken the wind out of the Falun Gong sails; protests petered out. Government repression of this religious dissent and the actions of Falun Gong believers themselves had accomplished the party-state's goals. The West looked at the government reaction to the sect with disbelief: How could the government so overreact? But Chinese leaders were well aware that the rise of religious sects had, more than once in the Chinese past, come at a time when the regime in power was starting to lose the Mandate. Historical memory made it absolutely essential to nip any such threat in the bud.

As for political dissent, the 1990s saw a continuing on-again, off-again cycle of repression, with periodic roundups of dissidents, then their release from prison. In part this seemed to reflect the government's effort to respond to foreign criticism of its human rights policy so as to avoid various penalties that foreign nations might apply. On the other hand, the erratic policy reflected the continuing distrust and fear among the leadership about the potential for political trouble if a more liberal policy were adopted. Thus, for example, one of the 1989 student leaders, Wang Dan, was sentenced to four years in prison in 1991 but he was released in 1993. Later he was re-imprisoned before being allowed to leave China in 1997. Similarly, the most famous dissident to that point, Wei Jingsheng, imprisoned since the Democracy Wall episode of 1979, was freed in 1993, re-imprisoned in 1995, and in 1998 released and allowed to leave China. A remarkable nationally televised debate between Chairman Jiang Zemin and President Bill Clinton in June 1998 that dealt with human rights issues, among others, raised hopes that the government might be starting to change its views. But late in 1998, a series of arrests of dissidents trying to form an alternative political party once again dashed hopes that any such change was occurring.

For this record, China was pilloried in the West, especially in the United States, where the issue gave rise to much China bashing and held up trade status and agreements, as well as China's entrance into international organizations such as the World Trade Organization. China's (and much of Asia's) response was that many of the individual rights laid down by Western nations in the Universal Declaration were culture-specific and did not apply in the same way in all cultures and countries. In China, traditionally the individual did not have *rights* but rather *responsibilities* to the collective (the family, the larger society, or the state). In such a culture, the Chinese asserted, the rights of the collective were what were properly called human rights. Further, they argued that when the West talked about human rights, it focused on rather narrow political and civil rights. China argued that economic and social rights had to precede political rights: What good is the right to assemble when one is too poor to have food to eat? What good is free speech when one is too poor to afford medical treatment? Finally, the Chinese emphasized state sovereignty whenever they were attacked for their human rights record. States signed the UN charter; thus, the human rights entailed in being a UN member were granted in sovereign states.

Before a UN World Conference on Human Rights in Vienna in 1993, Asian states met in Bangkok (March 29–April 2, 1993) to clarify their position on human rights and to assert their way of looking at the problem. The Bangkok Declaration issued at the end of the meeting was Asia's official view of human rights (not the view of the many nongovernmental Asian groups that attended). Its crucial ideas were set forth in Vienna by the Chinese delegate to that meeting. The declaration bears careful reading, for it makes the Chinese point of view very clear:

> The concept of human rights is a product of historical development. It is closely associated with specific social, political, and economic conditions and the specific history, culture and values of a particular country. Different historical development stages have different human rights requirements. ... Thus, one should not and cannot think the human rights standards and models of certain countries as the only proper ones and demand all other countries to comply with them. ... For the vast number of developing countries, to respect and protect human rights is first and foremost to ensure the full realization of the rights to subsistence and development. ... To wantonly accuse another country of abuse of human rights and impose the human rights criteria of one's own country or region on other countries or regions are tantamount to an infringement upon the sovereignty of other countries and interference in the latter's internal affairs. ... State sovereignty is the basis for the realization of citizens' human rights. If the sovereignty of a state is not safeguarded, the human rights of its citizens are out of the question, like a castle in the air.[7]

Many scholars, legal experts, and human rights specialists attacked outright the cultural relativist arguments that Western legal traditions infusing the "human rights regime" were inappropriate for non-Western countries. They argued that the regime had truly become universal.

> Human rights is the idea of our times. ... The principal covenants and conventions ... have been subscribed to by many nations, of every ideological complexion and political or economic commitment—Western and Eastern, developed and developing, democratic, authoritarian, and totalitarian, rich and poor, free enterprise and socialist."[8]

Others argued that Confucianism itself held values that were in close harmony with human rights, so that the cultural relativist arguments hardly applied.

Executions and Torture

It is interesting that Deng's reforms placed much more emphasis on the individual; it was individuals, after all, who were getting rich; the role of the state had been reduced. And yet, no new legal protections for the individual had been developed; the right of due process, for example, was still frequently violated. In the 1980s and 1990s there were frequent anticrime campaigns, with widespread executions: between August and October 1983, for example, there were 600 executions; and in 1990, 750 of 960 death sentences were carried out—totaling a third of the world's executions that year. (When judging such things, one must take care: in 1999, the United States was incarcerating 2 million people, fully one-quarter of the world's prison population.)

One of China's practices was to talk the human rights game but continue to walk along its old repressive path. A look at torture cases reveals the pattern. Torture was traditionally a common method to extract confessions from persons accused of or charged with a crime. In the anticrime campaign of 1983, torture was widespread. From 1985 to 1989 the state conducted an anti-torture campaign in which the number of torture cases actually increased, and it was during this same period that "China signed (12 December 1986), ratified (4 October 1988), and "enforced," (3 November 1988) the Convention Against Torture."[9] Indeed, China claimed to have been a leader in drafting the convention. Yet report after report of conditions relating to torture in China showed little improvement, if any. In April 1990, the International League for Human Rights claimed that torture was a "routine part of the modus operandi of [China's] law enforcement officials."[10] A 1995 Amnesty International report stated that

> seven years after it ratified the Convention against Torture, the government still has not taken measures to prohibit all acts of torture by law. … The ineffectiveness of the measures taken by the government is demonstrated by the continuing high incidence of torture in China.[11]

Hundreds of such complaints continued to come from China. In May 1996, the United Nations' Committee against Torture (CAT) made nine recommendations to China about its torture record. Basically, the committee told Beijing to clean up its act. But China's defensive response came straight from the substance of the Bangkok Declaration: "[A]s the proceedings before the CAT ended, the Chinese Ambassador excoriated the Committee for failing to understand China's cultural conditions and the problems faced by the Chinese government."[12] More government decrees in January 1998 calling for the end of torture by police indicated that the problem continued.

Yet, China continued to sign human rights documents. Near century's end, it signed two covenants, expansions of the Universal Declaration—the three documents are now often referred to as the International Bill of Rights. In October 1997, China signed the International Covenant on Economic, Social, and Cultural Rights, and in October 1998, it inked the Covenant on Civil and Political Rights. In early 2001, China ratified the first covenant on economic, social, and cultural rights, though it insisted on placing a reservation on Article 8, which specified the right to form labor unions and the right to strike. Twenty years after it had signed the Covenant on Civil and Political Rights, it still had not ratified it, meaning that it is not yet subject to the committees that monitor compliance with that covenant.

LIU XIAOBO AND CHARTER 08

Despite its signing international agreements on human rights and despite international pressure on China to hew to the human rights ideal, China's overall record has not been good. The most famous and outspoken dissident from 1989, when he participated in the Hunger Strike in Tiananmen Square until his death in July 2017, was Liu Xiaobo. A popular professor at Beijing Normal University, he became visiting scholar at three universities abroad and a "public intellectual," writing political and social essays, articles, and critiques on contemporary China. He wrote,

June 1989 has been the major turning point in my life. ... [at that time] I had chosen to return to China from the U.S. [at Columbia University] to join the protest movement, and then was thrown into prison for "the crime of spreading and inciting counterrevolution."[13]

During and after Beijing's Olympic Games, in the summer and fall of 2008, Chinese human rights activists drafted a platform for human rights, the rule of law, and moves toward a democracy. Calling themselves the Chinese Human Rights Defenders, they used as a model Charter 77, which had been a statement sent by Czech human rights advocates to the Czech government in January 1977 to criticize the Communist government for thumbing its nose at human rights despite various conventions and treaties it had signed that obligated it to do so. The drafters of Charter 08 did not "petition" the government, but meant the statement, presented to the public, as a platform for political reforms. Although Liu Xiaobo had not been the primary drafter of Charter 08, he became known as its foremost supporter, actively seeking more signatures. When the charter was formally made public on December 10, 303 people had signed, and thus endorsed, Charter 08; signers were not only the activists and other intellectuals but heads of farmers' and workers' organizations, and even government officials. After the activists posted Charter 08 on the internet, over 12,000 more added their names.[14]

The Charter advocated nineteen recommendations "on national governance, citizen's rights, and social development."[15] They included a new constitution that called for the separation of legislative, executive, and judicial powers, that granted the central government certain powers, with all other powers belonging to local governments (provincial and county).[16] It would be a federated Republic, with legislators directly elected by the people on the principle of "one person, one vote." An independent judiciary would be established with a supreme court that had powers of constitutional review. Human rights would be strictly guaranteed as the system of "re-education through labor" would end; and rural and urban equality would be sought through the abolition of the "two-tier household registry system" (the *hukou* system) that favored urban residents and treated rural residents almost as though they were second-class citizens. There would be fundamental freedoms: to assemble, to speak freely, to practice freedom of religion, to form non-governmental groups without having to get governmental approval. Student political indoctrination would be replaced with civic education courses to advance universal values and citizens' rights. The natural environment and private property would be protected; state-owned enterprises would be transferred to private ownership; and farmers could own, buy, and sell land. Mandatory was "a fair and adequate social security system," covering "all citizens" and providing "basic access to education, health care, retirement security, and employment."[17] Finally there must be a policy of

truth in reconciliation: All political prisoners and prisoners of conscience must be released. There should be a Truth Investigation Commission charged with finding the facts about past injustices and atrocities, determining responsibility for them, upholding justice, and, on these bases, seeking social reconciliation.[18]

Charter 08 was remarkable for its clearly-presented and rational tone; it was offered "in a spirit of [our] duty as responsible and constructive citizens."[19] It was not an emotional rant; it did not use inflammatory words. In its recommendations, it did not accuse, challenge, or threaten the government. It simply sets out the principles that Liu and others cherished. On the face of it, there seemed nothing at which a government should take umbrage. But undoubtedly, the government saw Charter 08 as not simply points to ameliorate some problems in the Chinese polity, but as the attempted overturning of the whole communist–capitalist status quo.

The Charter's penultimate paragraph did throw down the gauntlet:

> China, as a major nation of the world, as one of the five permanent members of the United Nations Security Council, and as a member of the UN Council on Human Rights, should be contributing to peace for humankind and progress toward human rights. Unfortunately, we stand today as the only country among the major nations that remains mired in authoritarian politics. Our political system continues to produce human rights disasters and social crises, thereby not only constricting China's own development but also limiting the progress of all of human civilization. This must change, truly it must. The democratization of Chinese politics can be put off no longer.[20]

The formal announcement of Charter 08 was timed to coincide with the sixtieth anniversary of the UN's Universal Declaration of Human Rights on December 10, 2008. When Charter 08 was placed on the internet, the government deleted it and began a crackdown using detention, harassment, and intimidation of those involved in writing Charter 08 and in seeking signatures for it. Beijing police came to Liu's apartment at 11 p.m. on December 8, 2008, two days before the Charter was made public. They took him, detained him until June 23, 2009 (168 days), and then formally "arrested" him on "suspicion of instigating subversion of state power."[21] Charter 08 was the main evidence against him at his sham trial on December 23, 2009. Liu had prepared a final statement, entitled "I Have No Enemies"; but the presiding judge stopped him after reading it for only fourteen minutes, because he arbitrarily ruled that Liu could not take more time than the prosecutor did in making his case. The last paragraph, which Liu did not get to read, indicated his perspective and his fatalism.

> I feel it is my duty as a Chinese citizen to try to realize in practice the right of free expression that is written in our country's constitution. There has been nothing remotely criminal in anything that I have done, yet I will not complain, even in the face of the charges against me.[22]

The court sentenced him to prison for eleven years.

It is not without considerable irony that two years to the day of the announcement of Charter 08 (December 10, 2010) Liu Xiaobo was awarded the Nobel Peace Prize in Oslo "for his long and non-violent struggle for fundamental human rights in China."[23] The Chinese government was furious and broke off diplomatic relations with Norway; those relations were not restored until December 2016. The Chinese Foreign Ministry tried to browbeat diplomats around the globe from attending the Award Ceremony. They barred Liu and his wife and his activist peers and friends from going to Oslo. In place of a Nobel speech that Liu was to have delivered, Norwegian actress Liv Ullman read Liu's essay, "I Have No Enemies," written for his trial. On the day the prize was granted, the Nobel certificate and the prize itself were placed on an empty chair on stage in a folder marked with the initials LXB. So paranoid was the Chinese government about the whole affair that they almost immediately banned the phrase "empty chair" or images of empty chairs from the Chinese internet. International media televised the ceremony, but China blocked the broadcast signals of CNN and the BBC. A Chinese official set forth China's position: "Liu Xiaobo is a criminal who has been sentenced by Chinese judicial departments for violating Chinese laws." Awarding the prize to Liu "runs completely counter to the principle of the prize and is also a blasphemy to the peace prize."[24]

FIGURE 21.1   Since the PRC's government did not allow Liu to go to Oslo to receive his Nobel Peace Prize, the Nobel Committee decided to represent him by an empty chair on which was placed his Nobel diploma and medal. The empty chair became a symbol of Chinese government autocracy, a turn that outraged the Beijing party and government.

Source: Junge, Heiko/AFP/Getty Images.

THE RULE OF GENERAL SECRETARY XI JINPING (2012–?)

In October 2016, the Central Committee of the CCP declared Xi Jinping "the leadership Core," that is, central to the leadership of the Communist Party; he thus joined only three other previous leaders of the party-state: Mao, Deng, and Jiang Zemin as holders of the name, not a formal title, but clearly connoting "a vital center." He had come into power in 2012 like a bulldozer, undertaking, as we have seen, his strong anti-corruption campaigns, which doubled as a vehicle to root out opposition men and even factions. His stature soared at the Nineteenth Party Congress in October 2017 when it was decided that his theoretical and practical contribution and legacy to the party-state, "Socialism with Chinese Characteristics for a New Era" was to be enshrined in the constitution. These words are described as "Xi Jinping Thought." Of the last five leaders of the party-state (Mao, Deng, Jiang, Hu, and Xi) the contributions of Jiang ("three represents") and Hu ("scientific approach to development" and "harmony") are placed in the constitution, but they are not attributed to any person who had a larger "thought" or "theory." Xi was now linked after only five years of rule (as with the word "core") with Mao and Deng, in that the constitution names each with their ideological contributions: Mao Zedong Thought ("mass line"), Deng Xiaoping Theory ("seeking truth from facts"), and Xi Jinping Thought. At the party congress in October 2017, 2,289 delegates voted unanimously to align Xi with Mao and Deng. Xi Jinping Thought was described by the Hong Kong and foreign press, respectively as "a nationalist appeal to return the country to historical greatness" and an "unabashed program of national revival backed up by increasing military power."[25]

He and Premier Li Keqiang restructured and rebalanced the economy: shifting prime importance from exports to the home market, reconfiguring the industrial structure, developing and encouraging domestic consumption; allowing private capital to enter the financial sector; taking away privileges from SOEs and strengthening the private sector; encouraging Chinese investments abroad; and stressing environmental and ecological improvement.[26] These were "the boldest set of economic and social reforms since 1978."[27]

FIGURE 21.2 The fifth leader of the PRC since its 1949 establishment, Xi (b. 1953) has already been named a Core Leader, and the CCP has agreed that he will not be bound by ten-year official party terms. His "China Dream" sees China a global power by 2050; his utopian international plans with many plausible opportunities seem almost counter-intuitive when paired with his increasing domestic suppression and authoritarian control.
Source: Government of India, licensed under the Government Open Data License—India (GODL) via Wikimedia Commons.

Although the release of Charter 08 and Liu's sentencing and arrest came under the leadership of Hu Jintao, who kept a steadily repressive hand on dissenters, Xi Jinping brought "a new authoritarianism," moving quickly to curb free speech and personal freedoms.[28]

The chill that has descended across Chinese civil society, especially over the last 12 months, has become one of the defining aspects of Xi Jinping's presidency, alongside his own rapid consolidation of power over the party, the government, and military. As China's most powerful party and state leader since Deng Xiaoping, Mr. Xi has presided over a crackdown without precedent since the repression that followed the 1989 Tiananmen Square massacre.[29]

THE INTERNET

The government maintained three key weapons to keep dissent and social unrest subdued: information control, exercise of coercive power, and improvement of local governance. The internet, which began to operate permanently in China in 1994, loomed as an increasingly large and powerful force in Chinese life. The government, which owned the online access routes, almost immediately saw it as the potential political threat that it was; the Ministry of Public Security took the first general steps to control internet use in 1997. In November 2000, the regime launched the Great Firewall, called formally by the government, the Golden Shield Project. The two were really one censorship vehicle, with differing functions. The Firewall filtered foreign websites and was a tool for the propaganda system while the Shield monitored the domestic internet and was a device for the public security system. Together they blocked website contents and monitored internet access of individuals. The Firewall and the Shield were initiated, developed, and directed by the Ministry of Public Security. In 2009, the Ministry proposed that new personal computers bought in China or abroad had to have pre-installed software called the Green Dam Youth Escort to filter out pornography. There was a hue and cry from Chinese "netizens" that they did not want the software and would not use it; that very negative response seemed to give the government pause and it temporarily postponed the action. It was thought that the software could spot pornography by picking up and analyzing skin-color; but it could not detect black skin, only fair skin or lighter skin. It filtered out and censored as pornographic a children's book, *Garfield: A Tail of Two Kitties*, because of the light yellow in the drawings of the kittens. And the software detected and censored pictures of Chinese political leaders as pornography. Needless to say, the Ministry dropped the software idea.

A study in late 2002 said that the Chinese government had blocked 18,931 websites.[30] As of September 2017, over 3,000 were blocked. Some of the more well-known sites included g-mail, Google, Facebook, Twitter, YouTube, Instagram, Pinterest, Vimeo, Dropbox, Chinese Wikipedia, Bloomberg, *New York Times*, Tumblr, Voice of America, *ABA*, *Wall St. Journal*, Reuters, *Time*, *The Economist*, Radio Australia, All Movie, Wiki-leaks, *Le Monde*, *Le Soir*, and most blogging sites. For China's 772 million internet users (at the end of 2017), such a situation could be more than frustrating. In addition, material on certain topics was simply blocked out, such as the Tiananmen massacre, Tank Man, police brutality, pro-democracy activists, freedom of speech, Taiwan, Tibet, the Dalai Lama, criminal activity, and obscenity and pornography. In the case of Liu Xiaobo, keywords and images of him and his wife were blocked out of the internet both when he received the Nobel Peace Prize in 2010 and for days after his death in 2017.

An estimated 90 million Chinese were able to slip past the Great Firewall with the use of VPNs (Virtual Private Networks). These were networks that were constructed using the internet to connect remote users to a company's private internal network. A user connected with the private network, used encryption and other security devices; only authorized users could enter the network. The data, furthermore, could not be intercepted; there was unfettered access to any website; and users gained privacy because the VPN hid "browsing activities from internet service providers."[31]

But from January to October 2017, the government issued new regulations to tighten even further its control over the internet. Starting with actions on VPNs, Beijing ordered China's largest telecommunications firms, China Mobile, China Telecom, and China Unicom, to ban the use of VPNs by February 1, 2018. The government was apparently spooked, for example, by the role that social media (specifically, Facebook, Twitter, and YouTube) had played in Egypt's Arab Spring in 2011 in organizing revolutionary efforts and disseminating reports of developments in the overthrow of President Mubarak. Wael Ghonim, a young Google executive whose Facebook page was credited with touching off the initial protest, put it succinctly, "If you want to liberate a country, give them the internet."[32] Facebook, Twitter, and YouTube were, of course, blocked websites in China, but VPNs had no blocked websites. Thus, the urgency of the government to gain a firmer grip on fine-tuning their censorship machine.

No one knew what the total impact of eliminating the possibility of VPNs would be, especially for academic, business, scientific, and technological elites, who depended on the internet. The government announced that approved VPNs would be available, but speculation on how that would work was largely negative. The application process would likely be bureaucratic, and therefore, lengthy; the context, paranoid; and, in the end it would likely be limited to one single location, that is, not to be taken home for work or not to be taken for work while traveling.

It was not only the VPN ban that 2017 brought as far as new, tougher internet regulations. China's Ministry of Industry and Information Technology (MIIT) announced that it would "clean up" the domestic internet by March 31, 2018. What cleaning up specifically entailed was not spelled out. The Cyberspace Administration of China established new restrictions, requiring online news programs to be controlled and managed by editorial staff sanctioned by the CCP. Foreign businesses in China were required to store crucial data on local servers, a move that brought worries about possible surveillance. The government banned streaming of "dramatic video content" if it did not have government permission. The government set forth new rules that internet chat service providers must verify the identities of users and keep a record of group chats; managers of chat groups must monitor the online activity of fellow chat group members. New regulations required internet users to sign up with their real names when participating in online chats.

For several years, Xi Jinping called for internet sovereignty, or, as he preferred to call it, "cyber sovereignty," by which he meant that all countries had the right to censor and regulate the internet within their own borders. This control of cyberspace, in Xi's view, was as crucial as a nation's territorial sovereignty. Laughable on the face of it, a recent Chinese decision on content censorship banned online users from eating bananas in a provocative way during live stream web casts; and, as one writer noted ironically, this ban "encapsulate[d] Beijing's view of cyber sovereignty." Though people the world over would like to conceive of a global internet community, the Chinese government concluded that "cyberspace must still respect the culture, customs, and governance of the physical space defined by a country's borders."[33]

In the arena of the internet, two "Cs" function as most important in Xi Jinping's China: control and censor. An internet army of police scoured the internet to censor or block out websites that contained key words, subjects, issues, developments, complaints about the party-state, Western ideas and practices—and all other points that the Ministry had found offensive because they posed a potential or perceived threat to government and party control. Reports indicate that the estimated numbers of internet police soared during the 2000s and 2010s.

In 2002, there were thirty to fifty thousand; but by 2013, the BBC reported that China's state media revealed that there were two million. Amnesty International reported that China "ha[d] the largest recorded numbers of imprisoned journalists and cyber-dissidents [in the world]." Further, Reporters Without Borders, based in Paris, in both 2010 and 2012 announced that "China is the world's biggest prison for netizens."[34]

Beyond internet activists and dissidents, the government certainly used the internet to tout itself, set up government discussions, arrange meetings with their factions, and strategize about putting their preferred policies into action. A 2017 study by three American academics estimated that the government itself fabricated and posted about 448 million political and social comments per year. In what was obviously a massive and secretive operation, the government and party were to extol their actions and/or "to distract the public and change the subject."[35] But there was also the work of factions, sparring with each other for power, influence, and the control of the policy agenda. Before Xi Jinping's rise to power in 2013, the two most powerful factions had been the "princelings," offspring of the first generation leaders of the PRC, the "elitists"; and those who had advanced their careers through the Communist Youth League (the "league faction"), the "populists." This post-Deng "one party, two coalitions" political reality was a marked departure from the all-powerful strongman model, seen in Mao and Deng. Although the strong leadership and policies of Xi Jinping from 2013 on suggested to some that the "Xi faction" might become THE unifying body that would subsume the two factions or coalitions into one. But the results of the Nineteenth Party Congress in October 2017 showed that the two factions were still alive, though diminished. The American Brooking Institute's accounting showed that of the twenty-five-member Politburo, fifteen were of Xi's faction (the princeling or elitist faction) and ten were of Hu Jintao's faction (the "league" or populist faction).[36] With all the 2017 stiffer censorship changes, it is almost certain that the internet does play an important role in factional dealings and interactions. As one scholar reflected on the stringent new internet regulations,

> This is a significantly escalated form of internet control and shows there is unprecedented urgency and desperation at the top of the government. This is clearly about the highest levels of political struggle and the different factions using the internet as their battlefield.[37]

The Crackdown against Lawyers

Since Xi became president and the party general-secretary, the pace of repression against political activists, journalists, artists, writers, professors, religious groups, and lawyers has quickened. Any potential threat to the party's monopolistic hold on power, however minor that challenge was, could be crushed by the party's iron fists. Professor Zhang Xuezhong of East China University in Shanghai, a champion of free speech and the rule of law, was sacked in 2013; he said, "I'm just a university faculty member who expresses his own opinions, thoughts, and proposals, which is absolutely my right. This is an out-and-out witch hunt."[38] Article 35 of China's constitution explicitly protects the right of freedom of expression.

But it was the state's crackdown against lawyers that was unprecedented in scope. On July 9, 2015, Chinese police seized 248 human rights lawyers, legal assistants, and political activists and brought them in for questioning and more. The government described the operation, dubbed the "709" crackdown for the date it began, as an attempt to destroy a "major criminal gang." The pattern was the same as the detention and arrest of Liu Xiaobo in 2009: seize, detain for a long period of time (up to eighteen months or more), then formally arrest, and move toward trial. During that lengthy time, typically the families of those arrested would not be told of their whereabouts or be able to talk or visit with them. Government techniques to get prisoners to talk centered on physical and psychological torture: beatings, indefinite isolation, prolonged sleep deprivation, threats to their families and to revoke their lawyers' licenses. One of the tenets in Xi Jinping Thought was "ensuring every dimension of governance is law-based," that is, that the rule of law is essential.[39] But in actuality, the rule of law meant that the Communist Party made the law, was above the law, and destroyed anyone who dared to question the party's monopoly of power. It is, we might say, "the rule of law with Chinese characteristics."

Beijing continued to sentence lawyers to prison. In late November 2017, Jiang Tianyong, called the "soul of the 709 rescue effort" for his determination to help embattled colleagues, was sentenced to two years, a fairly typical prison term for the lawyers. However, at the end of December 2017, Wu Gan was sentenced to eight years imprisonment, the longest term any lawyer received since the crackdown began. Wu, whose online handle was "Super Vulgar Butcher," used social media and often bizarre performance art to shame and humiliate CCP members. For instance, he photo-shopped faces of three Henan officials onto pigs and posted the image on social media with the caption: "World Most Wanted, Three Fat Pigs." He tried to humiliate the judge trying his case by hanging a photograph of the judge with a Hitler mustache outside the courtroom. After the harsh sentence was read, Wu gave a long statement, the first paragraph of which follows:

> For those living under a dictatorship, being given the honorable label of one who "subverts state power" is the highest form of affirmation for a citizen. It's proof that the citizen wasn't an accomplice or a slave, and that at the very least he went out and defended, and fought for, human rights.[40]

Two married human rights lawyers Wang Yu and her husband Bao Longjun were detained in the 709 suppression at "black jails" (extralegal detention centers where deprivation, isolation, and torture were common). Wang was one of the most famous of the women human rights activists. Wang and Bao were formally arrested in January 2016, then placed on parole in August after Wang's government-forced confession of the wrongness of her activity. They and their son were forced to live in an Inner Mongolian city, under continuous watch and, when out of their apartment, accompanied by government deputies constantly. The government frequently harangued her, attacking her work and character, using similar diatribes to characterize and tear down all activists: "Wang Yu is an 'arrogant convict of a woman'; 'a hypocritical and false lawyer'; 'a shrew'"; the Chinese state media accused her of "blabbering about the rule of law and human rights" before she was detained.[41]

In August 2016, Wang received in absentia the first American Bar Association's International Human Rights Award. The citation read, "Wang Yu committed herself to represent some of China's most underserved and marginalized in their struggle to access justice and worked to expand legal pathways for justice for women and girls." She took up a fiery defense of Ilham Tohti, the best known intellectual activist for Uighur human rights. In early 2015, she protested against government expropriations of cropland and properties northwest of Shanghai. She served the women's rights group, the "Five Feminists" (see below). She took on the thankless task of representing the outlawed Falun Gong. In 2013, six elementary girls, ages 11 to 13, in Hainan province were raped by their elementary school principal and a local government housing official. At first the local police maintained that sexual molestation had not occurred when the two men took the girls to a hotel overnight. Then, when physical exams showed that they had raped all the girls, word spread that the rapists would get very light sentences. Wang and her group, led by feminist Ye Haiyan traveled to Hainan to put pressure on authorities to act fairly and according to the law in sentencing these men. This episode was captured in the award-winning documentary *Hooligan Sparrow*—a nickname of the maverick Ye. In the end, the principal was sentenced to prison for thirteen and a half years and the housing official for eleven and a half years.

THE ROLES AND STATUS OF WOMEN IN THE ERA OF REFORM

As a whole, the position and status of women during the years of reform deteriorated from what had been. At least ideologically during the Mao years, the equality of men and women was seemingly a given. The Chinese Constitution of 1954 specified that women and men had equal rights and opportunities and that there should be policies to make sure that among males and females there should be equal pay for equal work. Mao's famous dictum in 1968 was that "women hold up half the sky": women were as important as men. These were the "ideal" ends to be worked for, but there were many gaps between the ideal and the real. "While the Communist revolution brought women more job opportunities, it also made their interests subordinate to collective goals": in short, the triumph of socialism and then Communism swallowed up the agenda of many women, for whom women's liberation was a key goal.[42] This had been at issue in the 1930s and 1940s between Communist Party leaders and women cadres. Women's role in rural collectivization in the 1950s empowered them to the degree that it offered them employment but in the process, women very rarely rose to positions of responsibility and leadership. While they routinely did heavy manual labor, they were paid less than men. They lived, as it were, as outsiders in communes organized around village relationships and often their husband's family. Naihua Zhang, a sent-down girl in the Cultural Revolution, spent years in the countryside; later, on reflection as a university professor, she "equated rural marriage with a total erasure of women's identity."[43] In urban settings, women worked in dismal small workshops with very little pay, while men were most often at work in big-factory and state-enterprise jobs. The reason often given for this workplace reality revealed deeply-entrenched gender prejudices: women naturally had a weaker constitution and a gentler temperament, and were therefore unfit for manning factory floors and operating heavy machinery.

In rural settings, women had to contend with life under the reforms: in many cases that meant that husband and adolescent sons were in urban areas trying to make more money to help relieve the poverty that many in the country experienced. The wife, her daughter-in-law, and daughters were left with the farming and the livestock. Because of this reality, scholars have begun to speak of the "feminization of agriculture." Here is a scholar-produced composite picture of the life of a rural woman in the first decade of the twenty-first century.

> A 45-year-old woman, performing agricultural and domestic tasks for her family while her husband and son are in the county seat trying to earn some money, and she and her daughter-in-law try to manufacture some small items, produce their requisite amount of grain, raise pigs, chickens, and ducks, embroider, watch the two children, saving money for taxes and education and health care … Maybe her mother-in-law, 67, has a broken hip. There is no money to spare for her treatment, so they just try to give her broth … Some houses in the hamlet even have electricity. There they can all watch TV in the evening, doing mending by its dim light.[44]

Women benefited during the years of reform after 1978 in the sense that a rising economic tide lifts all boats, but these last forty years saw the loss of ground in the movement for equal rights for women. In the closing or restructuring of SOEs (1998–2003), between 28 and 30 million people lost their jobs; many of these were women. In 1997, women accounted for only 39 percent of China's workforce, but they made up 61 percent of laid-off-workers, who lost their benefits as well. One unemployed woman was interviewed at a Tianjin unemployment center: "At our factory everyone who was laid off was a woman. Look around you. Everyone here is female. Now what can we do? We're not young enough."[45] Being hired again after being laid off was not easy: 75 percent of laid-off women were still unemployed after one year. Throughout initial hiring, being laid off, and trying to be rehired, women faced gender discrimination—continually still branded as "the weaker sex." If a woman took action in cases of clear employment discrimination, she might ironically find herself in trouble with the law. In June 2015 Gao Xiao applied to be a line cook at a restaurant, which refused to hire her because of her gender. They told her, "Men prepare the food; women only serve it." Gao filed a lawsuit, which in turn led to the police coming to her apartment for a visit. Since her bringing the lawsuit, officials issued her threats, badgered her parents, and hounded her landlord who, in turn, evicted her from her apartment. In the end, she won the lawsuit; the court gave her a paltry sum of $300 RMB (about 48 USD). She found work at a bakery; yet she was dissatisfied that the restaurant management never apologized and, on principle, launched an appeal.[46] Official actions betrayed the Communist fear of an individual demanding rights in the one-party state—especially if that person had many potent social connections that could be used to drum up an activist protest.

In addition to issues of employment, there were further indicators that the position of women was not good and was not improving; the hopes of the twentieth century in this regard seemed to be shriveling in the first two decades of the twenty-first. There was the obvious political glass ceiling for women. After the nineteenth meeting of the National Congress of the Communist Party of China in October 2017, there were no women on the most important party-state body, the seven member Standing Committee of the Politburo; there were two women on the twenty-five-membered Politburo; there was one woman on the sixteen full-membered Party Central Committee; there was one woman of 120 managers of centrally-run, state-owned companies; and finally, on the 2,280 member National People's Congress, there were just over 20 percent women (456)—a percentage that has been flat-lined for decades.

The income gap between men and woman widened. In 1990 urban women made 77.5 percent of what urban men made; that year in rural China, women made 79 percent of what men made. Twenty years later (2010) after years of economic expansion and the reform program, urban women received in wages 67.3 percent of what men had received—10.2 percent less than in 1990; in rural China, women in 2010 made 56 percent of what men had made, 23 percent less than in 1990. Then there were attitudes that underlie the gender bias—on the part of both women and men, biases that are extraordinarily difficult to change. The assumption: "Men belong in public life and women belong at home." In 2000, 54.3 percent of men agreed, but over half (50.6 percent) of women also agreed. If we took the same assumption set forth in 2010, 67.3 percent of men agreed (an increase of 7.7 percent) and 55 percent of women also agreed (an increase of 4.4 percent). It seems from this poll that the traditional gender bias negative to women had become more entrenched as reform progressed, departing more and more from the ideological stance of the Mao years and sharing more the traditional Chinese way of seeing superior men and subordinate women.

In September 2011, the Supreme Court of China ruled that "property bought before marriage either outright or on mortgage reverted to the buyer upon divorce"—it had previously been considered joint property. Since it was traditional that the groom and his family paid for the house, this ruling clearly discriminated against the wife and "guarantee[d] that the woman receive[d] nothing upon divorce." This law simply reinforced the old patriarchal power structure and system by placing the power in marriage into the husband's hands. The law also made it less likely that the wife would get custody of the children, for her husband would have the house where the children could live and she would be at least temporarily homeless. One Marxist commentator rued the decision and fondly looked back to the days of Mao: "Battles over property occur because of inequality. Situations such as these were virtually unheard of in Revolutionary China. Under socialism, all were guaranteed homes; it was never necessary to fight over who keeps a place to live."[47]

A 2013 UN survey of 10,000 men in Asia and the Pacific was entitled "Why Do Some Men Use Violence Against Women and How Can We Prevent It?" At least one of the sites of the interviews was in rural China, where over 80 percent of those who admitted to rape explained it as "sexual entitlement," that men have a right to have sex with women regardless of their consent. The study's overall findings "reaffirm that violence against women is an expression of women's subordination and inequality in the private and public spheres." The impetus, even compulsion for male violence against women "is associated with men's personal histories and practices, within a broader context of structural inequalities." At the China site, over 65 percent of violence-prone men reported experiencing physical, sexual, or emotional abuse as a child or witnessed the abuse of their mother: "these men were at least twice as likely to use violence against a woman partner."[48]

Chinese divorce rates continued to rise dramatically: from 1.3 million couples in 2003 to 2.7 million in 2010 to 4.8 million in 2016. The two reasons most commonly given were domestic violence and extramarital affairs. Reports from China in the last decade indicate that sexual harassment is ubiquitous and that domestic and sexual violence is commonplace. The development of an increasingly vibrant and active feminism is one response. In March 2015, the police arrested five women who had planned a protest against sexual harassment on subways and buses in Beijing, Guangzhou, and Hangzhou; they had hoped to carry anti-harassment signs and hand out stickers. This was not a protest or a demonstration (both are banned), or a criminal plot, but an attempt to make people aware of the issue. The arrest of the "Feminist Five," their detention for a month, the monitoring of their phones and emails, and their remaining "criminal suspects" for over a year after their release were further evidence of the government's being frightened that young women, grounded in social media, could very well be able to mobilize a huge network of fellow female activists. The tactics that the feminists took in light of the bans on protest demonstrations was performance art, the same method used by the lawyer Wu Gan. In 2012, three women donned wedding dresses spattered with fake blood and walked down a street in Beijing's main shop district, "carrying signs that read 'Love is not an excuse for violence' and calling people to be on guard against domestic abuse." The group set up an "Occupy Men's Toilet" campaign to call attention to what women considered a discriminatory proportion of male to female toilet facilities in public restrooms. In yet another act of performance art, the group shaved their heads to protest the discrimination against women in college admissions. Feminists won a victory, as it were, when the National People's Congress passed a Domestic Violence Law that took effect on March 1, 2016. But it has had many problems; the law promises the issuance of restraining orders to protect from abuse; yet the bureaucratic red-tape sometimes had what should be a 72-hour process take up to four weeks, in effect gutting the whole purpose of the order. Even worse were the sexist attitudes of the police and courts who, even in direly threatening situations where a husband has repeatedly beaten his wife, told her to go home and work it out.

Finally, the frequent response of the party-state to women's demands—to tell them to go back home and make babies—raised the hackles of many women. In October 2015, the government ended its thirty-six-year policy of one child per family and from that point instituted a two-child per family policy. The state's goal in this matter was dealing with the issue of China's aging population; without a strong economic and social safety net for retirees and the elderly and the availability of younger and middle-aged taxpayers to finance it, China would be hard-pressed to deal with what seems an oncoming crisis. But women activists refused to be held hostage for party-state policies. In the rapidly growing middle class (which made up roughly 68 percent of the urban population), some women began to break away from the traditional long-held expectations of compulsory marriage. They resented being seen as "reproductive tools" to help solve China's demographic problems. In the words of one feminist, "[T]he feminist movement's message of resistance to the traditional feminine roles of wife and mother pose[d] a unique threat to the Communist Party's vision of a patriarchal family at the core of a strong paternalistic state."[49] In all the government's dealing with dissenting groups or individuals, "[T]he priority of the authorities is not justice for victims but [instead] social stability."[50]

THE SPECTER OF MAO

The opening ceremonies of the 2008 Olympic Games showcased the genius of China's traditional culture, leaving out the twentieth century and, most notably, Mao Zedong. This followed a 2006 junior high and high school textbook revision in Shanghai (which often set nation-wide trends). In notes to the teacher in the junior high text: "Mao, the Long March, colonial repression of China and the Rape of Nanking [are] taught only in a compressed history curriculum." The senior high textbook mentioned Mao only once—and that "as part of a lesson on the custom of lowering the flag to half-staff at state funerals, like Mao's in 1976." Was Mao, in the first decade of the twenty-first century, being not only sidelined but erased as the reform movement picked up even more momentum?

The answer was loudly "NO." The 1990s saw the first strong appearance of a negative Neo-Maoist reaction against some aspects of the reform movement itself. The first stirring of a more critical view of the marketization of China appeared in 1993, the year after Deng's trip to Shenzhen, where he bolstered the reform effort. But it was not until the death of Deng in 1997 that the labels "New Left" (or "neo-Maoist") came to be considered de rigueur—with those groups generally holding positions outside the reform consensus. Its goal was to argue for an alternative to the reformist route to modernization and included the following principles: a renewed spirit of collectivism with a de-emphasis on individualism; a more significant role for state planning and a greatly diminished role for the private sector; the preservation of state-owned enterprises; and increased Chinese nationalism as opposed to the forces of globalization.

Among the most upsetting realities in the reform period to the neo-Maoists were the rapidly worsening inequality of wealth and income and the rampant corruption. Many neo-Maoists felt left behind in China's economic boom, marginalized by greedy capitalists. Nostalgically, they looked back and saw Mao's time as being simpler and "fairer," a time when everyone was poor, but very nearly equally poor. Embedded in this reaction was an extreme resentment toward elites. Key also in the New Left's outlook was the sense that the reformers had bought into Western values—the rule of law, a civil society, individualism—and were trying to emulate the Western processes of modernization, thus betraying Chinese values, especially Maoist values of the law as it related to the party and the ideals of the collective. Highly inflammatory to the New Left was any perceived criticism of or perceived aspersions on Mao himself or Mao Zedong Thought. For the neo-Maoists, Mao had taken on a religious aura; his home in Shaoshan, Hunan became the object of pilgrimages for those bound in their faith in Mao. The number of pilgrims visiting Mao's home is a measure of how quickly Mao the myth, the religious icon had grown in people's minds through the reform period: in the mid-1980s barely 60,000 made the trek to Shaoshan whereas in 2015 seventeen million pilgrims went.[51]

> They pounce[d] on bloggers who dared mock their beloved Chairman Mao. They scoured the nation's classrooms and newspapers for strains of Western-inspired heresies. And they took down professors, journalists, and others deemed … insufficiently red."[52]

The city of Luoyang in Henan province became a hotbed of sorts for neo-Maoists. Nearly every day, the old, the poor, the marginalized, retired and unemployed workers, and retired veterans appeared in the main public square of the city, professing nostalgia for the Cultural Revolution and dismissing the idea that there were ever brutal excesses and mass killings. They sang odes to Mao and read essays pinned to clotheslines, that both condemned the past thirty years of liberalization or positively reappraised the Cultural Revolution.[53]

In the 2013 run-up to the celebrations of the hundred and twentieth anniversary of Mao's birth, Maoists in Luoyang became active in protests over the policies of Xi. On May 27 approximately one hundred people, carrying Mao's photograph and the flag of the Communist Party, met at a Luoyang plaza to criticize the reforms and the "opening up" of China to the world. Organized by a group of farmers and retired workers on the pretext of having a forum to oppose genetically modified foods, the gist of the meeting was to discuss the case of neo-Maoist Bo Xilai, mayor of Chongqing, and to castigate Premier Wen Jiabao as the "traitor," who allegedly led the attack on Bo. In its blog, the group called for public gatherings and discussions in a dozen places including Luoyang, Wuhan, and Changsha.[54]

In February 2015, a group of neo-Maoists from thirteen provinces and cities held a two-day meeting in Luoyang. The manifesto they placed online "was nothing less than a call for revolution to overthrow the current system, which they claimed had evolved into a 'bourgeois fascist dictatorship led by bureaucrat monopolist capitalists.'" In a clarion call for action, they stressed that "a new socialist revolution is the only method to reverse the restoration of capitalism."[55] The first step was to mobilize the masses, especially workers and farmers. Those who have studied the neo-Maoist movement generally think that it has become the most significant political movement in China and that it constituted a large, looming threat to Xi's Communist Party. Such a reality has prompted Xi to rely on local police who began to obstruct the meetings.

Xi is certainly acutely aware of the potential danger. One irony is that he has probably done more than anyone to rev up the New Left movement. Since he became president, he has quoted Mao frequently and at great length, and he has commanded party officials to "hold high the banner of Mao Zedong Thought forever."[56] He has gone farther in his praise of Mao than Deng, Jiang, and Hu. He has drawn attention to himself making pilgrimages to revolutionary sites, including Mao's mausoleum. One of the New Left's leaders pointed out, "You can see that [Xi] is very familiar with Mao's work and Mao's thought and he worships it very much."[57] Xi seemed to put policies similar to Mao's into effect, even using the same names as Mao had. In 2013–2014, for fifteen months, Xi had his own "mass line" campaign (for Xi, part of his anti-corruption effort). The *South China Morning Post* reported in December 2014 that state media announced that "China is to send artists, filmmakers, and television staff to live among the masses in the rural areas in order to 'form a correct view of art.'" This seemed a loud echo from Mao's ideological effort in his "sent down" movement during the Cultural Revolution and is very close to a statement Mao made in a 1940 speech. And again, orders from "China's Media Watchdog" were that film and TV series production staffs must on a quarterly basis "go to grassroots communities, villages, and mining sites to do field study and experience life." Furthermore, scriptwriters, directors, broadcasters and TV presenters must "live for at least 30 days 'in ethnic minority and border areas, and areas that made major contributions to the country's victory in the revolutionary war.'" To some, it seemed that Xi was resurrecting Mao's "rectification campaigns" to stifle potential critics and to emphasize, as Mao did, the necessary "integration of ideology and artistic values."[58]

Xi has said, "Mao is a great figure who changed the face of the nation and led the Chinese people to a new destiny."[59] Hu Jia, a dissident who detests what Mao did to China and what both the neo-Maoists and Xi are doing today, told the British newspaper *The Guardian*:

> [S]imilarities between Mao Zedong and Xi Jinping are so strong that the Little Red Book could serve as a good guide to contemporary Chinese politics. We call Xi "Mao Jinping" or "Xi Zedong." As a Chinese person, I can tell you that Xi Jinping is a big Maoist, both in ideological terms and in how he tries to control Chinese society.[60]

Whatever his motives relating to the neo-Maoists, Xi tried to strike a balance between both views: in a speech he gave to mark the hundred and twentieth anniversary of Mao's birth, he said, "Revolutionary leaders are not gods but human beings. We cannot worship them as gods." But "neither can we totally repudiate them and erase their historical feats just because they made mistakes."[61] Xi and the party were stuck between a rock and a hard place. "Crush the neo-Maoists, and thereby negate your own revolutionary roots, or allow them to operate untethered, in the end, risking a dangerous populist revolt that could lead to your demise."[62]

Whither China? This two-word question reverberated throughout the twentieth and the early twenty-first centuries in the midst of revolution, nation-building, violence, reform, and repression. The question was raised in January 1940 by Mao Zedong himself as the title of his first "chapter" in his "On New Democracy." In that chapter he wrote, "The question once again rises. What is to be done? Whither China?" His concern was the Resistance War against Japan.

A spate of at least five books, entitled "Whither China," came during the violence and uncertainties of the Cultural Revolution and its aftermath and several appeared in the wake of Mao's death—all raising the question in the midst of social and political chaos and after the death of Mao who had been seen by many as synonymous with the revolution. At least another five were published in the 1990s in the aftermath of the Tiananmen street violence and the factional struggles in the party, experiences that indeed placed an urgency to the "Whither China" question. In the early twenty-first century, there was an avalanche of at least sixteen books and articles with the title "Whither China." The first came in 2003, a year after Jiang's "Three Represents" allowed capitalists to enter the CCP. The emergence of the New Left in the late 1990s and their further development in the 2000s and 2010s with their challenge to the "orthodox" reformers presented a strong new source of antagonism that had ominous implications for the future. The wild card in the party-state deck was Xi Jinping; with his openness to the neo-Maoists, his increasingly harsh societal repression, his personal aims and goals, grabbing more and more power in his hands, and possibly establishing his own personality cult—all posed worrisome possibilities and problems about where China is headed.

In his edited 2001 book *Whither China?* Zhang Xudong summarized the situation well:

> Today in media and academic discourses around the world, the image of China overwhelms our appetite for contradictory descriptions and frustrates our established analytical and conceptual framework. Amid dizzying change and radical uncertainty. ... [e]veryone agrees that this period is transitional. No one is certain about where it is leading and what it really means, either for China or the rest of the world."[63]

And then. ... On February 18, 2018, President Xi let it be known that he would not abide by the two-term limit for the presidency, that apparently he would serve as president for life. He thumbed his nose at the constitution and put thumbs down on the collective leadership model that had had been established by Deng Xiaoping and carried out by Jiang Zemin (reluctantly) and very cordially and smoothly by Hu Jintao. Now to one-man rule. The Asia Editor at the prestigious journal, *Foreign Policy*, was blunt in his evaluation of Xi's actions:

> This switch should leave everyone very worried, both inside and outside China. A country that once seemed to be clumsily lurching toward new freedoms has regressed sharply into full-blown dictatorship—of a kind that's likely to lead to dangerous and unfixable mistakes.[64]

Another writer for *Foreign Policy* took an even harder view of the Chinese future:

> China has broken a path toward a new form of totalitarianism in which one man will sit atop a police state with access to ubiquitous data gathered about citizens by social media and

online shopping platforms and a vast human and electronic surveillance apparatus to track their every move.[65]

He warned that Beijing has already developed a "social credit score" system to be instituted for every person or unit (such as factories, schools, and corporations) in 2020.

Chinese citizens will have their daily activities continually monitored and judged on what, for examples, they purchased at stores and online; where they were at any given random time; the identities of their friends and the nature of their activities; was online time spent on internet content or in video games; and the bills and taxes they paid. After such intense surveillance, their behaviors were to be evaluated, according to government regulations, as positive or negative; then those scores would be distilled into one number, which would be one's Citizen Score. That score would presumably tell everyone whether he/she would be trustworthy. One's Citizen Score might also determine his eligibility for a mortgage or her eligibility for a job or where their children could go to school. Only the government can tell. Was this 1984 all over again? No, it was 2020 and Xi-ism. Whither China? In 2019, the future indeed seemed dicier and more dangerous than it appeared in the first decade of this century.

Notes

1 Ann Kent, *China, the United Nations, and Human Rights* (Philadelphia, PA: University of Pennsylvania Press, 1999), p. 2.
2 Louis Henkin, "The Human Rights Idea in Contemporary China: A Comparative Perspective," in *Human Rights in Contemporary China*, ed. Randle Edwards, Louis Henkin, and Andrew Nathan (New York: Columbia University Press, 1986), p. 8.
3 Ibid., p. 9.
4 Kent, *China, the United Nations, and Human Rights,* p. 29.
5 Ibid., p. 30.
6 *The Chicago Tribune* (July 20, 2000), Section 1, p. 9.
7 Dali L. Yang, "China in 2001: Economic Liberalization and Its Political Discontents," *Asian Survey* 42, no. 1 (January–February, 2002): 21. © 2002 by the Regents of the University of California. Published by the University of California Press.
8 Speech by Li Huaqiu (Vienna: Permanent Mission of the PRC to the United Nations in Vienna, June 15, 1993), quoted in Michael Davis "Chinese Perspectives on Human Rights," in *Human Rights and Chinese Values*, ed. Michael C. Davis (Hong Kong: Oxford University Press, 1995), p. 17.
9 "Preface" in Edwards, Henkin, and Nathan, *Human Rights in Contemporary China*, p. 1.
10 Kent, *China, the United Nations, and Human Rights*, p. 85.
11 Ibid., p. 94.
12 Ibid., p. 101.
13 Liu Xiaobo, "I Have No Enemies" in *No Enemies, No Hatred: Selected Essays and Poems*, ed. Perry Link, Tienchi Martin-Liao, and Liu Xia (Cambridge, MA: The Belknap Press of Harvard University Press, 2012), pp. 321–2.
14 "Charter 08," Ibid. See the brief historical synopsis by Perry Link, pp. 300–01.
15 Ibid., p. 301.
16 Ibid., p. 305.
17 Ibid., p. 308.
18 Ibid.
19 Ibid., p. 305.
20 Ibid., pp. 309–10.
21 Ibid., p. 301.
22 Ibid., p. 326.

23 www.nobelprize.org/prizes/peace/2010/press-release

24 Tania Branigan, "Liu Xiaobo Nobel Win Prompts Chinese Fury," *The Guardian* (October 8, 2010). www.theguardian.com/world/2010/oct/08/nobel-peace-prize-liu-xiaobo

25 See Nectar Gan, "Xi Jinping Thought—The Communist Party's Tighter Grip on China in 16 Characters," *South China Morning Post* (October 25, 2017); Salvatore Babones, "The Meaning of Xi Jinping Thought," *Foreign Affairs* (November 5, 2017). www.foreignaffairs.com/articles/china/2017-11-05/meaning-xi-jinping-thought

26 Thomas Heberer, "The Chinese Dream's Domestic and Foreign Policy Shifts," *Asian Survey* 54, no.1, (January–February, 2014), p. 116.

27 Ibid., p. 113.

28 Simon Tisdall, "Chinese Repression of Dissent Intensifies under Ruthless Xi Jinping," *The Guardian* (December 30, 2014). www.theguardian.com/world/2014/dec/30/china-repression-dissent-xi-jinping

29 Tom Mitchell, "Xi's China: Smothering Dissent," *Financial Times* (July 27, 2016). www.ft.com/content/ced94-4db5-11e6-88c5-db83e98a590a

30 Jonathan Zittrain and Benjamin Edelman, "Empirical Analysis of Internet Filtering in China," cyber.harvard.edu/filtering.china

31 "China has launched another crackdown on the Internet—but it's different this time," CNBC, October 26, 2017. www.cnbc.com/.../china-launched-another-crackdown--0514002...

32 Sam Gustin, "Social Media Sparked, Accelerated Egypt's Revolutionary Fire," *Wired* (February 11, 2011). www.wired.com/2011/02/egypts-revolutionary-fire

33 Paul R. Burgman, Jr., "Securing Cyberspace: China Leading the Way in Cyber Sovereignty," *The Diplomat* (May 18, 2016). https://thediplomat.com/.../securing-cyberspace-china-leading-the-way-in-cyber-sovereignty

34 See www.internetfreedom.org/Background.html and Miles Yu, "Inside China," *Washington Times* (February 8, 2012).

35 www.theeconomist.com/.../21711902-worrying-implications-its-social-credit-project

36 Cheng Li, "The Powerful Factions among China's Rulers," The Brookings Institute (November 5, 2017). www.brookings.edu/articles/the-powerful-factions-among-china's-rulers

37 Benjamin Haas, "China Seeks to Block Internet VPNs by February 1, 2018," *The Guardian* (July 11, 2017). www.the guardian.com/world/.../china-moves-to-block-internet-vpns-from-2018

38 Simon Tisdall, "Chinese Repression of Dissent Intensifies under Ruthless Xi Jinping," *The Guardian* (December 30, 2014). www.theguardian.com/world/2014/dec/30/china-repression-dissent-xi-jinping

39 "In China, Rule by Fear and Force," *The Washington Post* (November 25, 2017).

40 "The Clarity and Courage of Wu Gan," *The Washington Post* (December 29, 2017).

41 See Abby Seiff, "China's Latest Crackdown on Lawyers Is Unprecedented, Human Rights Monitors Say," *ABA Journal* (February 2016); and Deborah Cassens Weiss, "Detained Chinese Lawyer to Receive the Inaugural ABA International Human Rights Award," *ABA Journal* (July 8, 2016).

42 Helen Gao, "How Did Women Fare in China's Communist Revolution?" *New York Times* (September 25, 2017). https://nyti.ms/2jWp66e

43 Ibid.

44 Susan Blum, "Rural China and the WTO," *Journal of Contemporary China* 11 (32), 2002, p. 472.

45 "Working Women in China: Second Class Workers," in *China Labour Bulletin*.

46 Jonathan Kaiman, "In China, Feminism is Growing—and So Is the Backlash," *Los Angeles Times* (June 15, 2016). www.latimes.com/world/asia/la-fg-china-feminist-activists-20160614-snap-story.html

47 All quotations in this paragraph come from Jason Unruhe, "New China Marriage Law: Patriarchy and Property," *Maoist Rebel News*, YouTube. https://maoistrebelnews.com/2011/.../new-china-marriage-law-patriarchy-and-property

48 All quotations in this report are based upon the Report of the United Nations Development Programme (September 10, 2013): "UN Survey of 10,000 Men in Asia and the Pacific Reveals Why Some Men Use Violence against Women and Girls."

49 Leta Hong Fincher, "China's Feminist Five," *Dissent* (Fall 2016). www.dissentmagazine.org/article/china-feminist-five

50 Li Maizi, "I Went to Jail for Handing Out Feminist Stickers in China," *The Guardian* (March 7, 2017). www.theguardian.com/.../mar/.../feminist-stickers-china-backlash-women-activists

51 Jamil Anderlini, "The Return of Mao: A New Threat to China's Politics," *Financial Times* (September 29, 2016). www.ft.com/content/63a5a9b2-85cd-11e6-8897-2359a58ac7a5

52 Chris Buckley and Andrew Jacobs, "Maoists in China, Given New Life, Attack Dissent," *New York Times* (January 4, 2015). www.nytimes.com/2015/01/.../chinas-maoists-are-revived-as-thought-police.html

53 "China's Maoists Still a Force 50 Years after the 1966–76 Cultural Revolution," *The Japan Times* (May 15, 2016). www.japantimes.co.jp/.../chinas-maoists-still-force-50-years-1966-1976-cultural-revolution

54 Jeffrey Hays, "Xi Jinping, Maoism and Confucius," *Facts and Details* (September 2016). http://factsanddetails.com/china/cat2/4sub5/entry-5542.html

55 Anderlini, p. 3.

56 Hays.

57 Anderlini, p. 2.

58 Hays.

59 Ibid.

60 Tom Phillips, "Uh-oh!: Bemused Chinese React to John McDonnell's Chairman Mao Speech," *The Guardian* (November 26, 2015). www.theguardian.com/2015/nov/26/uh-oh-bemused-chinese-react-to-john-mcdonnell's-chairman-mao-speech

61 Anderlini, p. 3.

62 Ibid.

63 Zhang Xudong, *Whither China? Intellectual Politics in Contemporary* China (Durham, NC: Duke University Press, 2001), p. 1.

64 James Palmer, "China's Stability Myth is Dead," *Foreign Policy* (February 26, 2018).

65 Emile Simpson, "Globalization Has Created a Chinese Monster," *Foreign Policy* (February 26, 2018).

Suggestions for Further Reading

Brown, Kerry and Simone Nieuwenhuizen. *China and the New Maoists* (London: Zed Books, 2016). This concise, lucid, and absorbing exploration of the presence of Mao and the New Left in China since the mid-1990s raises the question of how the party-state might deal with this potentially destabilizing force.

DeLisle, Jacques, Avery Goldstein, and Guobi Yang, eds. *The Internet, Social Media, and a Changing China* (Philadelphia, PA: University of Pennsylvania Press, 2016). These essays focus on such topics as the internet and authoritarianism, the potential of social media for political change, the roles of law in internet issues, and the roles of the internet in domestic and foreign policy.

Economy, Elizabeth. *The Third Revolution: Xi Jinping and the New Chinese State* (New York: Oxford University Press, 2018). This clear, engaging, and deeply researched study of Xi's domestic and foreign policies provides a valuable and cogent analysis of the new China and the man who will likely lead it for the foreseeable future.

Kent, Ann. *China, the United Nations, and Human Rights* (Philadelphia, PA: University of Pennsylvania Press, 1999). This study analyzes China's evolving human rights policies and the interaction of the PRC with human rights organs of the United Nations.

Lu Xiaobo. *No Enemies, No Hatred: Selected Essays and Poems*, edited by Perry Link, Tienchi Martin-Liao, and Liu Xia (Cambridge, MA: The Belknap Press of Harvard University Press, 2012). Liu's impressively thoughtful writings cover a wide-range of topics under the themes of "Politics with Chinese Characteristics," "Culture and Society," "China and the World," and "Documents." In the last, editors include material on Charter 08 and documents relating to his trial, including his final statement and the court's verdict.

22

Nationalism and Globalization, 1988–2018

According to the World Bank, since 1978 more than 800 million Chinese were lifted out of poverty. The transformation has been spectacular: in the twenty years between 1995 and 2015, per capita gross domestic product (GDP) rose from $700 to $7,683. Over 129 million homes were built in that period, together with a high-speed railway network extending over 11,000 miles, and 136 new airports projected to be completed by 2025. Individual cities have soared in size and productivity, so that their economies match those of entire countries. The GDP of the city of Chengdu is about the same size as that of Norway, that of Shenzhen similar to Sweden, while the size of the economy of metropolitan Guangzhou equals that of Switzerland.

It is clear that a large part of Chinese foreign policy and diplomacy focused on growing the Chinese economy and on making foreign policy more significant than in the period 1949 to 1978. In October 2017, Yang Jiechi, Minister of Foreign Affairs, was promoted to the Politburo. None of the foreign affairs ministers after 2003 had served on this important policy-making body. Commentators noted that elevating Yang was a sign of an "unprecedented transition of China's role, which will not be confined to domestic issues but demonstrate more interest in having a greater say on global issues."[1]

GLOBALIZATION, THE UNFOLDING DRAMA

China's domestic economic development and foreign policies were part and parcel of the ambitious goals of a new China, called by some, China's "Third Revolution," following Mao's and Deng's.[2] Development and diplomacy were inextricably tied together. Since the mid-1980s, this policy has been through five major stages. From the mid-1980s to 1989 came the initial development of coastal regions. In the 1980s, the special economic zones on or near the Pacific coast grew rapidly and, more importantly, revved up China's economy. The goals of the policy were to quicken the flow of foreign direct investment to China and to extend foreign trade to a wider area.

As premier, Zhao Ziyang oversaw these developments; and when he became general secretary of the CCP in 1987, he pushed an ambitious coastal development strategy that was aimed at turning the SEZs on China's coast into generators for the country's growth through international trade. The central government expanded the coastal area by establishing the following open economic zones (listed north to south): Liaodong Peninsula, Hebei Province (which surrounds Beijing

FIGURE 22.1 Although Zhao's contributions to the early reform successes were immeasurably important, his openness to the students' issues was apparently too despicable for the old guard to stomach. He was kept under house arrest until his death. The degree of animus against Zhao by his successors is on the whole quite mysterious. Whereas Hu Yaobang was clearly more politically liberal than Zhao, Hu was rehabilitated. Zhao was not.
Source: AP Photo/Xinhua/Shutterstock.

and Tianjin), Shandong Peninsula, the Yangzi River Delta, Xiamen- Zhangzhou-Quanzhou Triangle in southern Fujian Province, Pearl River Delta, and Guangxi Province. This strategy became the driving force behind China's economic boom. Although Deng Xiaoping ruled China unofficially throughout the 1980s and 1990s, it was Zhao "rather than Deng who was the actual architect of reform."[3] Zhao's decision to oppose martial law in the 1989 Tiananmen crisis cost him Deng's support. Conservatives, who opposed the economic reforms as envisioned by Zhao, attacked Zhao's record, airbrushing him out of photos and deleting his name from official documents. In the years after 2012, as President Xi Jinping systematically strengthened both the party and his own authority, he self-consciously developed a history of the CCP that reflected his goal of China's "great rejuvenation." It is especially notable that, in spite of Zhao's indispensable contributions to the core of what China's economy became, Xi did not include Zhao in his history. Unlike Zhao's fellow reformer, Hu Yaobang, who was purged in 1986 and rehabilitated in 2005, Zhao was not posthumously rehabilitated.

The Tiananmen massacre of June 4, 1989, gave rise to a period when the chief governmental concern was the regime's very survival. It was the second period in the crucial policy's evolution, when, as in Deng's phrase, the government "bided time and built capabilities"[4]: developing many global and regional linkages to make economic growth more rapid; resolving the long-standing dispute with the Soviet Union; and trying to deal with U.S. dominance in the Pacific and much of East Asia.

Jiang Zemin's leadership, from 1989 until 2002, marked a new phase of policy evolution. While the U.S. remained the principal power in the East Asian-Pacific region, China was rising swiftly. Jiang not only inserted China into multi-lateral regional organizations but also backed bilateral agreements with former Soviet states in Central Asia. Perhaps most important, in 2001 Jiang established a regional multi-lateral forum, the Shanghai Cooperation Organization (SCO) whose original members were China, Kyrgyzstan, Kazakhstan, Tajikistan, Uzbekistan, and Russia. India and Pakistan were added in 2017. The forum focused on issues of security, intelligence sharing, counter-terrorism, crime, drug trafficking, and increased military cooperation with annual joint military exercises, of which there were twenty-two between 2002 and 2016. One issue that faced SCO was its relationship with the CSTO (Collective Security Treaty Organization) formed by Russia in 1992. In 2017, four SCO countries were also in the CSTO: Kazakhstan, Kyrgyzstan, Tajikistan, and Russia. With Russia leading the CSTO and China, the SCO, Russia and China vied for stronger allegiance from the other three countries.

In his foreign policy, Hu Jintao, one of whose watchwords during his ruling years (2002–2012) was "harmonious society," called for peaceful development, for a harmonious world instead of uni-lateralism impelled by hegemonic lust. While Jiang had gotten multi-lateral agreements under way, some have seen Hu's years as a clear transition from Deng's "biding and building" to a stronger foreign policy that was designed to "[strike] some successes while maintaining the overarching goal of economic modernization and development."[5] These included negotiations for more com-prehensive regional economic agreements, building two natural gas pipelines from Turkmenistan, and establishing economic and geopolitical bases in Africa and Latin America.

Xi Jinping, flaunting self-confidence and his trust in his "China Dream," claimed that it would usher in the "great national rejuvenation" to benefit, not only China, but also the world. This national renewal would be realized through the principles of "peace, development, cooperation and win–win relations." Especially through his amazingly bold Belt and Road Initiative, he would "place China on par with the U.S. as a great global power, [which would be capable of provid-ing leadership to the international system,] [and] demonstrate [in the process] the success of the Chinese developmental model."[6]

The Chinese reform movement was grounded in globalization, which in its most fundamen-tal sense is the elimination of barriers to trade, communications, and cultural exchanges. As one scholar described the power of revolutionary globalization, "Once history breaks the ties that bind people to places, everything else on the globe comes loose."[7] This turning of the world upside down drove some people to hold more tightly to what they had or thought they had had: the nation, for example. In the face of globalization, the Chinese neo-Maoists focused on China rather than the international community, championed Mao, the founder of the nation, and proposed homegrown Chinese (neo-Maoist) paradigms as future policy guides. This is not to say that Xi Jinping and the government, leading China's globalization, were not nationalistic. In the absence of a strong func-tioning ideological component in its actions at home or abroad, upholding the Chinese nation and raising the flag of nationalism became a crucial aspect of Chinese relations with other nations. But unlike the xenophobic nationalism of the neo-Maoists, China under Xi strode onto the world stage with confidence, pragmatism, and "maturity."[8]

Bilateral and Multi-Lateral Free Trade Agreements

At the turn of the twenty-first century, the global trend toward free trade agreements was the rage. At the end of 2017, there were more than 669 global bilateral and multi-lateral trade agreements in a "complex system of multiple overlapping agreements," called by one social scientist "the spa-ghetti bowl."[9] Apart from its own regional economic imperatives, China's efforts to initiate its proj-ects of globalization corresponded to world trade trends. Vice Minister of Finance Zhu Guangyou explained, "Our position is clear: As China becomes more open, it's important for us to be inte-grated in the global trade system."[10]

As part of this integration, China signed and was a participant in numerous bilateral and multi-lateral free trade agreements (FTAs). At the beginning of 2018, China had working FTAs with twelve countries in Asia, Europe, Latin America and three entities (ASEAN, Hong Kong, and Macau). At the end of 2017, China had eight FTAs undergoing negotiations with three existing FTAs negotiating upgrades.; there were nine more under consideration, undergoing "joint feasibility studies."[11] In addition, there were in the world 2,673 bilateral treaties to set down processes of investing in the other country. China negotiated these treaties with 130 of the world's 193 countries, that is, 67 percent of the total.[12] Indeed China set itself up well as globalization picked up momentum; its stance vis-à-vis the world has shown a remarkable revolution since 1978 and especially since the 1990s.

One of the secrets of China's smashingly successful modernization was the vast amount of foreign direct investment (FDIs) coming into China's coffers. These were investments that an individual or company from one country makes in the business of another country—either in the form of acquiring business assets (like the controlling interest in a foreign company) or in becoming an owner of new business operations. Since the early 1990s, China became the major recipient of FDI in the world; indeed, from 2000 to 2010, China received about 20 percent of all the FDI money sent to developing countries around the globe. In 2016, China was the recipient of a record high 139 billion USD, the third highest in the world after the U.S. and the U.K. Both roles, receiving FDI funds and investing them in other countries, were a win–win situation; China utilized incoming FDI for its own reform and modernization and utilized outgoing FDI to win friends and gain favor with those countries. FDI outflows exceeded inflows only for the first time in 2016, when inflows were 44 billion USD less than the 183 billion USD outflows.

Regional Multi-Lateral Associations: International Players

Regional multi-lateral agreements, while harder to negotiate, played a greater role not only in economic matters such as free trade, but in geopolitical issues and in the process of integrating the regions of East, Southeast, South Asia, and the Pacific Rim. Chronologically, the first major regional grouping, the Association of Southeast Asian Nations (ASEAN), was formed during the Cold War in 1967, while the American War in Vietnam raged and China was viewed as a crazed entity during the Cultural Revolution. The original member-states were: Singapore, Thailand, Malaysia, the Philippines and Indonesia. Added later were Brunei (1984), Vietnam (1995), Laos and Myanmar (1997), and Cambodia (1999). Free trade was established between the nations in ASEAN beginning in 1993; its goals: achieving economic growth, social progress, and cultural development.

In 1997, China, Japan, and South Korea became attached to ASEAN in what was called ASEAN+3; its primary goal was to advance the economic integration of East Asia. In 2005, free trade between China and ASEAN became a reality. Between 2005 and 2014, the value of Asian intra-regional trade grew roughly from one to three trillion USD, and accounted for 50 percent of the foreign trade of all the countries in the region.[13] In terms of people-to-people exchanges, in 2016, 19.8 million Chinese tourists visited Southeast Asian countries while 10.3 million Southeast Asians visited China. At the ASEAN 2017 summit, marking the fiftieth anniversary of the body, the chairman's final report stated that "ASEAN–Chinese relations have been strong, stable, and mutually beneficial. Over the years the strategic partnership [between ASEAN and China] has grown rapidly to become one of ASEAN's most substantive dialogue partners."[14] In 2015, three more countries, India, Australia, and New Zealand were added to ASEAN+3 to create the organization ASEAN+6 with the same goal as ASEAN+3.

One geopolitical reality in East Asia in the early twenty-first century was the history of the twentieth-century dominance of the United States in the region, even though a geographically-based outsider. Its "Western, liberal internationalist" worldview now came to meet (and perhaps clash) with the second geopolitical reality, the emergence of the "local boy, made good" *at last*, China with its suddenly amazing wealth and power. At a time when the globe seemed to be obsessed with connectivity, free trade agreements (FTAs), and regional integration as a way of making sense of globalization, the competition between China and the United States for predominance in the East Asian–Western Pacific region tended logically to newer, more comprehensive regional bodies.

The United States led the formation of the Trans-Pacific Partnership (TPP) first broached after the turn of the twenty-first century. It was designed to be a partnership of twelve countries: the U.S., Australia, Brunei, Canada, Chile, Japan, Malaysia, Mexico, New Zealand, Peru, Singapore, and Vietnam, *minus China*. It would be a "comprehensive and high quality" FTA that would liberalize trade in goods and services, promote investments, and sponsor economic development. Appearing at the same time (2011) and with comparable goals was the Regional Comprehensive Economic Partnership (RCEP), led principally by China, *minus the U.S.* A key purpose of the RCEP was integrating two long-lived proposals, the East Asian FTA (ASEAN+3) with the Comprehensive Economic Partnership (ASEAN +6). Negotiations began in 2013 on a strengthened and more coherent structure for free trade among the ASEAN+6 grouping. Although the goal of TPP and RECP negotiators was to finish by 2015, the complex negotiations could not be rushed. The projected date of RCEP conclusion became late 2018 or 2019.

The TPP fell upon harder times. Negotiations concluded and the agreement was signed in February 2016. But in January 2017, U.S. President Donald Trump withdrew from the TPP for domestic political purposes, the very FTA that the U.S. had sponsored and led and which most had seen as a foil to the China-led RCEP. Trump's ill-informed ideological decision was, in effect, a green light for China to follow whatever policies it wanted in the East Asian-Pacific region, essentially turning all initiatives in East Asia over to China. When the withdrawal occurred, the eleven members remaining in the TPP assumed that the effort was likely dead; but in spring 2017, they revived it, and it was on track to be signed and to go into effect in March 2018.

THE BELT AND ROAD INITIATIVE

One of history's most audacious and staggeringly gutsy strategies of economic, political, and cultural development was the Belt and Road Initiative (BRI) that Xi announced in the early fall of 2013. It was conceived as one of the largest infrastructure and investment projects in history, involving sixty-nine countries with 65 percent of the world's population and, as of 2017, holding 40 percent of the world's GNP. It grabbed the historical imagination as a brilliant way forward toward an all-encompassing globalization for China, with its hearkening back to its glorious past as the prelude to what may yet come. It was a dual project: first, to build an "economic belt" along the historical Silk Road with partner-countries in order to create cooperation and bolster development in the Eurasian region; and second, to work with Southeast Asian nations to develop the twenty-first-century Maritime Silk Road. The initial outlays gave evidence of a strong commitment: 40 billion USD for the Silk Road Economic Belt; 25 billion USD for the Maritime Silk Road; 50 billion USD for the Asian Infrastructure Investment Bank (AIIB) to provide funding for the BRI; and 40 billion USD for the Silk Road Fund to further assist with finances. Embodying Xi's idealistic vision, the BRI would, he declared, essentially change the world: "Exchange will replace estrangement, mutual learning will replace clashes, coexistence will replace a sense of superiority."[15]

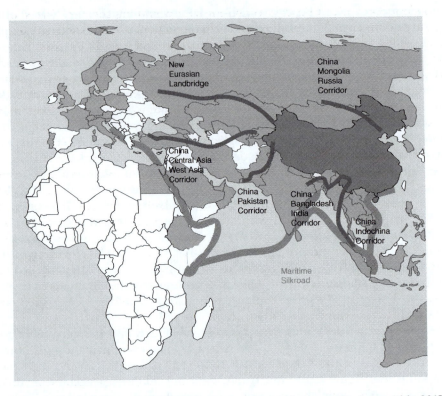

MAP 22.1 Belt and Road Initiative. This bold initiative was proposed by party Chairman Xi in 2013. It is a development strategy undertaken by the Beijing government involving infrastructure development and investment in Europe, Asia, and Africa.

The BRI was more than just reaching out to Central Asia, West Asia, Europe, and Africa; it was also a way for far western and southwestern China to be brought more closely into the Chinese political and cultural orbit. The ethno-political troubles in Xinjiang and Tibet from the 1980s on were often matched by Chinese police-state tactics (see p. 433). The economic approach through the BRI was an attempt to use "soft power" in pulling those disaffected regions closer to Beijing and to Central Asian countries as well. A precursor of the BRI in this regard was Jiang Zemin's Great Western Development Campaign launched in 1999. It focused on six provinces (Gansu, Guizhou, Qinghai, Shaanxi, Sichuan, and Yunnan), five autonomous regions (Guangxi, Ningxia, Inner Mongolia, Tibet, and Xinjiang), and one municipality (Chongqing). The goal: to undertake major infrastructural work and to create urban trade "hubs" such as Kashgar and Urumqi that could serve as nodes linked more clearly to Beijing.

The BRI itself called for the construction of six land "corridors" and the maritime route where, except in the latter, the railroad became the prime mover of cargo and people. Products could be shipped by rail to and from cities in China and Europe in about a quarter of the time that it took to ship by sea, and at a cost that was 65 to 70% less than shipping by air. While a month or two for ocean freight was acceptable for most industries, there were some high-tech and high-end fashion companies that needed their products to arrive as fast and cheaply as possible.

In the conception of BRI, one of two pre-eminent corridors, the New Eurasian Land Bridge, started in Yiwu City in Zhejiang province, a city famous for its 75,000 shops. The first shipment of goods from Yiwu traveled 7,375 miles through Kazakhstan, Russia, Belarus, Poland, Germany, Belgium, and France. It passed through the Chunnel under the English Channel and arrived in Barking, East London in early 2017, completing the journey in eighteen days. This Land Bridge route served thirty countries. Other European hubs for trains beginning from various sites in China included Hamburg and Duisburg, Rotterdam, Madrid, and Warsaw, and from the Maritime Silk Road route, Athens and Venice. From January through November, 2017, China sent 3,271 trains westward with plans to send 4,000 in 2018. Whereas in 2012, 2,500 cargo containers were sent to Europe, the projected estimate for 2020 was a mind-boggling 7.5 million containers.

The other five BRI corridors were China–Mongolia–Russia (northern China to eastern Russia); China–Central Asia–Western Asia (western China to Turkey); China–Indochina Peninsula (southern China to Hanoi and Singapore); China–Myanmar–Bangladesh–India (southern China to Myanmar); China–Pakistan (Xinjiang to Gwadar, Pakistan); and the Maritime Silk Road (Chinese Coast through Singapore to the Mediterranean). In addition to the railways, four natural gas pipelines were built, three from Turkmenistan in 2009, 2010, and 2014; the last from Kazakhstan was still under construction in 2018. The immensity of the BRI was shown also by the startling reality that it had specified and charted 900 separate developmental projects, earmarked at a cost of 900 billion USD.[16] One further Chinese rationale for the project was that the countries along the New Silk Road and those contiguous to it were resource rich.

If there were railways traversing the Eurasian continent, there had to be hubs where passengers and cargo were exchanged between trains or other modes of transport. Along the New Silk Road, cities were being constructed from scratch as hubs where trains loaded and unloaded travelers and freight. One was the Lanzhou New Area, a new city in the province of Gansu, 30 kilometers from Lanzhou, the capital of the province and an important city on the Old Silk Road. The Old Lanzhou, with a population of 3.6 million, had the "honor" of being recently ranked as one of the worst polluted cities in the world. Before Lanzhou New Area City could begin, bulldozers had to level off hundreds of mountains and destroy numerous villages to clear the way for this city—whose area was to cover 315 square miles. The new city would be surrounded by tens of thousands of kilometers of roads and railways. They began building the city in 2012. The population in 2017 was close to 100,000. The planners said that by 2020 the city should have five hospitals, seventy-five schools, and a GDP of 100 billion yuan. By 2030, the population should be a million with a GDP of 270 billion yuan. Was this a pipe dream? A mirage? Whatever one might say and however it turned out, it was a jawdroppingly bold project.

"Khorgos is a perfect symbol of a new world that is unknown, unfamiliar, and obscure: An oasis that is rising from the sands."[17] The soon-to-be city on the border between Xinjiang province and Kazakhstan is the "linchpin" in Xi's grand scheme of things.[18] It is hundreds of kilometers from any established city; and, although it was designated as a "port," it is almost the farthest point on the globe away from an ocean. Specifically, Khorgos was "the transport hub between the markets of China, Central Asia, South Asia, and Europe." It was, as one writer put it, in the process of "transitioning from the 'middle of nowhere' to the 'center of the world.'" In 2014 there was no city at all: "it was a border post, a village, and some lavender fields on the farthest fringe of Xinjiang." Each year trade worth at least 8 billion USD passed through Khorgos; and at the new city on the Kazak side of the border, there was the "dry port" and a huge free trade zone where about 30,000 traders came every day. There was to be a residential area for up to 50,000 people. Trains had to stop at the border since the train track gauge between China and the former Soviet republics differed; rather than changing the bogies, the containers were moved onto a train with the wider gauge railroad. On the Chinese side of the border was the town of Khorgas and its "port" of Horgos where, it was projected, the future population would be 200,000.

In China's eyes the flagship undertaking of the whole BRI project was the China–Pakistan Economic Corridor (CPEC). Foreign Minister Wang Yi took this "crown jewel" of the BRI and floridly compared it in simile to the artistic: "If 'One Belt, One Road' is like a symphony involving and benefiting every country, then construction of the China–Pakistan Economic Corridor is the sweet melody of the symphony's first movement."[19] The end point of this corridor was the deep-water seaport of Gwadar on the Arabian Sea, about 75 miles from the Iranian border and 333 miles west of Karachi, Pakistan's largest city. It was a link between the land "belt" and the maritime "road" in the BRI. Most important from China's perspective was that Gwadar would serve as the port for western China, particularly for Xinjiang, Qinghai, and Tibet. Kashgar in southwest Xinjiang province, the China hub of the CPEC, is 2,781 miles from Tianjin New Port on the Yellow Sea, the largest port in mainland China. But the distance from Kashgar to Gwadar, Pakistan is only 1,263 miles, less than half as far. As a geopolitical plus for China, the port of Gwadar would provide the PRC a way to circumvent the Straits of Malacca where 80 percent of China's oil passes through and which, in case of war with a hostile power, might be seized or blocked. In economic terms, the better and easier access to western China would likely have the potential to draw public and private developmental investments to that region.

China announced in 2015 that it would invest 46 billion USD in the CPEC project; by April 2017, that figure had ballooned to 62 billion. The Chinese had much necessary infrastructure to complete before the Gwadar Port project operated fully. The sea bed had to be dredged in its

FIGURE 22.2   The Chinese see Gwadar functioning as Western China's port as it is substantially closer to Xinjiang, Tibet, and other Western provinces than China's East Coast. China's hope was that Xinjiang and other disaffected ethnic areas could benefit from investments and help them feel part of the nation in this way.
Source: SM Rafiq Photography/Getty Images.

approaches to the docks and berths from 11.5 meters, then down to 14 and at last to 20 meters for larger ships. Multi-purpose berths and cargo terminals needed to be built. A breakwater around the port as protection from the pounding power of waves cost 132 million USD. The Chinese had to construct a desalinization plant to provide the city drinkable water. A 360 million USD coal power plant was constructed. The Chinese would build a 100 million USD, 300-bed hospital. They would set up a Special Economic Zone, modeled on China's own SEZs, and would include logistics hubs, manufacturing zones, supply centers, and warehouses and employ about 40,000 people. The Chinese built the 230 million USD Gwadar International Airport. Then, perhaps with an ironic memory of their own historical experience of leasing land to nineteenth-century imperialists, China requested and Pakistan acceded to officially leasing the port of Gwadar to China for forty-three years, until 2059.

BUILDING BASES IN AFRICA AND LATIN AMERICA

China's record in Africa is longstanding. During the Cold War, Mao Zedong cozied up to African nations in anti-colonial brotherhood and undertook construction of some engineering works, like the almost 2,000-kilometer railway from Zambia to the Tanzanian coast. One of the most significant things about China's approach in the BRI, Africa, and Latin America was China's positive "win–win" appeal: both the developer and the developed would come out on top: no zero-sum game here. China's policy of "non-interference" in domestic affairs made it an appealing approach for African countries, who tired of experiences with Western nations who always had agreements with "strings attached," and who patronizingly lectured former colonial underlings about human rights and/or democracy.

In the twenty-first century, the level of Chinese engagement in Africa's development "put centuries of previous contact in the shade," mainly because of China's awareness of its contemporary opportunities, given the West's decreasing engagement because of Africa's perceived instability, migration issues, and terrorism. For China, the opportunities were threefold: Africa's rich natural resources—oil from Angola, Namibia, and Sudan; copper from Zambia and the Democratic Republic of the Congo; cobalt from South Africa, Congo, and Zambia; and iron from Senegal. Second, it provided markets for Chinese manufactured goods and for construction companies; and third, it was an auspicious vehicle for Chinese geopolitical significance.

As for trade and investment, numbers tell the story. The value of China–Africa trade between 2000 and 2014 rose from 10 billion USD to 220 billion. China became Africa's largest trading partner when it surpassed the U.S. in 2009. Since 2000 to 2014, China's foreign direct investment stocks have soared from only 2 percent of the levels of U.S. investment to 55 percent of that investment. China contributes about 16.7 percent of all lending to Africa. Chinese banks worked with four major regional development organizations in Africa, as its commitment to aiding Africa's transformation. China was willing to work with Africans, not only on China-financed projects, but on homegrown development plans of the African Union's Agenda 2063; and on its own, it built the African Union's 200 million USD headquarters building in Addis Ababa, Ethiopia in 2013.

Some Africans harbored suspicions about China's motives; some complaints arose about Chinese companies using not enough locals in their work (though a poll by Johns Hopkins University found that 80 percent of workers on Chinese projects were African), about mistreatment of African workers it used, and about Chinese disregard of environmental issues. But a 2016 poll taken in thirty-six African countries showed that 63 percent of Africans said the Chinese presence and influence was "somewhat" or "very" positive.[20] A Pew Research Center poll found that 76 to

78 percent of respondents in Nigeria, Kenya, and Senegal viewed China favorably.[21] There was a general sense in Africa that the Chinese because of their proven record of completing large projects (airports, railways, roads and highways, ports, dams, and telecommunications networks) could and would transform Africa. Fifty-two of fifty-four African countries recognized the PRC diplomatically; two still recognized Taiwan: Swaziland and Burkina-Faso. In 2017, Beijing had fifty-two embassies in Africa compared to Washington's forty-nine. As of 2013, China had the most UN peacekeeper troops in Africa (1,500) of any other member of the UN Security Council.[22]

In Latin America, China was consistent with its African approach in handling trade and investment. First on the docket of negotiations was the promise that China would never impose any political conditions on its technical and economic assistance—there would be none of the "strings attached mode" of negotiations. China would be the model for development and the goal and strategy would be, as elsewhere in Chinese development programs, cooperation and "win–win." As indicative of the kind of special interest China would show in Latin America were the eight trips China's presidents made between 2001 and 2014: two by Jiang in 2001 and 2002; four by Hu: 2004, 2005, 2008, and 2010; and two by Xi (2013 and 2014) plus two by Xi as vice-president, 2009 and 2011. During the Hu administration, then, top-ranked Chinese leaders visited six times between 2004 and 2011.[23]

In 2015, Xi pledged 250 billion USD to the Latin American region by 2019. In early 2018, Latin America was already the second largest recipient of Chinese overseas investments.[24] It was in the explosion of trade where the take-off of the China–Latin American connection burgeoned. The raw trade data between 2005 and 2015 is compelling. In 2005, no Latin American country named China as its main export partner. However, by 2015, China had passed the U.S. as the main destination for exports from seven Latin American countries. For five countries—Brazil, Chile, Cuba, Peru, and Uruguay—China was the largest export market. For twenty countries (out of thirty-two) in South America, Central America, and the Caribbean, China was in their top five export markets. In 2018, eight Latin American countries imported more from China than they did from the U.S.; and six—Bolivia, Brazil, Chile, Peru, Cuba, and Uruguay—imported more from China than from any other country.[25] In looking at the Latin American context and its long mostly unhappy history with the U.S., four countries were most eager to embrace China as a trading partner specifically as an anti-U.S. alternative—Cuba, Venezuela, Bolivia, and Ecuador.

Finally, as in Africa, China offered support to regional Latin American groupings, often using these organizations to take the lead or to sponsor various developmental projects. In one, China was a participant: the Community of Latin American and Caribbean States (CELAC), which had its first ministerial meeting in Beijing in January 2015; one of its goals was to work toward the integration of regional trade. At that meeting China broached two possible long-term development projects: the Nicaragua Canal and a Brazil to Peru Railway that would cross both the Amazon and the Andes.[26] In addition, China had economic discussions with four other South American regional bodies.

GLOBALIZATION AND SOFT POWER

The image of itself that China wanted to project to the world was as worker for mutual respect and promoter of harmonious win–win cooperation; completely not in the vocabulary in speaking to other nations were words such as competition, conflict, or confrontation. The vehicle for this image was Confucius Institutes (CI), established beginning in 2004 at educational institutions (universities and primary and secondary schools) around the globe. Their mission was to teach Chinese language and traditional culture. It was, in fact, the largest language- and culture-promoting initiative that the world had ever seen. In May 2017, there were 513 in the world with 1,000 smaller classrooms in the primary and secondary schools. The approach in all the CI was to steer clear of any troubling Chinese actions or policies, for example, the 1989 Tiananmen massacre or the treatment of the Falun Gong. A Confucius Institute teacher must be Chinese by nationality; generally an American university followed Confucius' Institute guidelines on hiring teachers and staff, where the Chinese government vetted and selected a pool from which CIs chose its employees.

In 2017 and 2018, a trenchant criticism of CI arose from American journalists and some educational institutions. The concerns focused on two elements of the CI set-up: the stifling of academic freedom by CI guidelines that specified what can be brought up about China and discussed in classrooms and the control that China, a foreign power, wielded in classrooms composed mostly of students from the U.S. Part of this reaction no doubt reflected the animus against globalization that flowered in the early twenty-first century. But the Braga (Portugal) Incident of July 2014 raised questions in many minds about the motives of the CI and of China's larger view of its actions in the world.[27] Attending the conference of the European Association of Chinese Studies (EACS) was Xu Lin, the executive director of the Beijing CI headquarters. Xu, without consulting anyone, ripped out four pages from the conference program. One page mentioned the Chiang Ching-kuo Foundation for International Scholarly Exchange, based in Taiwan and named for a president of the Republic of China; the foundation had sponsored EACS meetings for two decades. The EACS dealt with the matter gingerly, but the incident left a bitter taste in the mouths of American, European, and Australian academics. Later in a BBC interview, Xu objected when the Braga Incident was brought up and, after the interview demanded that large portions of the interview text be deleted. She asserted that Taiwan belonged to China and that outsiders had no business interfering. When the BBC refused to go along with her censorship demand, Xu refused to answer questions she considered "difficult." Soft power apparently had a hard edge.

THE SOUTH CHINA SEA CONTROVERSY

It is not until one looks at China's record in the conflict in the South China Sea (SCS) that the harder edges of both confrontation and conflict found their way back into the Chinese vocabulary. Of increasing concern in the middle to late 1990s was China's aggressive stance regarding the Spratly Islands in the SCS. Under a loose interpretation of the 1982 Law of the Sea Convention, China claimed that almost all of the SCS fell under its sovereignty, specifically that it had a 200-mile "exclusive economic zone" around each of the Spratly Islands. Thus, China claimed that it owned the reportedly rich oil reserves off these islands. The "prize" was huge: there was an estimated 24.7 trillion cubic feet of natural gas and 4.4 billion barrels of oil under the SCS. The difficulty was that the islands were also claimed by Taiwan, the Philippines, Malaysia, Brunei, and Vietnam. China was quite aggressive in making its claims, seizing six atolls from Vietnam in 1988 and establishing outposts on many of the islands.

A 2002 agreement called on all claimants to the Spratlys to refrain from any action that would heighten tensions in the area. Yet China's every action in the SCS heightened tensions. The cat-and-mouse games played mostly by China, Vietnam, and the Philippines were frequent in the period 2011 to 2017. As an example, in spring 2012, the Chinese Vice-Foreign Minister declared that the waters around the Scarborough Shoal were "an integral part of [Chinese] territory"—even though the shoal was 140 miles from the Philippines and 406 miles to Hainan Island in China. In May, the Chinese built a barrier to the entrance of the shoal with one stationary Chinese guard ship to keep other ships away. In the months ahead, the Chinese ship turned away many Filipino ships. China then announced it would interdict and board any foreign vessel that was within 12 nautical miles of its baselines.

In Xi Jinping's presidency, there were two events in the SCS that gave China the image of spitting in the face of international norms and law—and therefore hugely confrontational and with absolutely no concern for win–win cooperation or mutual respect. In March 2014, the Philippine government submitted a case to the Permanent Court of Arbitration in The Hague, known either as *Philippines v. China* or *The South China Sea Arbitration*. The court was to rule specifically on the legality of China's "nine-dash-line," a vague and arbitrary line that had been drawn in 1947

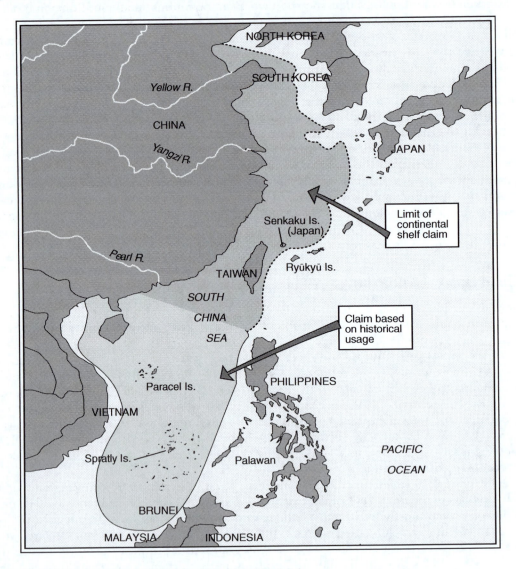

MAP 22.2   China's Maritime Territorial Claims in Regional East Asia.

by the Republic of China to enclose almost all the SCS that China now claimed as its own; it was neither scientific nor reflective of reality. In July 2016, the Court rejected the nine-dash line, ruling that "there was no legal basis for China to claim historic rights to resources within the sea areas falling within the 'nine-dash line.'"

But it was not only the ruling on the nine-dash line: the Court nailed China to the wall for other infractions as well. It found, reviewing the Scarborough Shoal incident,

> that China had violated the Philippines' sovereign rights in its exclusive economic zone by (a) interfering with Philippine fishing and petroleum exploration; (b) by constructing artificial islands; and (c) by failing to prevent Chinese fishermen from fishing in the zone.

In addition, it pointed out that "fishermen from the Philippines (like those from China) had traditional fishing rights at Scarborough Shoal and that China had interfered with those rights in restricting access." Finally, it found that in China's large-scale land reclamation and construction of artificial islands, "China had caused severe harm to the coral reef environment and violated its obligation to preserve and protect fragile eco-systems and the habitat of depleted, threatened, or endangered species."[28] China's reaction? It immediately declared the ruling null and void.

Even more brazenly aggressive was China's militarization of the waterway in the SCS. At a time when ownership and rights in the area were not at all yet clarified or agreed upon, China decided on its own to build military bases on the seven artificial islands that it had seized and restructured. Between June and December 2017, Chinese construction activities stretched across the whole Spratly Archipelago; it defended its construction of ammunition depots, sophisticated electronic intelligence equipment and 3,000-foot runways on these disputed islands as "normal."

UPS AND DOWNS IN EAST ASIAN RELATIONS

Japan

The relations between China and Japan in the late twentieth and early twenty-first centuries could be summed up in American writer William Faulkner's famous aphorism: "The past is never dead. It's not even past." The elephant in the diplomatic room for the two nations remained World War II and its seventy-five-year-old memories. The one near constant positive reality amid a period of one political dispute after another was the generally good health of the trading relationship. The amount and value of the trade kept growing with minor fluctuations due to negative political issues. The overall amounts were much stronger once the Chinese economy came into its own during the reforms.

Memories of World War II continued to have the effect of salt rubbed into still partially open wounds. As seen through Chinese (and South Korean) eyes, Japan seemed obsessively unwilling to accept full responsibility for its actions. Prime Ministerial visits to Yasukuni Shrine, where fourteen Class A Japanese war criminals were buried, brought harsh Chinese rhetoric, often violent street demonstrations, and cancellation of important planned diplomatic, economic, political and military meetings, conferences, and exchanges. Analysts have suggested that a prime minister might have chosen to visit the shrine for domestic political reasons and that he might simply discount any diplomatic ramifications.

The political nadir of China and Japan's political relationship in the late twentieth and early twenty-first centuries came during the administration of Prime Minister Koizumi Junichirō

(2001–2006); and it stemmed in large part from Yasukuni Shrine visits. After the war criminals had been secretly interred in 1978, Emperor Hirohito refused to go the shrine again; Emperor Akihito never went. A few prime ministers had visited the shrine in the past; however, it was only once in their official term as prime minister. But Koizumi insisted on visiting the shrine six times, once every year of his tenure. He claimed he visited for personal not governmental reasons, a difference the Chinese could not fathom since he was obviously Japan's official government leader. Chinese suspected that the shrine visits were indicative of a lack of normal human empathy among the Japanese, of being unrepentant over its wartime actions, and perhaps of being the first step to revival of the militaristic and aggressive attitudes that Japan sported during the war. Undoubtedly, these issues spurred to some degree the Chinese opposition to Japan's becoming a permanent member of the UN Security Council in early 2005. An internet petition to keep Japan off the council was signed by over ten million Chinese citizens in a few weeks. In April, Premier Wen Jiabao declared Beijing's opposition, citing "Japan's failure to treat history correctly."[29]

At a Beijing meeting with President Hu, the General Secretary of Japan's Liberal Democratic Party minced no words in bluntly telling Hu that Chinese objections to Koizumi's visits to Yasukuni "constituted interference in Japanese affairs."[30] Hu retorted that the three important issues that most affected Sino-Japanese relations were Yasukuni Shrine, Japanese history textbooks, and Taiwan—and that the relationship could be undermined by an incorrect attitude to any of the three. In March 2006 in a speech to a Japanese delegation, Hu explicitly declared that any resumption of bilateral summits between the two nations would occur only if no future prime minister would visit the shrine. Five months later, Koizumi visited the shrine on August 15, the highly symbolic day of war's end, a choice that rankled the Chinese. The Chinese press strongly condemned Koizumi for "trampling over human conscience and casting a shadow over a potential thaw in Chinese–Japanese relations."[31]

Koizumi's successor was Abe Shinzō, grandson of Kishi Nobusuke, who had been arrested by the United States as a Class A war criminal, but was found not guilty and later served as prime minister. In his second prime minister-ship Abe did visit the shrine in December 2013. "Abe insisted he had 'no intention' of hurting the feelings of the Chinese or South Korean people."[32] No intention? Did he not remember the reactions of China and South Korea to Koizumi's visits? Did he not remember that Sino-Japanese relations plummeted into the doldrums primarily over the Yasukuni question? A Chinese Foreign Minister spokesman presented Beijing's reaction: "Instead of reining in his acts, the Japanese leader has gone out of his way to once again create a serious incident on the issue of history, thus erecting a new, major, political barrier to the improvement and development of bilateral ties."[33] While Koizumi by all accounts was not a revisionist nationalist (that is, he did not want to rewrite Japan's war history in a more positive light), Abe was such a nationalist who expressed his desire to revise Japan's "peace constitution" and increase military spending. For the first time in the continuing Yasukuni story, the U.S. noted how upset it was about Abe's decision and action "that will exacerbate tensions with Japan's neighbors."

It is difficult to know how to take the Japanese obsession with Yasukuni Shrine and their awareness and perception of the violent reactions it stimulated in China, South Korea, and Southeast Asia. But yet Japanese leaders continued to visit it and claimed with straight faces that they had "no intention" of upsetting the countries Japan had bombed, attacked, brutalized, and occupied during the war. Japanese politicians' visits to Yasukuni became a crucial issue in East Asian regional diplomacy. As one scholar has said, "Geostrategic change [in East Asia] ha[d] turned revisionist sentiment in Japan into a strategic risk."[34]

Another World War II-related continuing source of enmity between China and Japan was the coverage of the war itself in middle and high school history textbooks. The Japanese government's

approved textbooks included revisions required by the government that downplayed and rationalized Japan's wartime roles. New textbooks published in 2005 whitewashed Japanese wartime
atrocities, including the Rape of Nanjing in 1937–1938, the forced recruitment of comfort women
(sex slaves), and the deadly use of biological weapons on whole villages. The government was
creating generations who would never know what Japan had done or what their actual past had
been. In cities around the country the Chinese took to the streets first in peaceful demonstrations
that almost inevitably turned violent with destructive attacks on Japanese businesses, on Japanese
consulates and the embassy in Beijing, and on Japanese themselves, beaten by cursing crowds.

In the early years of the twenty-first century, China's relations with Japan were endangered by
disputes over the ownership of the Diaoyu Islands or Senkaku Islands in the East China Sea. The
islands are made up of five uninhabited islets and three barren rocks for a total area of 5 square
kilometers. At stake in the dispute, however, were 200 million cubic meters of natural gas reserves
in four oil and gas fields over 1,100 feet below the ocean's surface. Japan based its position on the
UN Convention of the Law of the Sea (that both countries had signed) which allowed coastal countries to claim economic zones up to 370 kilometers from their shores. China, on the other hand,
based its claim on the 1958 Geneva Convention of the Continental Shelf, which allowed coastal
countries to extend their borders to the edges of their undersea continental shelves. Between 2004
and 2007, there were eleven rounds of talks to settle the issue; in June 2008, the two countries
agreed to develop gas fields jointly in disputed areas. They began talks then about the aim of improving cooperation; but the talks broke down in 2010 and have not been resumed. China began
drilling in an area that is China's zone; as of summer 2017, they had built sixteen drilling platforms.

But in the decade since 2008, incidents occurred that showed how tense the situation was.
In September 2010, a Chinese trawler collided with a Japanese Coast Guard ship near the disputed
islands; the Japanese, who claimed that the trawler purposefully rammed the Japanese ship, arrested the captain and detained him for more than two weeks. Tempers in both China and Japan
flared; various China–Japan related events were cancelled as were large-scale tourist groups to
both countries.

In August 2012 activists both from Hong Kong and Japan sailed to the islands and disem-
barked, ratcheting up even more the tautness of the situation. On September 10, the Japanese government announced that it had purchased the disputed islands from its private Japanese owner, in
what Tokyo said was an effort to defuse tensions. Four days later, six Chinese surveillance ships
sailed into waters around the islands to assert China's territorial claims. For the next two days the
largest anti-Japanese protests since the normalization of diplomatic relations (1972) erupted in
cities across China. In Beijing, thousands of protesters surrounded the Japanese embassy, pelting
it with rocks, bottles, and eggs. The second day was even worse: protesters battled police in the
streets, attacking Japanese-made cars and smashing up Japanese businesses and restaurants. Some
major Japanese companies—Toyota and Honda—temporarily closed their factories and offices
across China after a Toyota dealership was looted. A poll showed that 91 percent of those Chinese
surveyed approved using military force to enforce China's sovereignty over the islands.

Since the nationalization of the islands through the Japanese government's purchase, China
has regularly sent government vessels into the territorial waters to demonstrate China's determination that its claim of sovereignty would in the end be recognized. Japan owned the islands, but the
territorial issues had not yet been settled. In 2013 China unilaterally set up an air defense identification zone over the East China Sea, including air space over the islands. In August 2016, a Chinese flotilla of 230 fishing boats escorted by seven Coast Guard ships encircled the Senkakus for
a week, sailing in and out of Japan's territorial waters. By such a display, China upped the stakes
of the territorial dispute. A Chinese Foreign Ministry spokesperson, in speaking of this incident,

made China's position clear: "China has indisputable sovereignty over [the islands] and the adjacent waters."[35] A diplomatic breakthrough of sorts in December 2017 established a crisis management hot-line after years of fruitless negotiating. The dispute continued to simmer.

Korea

China remained an ally of North Korea, though it made it clear that it would not step in to provide support when the Soviet Union fell in 1991. In the first years of the twenty-first century, its relationship with the North Korean regime became increasingly testy. For many years, China had become a home to Koreans fleeing the Pyongyang regime's repression and famine. In 2002, over one hundred of these immigrants made their way to foreign embassies in Beijing to ask for asylum in South Korea. When China permitted this, North Korea was incensed. China, in turn, was more than annoyed at Kim Jong-il's admission that Pyongyang was developing nuclear weapons in clear violation of international agreements.

In 2003, North Korea withdrew from the Nuclear Non-Proliferation Treaty and the Six-Party Talks began (the participants were China, the United States, North and South Korea, Japan, and Russia). Hosted by Beijing, the talks focused on dismantling the North's nuclear program. In 2005, China's mediation brought together the fourth round of the talks, a round which ended with Pyongyang's agreement to give up its nuclear quest. Despite this apparent agreement, North Korea in July 2006 held several missile tests and in October 2006 conducted a nuclear test. Beijing, whose main concern was the stability of the Korean peninsula, became increasingly displeased with the Pyongyang government; its greatest fear was that the Kim regime (Kim Jong-il (1994–2011) and Kim Jong-un (2011–)) might collapse and, if so, China would likely have hundreds of thousands of refugees on its hands. For that reason, Beijing again pressed Pyongyang to rejoin the talks for a sixth round—which seemed to end positively when the North agreed in October 2007 to end its nuclear program and to dismantle its main production facility. But in April 2009, the North once again quit the talks, announcing it would restart its nuclear facilities. When it conducted a nuclear test in May 2009, the United States pushed for tougher UN sanctions against Pyongyang. In February 2013, the North staged its third nuclear test followed by more UN sanctions. Seven months later, China banned exports to the North of any items that could be used to make missiles or nuclear, chemical, or biological weapons.

In many ways the North was totally dependent on China. Beijing provided the Pyongyang regime with most of its food and energy supplies. Their bilateral trade increased tenfold from 2000 to 2015; China accounted for over 90 percent of the North's total trade volume. In late 2016 after North Korea had set off its fourth and fifth nuclear tests (in January and September), the UN cut the amount of coal the North could export by 60 percent; coal briquettes were the North's major export by far: in 2015, coal accounted for 68 percent of the North's total value of exports. On its own, China suspended coal imports from the North for much of the year and fuel sales to the North at several times during the year. In August 2017, China announced that it would implement UN sanctions and ban the importation of coal, minerals, and seafood from the North. In 2017 the volume of trade between China and the North fell sharply mostly because of UN sanctions. North Korea exploded its sixth nuclear test in September 2017; it was reportedly four to sixteen times larger than the fifth test. The North Koreans followed that test by launching in November an intercontinental ballistic missile that fell 621 miles away in the Sea of Japan. That act led to the UN decision to prohibit almost 90 percent of refined petroleum exports to North Korea. China announced in January 2018 that it would limit exports of crude oil, refined oil products, steel and other metals to the North. In actuality, the China–North Korean alliance is, as a Brookings Institute scholar put it, "a thing of the past." Beijing was ambivalent about defending Pyongyang; a 1961 treaty between the two countries specified that China is obligated to do so. Given the state of their relations, it was unclear what China would do in such a case.

Ironically, as China's relationship with the North turned sour, China's relationship with South Korea in the 1990s became closer. Attracted by possibilities of technical assistance, given South Korea's level of economic development, China and the Seoul regime established diplomatic relations in 1992. Trade grew rapidly, as South Korea poured much of its substantial China investment into Shandong province. In 2003, China surpassed the United States as the leading market for South Korean exports. South Korea was Beijing's top trading partner in 2017 and China was the destination for 25 percent of the South's exports. Among China's trade partners, South Korea ranked fourth. The only fly in the diplomatic ointment that seemed an ideal bilateral relationship came in 2017 when the South Korean government chose to adopt an American defense missile system over Chinese warnings and advice. The South saw the defensive system as a way to deflect possible North Korean missile attacks, but China believed that the system could be a threat to Chinese interests. After Seoul's choice, Beijing retaliated economically: banning the sale of some South Korean products, including video games; canceling the gigs of K-pop groups; closing some Korean companies doing business in China; boycotting Hyundai and Kia; ordering travel agencies to stop selling package tours. It was the last that had the greatest impact: the number of tourists in 2017 was about four million; in 2016, it had been a little over eight million. In October 2017, talks between Beijing and Seoul got on track to restore their relationship.

Vietnam

In the years before the Cultural Revolution, China had given advice and assistance to North Vietnam in its American war. But in the 1970s relations turned frigid over the issue of Cambodia. In that decade China had established an alliance with Cambodia's Communist Khmer Rouge. When the Khmer Rouge took power in 1975, they unleashed a reign of terror, now often referred to as a "holocaust," that led to the killing of ethnic Vietnamese living in Cambodia and to increasingly bad relations between Cambodia and Vietnam. Vietnam consequently invaded Cambodia in late 1978 to establish a regime that it could control. This takeover, and especially the brutality of the Vietnamese regime toward ethnic Chinese, enraged the Beijing leadership. In 1978, China cut off all its aid to Vietnam; and in February 1979, it invaded Vietnam "to teach it a lesson." The campaign was over in a month, with China's having been taught the lesson. It had nothing to show for the effort except high Chinese casualties and evidence that the PLA was, as one critic put it, "deficient in modern warfare."[36]

The November 1991 visit of Vietnam's prime minister and party general secretary to Beijing led to the normalization of relations. Since then, ongoing state visits of government leaders led to much better relations. Despite rivalry over the Spratly Islands, Chinese Politburo member Jia Qinglin, on a state visit to Hanoi in March 2006, said their relations were "in one of the best times in history."[37] But less than a decade later in May 2014 occurred the most violent anti-Chinese riots in Vietnam since before the 1979 war.[38] At issue was the Chinese decision to deploy a gigantic state-owned oil rig in fiercely-contested waters near the western edge of the Paracel Islands less than 150 miles from the Vietnamese shore line. In Binh Duong province just to the north of Ho Chi Minh City, thousands of frenzied rioters marched through industrial parks, setting on fire more than a dozen factories allegedly owned by Chinese, and burning to the ground a foreign-owned steel project. In Binh Duong only 14 of the 357 factories damaged, looted, or destroyed were owned by Chinese corporations. Similar rioting occurred in Ha Tinh province on the north-central coast. Vietnamese called the Chinese arrogant, slanderers of Vietnam on social media, and escalators of tension; some called for Chinese blood. On sea, the Chinese sent 80 ships to guard the rig. They engaged in a high-stakes game of chicken, battling with water cannon and ramming each other. The Chinese took the rig back to Hainan Island on July 16. The problem was temporarily over, but it was not until 2017 that some degree of normal bilateral relations occurred. In November a memorandum of understanding was signed in Hanoi in which both sides promised to settle problems in the SCS peacefully without reliance on force.

DEALING WITH WORLD REGIONS

By the 1990s, the PRC had important global credentials. It was a permanent member of the United Nations Security Council; it participated in the World Bank, the International Monetary Fund, and the Asian Development Bank; and it possessed a nuclear arsenal and its means of delivery.[10] Its relations with the global powers, the United States and the Soviet Union until its collapse in 1991 (and Russia afterward), ranged from warm to chilly from the 1980s into the 2000s.

The United States

The 1989 Beijing tragedy poisoned relations with the United States throughout the 1990s. It placed the trading relationship in jeopardy, as the U.S. Congress debated annually whether to bestow on the PRC "most favored nation status," which would permit it to trade at the normal tariff level enjoyed by U.S. trading partners. The U.S. government carped about China's record on human rights, technology transfers, trade, and various strategic issues. Beijing's response to the frequent criticism was that the United States was trying to contain and isolate China as it tried to assert its own hegemony; indeed, a mid-1996 poll of Chinese college students found that 95.7 percent agreed with that proposition.

U.S. policy toward Taiwan, the touchiest of all Chinese issues, was a constant irritant (see Chapter 23). The U.S. sale of planes and other military hardware to Taiwan, and especially U.S. deployment of ships in the vicinity of military exercises off Taiwan in the spring of 1996, stirred up anti-American feelings. The U.S.–Japan security agreement in 1996 was also seen as threatening because it put Taiwan in the "sphere of common defence [sic] interests" of the two countries. A spokesman for Jiang stated that "[t]his can absolutely not be accepted by the Chinese government and the Chinese people."[39] State visits by Jiang in 1997 and President Bill Clinton in 1998 seemed to warm up the often chilly relationship.

But in 1999 that thaw was followed by a freeze, taking the relationship to its iciest level since the establishment of diplomatic relations two decades earlier. In May, during the war in Kosovo, NATO planes bombed the Chinese embassy in Belgrade, destroying the building and killing several Chinese journalists. The United States called the bombing a mistake, attributing it to faulty maps. The Chinese sneered at what seemed to them a lame excuse. They argued that the bombing was intentional and that the U.S.-led West was trying to send a message to China: Don't try to deal with ethnic problems in Xinjiang and Tibet the way Serbia's leader had done against ethnic Albanians, that is, by killing them. Chinese students reacted violently to the embassy bombing by taking to the streets and attacking the U.S. embassy. The bombing seemed to crystallize the feeling that the United States would not allow China to take its rightful place among the nations of the world. China specifically demonized the United States as the neo-imperialist bogeyman behind its problems with Taiwan and Tibet.

On April 1, 2001, a U.S. EP-3 spy plane collided with a Chinese fighter jet along the Chinese coast. The spy plane made an emergency landing on Hainan Island, while the Chinese plane and pilot were lost. Crewmembers were permitted to leave after eleven days, but the incident strengthened the Chinese belief that the United States was trying to contain China. This chill in relations was relieved by the September 11 terrorist attacks in the United States. In the aftermath, for most Americans, terrorism replaced China as the main threat to the United States. With its own fears of Islamic separatism and terror, China became an ally of sorts with the United States in its war on terrorism.

In May 2015 at a meeting on Asian security, the U.S. called on China to halt its controversial land reclamation effort in the South China Sea, spelling out that the U.S. opposed any further militarization of the disputed territory. China had reclaimed seventeen times more than all the other countries reclaimed land combined.

Despite the ongoing concern with the SCS situation, the underlying source of deepest friction remained trade and economic relations. In September 2008, China became the largest U.S. foreign creditor, the holder of U.S. debt in treasury notes. At that time the debt was around $600 billion; in November 2017, the debt had doubled to $1.2 trillion. By 2005 China was the United States' third largest trading partner, its second largest source of imports, and its fifth largest export market. In 1985, the trade deficit with China was $6 million; in February 2000, it was 5.6 billion; however, in 2017, it totaled a gigantic $375 billion. U.S. resentments over the ever-towering trade deficit led to charges and countercharges of Chinese abuses of WTO rules.

In a case of intellectual property theft in 2014, a U.S. court indicted five Chinese from the PRC, allegedly with connections to the PLA, on charges of stealing trade technology from U.S. companies. Beijing responded by suspending its cooperation in the U.S. cybersecurity working group. And yet again in 2015, U.S. authorities pointed to evidence that Chinese hackers were the agents in a major online breach of the government's Office of Personnel Management and the theft of data from 22 million current and former federal workers. The issue of intellectual property theft loomed large in U.S. grievances about Chinese practices.

The Soviet Union (Russia after 1991)

The hostility with the Soviet Union that had produced the Sino–Soviet split in 1960 and brief outright skirmishes in early 1969 did not begin to subside until the presidency of Mikhail Gorbachev. In 1985, as expanded trade and cultural contacts began to relieve tensions, consulates were re-opened in Shanghai and St. Petersburg; China also purchased Soviet aircraft. Gorbachev's trip to Beijing in May 1989, at the time of the democracy demonstrations, formally healed the rupture that had existed between the two countries for three decades. The Soviet Union's collapse in 1991 left an impotent Russia; though Russia was no longer an immediate threat, the long border they shared made Russia an important player in Chinese strategic considerations. On Jiang's third visit to Russia between 1992 and 1996, he and Boris Yeltsin signed agreements that put to rest long-simmering border disputes. The Russians offered assistance in the Three Gorges Dam project and were eager to sell excess military equipment to China. Indeed, near the end of 2000, the two countries announced that China had committed itself to purchase weapons worth 15 billion USD from Russia over five years, "the largest single arms deal in Russian history."[40]

The exchanges of visits between leaders of the two countries showed a growing warmth and spirit of cooperation. From 2001 to 2011, there was at least one state visit each year; since 2012 when he took office, Xi Jinping met with Vladimir Putin more than twenty times. The 2008 and 2009 agreements for "long-term energy cooperation" underscored the closer relationships. Oil from a pipeline built from Russia to the border of Heilongjiang Province began flowing at the end of 2010, in the amount of 15 million tons a year; China in turn provided Russian oil companies $25 billion in loans. This was an energy marriage of the second largest oil producer in the world with the second largest oil consumer.

After Western sanctions were imposed on Russia in 2014 for its aggressive actions in Ukraine, Russia "pivoted" to Asia, and particularly to China. In a 30-year showpiece deal, Russia in that same year agreed to supply China with 38 billion cubic meters of natural gas per year worth an overall amount of 400 billion USD. But apart from this deal, there has been little to show for the "special relationship." Russia trades more with the European Union than with China, sending 9.6 percent of its 2016 exports to China, up from 7.5 percent in 2014; Russia is notably not among China's top ten trading partners. Similarly, Chinese investments in Russia have been of little import. In July 2017, China signed on to an 11 billion USD investment for Russian infrastructure; but this is like a drop in the bucket compared to the trillion dollar BRI investment where much money will go to former Soviet republics.

Regained Colonies: Hong Kong and Macao

In the early 1980s, China clarified that Britain could not renew the ninety-nine-year leasehold over the Hong Kong New Territories, ending in 1997. It also wanted to negotiate the return of the other two parts of Hong Kong—Hong Kong Island and Kowloon. The British agreed to negotiations that led to an agreement whereby Britain returned Hong Kong on July 1, 1997. According to Hong Kong's Basic Law, the Chinese stipulated that for fifty years after that date, Hong Kong retained a capitalist economy, becoming a "special administrative region" (HKSAR) under the formula of "one country, two systems." English remained the official language; Hongkongers paid no taxes to China; and the city's economy remained generally autonomous. Beijing controlled Hong Kong's defense and foreign policy.

Trickier was the long-term political relationship between Beijing and Hong Kong's authorities. In 2003, Beijing's handpicked Chief Executive of the city announced plans to enact an anti-subversion law that many viewed as a threat to freedom. Half a million people demonstrated against the proposal; bowing to people power, the Executive withdrew the bill. Many Hongkongers called for full democracy. The Basic Law stated that universal suffrage was an eventual goal but gave no timetable. Since then, Beijing ruled out direct elections for the Chief Executive until 2017 and for the Legislative Council (the legislature of the HKSAR), or Legco, until 2020. Each year on July 1 came a march for democracy, usually with tens of thousands participating. The period from 2004 until 2018 saw a continual jockeying back and forth over elections for Legco. In 2004 China ruled that it had to approve any changes in Hong Kong election laws, asserting its veto power against any moves to greater democracy. In late 2007, Beijing announced that it would allow the Chief Executive to be directly elected in 2017 and Legco in 2020.

But the Hong Kong situation became tenser in 2014. In June more than 90 percent of the 800,000 people who took part in an unofficial referendum voted in favor of giving the public a voice in shortlists for future elections of the Chief Executive. Beijing condemned the vote as illegal. In July tens of thousands turned out in a pro-democracy rally. In August, Beijing, overturning its own ruling from 2007, struck back, saying there would be no direct election for the Chief Executive in 2017 and that only candidates that Beijing approved could run. In reaction, for weeks from

September into November, one hundred thousand pro-democracy demonstrators, in what has come to be called the Occupy Central protests, occupied the city center. The city center (which was called the "Civic Space') was closed to the public from the end of 2014 until January 2018. In 2016 a number of pro-independence activists were elected to Legco. Beijing moved to oust them, but it was the High Court that officially removed them. Beijing was pushing, ever pushing; in an unprecedented move the Beijing government ruled that part of a high-speed railway station being built in Hong Kong would be regarded as mainland territory governed by mainland laws. In the wake of this ominous development, mostly middle-aged and elderly marched with banners reading "Protect Hong Kong!" Xi Jinping had the last word for the moment: "Beijing still holds supreme authority over the city and won't tolerate any challenge to its authority."[41]

In 1985 came negotiations with Portugal over the return of Macao. The small peninsula, occupied in 1557 and controlled since then with tacit Chinese consent, was the Chinese territory held the longest by a foreign state, almost four and a half centuries. Less significant economically and strategically than Hong Kong, it was nevertheless of great symbolic importance, and it reverted to Chinese control in December 1999.

INTERNAL OTHERS: TIBET AUTONOMOUS REGION

Relations between China and Tibet since the Cultural Revolution have alternated between periods of relative quiet punctuated by paroxysms of violence brought on by Chinese efforts to assert more stringent political or religious control over Tibetans. During the Cultural Revolution, Tibet saw the same brutal chaos and trashing of traditional culture as in China proper. Calling it a time when "the sky fell to the earth," Tibetans found at revolution's end, that all "expression of Tibetan identity and culture was forbidden with the single exception of the language."[42]

There was a general relaxation of Chinese controls from 1979 to 1987, wherein traditional customs and cultural practices emerged from the dustbin into which they had been thrown during the Cultural Revolution. Under Deng's economic reforms, China's policy was more conciliatory; Hu Yaobang himself went to Lhasa to announce the reforms, which, when instituted, were immediately successful: From 1979 to 1981, the per capita income of Tibetan peasants rose 73 percent. There were even negotiations to try to arrange the Dalai Lama's return to Tibet. Further, in 1986 a new first party secretary liberalized the party's policy toward religion, allowing a certain religious ceremony for the first time since its cancellation in 1967. Many Tibetans seized the day, putting up photographs of the Dalai Lama and defying Chinese laws restricting the number of monasteries and the numbers who could enter them.

In late September 1987, having tasted some greater freedom, Tibetan monks demonstrated for independence. Their arrests and beatings produced more demonstrations and confrontations with Chinese police. The largest anti-Chinese demonstration since the 1959 flight of the Dalai Lama erupted on March 5, 1989, followed by three days of street battles in which hundreds of Tibetans were killed or wounded. The Chinese put martial law in place for a year. Tibetans in every case reacted to Chinese draconian rule with antipathy, but they reacted to religious repression more quickly and violently than to simple political oppression. The possibility of greater religious freedom had set in motion the troubles of 1987 to 1989. The Chinese "take" on this Tibetan response was to clamp down even harder on religious issues in order to maintain stability.

Thus, when the tenth Panchen Lama (the second most important spiritual figure after the Dalai Lama) died in January 1989, the Chinese tried to control the naming of his successor, a role traditionally played by the Dalai Lama, who, in this case, named the eleventh Panchen Lama.

The Chinese government denounced the action as "illegal and a political plot by the Dalai clique to split the Motherland."[43] With the support of some Tibetan monks, in November 1995, the Chinese did select the new Panchen Lama, in effect ousting the person named by the Dalai Lama. Chinese actions, however reprehensible, were a continuation of their historical interference in Tibetan religious practices during the Qing dynasty and the Republic. In the spring of 1996 the Chinese launched a new campaign against the Dalai Lama, whom they described as "not a religious leader" but a "political fugitive."

At the turn of the twenty-first century, two destabilizing elements in Sino-Tibetan relations were the influx of large numbers of Han Chinese immigrants and economic development. Beginning in the late 1980s, the Chinese government encouraged ethnic (Han) Chinese to settle in Tibet in order to overwhelm Tibet with tens of thousands of Chinese. They ranged from laborers to professionals to demobilized troops. The huge population transfer continued into the 1990s and 2000s: it was part of the economic development plan and the political-control plan to make Tibet a more integral part of China. China provided subsidies and housing as incentives to Han Chinese settlers. Since Chinese downplayed the numbers while Tibetans exaggerated them, the factual numbers were hard to determine. Some Tibetans feared that they soon might become a minority in their own country. In 1994 Beijing called for speeded-up economic development in Tibet, emphasizing light industry and energy resources. China opened the Lhasa Stock Exchange in order to build a foundation for a market economy. Capital began to pour into the country and into enterprises, often headed by Chinese. Development continued apace throughout the 1990s, with an urban growth rate (mostly benefiting Chinese) of 10 percent and a rural growth rate of 3 percent. In 2001, work began on the Qinghai–Tibet railway, Tibet's first and the world's highest, reaching an altitude of 15,640 feet. Given that altitude for working conditions, it was a tremendous engineering feat. Running from Xining, the capital of Qinghai, the 1,956-kilometer railroad began passenger service on July 1, 2006. "The trains [were] equipped with pressurized wagons and [were] serviced by doctors and nurses. Passengers [were] provided with oxygen masks."[44]

In March 2008, another periodic round of anti-Chinese violence rampaged through Lhasa with Tibetan demonstrators torching Chinese businesses and police cars and then being shot by police. This outburst was the first that spread beyond Tibet itself. There were riots in counties and towns in Gansu, Qinghai, and Sichuan where many Tibetans lived. Dozens of Tibetans and Tibetan demonstrators elsewhere were killed. In the aftermath of this violence, from February 2009 to June 2017, a wave of self-immolations both in Tibet and among Tibetans in neighboring provinces swept the region. At least 150 Tibetans, some teenagers but mostly monks and nuns, burned themselves to death. Many commentators claimed that these dramatically tragic individual deaths had a greater impact than did all the group protests.

More ominous with regard to Tibetan religious practices and culture, in 2016 and 2017, was the scale of actions China undertook at very large Tibetan monasteries and Buddhist academies to ensure the CCP's harsh, even brutal control. Larung Gar (a gar is a monastic settlement) in Sichuan province was the largest Buddhist Institute in the world, housing between 10,000 and 40,000 monks, nuns, and visiting students. In June 2016, Beijing ordered that the site had become overcrowded and that the population had to be reduced to 5,000 by October 2017 in a program of mass expulsion of the monastics and the demolition of their residences—a crushing impingement by the party-state on the lives of Tibetan Buddhists, a forced secularization of religious institutions. The plan: divide the monastery into two parts, separated by a wall, the first being the academy or institute with a maximum of 1,500 students; the second a monastery with a maximum of 3,500 residents, mainly nuns. In the future 60 percent of the management at the Larung Gar would be CCP cadres, who were at least theoretically atheist; many cadres would also be installed at every level and in each section of the gar. Cadres would hold nearly half of positions on most committees and, in most cases, the key positions. The prefectural deputy police chief would be the party secretary and the principal of the Institute; three of his seven deputy principals would be cadres, and the six "sub-area management" units that supervised the monks at the Institute would be headed by a cadre, not a monk.

From then on, 40 percent of the classes must be in politics and other non-religious subjects. The most important criterion for accepting students was whether they "have a firm political stance, accepting the Great Motherland, the Chinese people, Chinese culture, the CCP, and socialism with Chinese characteristics"—nothing at all, for examples, on their previous study of Buddhism or their religious knowledge and interests.[45] A new government regulation stipulated that only residents of Sichuan could apply; the Larung Gar's previous application pool had been monastics who were not residents of Sichuan. Beijing's goal in in this unprecedented secular takeover of the administration of a religious institution was to ensure political stability in the monastery by intensifying the official management. Sophie Richardson, China Director of Human Rights Watch, noted, "The Chinese government's latest inroads at Larung Gar show a pernicious intent to exercise extreme control over religious practice. This is an immediate threat to the religious freedom of all Tibetans, but a long-term threat to all Chinese."[46]

XINJIANG-UIGHUR AUTONOMOUS REGION

In the first years of the twenty-first century, the most potentially explosive autonomous region was Xinjiang. Oil- and mineral-rich, with the lowest population density in the country, Xinjiang was the home of millions of Muslims, many of whom had only feeble allegiance to Beijing. Tensions and animosities between Chinese authorities and local ethnic groups festered for decades. The great fear of Beijing was that Islamic fundamentalism might take root in former Soviet Central Asia, spread across the border, and spearhead a Muslim separatist movement. In April 1990, rumors spread that Uighurs had smuggled in weapons from Afghanistan for a jihad, or holy war, to free Xinjiang from China. When Chinese troops tried to break up a rally of some 2,000 Uighurs at a town near Kashgar, violence erupted. Dozens were killed and hundreds injured in the clash. Following this incident, the Chinese substantially upped the number of troops they had in Kashgar, Urumqi (the provincial capital), and elsewhere in Xinjiang. Rumors abounded that secessionists were aiming at the establishment of an East Turkistani republic that would incorporate Uighurs from China and Russia.

The 1990s were the most volatile decade to that point in recent history, with a sporadic campaign of bombings and assassinations. In the mid-1990s, Xinjiang leaders asked Beijing for more autonomy, but Chairman Jiang was determined not to give an inch to what he called "splittists." In March 1997, the separatists (or, if seen from their point of view, "freedom fighters") answered that hard line, reaching into Beijing itself in a series of bombing attacks. After September 11, 2001, the Chinese government in the name of anti-terrorism arrested many and undertook repressive measures. As in Tibet, the government encouraged Han Chinese settlement of the area. The composition of the population had undergone a stunning change: in 1953 Han Chinese made up only 7 percent of Xinjiang's population; in the 2010 census the Han Chinese constituted 40.5 percent of the population with the Uighurs at 45.8 percent. In the years after, the population percentage stabilized at roughly the same level as in 2010. Nevertheless, widespread feelings among the Uighurs continued that they were being slowly dispossessed of what they considered their own territory. The problem of ethnic competition only exacerbated the tensions that plagued Xinjiang.

But July 2009 brought the worst ethnic violence in China in decades; it led to 197 deaths, over 1,600 wounded, and hundreds arrested in Urumqi. The Chinese blamed exiled Uighur dissident, Rebiya Kadeer, for orchestrating the unrest, while the Uighurs accused Chinese authorities for provoking violence. It is instructive to see the causes of this socio-political explosion as the context and dynamics of Xinjiang's unrest.[47] Short-term factors included the impact of the 2008 protests in Tibet and the possibility that it emboldened Uighur activists. Another short-term factor was the murder of two Uighurs at a Guangdong factory by a Han Chinese because of rumors that the Uighurs had raped a Han woman. What especially increased the ire of Xinjiang Uighurs was the almost incredible slowness with which the Han Chinese government in Guangdong handled the rape and their surmising of how that indifference reflected Han Chinese judgment of Uighurs as unimportant and subordinated.

There were long-term causes as well. The Uighurs were disgruntled about the government's sending some of them to work in factories in eastern provinces both to provide needed workers there and to make more jobs available for Uighurs in Xinjiang where unemployment was rampant. Almost all the sent Uighurs at the beginning of the project were seventeen- and eighteen-year-old girls. Many Uighurs could not understand why. One elderly man hypothesized, "60 percent of these girls will wind up as prostitutes; the other 40 percent will marry Han Chinese." Such propositions led to great disgust about what the Han Chinese were doing to Uighur women. Another important context for this particular episode as well as other violent incidents in the period from 2009 to 2017 was a rising sense of rapidly expanding disparities in wealth and unemployment. The employment market in special sectors among Uighur workers was especially serious; for example, Uighur teachers who did not know much Chinese could not count on getting any sort of teaching position. Income disparities screamed out loudly in comparisons between urban and rural families: in 1980, the urban income was 2.1 times the rural; whereas in 2007, the urban income was 3.24 times the rural. The life expectancy in 2009 for Han Chinese all across the country was 73.34 years; for the Uighurs, it was 63 years.[48]

In the relations between Uighur and Han the intangible elements—ways of thought, assumptions about the Other, stereotypes of how the Other acts and reacts, dismissals of the Other as sneaky and manipulative or as weak and feeble-minded—created auras about the Other that boded no good in three ways. First, springing from the intangible elements was a complete lack of trust and empathy between the two that poisoned any relationship, all expectations, and every judgment of the Other. Second, the Chinese apparently fell into an obsessive paranoia, where their only "comfort" and satisfaction seemed adding more controls—high-tech and otherwise—on cultural-religious issues and on day-to-day living patterns. Examples from 2017: in April a Chinese law prohibited the wearing of "abnormal beards" or veils in public. Also an April rule banned parents from naming children with names with religious connotations—like Saddam or Medina—on the basis that they could "exaggerate religious fervor."

Since October 2016, there was an arbitrary recall of passports from Xinjiang; and since early 2017, thousands of Uighurs and other Muslims had been detained in centers where they were forced to undergo "patriotic education." Uighurs studying in Egypt were ordered to return to Xinjiang; some did so; twenty had to be forcibly repatriated. One Hebibulla Tohti was a well-known Islamic scholar, fluent in Uighur, Mandarin, English, and Arabic, who had the backing of the Islamic Association in China, an organization sanctioned by the Beijing government. When he finished his dissertation and received his Ph.D., he returned, only to be detained. He was put on trial on trumped-up charges and given a ten-year prison sentence. The government never said what his exact crime was. Unsuspecting Uighurs were often victims of such zemblanities. One other: in

April 2017 security officials at UN headquarters ejected from the premises Dolkun Isa, an ethnic Uighur rights activist. He was accredited as an NGO participant in a UN Forum. He never received any explanation of what happened.

China feared that external forces from the Middle East and central Asia might join disaffected Uighurs in an Islamic separatist movement to gain independence for Xinjiang. But there has been no large-scale effort. The protests and violence most often came spontaneously as incidents have developed or led by individuals or small groups. In April 2017, a video thought to be released by ISIS showed Uighur fighters who reportedly pledged to return to China and "shed blood like rivers." A 2016 report had said that at least 114 Uighurs had joined ISIS, but this report could not be confirmed.[49] It is clear that the future here is fraught with unknowns and hidden dangers.

Notes

1 "It's a Good Day for China's Diplomats as Foreign Policy Chief Lands Seat on Politburo," *South China Morning Post* (October 25, 2017). www.scmp.com/news/china/policies-politics/article/...
2 See Elizabeth Economy, *The Third Revolution: Xi Jinping and the New Chinese State* (New York: Oxford University Press, 2018).
3 Roderick MacFarquhar, "Foreword" to *Zhao Ziyang, Prisoner of the State: The Secret Journal of Premier Zhao Ziyang* (New York: Simon & Schuster, 2010).
4 Michael Clarke, "The Belt and Road Initiative: China's New Grand Strategy?" in Roundtable: "China's Belt and Road Initiative: Views from along the Silk Road" *Asia Policy*, 24 (July 2017), p. 75. www.nbr.org/publications/asia-policy/free/ap24/AsiaPolicy24_BRI_July2017.pdf
5 Clarke, pp. 76–7.
6 Ibid., pp. 77–8.
7 Doug Guthrie, *China and Globalization: The Social, Economic, and Political Transformation of Chinese Society*, Revised Edition (New York: Routledge, 2009), p. xii.
8 Le Dinh Tinh, "The 2017 APEC Summit: A Game Changer for the Asia-Pacific," *Asia Pacific Bulletin* (November 15, 2017). https://scholarspace.manoa.hawaii.edu/handle/10125/49520
9 Joaquin Trace and Matthew Shearer, "What's the Future of Free Trade Agreements?" in "Beyond Borders: Integration and Trade" (March 1, 2017). blogs.iadb.org/integration-trade/en/welcome-to-beyond-borders-a-new-blog-created-by-the-integration-and-trade-sector
10 Keith Bradsher, "Once Concerned, China is Quiet about Trans-Pacific Trade Deal," *New York Times* (April 28, 2015). www.nytimes.com/2015/04/29/business/international/once-concerned-in-trade-deal.html
11 World Trade Organization: "Regional Trade Agreements." www.wto.org/english/tratop_e/region_e.htm
12 International Investment Agreements Navigator. www.investopedia.com/terms/f/fdi.asp
13 www.fmprc.gov.cn/mfa_eng/wjdt_665385/zyjh_665391/t1212272.shtml
14 "Chairman's Statement of the 20th Annual ASEAN-China Summit," www. asean.org/storage/2017/11/FINAL-Chairmans-Statement-of-the-2[0th]-ASEAN-Summit-13-Nov-2017-Manila1.pdf
15 Charlie Campbell, "Ports, Pipelines, and Geopolitics: China's New Silk Road Is a Challenge for Washington," *Time* (October 23, 2017).
16 Ibid.
17 Peter Frankopan, "China's New Silk Roads," *Sunday Times Magazine* (December 10, 2017) www.thetimes.co.uk/.../china-silk-road-peter-frankopan-tat-and-tinsel-trail-nh0rm...
18 "Linchpin" is in Campbell.
19 Tai Wei Lim, Henry Chan, Katherine Tseng, and Wen Xin Lim, *China's One Belt Road, One Road Initiative* (Kensington, London: Imperial College Press, 2016), pp. 285–6.
20 Ibid.
21 Julia Breuer, "Two Belts, One River? The Role of Africa in China's BRI" (Asienhaus Stiftung (July 2017). www.asienhaus.de/uploads/tx_news/Blickwechsel_OBOR_Afrika_01.pdf
22 Ambassador David H. Shinn, "China and Africa in the Xi Jinping Era," *The Diplomat* (March 25, 2013). https://thediplomat.com/2013/03/china-and-africa-in-the-xi-jinping-era/

23 Tom Piccone, "The Geopolitics of China's Rise in Latin America," *Geoeconomics and Global Issues*, paper 2, Brookings Institution (November 2016).

24 Stephen Kaplan, "China is Investing Seriously in Latin America. Should You Worry?" *Washington Post* (January 24, 2018).

25 See the analysis by William Naylor, "A Shifting Trade Landscape in Latin American Favors China and Globalization" in *Global Americans: Smart News and Research for Latin America's Change Makers* (July 10, 2017).

26 David Dollar, "China's Investment in Latin America," *Geoeconomics and Global Issues*, paper 4, Brookings Institute (January 2017).

27 For this episode, see www.revolvy.com/main/s=BragaIncident

28 "READ: Arbitral Court's Ruling on Philippines vs China" (ABC–CBN News (Posted on July 12, 2016).

29 Ed Griffith, "The Three Phases of China's Response to Koizumi and the Yasukuni Shrine Issue: Structuration in Sino-Japanese Relations," EOPS No.0007 (August 2012). European Research Center on Contemporary Taiwan. Eberhard Karls, Universitat Tubingen. www.ercct.unituebingen.de/.../EOPS7%2%20Ed%20 Griffith,%20China%20Yasukuni%20Shrine%

30 Ibid., p. 21.

31 Ibid., p. 23.

32 Justin McCurry, "Japan's Shinzo Abe Angers Neighbors and U.S. by Visiting War Dead Shrine," *The Guardian* (December 26, 2013).

33 Chico Harlan, "Japanese Prime Minister's Visit to Yasukuni War Shrine Adds to Tensions in Asia," *Washington Post* (December 26, 2013).

34 Sheila Smith, *Intimate Rivals: Japanese Domestic Politics and a Rising China* (New York: Columbia University Press, 2015), p. 100.

35 Ankit Panda, "Japan: 7 Chinese Coast Guard Ships, 230 Fishing Boats in Disputed East China Sea Waters," *The Diplomat* (August 8, 2016).

36 Craig Dietrich, *People's China* (New York: Oxford University Press, 1994), p. 265.

37 www.highbeam.com/doc/1P2-16008810.html

38 Per Liljas, "Anti-China Riot in Vietnam Leaves at Least 21 Dead," *Time* (May 15, 2014). time.com/100492/ Vietnam-anti-china-riots-21-dead

39 Ibid., p. 388.

40 Li Cheng, "China in 2000: A Year of Strategic Rethinking," *Asian Survey* 41, no. 1 (January–February, 2001): 77.

41 James Pomfret, "After Tough Years, the Hong Kong Democracy Protesters Sound Warning to China on New Year's Day," *Reuters* (January 1, 2018).

42 Tsering Shakya, *The Dragon in the Land of Snows* (New York: Columbia University Press, 1999), pp. 347–8.

43 Ibid., p. 440.

44 *The Straits Times* (Singapore), June 29, 2006, 7.

45 Human Right Watch, "China, Events of 2016." www.hrw.org/world-report/2017

46 Ibid.

47 This analysis follows that of Colin Mackerras in "Causes and Ramifications of the Xinjiang July 2009 Disturbances," *Sociology Study*, Vol. 2, no.7 (July 2012), 496–510. https://reserch-repository.griffith.edu.au/ bitstream/handle/10072/.../82072_1.pdf

48 Ibid.

49 Ibid.

Suggestions for Further Reading

Gillette, Maris Boyd. *Between Mecca and Beijing: Modernization and Consumption among Urban Chinese Muslims* (Stanford, CA: Stanford University Press, 2000). This study of the Hui community in Xi'an explores its changing identities and relations to the state during the reform era.

Guthrie Doug. *China and Globalization: The Social, Economic, and Political Transformation of Chinese Society* (London: Routledge, 2009). The tone of this analysis is both informal and contentious; its coverage is almost encyclopedic, though it is framed in compelling and theoretical sociologically-based parameters. It has been called "the best short introduction to how China's economy is changing."

Kaplan, Robert D. *Asia's Cauldron: The South China Sea and the End of a Stable Pacific* (New York: Random House, 2014). Having been described as riveting, compelling, and disturbing, this book argues that the South China Sea in the years ahead is likely "to become the flashpoint for future regional power struggles with serious international consequences."

Manicom, James. *Bridging Troubled Waters: China, Japan, and Maritime Order on the East China Sea* (Washington, D.C.: Georgetown University, 2014). This balanced analysis is one of the best accounts of the complicated history of China's and Japan's standoff over tiny islets and rocky outcrops in the East China Sea.

Miller, Tom. *China's Asian Dream: Empire Building Along the New Silk Road* (London: Zed Books, 2017). Well-researched and well-written with striking insights and arresting stories, this is basically a "guide" to the utopianism, personalities, institutions, and approaches that ground Xi Jinping's Belt and Road Initiative.

23

A Question of Identity
The Republic of China on Taiwan since the 1970s

The identity of a nation is based on a plethora of attributes that are shared by a people: common historical experiences; common culture and goals; racial, ethnic, and religious make-up; common heroes, villains, and mythical figures. When he died in April 1975, Chiang Kai-shek left behind a booming economy and the government that he and Kuomintang mainlanders had installed in the late 1940s. Those accomplishments, founding and shaping a new "state" and establishing a growing and thriving economy, were obviously two feathers in his military cap. But the downside: he did not allow the 90 percent of the population composed of native Taiwanese any political role; and his White Terror (basically from 1948 to the end of martial law in 1987—thirty-eight years and fifty-seven days), aimed ostensibly against the Communists, actually targeted any dissent whatsoever in a brutal dictatorial regime. With which of Chiang's identity "markers" would a mainlander's offspring or a Taiwanese likely identify?

In April 1980, five years after his death, a Taiwanese newspaper, noting that the Memorial Hall for Chiang was dedicated and opening, ruminated about his meaning for the people of Taiwan.

> Even after half a decade, the nation still has difficulty in accepting [his] loss. ... [At the memorial hall] the beauty of the site and the memorial structure give indication of the place the Generalissimo holds in the hearts of the Chinese people. ... Chiang ... did not live to see the culmination of his efforts, but the credit will be writ large in his name at the ... Memorial Hall. ... There his towering statue smiles down on the people he served so well.

There is little doubt that these are the thoughts of someone connected with the mainlander immigrants. But the thirty-three years since his death have seen great changes on Taiwan, changes that have substantially changed Chiang's identity and image—and Taiwan's.

BIRTH OF A DEMOCRACY

Chiang's son, Ching-kuo, became premier in 1971; he was the power behind many crackdowns on dissidents. But Chiang Ching-kuo was also responsible for beginning what has been called "Taiwanization," that is, opening up the political system (slowly to be sure) to Taiwanese, as opposed to mainland immigrants and their descendants. By 1970, increasing numbers of Taiwanese had been appointed to party posts at the county and municipal levels. It was the beginning of a policy of co-optation, of buying the opposition off by dangling political goodies before them. Some Taiwanese wanted more than simply being co-opted. In 1975 and 1976 Taiwanese opposition (known as "nonparty" [*dangwai*]) tried to challenge the party in elections and demanded fundamental changes in the political system. The Kuomintang government reacted as it always had done on the mainland, with repression and widespread arrests, determined to keep its monopoly of power.

At stake throughout these years was the identity of the state and its people. Was the government headquartered in Taipei the Republic of China (ROC) temporarily in exile or should the regime more appropriately be called the Republic of Taiwan? Until 2000 the identity was always determined by the mainlander Kuomintang, which held political and military power; they continued to monopolize the military and security bureaucracy known as the Garrison Command.

The Challenges of the Late 1970s

Chiang Ching-kuo took over the presidency in 1978 and met the heat of a growing protest movement. In 1979, the core of nonparty leaders published a political journal, in English called *Formosa*, in Chinese *Mei-li-tao*. The nonparty leaders hoped through its essays to inspire street demonstrations and mass rallies that could foster island-wide networks of politically active people. The government tried to keep the nonparty leaders "off balance, harassed them whenever possible, and leaked stories to the press about their personal lives that contained details of prurient interest"—a time-honored Chinese tactic to besmirch one's opponents.[1] The leaders were subject to more and more intense surveillance: Their telephones were tapped. With its control of the press, the Kuomintang government was always able to put its own spin on events as they occurred.

On December 10, 1979, nonparty leaders planned a rally in the southern port of Kaohsiung to celebrate the anniversary of the Universal Declaration of Human Rights. An attack on a *Mei-li-tao* staff member a day earlier by Kuomintang-hired thugs was a hint that the government clearly wanted to destroy nonparty leaders by orchestrating a riot and then using it as an excuse to crack down on dissenters. Many, like the feminist Lu Hsiu-lien, were aware that plots were underfoot:

> I sensed [she remembered] that something dangerous would happen that night. Things were out of control. If I were smart enough, I could have left right away, but of course I didn't … all we could do was wait and see.[2]

Nonparty leaders riding on the platform of a truck and followed by their supporters, some 30,000 strong, were met by attacking police who hemmed the crowd in, keeping it from moving and sporadically firing tear gas. While the leaders urged calm from their truck platform microphones, "persons unknown to the rally organizers" and rumored to be hired by party rightists attacked the police, injuring over one hundred.[3]

Three days after the incident, the government, with President Chiang reportedly saying, "We cannot afford dissent," cracked down. Over 150 people were arrested; forty-one nonparty leaders were tried and sentenced to prison terms. Among them was the chief strategist for the movement, Shih Ming-teh, who had already served many years in prison for plotting against the government; he had initially avoided capture because he was hidden by leaders of the Presbyterian Church on Taiwan (PCT), which had been active in the Taiwanese cause. This time Shih was sentenced to life imprisonment in the notorious prison on Green Island, southeast of Taiwan; the general secretary of PCT was also sent there for harboring Shih. Lu Hsiu-lien, who could have left before the rally but did not, was imprisoned. Many of those hauled in were subject to beatings and psychological torture. The government closed fifteen publications, including *Formosa*. All prisoners except Shih were released in the 1980s while Chiang was still president; Shih was freed in 1990.

The Opening of the Breach

Street protests did not cease in the generally repressive early 1980s, but they were no longer simply the political theater of the nonparty Taiwanese. Advocates of other causes—ecology, women's rights, workers' rights, veterans' welfare, and consumers' rights—took to the streets. Aware that the proponents of all these issues simply could not be prosecuted and that the changing times required new policies, Chiang in 1986 initiated various reform efforts that, in retrospect, marked the "transition from authoritarian rule to some kind of participatory democracy."[4] Chiang exhibited considerable courage, given the continued strength of conservatives within his party and their opposition to many of the proposals that he supported. Yet he did jail some opposition leaders, including Chen Shui-bian, then a Taipei city councilman, as sacrificial lambs to the conservatives.

But the nonparty group was not to be intimidated. On September 28, 1986, shucking off forever their nonparty status, 135 of the nonparty leaders, in blatant defiance of the longtime ban on forming other parties, announced the establishment of their party, the Democratic Progressive Party (DPP). In response, Chiang, the longtime repressor, became a supporter of change. He pressured his party's conservatives to accede to an evolution toward greater democracy, arguing that he had called for such change. Specifically, he was able to get agreement on the abolition of martial law, which had been in place since the late 1940s, as well as removal of the ban on the formation of opposition parties. Those remarkable changes came on October 15, little more than two weeks after the founding of the DPP—the first breach in the dike of authoritarian rule.

More breathtaking initiatives were in the offing. The Taipei government lifted all restrictions on travel to the PRC, making it possible for hundreds of thousands of mainlanders to visit their mainland homes for the first time since 1949.

The Presidency of Lee Teng-hui

Chiang died in January 1988. He passed on to his chosen successor, the native Taiwanese Lee Teng-hui, a Taiwan that "was a thriving economic entity that possessed a sophisticated and stable, but still evolving, political system."[5] Of Hakka ethnicity, Lee had studied agricultural economics, receiving a Ph.D. from Cornell University; he taught for many years at Taiwan National University (Taida) and served for two decades on the Sino-American Joint Commission on Rural Reconstruction. He was mayor of Taipei from 1978 to 1981, governor of Taiwan province from 1981 to 1984, and became Chiang's vice-president in 1984. Lee took office at a time when the democratic changes initiated by Chiang were starting to flower. In the December 1989 legislative elections, the first of the full-fledged two-party system, the DPP challenged the Kuomintang. Even though the Kuomintang won, the DPP made a creditable showing, taking enough seats in the Legislative Yuan to be able to introduce legislation. The constitution of 1946, under which the government was operating, had established the Legislative Yuan as the national legislature.

Lee's leadership was remarkable in hastening the Taiwanization of the political system. Taiwanese made up 85 percent of the population, but the number of official posts they held was a drop in the bucket. Mainlanders generally monopolized leadership in the military and police. Taiwanese composed 75 percent of the rank-and-file of the military, but Taiwanese generals comprised only about 17 percent of the total and Taiwanese officers with a rank of lieutenant colonel

FIGURE 23.1 Lee Teng-hui, the first Taiwanese president of the Republic of China, expanded democracy and set out to strengthen ties with the PRC. His administrations were marked, however, by tensions with the PRC. *Source*: AP Photos/Shutterstock.

or above made up only 4.3 percent. Similarly, Taiwanese numbered only 7.3 percent of the 150 high-ranking police officers throughout the island. Lee began to remedy this situation. In July 1988, when he was elected chair of the Kuomintang, he named thirty-one members to the party's Central Committee, sixteen of them Taiwanese. Overall, Taiwanese made up 40 percent of the new Central Committee compared to only 18 percent of the Central Committee formed in 1982. For his cabinet, Lee chose many younger Taiwanese; no fewer than fourteen held a Ph.D., with eleven from American institutions.

Lee had much trouble with various groups in the Kuomintang. Being Taiwanese was the first strike against him for many mainlanders; furthermore, they deeply resented his policy of Taiwanization, chalking it up simply to biased favoritism. Second-generation mainlanders were young Turks who did not want to submit to old Kuomintang procedures and policies, nor did they want Lee. Neanderthalic conservatives opposed Lee's domestic and foreign policies, especially his initiatives regarding the mainland. In the words of one scholar, they

> seem[ed] not to have noticed that authoritarianism had gone out of fashion. Their passion for order and control, their willingness to manipulate the organs of government to execute their will, and their visceral distrust of anyone who disagree[d] with them reflect[ed] values that [ran] deeply in Chinese political history.[6]

Under the constitution, the National Assembly was the parliamentary body established to elect the president and to adopt or amend the constitution. In the 1990 presidential election, anti-Lee forces in the National Assembly, having had enough of Lee's reforms, came together to try to block his election. Lee avoided being undone by the conservative mainlanders by naming as premier a mainlander, a career military man, and chief of staff from 1981 to 1989—Hau Pei-tsun. Hau quickly became the rallying point for mainlanders, who generally tended to be far more conservative in their views of both domestic and foreign policy. In contrast to Lee's "mainstream" faction, they became known as the "nonmainstream" faction, the formation of which was encouraged by Madame Chiang Kai-shek, who maintained homes both in Taipei and in New York City.

Taipei Spring

The wheeling and dealing of conservatives in the National Assembly to derail democratic reforms and to deny Lee the presidency brought an unexpected reaction from students at Taida and other universities. They copied a page from the student Democracy Movement in the PRC in 1989. From March 16 to March 22, 1990, they occupied the grounds of the Chiang Kai-shek Memorial in downtown Taipei, donned headbands with various political slogans, made demands, and even went on hunger strikes. In contrast to the generally unfocused Beijing student demands a year earlier, the Taiwan students had much more specific and direct goals:

> the disbanding of the electoral college [National Assembly], the suspension of the Temporary Provisions that froze aging Mainlanders in office ["old thieves," as they were called by the students], a timetable for full democratization, and a complete revamp of the Constitution.[7]

But the chief difference from the Beijing Spring of a year earlier was that the government of Lee Teng-hui was open to talking about the issues; indeed, since most of the students' agenda coincided with his own, it was a pleasure for him to do so.

On the day of his election, March 21, Lee himself went to the Chiang Kai-shek Memorial to talk with the students. He promised them that he would sponsor a "broad-based, high-level" conference to chart the course for the country's future. Four months later, he convened a National Affairs Conference that brought together a diverse group of 136 political and academic leaders. From June 28 to July 4, 1990, they discussed and debated the course of "Taiwan's political development and offer[ed] recommendations for democratization."[8] Lee, to his great political credit, was able to take the recommendations of the National Affairs Conference as a mandate and a map to move to further democratization—at the heart of which was constitutional reform, a revamped National Assembly and Legislative Yuan, and other political changes.

Constitutional Revolution

In essence, because of the insistence of the Kuomintang that the National Assembly had to keep representatives from all Chinese provinces and that Taiwan was only one represented province, the National Assembly actually represented China as it was in 1947, not Taiwan in the early 1990s. Under the reforms envisioned in the National Affairs Conference, the 1991 National Assembly would convene and, amid its other work, legislate itself out of existence. The question that emerged near the end of the assembly's session was whether it would play any role before its demise in charting constitutional changes. DPP representatives in both the Assembly and Legislative Yuan wanted no participation by the old-style Assembly because it was composed almost completely of mainlanders. They favored a new National Assembly's taking up any constitutional changes. Relations between the Kuomintang and the DPP in the 1991 Assembly and the Legislative Yuan were notoriously rancorous. Name-calling, fist fights, hair pulling, thrown ashtrays, and outright brawls frequently punctuated these sessions. A central issue that fueled the animosity was reunification with the mainland—the Kuomintang position—versus Taiwanese independence—the DPP position.

In April 1991, when it became apparent that the Kuomintang was reneging on the earlier pledge that only a new Assembly would take up constitutional issues, DPP representatives in the Assembly and the legislature walked out. Supported by 10,000 of their followers, they staged a huge demonstration march through Taipei punctuated by frequent confrontations with police. DPP leaders called off any further action when the Kuomintang offered minor concessions, but they boycotted the remainder of the session.

It was a momentous session. The "Temporary Provisions," which had been the basis for the Kuomintang's dictatorship, giving the president the right to rule under emergency conditions during the state of war with the PRC, were abolished. Both the National Assembly and the Legislative Yuan were reduced in size. All senior deputies in the two bodies would retire at the end of the session. From that point on, two-thirds of the bodies would be composed of representatives elected on Taiwan and one-third would be made up of representatives of overseas Chinese. The latter arrangement originated with the ideas of Sun Yat-sen, who had stressed the help that overseas Chinese had provided in the republican revolution and thus saw them as "part of the political community. According to ROC law, individuals who are born to Chinese parents are considered citizens of the republic regardless of where they actually were born, or where they reside."[9]

The remarkable democratic revolution of the late 1980s and 1990s continued with changes in the constitution in 1994. According to amendments, from that point on, presidents would be elected directly by voters; thus, the 1996 elections were the first under the new system. Presidential powers were strengthened with the decision that the premier's countersignature was no longer needed on presidential appointments. The terms of legislators were set at four years. The offices of speaker and deputy speaker were established for the National Assembly. In light of the frequent physical turmoil and unruliness in parliamentary bodies in the early years of the 1990s, the constitution was amended to limit parliamentary immunity of speech. In addition to the constitutional changes, the Legislative Yuan in the summer of 1994 passed legislation making the provincial governor and the mayors of Taipei and Kaohsiung elected directly by the people.

The constitutional amendment that gave the people the right to elect the president directly took away the National Assembly's primary task. After 1990, its main function was to amend the constitution. Increasingly searching for things to do, in the late 1990s the Assembly clashed more frequently with the Legislative Yuan over power sharing and carrying out such responsibilities as budget review. Therefore, in April 2000, a constitutional amendment transferred most of the National Assembly's powers to the Legislative Yuan. The Legislature's new purview included such items as constitutional amendments and impeachment of the president and vice-president. Once initiated by the Legislature, the National Assembly would be convened to vote on these matters. Most commentators believed that the once-powerful Assembly would soon fade from the scene.

THE ELEPHANT IN THE ROOM: TAIWAN'S RELATIONSHIP WITH THE PRC

In the period from 1987 until 1995, the pace of Cross-Strait relations was rapid with significant gains in the beginning integration of ROC and PRC in economic relations.

1987—The ban on Taiwanese traveling to the PRC was steadily relaxed.
1988—Indirect mail and indirect trade with the PRC began.

1989—Indirect telephone links began.

1990—A National Unification Council was formed to plan and advise on policy.

1991—Taiwan (February) set up the Straits Exchange Foundation (SEF) and Beijing set up its counterpart Association for Relations Across the Taiwan Strait (ARATS) to deal with "commercial, legal, and administrative matters" emerging between the two.

1992—Between the two, there were 24.11 million items of mail, 14.72 million telephone calls, and 62,000 telegrams. Officially declared indirect investment in the PRC totaled 20 percent of all Taiwan investment—in enterprises numbering between 10,000 and 15,000.

1993—The first meeting (April 27) of SEF and ARATS occurred in Singapore.

1995—Direct shipping links were established.

Though all gains underscored the increasingly positive relationship, the key events came with the establishment of SEF and ARATS, the chief negotiating bodies in Cross-Strait relations and the 1995 decision for direct shipping links. Until that year, only indirect trade, that is, through a third party as go-between, could be practiced. The meeting of SEF and ARATS in April 1993 was the first high-level meeting between the PRC and Taiwan since 1949. SEF's deputy secretary-general, perhaps hyperbolically, called it "one of the historic moments of the century," but it did symbolize "the fundamental shift in the relationship between the two political entities from confrontation to co-operative coexistence."[10] SEF and ARATS were to meet every three months, alternating between Beijing and Taipei, though that schedule was frequently altered by several rocky points in their relationship. A dialogue on issues such as cultural, technological, and scientific exchanges, investment rights, fishing disputes, protecting intellectual property rights, and resource and energy cooperation could not help but bring the region a greater sense of stability.

But, starting in 1995, both sides tumbled back into a state of tension that had not been felt for several decades. In part Lee and much of Taiwan's population had begun to shift away from supporting unification with China. Lee's own Taiwanese identity made the Beijing regime instinctively suspicious of all of his actions despite the fact that Lee was the KMT leader and had been handpicked by Chiang Ching-kuo. He stressed that he did not sympathize with the Taiwan independence movement, but during his second term as president, his actions began to suggest that he increasingly saw Taiwan as an independent nation-state. In part to soften the impact such a direct policy might make, he set out to strengthen ties to the mainland. He lifted all restrictions for Taiwanese who wished to travel to the PRC; within several months, the number of Taiwanese traveling to the mainland reached 10,000 per month. Taiwan businessmen now participated directly in PRC economic development, no longer having to work through their former Hong Kong agents. As for Taiwan's relationship to China, Lee continued to acknowledge that there was only one China.

The problem in the Taiwan–China relationship was that each side had a different goal. For China, Cross-Strait talks were about paving the way for reunification, while for Taiwan talks were a way to normalize relations between two states. Both sides had agreed in 1992 that a "one-China" policy was most appropriate in masking questions that were still undecided. The 1972 Shanghai Communique had stated pithily, "the United States acknowledges that Chinese on either side of the Taiwan Strait maintain there is but **one China** and that Taiwan is a part of **China**. The United States does not challenge that position." The heart of the problem was that the PRC and Taiwan did not agree on the most basic question—which "China" was in the formula? Under Lee Teng-hui's presidency, he and Taiwan publicly agreed with the one-China policy.

When constitutional reform had been underway, firebrands in the DPP had set out to put together a constitution so that when the 1992 National Assembly met on constitutional matters, the DPP would not only be able to move to scrap the old constitution but would have a proposed new one ready. The first article of the draft baldly set forth the party's position on the political identity of the island. It read, "Taiwan is a democratic republic of the people, by the people, and for the people whose name is the Republic of Taiwan."[11] President Lee Teng-hui exploded, calling it a "reckless and irresponsible move" and stressed that "there is only one China."[12] The official *People's Daily* in Beijing bitterly condemned the DPP's draft. In a public opinion poll, 60 percent of the respondents disapproved of the term *Republic of Taiwan*. Election results for the National Assembly in December 1991 also showed that the people did not favor the free Taiwan rhetoric, for the Kuomintang took 71 percent of the vote, with the DPP garnering only 24 percent. Vote totals notwithstanding, the issue nevertheless would not go away.

In early 1995, in a masterful stroke, President Lee acted to end some of the bitterness that existed among Taiwanese toward mainlanders because of the February 28, 1947, incident (see Chapter 15). Three years earlier, in winter 1992, Lee had had the official government report of the incident released with much fanfare in an attempt to "confront the ghosts of the past" and inaugurate a period of freer reporting by the media. On February 28, 1995, Lee dedicated a memorial to the victims of the incident in the capital's New Park. In the ceremony, Lee, the Taiwanese Hakka, formally apologized to the victims' families in his capacity as Kuomintang chairman and ROC president.

The position of many Taiwanese, especially the DPP, was that reunification would never occur; they argued that there was one China and one Taiwan, or two Chinas; independence for Taiwan would be a ratification of the reality that had developed in fact, if not in name, since 1949— that Taiwan was a separate nation. This DPP position was anathema to the government in Beijing; even bringing it up threw Communist officials into something approaching apoplectic rage. The DPP took the position that the 1946 constitution had to be discarded, not amended. "In their eyes, the entire political system the constitution ha[d] been used to justify *reflect[ed] the interest of the Mainlanders, with scant regard for the interests of the Taiwanese* [italics, mine]."[13]

Anything that suggested a tilt toward greater independence for the Taiwan regime reverberated loudly in Beijing. In June 1995, Lee received a visa to attend an alumni reunion at Cornell University. Since the 1972 Shanghai Communiqué's statement of the one-China policy, no top Taiwan government official had been allowed to visit the United States in a public capacity. But the U.S. Congress and President Clinton buckled under political pressure. Though Lee came for his own private purpose, the trip was "very public and highly publicized."[14] PRC editorials portrayed Lee as "traitorous to the cause of Chinese nationalism and [as] putting personal ambition above the safety and security of the Chinese citizenry."[15] Jiang Zemin suspended talks with Lee, and in July and August the PRC conducted missile tests off the northern coast of Taiwan to show their displeasure with Lee's actions.

More missile tests in December 1995 off the Fujian coast 170 kilometers north of the island failed to intimidate voters in Legislative Yuan elections. The Kuomintang won over 46 percent of the vote, about 7 percent less than in 1992; the DPP won over 33 percent and the New Party about 13 percent (The New Party was a break-away KMT splinter group, formed in 1993, which was rigidly right-wing). Before the presidential elections in March 1996, Beijing engaged in war games with live ammunition for nine days off the coast of Fujian. Its forces fired surface-to-air missiles into two target zones, one 35 kilometers northeast of Taiwan, the other 52 kilometers southwest of Kaohsiung. Beijing was seemingly terrified that an advocate of independence might be elected, distrustful as it already was about Lee and his intent. But Beijing's actions brought military reaction from the United States, which sent two nuclear-armed aircraft carrier fleets into waters in the western Pacific. Though both Beijing and Washington pulled back, the volatility of the continued face-off between Taiwan and the mainland was evident. The war scare had little effect on the elections:

Lee won, taking 54 percent of the vote; the DPP candidate won 21 percent. The tensions produced in the 1995–1996 election campaigns and the aggressiveness shown by the PRC underscored the raw sensitivity and sometimes almost panicked nature of situations that developed in the Strait.

THE REMARKABLE ELECTION AND BARREN PRESIDENCY OF CHEN SHUI-BIAN

On March 18, 2000, the Kuomintang, the party of Sun Yat-sen and Chiang Kai-shek, went down to a shocking political defeat in the presidential election. Little more than thirteen years after the first legal two-party election in Taiwan, the rebel Democratic Progressive Party won the election, sending the Kuomintang into shock and disarray. The former mayor of Taipei, Chen Shui-bian, jailed in 1986 for opposition to the government, was elected president. His running mate and new vice-president was Lu Hsiu-lien, the feminist activist who had been jailed in the 1979 Kaohsiung incident.

Chen's 2000 election was historic. Although he received only 39 percent of the vote, he defeated the New Party's candidate with 37 percent, and the Kuomintang candidate, with 23 percent. The election ended the Kuomintang's fifty-five-year dictatorship on Taiwan. Chen hit the nail on the head: "This is the greatest victory of Taiwan's democracy movement," he said.[16] One could almost call Chen's victory a storybook event in the history of Taiwan's democracy movement. In the same 1993 interview expressing his linkage of democracy and independence, he said:

> Over the past forty years, to pursue party politics and democracy, our predecessors went through the 2–28 Incident, the period of white terror, the Kaohsiung Incident, and many bloody and horrifying assassinations. Even I have experienced this: my wife has to use a wheelchair for the rest of her life because of a "political car accident." [Chen's wife was paralyzed after being hit by a truck—an accident both believe was arranged for political purposes.] I have also been jailed … it has been a rough road. … We have given our blood and sweat for the lifting of martial law, for the easing of restrictions on the formation of political parties, for the liberalization of media restrictions, and [for] the election of the legislature.[17]

Mainland–island relations regarding the 2000 presidential elections were especially tense, with Beijing once again threatening to hold war games to remind Taiwanese voters of the dangers of voting for anyone who might move toward independence. Many were shocked at Chen's election; as a result, Beijing had to cope with a Taiwanese leader who had said in a 1993 interview "[D]emocracy is the process and independence is the goal."[18] Despite its almost rabid pre-election rhetoric, the PRC adopted a wait-and-see attitude, and Chen immediately waved olive branches in Beijing's direction. In July 2000, PRC Defense Minister Chi Haotian told the U.S. defense secretary, "although China reserves the right to use force against Taiwan, that does not mean it intends to do so."[19] But Beijing entered a period of "strategic disengagement" from Taiwan. The central issue became the one-China formula that had been the core of PRC–U.S.–ROC understanding since the early 1970s. Beijing argued that before further negotiations with Chen, he had to accept the one-China formula; Chen would not do so. Therefore, from 2000 to 2008, there was a complete impasse despite the fact that Chen himself undertook various cross-Strait initiatives. Chen antagonized the PRC further with statements in 2002 about Taiwan "go[ing] its own way" if Beijing did not respond to Chen's advances and that there was "a country on each side" of the Taiwan Strait.[20] Further, in 2003, Chen began talking about formulating a new constitution and using referenda to decide significant state issues (in the midst of political stalemate). Beijing took both as backdoor ways to begin to move Taiwan to independence. Chen did nothing well—except perhaps rattling the mainland's cages.

Despite repeated warnings by the PRC and the United States, Chen placed two referenda on the March 2004 ballot. The first read:

> The people of Taiwan demand that the Taiwan Strait issue be solved through peaceful means. Should mainland China refuse to withdraw the missiles it has targeted at Taiwan and to openly renounce the use of force against us, would you agree that the Government should acquire more advanced anti-missile systems to strengthen Taiwan's self-defense capabilities?

The second read:

> Would you agree that our Government should engage in negotiations with Mainland China on the establishment of a "peace and stability" framework for cross-Strait interactions in order to build consensus and for the welfare of peoples on both sides?

In order to pass, over 50 percent of the voters had to vote in the referendums. Though over 7 million people voted on each referendum, with over 80 percent agreeing to each, this totaled only about 45 percent of the voters, so neither measure passed.

Unfortunately, the election in 2000 was the high point of Chen's two terms as president: it was all downhill after that. After the election, he had to govern with a party that had never held power and thus did not have access to many of the political resources that the Kuomintang had. He had to deal with a legislature and a military still fully controlled by a hostile Kuomintang, and he was faced with an enraged regime across the Taiwan Strait. His first four-year term was marked by almost total governmental stalemate between the Kuomintang-dominated legislature and the DPP president, by the worst economic period since World War II, and by a PRC that refused to deal directly with Chen, thereby casting cross-Strait relations into the deep-freeze. His second term was also marked by complete deadlock, as he spent almost all his time trying to fend off accusations of his corruption, that of his wife, son-in-law, and his associates.

The feud between Chen and the Legislative Yuan affected every governmental decision. To continue producing sufficient electric power, three nuclear power plants had been constructed, and the construction of a fourth was underway. The administration's decision to scrap this fourth plant poisoned the political atmosphere and led political opponents to move to impeach Chen—within months of his election. In the end, Chen yielded and in 2001 the power plant construction was resumed, but the political damage had been done. Chen's opponents were the Kuomintang and political parties that were breakaway factions of the Kuomintang, the New Party and the People's First Party (PFP), the latter formed by an erstwhile presidential candidate. (By 2001, the New Party had been substantially swallowed up by the PFP.) Because the main color in the Kuomintang flag was blue, this coalition of Chen's opponents was called the "pan-blue parties." The DPP and a small Taiwan Solidarity Union (established by former president Lee Teng-hui), favoring environmental protection in their agendas, were denoted the "greens." In parliamentary elections in late 2001, the greens increased their strength in the legislature to 100 members, but the pan-blue coalition maintained control with 114.

The pan-blue parties saw the March 2004 presidential election as a chance to end the stalemate. But it was not to be. Chen and Lu defeated their opponents by 29,518 votes out of about 13 million votes cast, a margin of 0.24 percent. The pan-blues yelled foul: Chen and Lu had been slightly wounded in an assassination attempt in the city of Tainan the day before the election. When time passed and there were no suspects or even solid leads, the pan-blues accused Chen and Lu of staging the attack to win sympathy votes in what had been predicted to be a very tight race. The summer of 2004 saw accusations and counter-accusations about the election and about how to proceed in the matter of governing. The situation went from bad to worse. When Chen left the presidency, he lost immunity from prosecution. He was indicted in December 2008 for embezzlement, bribe taking, and laundering funds. His trial ended in late July 2009. Found guilty, he faced life imprisonment. The soaring hopes of 2000 had collapsed in a heap of political rubble.

THE KUOMINTANG RETURNS: THE ONE-NOTE PRESIDENCY OF MA YING-JEOU

In the 2008 elections, the Kuomintang returned to power. Ma Ying-jeou, two-term mayor of Taipei and former chair of the KMT, won with a landslide 58 percent of the vote. With a turnout of 76.3 percent of the vote, the KMT even carried the DPP stronghold of southern Taiwan. Ma's election and the return of the KMT to power promised warmer relations with the PRC; Ma immediately inaugurated a more conciliatory Cross-Strait policy. Leaders of the KMT and its offshoot blue parties met Hu Jintao in spring and summer of 2005 and in April 2008 after their election victory. Cross-Strait talks were resumed for the first time since 1995. In November 2008, the PRC and ROC conducted their highest level visit in decades.

An obvious pattern of the Taiwan–China Cross-Strait relationship is that when the KMT party ruled (1987–1995 and 2008–2016) great progress was made in developing more connections, building more integration. But the minute the DPP was elected and ruled (2000–2008, 2016–), everything shut down, even when Chen Shui-bian tried to stimulate his own Cross-Strait initiatives without success and considerable humiliation because Beijing stopped playing the game it controlled. It was obvious that China dominated the game and would allow it to be played only if two phrases could echo throughout the room: "one-China policy" and "1992 consensus." If a timeline is made of Cross-Strait agreements and treaties, there was a flurry of twenty-three such agreements and treaties from 1987 to 1995 and from 2008 to 2013—agreements, for example, that tripled the number of weekly direct passenger flights, allowed cargo shipment between ports, established more direct postal links, and set up a food safety alert system. But there were absolutely no agreements or treaties in the years of DPP control.

One of the most significant agreements of the whole series was the signing of the Economic Co-operation Framework Agreement (ECFA) in June 2010. It was a Free Trade Agreement that abolished or reduced hundreds of tariffs from both sides. At the end of June, the "Early Harvest Program" was signed, listing the tariff concessions that were covered by the ECFA: there were 539 Taiwanese products worth 13.8 billion USD and 267 Chinese products. There were three main categories that composed 97 percent of the trade in petro-chemicals, steel, and optical-related items. Only 3 percent were agricultural products or textiles. The establishment of the ECFA was the most important of the Cross-Strait agreements. With his openness to dealing with Beijing, Ma oversaw a long string of Cross-Strait treaties—twenty-three negotiated and signed in ten rounds of talks, with three of those remaining unratified.

Negotiated and signed in June 2013, but not ratified by Taiwan's legislature, was the Cross-Strait Services Trade Agreement, which allowed the two sides to invest much more freely in the other's services market. That market included banking, health care, tourism, film, telecommunications, and publishing. These areas would be open to investment; businessmen would be able to retain indefinitely renewable visas for the other territory. It would greatly facilitate businesses to set up offices and branches in the other territory and for large amounts of holdings to be sold to the other party's investors.

This agreement spurred opposition in the Sunflower Student Movement, a coalition of students and civic groups, in the spring of 2014. The immediate concern of the movement was the perception that, after SEF and ARATS had negotiated and signed the treaty, the KMT government attempted ratification through what students considered undemocratic processes. Several hundred students occupied the Taiwan legislature from March 18 to April 10; there were also many street protests and rallies. The larger issues were the meaning and impact of the agreement for Taiwan and the Taiwanese. There was one obvious reason to ratify: increased Chinese investment in Taiwan would boost its economy. In addition, legislators prodded those opposed by arguing that unworked-out details on how the agreement would be implemented could be structured favorably for Taiwan. Others contended that pulling out of a signed treaty negotiated in part by Taiwanese would likely damage Taiwan's international credibility.

But there were powerful reasons to oppose the agreement. The treaty would benefit large companies with investment moneys, while it could possibly put small and medium-sized businesses into bankruptcy. Furthermore, Chinese investments in the publishing industry plus its already currently substantial investment in the news media could likely endanger free speech in Taiwan. Finally, and this was the continual DPP lament, the treaty would in effect lay the groundwork in specific ways for eventual political unification with the PRC. A May 2014 poll by Taipei's National Chengchi University, one of Taiwan's most prestigious and prominent universities, showed that public opinion was very sharply divided on the agreement: 43 percent supported it, while 40 percent opposed it. It had not yet been ratified by early 2018. In part the agreement's not being

FIGURE 23.2 Note the disarray and chaotic results of the occupation of the Legislative chambers by those in the Sunflower Student Movement. At the bottom of the picture of Sun Yat-sen is the number of hours (582) of the occupation.

Source: SAM YEH/AFP/Getty Images.

ratified stemmed from Ma's political weakness. Indeed, Ma's two terms (2008–2016), apart from the Cross-Strait agreements, were largely devoid of success.

Ma and his administration never recovered from Typhoon Morakot, which slammed into southern and central Taiwan in early August, 2009, fifteen months after he became president. Morakot was the deadliest typhoon to hit Taiwan in recorded history. Ma clearly underesti- mated the scale of the disaster, waiting three days before acting in the wake of the storm that killed at least 673 and caused catastrophic damage in the amount of 6.2 billion USD. Rain- fall in many places was more than 100 inches (in one county, 109.3 inches); mudslides were deadly and common in the southern mountain region. Critics said that Ma should have initially declared a national emergency to get the military involved immediately. As it was, when Ma acted, he only deployed about 2,100 soldiers, an incredibly small number for such a major task of rescuing survivors; he later increased the deployed to 46,000. He also first turned down all offers of foreign aid, a surprising and tragic decision. The *China Times*, normally a Ma sup- porter, editorialized, "Ma has been distant and arrogant, and he has only made [victims angrier] instead of comforting them. He has not shown decisiveness required in a leader when facing a sudden disaster."[21]

The centerpiece of his campaign in 2008 was his "6–3–3" pledge: his policies would produce 6 percent economic growth per year, an unemployment rate of less than 3 percent, and a per cap- ita income of more than 30,000 USD. In terms of economic growth from 2010 through 2016, the figures are

2010, **10.6%**   2014, **3.8%**
2011, **3.8%**   2105, **0.7%**
2012, **2.1%**   2016, **1.5%**
2013, **2.2%**

The average growth per year was 3.5 percent, not close to the 6 percent he had pledged. As for pledging an unemployment rate of under 3 percent, the rates of unemployment during the Ma years ranged from 3.9 to 6.0 percent, with an average of 4.4 percent. And in per capita income with a goal of over 30,000 USD, the per capita income ranged from 16,960 USD in 2009 to 22,497 USD in 2016. The average during the Ma years was 20,654 USD. In none of his pledges did he come close to his goals. Perhaps he meant the figures as goals to try to reach. But the fact that he was so far off the mark he had set angered the opposition whose views, perhaps legitimately, centered on that campaign pledge.

In one evaluation of Ma as president, one Alfred Tsai wrote a piece in the May 25, 2015 edi- tion of *Taipei Times*, entitled "Ma's Golden Decade of Achievement." Whether the purpose of this editorial was sarcasm is uncertain (certainly the title is sarcastic), but, apart from the Cross-Strait successes, the essay spins off a long list of Ma's governing failures. He did not excel as a political leader. He had led the KMT into major defeats in 2014's local elections. In 2015, his approval rating in the country was 16 percent, though in September 2013 it had been at only 9 percent. He did not begin to solve long-standing issues that should have been at least broached: food safety, stagnant wages, nuclear energy issues, some constitutional revisions, and social welfare issues which were crying out for changes. The editorial was most compelling when he named fundamental problems in Taiwanese politics, society, and culture that no one person could possibly fix alone. Perhaps these points helped to account for Ma's apparent ineffectiveness as president. The editorialist called them Taiwan's "underlying political gridlock."

THE FIRST FEMALE PRESIDENT, THE DPP'S TSAI ING-WEN

The upshot of Ma's lackluster and highly unpopular presidency was a huge win for the opposition DPP in the 2016 presidential election. Tsai Ing-wen was the first woman elected president in the history of the Republic of China. Not only the first woman, but she was also the first president of both Hakka and aboriginal descent, the first unmarried president; and in terms of electoral history, the first never to have held an elected executive post before the presidency and the first popularly elected president without having served as mayor of Taipei. She was a law professor, holding degrees from prestigious Taiwan universities, as well as advanced degrees in law and international trade from Cornell University and the London School of Economics. But, like Chen and Ma, she had a rough start, primarily because, as leader of the DPP, she did not support the one-China policy. Beijing simply deep-sixed the Cross-Strait dialogues; in short, no more agreements. When the DPP took over, China automatically, almost as in a Pavlovian response, closed the spigot. As in the case of tourism which flourished in the Ma years: Beijing cut back on the number of group tours allowed to go to Taiwan. Chinese tourists on the island dropped by 30 percent from the previous year. That loss in itself caused problems for an anemic economy.

Other economic issues also raised discontent with Tsai; there was a general cry for higher wages, cheaper housing, and job creation, especially for youths. The monthly wages for entry-level engineers was about 1,300 USD; as crucial in the success of Taiwan's giant tech industry, they had to be employed in Taiwan. But salary levels forced many to leave Taiwan for more moneyed opportunities. In the Ma years tariffs were dropped on about 800 goods; Ma had proposed a "trade-in-goods agreement" by which close to 1,000 more products would have had their tariffs cut. But that was put on hold since the two sides were no longer talking. Because of the economic problems, many people were therefore disgruntled about the Cross-Strait stalemate; and yet, polls showed that 57 percent of Taiwanese still wanted Tsai to resist China's demands to say that both sides belonged to one China. Taiwan was bound up in a "Catch-22" situation.

FIGURE 23.3 Here President Tsai gives an address on the decision of the Republic of Panama to end diplomatic relations with the Republic of China (Taiwan). Panama's choice to recognize the PRC instead was painful to the ROC, since they had maintained diplomatic relations since the 1920s.
Source: Presidential Office, Taiwan, via Wikimedia Commons.

Another possible option for Taiwan to entertain was to begin what Tsai called the "New Southbound Policy." Instead of being stymied by Beijing's control of the strait situation, there might be possibilities to build greater regional connectivity with eighteen countries in Southeast and South Asia, along with Australia and New Zealand. Trade, investment, and tourist industry opportunities possibly beckoned. In 2016, tourists in Taiwan from South and Southeast Asia had totaled 1.65 million; perhaps they could make up the Beijing-caused tourist slack. But such a policy was one that would only work, if at all, in the long term. Given China's increasing ability to play hardball, the long term might never come into play. And there were intimations that it might not work at all. In the 1990s, Taiwan had signed ten bilateral investment agreements with Southeast Asian countries. Tsai and the DPP wanted to renew and possibly refine these agreements in order to invigorate present and future possibilities. But none of the ten responded positively or indicated that they wanted to renew or upgrade these agreements.[22] Even more ominously, China had begun to pressure Southeast Asian countries—Vietnam and Singapore, specifically—to commit in their dealings with China and Taiwan to the one-China policy. China acted in this way to weaken Taiwan's international presence and to build up as much anger in Taiwan over DPP rule so as to move the island's populace to a more open opinion about unification with China.[23]

THE CHANGING FACE OF THE ECONOMY AND RELATED ISSUES

The economy, once seen as nothing short of a miracle, went south during the presidencies of Chen and Ma and was off to a slow start with Tsai. Not only did Chen seem unable to govern, given the decision-making deadlock, but the economy tanked: the stock market dropped over 50 percent, unemployment rose to unprecedented heights, and imports and exports shrank. Ma had to face the global recession that hit only a few months after his election: his April 2008 approval rating—60.5 percent—collapsed to 24.9 percent in September.

But until the early twenty-first-century downturn, Taiwan had known years of economic growth driven by the expansion of exports, which were also the crucial source of its rapid industrialization. Export processing zones, with their electronic industries and cheap labor (workers made 15 percent of what comparable workers made in the United States and 20 percent of those in Japan), were the cornerstones of economic success. And it was generally American and Japanese investment that stimulated the electronic and electrical appliance industries. But electronics were only part of the export success story. Beginning in the 1970s, Taiwan had moved into the machine-tool and transportation-equipment industry, and in the 1980s it had aggressively entered the computer/information technology industry.

Supporting the expansion into these industries was a government commitment to supporting research and fostering development of scientific and technological innovations that were "cutting edge" and "state of the art". A bill passed in 1979 set guidelines for "science-based industrial parks" that would include laboratories and research units, commercial enterprises, even residential accommodations. The most famous such park, opened in late 1980, was the Hsinchu Science Park. By 1990 it was generally acknowledged to be one of the most important research and development centers in East Asia—the Asian "Silicon Valley." In 1995 it had 134 firms involved primarily in computers, telecommunications, integrated circuits, semiconductors, opto-electronics, biotechnology, and automation. Two other science parks, the South Taiwan Science Park in Kaohsiung and Tainan, opened in 2000, and the Central Taiwan Science Park in the Taichung area, starting in 2003. All three science parks were involved in the same fields as the Hsinchu Park, but, in addition the South Park was involved in exploring green energy possibilities.

The search for green energy came in large part from the decision of both major political parties to make Taiwan a "nuclear-free homeland." Dependent in its early modernizing period on three nuclear power plants, Taiwan had plans to construct a fourth plant in the early twenty-first century. To that point, the KMT had been staunch advocates and supporters of nuclear energy. When the DPP was established, it vowed to challenge the KMT on this issue. One of Chen Shui-bian's first acts as president was to stop construction of the fourth nuclear power plant. The project, however, was later reinstated. "A decade of monumental cost overruns" that featured lawsuits among various contractors and sub-contractors, charges of shoddy construction, and many other assorted problems "made the plant a lightning rod for anti-nuclear sentiment."[24] As President Ma's popularity

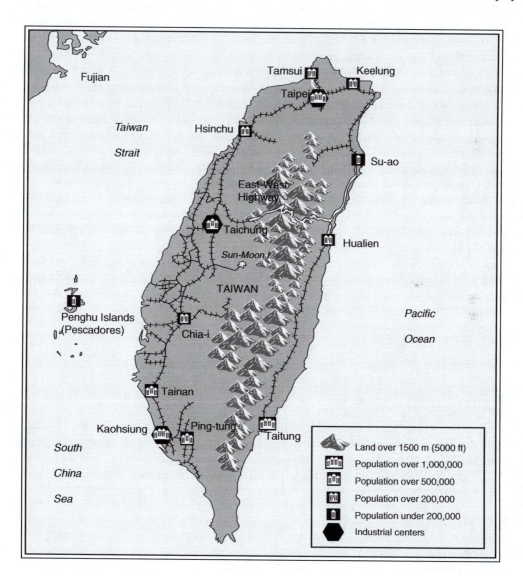

MAP 23.1 Taiwan, 2018.

waned, his support of the fourth plant scared many citizens. Then came the tragedy at Fukushima, Japan. On March 11, 2011, a 9.0 magnitude earthquake on the ocean floor about 130 miles east of Japan resulted in a 50-foot tsunami that, in turn, disabled the power supply and cooling of three nuclear reactors, causing a nuclear accident. Taiwanese knew that Taiwan, like Japan, lay on the Pacific seismic belt, prone to earthquakes and any tsunami aftermath. The Central Weather Bureau Seismic Network reported that Taiwan from 1991 to 2006 had 18,500 earthquakes per year, with about 1,000 felt by people. In light of the Fukushima accident, Taiwanese began to mobilize themselves in massive protests about the fourth nuclear power plant in 2012, 2013, and 2014. In 2014, the government suspended construction on the plant, though it was 90 percent completed at a cost of 9.3 billion USD. In the end, the government would leave the fate of the plant in the hands of the people who would decide by referendum what it would be. No referendum was scheduled.

More and more people left the farms to enter this export-oriented economy. The 1980 profile of the workforce was 75 percent industrial and manufacturing, 38 percent in services, and 20 percent agricultural. The breakdown in 2017, in sharp contrast, was 59 percent in services, 36 percent in industrial-manufacturing, and only 5 percent in agriculture. As agriculture declined in importance, new forms of agriculture appropriate for the export market began to appear. The cultivation of flowers and decorative plants emerged in the 1970s and grew steadily into the 2010s. Taiwan was the largest exporter of orchids in the world, in 2015 exporting 193.62 million USD worth of those flowers primarily to the United States, Japan, and the EU but in 2017 orchid seedlings were exported to 87 countries and territories. In 2008, a hectare (2.47 acres) of flowers brought a grower up to $24,000 (U.S.), whereas that same hectare producing rice brought only $3,000. The government offered assistance to grow the orchid industry. In 2003 it began the Taiwan Orchid Plantation (TOP), a 175 hectare (434 acres) tract of land with state of the art infrastructure: a quarantine station, and packing, shipping, and customs facilities. Fully operational in 2012, TOP used technology such as genetic engineering to improve yields, produce hardier varieties and gain greater control over the appearance of new varieties. Aquaculture was another export-oriented agricultural activity: carp, eel, tilapia, grouper, clams, oysters, and sea cucumbers were grown in both brackish and freshwater ponds.

DIPLOMACY: SEEKING RESPECT

Taiwan was a nation-state in fact but not in name. Ousted from the UN in 1971 and with countless nations breaking diplomatic relations with it to embrace the PRC, Taiwan, like the late American comedian Rodney Dangerfield, "got no respect." Taiwan campaigned almost yearly since 1993 to be readmitted to the UN, but it has not yet succeeded. Before May 2009, Taiwan tried thirteen times to attain "observer status" at the World Health Organization (WHO); each time the PRC applied pressure on nations to refuse. Over time both Beijing and Taipei have competed for diplomatic recognition from various countries. The number of countries with which Taiwan had diplomatic relations by early 2018 numbered only twenty (nineteen countries out of the 193 countries in the UN plus the Vatican). The competition goes under the euphemistic name "checkbook diplomacy"; but its blunt name is bribery. Beijing has played the money game better than Taipei, freely doling out funds to states for infrastructure projects.

A few examples from countries in the Caribbean Basin are instructive. Bahamas (1997): the PRC donated 14 million USD to build docks and three resorts in Nassau; (2011): the PRC donated 3.4 billion USD for a gaming and entertainment resort. Saint Lucia (1997): the PRC loaned 15 million USD for the construction of a cricket stadium and 10 million USD to build a psychiatric hospital. However, in a classic instance of how checkbook diplomacy worked, in 2007 because Taiwan provided more generous funds, St. Lucia switched to re-recognizing Taipei. Costa Rica (2007): the PRC gave $300 million USD so that the nation could lower its national debt.[25]

Relations with the United States

As we have seen, on January 1, 1979, the United States, one of Taiwan's closest allies and the one that had done most to create the island's modern economic miracle, severed diplomatic relations with Taipei as it established relations with Beijing. The mutual defense treaty between Taiwan and the United States was also abolished. But in April 1979, the U.S. Congress passed the Taiwan Relations Act, which, in effect, accorded Taiwan "treatment equivalent to a sovereign state." Agreements over trade, fishing, copyrights, aviation, education, and defense technology between the two were handled by two offices, the Taipei Economic and Cultural Representative Office in Washington, D.C., and the American Institute in Taiwan. Staffed by professional diplomats, these offices were like the embassies before 1979. Indeed, Taiwan had twelve consular-like offices in U.S. cities—more than it had in 1979. With relations like these, who needs diplomatic relations?

Even more, the Taiwan Relations Act made strong commitments to Taiwan: any threat to Taiwan would be of grave concern in the U.S.; the U.S. would provide arms "of a defensive character"; and the U.S. would remain prepared to resist actions of force or coercion that would endanger the security and well-being of the Taiwanese people.[26] Given the tense relationships between the PRC and Taiwan, the Taiwan Relations Act could come back to haunt the United States. "The Act left open the possibility of renewed United States military protection and assistance to safeguard Taiwan's interests and deter mainland China if and when it was deemed necessary."[27]

Thus, the United States continued to sell arms and planes to Taiwan—from George H.W. Bush's sale of F-16 fighter planes and surface-to-air missiles in 1992 to Bill Clinton's 1997 sale of long-range early-warning radar systems and advanced antimissile systems such as the Patriot and Aegis-class destroyers. The administration of George W. Bush espoused an even more aggressive position, declaring that the United States would "do whatever it took" to help Taiwan defend itself. He offered four destroyers, eight diesel-electric submarines, up to a dozen antisubmarine aircraft, and a long-range radar system to detect ballistic and cruise missiles. Because of the economic hard times, Taiwanese negotiators did not make it to Washington to discuss an arms package until July 2004. Mainland China's reaction was that such sales only made Cross-Strait tensions worse and that they violated a joint communiqué signed by China and the United States in August 1982, which read in part "[The U.S.] does not seek to carry out a long-term policy of arms sales to Taiwan … and that it intends gradually to reduce its sale of arms, leading, over a period of time, to a final resolution."]28 The administration of Barack Obama continued the pattern of arms sales, sending Taiwan three "packages" of various missiles, amphibious assault vehicles, Black Hawk helicopters, advanced radar systems, guided bombs, and other military weapons. The arms packages were sent in 2010 (6.4 billion USD); 2011 (5.8 billion USD); and 2015 (1.83 billion USD).

SOCIETY IN FLUX

Higher Education

Undergirding both economic and political change was an expanding and successful educational system that provided a well-educated workforce and citizenry. Compulsory education was raised to twelve years in 2014. As a result, the literacy rate shot up from 45 percent in 1949 to 93 percent in 1990 and to 98.7 percent in 2017. Students could choose to go to academic or vocational high school or to get a job. As for higher education, in 1995 Taiwan had 117 schools of higher education, forty-two universities and seventy-five polytechnic schools. It was in the mid-1990s when higher education began an unprecedented expansion; before then, it was promoted to serve economic development and the focus was the elite who had early on been the main clientele.

About 1995, the model shifted away from focusing on elites to the "massification" or universal model, where all could go to study.[29] This change came as a response to global competition, domestic political issues, and rapid social change. As in its work with research and development in the industrial and agricultural worlds, the government was ready to step in with programs and money to build excellence into the system. Plans to work toward this excellence came into being in 2003, 2005, and 2011.

In early 2018, university and colleges numbered 155 and junior colleges, 191, for a total of 346.[30] University acceptance rate underscores the new educational goals: before the 1970, it had been about 20 percent; in the mid-'90s it was 49 percent; and by 2006, it was over 90 percent. Numbers of students tell the same story: In 1950, 6,665; in 1986, 345,736, a 52-fold increase; in 2012, 1,259,490, a tripling from 1986. Projections suggested that the student population would begin to decrease due to a consistently lower birth rate and a rapidly aging population and that, as a result, up to a third of colleges and universities may have to eventually close or merge. In order to bolster the number of students as the Taiwanese pool diminishes, stress has been placed on bringing foreign students to study. Mainland Chinese began to come to Taiwan to study in 2011. The following numbers of PRC students studying in Taiwan underscore how important such an influx can be for the health of Taiwanese higher education.

2011—12,155   2014—32,911
2012—17,454   2015—41,927
2013—24,787   2016—41,975

One other downside of the "massification" of higher education is that so many more young people were graduates that competition for jobs became stiff. Nearly 70 percent of Taiwan's eighteen- to twenty-two-year-olds were studying—the second highest rate in the world after South Korea. An inability to find satisfactory employment could lead to bitter social disgruntlement. Only 25 percent of graduates in the years from 2008 to 2013 found work. The unemployment rate for this population was 2.7 percent in 1993; by 2012, it was 5.8 percent.

WOMEN AND GENDER ROLES

Education allowed women to emerge as they never had in traditional Chinese society. In the new Taiwan, women often started to enter the workforce before marriage, thereby gaining independence from family before marriage. After marriage, their wages and salaries put them more on par with their husbands, and often led to situations where they participated more in decision making than they had in traditional marriages. Work after marriage also generally meant smaller families. It was not only in the economic arena that the position of women improved. More educated women were more aware of their legal rights (vis-à-vis men) and of political rights and opportunities in general; they were also more likely to participate in social causes.

The founder of the movement to raise women's consciousness in Taiwan was Lu Hsiu-lien (Annette Lu), who served as vice-president of the ROC from 2000 to 2008. Educated at Harvard Law School, she inaugurated the Taiwan feminist movement with essays she wrote in the early

1970s. Her major work, *New Feminism*, was published in 1974. At once a history of women's movements around the world and an account of the traditional role of women in China, the book argued that the real glass ceiling for women was not economic oppression but the "invisible concepts of patriarchal values [that] continue to control Chinese women's fates."[31] Lu was jailed for her participation in the 1979 Kaohsiung Incident, but many suspect that her real "crime" was her strong feminist activity. She reported that during the interrogation following her arrest, one of her questioners said, "Your motivation to launch such a movement is to destabilize the society."[32] The landslide election of Tsai Ing-wen in 2016 was the grandest victory for women in the modern period. She came to the presidency with no political "dowry" from a former male political figure or head of state and no well-known family name. As one commentator wrote, her victory "engenders hope for the dawn of greater gender equality in the whole of Asia."[33]

The women's movement did not remain in the realm of the elites or the activists. From the mid-1970s to the mid-1990s, no fewer than ninety-six popular magazines were published for female readers; they discussed women's roles, family issues, and sexuality. Often the double standard was evident in talking about husbands and wives, whether the subject was who did the housework when both spouses had jobs or the permissibility of extramarital affairs for husbands but never wives. Even though divorce was possible, the divorce rate was very low. Children were part of the husband's family line; women who divorced were hardly ever left with any custody rights. Divorce, therefore, might mean that a woman would never see her children again. Also, if a woman initiated a divorce, it was likely that she would not be given alimony.

Taipei's LGBT community was for many years a lively presence in Asia's most friendly LGBT city. In 2003 it held its first annual Pride Parade, what has become the largest gay pride parade in Asia. The 2017 version drew an estimated 123,000 participants. who were especially celebratory and euphoric. Five months before, on May 24, the highest court in Taiwan, the Judicial Yuan, had ruled that denying same-sex couples the right to marry violated their right to equality under the Taiwanese constitution. The decision, one commentator said, is "a testament to the robust democracy that the Taiwanese have built in a region often lacking in the rule of law and pluralistic values." Taiwanese pluralism and tolerance makes it "a beacon of liberal values."[34] The government also played a role in making the island's culture diversified: it reformed the state education curriculum to de-emphasize traditional Confucian moral guidance in favor of pluralistic values.

THE ENVIRONMENT

Environmental pollution was the price of economic development and one of the most serious of Taiwan's problems. There were biologically active wastes, including food wastes, human and animal wastes, and carcasses. The horrifying statistics were that

> in all of Taiwan, less than 1 percent of human excrement receive[d] even primary sewage treatment; in Taipei City the figure [was] less than 3 percent. Not surprisingly, Taiwan had among the highest incidence of hepatitis B in the world.[35]

There were also pollutants consisting of inert and semi-inert substances—plastics, metal, and glass in ordinary trash. These were usually dumped into landfills, but appropriate landfill sites no longer existed.

The most toxic of all pollutants were hazardous wastes: pesticides, caustic chemicals, and radioactive wastes. Air pollution was easily the most visible of all—"the ugly brown pall"—caused by an eye-watering mix of industrial pollution, motor vehicle emissions, aerosols, and burning waste.

Finally, there was noise pollution: noise levels above 80 decibels were often registered on Taipei streets; the chief culprit here, with an overall negative effect on the quality of life, was indiscriminate, constant horn honking.

In addition to these pollution problems, there were other serious environmental concerns. As in the PRC, the amount of land available for agriculture was declining at an alarming rate; even worse than the outright decline was that close to half of the land that was now farmed was considered marginal. Soil erosion in many areas was a serious problem. There was also a potentially serious water shortage. Most island wildlife had been killed off. All in all, Taiwan, like the PRC, was on many levels an environmental nightmare.

WHITHER TAIWAN? A CHOICE OF IDENTITY?

From the late 1940s until the 1990s, the Kuomintang had attempted to socialize the Taiwanese into being citizens of the ROC rather than citizens of Taiwan. Thus, only the Mandarin dialect, the "national language" of China, not Taiwanese, was used in schools, as well as on radio and television. Junior high and elementary students learned little about Taiwan. Reports showed that of about 1,200 pages of required elementary social studies texts, only thirty mentioned Taiwan. In the 1987 college entrance examinations, four of forty-two questions on geography were concerned with Taiwan and one of thirty-two questions on history was on Taiwan. The imbalance in curricular materials was an irritant among Taiwanese already upset by the attitudes and approaches of the mainlanders. The DPP-controlled government in 2002 announced that new passports would have the words "Issued in Taiwan" added.[36]

But this "Republic of China" perspective began to shift dramatically in the 1990s: the Taiwanization emphasis and efforts of Lee Teng-hui followed by Chen Shui-bian's presidency after the DPP's dramatic electoral victory in 2000. Ironically, the trend was solidified and even hastened by the more "open to China" presidency of Ma Ying-jeou, whose favorable poll numbers fell to single digits because of his China policy. A June 2013 DPP telephone survey, that collected 1,149 samples and had a margin of error of 2.95 percentage points, showed an overwhelming 77.6 percent identified themselves as exclusively Taiwanese. A 1991 poll, in contrast, showed that only 17.7 percent identified themselves as exclusively Taiwanese. In 1991, about 25 percent identified themselves as exclusively Chinese, but in 2017 only 3 percent saw themselves as exclusively Chinese.

On the independence–unification issue, the survey found that, overall, 59 percent supported independence, 25.9 percent said they supported unification, and 10.3 percent preferred the "status quo." For Taiwanese under forty, fully 84 percent were pro-independence. When all Taiwanese were considered, only one-third supported unification, down from 60 percent in 2003. When all respondents were considered, fully 75 percent would support independence if it would not cause a war.

When asked whether Taiwan and China were parts of one country, the survey found that 78.4 percent disagreed, while 15 percent agreed. As for whether Taiwan and China were two districts in one country, 70.6 percent disagreed, while 22.8 percent agreed. When asked which among four descriptions—"one country on each side," "a special state-to-state relationship," "one country, two areas," and "two sides are of one country"—they found the most acceptable, 54.9 percent said "one country on each side," 25.3 percent chose "a special state-to-state relationship," 9.8 percent said "one country, two areas" and 2.5 percent favored "two sides are of one country." The trend is clear: as Taiwanese aged, those who experienced Taiwan up to the reform period began to die. Younger people would set the pace for the future, and the vast majority, were opting to become Taiwanese rather than Chinese.[37] What that decision would mean for policymakers in the PRC, of course, cannot possibly be known.

One other force that is operative in propelling the Taiwanese track was the campaign against Chiang Kai-shek and his dictatorial authoritarianism. Memorials honoring Chiang were mostly statues in the hundreds, located in schools, government and other office buildings, and parks. The effort to destroy them or get them moved out of the public eye began in earnest during the administration of Chen Shui-bian. A law passed in late 2017 called for the "mandatory axing of symbols of its authoritarian past and argued that this "transitional justice bill" specify that "authoritarian rule should be stripped of legitimacy" as it violated freedom and democracy.[38] Public statues of Chiang were attacked, pelted with paint and eggs, even decapitated, and deposited randomly around Chiang's mausoleum. Streets and schools were renamed; the name of Taiwan's international airport was changed, and Chiang's image was removed from banknotes. Through these techniques, Chiang's public image was steadily eroded and he was left primarily with the major murderous legacy of the February 28, 1947 massacre and the bleak years of the White Terror (1948–1975). A historian at Academia Sinica explained the newfound contempt for Chiang: "We don't want to be part of China, and Chiang Kai-shek represents the idea that China possesses Taiwan."[39]

One last anecdote, to emphasize the combustible feelings coming from small incidents in both Taiwan and the PRC with implications on the issue of unification or independence. In 2016, a sixteen-year-old Taiwanese singer in a south Korean K-pop group (Chou Tzu-yu) attracted attention on a South Korean variety show when she introduced herself and waved the flag of the Republic of China, alongside those waving South Korean and Japanese flags. When a Taiwanese-born male singer based in China saw the television clip, he accused Chou of being a "pro-Taiwanese

FIGURE 23.4 In the interest of "axing" all Chiang Kai-shek memorials, this garden has become the dumping ground for those things which resurrect in memory the brutal authoritarianism of his regime. This action is taken in stated support of freedom and democracy.
Source: Henry Westheim Photography/Alamy Stock Photo.

independence activist." There followed an uproar which resulted in Chou reading an apology: all this happened the day before Tsai Ing-wen's presidential election. The apology said,

> There is only one China. The two sides of the Taiwan Strait are one entity. I feel proud being a Chinese. I, as a Chinese have hurt the company and netizens feelings due to my words and actions. … I feel very, very sorry and also very guilty.

Many Taiwanese were horrified by her apology, seeing it as "humiliating and a sign of Taiwan's predicament that Chou had to apologize for expressing her Taiwanese identity and for showing her nation's flag."[40] In her victory speech, President Tsai said that the episode had "angered many Taiwanese people, regardless of their political affiliation."

With the DPP's electoral victories and the obvious shifts of Taiwanese public opinion posed against Beijing's decision to have nothing to do with DPP leaders, it seems that the hour is drawing near when the ultimate choice—independence or unification—will be compelled. With the PRC's wealth and power and its will and determination to browbeat countries such as Panama into doing its bidding, it appears that the deck is stacked against the Taiwanese. But one crucial lesson of history is that nothing is inevitable: so there yet lies hope for the people on Taiwan, whatever the ultimate decision.

Notes

1 Murray A. Rubinstein, "Political Taiwanization and Pragmatic Diplomacy: The Eras of Chiang Ching-kuo and Lee Teng-hui, 1971–1994," in *Taiwan: A New History*, ed. Murray A. Rubinstein (Armonk, NY: M.E. Sharpe, 1999), p. 441.
2 Quoted in ibid., p. 442.
3 Marc J. Cohen, *Taiwan at the Crossroads* (Washington, D.C.: Asia Resource Center, 1988), p. 39.
4 Hung-mao Tien, "Taiwan's Evolution Toward Democracy: A Historical Perspective," in *Taiwan, Beyond the Economic Miracle*, ed. Denis Fred Simon and Michael Y.M. Kau (Armonk, NY: M.E. Sharpe, 1992), p. 9.
5 Rubinstein, "Political Taiwanization and Pragmatic Diplomacy," p. 447.
6 Alan M. Wachmann, "Competing Identities in Taiwan," in *The Other Taiwan: 1945 to the Present*, ed. Murray A. Rubinstein (Armonk, NY: M.E. Sharpe, 1994), p. 24.
7 Alan M. Wachmann, *Taiwan, National Identity and Democratization* (Armonk, NY: M.E. Sharpe, 1994), pp. 151–2.
8 Ibid., p. 152.
9 Ibid., p. 200, n. 55.
10 Ibid., p. 194.
11 *Free China Journal*, October 18, 1991, p. 1.
12 Wachman, p. 195.
13 Ibid., p. 193.
14 Maurice Meisner, *Mao's China and After* (New York: Free Press, 1999), p. 530.
15 John Bryan Starr, "China in 1995: Mounting Problems, Waning Capacity," *Asian Survey*, 36, no. 1 (January–February 1996): 23.
16 Terry McCarthy, "Taiwan Takes a Stand," *Time* 155, no. 12 (March 27, 2000): 52. www.cnn.cp,/ASIANOW/time/magazine/2000/0327/cover1.html
17 Wachmann, *Taiwan*, p. 256.
18 Ibid., p. 162.
19 www.s-t.com/daily/07-0007-13-00/a02wn.002.htm
20 Shelley Rigger, "Taiwan in 2002: Another Year of Political Droughts and Typhoons," *Asian Survey* 43, no. 1 (January–February, 2003): 47.

21 Tania Branigan, "Taiwan Cabinet Members Offer to Resign over Typhoon Morakot Response," *The Guardian* (August 19, 2009).

22 Huang, Kwei-bo, "Taiwan's Southward Integration Faces a Long Uphill Battle," *EASTASIAFORUM* (October 17, 2017).

23 See Ralph Jennings, "Taiwan President Marks First Anniversary as Discontent Grows," *Voice of America News* (May 19, 2017). www.voanews.com/a/taiwan-president-marks-first-anniversary-as-discontent-grows/3862126.html

24 Timothy Ferry, "Phasing Out Nuclear Power in Taiwan," *Taiwan Business Topics* (September 15, 2015).

25 "Checkbook Diplomacy: The Economics of Sino-Caribbean Relations," COHA (Council on Hemispheric Affairs (August 19, 2013). Source of Figures 1 and 2, Elise Lefeuvre.

26 Gary Klintworth, *New Taiwan, New China: Taiwan's Changing Role in the Asia-Pacific Region* (New York: St. Martin's Press, 1995), p. 63.

27 Ibid., p. 64.

28 "U.S. Conventional Arms Sales to Taiwan," Arms Control Association; available at www. armscontrol.org/factsheets/taiwanarms.asp

29 Sheng Ju-Chan and Liang Wen-Lin, "Massification of Higher Education in Tawian: Shifting Pressure from Admissions to Employment," *Higher Education Policy* 28 (1) (March 2015).

30 Chuing Prudence Chou, "Education in Taiwan: Taiwan's Colleges and Universities," Brookings Institution (November 12, 2014).

31 Catherine S. Farris, "The Social Discourse on Women's Roles in Taiwan: A Textual Analysis," in Rubinstein, *The Other Taiwan*, p. 311.

32 Ibid.

33 Andreea Brinza, "Tsai Ing-wen: A New Type of Female Leader in Asia," *The Diplomat* (May 26, 2016).

34 Trevor Sutton and Brian Harding, "Why Taiwan's Gay Marriage Law Matters," *The Diplomat* (June 1, 2017).

35 Jack F. Williams, "Paying the Price of Economic Development in Taiwan: Environmental Degradation," in Rubinstein, *The Other Taiwan*, p. 241.

36 Monique Chu and Ko Shu-ling, "Chang Gives His Approval to Passports," *Taipei Times* (January 15, 2002). www.taipeitimes.com/News/front/archives/2002/01/15/119980

37 Compare the results of two polls by the *Taipei Times* in 2013 and 2015. See Chris Wang, "Taiwanese Prefer Independence over Unification: Survey" (October 31, 2013) and Tseng Wei-chen and Chen Wei-han, "Unification Support Dives: Poll" (July 26, 2015).

38 "Taiwan Votes to Erase Chiang Kai-shek's Authoritarian Legacy with New Law," *South China Morning Post* (December 6, 2017). Austin Ramzy, "Divisive Monuments? Put Them All in a Taiwan Park," *New York Times* (August 22, 2017).

39 Austin Ramzy, "Divisive Monuments? Put Them All in a Taiwan Park," *New York Times* (August 22, 2017).

40 Chris Buckley and Austin Ramzy, "Singer's Apology for Waving Taiwan's Flag Stirs Backlash of Its Own," *New York Times* (January 16, 2016). www.nytimes.com/2016/01/17/world/.../taiwan-china-singer-chou-tzu-yu.htm

Suggestions for Further Reading

Brown, Melissa J. *Is Taiwan Chinese? The Impact of Culture, Power, and Migration on Changing Identities* (Berkeley, CA: University of California Press, 2004). Arguing that identity is based on social experience, not culture or ancestry, Brown probes the discrepancies between the cultural identities in Taiwan and China and their impacts on political issues and goals.

Hughes, Christopher. *Taiwan and Chinese Nationalism: National Identity and Status in International Society* (London: Routledge, 1997). This careful look at the relations between the PRC and ROC links Taiwan's status to the development of nationalism on the mainland.

Roy, Denny. *Taiwan: A Political History* (Ithaca, NY: Cornell University Press, 2003). This is a lively and insightful survey from the fifteenth century to 2001.

Rubinstein, Murray A., ed., *Taiwan: A New History*, 2nd edition (Philadelphia, PA: Taylor & Francis, 2007). An especially rich collection of essays covering the period from the late Ming to the present, as well as topics such as aborigines, religion, and literature.

Zhao, Suisheng, ed., *Across the Taiwan Strait: Mainland China, Taiwan, and the 1995–1996 Crisis* (New York: Routledge, 1999). This study examines aspects of the tense Beijing–Taipei relationship and provides insights into the perspective of the United States.

PRONUNCIATION GUIDE

The following is a list of common people (many of which are included in *Revolution and Its Past*) and place names with their Pinyin spelling and phonetic pronunciations.

People Pinyin	Phonetic
Ai Qing	eye ching
Bai Hua	bigh hwah
Cai Yuanpei	tsigh you-en pay
Chai Ling	chigh leeng
Chen Duxiu	chun doosheeoh
Chen Shuibian	chun shway bee-en
Chen Yi	chun ee
Chiang Ching-kuo	jee-ahng jeeng-gwo
Chiang Kai-shek	jee-ahng kai shek
Cui Jian	tsway jee-en
Daoguang emperor	dow gwahng
Deng Xiaoping	dung she-ow peeng
Empress Dowager Cixi	tsi she
Fang Lizhi	fahng lee jer
Feng Guifen	fung gway fun
Feng Yunshan	fung you-n shahn
Feng Yuxiang	fung you shee-ahng
Guangxu emperor	gwahng shu
H. H. Kung	gung
Hai Rui	high ray
Hong Xiuquan	hung she-o chew-on
Hou Dejian	hoe duh jee-en
Hu Feng	who fung
Hu Jintao	who jin tao
Hu Shi	who sher
Hu Yaobang	who yao bahng
Hua Guofeng	hwah gwo fung
Huang Shaoxiong	hwahng shaow sheeong
Huang Xing	hwahng sheeng
Jiang Qing	jee-ahng ching
Jiang Zemin	jee-ahng dzi-mean
Kang Youwei	kahng you way
Kangxi emperor	kahng she
Lao She	lao shuh
Lee Tung-hui	lee dung hway
Li Dazhao	lee dah jao
Li Hongzhang	lee hung jahng
Li Hongzhi	lee hung jer
Li Kuo-ting	lee gwo teeng
Li Peng	lee pung
Li Yizhe	lee ee juh
Li Zongren	lee dzung ren
Liang Qichao	lee-ahng chee chow

(Continued)

People Pinyin	Phonetic
Liao Zhongkai	lee-ow jong kai
Lin Biao	lin bee-ow
Lin Yutang	lin you tahng
Liu Shaoqi	lee-o shaow chee
Lu Hsiu-lien	loo she-o lee-en
Lu Xun	lu shwun
Mao Zedong	mao dzi dung
Peng Dehuai	pung duh why
Peng Zhen	pung jun
Qianlong emperor	chee-en lung
Qiu Jin	chee-oh jeen
Qu Qiubai	chew chee-oh by
Shen Congwen	shun tsong one
Shen Dingyi	shun deeng ee
Shi Dakai	sher da kai
Song Jiaoren	soong jee-ow ren
Soong Meiling	soong may ling
Sun Yat-sen	suhn yat sen
Wang Dan	wahng dahn
Wang Guangmei	wahng gwahng may
Wang Jingwei	wahng jeeng way
Wang Shiwei	wahng sher way
Wang Shuo	wahng shu-ough
Wang Tiendeng	wahng tee-en dung
Wen Jiabao	one jee-ah bao
Wei Jingsheng	way jeeng shung
Wen Yiduo	one yee dwo
Wu Peifu	woo pay foo
Wu'er Kaixi	woo-er kai she
Xianfeng emperor	she-en fung
Xiao Chaogui	she-ow chow gway
Xu Xilin	shu she lin
Yan Xishan	yen she shahn
Yang Xiuqing	yahng she-o cheeng
Ye Jianying	yeh jee-en yeeng
Ye Wenfu	yeh one foo
Yin Chung-yung	yin jong yung
Yuan Shikai	yu-en sher kai
Zeng Guofan	dzung guo-fahn
Zhang Guotao	jahng gwo tao
Zhang Xueliang	jahng shweh leeahng
Zhang Zhidong	jahng jer dung
Zhang Zongchang	jahng dzung chahng
Zhang Zuolin	jahng dzwo lin
Zhao Ziyang	jao dzi yahng
Zhou Enlai	jo en lai
Zhu De	joo duh
Zhu Rongji	joo rong jee
Zou Rong	dzoh ruong
Zuo Zongtang	dzwo dzung tahng

Place Pinyin	Phonetic
Anhui	ahn hway
Changsha	chahng sha
Chengdu	chung doo
Chongqing	chong ching
Dagu	dah goo
Dalian	dah lee-en
Dongbei	dong bay
Eyuwan	uh you wahn
Fujian	foo jee-en
Gansu	gahn su
Guangdong	gwahng dung
Guangxi	gwahng she
Guangzhou	gwahng jo
Guizhou	gway jo
Hainan	high nahn
Hangzhou	hahng jo
Hebei	huh bay
Heilongjiang	hay lowng jeeahng
Henan	huh nahn
Hubei	who bay
Hunan	who nahn
Jiangsu	jeeahng su
Jiangxi	jeeahng she
Jilin	jee lin
Kaohsiung	gao she-ung
Keelung	jee lung
Kunming	kwun meeng
Liaodong	lee-ow dung
Liaoning	lee-ow neeng
Loyang	lwo yahng
Nanjing	nahn jing
Ningbo	neeng bwo
Peiping	bay ping
Penglai	pung lie
Qingdao	ching dao
Quzhou	chew jo
Rehe	ruh huh
Ruijin	ray jin
Shaanxi	shen she
Shandong	shahn dung
Shanhaiguan	shahn high gwahn
Shanxi	shahn she
Shaoxing	shao shing
Shenyang	shun yahng
Shenzhen	shun jun
Sichuan	si chew-ahn
Subei	soobay
Tianjin	tee-en jeen
Wuchang	woo chahng
Wuhan	woo hahn

(*Continued*)

Place Pinyin	Phonetic
Xi'an	she ahn
Xiang-exi	shee-ahng uh she
Xikang	she kahng
Xinjiang	sheen jee-ahng
Xunwu	shwun woo
Xuzhou	shoo jo
Yan'an	yen ahn
Yunnan	yuwn nahn
Zhejiang	juh jeeahng
Zhili	jer lee
Zhongnanhai	jong nahn high

INDEX

Note: **Bold** page numbers refer to tables; *italic* page numbers refer to figures and page numbers followed by "n" denote endnotes.